Elegant Pumpkin-Walnut Layered Pie, page 244

Carrot-Pecan Casserole, page 282

Cranberry Relish, page 276;
Pork Loin With Raisin Sauce, page 278

Meet the *Southern Living*® Foods Staff

On these pages we invite you to match the names and faces of the people behind these pages (left to right unless otherwise noted).

Assistant Foods Editors:
JOY E. ZACHARIA
CYBIL BROWN TALLEY

VICKI POELLNITZ, *Assistant Foods Editor;*
SUSAN DOSIER, *Executive Editor*

REBECCA KRACKE GORDON, *Test Kitchens staff;* MARY ALLEN PERRY, *Recipe Development Director;*
VANESSA A. MCNEIL, JAMES SCHEND, VIE WARSHAW, *Test Kitchens staff;*
LYDA H. JONES, *Test Kitchens Director*

ANDRIA SCOTT HURST, *Foods Editor;*
SHIRLEY HARRINGTON, *Associate Foods Editor;*
SCOTT JONES, *Foods Editor;* DONNA FLORIO, *Senior Writer*

Assistant Foods Editors: KATE NICHOLSON,
SHANNON SLITER SATTERWHITE,
CYNTHIA ANN BRISCOE

Photographers and Photo Stylists: (sitting) CARI SOUTH
(standing) BETH DREILING, CINDY MANNING BARR, WILLIAM DICKEY

3

Molasses Pork Tenderloin With Red Wine Sauce, page 290;
Broccoli With Pimiento Cheese Sauce, Pepper Jelly-Glazed
Carrots, page 291; Cranberry Congealed Salad, Two-Seed
Bread Knots, page 292

Southern Living®

2002 ANNUAL RECIPES

Oxmoor
House®

© 2002 by Oxmoor House, Inc.
Book Division of Southern Progress Corporation
P.O. Box 2463, Birmingham, Alabama 35201

Southern Living®, *Summer Suppers®*, and *Holiday Dinners®* are federally registered trademarks of Southern Living, Inc.

ISBN: 0-8487-2540-9
ISSN: 0272-2003

Printed in the United States of America
First printing 2002

To order additional publications, call 1-800-633-4910.

We Want Your FAVORITE RECIPES!

Southern Living cooks are the best cooks of all, and we want your secrets! Please send your favorite original recipes for main dishes, desserts, and everything in between, along with any hands-on tips and a sentence about why you like each recipe. We can't guarantee we'll print them in a cookbook, but if we do, we'll send you $20 and a free copy of the cookbook. Send each recipe on a separate page with your name, address, and daytime phone number to:

Cookbook Recipes
Oxmoor House
2100 Lakeshore Drive
Birmingham, AL 35209

For more books to enrich your life, visit
oxmoorhouse.com

Southern Living®

Executive Editor: Susan Dosier
Senior Writer: Donna Florio
Foods Editors: Andria Scott Hurst, Scott Jones
Associate Foods Editor: Shirley Harrington
Assistant Foods Editors: Cynthia Ann Briscoe, Kate Nicholson,
    Vicki Poellnitz, Shannon Sliter Satterwhite, Cybil B. Talley,
    Joy E. Zacharia
Test Kitchens Director: Lyda H. Jones
Recipe Development Director: Mary Allen Perry
Test Kitchens Staff: Rebecca Kracke Gordon, Vanessa A. McNeil,
    Jan Moon, James Schend, Vie Warshaw
Administrative Assistants: Brenda Carling, Sandra J. Thomas
Photography and Color Quality Director: Kenner Patton
Senior Foods Photographers: Tina Cornett, Charles Walton IV
Photographers: William Dickey, Beth Dreiling
Senior Photo Stylists: Cindy Manning Barr, Buffy Hargett
Assistant Photo Stylists: Lisa Powell, Cari South
Photo Librarian: Tracy Duncan
Photo Assistant: Catherine Carr
Production Manager: Katie Terrell Morrow
Production Coordinator: Jamie Barnhart

Oxmoor House, Inc.

Editor-in-Chief: Nancy Fitzpatrick Wyatt
Executive Editor: Susan Carlisle Payne
Art Director: Cynthia R. Cooper
Copy Chief: Catherine Ritter Scholl

Southern Living® 2002 Annual Recipes

Editor: Catherine Ritter Scholl
Copy Editor: Donna Baldone
Editorial Assistant: Jane Lorberau Gentry
Director, Production and Distribution: Phillip Lee
Books Production Manager: Theresa L. Beste
Production Assistant: Faye Porter Bonner

Contributors

Designer: Carol O. Loria
Indexer: Mary Ann Laurens
Editorial Consultant: Jean Wickstrom Liles

Cover: Fresh Orange Italian Cream Cake, page 294
Page 1: Pork Loin With Raisin Sauce, page 278; Carrot-Pecan
    Casserole, page 282; Cranberry Relish, page 276;
    Elegant Pumpkin-Walnut Layered Pie, page 244

Contents

Our Year at Southern Living

Dear Friends,

Greetings from the Foods staff! A friend once told me that when you make brownies for your family, more is cooking than a great dessert. I think this wise woman knew that when you cook, you feed the appetite. But when you cook for others, you feed the soul.

We hope this year's cookbook does exactly that for you. With each page, we offer ideas for mealtime survival. (Check out our "What's For Supper" and "Quick and Easy" columns.) And hopefully, the recipes also fill yet another need for your family and friends—the closeness

"When you cook for others, you feed the soul."

that comes when you eat dinner together. I sense that need to eat together now more than ever. My youngest has started school, and the afternoons and evenings are a blaze of homework and activity. Dinnertime is a chance for us to stop as a family and catch up.

This year's book celebrates an important event for our staff and readers. For the first time ever, we showcase the results of our $100,000 *Southern Living* Cook-Off 2002. After the winner was announced in Orlando in September, the news was transmitted to our home offices in order to meet our press deadlines. All 15 finalists recipes and brand winners are included as a bonus in this book. If you're eager for more contest coverage, see our January, 2003, special section in the magazine. If you want to be $100,000 richer, enter our Cook-Off 2003 contest at **www.southernlivingcookoff.com,** see the ads in the magazine, or call toll free at 1-866-587-3353.

We also include in this book the recipes from "*Southern Living* Favorites." This was our second time to produce this 13th issue which captures the very best flavors of the South. And don't miss the *Southern Living* Cooking School special section in September's chapter. It gets us all ready for back-to-school cooking and the pleasures of the fall table.

So let us know what feeds your soul and your family. To send a recipe, go to **www.southernliving.com/food/survey_readerrecipes.asp** or mail it to *Southern Living* Foods Editor, 2100 Lakeshore Drive, Birmingham, AL 35209. If you have questions or story ideas, e-mail me at **susan_dosier@timeinc.com** And don't forget to enter our Cook-Off! You have almost a whole year to test and perfect your entries.

Cheers!

Susan Dosier

Executive Editor

Best Recipes of 2002

Members of our Foods staff gather almost every day to taste-test recipes and rate them based on taste, overall appeal, ease of preparation, and even cost. Here we share our very favorite recipes.

Blackberry Cobbler (page 17) Frozen berries and premade piecrust makes this 10-minute dessert a year-round hit.

Creamy Macaroni and Cheese (page 26) Two kinds of Cheddar smother old-fashioned elbow macaroni in this homage to Mom's comforting classic.

Quick Whipping Cream Biscuits (page 27) These buttery, flaky, pillowlike treats require only four ingredients and 25 minutes.

Cordial Cherries (page 30) These brandy-spiked chocolate treats explode with flavor. They're love at first bite!

Chocolate-Dipped Caramels (page 30) Rich homemade caramel crouches under a chocolate shell in these bite-size candies so good you'll want to eat them by the handful.

Classic Cream Scones (page 41) A sugar crust coats these sweet versions of the teatime favorites, ready to hit the table in less than a half hour.

Date-Orange-Nut Spread (page 59) Honey adds a hint of sweetness while almonds and walnuts supply a toasty crunch to this chunky appetizer spread.

Strawberry Meringue Parfaits (page 62) This impressive dessert boasts layers of silky custard, sweet strawberries, and delicate meringue. Serve it in stemmed glassware for a festive flair.

Meringues (page 62) With only four ingredients, light-as-air meringue cookies are a great low-fat snack or special addition to a creamy dessert.

Spicy Red Beans and Rice (page 56) This slow-cook staple combines bacon, smoked sausage, and salt pork to yield a distinct down-South flavor.

Semitas (page 81) Anise seeds impart subtle flavor to these small, sweet loaves that have a texture similar to that of kaiser rolls.

Molletes (page 83) A kitchen tool called a *dulce* marker creates the characteristic scalloped design on these traditional Mexican sweet breads. Four variations provide ample opportunities for you to hone your baking skills.

Coco Loco Custard (page 89) Toasted coconut and rum form a silky-sweet alliance in this subtle dessert sure to please a crowd.

Coconut Cream Pie (page 92) Cream of coconut and cheesecake pudding mix enhance the luscious filling nestled in a crumb crust and topped with billowy clouds of whipped topping.

Kentucky Hot Browns (page 94) This Louisville creation pairs the legacy of the turkey sandwich with ripe tomatoes and crunchy bacon for a little-known but much-loved open-faced meal, served hot from the oven.

Cream Cheese Pound Cake With Strawberries and Cream (page 104) The simplicity of pound cake takes on a splashy new character when paired with the dynamic strawberry. It's the ultimate salute to spring.

Party-Perfect Strawberry Shortcakes (page 105) Nothing says summer better than these petite shortcakes, spread with minted jam, the freshest berries, and a dollop of freshly whipped cream.

Our Best Southern Fried Chicken (page 106) An overnight soak ensures an irresistibly crispy crust that encases the juicy chicken.

Hot-Water Cornbread (page 107) Five versions of this Southern-fried classic recall the memories of Sunday meals back home and bring a new generation to the dinner table.

Fresh Mozzarella-Tomato-Basil Salad (page 110) Chill this super-quick herbed tomato mix before serving for a fresh take on the typical tossed salad.

Buttermilk Batter-Fried Onion Rings (page 131) Sweet onions and buttermilk prove an irresistible combination, especially when served sizzling hot in your own kitchen.

Beef Tenderloin in Wine Sauce (page 136) A splash of dry red wine and the flavors of mushrooms, Worcestershire sauce, and Italian seasoning enliven this choice beef cut.

All of our winning recipes in Cook-Off 2002 received our highest rating as well. These recipes begin on page 318.

Taste of the South

*Each month this magazine column features signature Southern recipes
celebrating our region's rich heritage and traditional fare.*

Macaroni and Cheese (page 26) Our entire staff agrees that this cheesy casserole is one of the South's favorite comfort foods, but that's about all we agree on regarding this subject. The creamy vs. custard-style debate raged around our table. You be the judge.

Spicy Red Beans and Rice (page 56) This New Orleans staple relies on smoked sausage and bacon for its rich flavor.

Kentucky Hot Browns (page 94) Savor Louisville's signature dish—an open-faced turkey sandwich smothered with a delicate cheese sauce and topped with crisp bacon strips—and try each of the three tasty variations.

Southern Sunday Dinner (page 106) Relish some of our region's most treasured dishes in this oh-so-Southern menu featuring crunchy fried chicken, soulful black-eyed peas, tender turnip greens, and mouthwatering hot-water cornbread.

Buttermilk Batter-Fried Onion Rings (page 131) A light, crispy batter encases these addictive golden gems.

Fipps Family Potato Salad (page 138) Take the summertime family favorite back to the basics with this time-honored recipe.

Sweet-Tart Lemonade (page 160) and **Tea Cakes** (page 161) Quench your thirst and your Southern sweet tooth at the same time with this nostalgic duo so welcome in the dog days of summer.

Coca-Cola Cake (page 181) Serve this chocolaty cake with its fudgy frosting for a sweet slice of Southern tradition. A glass of cold milk is optional.

New Orleans Barbecue Shrimp (page 201) This Crescent City classic bathes succulent shrimp in a buttery, spicy, sauce poised for French bread dunking.

Classic Peanut Brittle (page 223) Today this old-timey nutty, crunchy confection can come from your cooktop or your microwave.

Cornbread Dressing (page 249) Tender cornbread creates the base for this quintessential Southern dressing. It's a must-have for any holiday feast.

Sweet Potato Casserole (page 309) Toasty pecans, crunchy cornflakes, and gooey marshmallows top this sweet side dish that's essential to any holiday feast.

Quick & Easy

*It seems like we're always in a rush to get dinner on the table.
We hope these one-dish meals and streamlined weeknight favorites
ease the pace and please the palate.*

■ Mama Mia! A fast *and* flavorful Italian meal: spaghetti and meatballs, complete with salad and garlic bread. (page 25)

■ Ten minutes are all it takes to have any of these breakfast breads in the oven. (page 41)

■ Use jarred minced garlic to chop up your prep time in a flavorful way. (page 61)

■ Enjoy making and serving delectable chicken dishes that all take 30 minutes or less to prepare. (page 91)

■ This trio of our personal favorites delivers fantastic flavor without the fuss. (page 108)

■ South-of-the-border recipes that minimize prep time and maximize flavor. (page 143)

■ Three fast and fresh pasta recipes to satisfy your carb cravings. (page 161)

■ Seven ingredients or less is all it takes for these simple sides and main dishes that highlight pasta's versatility. (page 186)

■ Savor end-of-season tomatoes in a variety of quick and tasty dishes. (page 213)

■ Frozen veggies offer convenience, affordability, and great flavor in snappy side dishes. (page 234)

■ Glazes and sauces take these vegetables to new heights. (page 283)

■ Creamy chowders make fast, hearty meals and can be prepared ahead for entertaining ease. (page 305)

Living Light

*Each month we focus on different foods and timely concepts
to help you make healthy choices for your family.*

♥ Fresh-squeezed citrus juice in healthy, hearty dishes will chase away the winter blues. (page 22)

♥ Spectacular spuds produce crispy fries and creamy casseroles that are as satisfying as they are nutritious. (page 34)

♥ Turn your plate into a palette of beautiful flavors with these fresh recipes featuring fruits and vegetables. (page 68)

♥ Citrus makes a splash in everything from entrées to desserts. (page 84)

♥ Cooking with low-fat dairy products proves that silky texture and satisfying taste don't equal a diet disaster. (page 123)

♥ A Low Country chef shares her love of cooking as well as her inviting, healthful recipes. (page 144)

♥ Healthy blueberries lend sweet, tangy flavor and vivid color to salads, muffins, and more. (page 177)

♥ Hearty entrées featuring low-fat cuts of meat are lusciously lean. (page 193)

♥ Stir up good nutrition with tasty dishes containing protein-packed legumes. (page 202)

♥ Popular ingredients in many Southern kitchens bring a taste of the Mediterranean to your table in a healthy way. (page 236)

♥ Healthy holiday fare is no longer a contradiction in terms with these lightened seasonal favorites. (page 284)

♥ Enjoy rich and hearty versions of weeknight-friendly chicken dishes that guarantee wholesome success. (page 308)

Top-Rated Menus

*This popular column showcases award-winning classics
from the* Southern Living *Recipe Hall of Fame.*

■ Charm your sweetheart with a **Valentine's Day Dinner.** A spicy Creole sauce enlivens plump chicken cakes, and fresh basil adds a bright note to Cherry Tomato-Caper Salad. Simple shortbread dotted with raspberry preserves and drizzled with a sweet glaze is a fitting finale. (page 32)

■ Impress your guests with **A Friendly Feast.** Creamy goat cheese mingles with crisp-tender asparagus and roasted beets in a stunning salad, and a robust marinade infuses juicy lamb chops with bold flavors, while Chipotle and Cilantro Oils finish the dish. Creamy Onion Risotto makes a stellar accompaniment for the meaty chops, and a ginger-tinged pound cake ends the meal on a sweet note. (page 96)

■ Showcase our region's cuisine in this **Southern Classics** combo. Tender pork chops stuffed with smoky bacon and fontina cheese are an enticing entrée, and grits get a new attitude when cooled, shaped, and stacked for a striking presentation. A side of sweet creamed corn completes the plate. (page 204)

■ Enjoy an autumn evening with our **Casual Weeknight Supper.** Canned tomato soup gets a boost from fresh basil in creamy Tomato-Basil Bisque, and cashews add crunch to a colorful salad featuring apples and baby spinach tossed in a tangy vinaigrette. The classic BLT acquires an Italian accent when piled high with salami, mortadella, and provolone, and oatmeal cookies sweetened with sorghum will satisfy your sweet tooth. (page 230)

■ Savor the season with a holiday **Feast Without Fuss.** Tender pork loin benefits from a sweet-and-tangy mustard glaze, while carrots are elevated to stately status in a sweet side casserole strewn with pecans and kissed with orange zest. Crisp-tender sugar snap peas tossed with fresh basil and lemon make a fast and colorful accompaniment. (page 282)

■ Pull out all the stops when you celebrate with this **Lasting Impressions Dinner.** Crumbles of Stilton cheese and slices of portobello mushrooms unite in a rich, sumptuous sauce that enhances fork-tender beef tenderloin fillets. Silky Sweet Onion Pudding and an herb-infused potato medley provide the perfect pairing for the elegant entrée. A buttery bakery apple strudel makes an easy and tempting finale to this grand menu. (page 310)

January

Southern Favorites Made Simple

Convenience products let you whip up regional dishes fast. These recipes are as good as their labor-intensive counterparts and take 10 minutes or less of preparation time.

Chicken and dumplings to the table in 35 minutes? *Southern Living* Foods Editors were astonished when they heard the preparation and cooking times for this traditional favorite.

Assistant Foods Editor Kate Nicholson assured them that this and the other recipes featured here deliver authentic Southern flavor in a flash. They make the most of frozen foods and the seasonings you keep in your pantry, resulting in preparation times of 5 to 10 minutes.

Several readers contributed terrific recipes, while Mary Allen Perry of our Test Kitchens rounded out the mix with her twists on regional classics. Take advantage of these timesaving choices, and serve a Southern favorite tonight.

PAN-FRIED PORK CHOPS

MAKES 6 TO 8 SERVINGS

These tasty chops go from pan to plate in under 20 minutes. *(pictured on page 39)*

- ½ cup all-purpose flour
- 1 teaspoon salt
- 1 teaspoon seasoned pepper
- 1½ pounds wafer-thin boneless pork chops
- ¼ cup vegetable oil

COMBINE first 3 ingredients in a shallow dish, and dredge pork chops in flour mixture.

FRY pork chops, in 3 batches, in hot oil in a skillet over medium-high heat 1 minute on each side or until browned. Drain on paper towels. **Prep: 10 min., Cook: 6 min.**

BOBBY LOU ARMSTRONG
NEW ORLEANS, LOUISIANA

SUCCOTASH

MAKES 6 TO 8 SERVINGS

Crispy crumbles of smoky bacon top this down-home dish. *(pictured on page 39)*

- 1 (10-ounce) package frozen petite lima beans
- 1 (16-ounce) package frozen white shoepeg corn
- 2 tablespoons butter or margarine
- 2 tablespoons all-purpose flour
- 1 teaspoon sugar
- ½ teaspoon salt
- ½ teaspoon seasoned pepper
- 1¼ cups milk
- Garnish: cooked and crumbled bacon

COOK lima beans according to package directions; drain.

PULSE corn in a food processor 8 to 10 times or until coarsely chopped.

MELT butter in a large saucepan over medium heat; add flour, stirring until smooth. Cook, stirring constantly, 1 minute; stir in sugar, salt, and seasoned pepper. Gradually add milk, stirring until smooth.

STIR in corn, and cook, stirring often, 12 to 15 minutes or until corn is tender and mixture is thickened. Stir in drained lima beans. Garnish, if desired, and serve immediately. **Prep: 10 min., Cook: 20 min.**

CREAMED CORN: Prepare recipe as directed, omitting lima beans.

QUICK CHICKEN AND DUMPLINGS

MAKES 4 TO 6 SERVINGS

One roasted whole chicken or six skinned and boned cooked chicken breast halves yield about 3 cups chopped meat.

- 4 cups water
- 3 cups chopped cooked chicken
- 2 (10¾-ounce) cans cream of chicken soup, undiluted
- 2 teaspoons chicken bouillon granules
- 1 teaspoon seasoned pepper
- 1 (7.5-ounce) can refrigerated buttermilk biscuits

BRING first 5 ingredients to a boil in a Dutch oven over medium-high heat, stirring often.

SEPARATE biscuits in half, forming 2 rounds; cut each round in half. Drop biscuit pieces, 1 at a time, into boiling mixture; stir gently. Cover, reduce heat to low, and simmer, stirring occasionally, 15 to 20 minutes. **Prep: 10 min., Cook: 25 min.**

TO LIGHTEN: Use reduced-sodium, reduced-fat cream of chicken soup; reduced-fat biscuits; and chopped, cooked chicken breast halves.

JUDITH VEST
BRISTOL, VIRGINIA

MASHED POTATOES WITH TOMATO GRAVY

MAKES 6 TO 8 SERVINGS

These rich, creamy spuds benefit from the herb-infused Tomato Gravy. *(pictured on page 39)*

- 1 (22-ounce) package frozen mashed potatoes
- 2⅓ cups milk
- ½ (8-ounce) package cream cheese, softened
- 1 teaspoon salt
- 1 teaspoon seasoned pepper
- Tomato Gravy

STIR together potatoes and milk in a large bowl. Microwave at HIGH 8 minutes; stir and microwave 5 to 7 more minutes. Let stand 2 minutes.

STIR in cream cheese, salt, and seasoned pepper, stirring until cheese melts and mixture is blended. Serve with Tomato Gravy. **Prep: 5 min., Cook: 15 min., Stand: 2 min.**

TO LIGHTEN: Use fat-free milk and reduced-fat cream cheese.

Tomato Gravy:

MAKES ABOUT 2½ CUPS

- 2 tablespoons butter or margarine
- 2 tablespoons all-purpose flour
- ½ cup chicken broth
- 1 (14½-ounce) can diced tomatoes with basil, oregano, and garlic
- 1 teaspoon sugar
- ½ teaspoon seasoned pepper

MELT butter in a large saucepan over medium heat; add flour, stirring until smooth. Cook, stirring constantly, 1 minute. Add broth, stirring until smooth. Add diced tomatoes, sugar, and pepper, and cook, stirring often, 3 to 5 minutes or until thickened. **Prep: 5 min., Cook: 6 min.**

MARGARET CAMPBELL
FORT WORTH, TEXAS

TURNIP GREENS STEW

MAKES 6 TO 8 SERVINGS

Frozen seasoning blend is a mixture of diced onion, red and green bell peppers, and celery. *(pictured on page 38)*

- 2 cups chopped cooked ham
- 1 tablespoon vegetable oil
- 3 cups chicken broth
- 2 (16-ounce) packages frozen chopped turnip greens
- 1 (16-ounce) package frozen seasoning blend
- 1 teaspoon sugar
- 1 teaspoon seasoned pepper

SAUTÉ ham in hot oil in a Dutch oven over medium-high heat 5 minutes or until lightly browned. Add chicken broth and remaining ingredients; bring greens mixture to a boil. Cover, reduce heat to low, and simmer, stirring occasionally, 25 minutes. **Prep: 5 min., Cook: 30 min.**

NOTE: For testing purposes only, we used McKenzie's Seasoning Blend.

COLLARD STEW: Substitute 1 (16-ounce) package frozen chopped collard greens and 1 (16-ounce) can black-eyed peas, drained, for 2 packages turnip greens, if desired. Prepare recipe as directed, cooking collard greens 15 minutes; add black-eyed peas, and cook 10 more minutes.

BLACKBERRY COBBLER

MAKES 6 TO 8 SERVINGS

Serve Sugared Piecrust Sticks alongside this juicy fruit dessert to delight the cobbler crust fans in your family.

- 1⅓ cups sugar
- ½ cup all-purpose flour
- ½ cup butter or margarine, melted
- 2 teaspoons vanilla extract
- 2 (14-ounce) bags frozen blackberries, unthawed
- ½ (15-ounce) package refrigerated piecrusts
- 1 tablespoon sugar
- Vanilla ice cream (optional)
- Sugared Piecrust Sticks (optional)

STIR together first 4 ingredients in a large bowl. Gently stir in blackberries until sugar mixture is crumbly. Spoon fruit mixture into a lightly greased 11- x 7-inch baking dish.

CUT 1 piecrust into ½-inch-wide strips, and arrange strips diagonally over blackberry mixture. Sprinkle top with 1 tablespoon sugar.

BAKE at 425° for 45 minutes or until crust is golden brown and center is bubbly. If desired, serve with ice cream and Sugared Piecrust Sticks. **Prep: 10 min., Bake: 45 min.**

SUGARED PIECRUST STICKS: Cut 1 refrigerated piecrust into ½-inch-wide strips. Sprinkle strips with 1 tablespoon sugar; place on a lightly greased baking sheet. Bake at 425° for 6 to 8 minutes or until golden brown.

Food, Fun, and Family

Enjoy dinnertime togetherness by getting the whole family involved in preparing the meal.

Family Night

Serves 4 to 6

Vegetable Dip   Sliced fresh vegetables

Rainbow Salad with Dijon Vinaigrette or
Lite Herb Dressing

Healthy Chicken Enchiladas   Black beans   Rice

Fresh fruit   Iced tea

Busy schedules make it difficult to fit in even simple things, such as regular family dinnertime. Long revered in the South as the rule rather than the exception, supper is the ideal time to gather for a nourishing meal and to share the day's experiences. It's also a great opportunity for parents and children to give each other undivided attention. "Interacting as a family in an atmosphere of caring and love can be very dynamic. Food is a manifestation of love, and that can be reflected at the table," says Dr. Rama Pemmaraju Rao, a physician of psychiatric medicine at UAB and Children's Hospitals in Birmingham.

Our advice: Instead of waiting to gather around the table, get the entire crew into the kitchen ahead of time. Involve everyone in the meal's preparation for an enjoyable learning experience and family bonding. Here are some family-friendly recipes that will get you moving in the right direction. See "Wellness Pantry" at right for foods to keep on hand for quick and nutritious meals.

VEGETABLE DIP

MAKES 1½ CUPS

> 1 cup low-fat sour cream
> ½ cup low-fat mayonnaise
> 1 green onion, chopped
> 2 tablespoons chopped pimiento
> 1 tablespoon prepared horseradish
> ½ teaspoon dried parsley
> ½ teaspoon dried dillweed
> ½ teaspoon salt
> ¼ teaspoon celery seeds
> Sliced fresh vegetables

COMBINE first 9 ingredients; cover and chill 8 hours. Serve with sliced fresh vegetables. **Prep: 10 min., Chill: 8 hrs.**

BETTY DUNSIRE
THE VILLAGES, FLORIDA

RAINBOW SALAD

MAKES 10 CUPS

> ½ (10-ounce) package finely shredded cabbage
> ½ head romaine lettuce, chopped
> 2 medium carrots, grated
> 2 celery ribs, chopped
> 2 green onions, chopped
> 1 tomato, chopped
> 1 cucumber, chopped
> ½ red bell pepper, diced
> ½ cup shredded Parmesan cheese
> ½ teaspoon salt
> ⅛ teaspoon pepper
> Dijon Vinaigrette or Lite Herb Dressing

COMBINE first 11 ingredients in a large bowl; cover and chill 1 hour. Toss salad with Dijon Vinaigrette or Lite Herb Dressing before serving. **Prep: 15 min., Chill: 1 hr.**

SHERRIE YARBRO
CLARKSBURG, TENNESSEE

Dijon Vinaigrette:

MAKES 1½ CUPS

> 1 cup olive oil
> ½ cup cider vinegar
> 1 tablespoon Dijon mustard
> 1 teaspoon dried dillweed
> ½ teaspoon salt
> ¼ teaspoon sugar
> ¼ teaspoon pepper

WHISK together all ingredients. Cover and chill until ready to serve. **Prep: 5 min.**

NORA HENSHAW
OKEMAH, OKLAHOMA

Lite Herb Dressing:

MAKES 1¼ CUPS

> 1 cup plain yogurt
> 2 tablespoons fat-free buttermilk
> 1 tablespoon lemon juice
> ¼ teaspoon dried mint
> ¼ teaspoon dried chives
> ¼ teaspoon dried dillweed
> ¼ teaspoon pepper
> ⅛ teaspoon salt

WHISK together all ingredients in a small bowl. Cover and chill until ready to serve. **Prep: 5 min.**

CYNTHIA ENGELHARDT
COLUMBIA, SOUTH CAROLINA

HEALTHY CHICKEN ENCHILADAS

MAKES 4 TO 6 SERVINGS

5 small tomatillos, coarsely chopped
2 plum tomatoes, coarsely
   chopped
½ medium-size yellow onion,
   coarsely chopped
1 (10-ounce) can diced tomatoes and
   green chiles, drained
2 cups (8 ounces) shredded fat-free
   Cheddar cheese, divided
2 cups (8 ounces) shredded fat-free
   mozzarella cheese, divided
2 (8-ounce) packages fat-free cream
   cheese, softened
2 jalapeño peppers, seeded and
   chopped
½ cup chopped fresh cilantro
½ cup low-sodium chicken broth
2 cups chopped cooked chicken
10 (7-inch) flour tortillas

PROCESS first 4 ingredients in a food processor or blender, stopping to scrape down sides. Set aside tomato sauce.
STIR together half of Cheddar, half of mozzarella, cream cheese, and next 3 ingredients. Stir in chopped chicken. Spoon mixture evenly onto 1 side of each tortilla; roll up, and place seam side down in an 11- x 7-inch baking dish. Sprinkle with remaining cheeses; top with tomato sauce.
BAKE at 350° for 35 minutes. Serve with black beans and rice. **Prep: 15 min., Bake: 35 min.**

NOTE: If you don't have time to spare for the prep work, you can easily make this dish ahead. Cover and chill enchiladas up to 8 hours before baking, if desired. To serve, uncover and bake at 350° for 40 to 45 minutes or until thoroughly heated.

ERIS MOUTON
HOUSTON, TEXAS

Wellness Pantry

Keep these foods on hand for quick and healthy meals.

Canned Salmon and Water-packed Tuna: Think beyond salmon croquettes and mayo-loaded tuna sandwiches. Canned tuna and salmon are packed with flavor and nutrients and may be stored in your pantry for about a year. Either fish may be sprinkled over a green salad for a tasty one-dish meal.

Couscous: Talk about quick. This teeny-weeny pasta is ready in about 5 minutes. Plain or flavored couscous makes a great rice or potato alternative. It's low in fat and an excellent source of carbo-hydrates. Cook as directed; then stir in chopped onion, mush-rooms, and roasted peppers for a healthy and delicious side dish. Add chopped cooked chicken or tofu, and you've got dinner.

Canned Beans: Combine a variety of beans, such as navy, kidney, and black, for the basis of a quick meatless chili. Create bean salads in minutes with just a few extra pantry staples, such as salsa and corn. Mash pinto or black beans for burritos, and add your favorite toppings. Beans are also a great source of protein and iron.

Pasta Sauces: Years ago there were two types of pasta sauce—with or without meat. Nowadays you can get jazzed-up varieties with dried tomatoes or multi-cheese medleys. Pair a flavorful sauce with pasta, and you'll have dinner ready in 15 minutes; or spoon sauce over a baked (or microwaved) potato, and sprinkle with part-skim mozzarella for a hearty spud.

Great Grill

In the South, even cold weather works for grilling if you choose quick-cooking meats like flavorful flank steak.

GRILLED FLANK STEAK WITH HORSERADISH SAUCE

MAKES 6 SERVINGS

1 (2-pound) flank steak
Basic Marinade
6 cups gourmet salad greens
Horseradish Sauce

PLACE steak in a heavy-duty zip-top plastic bag; add marinade. Seal bag; chill 8 hours, turning occasionally. Remove steak from marinade, discarding marinade.
GRILL, covered with grill lid, over medium-high heat (350° to 400°) 8 to 10 minutes on each side or to desired degree of doneness. Cut diagonally across the grain into thin strips. Serve over greens with sauce. **Prep: 15 min., Chill: 8 hrs., Grill: 20 min.**

Basic Marinade:

MAKES 1½ CUPS

1 small onion, diced
3 garlic cloves, minced
½ cup olive oil
¼ cup white wine vinegar or lemon
   juice
2 tablespoons Worcestershire sauce
2 teaspoons sugar
1 teaspoon salt
1 teaspoon pepper

STIR together all ingredients. **Prep: 5 min.**

Horseradish Sauce:

MAKES 1½ CUPS

1 (8-ounce) container sour cream
3 to 4 tablespoons prepared
   horseradish
2 tablespoons white wine vinegar
1 tablespoon mayonnaise
1 tablespoon chopped fresh parsley
½ teaspoon salt
⅛ teaspoon pepper

STIR together all ingredients. **Prep: 5 min.**

A Trio of Chili Colors

No matter how you like this comforting all-in-one meal, we have a recipe for you.

What's your chili choice? Whether you're a fan of black beans, red beans, or white beans, we have your preference covered. Beef or chicken? We've taken care of that, too. Don't fret over the long lists of ingredients—these recipes are easy to prepare and freeze splendidly. So go ahead and take your pick.

WHITE BEAN CHILI

MAKES 4 QUARTS

- 1 medium onion, chopped
- 1 tablespoon olive oil
- 2 garlic cloves, minced
- 8 skinned and boned chicken breast halves, cut into bite-size pieces
- 3 cups water
- 1 teaspoon salt
- 2 teaspoons ground cumin
- 1 teaspoon chili powder
- 1 teaspoon pepper
- 1 teaspoon dried oregano
- 4 (15-ounce) cans cannellini or great Northern beans, rinsed, drained, and divided
- 1 (14½-ounce) can chicken broth
- 1 (16-ounce) package frozen shoepeg white corn
- 2 (4.5-ounce) cans chopped green chiles
- 3 tablespoons lime juice
- Garnish: fresh cilantro sprigs

SAUTÉ chopped onion in hot oil in a large Dutch oven over medium-high heat 7 minutes; add garlic, and sauté 2 to 3 minutes.

STIR in chicken pieces, and cook, stirring constantly, until chicken is lightly browned. Stir in 3 cups water and next 5 ingredients; reduce heat, and simmer, stirring often, 10 minutes or until chicken is done.

PLACE 2 cans of beans in a blender; add broth, and process until smooth, stopping to scrape down sides.

STIR bean puree, remaining 2 cans of beans, corn, and chiles into chicken mixture in Dutch oven; bring to a boil over medium-high heat. Reduce heat, and simmer, stirring often, 30 minutes or until thoroughly heated. Stir in lime juice just before serving. Garnish, if desired. **Prep: 25 min., Cook: 1 hr.**

NOTE: Use a handheld submersion blender to puree the beans and broth, if desired.

HARRIET CARROLL
DALLAS, TEXAS

RED BEAN CHILI

MAKES 8 CUPS

Reader Denise Parisher's dad dislikes tomatoes, so she and her mother developed this recipe using tomato juice and soup instead. Serve this hearty classic with cornbread or crackers.

- 2 pounds lean ground beef
- 1 large onion, chopped
- 2 (15-ounce) cans light red kidney beans
- 1 (12-ounce) can tomato juice
- 1 (10¾-ounce) can tomato soup
- 2 tablespoons chili powder
- 1 teaspoon salt
- 1 teaspoon pepper
- Garnish: chopped onion

COOK beef and onion in a large Dutch oven over medium-high heat 10 to 12 minutes, stirring until beef crumbles and is no longer pink. Drain and return beef mixture to Dutch oven.

STIR kidney beans and next 5 ingredients into beef mixture; reduce heat, and simmer, stirring occasionally, 1 hour. Garnish, if desired. **Prep: 10 min.; Cook: 1 hr., 12 min.**

SLOW-COOKER RED BEAN CHILI: Cook ground beef and onion according to recipe directions; drain and place in a 4½-quart slow cooker. Add beans and next 5 ingredients. Cover and cook at HIGH 5 hours. Garnish, if desired. **Prep: 15 min.; Cook : 5 hrs., 12 min.**

DENISE J. PARISHER
HOUSTON, TEXAS

BLACK BEAN CHILI

MAKES 12 CUPS

- 1 pound boneless top sirloin steak, cut into 1-inch cubes
- 2 onions, chopped
- 1 medium-size green bell pepper, chopped
- 1 jalapeño pepper, seeded and chopped
- 3 to 4 garlic cloves, minced
- 1½ teaspoons salt, divided
- 3 tablespoons olive oil
- 1 (28-ounce) can crushed tomatoes
- 1 (12-ounce) bottle dark beer
- 2 tablespoons chili powder
- 1 tablespoon ground cumin
- 2 teaspoons dried oregano
- 1½ teaspoons ground black pepper
- 1 teaspoon sugar
- ¼ teaspoon ground red pepper
- 2 cups beef broth
- 3 (15-ounce) cans black beans, rinsed and drained
- Garnish: shredded Cheddar cheese

COOK first 5 ingredients and ½ teaspoon salt in hot oil in a large Dutch oven over medium-high heat, stirring constantly, 8 minutes or until beef browns and vegetables are tender.

STIR in remaining 1 teaspoon salt, crushed tomatoes, ½ cup beer, and next 6 ingredients, and simmer, stirring occasionally, 30 minutes. Stir in remaining 1 cup beer, broth, and beans, and simmer, stirring occasionally, 45 minutes or until thoroughly heated. Garnish, if desired. **Prep: 25 min.; Cook: 1 hr., 30 min.**

MARY ELLEN BUTLER
TYBEE ISLAND, GEORGIA

Sweet Potato Tartlets

Julyette Marshall of Houston is a woman of many talents. Besides being an avid gardener, she is also a business-woman with a distinguished history of community service. The multifaceted former fashion model also loves to cook. Here she shares an African-flavored recipe with us.

ZAMAANI'S NUTTY YAM TARTLETS

MAKES 4 DOZEN

This recipe makes a generous number, but the tartlets freeze beautifully, allowing you to keep some on hand.

> 2 pounds sweet potatoes
> ¼ cup butter or margarine
> 3 large eggs, lightly beaten
> 1 cup chopped pecans, toasted
> ½ cup sugar
> ½ cup firmly packed dark brown sugar
> ⅓ cup coconut milk
> ¼ cup sweetened flaked coconut
> ¼ cup honey
> 1 teaspoon light or dark rum
> ¼ teaspoon ground nutmeg
> ¼ teaspoon ground allspice
> ¼ teaspoon ground cinnamon
> ¼ teaspoon vanilla extract
> 4 (10-ounce) packages frozen tart shells*
> Whipped cream

COOK potatoes in boiling water to cover in a Dutch oven 1 hour or until tender; drain. Peel potatoes, and discard skins.

MASH potatoes with a potato masher. Stir in butter until melted. Stir in eggs and next 11 ingredients, blending well. Spoon about 2 tablespoons mixture into each tart shell.

BAKE at 350° for 45 minutes or until set. Store in an airtight container in freezer, if desired. Serve tartlets with whipped cream. **Prep: 15 min., Cook: 1 hr., Bake: 45 min.**

*Substitute 2 unbaked 9-inch pastry shells, if desired. Spoon potato mixture evenly into pastry shells; bake as directed.

Sweet and Simple Quick Breads

These oven-fresh recipes make great snacks or welcoming gifts.

BLUEBERRY-ORANGE BREAD

MAKES 1 LOAF

> 1 cup bran cereal, crushed
> ¾ cup water
> 1 tablespoon grated orange rind
> ¼ cup fresh orange juice
> ½ teaspoon vanilla extract
> 2 cups all-purpose flour
> 1 cup sugar
> 1½ teaspoons baking powder
> ½ teaspoon baking soda
> ½ teaspoon salt
> 1 large egg
> 2 tablespoons vegetable oil
> 1 cup frozen blueberries, thawed

STIR together first 5 ingredients in a large bowl; let stand 10 minutes or until cereal softens.

STIR in flour and next 6 ingredients just until dry ingredients are moistened. Gently fold in blueberries. Pour batter into a greased 9- x 5-inch loafpan.

BAKE at 350° for 1 hour or until a long wooden pick inserted in center comes out clean. Cool on a wire rack 10 to 15 minutes; remove from pan, and cool completely on wire rack. **Prep: 20 min., Bake: 1 hr., Cool: 15 min.**

JUDY CARTER
WINCHESTER, TENNESSEE

TIPSY PEACH BREAD

MAKES 1 LOAF

> 1 (16-ounce) package frozen sliced peaches, thawed
> ½ cup dark rum
> 1¾ cups all-purpose flour
> 1 cup sugar
> 1 teaspoon baking powder
> 1 teaspoon baking soda
> ½ teaspoon salt
> ½ teaspoon ground cinnamon
> ¼ teaspoon ground allspice
> ⅛ teaspoon ground cloves
> 1 large egg, lightly beaten
> 3 tablespoons butter, melted
> 1 teaspoon vanilla extract
> ¾ cup chopped almonds

COOK thawed peaches and rum in a saucepan over medium-high heat, stirring often, 15 minutes or until peaches are tender.

PROCESS peach mixture in a blender until smooth.

COMBINE flour and next 7 ingredients in a large bowl. Stir in peach puree, egg, melted butter, and vanilla; blend well. Stir in almonds. Pour into a greased and floured 8½- x 4½-inch loafpan.

BAKE at 350° for 30 minutes. Cover with aluminum foil, if necessary, to avoid excessive browning, and bake 15 more minutes or until a long wooden pick inserted in center comes out clean. Cool on a wire rack 10 to 15 minutes; remove from pan, and cool completely on wire rack. **Prep: 30 min., Bake: 45 min., Cool: 15 min.**

JOSEPHINE N. JONES
CHARLESTON, SOUTH CAROLINA

Twist of Citrus

These fresh recipes are sure to chase away the winter blues.

Fragrant citrus lends amazing flavor and aroma to breads, beverages, marinades, pasta salads, frostings, and even soups. It's also packed with such antioxidants as vitamin C and folic acid, as well as potassium and fiber, all of which may help prevent cancer and heart disease. The peak season for citrus runs from January through June, making now just the right time to enjoy these great-tasting and satisfying dishes.

WINTER FRUIT CUP

MAKES 6 SERVINGS

2 Red Delicious apples, chopped
4 grapefruit, peeled and sectioned
3 oranges, peeled and sectioned
½ cup firmly packed brown sugar, divided
1 tablespoon butter or margarine
½ cup nonfat sour cream
½ teaspoon vanilla extract

COMBINE fruit and ¼ cup brown sugar, tossing to coat. Cover and chill 8 hours, stirring occasionally.
MELT butter in a saucepan over medium heat; add remaining ¼ cup brown sugar, and cook, stirring constantly, until sugar dissolves and mixture is bubbly. Remove from heat; gradually stir in sour cream and vanilla. Serve with fruit mixture. **Prep: 25 min., Chill: 8 hrs.**

SUSAN COOK
BROWNSBURG, INDIANA

Per serving: Calories 246 (9% from fat); Fat 2.4g (sat 1.4g, mono 0.6g, poly 0.1g); Protein 3g; Carb 58g; Fiber 11g; Chol 7mg; Iron 0.5mg; Sodium 24mg; Calc 104mg

LIME-POTATO SALAD

MAKES ABOUT 8 CUPS

The piquant dressing imparts a slightly spicy Southwestern flavor.

3 pounds small red potatoes, cut into ¾-inch cubes
Vegetable cooking spray
2 teaspoons salt
½ cup plain nonfat yogurt
¼ cup reduced-fat mayonnaise
1 (4.5-ounce) can chopped green chiles
3 tablespoons chopped fresh cilantro
2 teaspoons sugar
2 teaspoons grated lime rind
¼ cup fresh lime juice
¾ teaspoon ground cumin
¼ teaspoon ground red pepper
½ small purple onion, minced

PLACE potato on an aluminum foil-lined baking sheet. Coat potato with cooking spray; sprinkle with salt.
BAKE at 450° for 40 minutes or until tender. Let cool 15 minutes.
STIR together yogurt and next 8 ingredients; reserve half of dressing.
COMBINE potato and onion in a large bowl; add remaining dressing, tossing gently to coat. Cover and chill 2 hours. Toss with reserved dressing just before serving. **Prep: 25 min., Bake: 40 min., Chill: 2 hrs.**

Per 1 cup: Calories 232 (11% from fat); Fat 2.9g (sat 0.5g, mono 0g, poly 0.1g); Protein 5g; Carb 48g; Fiber 4.8g; Chol 3mg; Iron 2.5mg; Sodium 726mg; Calc 74mg

LIME-ORANGE CATFISH

MAKES 6 SERVINGS

Grilled or broiled, this entrée is loaded with tangy flavor.

¼ cup fresh lime juice
⅓ cup orange juice
2 teaspoons sugar
1 garlic clove, pressed
¼ teaspoon salt
½ teaspoon dry mustard
½ teaspoon paprika
¼ teaspoon pepper
2 tablespoons olive oil
6 (4-ounce) catfish fillets
Vegetable cooking spray
Garnishes: lime and orange slices, fresh parsley sprigs

WHISK together first 8 ingredients; gradually whisk in olive oil until well blended. Remove half of marinade, and set aside.
PLACE catfish in a shallow dish or heavy-duty zip-top plastic bag; pour remaining marinade over catfish. Cover or seal bag, and chill 15 minutes, turning catfish once.
REMOVE catfish from marinade, discarding marinade.
COAT grill rack with cooking spray; place on grill over medium-high heat (350° to 400°). Place catfish on rack, and grill 5 minutes on each side or until done. Remove to a serving platter; drizzle with reserved marinade. Garnish, if desired. **Prep: 15 min., Chill: 15 min., Grill: 10 min.**

Per serving: Calories 183 (54% from fat)*; Fat 11g (sat 2.3g, mono 5.8g, poly 2g); Protein 18g; Carb 2g; Fiber 0g; Chol 53mg; Iron 0.7mg; Sodium 109mg; Calc 13mg

NOTE: To broil catfish, follow recipe up to removing fish from marinade. Place fish on a rack coated with cooking spray; place rack in a broiler pan. Broil, 3 inches from heat, 7 to 8 minutes or until golden brown. Remove to a serving platter; drizzle with reserved marinade. Garnish, if desired.

*Most of the fat calories come from omega-3 fatty acids (in catfish) and monounsaturated fat (in olive oil), both of which are associated with lowering LDL (bad) cholesterol and increasing HDL (good) cholesterol.

APRICOT CHICKEN WITH ROASTED POTATO THINS

MAKES 4 SERVINGS

  4 skinned and boned chicken breast
    halves
  ¼ teaspoon salt
  1 (16-ounce) can apricot halves,
    undrained
  ½ cup orange juice
  2 tablespoons lite soy sauce
  1 garlic clove, minced
  1 teaspoon dark sesame oil
  ¾ cup all-purpose flour
  ¼ to ½ teaspoon ground red pepper
  2 teaspoons vegetable oil
  6 green onions, thinly sliced
  ¼ cup chopped fresh cilantro
    Roasted Potato Thins

PLACE chicken between 2 sheets of plastic wrap. Flatten to ½-inch thickness, using a meat mallet or rolling pin. Sprinkle with salt.

DRAIN apricots, reserving liquid. Coarsely chop apricots.

STIR together reserved liquid, apricots, orange juice, and next 3 ingredients.

COMBINE flour and pepper; dredge chicken in flour mixture.

COOK chicken in hot vegetable oil in a large skillet over medium-high heat 3 minutes on each side. Reduce heat to medium; stir in apricot mixture. Cook 3 to 5 minutes. Add onions, and cook 1 minute. Sprinkle with cilantro. Serve with Roasted Potato Thins. **Prep: 15 min., Cook: 12 min.**

Per serving, including Roasted Potato Thins: Calories 368 (28% from fat); Fat 11.4g (sat 2.5g, mono 4.9g, poly 2.9g); Protein 33g; Carb 33g; Fiber 3.2g; Chol 82mg; Iron 2.8mg; Sodium 490mg; Calc 55mg

Roasted Potato Thins:

MAKES 4 SERVINGS

  1 large unpeeled baking potato
    Vegetable cooking spray
  ¼ teaspoon salt

CUT potato into thin slices; arrange on an aluminum foil-lined pan coated with cooking spray. Lightly coat potato slices with cooking spray. Sprinkle with salt. Bake at 400° for 30 minutes or until golden brown. **Prep: 5 min., Bake: 30 min.**

Per serving: Calories 65 (17% from fat); Fat 1.2g (sat 0.1g, mono 0.7g, poly 0.4g); Protein 1g; Carb 13g; Fiber 1.2g; Chol 0mg; Iron 0.7mg; Sodium 149mg; Calc 5mg

Healthy Lifestyle Changes

Use these strategies for starting—and keeping—a healthy lifestyle.

■ First, make health, not appearance, your weight management priority. A healthy weight may not be your "ideal" weight, but it will be easier to maintain.

■ Losing weight boils down to simple math: You need to eat fewer calories than you burn. If you overeat or underexercise, you'll either maintain or gain weight. So here are your choices: Eat less, exercise more, or even better—both.

■ Be specific in your goals. Don't say, "I'm going to eat fewer fatty foods." Instead, plan to eat a grilled chicken sandwich and salad with vinaigrette instead of a fried chicken sandwich and curly fries. Say "I'll walk Fido 30 minutes on Tuesdays, Thursdays, and Saturdays," as opposed to "I'm going to be more physically active."

■ Be realistic with your self-talk. Skip absolutes such as "always," "never," and "should." This will only sabotage your efforts. Instead, expect to be successful by using positive self-talk for every step you've taken towards your goal. If you get in only a 10-minute walk today, that's great. Tomorrow you might be able to walk 15 minutes and perhaps 25 the next day.

■ Serve yourself half of your normal portion size, and keep serving dishes in the kitchen. You'll be less likely to go back for seconds.

■ Don't prepare different foods for other family members. Your spouse and kids need the veggies, grains, and beans, too. Teach your kids healthy eating and exercise habits early.

■ Remember that many activities count as exercise. Gardening, raking leaves, doing household chores, and dancing in the living room are all forms of exercise.

■ Sit down to eat. Respect yourself enough to take the time to enjoy your meals. Food is never as satisfying standing or doing other chores as it is when you give a meal your undivided attention. To learn more terrific exercises on self-respect and mindful living, read *Taming Your Gremlins: A Guide to Enjoying Yourself,* by Richard David Carson or *When You Eat at the Refrigerator, Pull Up a Chair,* by Geneen Roth. Both books can be ordered at **www.barnesandnoble.com**

■ Figure out your eating triggers. If something triggers your urge to eat, even when you're not hungry, find out why. Learn to differentiate between physical hunger and other emotionally driven hungers. Keeping a journal will help you notice patterns. Try trigger busters such as walking your dog, planting flowers, or renting a movie.

■ For other reliable nutrition- and exercise-related Web sites, log onto the American Dietetic Association at **www.eatright.org,** the American Council on Exercise at **www.acefitness.org,** or Shape Up America at **www.shapeup.org**

Speedy Salads

Liven up your weeknight meals with these easy salads.

People often say that the most difficult part of planning a menu is selecting the side dishes. This time of year, many vegetables are not at their peak, so salads are a great choice. These recipes are versatile and easy to make. Serve Quick Greek Salad with grilled fish and pasta, or Ramen Noodle Salad with fresh fruit for a fast weeknight supper. Classic Broccoli-Raisin Salad makes an ideal side for brunch, lunch, or dinner.

CLASSIC BROCCOLI-RAISIN SALAD

MAKES 6 SERVINGS

You've probably seen many versions of this old standby. It's so good, we're trying it again. The recipe easily doubles to serve 12.

- 1 medium-size purple onion
- 1 (16-ounce) package fresh broccoli florets
- 1 (3.75-ounce) package sunflower kernels
- 1 cup golden raisins
- 1 cup mayonnaise
- 4 bacon slices, cooked and crumbled
- 3 tablespoons red wine vinegar

CUT onion into thin slices; cut onion slices in half.

STIR together onion and remaining ingredients. Chill at least 2 hours. **Prep: 10 min., Chill: 2 hrs.**

NOTE: For a lighter version, substitute turkey bacon and low-fat mayonnaise.

CHARLENE PITTS PADGETT
PACE, FLORIDA

QUICK GREEK SALAD

MAKES 4 TO 6 SERVINGS

Balsamic vinegar, fresh oregano, and artichoke marinade create the zesty dressing for this colorful salad.

- 8 plum tomatoes
- 1 medium cucumber
- 1 large green bell pepper
- 1 small onion
- 1 (12-ounce) jar marinated artichoke heart quarters
- 3 tablespoons lemon juice
- 1 tablespoon balsamic vinegar
- 1 teaspoon chopped fresh oregano
- ½ teaspoon salt
- ½ teaspoon coarsely ground pepper
- 1 teaspoon sugar (optional)
- 1 head Green Leaf lettuce, torn
- 8 to 10 pitted ripe olives
- ¼ cup crumbled feta cheese
- Pita wedges (optional)

CUT tomatoes into wedges, and seed. Cut cucumber into thin slices; cut bell pepper into thin strips. Cut onion into slices, and separate into rings.

DRAIN artichoke hearts, reserving ¼ cup marinade.

WHISK together reserved artichoke marinade, next 5 ingredients, and, if desired, sugar in a large bowl. Add cut vegetables, artichokes, lettuce, and olives, tossing to coat. Cover and chill at least 30 minutes. Sprinkle with feta cheese just before serving. Serve with pita wedges, if desired. **Prep: 10 min., Chill: 30 min.**

PATSY BELL HOBSON
LIBERTY, MISSOURI

RAMEN NOODLE SALAD

MAKES 8 TO 10 SERVINGS

- 1 (3-ounce) package ramen noodle soup mix
- ¼ cup butter or margarine
- 1 cup walnuts or pecans, chopped
- 1 (16-ounce) package fresh broccoli florets
- 1 head romaine lettuce, torn
- 4 green onions, chopped
- Sweet-and-Sour Dressing

REMOVE seasoning packet from ramen noodles, and reserve for another use. Break noodles into pieces.

MELT butter in a large skillet over medium-high heat; add ramen noodles and walnuts, and sauté until lightly browned. Drain on paper towels.

TOSS together noodle mixture, broccoli, lettuce, and green onions in a large bowl; add ¼ cup Sweet-and-Sour Dressing, tossing to coat. Serve with remaining dressing. **Prep: 30 min.**

Sweet-and-Sour Dressing:

MAKES 1 CUP

- ½ cup vegetable oil
- ¼ cup sugar
- ¼ cup red wine vinegar
- 1 tablespoon soy sauce
- ½ teaspoon salt
- ¼ teaspoon pepper

WHISK together all ingredients. **Prep: 5 min.**

JOY KLOESS
BIRMINGHAM, ALABAMA

Marvelous Meatballs

Your family's favorite meal just got easier.

Spaghetti and Meatballs Dinner
Serves 6 to 8

Country-Style Spaghetti   Baked Meatballs
Tossed green salad   Vinaigrette Salad Dressing
Buttery Garlic Bread

Try these shortcuts for good old-fashioned spaghetti and meatballs. Make and freeze Baked Meatballs, or buy frozen ones. Serve them with a bottled sauce or in our Country-Style Spaghetti. If you're lucky enough to have leftovers, freeze them in single servings for delicious, quick meals on-the-run.

COUNTRY-STYLE SPAGHETTI

MAKES 6 TO 8 SERVINGS

2 (28-ounce) cans diced tomatoes
1 (6-ounce) can tomato paste
1 cup water
1 teaspoon dried basil
1½ teaspoons salt
¼ teaspoon black pepper
⅛ teaspoon dried oregano
⅛ teaspoon ground red pepper
3 dozen frozen, cooked Italian-style meatballs, thawed
16 ounces spaghetti, cooked

STIR together first 8 ingredients in a large saucepan over medium-high heat. Reduce heat, and simmer, stirring occasionally, 40 minutes. Add meatballs; simmer 20 minutes. Serve over pasta. **Prep: 10 min., Cook: 1 hr.**

SUZAN L. WIENER
SPRING HILL, FLORIDA

BAKED MEATBALLS

MAKES 4 DOZEN

1½ pounds ground beef
1 large egg, lightly beaten
¾ cup uncooked quick-cooking oats
¾ cup milk
1 teaspoon salt
1 teaspoon Italian seasoning
¼ teaspoon pepper
3 tablespoons all-purpose flour
1½ teaspoons paprika
½ teaspoon salt

COMBINE first 7 ingredients; shape into 1-inch balls. Combine flour, paprika, and salt. Gently roll meatballs in flour mixture, and place on a lightly greased rack in a foil-lined 13- x 9-inch pan.

BAKE at 400° for 25 to 30 minutes. Drain on paper towels. Serve with your favorite sauce. **Prep: 20 min., Bake: 30 min.**

NOTE: To freeze, cool completely, and seal in an airtight container. To serve, place in a single layer on a baking sheet; bake at 400° for 10 to 15 minutes.

JANICE M. FRANCE
DEPAUW, INDIANA

VINAIGRETTE SALAD DRESSING

MAKES 1½ CUPS

½ cup apple cider vinegar
3 tablespoons chopped onion
2½ tablespoons sugar
1 large garlic clove
1 teaspoon salt
1 teaspoon dry mustard
½ teaspoon pepper
1 cup vegetable oil

PROCESS first 7 ingredients in a blender until smooth. With blender running, add oil in a slow, steady stream; process until smooth. Cover and chill. **Prep: 5 min.**

PAT CAMPBELL
TEMPLE, TEXAS

BUTTERY GARLIC BREAD

MAKES 8 SLICES

½ cup butter or margarine
4 garlic cloves, pressed
½ teaspoon salt
1 (16-ounce) Italian bread loaf
1½ teaspoons Italian seasoning
¼ cup freshly grated Parmesan cheese

MELT butter in a skillet over medium-high heat; add garlic and salt, and sauté 2 minutes. Cut bread into 1½-inch slices, and dip into butter mixture, coating both sides. Place on a baking sheet.
STIR together Italian seasoning and Parmesan cheese; sprinkle on 1 side of each bread slice. Broil 5 inches from heat 4 minutes or until cheese melts. **Prep: 15 min., Broil: 4 min.**

JANE LEAHY
TANEYTOWN, MARYLAND

Macaroni and Cheese

Serve up some comfort with this favorite dish.

There are rigorous standards for the perfect macaroni and cheese—just ask the *Southern Living* Foods staff. Whether the macaroni is bathed in cheesy sauce or layered with cheese, topped with eggs and milk, then baked (custard style), this dish's sturdy simplicity offers a happy reminder that no matter how rough the day has been, there is comfort to be found. The custard vs. creamy debate raged at the tasting table for days, with advocates on both sides advancing their causes.

Here are some of the other dividing lines: Bake it in a deep bowl or a shallow dish? Stir in a sleeve of crumbled saltines to help give it body or not? Cheddar cheese, Velveeta, or a combination of Cheddar and American? (They concluded that good-quality sharp and extra-sharp Cheddar give the best results to both creamy and custard-style versions.) Finally, they considered whether to put the cheese on top at the last minute or bake it the whole time to make it crusty.

The cook's style and skill, though, are the most important factors. Custard versions can be dry without enough cheese or milk-and-egg mixture, or if they're overbaked. Other cooks take a more-is-better approach, loading their recipes with extra cheese and butter, producing an oil slick of a sauce. *Southern Living* Foods Editors don't mention in polite company those folks who include such foreign ingredients as mushrooms, fresh herbs, or pimiento. (Well, okay. They might allow a little pimiento.)

In the end, your mac 'n' cheese preference bakes down to what you grew up with. All the discussion and research in the world won't change the fact that your mama's recipe is the best—at least in your eyes. With that in mind, here are two stellar examples: one custard style, the other creamy. Go ahead and serve them to your mama—she'll be impressed.

BAKED MACARONI AND CHEESE

MAKES 8 TO 10 SERVINGS

The eggs and milk form a custard base in this version. Crackers thicken it.

- 1 (8-ounce) package large elbow macaroni, cooked
- 16 saltine crackers, finely crushed
- 1 teaspoon salt
- 1 teaspoon seasoned pepper
- 1 (10-ounce) block sharp Cheddar cheese, shredded
- 1 (10-ounce) block extra-sharp Cheddar cheese, shredded
- 6 large eggs, lightly beaten
- 4 cups milk

LAYER one-third each of macaroni, crackers, salt, pepper, and cheeses into a lightly greased 13- x 9-inch baking dish. Repeat layers twice.

WHISK together eggs and milk; pour over pasta mixture.

BAKE at 350° for 55 to 60 minutes or until golden and set. Let stand 10 minutes before serving. **Prep: 20 min., Bake: 1 hr., Stand: 10 min.**

NOTE: For testing purposes only, we used Kraft Cracker Barrel cheeses.

CREAMY MACARONI AND CHEESE

MAKES 6 TO 8 SERVINGS

- ½ cup butter or margarine
- ½ cup all-purpose flour
- ½ teaspoon salt
- ½ teaspoon ground black pepper
- ¼ teaspoon ground red pepper
- ¼ teaspoon granulated garlic
- 2 cups half-and-half
- 2 cups milk
- 2 (10-ounce) blocks sharp Cheddar cheese, shredded and divided
- 1 (10-ounce) block extra-sharp Cheddar cheese, shredded
- 1 (16-ounce) package elbow macaroni, cooked

MELT butter in a large skillet over medium-high heat. Gradually whisk in flour until smooth; cook, whisking constantly, 2 minutes. Stir in salt and next 3 ingredients. Gradually whisk in half-and-half and milk; cook, whisking constantly, 8 to 10 minutes or until thickened.

STIR in half of sharp Cheddar cheese. Stir in extra-sharp Cheddar cheese until smooth. Remove from heat.

COMBINE macaroni and cheese mixture, and pour into a lightly greased 13- x 9-inch baking dish. Sprinkle with remaining sharp Cheddar cheese.

BAKE at 350° for 20 minutes (bake 15 minutes longer for a crusty top). **Prep: 35 min., Bake: 35 min.**

NOTE: For testing purposes only, we used Kraft Cracker Barrel cheeses.

Warm Biscuits and Sweet Marmalade

Start your own weekend breakfast tradition with these mouthwatering classics.

Concentrate really hard and you just might be able to smell the buttery, flaky biscuits pictured on page 37. The only way you could possibly improve on these pillowlike treats is to split them and spread them with a heaping spoonful of sweet orange marmalade.

Our Foods staff preferred the whipping cream version, but if you like a slightly tangy biscuit, substitute buttermilk mixed with a little sugar for the cream. Either way, they'll fly off the plate.

QUICK WHIPPING CREAM BISCUITS

MAKES 1 DOZEN

These rich, buttery biscuits can be on the table in 25 minutes. *(pictured on page 37)*

> ½ cup butter or margarine
> 2 cups self-rising flour
> ¾ to 1 cup whipping cream*
> ¼ cup butter or margarine, melted

CUT ½ cup butter into flour with a pastry blender or fork until crumbly. Add whipping cream, stirring just until dry ingredients are moistened.
TURN dough out onto a lightly floured surface, and knead lightly 3 or 4 times. Roll or pat dough to ¾-inch thickness. Cut with a 2-inch round cutter; place biscuits on a lightly greased baking sheet.

BAKE at 400° for 13 to 15 minutes. Brush biscuits with ¼ cup melted butter. **Prep: 10 min., Bake: 15 min.**

*Substitute ¾ cup buttermilk and 1 tablespoon granulated sugar, stirred together, for whipping cream, if desired.

SUNNY ORANGE MARMALADE

MAKES 5 PINTS

This recipe is a little time-consuming, but it's well worth the wait. See our "Breakfast Primer" (at right) for shortcuts. *(pictured on page 37)*

> 12 oranges (about 6 pounds)
> 2 lemons
> 4 cups water
> 9 cups sugar

PEEL oranges, and cut rind into thin strips. Chop pulp, discarding seeds. Cut lemons into thin slices, discarding seeds.
COMBINE orange rind, chopped pulp, lemon slices, and 4 cups water in a large Dutch oven; bring to a boil. Reduce heat, and simmer 15 minutes. Remove from heat; cover and chill 8 hours or overnight.
COMBINE fruit mixture and sugar in a Dutch oven; bring to a boil. Reduce heat, and simmer, stirring occasionally, 1½ hours or until a candy thermometer registers 215°.
PACK hot marmalade into hot, sterilized jars, filling to ¼ inch from top; wipe jar rims. Cover at once with metal lids, and screw on bands.
PROCESS in boiling water bath 5 minutes. **Prep: 45 min.; Chill: 8 hrs.; Cook: 1 hr., 45 min.; Process: 5 min.**

Breakfast Primer

■ Jan Moon of our Test Kitchens shared a helpful tip for a quicker marmalade: To save some prep time, she cut unpeeled oranges into quarters, then removed and discarded the seeds. She pulsed the oranges in a food processor until they were coarsely chopped and proceeded with the recipe.

■ Do not substitute all-purpose flour for self-rising in this biscuit recipe.

■ Stir dough just until dry ingredients are moistened.

■ If you're intimidated by rolling pins, simply pat the biscuit dough onto a floured surface to about ¾-inch thickness before cutting.

■ Dip your biscuit cutter into flour; this keeps the dough from sticking.

from our kitchen

In the Freezer

Whether you use a freezer to take advantage of economical bulk buys or to keep leftovers for quick meals, proper storage is very important. Foods Editor Andria Scott Hurst's favorite piece of kitchen equipment is Tilia's FoodSaver® (right). This vacuum-packaging appliance seals food airtight, preventing freezer burn. The sealed packages take up less room, so you can store more in a small space. Several models and sizes are available ranging from about $100 to $320. You'll find FoodSaver in department stores, kitchen shops, and Wal-Mart or at the company's Web site, **tilia.com**

If you freeze foods in plastic containers, make sure they're specifically designed for that purpose. Plastic storage containers won't protect foods from freezer burn, and they often crack or split when frozen. Be sure to select the right-size containers for the amounts of food you're freezing so there's as little air inside as possible. Two advantages of using containers: They stack well for neat storage, and they're reusable.

Sweet News

Because almond toffee bits (formerly called almond brickle chips) sometimes can be hard to find, we have discovered a good substitute—Werther's Original candies, unwrapped and crushed. Forty crushed candies equal 1 cup; 50 candies equal 1¼ cups. These work great in the Chocolate-Toffee Bars from *Christmas With Southern Living 2001,* page 30. (Call 1-800-884-3935 to order the book.)

From Your Freezer

Thanks to all of you for sharing hints on making the best use of freezers. Here are some of your ideas.

■ Hilda Nix of Atlanta writes, "When I buy a pound of bacon, I cook the entire pound, drain well, and quickly freeze in single layers in a plastic container. I can take as many slices out as needed and give them a quick zap in the microwave. This is especially convenient when cooking for one."

■ Dan Ward of Longwood, Florida, advises, "To maintain the quality and flavor of freshly caught fish, freeze it in a bag or container of water."

■ Peggy Metzger of Marshall, Texas, keeps uncooked bacon on hand in small portions. "At the end of a long strip of wax paper, place one piece of bacon, and

fold over. Repeat this process until all the bacon is placed. Store in a heavy-duty freezer bag. To use, unfold the amount needed, and cut the paper. Return the unused portion to the freezer."

■ Karen Widmyer of Catonsville, Maryland, cooks lean sausage, crumbling the meat as it cooks, drains it well, and freezes it in heavy-duty zip-top plastic bags. "I use the meat," Karen writes, "when I make Egg Beaters frittatas. It adds flavor without adding much extra fat. I also make taco meat and freeze it in small portions for a quick taco salad."

■ Hilda Forrest of Lexington, North Carolina, says, "I use the freezer to preserve foods from my garden, store hard-to-find produce and grocery items, and stock up on sale items I use frequently."

■ Polly Frye of Alexandria, Virginia, promptly freezes any cooked leftover poultry or meats. "Fried or roasted chicken is great for gumbo and jambalaya. The best, though, are steaks, prime rib, and pork roasts for chili."

■ Lynn Corbin of Brunson, South Carolina, suggests, "To prevent an avalanche of frozen items when opening an upright freezer, store items in plastic crates (available at home and discount stores) or resealable bags. Also, grate and freeze Cheddar cheese. For recipes, just measure out the amount you need."

Tips and Tidbits

■ When you don't have time to make cornbread, try Keebler's Harvest Bakery Corn Bread Crackers. They're great with the three kinds of chili featured on page 20.

■ Always window-shop at grocery and specialty stores when you're traveling. Stock up on ingredients you can't find at home.

■ Avoid cross-contaminating food by using an assortment of colored hard-plastic cutting boards—a yellow one for poultry and a red one for beef, for example.

■ Here are some good seasonal buys, plus storing suggestions.
Fresh cranberries: Freeze in their original bags.
Candied fruit: Freeze in airtight containers.
Almond brickle chips: Freeze in their original bags.
Raspberry morsels: Freeze in their original bags.

February

Chocolate Confections

So easy to make, so sweet to eat.

As the sweetest day of the year rounds the corner, add a heartfelt personal touch to a time-honored tradition by tempting your cherished Valentine with our chocolate lovers' treasures. These velvety handcrafted delights are guaranteed to evoke fond memories and offer lingering flavors.

The recipes are easy and fun to make, and they'll disappear in seconds. Plus, we've chosen a few mail-order sources for time-pressed folks (see "Southern Sweets" on facing page).

BOURBON BALLS

MAKES 25 BALLS

> 1 (16-ounce) package powdered sugar
> ⅓ cup bourbon
> ¼ cup butter, softened
> 50 pecan halves (about 1¼ cups)
> 2 cups (12 ounces) semisweet chocolate morsels
> 1 tablespoon shortening

STIR together first 3 ingredients until blended. Cover and chill 8 hours.
SHAPE mixture into 1-inch balls. Gently press pecan halves into 2 sides of each ball. Chill 8 hours.
MELT chocolate and shortening in a saucepan over medium heat. Remove from heat. Dip bourbon balls in chocolate, and place on wax paper.
CHILL 1 hour or until hardened. **Prep: 45 min., Chill: 17 hrs.**

NOTE: For testing purposes only, we used Woodford Reserve Distiller's Select Bourbon.

ROB CAUDILL
LOUISVILLE, KENTUCKY

CHOCOLATE-DIPPED CARAMELS

MAKES ABOUT 10 DOZEN

These creamy confections received our Test Kitchens' highest rating.

> 1 cup sugar
> 1 cup butter
> 1 cup dark corn syrup
> 1 (14-ounce) can sweetened condensed milk
> 1 teaspoon vanilla extract
> 2½ cups semisweet chocolate morsels
> 2 tablespoons shortening

BRING first 3 ingredients to a boil in a saucepan over medium heat; cook 7 minutes, without stirring. Stir in condensed milk, and bring to a boil; cook, stirring constantly, 10 minutes or until a candy thermometer reaches 245°.
REMOVE from heat, and stir in vanilla. Pour into a lightly greased aluminum foil-lined 8-inch square dish. Let stand 8 hours at room temperature.
CUT caramel into ½-inch squares, and shape into balls.
MELT chocolate and shortening in a saucepan over medium heat. Remove from heat. Dip balls into melted chocolate mixture; place on wax paper. Chill 8 hours. **Prep: 5 min., Cook: 17 min., Stand: 8 hrs., Dip: 1 hr., Chill: 8 hrs.**

CRACKER CANDY

MAKES 10 SERVINGS

> 2½ cups miniature round buttery crackers
> ¾ cup butter
> ¾ cup firmly packed brown sugar
> 2 cups milk chocolate morsels
> Chopped pecans (optional)
> Rainbow candy sprinkles (optional)

PLACE crackers in a lightly greased aluminum foil-lined 12- x 9-inch pan.
BRING butter and brown sugar to a boil in a medium saucepan, stirring constantly; cook, stirring often, 3 minutes. Pour mixture over crackers.
BAKE at 350° for 5 minutes. Turn oven off. Sprinkle crackers with chocolate morsels, and let stand in oven 3 minutes or until chocolate melts. Spread chocolate evenly over crackers. Top with pecans or candy sprinkles, if desired. Cool; break into pieces. Store in refrigerator. **Prep: 13 min., Bake: 5 min., Stand: 3 min.**

NOTE: For testing purposes only, we used Mini Ritz crackers.

CORDIAL CHERRIES

MAKES 2½ DOZEN

> 1 (10-ounce) jar maraschino cherries with stems
> ½ cup brandy (optional)
> 1 (8-ounce) package semisweet chocolate baking squares, chopped

DRAIN maraschino cherries, and return to jar. Pour brandy, if desired, in jar; cover with a lid, and freeze 8 hours. Drain cherries, and pat dry, reserving brandy for another use.
MELT two-thirds of chocolate baking squares in a saucepan over medium heat, stirring until a candy thermometer reaches 115°. Remove from heat; add remaining chocolate, and stir until candy thermometer reaches 89° and chocolate is smooth.
DIP cherries quickly into melted chocolate, coating well. Place cherries on wax paper, stem sides up, and cool. **Prep: 10 min., Freeze: 8 hrs., Cook: 10 min.**

MICROWAVE CHOCOLATE FUDGE

MAKES 3 DOZEN SQUARES

3 cups milk chocolate morsels
1 (14-ounce) can sweetened
    condensed milk
¼ cup butter or margarine, cut into
    pieces

COMBINE all ingredients in a 2-quart glass bowl. Microwave chocolate mixture at MEDIUM (50% power) 5 minutes, stirring at 1½-minute intervals. **POUR** into a greased 8-inch square dish. Cover and chill 8 hours; cut into 1½-inch squares. Store in refrigerator. **Prep: 5 min., Cook: 5 min., Chill: 8 hrs.**

Don't Spill the Beans

It's no mystery that canned beans often get a bad rap. We've uncovered a couple of recipes that just might change your mind about using beans such as canned cannellini and navy. We think you'll be especially pleased with our festive Red Pepper Hummus, which substitutes navy beans for the classic chickpeas. Try serving it as an appetizer at your next dinner party. Imagine—canned beans producing something that's not only elegant but delicious, too. This can be our little secret.

RED PEPPER HUMMUS

MAKES 2 CUPS

1 (15-ounce) can navy beans, rinsed
    and drained
2 garlic cloves, chopped
½ cup roasted red bell peppers,
    drained and chopped
⅓ cup tahini
¼ cup fresh lemon juice
¾ teaspoon salt
¼ teaspoon ground cumin
¼ teaspoon ground coriander
¼ teaspoon ground red pepper
2 tablespoons olive oil
1 tablespoon chopped fresh cilantro
Garnishes: lettuce, toasted sesame
    seeds, chopped green onions

PROCESS first 9 ingredients in a food processor or blender until smooth, stopping to scrape down sides. With processor running, pour oil through food chute in a slow, steady stream; process until smooth. Stir in cilantro; chill 1 hour. Garnish, if desired. Serve with tortilla or pita chips. **Prep: 15 min., Chill: 1 hr.**

WILL MULLINS
BATON ROUGE, LOUISIANA

WHITE BEAN-AND-TUNA SALAD SANDWICHES

MAKES ABOUT 4 CUPS

1 (15-ounce) can cannellini beans,
    rinsed and drained*
1 (12½-ounce) can solid white tuna in
    spring water, drained and flaked
4 bacon slices, cooked and crumbled
2 plum tomatoes, chopped
¼ cup chopped purple onion
¼ cup mayonnaise
3 tablespoons fresh lemon juice
2 tablespoons chopped fresh chives
2 teaspoons Dijon mustard
1 teaspoon minced fresh dill
¼ teaspoon pepper
Sourdough or rye bread
Lettuce leaves

STIR together first 11 ingredients; chill 1 hour. Serve on lightly toasted bread with lettuce. **Prep: 25 min., Chill: 1 hr.**

*Substitute 1 (15-ounce) can navy beans for cannellini beans, if desired.

MERLE DUNSON
TAYLORS, SOUTH CAROLINA

Beans, Beans, Good for Your Heart … and Much More

Scientists have known for some time that beans are low in fat and high in fiber and protein. Now researchers at Michigan State University also have found that beans are rich in antioxidants, much like those found in red wine. These substances have been linked to slowing the aging process as well as fighting cancer and heart disease.

Candlelight on a Budget

A memorable meal with your beloved doesn't have to break the bank.

Valentine's Day Dinner

Serves 4

Cherry Tomato-Caper Salad

Chicken Cakes With Creole Sauce

Raspberry Shortbread

Chardonnay

Celebrate Valentine's Day or other special occasions with our cozy menu. You could certainly spend big bucks at a trendy restaurant, but true romantics know that feasting doesn't have to cost a fortune. For less than $30 and a mere hour of your time, you can cook a fabulous meal that's straight from the heart.

Flowers bring a thoughtful touch to the dinner table. You can gather some greenery from your garden, pick up an inexpensive bouquet from the florist or grocery store, or arrange a few potted plants such as African violets as a centerpiece. Then light some candles and play your favorite songs as finishing touches, and spend a wonderful evening with the one you love.

CHERRY TOMATO-CAPER SALAD

MAKES 4 SERVINGS

Fresh basil adds a bright note to this colorful salad. *(pictured on page 40)*

> 2 tablespoons balsamic
>   vinegar
> 1 tablespoon drained small
>   capers
> 4 teaspoons olive oil
> ½ teaspoon pepper
> 1 pint cherry tomatoes, halved
> 6 fresh basil leaves, shredded
> Bibb lettuce leaves (optional)

COMBINE first 4 ingredients. Drizzle over cherry tomatoes, tossing to coat. Let stand at least 15 minutes or up to 1 hour. Sprinkle with basil. Serve over Bibb lettuce, if desired. **Prep: 15 min., Stand: 1 hr.**

CHICKEN CAKES WITH CREOLE SAUCE

MAKES 4 SERVINGS

To get a head start, refrigerate the shaped cakes overnight, and pan-fry them right before dinner. *(pictured on page 40)*

> 2 tablespoons butter or margarine
> ½ medium-size red bell pepper, diced
> 4 green onions, thinly sliced
> 1 garlic clove, pressed
> 3 cups chopped cooked chicken
> 1 cup soft breadcrumbs
> 1 large egg, lightly beaten
> 2 tablespoons mayonnaise
> 1 tablespoon Creole mustard
> 2 teaspoons Creole seasoning
> ¼ cup vegetable oil
> Creole Sauce
> Garnish: chopped fresh parsley

MELT butter in a large nonstick skillet over medium heat.

ADD bell pepper, green onions, and garlic, and sauté 3 to 4 minutes or until vegetables are tender.

STIR together bell pepper mixture, chicken, and next 5 ingredients in a bowl. Shape chicken mixture into 8 (3½-inch) patties.

FRY 4 patties in 2 tablespoons hot oil in a large skillet over medium heat 3 minutes on each side or until golden brown. Drain on paper towels.

REPEAT procedure with remaining 2 tablespoons oil and patties. Serve immediately with Creole Sauce. Garnish, if desired. **Prep: 20 min., Cook: 6 min. per batch**

Creole Sauce:

MAKES 1¼ CUPS

> 1 cup mayonnaise
> 3 green onions, sliced
> 2 tablespoons Creole mustard
> 2 garlic cloves, pressed
> 1 tablespoon chopped fresh parsley
> ¼ teaspoon ground red pepper

STIR together all ingredients until well blended. **Prep: 5 min.**

RASPBERRY SHORTBREAD

MAKES 6 DOZEN

1 cup butter, softened
⅔ cup sugar
2½ cups all-purpose flour
1 (10-ounce) jar seedless raspberry jam
1½ cups powdered sugar
3½ tablespoons water
½ teaspoon almond extract

BEAT butter and ⅔ cup sugar at medium speed with an electric mixer until light and fluffy. Gradually add flour, beating at low speed until blended.

DIVIDE dough into 6 equal portions, and roll each dough portion into a 12-inch-long x 1-inch-wide strip. Place 3 dough strips on each of 2 lightly greased baking sheets.

MAKE a ½-inch-wide x ¼-inch-deep indentation down center of each strip, using the handle of a wooden spoon.

BAKE in 2 batches at 350° for 15 minutes. Remove from oven, and spoon jam into indentations. Bake 5 more minutes or until lightly browned.

WHISK together powdered sugar, 3½ tablespoons water, and almond extract; drizzle over warm shortbread. Cut each strip diagonally into 12 (1-inch-wide) slices. Cool in pans on wire racks. Store in an airtight container. **Prep: 30 min., Bake: 20 min. per batch**

Wine Picks

Foods Editor Scott Jones, our wine expert, recommends the following wines with this menu.

■ 2000, Eberle, Chardonnay, California
■ 1999, Meridian, Chardonnay, Santa Barbara County, California
■ 2000, Hedges, Fumé-Chardonnay, Columbia Valley, Washington
■ 2000, Wolf Blass, Chardonnay, Southeast Australia

Hometown Favorites

We know how popular community cookbooks are in the Southern kitchen. Your family and friends will love these two terrific main-course recipes, courtesy of Junior League cookbooks from New Orleans and Austin.

FRENCH MARKET MEAT LOAF

MAKES 8 TO 10 SERVINGS

Ladle the rich Tomato Gravy, developed by Test Kitchens staffer Lyda Jones, over hearty slices of this sausage-studded meat loaf.

1 (8-ounce) package Cajun sausage links, diced
1 medium onion, diced
1 small green bell pepper, diced
2 garlic cloves, minced
2 teaspoons salt
1 teaspoon pepper
½ teaspoon dried thyme
½ teaspoon dried oregano
2 pounds ground beef
½ cup beef broth
½ cup tomato sauce
¼ cup soft breadcrumbs
1 large egg, lightly beaten
Tomato Gravy

COOK first 8 ingredients in a large non-stick skillet over medium-high heat, stirring often, 10 minutes or until vegetables are tender. Drain on paper towels; cool.

STIR together ground beef and next 4 ingredients in a large bowl; stir in sausage mixture. Shape meat mixture into an 11½- x 4-inch loaf; place in a lightly greased aluminum foil-lined 15- x 10-inch jellyroll pan.

BAKE at 375° for 50 minutes or until meat mixture is no longer pink in center; drain and let stand 10 minutes. Serve with Tomato Gravy. **Prep: 30 min., Cook: 10 min., Bake: 50 min., Stand: 10 min.**

CRESCENT CITY COLLECTION: A TASTE OF NEW ORLEANS
THE JUNIOR LEAGUE OF NEW ORLEANS
NEW ORLEANS, LOUISIANA

Tomato Gravy:

MAKES ABOUT 1 CUP

2 tablespoons butter or margarine
2 tablespoons all-purpose flour
⅓ cup beef broth
1 (8-ounce) can tomato sauce
¼ teaspoon salt
¼ teaspoon pepper

MELT butter in a small saucepan; whisk in flour, and cook, whisking constantly, 1 minute. Gradually whisk in broth and tomato sauce; reduce heat, and simmer until thickened. Whisk in salt and pepper. **Prep: 5 min., Cook: 5 min.**

ASIAN PORK TENDERLOIN

MAKES 6 SERVINGS

⅓ cup lite soy sauce
¼ cup sesame oil
⅓ cup packed light brown sugar
2 tablespoons Worcestershire sauce
2 tablespoons lemon juice
4 garlic cloves, crushed
1 tablespoon dry mustard
1½ teaspoons pepper
1½ to 2 pounds pork tenderloin

WHISK together first 8 ingredients. Place pork in a shallow dish; add marinade, turning pork to coat. Cover and chill 8 hours. Remove pork from marinade, discarding marinade. Place in an aluminum foil-lined roasting pan.

BAKE at 450° for 25 minutes or until a meat thermometer registers 160°. Let pork stand 5 minutes. **Prep: 20 min., Chill: 8 hrs., Bake: 25 min., Stand: 5 min.**

AUSTIN ENTERTAINS
THE JUNIOR LEAGUE OF AUSTIN
AUSTIN, TEXAS

Add Grits to the Menu

Potatoes: The Ultimate Comfort Food

Whether it's time for brunch or you need a hearty side dish for a crowd, Mexican Cheese Grits offers creamy comfort and great taste. Green chiles add a mild kick; red bell pepper lends color and sweetness. Process cheese and shredded Cheddar make the recipe doubly luscious and thick.

MEXICAN CHEESE GRITS

MAKES 6 TO 8 SERVINGS

You can make this dish ahead, but hold off sprinkling the cheese on top until time to reheat.

- 1 cup uncooked regular grits
- 1 (8-ounce) loaf pasteurized prepared cheese product
- ½ cup milk
- 2 large eggs
- 2 tablespoons butter or margarine
- 1 small onion, chopped
- 1 small red bell pepper, chopped
- 2 garlic cloves, pressed
- 1 (4.5-ounce) can chopped green chiles, drained
- 1 (12-ounce) package shredded Cheddar cheese, divided
- ¼ teaspoon ground red pepper

COOK grits according to package directions. Stir in cheese product until melted. Stir together milk and eggs; stir into grits mixture.

MELT butter in a large skillet over medium heat; add onion and next 3 ingredients, and sauté until tender. Stir onion mixture, 1 cup shredded cheese, and ground red pepper into grits mixture. Pour into a lightly greased 13- x 9-inch baking dish.

BAKE at 350° for 30 minutes; sprinkle with remaining shredded cheese, and bake 5 to 10 more minutes or until cheese melts. **Prep: 15 min., Bake: 40 min.**

NOTE: For testing purposes only, we used Velveeta Pasteurized Prepared Cheese Product.

Potatoes are like your favorite pair of khakis: comfortable and compatible with just about anything. Imagine a perfectly dressed baked potato alongside a juicy steak; hot, crispy fries dipped in cool ketchup; or creamy mashed potatoes ladled with savory brown gravy. These combinations just scream "comfort food."

At about 100 calories for a 5.3-ounce spud, potatoes are not only modest in calories but also very nutritious. So go ahead and put these and other potato recipes on your breakfast, lunch, or dinner plate.

SPICY OVEN FRIES

MAKES 6 SERVINGS

- 3 large baking potatoes (about 2 pounds)
- 2 tablespoons olive oil
- 2 tablespoons Creole seasoning
- Vegetable cooking spray

CUT each baking potato lengthwise into 8 wedges.

COMBINE olive oil and Creole seasoning in a zip-top plastic bag; add potato wedges. Seal bag, and shake to coat.

ARRANGE potato wedges, skin sides down, in a single layer on a baking sheet coated with cooking spray.

BAKE potato wedges at 450° for 20 minutes or until golden brown. **Prep: 8 min., Bake: 20 min.**

Per 4 wedges: Calories 181 (24% from fat); Fat 4.9g (sat 0.7g, mono 3.3g, poly 0.4g); Protein 3g; Carb 32g; Fiber 3.2g; Chol 0mg; Iron 1.7mg; Sodium 484mg; Calc 12mg

ORANGE-SPICE MASHED SWEET POTATOES

MAKES 10 SERVINGS

Save time by baking potatoes a day ahead. Cover and chill until ready to assemble.

- 3 pounds sweet potatoes
- ⅓ cup fresh orange juice
- ¼ teaspoon ground nutmeg
- ¼ teaspoon ground ginger
- Vegetable cooking spray
- ½ cup chopped pecans
- ½ cup firmly packed brown sugar
- 1 teaspoon grated orange rind
- 1 teaspoon ground cinnamon

BAKE potatoes at 400° for 1 hour or until tender; peel. Reduce oven temperature to 350°.

BEAT potatoes, orange juice, nutmeg, and ginger in a large mixing bowl at medium speed with an electric mixer until smooth. Spoon mixture into a 13- x 9-inch baking dish coated with cooking spray.

COMBINE chopped pecans and remaining 3 ingredients; sprinkle evenly over potato mixture.

BAKE at 350° for 20 minutes or until thoroughly heated. **Prep: 15 min.; Bake: 1 hr., 20 min.**

KENNETH MOYERS
BRIDGEWATER, VIRGINIA

Per ¾-cup serving: Calories 218 (19% from fat); Fat 4.8g (sat 0.5g, mono 2.5g, poly 1.5g); Protein 2.9g; Carb 42g; Fiber 3.2g; Chol 0mg; Iron 1.1mg; Sodium 21mg; Calc 42.6mg

CREAM CHEESE MASHED POTATOES

MAKES 8 SERVINGS

- 2½ pounds baking potatoes, peeled and quartered
- ½ (8-ounce) package fat-free cream cheese, softened
- 3 tablespoons reduced-calorie margarine, softened
- 1½ teaspoons sugar
- 1 teaspoon garlic salt
- ½ to 1 teaspoon pepper
- Vegetable cooking spray

COOK potatoes in boiling water to cover in a Dutch oven 25 minutes or until tender. Drain.

BEAT potatoes, cream cheese, and next 4 ingredients in a large bowl at medium speed with an electric mixer until fluffy. Spoon into a 9-inch square baking dish coated with vegetable cooking spray.

BAKE at 325° for 30 minutes or until thoroughly heated. **Prep: 30 min., Cook: 25 min., Bake: 30 min.**

PATRICIA KEITH
OCEANSIDE, CALIFORNIA

Per ½-cup serving: Calories 123 (19% from fat); Fat 2.6g (sat 0.5g, mono 0.1g, poly 0.1g); Protein 4.3g; Carb 21g; Fiber 1.7g; Chol 1mg; Iron 0.9mg; Sodium 355mg; Calc 34.5mg

CONFETTI TWICE-BAKED POTATOES

MAKES 8 SERVINGS

- 4 medium baking potatoes
- ½ cup fat-free sour cream
- ¼ cup fat-free milk
- 2 tablespoons butter or margarine
- ¼ cup chopped fresh basil
- ¼ cup chopped fresh parsley
- 2 green onions, chopped
- 2 garlic cloves, minced
- Butter-flavored vegetable cooking spray
- 2 plum tomatoes, chopped
- ½ cup (2 ounces) shredded reduced-fat sharp Cheddar cheese

BAKE potatoes at 375° for 1 hour or until tender; cool 10 minutes. Reduce oven temperature to 350°.

CUT potatoes in half lengthwise; carefully scoop out pulp into a large bowl, leaving shells intact. Stir together pulp, sour cream, milk, and butter; stir in basil and next 3 ingredients.

COAT insides of potato shells with cooking spray. Spoon potato mixture evenly into shells; sprinkle evenly with tomato and cheese.

BAKE potatoes at 350° for 10 minutes or until thoroughly heated and cheese is melted. **Prep: 15 min.; Bake: 1 hr., 10 min.**

NOTE: To make ahead, place unbaked stuffed potato halves, covered, in the refrigerator. Bring potato halves to room temperature before baking at 350°.

NANCY CHENE
NEW BALTIMORE, MICHIGAN

Per 1 potato half: Calories 129 (26% from fat); Fat 3.7g (sat 2.3g, mono 1g, poly 0.2g); Protein 4.6g; Carb 20g; Fiber 1.9g; Chol 11mg; Iron 1.2mg; Sodium 96mg; Calc 80mg

CREAMY POTATO-GARLIC SPREAD

MAKES 6 SERVINGS

Serve with baked pita chips, raw veggies, or low-fat crackers.

- 1 pound baking potatoes, peeled and cut into 2-inch cubes
- 3 tablespoons fresh lemon juice
- 1 tablespoon olive oil
- 1 teaspoon bottled minced roasted garlic
- ½ to 1 teaspoon grated lemon rind
- ½ teaspoon salt
- ½ teaspoon freshly ground pepper
- 1 green onion, chopped (optional)

COOK potatoes in boiling water to cover in a Dutch oven 15 minutes or until tender. Drain.

PROCESS potatoes, lemon juice, and next 5 ingredients in a food processor until smooth, stopping to scrape down sides. Transfer mixture to a serving dish, and sprinkle with onion, if desired. **Prep: 5 min., Cook: 15 min.**

NOTE: To make your own pita chips, cut 2 (6-inch) pita rounds into wedges; split in half at seams. Place on a baking sheet coated with vegetable cooking spray; coat wedges with cooking spray. Bake at 450° for 4 to 5 minutes or until crisp.

Per ¼-cup serving: Calories 76 (28% from fat); Fat 2.4g (sat 0.3g, mono 1.8g, poly 0.2g); Protein 1.2g; Carb 13g; Fiber 1g; Chol 0mg; Iron 0.2mg; Sodium 197mg; Calc 5mg

Let the Red Beans and Rice Roll

A longtime staple for Monday meals in New Orleans, red beans and rice are great any day of the week, especially during the busy time of Mardi Gras. Revelers descend into the Crescent City for masked parties, dozens of parades, and scenes of good-natured mayhem. So whether you plan to make the trip to New Orleans or just plan on throwing your own party at home, enjoy a taste of Mardi Gras with this Cajun classic.

RED BEANS AND RICE

MAKES 15 CUPS

Add a crisp green salad and crusty French bread for a soul-satisfying meal.

- 1 (16-ounce) package dried red beans
- 10 cups water
- 1 ham bone*
- 1 onion, chopped
- 1 green bell pepper, chopped
- 2 garlic cloves
- ½ teaspoon salt
- ¼ teaspoon ground black pepper
- ½ teaspoon ground red pepper
- 1 teaspoon hot sauce
- 1½ pounds smoked sausage, sliced
- Hot cooked rice

BRING first 10 ingredients to a boil in a Dutch oven. Reduce heat, and simmer 2½ hours, stirring occasionally.

BROWN sausage in a large skillet over medium-high heat; drain. Add to bean mixture; simmer 30 minutes or until beans are tender. Serve over hot cooked rice. **Prep: 10 min., Cook: 3 hrs.**

*Substitute ½ pound smoked ham hocks, if desired.

DARLENE BRUNSON
BOSSIER CITY, LOUISIANA

Make Meals Easy

Give weeknight cooking a helping hand with these one-dish dinners.

Do you need to take the edge off the dinnertime rush? We have the perfect solution for doable weeknight fare. Not just another baked casserole, a one-dish meal can be any recipe prepared in one skillet, Dutch oven, or baking dish, saving you money and time. All you need is a salad, bread, or simple vegetable to complete the meal. Because the majority of these dishes are prepared in one pot, you'll have less cookware to clean up. We've specifically chosen recipes with affordable, easy-to-find ingredients; many are pantry staples. These dishes yield plenty for leftovers; you can also double the portions for future meals. Here's to making your life a little easier. (For more great recipes and salad ideas, see "Supper Solutions" on page 44.)

BROCCOLI MACARONI AND CHEESE

MAKES 6 TO 8 SERVINGS

Stir in chopped cooked chicken if you want some meat in this dish.

- ¼ cup butter or margarine, divided
- 2 tablespoons all-purpose flour
- 2 cups milk
- 1 (8-ounce) package shredded Cheddar-American cheese blend
- ½ teaspoon salt
- ⅛ teaspoon ground red pepper
- 1 (10-ounce) package frozen broccoli, thawed and coarsely chopped
- 8 ounces elbow macaroni, cooked
- ¼ cup fine, dry breadcrumbs or ½ cup grated Parmesan cheese

MELT 2 tablespoons butter in a large saucepan over medium heat, and whisk in all-purpose flour; cook, whisking constantly, 2 minutes.

WHISK in milk gradually; cook, whisking constantly, 5 minutes or until mixture thickens. Remove from heat. Add shredded cheese, salt, and pepper, stirring until cheese melts. Stir in broccoli and pasta. Pour into a lightly greased 11- x 7-inch baking dish. Sprinkle with breadcrumbs; dot with remaining 2 tablespoons butter.

BAKE at 350° for 25 to 30 minutes. **Prep: 15 min., Bake: 30 min.**

TO LIGHTEN: Substitute equal portions reduced-calorie margarine, 2% reduced-fat milk, and 2% reduced-fat shredded sharp Cheddar cheese, and reduce salt to ¼ teaspoon. Cook as directed, and pour into baking dish. Stir together remaining margarine, melted, and breadcrumbs; sprinkle over pasta mixture. Bake as directed, and let stand 5 minutes before serving.

EMELIA MARX-CARMAN
LOUISVILLE, KENTUCKY

CHICKEN-AND-SAUSAGE JAMBALAYA

MAKES 6 TO 8 SERVINGS

We used a deli chicken to make this entrée easier. Be sure to remove all skin and bones.

- 1 (16-ounce) package Cajun-style smoked sausage, cut into ¼-inch slices
- 2 celery ribs, chopped
- 1 medium onion, chopped
- 1 medium-size green bell pepper, chopped
- 4 cups chopped cooked chicken
- 1 (32-ounce) container chicken broth
- 1½ cups uncooked long-grain rice
- 1 tablespoon Cajun seasoning
- Garnish: chopped fresh parsley

COOK smoked sausage in a Dutch oven over medium heat, stirring constantly, 3 minutes or until browned. Add celery, onion, and bell pepper, and sauté 6 to 8 minutes or until vegetables are tender.

STIR in chicken and next 3 ingredients; bring to a boil. Cover, reduce heat, and simmer 45 minutes or until rice is done and liquid is absorbed. Remove from heat, and let stand 10 to 15 minutes before serving. Garnish, if desired. **Prep: 20 min., Cook: 45 min., Stand: 15 min.**

NOTE: For testing purposes only, we used Conecuh Sausage (1-800-726-0507).

PIZZA SWISS STEAK

MAKES 6 TO 8 SERVINGS

- ⅓ cup all-purpose flour
- 2 teaspoons salt
- ¼ teaspoon pepper
- 1½ to 2 pounds cube steak, cut into bite-size pieces
- 2 tablespoons vegetable oil
- 1 medium onion, halved and sliced
- 1 medium-size green bell pepper, chopped
- 1 (4-ounce) can sliced mushrooms, drained
- 1 (15-ounce) can pizza sauce
- 1 (8-ounce) can basil-garlic tomato sauce
- ½ cup (2 ounces) shredded mozzarella cheese

COMBINE first 3 ingredients. Dredge steak in flour mixture.

BROWN steak, in batches, in hot oil in a large skillet over high heat 1 to 2 minutes on each side. Remove steak from skillet, and place in a lightly greased 13- x 9-inch baking dish.

SAUTÉ sliced onion, chopped bell pepper, and mushrooms in skillet over medium-high heat 5 minutes or until tender. Add pizza and tomato sauces, and simmer 15 minutes; pour over steak.

BAKE, covered, at 350° for 45 minutes. Uncover and sprinkle with cheese; bake 15 more minutes or until cheese melts. **Prep: 10 min., Cook: 25 min., Bake: 1 hr.**

JANICE M. FRANCE
DEPAUW, INDIANA

Quick Whipping Cream Biscuits,
Sunny Orange Marmalade, page 27

Turnip Greens Stew, Mashed Potatoes With Tomato Gravy, page 17;
Succotash, Pan-Fried Pork Chops, page 16; cornbread

Chicken Cakes With Creole Sauce, Cherry
Tomato-Caper Salad, rice pilaf, page 32

Start the Morning Right

Begin your day with these warm, inviting treats.

Breakfast doesn't have to be a complicated meal, as these great recipes demonstrate.

Reader Robyn Arnold of Houston used to fight the mall crowds on Christmas Eve just to buy cinnamon rolls for the next morning until she developed her fabulous recipe for Mama's Mini-Cinnis. Now, she says, "my family loves waking up to the smell of home-baked cinnamon rolls with just the right amount of fuss and very little cleanup." Our Classic Cream Scones, meanwhile, take just 25 minutes to prepare yet received our highest rating—meaning they're some of the best scones we've ever tried.

ENGLISH CHEESE MUFFINS

MAKES 8 SERVINGS

- 8 bacon slices, cooked and crumbled
- 1 (5-ounce) jar sharp process cheese spread
- ¼ cup butter or margarine, softened
- 1 green onion, chopped
- 4 English muffins, split
- Sliced tomato (optional)

STIR together first 4 ingredients; spread about 2 tablespoons cheese mixture on each muffin half.

BAKE at 325° for 15 minutes or until golden. Serve with sliced tomato, if desired. **Prep: 10 min., Bake: 15 min.**

LYDIA H. HAMPTON
BRENTWOOD, TENNESSEE

CLASSIC CREAM SCONES

MAKES 1 DOZEN

These luscious scones received a 3—our Test Kitchens' top rating. Try them topped with homemade jam or preserves for a sweet start to your day.

- 2 cups all-purpose flour
- 2 teaspoons baking powder
- ⅛ teaspoon salt
- ¼ cup sugar
- ⅓ cup butter or margarine, cubed
- ½ cup whipping cream
- 1 large egg
- 1½ teaspoons vanilla extract
- 1 egg white
- 1 teaspoon water
- Sugar

COMBINE first 4 ingredients. Cut in butter with a pastry blender until mixture is crumbly.

WHISK together cream, egg, and vanilla; add to flour mixture, stirring just until dry ingredients are moistened.

TURN dough out onto a lightly floured surface. Pat dough to ½-inch thickness; cut with a 2½-inch round cutter, and place on baking sheets.

WHISK together egg white and 1 teaspoon water; brush mixture over tops of scones. Sprinkle with additional sugar.

BAKE at 425° for 13 to 15 minutes or until lightly browned. **Prep: 10 min., Bake: 15 min.**

MAMA'S MINI-CINNIS

MAKES 2 DOZEN

This simple-to-prepare recipe doubles easily for a crowd.

- 2 (8-ounce) cans refrigerated crescent rolls
- 6 tablespoons butter or margarine, softened
- ⅓ cup firmly packed brown sugar
- ¼ cup chopped pecans
- 1 tablespoon sugar
- 1 teaspoon ground cinnamon
- ⅔ cup powdered sugar
- 1 tablespoon milk or half-and-half
- ¼ teaspoon almond or vanilla extract
- ⅛ teaspoon salt

UNROLL crescent rolls, and separate each dough portion along center perforation to form 4 rectangles; press diagonal perforations to seal.

STIR together butter and next 4 ingredients; spread evenly over 1 side of each rectangle. Roll up jellyroll fashion, starting at long end. Gently cut each log into 6 (1-inch-thick) slices, using a serrated knife. Place rolls, ¼ inch apart, into 2 greased 8-inch cakepans.

BAKE at 375° for 15 to 18 minutes or until golden. Cool 5 to 10 minutes.

STIR together powdered sugar and remaining 3 ingredients. Drizzle over warm rolls. **Prep: 10 min., Bake: 18 min., Cool: 10 min.**

NOTE: To make slicing easier, place unbaked rolls on baking sheet, and freeze for 10 minutes.

ROBYN ARNOLD
HOUSTON, TEXAS

Time-Savers With Big Flavor

Slow cookers work their magic while you're at the office.

If you think slow cookers are a thing of the past, think again. They come in lots of shapes and sizes, but the 5- to 6-quart models work just fine for most families.

The low heat helps tenderize and reduce shrinkage of lean, less expensive cuts of meat. However, when you use the low setting on larger cuts, such as roasts or whole chickens, the USDA recommends that your cooker maintain a minimum of 170° to ensure a safe final internal temperature.

You may be tempted to peek, but resist at all costs—lifting the lid lets precious heat escape, dramatically extending the final cook time.

Quick Tips for Slow Cooking

- Slow cookers don't brown food, so sear meat in a skillet for extra flavor before adding it to the pot.

- Fatty meats require less liquid. With chicken, use cuts such as thighs and legs rather than breasts, which tend to become dry.

- A slow cooker should never be more than two-thirds full.

- If the lid is too loose, the vacuum created during cooking will be affected, extending cook time.

CAMP STEW

MAKES 18 CUPS

Chock-full of meat and vegetables, this is the ideal cold-weather meal for your family.

1 pound ground beef
1 medium onion, chopped
2 large potatoes, peeled and diced
1 (16-ounce) package frozen speckled butter beans, thawed
1 (14¾-ounce) can creamed corn
1 (8¾-ounce) can whole kernel corn, drained
1 (10-ounce) can barbecued pork
1 (10-ounce) can white chicken in water, drained
2 (14½-ounce) cans stewed tomatoes
1 cup ketchup
1 cup water
2 to 4 tablespoons lemon juice
1 tablespoon Worcestershire sauce
1 teaspoon hot sauce
1 teaspoon salt
1 teaspoon pepper

COOK ground beef and onion in a large skillet over medium-high heat, stirring until beef crumbles and is no longer pink; drain.
LAYER potato, butter beans, beef mixture, creamed corn, and remaining ingredients in a 6-quart slow cooker.
COOK, covered, on LOW 8 hours or until potato is tender. **Prep: 15 min., Cook: 8 hrs.**

NOTE: For testing purposes only, we used Castleberry's Barbecue Pork.

KRISTIN CHAPPELL
OPELIKA, ALABAMA

SCALLOPED POTATOES WITH HAM

MAKES 6 SERVINGS

3 pounds medium potatoes, thinly sliced
1 medium onion, thinly sliced
1 cup diced cooked ham
1 cup (4 ounces) shredded American cheese
½ teaspoon salt
¼ teaspoon pepper
1 (10¾-ounce) can cream of mushroom soup, undiluted
¾ cup water
1 tablespoon chopped fresh chives (optional)

LAYER half each of first 4 ingredients in a 5-quart slow cooker. Sprinkle with salt and pepper; repeat layers with remaining potato, onion, ham, and cheese.
STIR together soup and ¾ cup water; spoon over potato mixture.
COOK, covered, on LOW 7 to 8 hours. Sprinkle with chives, if desired. **Prep: 20 min., Cook: 8 hrs.**

PATSY BELL HOBSON
LIBERTY, MISSOURI

FARM-STYLE PORK CHOPS

MAKES 4 TO 6 SERVINGS

¼ cup soy sauce
¼ cup orange marmalade
2 tablespoons ketchup
1 garlic clove, pressed
4 pounds boneless pork chops
2 tablespoons all-purpose flour

STIR together first 4 ingredients; brush sauce on both sides of pork. Place in a 5-quart slow cooker, and pour remaining sauce over pork.
COOK, covered, on LOW 7½ hours or until tender. Remove from slow cooker. Skim fat from sauce, and whisk in flour until slightly thickened. Serve over pork chops. **Prep: 10 min.; Cook: 7 hrs., 30 min.**

NORA HENSHAW
OKEMAH, OKLAHOMA

SLOW COOKER FAJITAS

MAKES 4 TO 6 SERVINGS

Tender flank steak makes a flavorful filling for fajitas.

- 1½ pounds flank steak, cut into 6 pieces
- 1 medium onion, chopped
- 1 green bell pepper, sliced
- 1 jalapeño pepper, seeded and chopped
- 2 garlic cloves, pressed
- 1 tablespoon chopped fresh cilantro
- 1 teaspoon chili powder
- 1 teaspoon ground cumin
- 1 teaspoon ground coriander
- ¾ to 1 teaspoon salt
- 1 (10-ounce) can diced tomatoes and green chiles, drained
- Flour tortillas
- Toppings: shredded Cheddar cheese and sour cream

PLACE steak in the bottom of a 5-quart slow cooker; top with onion and next 9 ingredients.

COOK, covered, on LOW 8 to 10 hours (or on HIGH 4 to 5 hours). Remove meat, and shred with a fork. Serve with tortillas and desired toppings. **Prep: 10 min., Cook: 10 hrs.**

Winter Vegetable Sides

Winter may not seem like the most prolific time for fresh produce, but we've elevated this season's harvest to new heights. Slow cooking works magic on sturdy winter vegetables, bringing out their natural sweetness; we also rely on a host of flavor enhancers from herbs to full-flavored cheeses. Serve any one of these sides as an appetizing complement to your next entrée, and taste the season's best flavors in these warming, delicious dishes.

GREEK GARBANZO STEW

MAKES 8 SIDE-DISH SERVINGS OR 3 TO 4 MAIN-DISH SERVINGS

Serve this zesty side over couscous for a hearty vegetarian entrée.

- 1 medium onion, diced
- 1 tablespoon olive oil
- 2 garlic cloves, minced
- 1 (28-ounce) can diced tomatoes
- 1 (15-ounce) can garbanzo beans, rinsed and drained
- 1 (14.5-ounce) can vegetable broth
- 2 tablespoons tomato paste
- ½ teaspoon dried rosemary
- 2 teaspoons dried oregano
- 1 teaspoon Greek seasoning
- ¼ teaspoon salt
- ½ teaspoon pepper
- 1 (6-ounce) package fresh baby spinach
- 2 tablespoons chopped fresh parsley
- Crumbled feta cheese (optional)

SAUTÉ onion in hot oil in a Dutch oven over medium-high heat 4 to 5 minutes or until tender. Add garlic, and cook 1 minute. Stir in tomatoes and next 8 ingredients. Bring to a boil; reduce heat to low, and simmer, stirring occasionally, 15 minutes. Stir in spinach and chopped parsley; cook 5 minutes. Top with crumbled feta cheese, if desired. **Prep: 10 min., Cook: 30 min.**

KAREN C. GREENLEE
LAWRENCEVILLE, GEORGIA

CREAMY PAN-BRAISED FENNEL

MAKES 8 SERVINGS

The distinctive flavor of fennel makes a terrific accompaniment with ham, roast beef, or pork.

- 4 large fennel bulbs
- 1½ cups whipping cream
- ½ teaspoon salt
- ½ teaspoon pepper
- ¼ teaspoon ground nutmeg
- ¼ cup fine, dry breadcrumbs
- ¼ cup shredded Parmesan cheese
- 1½ tablespoons butter or margarine

TRIM bases from fennel bulbs; cut into eighths, reserving fronds for another use.

Arrange fennel in a lightly greased 11- x 7-inch baking dish.

WHISK together whipping cream and next 3 ingredients, and pour over fennel slices. Sprinkle fennel slices with breadcrumbs and Parmesan cheese, and dot with butter.

BAKE, covered, at 425° for 20 minutes. Uncover and bake 20 more minutes or until fennel is tender and yields when a knife is inserted into the thickest slices. Serve immediately. **Prep: 15 min., Bake: 40 min.**

VANESSA GERONDALE
HOUSTON, TEXAS

BALSAMIC BABY CARROTS

MAKES 4 TO 6 SERVINGS

Crisp-tender carrots bathed in a tangy glaze add a vibrant touch to a winter meal.

- 3 cups water
- 1 pound baby carrots
- 2 large shallots, thinly sliced
- 1 medium-size red bell pepper, diced
- 1 tablespoon olive oil
- 3 tablespoons balsamic vinegar
- 1½ tablespoons sugar
- ½ teaspoon salt
- ¼ teaspoon freshly ground pepper
- 2 tablespoons chopped fresh Italian parsley
- Garnish: fresh Italian parsley sprig

BRING 3 cups water to a boil in a 3-quart saucepan; add carrots, return to a boil, and cook 4 minutes. Remove from heat; drain well.

SAUTÉ shallots and bell pepper in hot oil in a large skillet over medium-high heat 3 minutes or until crisp-tender. Stir in carrots, vinegar, and next 3 ingredients, and cook 4 to 5 minutes or until liquid is reduced and vegetables begin to glaze. Remove from heat; stir in chopped parsley. Garnish, if desired. **Prep: 10 min., Cook: 17 min.**

GLORIA PLEASANTS
WILLIAMSBURG, VIRGINIA

Supper Solutions

Here are more simple ways to get dinner on the table.

If you liked the recipes in "Make Meals Easy" (page 36), take a look at these additional main-dish and side-salad suggestions. Make the entrée selections ahead on the weekend, or stir them together on a weeknight.

SPINACH-BLACK BEAN LASAGNA

MAKES 6 SERVINGS

2 large eggs, lightly beaten
1 (15-ounce) container ricotta
    cheese
1 (10-ounce) package frozen chopped
    spinach, thawed and well drained
¼ cup chopped fresh cilantro
½ teaspoon salt
4 cups (16 ounces) shredded
    Monterey Jack cheese with
    peppers, divided
2 (16-ounce) cans black beans, rinsed
    and drained
1 (2-pound, 13-ounce) jar pasta sauce
½ teaspoon ground cumin
9 precooked lasagna noodles
Garnish: chopped fresh cilantro

STIR together first 5 ingredients and 1 cup Monterey Jack cheese; set aside.
MASH beans with a potato masher or fork in a large bowl; stir in pasta sauce and cumin. Spread one-third of bean mixture in a lightly greased 13- x 9-inch baking dish.
LAYER with 3 noodles, half of spinach mixture, and 1 cup Monterey Jack cheese; repeat layers. Spread with one-third bean mixture; top with remaining 3 noodles and remaining bean mixture.
BAKE, covered, at 350° for 1 hour; uncover and top with remaining Monterey Jack cheese. Bake 5 more minutes or until cheese melts. Garnish, if desired. **Prep: 25 min.; Bake: 1 hr., 5 min.**

TURKEY SCALOPPINE WITH ANGEL HAIR PASTA

MAKES 6 SERVINGS

We used tenderloins instead of a whole turkey breast to simplify this scrumptious recipe.

½ cup all-purpose flour
1 teaspoon salt
½ teaspoon pepper
2 turkey tenderloins, thinly sliced
    (about 1½ pounds)
4 bacon slices, chopped
2 tablespoons vegetable oil
1 (8-ounce) package sliced
    mushrooms
1 (14-ounce) can artichoke hearts,
    drained and quartered
2 tablespoons capers
1 cup whipping cream
1 (14½-ounce) can chicken broth
8 ounces angel hair pasta,
    cooked

COMBINE first 3 ingredients; dredge turkey slices in flour mixture.
COOK bacon in a Dutch oven over medium-high heat until crisp; remove bacon, and drain on paper towels, reserving drippings in pan. Add oil to drippings, and cook turkey, in batches, over medium-high heat 1 minute on each side. Remove from pan.
SAUTÉ mushrooms in pan 5 to 7 minutes or until tender. Add artichokes and capers, and sauté 5 minutes. Stir in cream and broth; reduce heat, and simmer 10 minutes. Stir in bacon, turkey, and pasta, and cook until thoroughly heated. **Prep: 30 min., Cook: 30 min.**

TO LIGHTEN: Combine ¼ cup flour, ½ teaspoon salt, and pepper, and dredge turkey slices in flour mixture. Cook turkey in a large nonstick skillet coated with vegetable cooking spray over medium heat 2 minutes on each side; remove turkey from skillet. Sauté mushrooms in skillet 5 to 7 minutes or until tender, and add 2 bacon slices, cooked and crumbled; add artichokes and capers, and sauté 5 minutes. Whisk together 1 (14½-ounce) can low-sodium, fat-free chicken broth and 2 tablespoons all-purpose flour; add broth mixture and 1 cup fat-free half-and-half to skillet. Stir in turkey and pasta, and cook until thoroughly heated.

CINDY RENO
NORRIS, TENNESSEE

A New Leaf

Try these quick ideas to accompany your one-dish meals.

■ Use bag salads. For the best flavor, soak the greens in cold water a few minutes; then spin them dry. They'll perk up after being refreshed, and salad dressings will cling to them better.

■ Boost commercial salad dressing by stirring in fresh mint, basil, oregano, garlic, or shallots.

■ Buy a bag of shredded coleslaw, and top with your favorite salad dressing (we like Russian, Thousand Island, or light Italian).

■ Serve vegetables such as baby carrots, celery sticks, and bell peppers with a low-fat dip. Kids will love this.

Versatile Broccoli and Cauliflower

Bring flowers to your winter table— the tops of broccoli and cauliflower, that is. They are actually the plants' flowers, and these recipes will make sure you eat them. The tender florets of these winter vegetables give meals healthy good taste. Both veggies respond to similar cooking methods; quick boiling, sautéing, and stir-frying create the best textures in either. They're also delicious when encased in a crisp, deep-fried crust.

When time is short, purchase bags of precut florets. If you purchase whole broccoli, save the stems to use in soups and stir-fries.

BROCCOLI-CAULIFLOWER FRITTERS

MAKES 6 TO 8 SERVINGS

- ½ **pound fresh broccoli florets**
- ½ **pound fresh cauliflower florets**
- 2 **cups boiling water**
- 2 **large eggs, lightly beaten**
- 1 **small onion, diced**
- ½ **cup chopped pecans, toasted**
- ½ **cup self-rising flour**
- ½ **teaspoon salt**
- **Vegetable oil**

COOK florets in 2 cups boiling water in a Dutch oven over medium heat 10 to 12 minutes or until very tender; drain.
MASH florets with a potato masher or fork in a large bowl. Stir in eggs and next 4 ingredients.
POUR oil to a depth of ¼ inch into a large skillet; heat to 350°. Drop broccoli mixture by tablespoonfuls into hot oil, and cook in batches 1 to 2 minutes on each side or until lightly browned. Remove to a wire rack on a baking sheet; keep warm. **Prep: 15 min., Cook: 4 min. per batch**

JEANNE GIBBONS-BLACKMON
FALKVILLE, ALABAMA

ALMOND BROCCOLI IN SHERRY SAUCE

MAKES 6 SERVINGS

A creamy sherry sauce and slivered almonds lend richness and crunch to the tender florets.

- 1½ **pounds fresh broccoli, trimmed and separated into florets**
- 4 **cups boiling water**
- 1 **chicken bouillon cube**
- ¾ **cup boiling water**
- ¼ **cup butter or margarine**
- ¼ **cup all-purpose flour**
- 1 **cup half-and-half**
- 2 **tablespoons sherry**
- 2 **tablespoons lemon juice**
- ½ **teaspoon salt**
- ¼ **teaspoon pepper**
- ¾ **cup shredded Parmesan cheese**
- ⅓ **cup slivered almonds, toasted**

COOK florets in 4 cups boiling water in a Dutch oven over medium heat 4 to 5 minutes or until crisp-tender; drain. Place florets in a lightly greased 2-quart baking dish, and set aside.
DISSOLVE bouillon cube in ¾ cup boiling water.
MELT butter in a large saucepan over medium-high heat. Whisk in flour, and cook, whisking constantly, 1 minute. Gradually whisk in bouillon mixture and half-and-half, and cook, stirring constantly, until mixture thickens and comes to a boil.
WHISK in sherry and next 3 ingredients. Pour over broccoli; sprinkle with cheese and almonds.
BAKE at 375° for 20 minutes or until bubbly. **Prep: 15 min., Bake: 20 min.**

BROCCOLI WITH SESAME SEEDS

MAKES 4 TO 6 SERVINGS

- ¼ **cup soy sauce**
- 4 **green onions, sliced**
- 2 **tablespoons sesame seeds, toasted**
- 2 **tablespoons brown sugar**
- 2 **tablespoons grated fresh ginger**
- 1 **large garlic clove, minced**
- ½ **teaspoon dried crushed red pepper**
- 2 **tablespoons sesame oil**
- 1 **pound fresh broccoli, trimmed and separated into florets**

STIR together first 7 ingredients.
HEAT oil in a large skillet or wok over medium-high heat. Add broccoli, and stir-fry 3 to 5 minutes or until crisp-tender; stir in soy sauce mixture until thoroughly heated, coating well. **Prep: 10 min., Cook: 5 min.**

15-Minute Sides

Pressed for time? These superfast recipes allow you to enjoy the flavor and health benefits of broccoli and cauliflower florets on the busiest weeknights.

Lemony Herbed Broccoli

MAKES 4 TO 6 SERVINGS

Melt ¼ cup butter or margarine in a large skillet over medium heat. Add 1 pound cooked fresh broccoli florets, 1 teaspoon grated lemon rind, 1 tablespoon fresh lemon juice, ½ teaspoon salt, and ¼ teaspoon dried basil. Cook broccoli mixture, stirring gently, 3 to 5 minutes or until thoroughly heated. **Prep: 10 min., Cook: 5 min.**

NORA HENSHAW
OKEMAH, OKLAHOMA

Cauliflower in Browned Butter

MAKES 4 TO 6 SERVINGS

Heat ¼ cup butter or margarine in a large skillet over medium heat 1 to 2 minutes or until lightly browned. Add 1 head cauliflower, separated into florets and cooked; 1 to 2 teaspoons minced roasted garlic; and ½ teaspoon salt. Cook, stirring gently, 2 to 3 minutes or until thoroughly heated. **Prep: 5 min., Cook: 5 min.**

ANGELA JEFFERS
JOHN'S ISLAND, SOUTH CAROLINA

from our kitchen

Assistant Foods Editor Cynthia Briscoe's story on chocolate (pages 30-31) is pure, sweet satisfaction. Making our recipes is easier than you think if you follow these tips.

Store chocolate wrapped and well sealed, in a cool, dry place; moisture and dramatic changes in temperature take a visual toll on chocolate. If you store it in the refrigerator, it may come out with a dull gray cast (known as "bloom"), but it'll still work fine in recipes. And don't worry if your stash has a slightly grainy texture—it won't affect the outcome of your cakes, cookies, or brownies.

For candy coating or decorations, melt chocolate gently; don't overheat it. This ensures a smooth consistency and shiny appearance. Make sure your double boiler or heavy saucepan is completely dry, because a stray water droplet can cause chocolate to "seize" into a grainy, lumpy mass. For best results, melt chocolate pieces of similar sizes and shapes. (Larger pieces will take longer to melt; smaller pieces may overcook.) Chocolate morsels are the sturdiest chocolate for melting. Squares are the next best option.

For quicker melting, microwave coarsely chopped chocolate at MEDIUM (50% power) for 30-second intervals until it starts to shine. Remove it from the microwave, and stir until completely smooth.

Quick Potatoes

Thank goodness there are so many ways to serve potatoes in a flash. You can buy them pan-ready fresh, frozen, dried, shredded, sliced, or mashed. The freezer case is crammed full of thick, thin, and crinkle-cut fries; nuggets; stuffed potatoes; and more. We particularly like frozen mashed potatoes, which can be cooked quickly in the microwave. Try them with flavored cream cheese, half-and-half, or extra butter for a satisfying side.

And if you haven't tried instant potatoes lately, you're in for a delicious surprise. Today, those familiar flakes and buds come alive with real potato taste and texture. Stir in a little cream, your favorite herb, or roasted garlic for terrific mashed potatoes. You can also use the dried flakes to coat fish or chicken, or to add body to soups and stews.

Scintillating Sauces

Pace Chunky Salsa has gotten sassier with the introduction of new flavors. Experience the rich, smoky flavor of Chipotle; the crisp tang of Lime & Garlic; the robust body of Grande Garlic; the mild kick of Fire-Roasted Tomato or Roasted Pepper & Garlic; and the authentic taste of Cilantro.

Use these salsas as marinades, ingredients, or toppings. Mix ½ cup of the Chipotle Chunky Salsa with 1 pound of ground beef for out-of-the-ordinary burgers. Sauté chicken strips in Cilantro Chunky Salsa for speedy fajitas. Give meat loaf more zing with Fire-Roasted Tomato Chunky Salsa: Mix ½ cup into the ground beef, and use the remainder for the sauce. Visit **www.pacefoods.com** for more ideas.

Want to taste the best recipes?

To receive a copy of the top-rated recipes for the past year, send a self-addressed, stamped, business-size envelope to Year's Best Recipes Editor, *Southern Living,* P.O. Box 523, Birmingham, AL 35201. Or visit **www.southernliving.com** to print out a copy of the recipes, entertaining tips, and more.

Tips and Tidbits

■ Stemmed glasses can be a nuisance to clean if the last drops of wine dry in the narrow bases. Madelyn Coar of Birmingham, Alabama, eliminates the problem this way: "After a big party, gather all glasses on a counter near the sink," she says. "Pour a little water in each glass. Whenever you're ready to wash them, they'll be easy to clean."

■ A loose or broken handle on a saucepan or skillet can be hazardous. The spin of a handle can send hot food flying across the kitchen, and you risk burning yourself in the process. Secure all handles on your cookware—if they can't be repaired, discard them.

■ Keep your pizza stone in the oven all the time. It conducts heat evenly, so casseroles, biscuits, and muffins brown on the top and bottom.

■ Don't let pots and pans tie your hands or block your creativity—our kitchen is full of multitalented equipment. So before you rush out to buy a specific bowl, casserole dish, or cakepan, look for substitutes. Bake a pie in a deep skillet, or shape a loaf of yeast bread in a clay roasting pot. Round cakes can be made square; layer cakes can become sheet cakes.

March

Easter Party Delights

Create a playful springtime celebration for the little "bunnies" in your life.

Give your children and their friends an Easter event fit for Peter Rabbit. Jan Moon of our Test Kitchens combined the bright spring colors and childlike whimsy of a tea party to create her delicious treats. For decoration, try Jan's Easter Egg Kaleidoscopes, which she says "are just like building a sandcastle, only with sugar."

COTTONTAIL PUNCH

MAKES 12 CUPS

- 6 cups peach-flavored white grape juice
- 1 (12-ounce) can frozen lemonade concentrate, thawed and undiluted
- 1 (1-liter) bottle club soda
- Lemonade Ice Cubes

STIR together first 3 ingredients in a large container; add Lemonade Ice Cubes. **Prep: 10 min.**

Lemonade Ice Cubes:

MAKES 2 TRAYS

- 1 (6-ounce) can frozen lemonade concentrate
- Red and green liquid food coloring

PREPARE lemonade according to package directions, and divide into 2 equal portions. Stir 2 drops red food coloring into 1 portion; pour into an ice cube tray, and freeze 8 hours. Repeat procedure with green food coloring and remaining lemonade. **Prep: 10 min., Freeze: 8 hrs.**

EASTER BUNNY PARTY SANDWICHES

MAKES ABOUT 2 DOZEN

- 1 (16-ounce) loaf white bread
- 1 (8-ounce) container chive-and-onion-flavored cream cheese
- 2 cups (8 ounces) shredded mozzarella cheese
- Decorations: red grape halves, blueberries

CUT bread slices using a 3- to 4-inch bunny-shaped cookie cutter. Spread 1 side of each slice with cream cheese; sprinkle with mozzarella cheese. Decorate with grape halves for eyes and a blueberry for the nose, if desired. **Prep: 25 min.**

DUCK PARTY SANDWICHES: Cut bread slices using a 3- to 4-inch duck-shaped cookie cutter. Spread 1 side of each slice with garden-vegetable cream cheese; sprinkle with shredded Cheddar. Decorate with olive slices for eyes, if desired.

FLOWER PARTY SANDWICHES: Cut bread slices using a 3- to 4-inch flower-shaped cookie cutter. Spread 1 side of each slice with strawberry cream cheese. Decorate flower with a strawberry slice in each petal and a blueberry in the center, if desired.

EASTER EGG PARTY SANDWICHES: Cut bread slices using a 3- to 4-inch egg-shaped cookie cutter. Spread 1 side of each slice with blueberry or strawberry cream cheese. Decorate Easter egg with strawberry slices or blueberries, and pipe with contrasting-colored cream cheese, if desired.

ROBIN'S EGG NESTS

MAKES ABOUT 2 DOZEN

- 6 (2-ounce) squares almond bark coating, melted
- Green food coloring paste
- 2½ cups crumbled shredded whole wheat cereal biscuits
- ¼ teaspoon orange oil flavoring (optional)
- Assorted jelly beans

STIR together melted coating and desired amount of food coloring paste; add cereal and, if desired, orange oil flavoring, stirring to combine.
DROP mixture by heaping tablespoonfuls onto wax paper; shape each spoonful into a bird's nest. Gently make a small indentation in center; fill with 3 jelly beans. Let dry completely. **Prep: 20 min.**

NOTE: Melt coating in the microwave for 3 minutes at MEDIUM (50% power), stirring once each minute.

EASTER EGG KALEIDOSCOPES

MAKES 1 EGG

Kids enjoy helping create these egg-shaped sugar shells that make a pretty centerpiece.

- 4 teaspoons cold water
- Red, green, or blue liquid food coloring
- 2 cups sugar
- Royal Icing
- Decorations: icing Easter animals, tiny candy blossoms

STIR together 4 teaspoons cold water and 2 drops of desired food coloring. Combine sugar and colored water in a zip-top plastic bag; blend well.
PACK sugar mixture firmly and evenly into 2 large half-egg molds; scrape off excess sugar mixture. Invert eggs onto a baking sheet; remove molds. Using a spatula, gently shave a flat edge on wide end of each egg to form a base.
BAKE at 200° for 15 to 20 minutes or until eggs harden. Remove from oven, cool, and scoop excess sugar from center of each egg half with a spoon or paring knife, leaving a ½-inch border.

Smooth edges with a spatula or spoon. Return to oven, and bake 10 to 15 minutes or until dried.

SCOOP out center of 1 egg half gently, all the way through, with a spoon or paring knife to form an oval window, leaving a ½-inch border. Smooth window edges with a spatula or spoon.

INVERT both egg halves onto a baking sheet. Pipe Royal Icing into egg half without window, and decorate Easter scene as desired.

PIPE Royal Icing around inside rim of window, and gently place on top of other half, forming a whole egg. Pipe a border around outside rim of window and seam of egg. Let stand at least 1 hour to dry. Store in an airtight container. **Prep: 1 hr., 15 min.; Bake 35 min.; Stand: 1 hr.**

FOR HORIZONTAL EGG KALEIDOSCOPES:
Prepare egg molds as directed, and invert onto a baking sheet, removing molds. Gently cut off 1 inch from narrow end of each egg half to form a window. Bake as directed. Scoop out center of each egg, leaving a ½-inch border. Decorate shells as desired. Pipe Royal Icing around inside rim of 1 shell, and gently place on top of remaining shell, forming a whole egg. Pipe a border around outside rim of window and seam of egg. Let stand at least 1 hour to dry.

Royal Icing:

MAKES ABOUT 3 CUPS

    1 (16-ounce) package powdered sugar
    3 tablespoons meringue powder
    6 to 8 tablespoons warm water

BEAT all ingredients at low speed with an electric mixer until blended.
BEAT at high speed 4 to 5 minutes or until stiff peaks form. If icing is too stiff, add additional water, ¼ teaspoon at a time, until desired consistency. **Prep: 6 min.**

NOTE: Icing dries rapidly; keep extra icing covered tightly at all times while working. Look for meringue powder and icing decorations at crafts stores and cake-decorating stores. We used an egg-mold kit from Wilton (1-800-794-5866 or **wilton.com**) and candy flowers from Sweet Celebrations (1-800-328-6722 or **sweetc.com**).

Here's a Toast to Spring

Celebrate winter's end with festive drink selections.

It's the beginning of spring, and that means celebrations galore. So we've gathered mouthwatering beverage recipes for entertaining or simply enjoying at home. Enjoy these offerings as you relish the season.

MINT JULEP

MAKES 4 CUPS

    2 cups bottled spring water
    ¾ cup sugar
    3 cups loosely packed fresh mint
        leaves
    2 cups bourbon

BRING first 3 ingredients to a boil in a large saucepan, stirring until sugar dissolves. Remove from heat. Cover; steep 30 minutes. Pour through a wire-mesh strainer into a pitcher, discarding mint leaves. Cool. Stir in bourbon. Serve over crushed ice. **Prep: 35 min.**

STANLEY DRY
NEW IBERIA, LOUISIANA

MARGARITA GRANITA

MAKES 5 CUPS

    3 cups water
    1 cup sugar
    ½ cup fresh lime juice
    ⅓ cup fresh lemon juice
    6 tablespoons orange liqueur
    6 tablespoons gold tequila
    2 teaspoons grated lime rind
    Sugar

BRING 3 cups water and 1 cup sugar to a boil in a saucepan, stirring mixture constantly. Pour into a large bowl; add lime juice and next 4 ingredients. Cover; freeze 8 hours.

PROCESS frozen mixture in a blender or food processor until slushy.

DIP margarita glass rims into water; dip rims in sugar. Spoon granita into glasses. **Prep: 15 min., Freeze: 8 hrs.**

NOTE: For a nonalcoholic version, omit liquors, and add ½ cup fresh orange juice.

PINEAPPLE FRUIT PUNCH

MAKES ABOUT 1½ GALLONS

    1 (46-ounce) can pineapple juice
    2 to 3 cups sugar
    2 (2.3-ounce) packages unsweetened
        lemonade drink mix
    3 quarts water
    1 (12-ounce) can frozen orange juice
        concentrate, thawed and undiluted
    ⅓ cup lemon juice
    1 quart ginger ale, chilled

STIR together first 3 ingredients in a large container until sugar dissolves. Stir in 3 quarts water, orange juice concentrate, and lemon juice; chill 4 hours. Stir in ginger ale just before serving. **Prep: 10 min., Chill: 4 hrs.**

NOTE: To make an ice ring, reserve 4 cups punch before chilling. Arrange assorted fruit in bottom of a 6-cup ring mold. Pour punch into mold, and freeze 8 hours.

ROSIE LEE HALL
TALLASSEE, ALABAMA

Sharing Food Fellowship

In these three Southern communities, home cooking is the tie that binds.

As Southerners, we know that food creates community. Dishes prepared and meals served for others create a comforting bond. Now more than ever, people appreciate the cheer, togetherness, and warmth of gathering and eating with friends. We visited with religious organizations from Texas, Georgia, and Oklahoma that exemplify the spirit of people reaching out to one another. Although distinctly different, the three groups share a common goal—nurturing others by offering not only food for the soul but lovingly cooked meals to satisfy the body as well.

Feeding the College Crowd

Every Wednesday, students at Northeast Texas Community College in Mount Pleasant, Texas, can enjoy a free hot lunch at the Baptist Student Ministries building just off campus. During the fall and spring semesters, some 15 Baptist churches in the area surrounding the college take turns preparing lunch for the young people. In addition, the pastor or a church member gives a short devotional so the collegians can stay connected to their faith. Volunteer cooks whip up crowd-pleasing dishes such as Jalapeño Chicken Casserole and Meatball Stroganoff.

JALAPEÑO CHICKEN CASSEROLE

MAKES 8 TO 10 SERVINGS

- 1 (10-ounce) package frozen chopped spinach, thawed
- 2 tablespoons butter or margarine
- 1 large onion, chopped
- 2 green onions, chopped
- 2 jalapeño peppers, seeded and chopped
- 1 (10¾-ounce) can cream of chicken soup, undiluted
- 1 (8-ounce) container sour cream
- 1 teaspoon ground cumin
- 1 (12-ounce) package nacho cheese-flavored tortilla chips
- 6 cups chopped cooked chicken
- 1 (8-ounce) package shredded Mexican four-cheese blend
- Garnish: green onions

DRAIN spinach well, pressing between paper towels.

MELT butter in a large skillet over medium heat. Add chopped onion, green onions, and jalapeño; sauté until tender. Remove skillet from heat; stir in spinach, soup, sour cream, and ground cumin.

LAYER half each of tortilla chips, chicken, spinach mixture, and cheese in a lightly greased 13- x 9-inch baking dish. Repeat layers, ending with spinach mixture.

BAKE at 350° for 10 minutes; sprinkle evenly with remaining cheese, and bake 10 more minutes or until cheese is melted. Garnish, if desired. **Prep: 20 min., Bake: 20 min.**

NOTE: For testing purposes only, we used Nacho Cheese Doritos.

MEATBALL STROGANOFF

MAKES 6 SERVINGS

Double this recipe for larger crowds.

- 1 pound lean ground beef
- 1 small onion, chopped
- 1 white bread slice, torn
- 1 large egg, lightly beaten
- 1 teaspoon minced garlic
- ½ teaspoon salt
- ½ teaspoon pepper
- 1 (10¾-ounce) can cream of mushroom soup, undiluted
- 1 (10-ounce) can beef broth
- 1 (3-ounce) package cream cheese, softened
- ½ cup sour cream
- 1 tablespoon chopped fresh or 1 teaspoon dried parsley flakes
- 1 (8-ounce) package wide egg noodles, cooked

COMBINE first 7 ingredients in a large bowl; shape mixture into 16 to 20 balls (about 2 tablespoonfuls each).

BROWN meatballs in a large skillet over medium heat. Remove meatballs from skillet; drain well, and set aside.

ADD soup, broth, and cream cheese to skillet, stirring until blended; return meatballs to skillet. Cover, reduce heat, and simmer, stirring occasionally, 10 minutes.

STIR together sour cream and parsley.

SERVE meatballs over noodles, and top with sour cream mixture. **Prep: 20 min., Cook: 20 min.**

TO FREEZE: Place cooked cream cheese mixture and noodles together in an airtight container, and freeze up to 1 month. Place cooked meatballs in an airtight container or large heavy-duty zip-top plastic bag, and freeze up to 1 month.

TO LIGHTEN: Substitute reduced-sodium, reduced-fat cream of mushroom soup; light sour cream; and 33%-less-fat cream cheese.

Preachers With Pans

In Marietta, Georgia, an annual clergy cook-off ignites the culinary talents of area ministers, who prepare their best dishes while onlookers buy samples. Each $1 purchase equals a vote; the pastor with the most votes wins the People's Choice Award. The event benefits The Extension, a nonprofit substance abuse center. Winning recipes include Barbecue Baked Catfish and Cumin-Celery-Scented Coleslaw.

CUMIN-CELERY-SCENTED COLESLAW

MAKES 7 CUPS

Cumin and celery seeds give this coleslaw a contemporary twist.

1 teaspoon cumin seeds
1 teaspoon celery seeds
1 cup mayonnaise
2 tablespoons white wine
   vinegar
¾ teaspoon salt
⅛ teaspoon ground red pepper
1 large cucumber, peeled
1 medium cabbage, finely shredded, or
   2 (10-ounce) packages angel hair
   cabbage
Garnish: fresh cilantro sprig

COOK cumin and celery seeds in a hot nonstick skillet over medium-high heat, stirring constantly, 2 minutes or until seeds are toasted.
PLACE seeds in a large bowl; whisk in mayonnaise and next 3 ingredients.
HALVE cucumber lengthwise; seed and cut into ¾-inch-thick slices. Place cucumber and cabbage in bowl with dressing; toss to coat. Cover and chill 4 hours. Garnish, if desired. Serve with a slotted spoon. **Prep: 27 min., Chill: 4 hrs.**

BARBECUE BAKED CATFISH

MAKES 5 SERVINGS

¾ cup ketchup
¼ cup butter or margarine
1 tablespoon balsamic vinegar
1 tablespoon Worcestershire sauce
1 teaspoon Dijon mustard
½ teaspoon Jamaican jerk seasoning
1 garlic clove, minced
10 (3- to 4-ounce) catfish fillets
⅛ teaspoon pepper
Garnish: chopped fresh parsley

STIR together first 7 ingredients in a small saucepan over medium-low heat; cook ketchup mixture 10 minutes, stirring occasionally.
SPRINKLE catfish with pepper; arrange in a lightly greased aluminum foil-lined broiler pan. Pour sauce over catfish.
BAKE catfish at 400° for 10 to 12 minutes or until fish flakes with a fork. Garnish, if desired. **Prep: 20 min., Bake: 12 min.**

A Passover Celebration

In Oklahoma City, a Jewish study group joins similar organizations in a women's dessert seder during Passover. "It's a time to invite others into our group who don't have family," says Marcy Moskowitz Price, program director of the Jewish Federation Center. The eight-day event is steeped in rituals; a feast of desserts, including those here, concludes the occasion.

THREE-FRUIT ICE

MAKES 8 CUPS

2 cups water
1 cup sugar
4 bananas, mashed
2 cups grape juice
⅓ cup fresh lemon juice (about 4
   lemons)
Garnish: fresh mint sprigs

COOK 2 cups water and sugar in a medium saucepan over medium heat, stirring constantly, 5 minutes or until sugar is dissolved. Remove from heat, and cool.
PROCESS sugar mixture, banana, and juices in a blender until smooth. Pour into a 13- x 9-inch pan, and freeze 3 hours or until almost firm.
BEAT banana mixture in pan at medium speed with an electric mixer until mixture is smooth. Cover and freeze 8 hours. Garnish, if desired. **Prep: 10 min., Freeze: 11 hrs.**

LEMONY PASSOVER CHEESECAKE

MAKES 10 TO 12 SERVINGS

1 cup crushed mandelbrot*
1 cup finely chopped pecans
¼ cup sugar
⅓ cup butter or margarine, melted
2 (8-ounce) packages cream cheese,
   softened
3 large eggs
1 (14-ounce) can sweetened
   condensed milk
2 teaspoons grated lemon rind
⅓ cup fresh lemon juice
1 (8-ounce) container sour cream
Garnishes: sour cream, lemon slices,
   lemon rind strips

STIR together first 4 ingredients, and press mixture in bottom and 2 inches up sides of a lightly greased 9-inch springform pan.
BEAT cheese at medium speed with an electric mixer 3 minutes or until light and fluffy. Add eggs, 1 at a time, beating just until blended. Gradually add milk, rind, and juice, beating until blended. Pour into prepared crust.
BAKE at 300° for 1 hour or until almost set. Turn off oven, and let cake stand in oven 30 minutes. Remove cake to a wire rack; spread evenly with sour cream, and let cool completely. Cover and chill 8 hours. Garnish, if desired. **Prep: 15 min., Bake: 1 hr., Stand: 30 min., Chill: 8 hrs.**

*Mandelbrot is a crisp, cookielike almond bread. Substitute 1 (8-ounce) package almond biscotti, crushed, if desired.

A Basket of Caring

Transform leftovers into charming gift packages
that are perfect for family and friends.

Food nourishes relationships in the South better than any place we know. Southerners just naturally welcome new neighbors, celebrate births, give comfort, and send their kids away to college with arms full of home-cooked food. We all know the next best thing to receiving such a package is giving one, and this story shows you how.

Many of these recipes take advantage of big meals that start with meats such as ham or roast beef, letting you turn those leftovers into a salad or sandwich with stylish sauces.

If you prefer, assemble the ingredients instead of furnishing a completely prepared dish. This eliminates any worries about delivery—you still have the pleasure of giving dinner, but the recipient enjoys the choice of when to serve it. However you deliver them, few presents are more thoughtful.

Be Prepared

It's easy to pack goodies from your kitchen when you keep these items on hand.

- disposable food cartons, plastic bags, baskets, and boxes
- assorted place mats and napkins you can use as gifts
- small jars or bottles with lids
- decorative wrapping paper and ribbon or raffia

HAM-STUFFED BAKED POTATOES

MAKES 8 SERVINGS

Use leftover ham to make these easy potatoes. Send them with a bag of assorted salad greens and carrot sticks.

> 4 large potatoes (about 3 pounds)
> 1 tablespoon butter or margarine
> 3 cups chopped cooked ham
> 1 small onion, diced
> 2 garlic cloves, minced
> ½ cup sour cream
> ¼ teaspoon salt
> ¼ teaspoon pepper
> ¾ cup shredded Parmesan cheese
> Garnish: chopped fresh chives

BAKE potatoes at 450° for 1 hour or until tender. Allow to cool to touch.
CUT potatoes in half lengthwise; scoop out pulp, and place in a bowl, leaving shells intact. Set pulp and shells aside.
MELT butter in a small skillet over medium-high heat; add chopped ham, diced onion, and minced garlic, and sauté until onion is tender.
MASH potato pulp; stir in ham mixture, sour cream, salt, and pepper. Stuff shells with potato mixture; sprinkle evenly with Parmesan cheese. Place in a 13- x 9-inch pan or casserole dish.
BAKE at 350° for 25 to 30 minutes. Garnish, if desired. **Prep: 20 min.; Bake: 1 hr., 30 min.**

WILD RICE-AND-CHICKEN SALAD

MAKES 4 SERVINGS

Roast one chicken for you and a second for the salad. If you're short on time, use a deli-roasted chicken from the supermarket.

> 1 (14-ounce) can low-sodium fat-free chicken broth
> 1 (6-ounce) package long-grain and wild rice mix
> 2 cups shredded cooked chicken
> 2 celery ribs, thinly sliced
> 1 green bell pepper, chopped
> 1 small purple onion, chopped
> Lemon-Mustard Dressing

BRING chicken broth to a boil in a medium saucepan; stir in rice mix and seasoning packet. Return to a boil; cover, reduce heat, and simmer 30 minutes or until rice is tender. Cool.
STIR together rice mixture, chicken, and remaining ingredients. Chill at least 30 minutes. **Prep: 10 min., Cook: 30 min., Chill: 30 min.**

Lemon-Mustard Dressing:

MAKES ABOUT ⅔ CUP

> ¼ cup olive oil
> ⅓ cup lemon juice
> 1½ teaspoons dry mustard
> ½ teaspoon pepper

WHISK together all ingredients. **Prep: 5 min.**

CAROLINE KENNEDY
NEWBORN, GEORGIA

SPICY THAI MAYONNAISE

MAKES 1⅓ CUPS

Give this to use as a dressing or sandwich spread. It enlivens potato salad, chicken, or roast-beef sandwiches.

> 1 cup mayonnaise
> 3 green onions, chopped
> 2 tablespoons chili-garlic paste
> 1 tablespoon chopped fresh cilantro
> 1 jalapeño pepper, seeded and chopped
> 1 teaspoon red wine vinegar
> ¼ teaspoon curry powder

PROCESS all ingredients in a blender or food processor until smooth, stopping to scrape down sides. Chill at least 1 hour. **Prep: 15 min., Chill: 1 hr.**

KATIE KELLY BELL
ATLANTA, GEORGIA

HORSERADISH SPREAD

MAKES 1¼ CUPS

Wrap sliced roast beef, chewy rolls, and a jar of this wonderful concoction in a basket. To round out the package, add chips and a couple of bottles of premium beer.

- 1 (5-ounce) package garlic-and-herb-flavored spreadable cheese
- 3 tablespoons prepared horseradish, drained
- ½ (8-ounce) package cream cheese, softened
- ¼ cup sour cream
- 1 tablespoon chopped fresh dill

STIR together all ingredients until blended. Cover and chill up to 7 days. **Prep: 5 min.**

NOTE: For testing purposes only, we used Rondelé Garlic & Herbs Gourmet Spreadable Cheese.

BEEF ROLLS WITH MUSTARD-HORSERADISH CREAM

MAKES 6 SERVINGS

- 1 medium onion, halved and sliced
- 1 yellow bell pepper, halved and sliced
- 1 teaspoon vegetable oil
- 6 sandwich rolls, split and toasted
- Mustard-Horseradish Cream
- 6 romaine lettuce leaves
- 1 pound roast beef, thinly sliced

SAUTÉ onion and bell pepper in hot oil in a skillet over medium heat 2 minutes or until tender.
SPREAD cut sides of each roll with 1 tablespoon Mustard-Horseradish Cream. Top bottom half with lettuce, onion, bell pepper, and roast beef. Spoon remaining Mustard-Horseradish Cream over beef; top with remaining rolls. **Prep: 20 min.**

Mustard-Horseradish Cream:

MAKES ABOUT 1 CUP

- 1 cup light sour cream
- 2 to 3 tablespoons prepared horseradish
- 1 teaspoon dry mustard
- ¼ teaspoon lemon rind

STIR together all ingredients. Chill until ready to serve. **Prep: 5 min.**

PORK TENDERLOIN SANDWICHES WITH BOURBON SAUCE

MAKES 3 DOZEN APPETIZERS

Help a friend prepare for a party—you marinate the pork tenderloins, make and bottle the Bourbon Sauce, and then let the host do the rest.

- 2 (¾-pound) pork tenderloins
- 3 garlic cloves, slivered
- ⅓ cup peanut oil
- ¼ cup bourbon
- 1 tablespoon Worcestershire sauce
- 1 tablespoon dried rosemary
- 1 teaspoon Greek seasoning
- Bourbon Sauce
- 3 dozen yeast rolls, split

CUT several small slits in pork; stuff garlic into slits.
COMBINE oil and next 4 ingredients in a shallow dish; add pork. Cover and chill 2 hours, turning occasionally.
BAKE at 325° for 55 minutes or until a meat thermometer inserted into thickest portion registers 160°. Remove from oven; cool. Cut into ¼-inch-thick slices. Pour Bourbon Sauce over pork; cover and chill 8 hours. Serve pork on split rolls. **Prep: 10 min., Chill: 10 hrs., Bake: 55 min.**

Bourbon Sauce:

MAKES 2 CUPS

- 1 cup ketchup
- ½ cup firmly packed dark brown sugar
- ½ cup bourbon
- 2 tablespoons Worcestershire sauce
- 1½ teaspoons Greek seasoning
- 1 teaspoon garlic salt

STIR together ketchup and next 5 ingredients. **Prep: 5 min.**

Bake a Batch of Cookies

Homemade sweets are always a treat. These will disappear quickly.

CARAMEL-FILLED CHOCOLATE COOKIES

MAKES 4 DOZEN

- 1 cup butter or margarine, softened
- 1 cup sugar
- 1 cup firmly packed brown sugar
- 2 large eggs
- 2 teaspoons vanilla extract
- 2¼ cups all-purpose flour
- ¾ cup unsweetened cocoa
- 1 teaspoon baking soda
- 1 cup chopped pecans, divided
- 6 (2-ounce) packages chocolate-caramel cookie bars, cut into 1-inch pieces
- 1 tablespoon sugar
- 2 (2-ounce) vanilla bark coating squares

BEAT butter at medium speed with an electric mixer until creamy; gradually add sugars, beating well. Add eggs, 1 at a time, and vanilla, beating until blended.
COMBINE flour, cocoa, and soda; add to butter mixture, beating at low speed until blended after each addition. Stir in ½ cup pecans. Shape 1 tablespoon dough around each candy piece, covering completely, to form balls.
COMBINE remaining ½ cup pecans and 1 tablespoon sugar. Gently press top of each ball into pecan mixture. Place balls, pecan sides up, 2 inches apart on baking sheets.
BAKE at 375° for 7 to 10 minutes. Cool on baking sheets 2 minutes. Remove from baking sheets; cool completely on wire racks. Melt coating squares in a saucepan over low heat, stirring constantly until smooth. Drizzle over cookies. **Prep: 20 min., Bake: 10 min., Cool: 2 min.**

NOTE: For testing purposes only, we used Twix Caramel Cookie Bars.

HAZEL M. STALEY
GAITHERSBURG, MARYLAND

Tasty Tortilla Treats

Flour tortillas are good for more than burritos and wraps. They're great for quick snacks, easy desserts, and dressed-up leftovers. These reader recipes require little more than your oven and a few staples from the refrigerator and pantry.

SOFT TACO STACKS

MAKES 6 SERVINGS

- 1 (16-ounce) can refried beans
- 9 (10-inch) flour tortillas, divided
- 1 (8-ounce) package shredded Mexican four-cheese blend
- 2 jalapeño peppers, seeded and chopped
- 1½ cups chopped cooked chicken
- 6 green onions, sliced
- 1½ cups shredded lettuce
- 1 (8-ounce) jar salsa
- 1 medium avocado, diced
- 2 medium tomatoes, seeded and chopped
- ⅓ cup chopped fresh cilantro

SPREAD beans on 1 side each of 3 tortillas; place tortillas, beans sides up, on a baking sheet. Sprinkle evenly with cheese and next 3 ingredients.
BAKE at 350° for 15 minutes or until cheese melts. Remove from sheet, and sprinkle evenly with lettuce.
TOP each with 1 tortilla. Spread each tortilla top with 2 tablespoons salsa, and sprinkle evenly with avocado, tomato, and cilantro; top with remaining 3 tortillas. Cut into quarters; serve with remaining salsa. **Prep: 30 min., Bake: 15 min.**

TO LIGHTEN: Use fat-free refried beans and 2% reduced-fat cheese.

JUDY OGLESBY
BRANDON, MISSISSIPPI

JUMPIN' JACK TORTILLAS

MAKES 8 SERVINGS

Serve with your favorite salsa or guacamole.

- 8 (8-inch) flour tortillas*
- Vegetable cooking spray
- 2 teaspoons chili powder
- ½ teaspoon salt
- 1½ cups (6 ounces) shredded Monterey Jack cheese with peppers

CUT tortillas into eighths; coat triangles with cooking spray, and place on a baking sheet.
COMBINE chili powder and salt; sprinkle over tortillas. Top with cheese.
BAKE at 400° for 15 minutes or until cheese melts and tortillas are golden brown. **Prep: 10 min., Bake: 15 min.**

*Substitute 8 (8-inch) corn tortillas for flour tortillas, if desired.

LOGAN GEORGIADIS
ORLANDO, FLORIDA

DESSERT QUESADILLAS

MAKES 6 SERVINGS

- 2 Granny Smith apples, thinly sliced
- ½ cup sweetened dried cranberries
- 1 teaspoon cinnamon sugar
- 1 teaspoon lemon juice
- 7 tablespoons butter or margarine, divided
- 6 (10-inch) flour tortillas
- 1 (8-ounce) package cream cheese, softened
- ¼ cup powdered sugar
- ½ cup caramel sauce
- ½ cup chopped pecans, toasted

TOSS together first 4 ingredients.
MELT 1 tablespoon butter in a large nonstick skillet over medium heat; add apple mixture, and sauté 5 minutes or until tender. Remove apple mixture, and set aside; wipe skillet clean.
SPREAD 1 tablespoon butter evenly on 1 side of each tortilla.
STIR together cream cheese and powdered sugar until smooth. Spread cheese mixture evenly on unbuttered side of each tortilla, and top evenly with apple mixture. Fold tortillas in half over apple mixture.
COOK quesadillas, in batches, in skillet over medium heat 2 minutes on each side or until golden brown. Drizzle with caramel sauce, and sprinkle with pecans before serving. **Prep: 5 min., Cook: 4 min. per batch**

EVA JONES
TOWER HILL, ILLINOIS

SWEET TORTILLA TRIANGLES WITH FRUIT SALSA

MAKES ABOUT 5 DOZEN

- ¼ cup sugar
- 2 tablespoons light brown sugar
- 1 teaspoon ground cinnamon
- ¼ cup butter or margarine
- ⅛ teaspoon vanilla extract
- 8 (8-inch) flour tortillas
- Fruit Salsa

COMBINE sugars and cinnamon.
MELT butter in a saucepan over medium heat; stir in vanilla. Brush 2 tortillas with butter mixture; sprinkle with about 1½ tablespoons sugar mixture. Cut into eighths, and place on a baking sheet.
BAKE at 450° for 5 minutes or until golden brown. Repeat with remaining tortillas. Serve with Fruit Salsa. **Prep: 15 min., Bake: 5 min. per batch**

SAVORY TRIANGLES: Omit sugars, cinnamon, vanilla, and Fruit Salsa. Brush tortillas with ¼ cup melted butter; sprinkle with ½ cup shredded Parmesan cheese, ¼ cup sesame seeds, and 1 tablespoon pepper. Proceed as directed.

Fruit Salsa:

MAKES 2½ CUPS

- 1 cup chopped fresh pineapple
- ½ cup chopped fresh mango
- 1 cup chopped fresh strawberries
- 1 tablespoon chopped fresh mint
- 1 tablespoon fresh lime juice

TOSS together all ingredients. Cover fruit mixture, and chill 1 hour. **Prep: 20 min., Chill: 1 hr.**

PAULA BIELER
AUSTIN, TEXAS

Bring Home the Bacon

Give dinner some sizzle with these irresistible dishes.

If the sound of bacon frying can awaken your early-morning senses, then why not give it a starring role at suppertime too? With so many options available, there's no need to wait for breakfast to enjoy its unmistakable taste. So move over, eggs and biscuits—bacon's gone mainstream.

STUFFED BANANA PEPPERS

MAKES 6 TO 8 SERVINGS

- 6 to 8 large banana peppers
- 2 cups (8 ounces) shredded sharp Cheddar cheese
- 1 small tomato, diced
- 1 medium onion, diced
- ½ small green bell pepper, diced
- 1 to 2 jalapeño peppers, diced
- ⅛ teaspoon salt
- ⅛ teaspoon pepper
- 12 to 16 bacon slices

CUT a slit lengthwise in each banana pepper, cutting to, but not through, other side. Remove seeds.
COMBINE cheese and next 6 ingredients. Spoon mixture evenly into each pepper, and wrap each with 2 bacon slices; secure with wooden picks. Place peppers on a rack in a broiler pan.
BROIL 5½ inches from heat 4 to 5 minutes on each side or until golden. **Prep: 15 min., Broil: 10 min.**

JEAN VOAN
SHEPHERD, TEXAS

SOUTHERN SMOTHERED GREEN BEANS

MAKES 6 TO 8 SERVINGS

- 4 to 6 bacon slices
- 3 celery ribs, chopped
- 1 pound fresh green beans, trimmed
- 1 medium onion, chopped
- 1 red bell pepper, chopped
- 3 plum tomatoes, seeded and chopped
- 2 garlic cloves, minced
- ½ teaspoon dried thyme
- ½ teaspoon dried basil
- ½ teaspoon paprika
- ¼ teaspoon black pepper
- 1½ teaspoons salt

COOK bacon in a large skillet until crisp; remove bacon, and drain on paper towels, reserving 2 tablespoons drippings in skillet. Crumble bacon, and set aside.
COOK celery and next 3 ingredients in hot drippings in skillet over medium-high heat 10 to 12 minutes. Add tomato and next 6 ingredients; cook, stirring often, 5 minutes or until beans are tender. Stir in bacon. **Prep: 10 min., Cook: 27 min.**

LINDA L. ROWLEY
THE WOODLANDS, TEXAS

BACON-FRIED TATERS

MAKES 6 TO 8 SERVINGS

- 8 bacon slices
- 2½ pounds baking potatoes, cooked and cut into ½-inch-thick slices
- 2 green onions, sliced
- 1 (4-ounce) jar diced pimiento, drained
- ¾ teaspoon salt
- ½ teaspoon pepper

COOK bacon in a large skillet until crisp; remove bacon, and drain on paper towels, reserving ¼ cup drippings in skillet. Crumble bacon.
COMBINE sliced potato, half of bacon, onions, and next 3 ingredients in skillet. Cook, covered, over low heat 15 minutes; uncover and cook 10 minutes or until golden brown on bottom. Sprinkle with remaining bacon. **Prep: 30 min., Cook: 25 min.**

DELLA TAYLOR
JONESBOROUGH, TENNESSEE

PEPPERED BACON-WRAPPED PORK TENDERLOIN

MAKES 8 SERVINGS

- ¼ cup butter or margarine
- ¾ pound fresh mushrooms, sliced
- 1 small onion, chopped
- ¼ cup chopped pecans, toasted
- 2 (¾-pound) pork tenderloins, trimmed
- 1 teaspoon salt
- 1 teaspoon ground black pepper
- 8 thick bacon slices
- ¼ cup firmly packed brown sugar
- 1 teaspoon cracked black pepper

MELT butter in a large skillet over medium-high heat; add mushrooms and onion, and sauté 8 minutes or until tender. Stir in pecans, and set aside.
PLACE pork between 2 sheets of plastic wrap; flatten to ¼-inch thickness, using a meat mallet or rolling pin. Sprinkle with salt and ground pepper.
SPREAD mushroom mixture evenly on 1 side of each tenderloin, leaving a ¼-inch border. Roll up, jellyroll fashion, starting with 1 long end. Wrap 4 bacon slices around each tenderloin, and secure with wooden picks. Place, seam sides down, on a lightly greased rack in a roasting pan. Rub evenly with sugar and cracked pepper.
BAKE, uncovered, at 450° for 15 minutes. Reduce temperature to 400°.
BAKE at 400° for 15 minutes or until a meat thermometer registers 160°. **Prep: 20 min., Bake: 30 min.**

Comforting Red Beans and Rice

This simple, satisfying dish is synonymous with home cooking in New Orleans.

Assistant Foods Editor Joy Zacharia was somewhat apprehensive to write an article on red beans and rice, knowing how persnickety New Orleans folks are about their native dishes. But after chatting with food experts and home cooks, she learned that no two recipes are alike.

"In New Orleans, you come out of the womb instinctually knowing how to cook red beans and rice. Really, only the nervous newlywed follows a recipe," says Poppy Tooker, a Louisiana native who is one of four U.S. international governors of Slow Food, an Italy-based organization dedicated to preserving world food traditions.

There's more to this dish than beans, though. For some cooks, ham hocks, andouille sausage, or bacon is a must; for others, it's pickled or salt pork.

Food writer Marcelle Bienvenu, who has collaborated with Emeril Lagasse on several cookbooks and who edits the cooking section of his Web site, says, "Some people like to serve fried pork chops with the red beans and rice; others omit the smoked sausage in the pot but serve a link of sausage with the red beans. Everyone has his or her version, depending on family traditions."

Southern Living Lifestyle Editor and New Orleans native Majella Chube Hamilton uses smoked turkey to give her red beans their characteristic flavor, while her mom, Merion Chube, sticks to smoked sausage and, sometimes, ham hocks. "It's not a seasoning I use often," Merion says, "but when I visit family in

Indianapolis, I know my son-in-law and his dad like my red beans cooked with smoked ham hocks."

Nobody knows exactly when the dish was born: "Red beans have been in-grained in the New Orleans landscape for about 200 years," Poppy says. It is well known that Louis "Satchmo" Armstrong loved them. In a letter to a fellow New Orleanian, Armstrong wrote, "It really shouldn't be any problem at all for you to figure out my favorite dish. We all were brought up eating the same thing, so I will tell you: Red Beans and Rice with Ham Hocks is my birthmark."

We should all be so lucky.

SPICY RED BEANS AND RICE

MAKES 2 QUARTS

- **2 pounds dried red kidney beans**
- **5 bacon slices, chopped**
- **1 pound smoked sausage, cut into ¼-inch-thick slices**
- **½ pound salt pork, quartered**
- **6 garlic cloves, minced**
- **5 celery ribs, sliced**
- **2 green bell peppers, chopped**
- **1 large onion, chopped**
- **2 (32-ounce) containers chicken broth**
- **2 cups water**
- **1 teaspoon salt**
- **1 teaspoon ground red pepper**
- **1 teaspoon black pepper**
- **Hot cooked rice**

PLACE kidney beans in a Dutch oven. Cover with water 2 inches above beans, and let soak 8 hours. Drain beans; rinse thoroughly, and drain again.

SAUTÉ bacon in Dutch oven over medium-high heat 5 minutes. Add smoked sausage and salt pork; sauté 5 minutes or until sausage is golden brown. Add garlic and next 3 ingredients; sauté 5 minutes or until vegetables are tender.

STIR in beans, broth, 2 cups water, and next 3 ingredients; bring to a boil. Boil 15 minutes; reduce heat, and simmer, stirring occasionally, 3 hours or until beans are tender. Remove salt pork before serving. Serve over rice. **Prep: 30 min.; Soak: 8 hrs.; Cook: 3 hrs., 30 min.**

NOTE: For quick soaking, place kidney beans in a Dutch oven; cover with water 2 inches above beans, and bring to a boil. Boil 1 minute; cover, remove from heat, and let stand 1 hour. Drain and proceed with recipe.

Top Dogs

Southerners love hot dogs—so much so that we have several cities on the National Hot Dog and Sausage Council's Top 10 Hot Dog Consuming American Cities list: Baltimore/Washington, D.C.; Birmingham/Montgomery; Miami/Fort Lauderdale; Houston; and San Antonio/Corpus Christi. These recipes are list-toppers too.

FRIED HOT DOGS

MAKES 4 SERVINGS

- **4 hot dogs**
- **¼ cup mayonnaise**
- **¼ cup mustard**
- **4 hamburger buns, toasted**
- **4 tomato slices**
- **4 onion slices**
- **4 lettuce leaves**

CUT a slit lengthwise through each hot dog, cutting to, but not through, other side. Place hot dogs, flat sides down, in a skillet, and cook 2 minutes on each side or until browned. Drain hot dogs on paper towels.

STIR together mayonnaise and mustard; spread evenly on hamburger bun halves. Place 1 hot dog on bottom half of each bun; top each evenly with tomato, onion, lettuce, and remaining bun halves. **Prep: 5 min., Cook: 5 min.**

JERRY LYNN ROGERS
KINGSPORT, TENNESSEE

Taco Dogs

MAKES 8 SERVINGS

8 hot dogs
1 cup refried beans
1 cup (4 ounces) shredded Cheddar
    cheese
½ cup salsa
8 (8-inch) flour tortillas
1 cup shredded lettuce
1 tomato, chopped

COOK hot dogs in boiling water to cover 5 minutes; drain.

COMBINE beans, cheese, and salsa in a glass bowl, and microwave at HIGH 2 minutes or until thoroughly heated, stirring once.

SPREAD mixture evenly on 1 side of each tortilla. Place hot dogs on tortillas; top hot dogs evenly with lettuce and tomato, and roll up tortillas. **Prep: 10 min., Cook: 7 min.**

Corn Dogs and Taters

MAKES 8 SERVINGS

16 (8-inch) wooden sticks,
    divided
8 hot dogs
2 baking potatoes, cut into ½-inch
    cubes (about ¾ pound)
¾ cup all-purpose flour
½ teaspoon baking
    powder
½ teaspoon salt
1 large egg
½ cup milk
1 tablespoon vegetable oil
Peanut oil

INSERT a stick into each hot dog, leaving about a 3-inch handle; set aside.

THREAD potatoes onto remaining sticks. Whisk together flour and next 5 ingredients; pour into a tall glass.

POUR peanut oil to a depth of 1½ inches into a large skillet; heat to 350°.

DIP hot dogs in batter, covering well.

FRY hot dogs and potatoes, in batches, 4 to 5 minutes or until golden brown. Serve with mustard or ketchup. **Prep: 10 min., Cook: 5 min. per batch**

NOTE: Substitute 1 (8-ounce) package hush puppy mix and ¾ cup milk or 1 (8½-ounce) package corn muffin mix, 1 large egg, and ⅓ cup milk for flour through vegetable oil.

Bourbon Sausage Dogs

MAKES 8 SERVINGS

⅔ cup firmly packed light brown sugar
⅔ cup ketchup
½ cup bourbon or cola soft drink
2 tablespoons minced onion
1 (16-ounce) package bun-length
    smoked sausage
8 hot dog buns
Coleslaw

STIR together first 4 ingredients in a large skillet over low heat; add sausage. Cover and simmer 30 minutes. Serve on buns with Coleslaw. **Prep: 10 min., Cook: 30 min.**

Coleslaw:

MAKES ABOUT 3 CUPS

1 (8-ounce) container sour cream
2 tablespoons sugar
2 tablespoons white vinegar
2 teaspoons celery seeds
1 teaspoon salt
¼ teaspoon ground cumin
1 (10-ounce) package finely shredded
    cabbage

STIR together first 6 ingredients in a large bowl; add shredded cabbage, tossing to coat. Cover and chill until ready to serve. **Prep: 5 min.**

CAROLYN M. HOWE
SHIPPENSBURG, PENNSYLVANIA

Try a New Stew

Mirliton, a squashlike fruit, tastes similar to yellow squash or zucchini. This stew is the perfect way to try it.

Mirliton Stew

MAKES 6 SERVINGS

1 pound Italian sausage
4 large mirlitons (chayotes), seeded
    and chopped*
1 medium-size green bell pepper,
    chopped
1 small onion, chopped
2 garlic cloves, pressed
½ teaspoon dried thyme
1 (18-ounce) jar spaghetti sauce
1 (16-ounce) can tomato sauce
3 cups water
½ teaspoon salt
1 (6.6-ounce) package polenta
1 cup milk
¾ cup shredded Parmesan cheese,
    divided

REMOVE and discard casings from sausage. Cook sausage in a skillet over medium-high heat, stirring until sausage crumbles and is no longer pink. Remove sausage from skillet; drain well, reserving 1 teaspoon drippings in skillet.

SAUTÉ chopped mirliton and next 4 ingredients in hot drippings in skillet 5 minutes or until onion is tender. Stir in sausage, spaghetti sauce, and tomato sauce; cover and cook over medium heat, stirring occasionally, 30 minutes or until mirliton is tender. Keep warm.

BRING 3 cups water and salt to a boil in a saucepan; gradually stir in polenta. Reduce heat, and cook, stirring constantly, 5 minutes. Stir in milk and half of Parmesan cheese; cook 3 minutes. Pour polenta onto a serving plate; spoon sausage mixture evenly over polenta, and sprinkle with remaining Parmesan cheese. **Prep: 30 min., Cook: 45 min.**

*Substitute 4 large yellow squash or zucchini, if desired.

Appetizers on Hand

When guests come by at a moment's notice, treat them to these festive bites.

Be prepared for an impromptu gathering by keeping these snacks in your freezer or refrigerator. When friends drop by, you'll only have to heat or slice the appetizers, place them on a serving dish, and stir together our Speedy Spring Cooler. Then you'll be free to enjoy the visit.

SPICY CHEESE-BEEF DIP

MAKES 2¼ CUPS

- 1 pound ground beef
- 2 green onions, sliced
- 1 (1¼-ounce) envelope taco seasoning mix
- 1 (16-ounce) jar salsa
- ¾ cup water
- 1 (8-ounce) loaf pasteurized prepared cheese product, cubed
- ¼ cup instant potato flakes

COOK ground beef in a large skillet, stirring until crumbled and no longer pink; drain. Return beef to skillet; stir in green onions and next 3 ingredients.
BRING to a boil; reduce heat, and simmer 5 minutes.
STIR in cubed cheese product until melted. Stir in potato flakes, and cook over low heat 5 minutes or until thickened. Serve warm with tortilla chips. **Prep: 10 min., Cook: 15 min.**

NOTE: To make ahead, cool, cover, and chill. To reheat, cook over low heat, stirring occasionally, about 15 minutes or until thoroughly heated.

KATHLEEN A. CHAVEZ
MONROE, NORTH CAROLINA

SNAPPY REUBEN ROLLS

MAKES 8 APPETIZERS

- 1 (8-ounce) package refrigerated crescent rolls
- 1 (10-ounce) can sauerkraut, drained
- 2 tablespoons Thousand Island salad dressing
- 1 teaspoon dry mustard
- 8 (½-ounce) thinly sliced deli corned beef slices
- 2 Swiss cheese slices, cut into 16 (½-inch) strips

UNROLL crescent rolls, and separate into 8 triangles. Roll each dough portion into a 7-inch triangle.
STIR together sauerkraut, salad dressing, and mustard. Place 1 corned beef slice across wide side of 1 triangle, folding to fit, if necessary.
SPREAD 2 tablespoons sauerkraut mixture over corned beef, and top with 2 cheese strips. Roll up, beginning with wide end of triangle. Repeat with remaining triangles, sauerkraut mixture, corned beef, and cheese. Place rolls, point sides down, on an ungreased baking sheet.
BAKE rolls at 375° for 15 to 17 minutes or until golden brown. **Prep: 15 min., Bake: 17 min.**

NOTE: Rolls may be baked and frozen. To reheat, thaw at room temperature 15 minutes; cover with foil, and bake at 375° for 25 minutes. Uncover and bake 4 minutes.

SUDI HATFIELD
EDISON, NEW JERSEY

SOUTHWESTERN CHICKEN SALAD SPIRALS

MAKES 40 APPETIZERS

Pine nuts add an unexpected crunch to these savory snacks. *(pictured on page 74)*

- 1 (7-ounce) jar roasted red bell peppers
- 2 cups chopped cooked chicken
- 1 (8-ounce) package cream cheese, softened
- 1 (0.4-ounce) envelope Ranch-style buttermilk dressing mix
- ¼ cup chopped ripe olives
- ½ small onion, diced
- 1 (4.5-ounce) can chopped green chiles, drained
- 2 tablespoons chopped fresh cilantro
- ½ teaspoon pepper
- ¼ cup pine nuts (optional)
- 8 (6-inch) flour tortillas
- Garnish: fresh cilantro

DRAIN roasted peppers well, pressing between layers of paper towels; chop.
STIR together roasted peppers, chicken, and next 7 ingredients. Cover and chill at least 2 hours.
STIR pine nuts, if desired, into chicken mixture. Spoon evenly over tortillas, and roll up. Cut each roll into 5 slices, securing with wooden picks, if necessary. Garnish, if desired. **Prep: 15 min., Chill: 2 hrs.**

JENNI DISE
PHOENIX, ARIZONA

SPEEDY SPRING COOLER

MAKES 6 CUPS

Stir up this three-ingredient cooler for a refreshing beverage anytime. *(pictured on page 74)*

- 1 (6-ounce) can frozen orange juice concentrate, thawed and undiluted
- 1 (12-ounce) can frozen unsweetened apple juice concentrate, thawed and undiluted
- 1 (1 liter) bottle club soda, chilled

COMBINE all ingredients, and serve over ice. **Prep: 5 min.**

Feta Squares

MAKES 20 APPETIZERS

    1 pound feta cheese, crumbled
    1½ (8-ounce) packages cream cheese,
      softened
    5 large eggs
    1 tablespoon chopped fresh dill
    ⅛ teaspoon salt
    ⅛ teaspoon pepper
    12 frozen phyllo pastry sheets, thawed
    ½ pound butter, melted

BEAT cheeses at medium speed with an electric mixer until blended. Add eggs at low speed, one at a time, until blended. Stir in dill, salt, and pepper.

CUT each pastry sheet into a 13- x 9-inch rectangle. Stack 8 pastry sheets in a lightly greased 13- x 9-inch pan, brushing with butter between sheets. Spread with cheese mixture; top with 4 more sheets, and brush with butter.

BAKE at 350° for 45 to 50 minutes or until golden brown. Let stand 10 minutes before cutting into squares. **Prep: 25 min., Bake: 50 min., Stand: 10 min.**

NOTE: Squares may be baked, covered with foil, and frozen. Thaw at room temperature 30 minutes. Bake squares at 350° for 25 minutes or until thoroughly heated.

MARIA LATTO
CHARLESTON, SOUTH CAROLINA

Wine Picks

Foods Editor Scott Jones recommends the following wines to enjoy with food or by themselves.

■ 2000, Wynns Coonawarra Estate, Chardonnay, Australia

■ 2000, Barossa Valley Estate, Shiraz, Australia

■ Nonvintage, Duval-Leroy, Brut, France

Honey Adds Flavor Anytime

Try these enticing recipes for an appealing appetizer and a citrus-spiked side dish.

Honey tends to evoke thoughts of a soothing accompaniment with breakfast foods such as oatmeal. This comforting ingredient, however, plays a grander role in many of the dishes served during the Jewish holidays. They're perfect for Passover, but we know you'll enjoy them year-round.

Carrots With Honey

MAKES 4 SERVINGS

    1 pound carrots, diagonally sliced
    ¼ cup fresh orange juice
    1 tablespoon fresh lime juice
    2 teaspoons butter or margarine
    ½ teaspoon salt
    ⅓ cup honey
    1 teaspoon minced fresh ginger
    ½ teaspoon grated orange rind
    ½ teaspoon grated lime rind

COOK first 5 ingredients in a 2-quart saucepan over medium heat, stirring often, 20 minutes or until carrot is tender.

REMOVE from heat; stir in honey and remaining ingredients. **Prep: 15 min., Cook: 20 min.**

Date-Orange-Nut Spread

MAKES 2 CUPS

Serve as an appetizer with matzo (crisp unleavened bread) or crackers.

    1½ cups chopped dates
    ½ cup raisins
    ½ cup sweet white wine
    ½ teaspoon grated orange rind
    1 large navel orange, peeled and cut
      into chunks
    ⅓ cup honey
    ½ cup almonds, toasted
    ½ cup walnuts, toasted
    ½ teaspoon ground cinnamon
    ¼ teaspoon ground cardamom

COMBINE dates and raisins in a bowl; add wine. Cover and chill 8 hours.

PROCESS date mixture, orange rind, and remaining ingredients in a food processor until slightly chunky and spreadable, adding more wine if needed. **Prep: 20 min., Chill: 8 hrs.**

NOTE: For testing purposes only, we used Sunsweet chopped dates and Mogen David white wine.

MICHELLE ZACHARIA
OMAHA, NEBRASKA

Simple Seafood Sandwiches

If you've had your fair share of chicken and beef entrées, try one of our tasty seafood sandwiches for a wonderful dinnertime alternative.

Do you need a new idea for a no-hassle meal? Try sandwich night. Start a weekly routine at your house with these uncomplicated recipes. Not only is seafood the star, but the breads and toppings also add new dimensions. Spread canned tuna on English muffins, and top with tomato and Swiss cheese slices. Crown Crab Cake Sandwiches with your favorite coleslaw. Chips, corn on the cob, or fresh fruit are great accompaniments for a relaxed dinner.

TUNA MELTS

MAKES 4 SERVINGS

- 1 (12-ounce) can white tuna in water, drained
- 2 celery ribs, chopped
- 3 tablespoons mayonnaise
- 2 tablespoons Dijon mustard
- 2 teaspoons lime juice
- ½ teaspoon pepper
- 4 English muffins, split
- 8 tomato slices
- 8 (1-ounce) Swiss cheese slices

STIR together first 6 ingredients; spread evenly on each English muffin half. Top each muffin half with 1 tomato slice and 1 cheese slice.
BROIL sandwiches 6 inches from heat 5 minutes or until cheese melts. **Prep: 20 min., Broil: 5 min.**

AMY STEIN
BIRMINGHAM, ALABAMA

FRIED CATFISH SANDWICHES

MAKES 4 SERVINGS

Serve these sandwiches with coleslaw and French fries for a casual weekend supper.

- ¾ cup yellow cornmeal
- ¼ cup all-purpose flour
- 2 teaspoons salt
- 1 teaspoon ground red pepper
- ¼ teaspoon garlic powder
- 4 catfish fillets (about 1½ pounds)
- ¼ teaspoon salt
- Vegetable oil
- 4 onion sandwich buns, split and toasted
- Cocktail or tartar sauce
- Lettuce leaves
- 4 tomato slices (optional)

COMBINE first 5 ingredients in a large shallow dish.
SPRINKLE fish with salt; dredge in flour mixture, coating well.
POUR oil to a depth of 3 inches in a Dutch oven; heat to 350°. Fry fish 4 to 5 minutes on each side or until golden brown. Drain on paper towels.
SERVE on sandwich buns with cocktail sauce, lettuce, and, if desired, tomato. **Prep: 15 min., Cook: 10 min.**

HENRIETTA RUSSELL
BIRMINGHAM, ALABAMA

CRAB CAKE SANDWICHES

MAKES 6 SERVINGS

Onion sandwich buns partner perfectly with the crispy, golden cakes. Substitute store-bought tartar sauce, if you like. *(pictured on page 75)*

- ¾ cup Italian-seasoned breadcrumbs
- 1 large egg
- 3 tablespoons mayonnaise
- 2 tablespoons chopped fresh parsley
- 1 tablespoon fresh lemon juice
- 1 teaspoon Dijon mustard
- ½ teaspoon salt
- ½ teaspoon ground red pepper
- 1 pound lump crabmeat, flaked
- ⅓ cup fine, dry breadcrumbs
- 2 tablespoons butter or margarine
- 6 onion sandwich buns, split
- Tartar Sauce
- Commercial coleslaw

COMBINE first 8 ingredients; gently fold in crabmeat. Shape crab mixture into 6 patties; dredge in ⅓ cup breadcrumbs. Cover and chill 1 hour.
MELT butter in a large nonstick skillet over medium-high heat; cook crab cakes, in batches, 3 minutes on each side or until golden brown. Drain on paper towels. Serve on buns with Tartar Sauce and coleslaw. **Prep: 20 min., Chill: 1 hr., Cook: 6 min. per batch**

Tartar Sauce:

MAKES ½ CUP

- ¼ cup sour cream
- 3 tablespoons mayonnaise
- 2 teaspoons grated lemon rind
- 1 tablespoon chopped fresh parsley
- 1 tablespoon minced green onions
- 1 teaspoon fresh lemon juice
- ¼ teaspoon hot sauce

STIR together all ingredients in a bowl. **Prep: 5 min.**

LILANN TAYLOR
SAVANNAH, GEORGIA

Garlic in a Jar Makes It Fast

Regular or roasted, this convenience product is a flavorful way to chop up your prep time.

Let's say your recipe calls for six cloves of minced garlic. Even with all the different gadgets that are available to accomplish the task, peeling and chopping fresh garlic has to be one of the least appealing aspects of preparation. Jarred minced garlic, often sold in the produce section, can make quick work of this. Generally, ½ teaspoon of prepared minced garlic equals 1 medium whole clove, but we find that 1½ teaspoons really suits our taste.

If you love the rich taste of roasted garlic but don't have time to prepare your own, you can buy it in a jar as well. Whichever variety you choose, buy it in small quantities, and keep it refrigerated once opened to prevent it from turning rancid.

GARLIC-PARMESAN PORK CHOPS

MAKES 4 TO 6 SERVINGS

- 6 (½-inch-thick) boneless pork loin chops
- ½ teaspoon salt
- ½ teaspoon pepper
- ¼ cup milk
- 2 tablespoons Dijon mustard
- 1 cup Italian-seasoned breadcrumbs
- ¼ cup butter or margarine, divided
- 1½ teaspoons jarred minced garlic
- ¾ cup whipping cream
- ⅓ cup white wine or chicken broth
- ½ cup grated Parmesan cheese

SPRINKLE pork chops evenly with salt and pepper.
STIR together milk and mustard. Dip pork chops in milk mixture; dredge in breadcrumbs. Place pork chops on a rack in a broiler pan.
BAKE pork chops at 375° for 30 minutes or until done.
MELT 1 tablespoon butter in a saucepan over medium-high heat; add garlic, and sauté 2 to 3 minutes. Stir in cream, wine, and cheese; reduce heat, and simmer 3 to 4 minutes (do not boil). Whisk in remaining 3 tablespoons butter until melted. Serve with chops. **Prep: 5 min., Bake: 30 min., Cook: 7 min.**

EASY PIZZA SQUARES

MAKES 6 SERVINGS

- 1 (10-ounce) package refrigerated pizza crust
- 1½ cups (6 ounces) shredded Mexican four-cheese blend, divided
- ⅔ cup mayonnaise
- 2 tablespoons chopped fresh basil
- 2 teaspoons jarred minced garlic
- ⅛ teaspoon salt
- ¼ teaspoon Italian seasoning
- 4 plum tomatoes, thinly sliced

FIT pizza crust onto a lightly greased 13- x 10-inch baking sheet.
BAKE at 350° for 10 minutes or until lightly browned.
STIR together 1 cup cheese, mayonnaise, and next 4 ingredients; spread mixture over pizza crust. Arrange sliced tomato over crust, and sprinkle with remaining ½ cup cheese.
BAKE at 375° for 15 minutes. Cut into squares. **Prep: 10 min., Bake: 25 min.**

ANNE DIXON
CHARLOTTE, NORTH CAROLINA

GREEN BEANS WITH GARLIC-HERB BUTTER

MAKES 4 SERVINGS

Accent your favorite entrée with this garden-fresh side dish.

- 1 pound fresh green beans, trimmed
- ¼ cup butter or margarine
- 1 small onion, minced
- 1 celery rib, minced
- 1½ teaspoons jarred minced garlic
- ¼ teaspoon chopped fresh or dried rosemary
- ¾ teaspoon salt
- ¼ cup chopped fresh parsley

BRING salted water to a boil in a large saucepan; add beans, cover and cook 10 to 15 minutes or until crisp-tender. Drain. Plunge into ice water to stop the cooking process; drain.
MELT butter in a saucepan over medium-high heat; add onion and celery, and sauté 5 minutes. Add garlic, and sauté 2 minutes. Stir in beans, rosemary, salt, and parsley; sauté 4 minutes or until thoroughly heated. **Prep: 10 min., Cook: 26 min.**

CHRISTINE MCDONALD
VICTORIA, TEXAS

Creamy Custard Creations

Dessert lovers marvel at the silky appearance and taste of custard, but they're often too timid to prepare it from scratch. Don't be.

These deceptively easy recipes require only a few basic ingredients: sugar, milk or cream, eggs, and sometimes cornstarch. Add chocolate or fresh fruit, and you'll have a treat for any occasion.

GRAHAM BANANA PUDDING

MAKES 6 TO 8 SERVINGS

    4 cups half-and-half
    4 large egg yolks
    1½ cups sugar
    ¼ cup cornstarch
    ¼ teaspoon salt
    3 tablespoons butter or margarine
    2 teaspoons vanilla extract
    1 (5-ounce) package graham crackers,
        divided
    4 large ripe bananas, sliced and
        divided
    2 cups whipping cream
    2 tablespoons sugar

WHISK together first 5 ingredients in a saucepan over low heat; cook, whisking constantly, 8 to 10 minutes or until thickened. Remove from heat; stir in butter and vanilla. Layer 5 graham crackers, half of bananas, and half of pudding in a 13- x 9-inch dish. Repeat layers. Cover pudding, and chill 6 hours.
BEAT whipping cream and 2 tablespoons sugar at medium speed with an electric mixer until soft peaks form. Spread over pudding. Chill until ready to serve. **Prep: 5 min., Cook: 10 min., Chill: 6 hrs.**

DORSELLA UTTER
LOUISVILLE, KENTUCKY

BLACK-AND-WHITE CRÈME BRÛLÉE

MAKES 6 SERVINGS

French for "burnt cream," crème brûlée sounds fancy, but it's really a simple custard with a crunchy sugar top. In this version, chocolate adds an extra layer of flavor.

    2½ cups whipping cream, divided
    1 cup semisweet chocolate morsels
    5 egg yolks
    ½ cup sugar
    1 tablespoon vanilla extract
    6 tablespoons light brown sugar

HEAT ½ cup whipping cream and chocolate morsels in a saucepan over low heat, stirring until chocolate melts. Cool slightly. Pour evenly into 6 (6-ounce) round individual baking dishes. Set aside.
WHISK together remaining 2 cups whipping cream, egg yolks, ½ cup sugar, and vanilla until sugar dissolves and mixture is smooth. Pour evenly into prepared baking dishes; place dishes in a 13- x 9-inch pan. Add hot water to pan to a depth of ½ inch.
BAKE at 275° for 1 hour and 10 minutes or until almost set. Cool custards in water in pan on a wire rack. Remove custards from pan; cover and chill at least 8 hours.
SPRINKLE 1 tablespoon brown sugar over each custard, and place custards in pan.
BROIL 5½ inches from heat until sugar melts. Let stand 5 minutes to allow sugar to harden. **Prep: 10 min.; Bake: 1 hr., 10 min.; Chill: 8 hrs.; Stand: 5 min.**

STRAWBERRY MERINGUE PARFAITS

MAKES 6 SERVINGS

You can substitute store-bought meringue cookies for the Meringues. (pictured on page 79)

    1 quart fresh strawberries, sliced
    1¾ cups sugar, divided
    ¼ cup cornstarch
    4 egg yolks
    3 cups milk or half-and-half
    ¼ cup butter or margarine
    2 teaspoons vanilla extract
    Meringues

SPRINKLE sliced strawberries with ¼ cup sugar.
COMBINE remaining 1½ cups sugar and cornstarch in a large saucepan over medium heat. Gradually whisk in egg yolks and milk; cook milk mixture, whisking often, 12 minutes or until thickened. Bring milk mixture to a boil, and cook, stirring constantly, 1 minute. Remove mixture from heat; stir in butter and vanilla extract. Cover and chill 6 hours.
SPOON half of custard into 6 parfait glasses; top with half of sliced strawberries and 3 Meringues. Repeat layers, ending with 1 Meringue on top of each serving. **Prep: 10 min., Cook: 15 min., Chill: 6 hrs.**

Meringues:

MAKES ABOUT 2½ DOZEN

    4 egg whites
    1 teaspoon cream of tartar
    ¼ teaspoon almond extract
    ¼ cup sugar

BEAT egg whites at medium speed with an electric mixer until foamy; add cream of tartar and almond extract, beating until blended. Gradually add sugar, beating until stiff peaks form and sugar dissolves.
PIPE or spread mixture into small 2-inch cookie shapes or other desired shapes onto a parchment paper-lined baking sheet.
BAKE at 200° for 2 hours. Turn oven off; let stand in closed oven with light on 8 hours. **Prep: 20 min., Bake: 2 hrs., Stand: 8 hrs.**

SANDRA MERRITT
KENNESAW, GEORGIA

Easy Pasta Suppers

There's no escaping the fact that today's busy lifestyle means time is at a premium. All these hearty pasta dishes can be prepared in 15 minutes or less with minimal fuss. Feel free to swap out the fusilli, elbow macaroni, or penne pasta in three of the recipes. Double the recipe for Chicken Macaroni and Cheese or Pasta With Sausage and Bell Peppers so you can freeze some for later.

EASY SKILLET BEEF 'N' PASTA

MAKES 6 TO 8 SERVINGS

- 2 pounds lean ground beef
- 3 cups water
- 8 ounces uncooked elbow macaroni
- 1 (26-ounce) jar pasta sauce
- 2 cups (8 ounces) shredded mozzarella cheese
- 1 cup (4 ounces) shredded Parmesan cheese
- 3 large green onions, chopped
- 1 (4½-ounce) can sliced ripe olives, drained

COOK ground beef in a large skillet over medium heat 8 minutes, stirring until it crumbles and is no longer pink; drain well, and return to skillet.

STIR in 3 cups water, and bring to a boil; stir in pasta. Reduce heat, cover, and simmer, stirring often, 15 to 18 minutes or until pasta is tender.

STIR in pasta sauce; sprinkle with half each of mozzarella cheese and Parmesan cheese. Sprinkle evenly with green onions and olives; sprinkle with remaining mozzarella cheese and Parmesan cheese. Cover and cook 4 to 5 minutes or until cheeses are melted. **Prep: 10 min., Cook: 30 min.**

ANNE LANDERS
HERNANDO, MISSISSIPPI

PASTA WITH SAUSAGE AND BELL PEPPERS

MAKES 8 SERVINGS

- 1 pound Italian sausage
- 1 large onion, chopped
- 1 red or green bell pepper, cut into strips
- 1½ teaspoons dried basil
- 1 (14-ounce) can Italian herb-seasoned chicken broth
- 1 (16-ounce) package fusilli, cooked
- 1 cup (4 ounces) shredded Parmesan cheese

REMOVE and discard sausage casings.
COOK sausage and next 3 ingredients in a skillet over medium-high heat, stirring until sausage crumbles and is no longer pink. Drain well; return to skillet. Stir in broth; cook, stirring often, 5 minutes or until thoroughly heated.

SPOON the sausage mixture over hot pasta; sprinkle with cheese, and serve immediately. **Prep: 10 min., Cook: 15 min.**

MARTHA C. SILLAY
CUMMING, GEORGIA

CHICKEN MACARONI AND CHEESE

MAKES 4 TO 6 SERVINGS

- 1 (16-ounce) loaf pasteurized prepared cheese product, cubed
- 1 (8-ounce) container sour cream
- ½ cup milk
- 2½ cups chopped cooked chicken
- 8 ounces penne pasta, cooked

COOK first 3 ingredients in a Dutch oven over medium-low heat, stirring constantly, 5 minutes or until cheese melts.
STIR in chicken and pasta; cook, stirring constantly, 5 minutes or until thoroughly heated. **Prep: 10 min., Cook: 10 min.**

SPICY CHICKEN MACARONI AND CHEESE: Substitute 2 (8-ounce) loaves Mexican-style pasteurized prepared cheese product, cubed, for regular cheese product.

TO LIGHTEN: Use light pasteurized prepared cheese product, light sour cream, and 2% reduced-fat milk.

FABULOUS TUNA-NOODLE CASSEROLE

MAKES 6 TO 8 SERVINGS

- ¼ cup butter or margarine
- 1 small red or green bell pepper, chopped
- 1 small onion, chopped
- 1 cup sliced fresh mushrooms
- ¼ cup all-purpose flour
- 2½ cups milk
- 2 cups (8 ounces) shredded Cheddar cheese
- 2 (9-ounce) cans solid white tuna in spring water, drained and flaked
- 1 (12-ounce) package egg noodles, cooked
- 2 teaspoons dried parsley flakes
- ½ teaspoon salt
- ½ teaspoon pepper
- ½ cup fine, dry breadcrumbs
- 2 tablespoons butter or margarine, melted

MELT ¼ cup butter in a large skillet over medium heat; add bell pepper, onion, and mushrooms, and sauté 5 minutes or until tender.

WHISK together flour and milk until smooth; stir into vegetable mixture, and cook, stirring constantly, 5 minutes or until thickened. Remove from heat; add cheese, stirring until melted.

STIR in tuna and next 4 ingredients; spoon into a lightly greased 13- x 9-inch baking dish.

BAKE, covered, at 350° for 25 minutes. Stir together breadcrumbs and 2 tablespoons melted butter; sprinkle over casserole, and bake 5 more minutes. **Prep: 15 min., Cook: 10 min., Bake: 30 min.**

BARBARA SHERRER
BAY CITY, TEXAS

Asparagus Welcomes Spring to Your Table

Many of us grew up on canned asparagus, but once you taste it fresh, you will eagerly await the arrival of spring's first spears.

Although asparagus is available year-round (canned, frozen, and through hot-house sources), the optimum season runs from February through June. The most tender stalks are apple green and pencil thin with purple-tinged tips; older, more mature plants have thicker spears. You might want to remove the tough outer layer on larger spears with a knife or a vegetable peeler.

When buying asparagus, choose firm, bright-green stalks with tight tips. It will keep, tightly wrapped in a plastic bag in the refrigerator, for three to four days, but it's best when cooked on the day of purchase.

ROASTED SHALLOT ASPARAGUS

MAKES 8 SERVINGS

    2 pounds fresh asparagus
    ¼ cup olive oil, divided
    1 shallot, minced
    2 tablespoons white wine vinegar
    ¾ teaspoon salt
    ½ teaspoon freshly ground pepper

SNAP off tough ends of asparagus. Toss asparagus with 2 tablespoons oil; place in a 15- x 10-inch jellyroll pan.
BAKE at 400°, stirring occasionally, 30 to 45 minutes or until tender.
STIR together shallot and next 3 ingredients; gradually whisk in remaining 2 tablespoons oil. Pour over asparagus, and serve immediately. **Prep: 15 min., Bake: 45 min.**

ALMOND ASPARAGUS

MAKES 8 SERVINGS

    2 pounds fresh asparagus
    2 tablespoons butter or margarine
    1 tablespoon lemon juice
    ¾ cup slivered almonds, toasted
    ½ teaspoon salt
    ¼ teaspoon pepper

SNAP off tough ends of asparagus. Cook asparagus in boiling water to cover 3 minutes or until crisp-tender; drain.
PLUNGE asparagus into ice water to stop the cooking process; drain.
MELT butter in a large skillet over medium heat; add asparagus, and sauté 3 to 5 minutes. Toss asparagus with lemon juice and remaining ingredients. **Prep: 15 min., Cook: 10 min.**

ETHEL C. JERNIGAN
SAVANNAH, GEORGIA

SESAME ASPARAGUS

MAKES 4 SERVINGS

    1 pound fresh asparagus
    2 tablespoons peanut oil,
        divided
    2 large shallots, minced
    1 tablespoon sesame seeds
    ⅛ teaspoon freshly ground pepper
    2 teaspoons soy sauce
    ½ teaspoon dark sesame oil

SNAP off tough ends of asparagus. Cook half of asparagus in 1 tablespoon hot peanut oil in a large skillet over medium-high heat 3 to 4 minutes on each side.
STIR together shallot and next 4 ingredients. Sprinkle half of shallot mixture over asparagus in skillet; cook 1 to 2 minutes or until shallot is tender.
REMOVE asparagus mixture from skillet, and keep warm. Repeat procedure with remaining asparagus, peanut oil, and shallot mixture. **Prep: 10 min., Cook: 10 min. per batch**

HANNAH YOUNGBLOOD
SMITHFIELD, NORTH CAROLINA

CHILLED GINGER ASPARAGUS

MAKES 4 SERVINGS

    ¾ cup rice vinegar
    1½ tablespoons minced fresh
        ginger
    2 tablespoons sugar
    1 pound fresh asparagus
    1 garlic clove, minced
    3 tablespoons vegetable oil
    2 tablespoons dark sesame oil
    1 teaspoon soy sauce
    ½ teaspoon salt

BRING vinegar and ginger to a boil in a small saucepan, and boil 7 minutes or until liquid is reduced by half. Remove from heat, and stir in sugar; set mixture aside.
SNAP off tough ends of asparagus. Place asparagus and water to cover in a large skillet, and bring to a boil; remove from heat, and drain.
PLUNGE asparagus into ice water to stop the cooking process, and drain. Arrange asparagus spears on a serving platter.
STIR together garlic and next 4 ingredients. Drizzle over asparagus; cover and chill 30 minutes. Drizzle vinegar mixture over asparagus; cover and chill 1 hour. **Prep: 20 min.; Chill: 1 hr., 30 min.**

Rediscover Iceberg Lettuce

If you haven't purchased iceberg lettuce recently, this story is for you. Despite the popularity of other lettuces, iceberg still has much to be admired. It adds cool crunch to salads and can serve as a sturdy base for appetizers such as Chicken Lettuce Wraps. This and our other inventive selections, created by Test Kitchens staffer Vanessa McNeil, can be prepared in less than an hour. You'll welcome their freshness at a time when many vegetables are just coming into peak season.

LETTUCE-WEDGE SALAD

MAKES 4 SERVINGS

Pair this salad with your favorite soup for a quick, delicious dinner.

    4 to 6 bacon slices*
    1 medium onion, sliced
    1 cup buttermilk
    ½ cup sour cream
    1 (1-ounce) envelope Ranch-style
        dressing mix
    ¼ cup chopped fresh basil
    2 garlic cloves
    1 large head iceberg lettuce,
        cut into 4 wedges
    Shredded basil (optional)

COOK bacon in a large skillet until crisp; remove bacon, and drain on paper towels, reserving 1 teaspoon drippings in skillet. Crumble bacon, and set aside.

SAUTÉ onion in hot drippings in skillet over medium heat 10 minutes or until tender and lightly browned. Remove from heat; cool.

PROCESS buttermilk and next 4 ingredients in a blender or food processor until smooth, stopping to scrape down sides. Stir in onion.

TOP each lettuce wedge with dressing; sprinkle with bacon, and top with shredded basil, if desired. **Prep: 30 min., Cook: 15 min.**

*Substitute turkey bacon, if desired.

CHICKEN LETTUCE WRAPS

MAKES 4 SERVINGS

Serve with frozen egg rolls for a quick meal.

    2 garlic cloves
    1 pound skinned and boned chicken
        breast halves, coarsely chopped
    2 tablespoons dark sesame oil
    ¼ cup chopped fresh mint
    2 green onions, chopped
    2 tablespoons soy sauce
    8 large iceberg lettuce leaves
    Garnish: fresh mint leaves

PULSE garlic in a food processor 3 times or until minced. Add chicken, and pulse 8 times or until ground.

COOK chicken mixture in hot oil in a large skillet over medium heat 8 to 10 minutes or until chicken is done. Stir in mint, onions, and soy sauce. Serve on lettuce; garnish, if desired. **Prep: 15 min., Cook: 10 min.**

MEXICAN LAYERED SALAD

MAKES 8 SERVINGS

This is a fresh twist on a favorite, adding Southwestern flavors such as green chiles, cilantro, cumin, and lime.

    1 (9-ounce) package cornbread mix
    1 (4.5-ounce) can chopped green
        chiles
    ½ cup light mayonnaise
    ½ cup chopped fresh cilantro
    ¼ cup lime juice
    1 teaspoon ground cumin
    ½ teaspoon salt
    1 head iceberg lettuce, shredded
    1 (15-ounce) can black beans, rinsed
        and drained
    1 (11-ounce) can whole kernel corn,
        drained
    1 (8-ounce) package reduced-fat
        shredded Cheddar cheese
    1 large red bell pepper,
        chopped
    3 green onions, chopped
    6 plum tomatoes, chopped
    Garnish: green onion curls

PREPARE cornbread mix according to package directions, adding chiles. Cool and crumble.

PROCESS mayonnaise and next 4 ingredients in a food processor or blender until smooth, stopping to scrape down sides.

LAYER a 4-quart bowl with half of shredded lettuce, half of crumbled cornbread, one-third of mayonnaise mixture, and half each of black beans, corn, shredded Cheddar cheese, and next 3 ingredients. Repeat layers. Top with remaining mayonnaise mixture. Cover and chill 1 to 2 hours. Garnish, if desired. **Prep: 40 min., Chill: 2 hrs.**

NOTE: Don't forget to buy the other ingredients that you'll need to make the cornbread.

COUSCOUS-AND-GARBANZO SALAD

MAKES 4 SERVINGS

    1 (14-ounce) can chicken broth
    1 cup uncooked couscous
    1 (15-ounce) can garbanzo beans,
        rinsed and drained
    4 green onions, sliced
    3 carrots, shredded
    1 red bell pepper, diced
    ½ cup pitted kalamata olives
    Mint Vinaigrette
    1 head iceberg lettuce, torn
    1 (4-ounce) package crumbled feta
        cheese (optional)

BRING broth to a boil in a saucepan. Add couscous; cover and remove from heat. Let stand 10 minutes.

TOSS together couscous, garbanzo beans, and next 4 ingredients in a large bowl. Drizzle with Mint Vinaigrette, tossing gently to coat.

TOSS in torn lettuce. Sprinkle with feta cheese, if desired, just before serving. **Prep: 20 min.**

Mint Vinaigrette:

MAKES ¾ CUP

    ⅔ cup chopped fresh mint
    3 tablespoons white wine vinegar
    2 garlic cloves
    1 teaspoon Dijon mustard
    ¼ teaspoon sugar
    ¼ teaspoon salt
    ⅛ teaspoon pepper
    ½ cup olive oil

PROCESS first 7 ingredients in a food processor until minced, stopping to scrape down sides. With food processor running, add oil in a slow, steady stream until blended. **Prep: 5 min.**

Try Lamb Chops Tonight

This quick-cooking alternative to steak or chicken is perfect for spring.

Whether for an appetizer or an entrée, lamb chops make a flavorful stand-in for beef or poultry. We tested these recipes using both rib chops and the slightly larger loin chops. It may be necessary to trim excess fat, leaving only a minimal amount at the top and bottom. Rib chops broil or pan-fry quickly and are best enjoyed medium rare; loin chops take a few minutes of additional cooking time.

FRIED LAMB CHOPS

MAKES 6 MAIN-DISH SERVINGS OR
18 APPETIZER SERVINGS

1 cup Italian-seasoned breadcrumbs
¼ cup grated Parmesan cheese
1 teaspoon salt
1 teaspoon garlic powder
1 teaspoon onion powder
1 teaspoon pepper
2 teaspoons paprika
18 (2- to 3-ounce) lamb rib chops*
1 cup all-purpose flour
2 large eggs, lightly beaten
Vegetable oil
Garnishes: lemon wedges, fresh
    rosemary sprigs

STIR together first 7 ingredients.
DREDGE chops in flour; dip in egg, and dredge in breadcrumb mixture.
POUR vegetable oil to a depth of ¼ inch into a skillet; fry chops, in batches, over medium-high heat 5 to 7 minutes on each side. Garnish, if desired. **Prep: 15 min., Cook: 14 min. per batch**

*Substitute 12 loin chops, if desired. Cook 3 more minutes on each side.

EASY BAKED LAMB CHOPS

MAKES 6 MAIN-DISH SERVINGS OR
18 APPETIZER SERVINGS

1 tablespoon all-purpose flour
½ teaspoon salt
¼ teaspoon pepper
18 (2- to 3-ounce) lamb rib chops*
1 (1-ounce) envelope onion soup mix
1 red bell pepper, thinly sliced
1 (8-ounce) package sliced fresh
    mushrooms
½ (14-ounce) can diced tomatoes,
    undrained
1 tablespoon steak sauce

COMBINE first 3 ingredients; set aside. Tear off 1 (28- x 18-inch) heavy-duty aluminum foil sheet. Place in a 13- x 9-inch pan.
PLACE chops in pan; sprinkle evenly with flour mixture. Top with soup mix and next 4 ingredients.
BRING up 2 long sides of foil sheet, and double-fold with about 1-inch-wide folds. Double-fold each end to form a packet, leaving room for heat to circulate inside packet.
BAKE at 375° for 45 minutes. **Prep: 20 min., Bake: 45 min.**

*Substitute 12 loin chops for rib chops, if desired. Bake 10 more minutes or to desired degree of doneness.

MARY BETH KINNEY
RUTLAND, VERMONT

GLAZED LAMB CHOPS

MAKES 6 MAIN-DISH SERVINGS OR
18 APPETIZER SERVINGS

¾ cup dry red wine
⅓ cup orange juice
4 garlic cloves, chopped
4 shallots, chopped
2 tablespoons minced fresh rosemary
1½ tablespoons minced fresh oregano
3 tablespoons olive oil
18 (2- to 3-ounce) lamb rib chops*
1 teaspoon salt
1 teaspoon pepper
2 tablespoons honey

WHISK together first 7 ingredients in a small bowl. Pour mixture into a large heavy-duty zip-top plastic bag, reserving ¼ cup; add lamb chops. Seal bag, and chill 2 hours.
REMOVE chops from marinade, discarding marinade. Sprinkle with salt and pepper. Place chops on a lightly greased rack in a broiler pan.
STIR together reserved ¼ cup wine mixture and honey.
BROIL chops 3 inches from heat 5 minutes on each side or to desired degree of doneness, basting with honey mixture after 3 minutes. **Prep: 25 min., Chill: 2 hrs, Broil: 10 min.**

*Substitute 12 loin chops for rib chops, if desired. Broil loin chops 3 more minutes on each side or to desired degree of doneness.

TWILA GINGER
LEESBURG, FLORIDA

A Blarney Good Breakfast

Get a jump on the leprechauns with a
St. Patrick's Day breakfast.

Leprechauns' Breakfast

Serves 6

Boxty

Applesauce   Bacon, ham, or sausage

Pan-Fried Tomatoes

Irish Bread

Coffee   Orange juice

There's something extra-comforting about a hearty breakfast. This St. Patrick's Day, why not perk up your dinner table with these hearty, easy-to-make Irish breakfast specialties? Add your favorite rasher (slices of bacon or ham) or sausage to round out the meal.

BOXTY

MAKES 6 SERVINGS

A side dish created with mashed and shredded potatoes, boxty is often served with applesauce.

**4 large potatoes (about 3 pounds),
    peeled and divided**
2 teaspoons salt, divided
3 green onions, diced
1 teaspoon caraway seeds
½ teaspoon pepper
1 large egg, lightly beaten
2 tablespoons whipping cream
1 cup all-purpose flour
6 tablespoons vegetable oil

CUT 2 potatoes into cubes; cook potato cubes and 1 teaspoon salt in boiling water to cover 15 minutes or until tender. Drain and mash with a potato masher; set aside.

SHRED remaining 2 potatoes; press between layers of paper towels to remove excess water.

COMBINE mashed and shredded potatoes in a large bowl; stir in remaining 1 teaspoon salt, onions, and next 4 ingredients. Gradually add flour to form a soft dough; shape into 12 patties.

FRY patties, in batches, in hot oil in a large skillet over medium-high heat 6 to 7 minutes on each side or until golden brown. Drain on paper towels. **Prep: 30 min., Cook: 30 min.**

LOIS BOMBA
HOUSTON, TEXAS

PAN-FRIED TOMATOES

MAKES 8 SERVINGS

4 large ripe tomatoes
1 teaspoon salt
½ teaspoon pepper
1 cup fine, dry breadcrumbs
¼ cup bacon drippings

CUT tomatoes into ½-inch-thick slices, and sprinkle tomato slices evenly with salt and pepper. Let tomato slices stand 30 minutes.

PAT tomato slices dry, and dredge in breadcrumbs.

COOK tomato slices, in batches, in hot bacon drippings in a large nonstick skillet over medium-high heat 2 minutes on each side or until golden brown. Drain on paper towels. Serve immediately. **Prep: 15 min., Stand: 30 min., Cook: 4 min. per batch**

IRISH BREAD

MAKES 1 (10½-INCH) ROUND

3 cups all-purpose flour
2 tablespoons baking powder
½ teaspoon salt
½ cup sugar
¼ cup shortening
¼ cup butter or margarine
1 cup raisins
1¼ cups milk
2 large eggs
1 tablespoon white vinegar

COMBINE first 4 ingredients in a bowl. Cut shortening and butter into flour mixture with a pastry blender or fork until mixture is crumbly. Stir in raisins.

WHISK together milk, eggs, and vinegar; add to flour mixture, stirring just until moistened. Pour batter into a greased 10½-inch cast-iron skillet.

BAKE at 350° for 35 to 40 minutes. **Prep: 15 min., Bake: 40 min.**

NOTE: Bread also may be baked in 2 greased 8-inch round cakepans for 30 to 35 minutes.

CHRISTINE JOHNSTON
WILMINGTON, MASSACHUSETTS

Bursting With Color

Enjoy a rainbow of color and fresh flavor
for breakfast, lunch, and supper.

You know the drill: Eat five or more servings of fruits and vegetables a day. What you may not know is that the color of those foods also matters.

According to the National Cancer Institute, the most intensely colored fruits and vegetables offer the highest nutritional bang for their buck. They're rich in phytochemicals, which not only guard plants from insects, sunlight, and bad weather but also may protect humans from disease. So eat a variety of brightly hued fruits and veggies at every meal.

We've gathered a bumper crop of recipes to turn your plate into a palette of beautiful flavors.

Fresh Fruit With Lime Sauce

MAKES 10 SERVINGS

    1 cup water
    1 tablespoon cornstarch
    1 cup sugar
    1 teaspoon grated lime rind
    ¼ cup fresh lime juice
    1 pineapple, cut into 1-inch
        pieces
    2 cups red seedless grapes
    1 large pink grapefruit, peeled and
        sectioned
    3 kiwifruit, peeled and sliced
    2 oranges, peeled and
        sectioned

WHISK together 1 cup water and cornstarch in a small saucepan. Whisk in sugar, rind, and juice.

COOK over low heat, whisking constantly, 10 minutes or until thickened; cool slightly. Chill 2 hours.

COMBINE pineapple and remaining ingredients in a large bowl, and drizzle with sauce, tossing to coat. Serve immediately. **Prep: 30 min., Cook: 10 min., Chill: 2 hrs.**

BLANCHE KRUSE
BELLVILLE, TEXAS

Per serving: Calories 153 (3% from fat); Fat 0.5g (sat .03g, mono .04g, poly .14g); Protein 1g; Carb 39g; Fiber 2.5g; Chol 0mg; Iron 0.4mg; Sodium 3mg; Calc 27mg

Butternut Soup

MAKES 6 SERVINGS

Serve this hearty soup with a vinaigrette-tossed, veggie-loaded salad or alongside your favorite sandwich.

    1 leek
    2 carrots, chopped
    2 celery ribs, chopped
    1 tablespoon chopped fresh ginger
    1 jalapeño pepper, chopped
    2 teaspoons olive oil
    1 medium butternut squash, cubed
    4 cups low-sodium chicken broth
    1 cup fat-free half-and-half
    ½ teaspoon salt
    ¼ teaspoon freshly ground pepper

DISCARD green top from leek; cut white portion of leek into thin slices.
SAUTÉ leek and next 4 ingredients in hot oil in a Dutch oven over medium heat 10 to 15 minutes or until tender.

STIR in butternut squash and chicken broth; bring to a boil. Reduce heat, and simmer 30 minutes or until squash is tender. Cool slightly.
PROCESS squash mixture, in batches, in a food processor or blender until smooth. Return to Dutch oven; stir in half-and-half, salt, and pepper.
COOK mixture over medium heat, stirring often, until thoroughly heated. Serve soup immediately. **Prep: 30 min., Cook: 45 min.**

ETHEL C. JERNIGAN
SAVANNAH, GEORGIA

Per 1½-cup serving: Calories 138 (12% from fat); Fat 1.8g (sat 0.3g, mono 1.2g, poly 0.3g); Protein 3.9g; Carb 25g; Fiber 5.6g; Chol 0mg; Iron 1.4mg; Sodium 563mg; Calc 109mg

Curried Pasta With Apple

MAKES 7 CUPS

This crunchy, colorful salad makes a delicious picnic side dish.

    1 (12-ounce) package tricolored
        rotini
    ⅔ cup plain fat-free yogurt
    ¼ cup light mayonnaise
    3 tablespoons fresh lime juice
    2 teaspoons sugar
    1½ teaspoons curry powder
    ½ teaspoon salt
    ¼ teaspoon ground red pepper
    ¼ teaspoon ground black pepper
    1 Granny Smith apple, diced
    ¼ cup dried cherries or sweetened
        dried cranberries
    4 green onions, thinly sliced
    2 carrots, grated
    ½ cup soy nuts* or slivered almonds,
        toasted

COOK rotini according to package directions, omitting salt and fat; drain.
STIR together yogurt and next 7 ingredients in a large bowl. Add pasta, apple, and next 3 ingredients, tossing to coat. Sprinkle with soy nuts. Serve immediately. **Prep: 25 min., Cook: 15 min.**

*Soy nuts may be found in the snack section of your supermarket or in health food stores.

Per 1-cup serving: Calories 280 (16% from fat); Fat 5g (sat 0.9g, mono 0.1g, poly 0.4g); Protein 11g; Carb 49g; Fiber 5g; Chol 4mg; Iron 2.3mg; Sodium 305mg; Calc 83mg

CREOLE-MARINATED VEGETABLES

MAKES 8 SERVINGS

- 1 pound fresh broccoli, trimmed and cut into florets
- 2 large carrots, sliced, or 2 cups baby carrots, sliced
- 1 (8-ounce) package fresh mushrooms, quartered
- 1 (14-ounce) can quartered artichoke hearts, drained
- ½ purple onion, thinly sliced
- 1 pint grape or cherry tomatoes, halved
- Creole Dressing

COOK broccoli and carrot in boiling water to cover 5 minutes; drain. Plunge into ice water to stop the cooking process; drain.

COMBINE broccoli mixture, mushrooms, and next 3 ingredients in a large bowl. Add Creole Dressing, tossing to coat. Cover and chill 2 hours. **Prep: 20 min., Cook: 5 min., Chill: 2 hrs.**

Per 1-cup serving: Calories 160 (55% from fat*); Fat 9.7g (sat 1.4g, mono 7.2g, poly 1g); Protein 4g; Carb 16g; Fiber 4g; Chol 0mg; Iron 0.9mg; Sodium 370mg; Calc 35mg

*We used very low-calorie vegetables in this recipe; most of the calories come from the dressing's oil, which is the healthful monounsaturated kind.

Creole Dressing:

MAKES ¾ CUP

- 2 tablespoons Creole mustard
- ⅓ cup red wine vinegar
- ⅓ cup olive oil
- 1½ tablespoons sugar
- ¼ teaspoon salt

WHISK together all ingredients; blend well. **Prep: 5 min.**

ROSE TURNER PATE
PITTSBORO, NORTH CAROLINA

GLAZED SALMON WITH STIR-FRIED VEGETABLES

MAKES 4 SERVINGS

- 2 carrots
- 1 parsnip
- 1 small red bell pepper
- 8 green onions
- 4 (4-ounce) skinless salmon fillets
- ¼ teaspoon salt
- Vegetable cooking spray
- ¼ cup apple jelly
- 3 tablespoons rice wine vinegar
- 2 tablespoons water
- 1 tablespoon lite soy sauce
- 1 teaspoon cornstarch
- ½ to 1 teaspoon chopped fresh dill (optional)
- 2 teaspoons vegetable oil
- Garnish: fresh dill sprigs

CUT first 4 ingredients into thin strips, and set aside.

SPRINKLE salmon fillets evenly with salt. Place on a rack in a broiler pan coated with cooking spray.

BROIL 6 inches from heat 10 to 13 minutes or until fish flakes with a fork.

WHISK together jelly, next 4 ingredients, and, if desired, dill.

COOK carrot and parsnip in hot oil in a large skillet over medium-high heat, stirring often, 2 to 3 minutes. Add bell pepper and onions; cook 1 to 2 minutes or until crisp-tender. Remove vegetables from skillet, and keep warm.

ADD jelly mixture to skillet, and cook, stirring constantly, 3 to 4 minutes or until thickened.

SPOON vegetables evenly onto serving plates. Drizzle with half of sauce. Top with salmon fillets, and drizzle with remaining sauce. Garnish, if desired. **Prep: 15 min., Cook: 22 min.**

JOANNA L. HAY
ARCADIA, FLORIDA

Per serving: Calories 348 (39% from fat*); Fat 15g (sat 2.7g, mono 5.8g, poly 5.2g); Protein 24g; Carb 28g; Fiber 3.5g; Chol 67mg; Iron 1mg; Sodium 399mg; Calc 52mg

*Only 7% of the total calories in this recipe comes from saturated fat. The remaining fat calories are from beneficial mono- or polyunsaturated oils.

Cheese Appetizers

These tasty options offer loads of flavor to whet your guests' appetites.

QUICK ARTICHOKE DIP

MAKES 2 CUPS

- ½ cup reduced-fat mayonnaise
- ½ cup reduced-fat sour cream
- 1 (0.6-ounce) envelope Italian dressing mix
- 1 (16-ounce) can quartered artichoke hearts, drained
- ¼ cup shredded Parmesan cheese

PROCESS first 3 ingredients in a food processor until blended, stopping to scrape down sides. Add artichokes and cheese, pulsing just until artichokes are coarsely chopped. Spoon into a bowl. Cover; chill 1 hour. **Prep: 5 min., Chill: 1 hr.**

JOSIE FLYNN
VIENNA, VIRGINIA

CHEESE PUFFS

MAKES 2 DOZEN

- 1 (16-ounce) loaf French bread
- ½ cup butter or margarine
- 1 cup (4 ounces) shredded sharp Cheddar cheese
- 1 (3-ounce) package cream cheese
- 2 egg whites

TRIM crust from bread; discard. Cut bread into 2-inch cubes; place in a large bowl.

MELT butter and cheeses in a saucepan over low heat; stir occasionally.

BEAT whites at high speed with an electric mixer until stiff peaks form; fold one-quarter of whites into cheese mixture. Fold into remaining whites. Pour over bread cubes, tossing to coat. Place in a single layer on an ungreased baking sheet. **BAKE** at 400° for 12 minutes. **Prep: 15 min., Cook: 5 min., Bake: 12 min.**

CLARISSA MCCONNELL
ORLANDO, FLORIDA

from our kitchen

Serving fresh vegetables is easier than ever with Ready Pac Produce. A delicious blend of shredded carrots and leafy greens—spinach, baby red chard, and red cabbage—is in a microwave-safe bag; the flavor is mild and slightly sweet. Just poke a few holes in the bag, cook in the microwave for two to three minutes on HIGH, and you've got beautiful vegetables with no mess. Snip open the bag; then pour the steamed greens into a serving dish. Sprinkle with a pinch of salt and pepper; add a little butter or olive oil, if you wish, and serve.

Spinach lovers will be thrilled to find Ready Pac baby spinach too. Cleanup is a breeze, and you won't have to deal with leftovers. Look for both products in the produce section with the bagged salad greens.

Enjoy Succulent Lamb

Lamb is a prominent item on many menus this time of year, but it's not always available in every market. Thanks to Jamison Farm, it's just a phone call away. Products include leg of lamb, chops, shanks, stews, and sausage. The company ships large and small orders; you'll get recipes and serving suggestions in each package. For more information call 1-800-237-5262, or visit **jamisonfarm.com**

Colored Margarines Are a Hit

Okay, grandma and the all-things-proper police will hate this, but your children will love it: Parkay Fun Squeeze margarines in Electric Blue and Shocking Pink. Our junior testers loved using the eye-popping colors to top green beans, corn on the cob, potatoes, and toast. They even ate steamed broccoli dipped into a puddle of pink. Kids have so much fun with these margarines, they'll forget they're eating something good for them. Heck, you may be tempted to try them too.

Tips and Tidbits

■ Patricia Haydel of Hammond, Louisiana, writes that regular or diet lemon-lime soft drinks, such as Sprite and 7 UP, can also do double duty as a food preservative. "To prevent apples or other fruit from turning brown after slicing, pour over sliced fruit if you're out of lemon. You can add a few ice cubes to help keep the fruit crunchy. The carbonated drink doesn't affect the taste at all."

■ Peggy Bonfield of Wilsonville, Alabama, makes weekend mornings special by adding a small can of crushed pineapple in its own juice to pancake batter. "Top warm pineapple pancakes with a scoop of ice cream for a wonderful brunch dessert," she says.

Start the Day Right

Here's morning fare that's perfect for Passover. For additional recipes to enjoy during this holiday (and year-round), see "Honey Adds Flavor Anytime" on page 59.

PECAN-COCONUT GRANOLA

MAKES 6 CUPS

Enjoy this sweet and crunchy treat with milk, or sprinkle it over yogurt or fresh fruit.

- ½ to ¾ cup firmly packed light brown sugar
- ½ cup canola oil
- ½ cup water
- ¼ cup butter or margarine
- ½ cup chopped pecans or almonds
- ½ cup sweetened flaked coconut
- 1 teaspoon ground cinnamon
- 1 (12-ounce) package matzo farfel*
- ⅓ cup raisins or chopped dates

COOK first 4 ingredients over medium heat in a large saucepan, stirring constantly, until butter melts.
STIR in pecans, coconut, and cinnamon. Add matzo farfel; toss well to coat. Spread in a lightly greased, aluminum foil-lined 15- x 10-inch jellyroll pan.
BAKE at 350° for 35 minutes or until golden brown, stirring occasionally. Remove from oven. Stir in raisins, and cool completely. **Prep: 15 min., Bake: 35 min.**

*Matzo farfel is coarsely crumbled matzo. If this recipe is not served for Passover, 1 to 1½ cups uncooked regular oats may be substituted.

JAMI GAUDET
MACON, GEORGIA

April

South-of-the-Border Eggs

Depart from the usual chicken or beef supper
with these Tex-Mex recipes.

Still mulling over tonight's dinner choice? Do the eggs in your refrigerator have a fast-approaching expiration date? If so, we've solved your problem. Using spicy Tex-Mex flavors, we offer clever ways to enjoy one of morning's main staples at night. You can swap out the cheeses in all these recipes and select the salsa heat of your choice. We bet the folks at your house will love our tasty twists on supper when they try these hearty, flavorful dishes.

HUEVOS RANCHEROS

MAKES 2 TO 4 SERVINGS

Huevos rancheros (WAY-vos ran-CHEH-rohs) is Spanish for "ranch-style eggs." *(pictured on facing page)*

- 4 (6-inch) corn tortillas
- 2 tablespoons vegetable oil, divided
- 4 large eggs
- ½ cup (2 ounces) shredded Monterey Jack cheese or Cheddar cheese
- 1 (8-ounce) jar pico de gallo or chunky salsa

FRY tortillas, 2 at a time, in 1 tablespoon hot vegetable oil in a large nonstick skillet 1 minute on each side or just until softened. Drain on paper towels. Arrange in an even layer in an aluminum foil-lined 15- x 10-inch jellyroll pan.
BREAK eggs in remaining 1 tablespoon hot oil in skillet, and cook 2 minutes on each side or until done. Place 1 egg in center of each tortilla; sprinkle with cheese, and spoon pico de gallo evenly over eggs.

BROIL 5½ inches from heat 1 minute or until cheese melts. **Prep: 10 min., Cook: 10 min.**

CAROLYN FLOURNOY
SHREVEPORT, LOUISIANA

POTATO-AND-EGG BURRITOS

MAKES 5 SERVINGS

For a lighter dish, substitute turkey bacon, and use vegetable cooking spray to cook the hash browns and onion.

- 10 (6-inch) flour tortillas
- 8 bacon slices
- 1 (16-ounce) package frozen shredded hash browns, thawed
- 1 medium onion, chopped
- 1 dozen large eggs
- 1 teaspoon salt
- ¾ teaspoon pepper
- Shredded Cheddar cheese (optional)
- Salsa (optional)

HEAT tortillas according to package directions; keep warm.
COOK bacon in a large nonstick skillet until crisp; remove bacon, and drain on paper towels, reserving 1 tablespoon drippings in skillet. Crumble bacon, and set aside.
COOK hash browns and onion in hot drippings over medium-high heat, stirring often, 10 minutes or until lightly browned and onion is tender.
WHISK together eggs, salt, and pepper. Pour into skillet, and cook, stirring gently, over medium heat 8 to 10 minutes or until eggs are cooked. Remove from heat, and stir in bacon.

SPOON egg mixture evenly down centers of tortillas, and top with cheese, if desired. Fold opposite sides of tortillas over filling, and serve immediately. Serve with salsa, if desired. **Prep: 15 min., Cook: 30 min.**

DEBBIE TYE
DALLAS, TEXAS

MEXICAN QUICHE CUPS

MAKES 1 DOZEN

We liked this with tomatillo salsa as well as traditional tomato salsa.

- 4 (4-inch) chorizo sausage links (about ¾ pound), chopped
- 2 (10-ounce) cans refrigerated pizza crust
- 1 cup (4 ounces) shredded Mexican four-cheese blend
- 5 large eggs
- ½ cup milk
- ½ teaspoon ground cumin
- ⅛ teaspoon pepper
- Salsa (optional)
- Sour cream (optional)

COOK chorizo sausage in a large skillet over medium heat 5 minutes or until browned. Drain and set aside.
ROLL or pat 1 can pizza crust dough into a 15- x 10-inch rectangle; cut into 6 (5-inch) squares. Press squares into a lightly greased 12-count muffin pan, skipping every other muffin cup. Repeat procedure with remaining 1 can pizza crust dough and another lightly greased 12-count muffin pan.
SPOON sausage evenly into prepared cups; sprinkle evenly with cheese.
STIR together eggs and next 3 ingredients; pour evenly over cheese.
BAKE at 375° for 20 minutes or until golden brown. Serve with salsa and sour cream, if desired. **Prep: 30 min., Bake: 20 min.**

MEXICAN PIZZA: Unroll 1 can pizza crust dough, and press into a lightly greased 15- x 10-inch jellyroll pan. Cook sausage as directed. Sprinkle sausage and cheese evenly over dough; top with egg mixture and 1 cup salsa. Bake at 400° for 20 minutes or until set. Makes 6 to 8 servings. **Prep: 10 min., Bake: 20 min.**

Huevos Rancheros with black beans and avocado salad, facing page

Southwestern Chicken Salad Spirals,
Speedy Spring Cooler, page 58

Crab Cake Sandwiches, page 60

Grilled Lamb Chops With Chipotle and Cilantro Oils, page 96;
Onion Risotto, page 97

Ginger Pound Cake, page 97

Bacon-Mandarin Salad, page 87

Chicken With Polenta, page 87

Strawberry Meringue Parfaits, page 62

Orange Dream Pie, page 93

Lemon-Blueberry Cream Pie, page 92

Discover the Sweet Secrets of South Texas

We've uncovered a hidden treasure: the irresistible handmade breads of the Rio Grande Valley.

Texans are proud of their strong food traditions, and for good reason. This culturally diverse state has everything from fresh Gulf seafood to a brisket barbecue that's nothing short of a beef lover's paradise. And let's not forget the almost inexhaustible supply of heavenly Tex-Mex cooking. Still, one of the tastiest foods unique to the Lone Star State has managed to go relatively unnoticed, and that's the alluring *pan dulce,* or sweet bread, of the Rio Grande Valley.

It's important to point out, though, that our definition of "sweet" is probably different from the one used by Hispanic bakers. Unlike traditional pastries, *pan dulce* gets most of its sweetness from fruit-based fillings and various pastes and glazes; the bread itself is only slightly sweet.

Folks line up—in many cases before dawn—to get the morning's first fresh-from-the-oven gems, which bear such lighthearted names as *cuernitos* ("little horns"), *cochinitos* ("little pigs"), and *orejas* ("ears"). Once inside, customers grab tongs and round aluminum trays (think pizza pans) before heading off to the polished glass cases to make their selections.

Although most recipes are closely guarded by individual proprietors, we were fortunate enough to find three bakeries—La Mexicana and Lara's in Harlingen and La Especial in San Benito—willing to share the secrets for several of their most popular breads.

Of course, the original recipes make hundreds of servings, so Justin Craft of our Test Kitchens went to work carefully adapting them for the home cook. Now you, too, can enjoy these treats that will have your family shouting for *más.*

SEMITAS

MAKES 1 DOZEN

These small, sweet loaves have a texture similar to that of kaiser rolls.

- 1 (¼-ounce) envelope active dry yeast
- 1 cup warm water (100° to 110°)
- ½ cup sugar, divided
- 5 cups bread flour
- 1 (2.3-ounce) jar anise seeds (½ cup)
- 6 tablespoons shortening
- 2 large eggs
- ¼ teaspoon salt

STIR together yeast, 1 cup warm water, and 2 tablespoons sugar in a 2-cup liquid measuring cup; let stand 5 minutes.

STIR together remaining 6 tablespoons sugar, flour, and next 4 ingredients in bowl of a heavy-duty electric stand mixer. Add yeast mixture, and beat at medium speed with electric mixer, using dough hook attachment, 6 minutes.

DIVIDE dough into 12 equal portions. Shape each portion into a round loaf, and place on 3 lightly greased baking sheets (4 loaves per baking sheet).

COVER and let rise in a warm place (85°), free from drafts, 2 to 3 hours or until doubled in bulk.

BAKE at 425° for 8 to 10 minutes or until golden brown. Cool on baking sheets on wire racks. **Stand: 5 min., Prep: 20 min., Rise: 3 hrs., Bake: 10 min.**

BOLILLOS

MAKES 1 DOZEN

This bread tastes and looks like a French roll.

- 2 (¼-ounce) envelopes active dry yeast
- 1 cup warm water (100° to 110°)
- 2 tablespoons sugar
- 3½ cups bread flour
- 2 tablespoons shortening
- 2 teaspoons salt

STIR together first 3 ingredients in a 2-cup liquid measuring cup; let yeast mixture stand 5 minutes.

STIR together flour, shortening, and salt in bowl of a heavy-duty electric stand mixer.

ADD yeast mixture, and beat at medium speed with mixer, using dough hook attachment, 6 minutes.

TURN dough out onto a lightly floured surface, and divide into 12 equal portions. Knead each portion 3 times.

SHAPE each portion into a 6-inch log, and place on 2 lightly greased baking sheets (6 loaves per baking sheet).

COVER dough, and let rise in a warm place (85°), free from drafts, 40 minutes (dough will not double in bulk). Cut a shallow slit, lengthwise, in top of each loaf.

BAKE at 425° for 10 minutes or until golden brown. Cool on baking sheets on wire racks. **Stand: 5 min., Prep: 25 min., Rise: 40 min., Bake: 10 min.**

PURO DE PIÑA

MAKES 1 DOZEN

This bread, along with the *Empanadas* and *Cuernitos* variations that follow, is made from the same basic *pan dulce* dough called *fino*.

- 3½ cups all-purpose flour
- 1 cup sugar, divided
- 1¾ teaspoons ground cinnamon, divided
- ½ teaspoon salt, divided
- 1 (¼-ounce) envelope active dry yeast
- ¾ cup water
- ¼ cup shortening
- ¼ teaspoon vanilla extract
- 1 (15¼-ounce) can pineapple tidbits
- 2 tablespoons cornstarch

STIR together flour, ¾ cup sugar, ½ teaspoon cinnamon, and ¼ teaspoon salt in bowl of a heavy-duty electric stand mixer. Add yeast and next 3 ingredients; beat at low speed with mixer, using dough hook attachment, 1 minute. **INCREASE** speed to medium, and beat 1 more minute. Cover dough with wax paper, and let stand 30 minutes.

STIR together pineapple, 2 tablespoons sugar, 1 teaspoon cinnamon, and remaining ¼ teaspoon salt in a saucepan over medium heat; simmer 1 minute.

PROCESS pineapple mixture in a blender or food processor until smooth, stopping to scrape down sides. Return to pan, reserving 2 tablespoons.

STIR together reserved 2 tablespoons pineapple mixture and cornstarch in a small bowl. Whisk cornstarch mixture into pineapple mixture in pan, and cook, whisking often, 2 minutes or until smooth and thickened. Remove pan from heat, and cool.

TURN dough out onto a lightly floured surface; divide into 12 equal portions.

ROLL each portion to a length of 10 inches, forming a 6-inch base and 2-inch top (shape resembles a triangle with a flat top). Spread 1½ tablespoons pineapple mixture on 1 side of each portion, leaving a border around edges.

ROLL up each portion, starting at 6-inch end, and place on 2 lightly greased baking sheets (6 portions per baking sheet). Combine remaining 2 tablespoons sugar and remaining ¼ teaspoon cinnamon; sprinkle evenly over dough.

COVER and let stand in a warm place (85°), free from drafts, 15 minutes (dough will not double in bulk). **BAKE** at 375° for 15 to 18 minutes. Cool on baking sheets on wire racks. **Prep: 1 hr., Stand: 45 min., Bake: 18 min.**

EMPANADAS: Stir together 1 (15-ounce) can unsweetened pumpkin, 2 tablespoons sugar, 1 teaspoon ground cinnamon, and ¼ teaspoon salt. Prepare dough as directed. After dough stands 30 minutes, divide into 12 equal portions, and shape into balls. Roll or flatten balls into 6-inch circles. Spoon 1½ tablespoons pumpkin mixture onto half of each pastry circle. Moisten edges with water; fold dough over pumpkin mixture, pressing edges to seal. Crimp edges of dough with a fork. Place on lightly greased baking sheets. Cover and let stand in a warm place (85°), free from drafts, 15 minutes. Bake at 375° for 15 to 18 minutes or until golden brown. Cool on baking sheets on wire racks. Makes 1 dozen. **Prep: 50 min., Stand: 45 min., Bake: 18 min.**

CUERNITOS: Prepare dough as directed. After dough stands 30 minutes, turn out onto a lightly floured surface, and divide into 12 equal portions. Roll each portion to a length of 10 inches, forming a 6-inch base and 2-inch top. Roll up each portion, starting at 6-inch end. Gently shape each portion into a crescent, and place on lightly greased baking sheets. Combine 2 tablespoons sugar and ¼ teaspoon cinnamon; sprinkle evenly over dough. Cover and let stand in a warm place (85°), free from drafts, 15 minutes. Bake at 375° for 15 to 18 minutes. Cool on baking sheets on wire racks. Makes 1 dozen. **Prep: 50 min., Stand: 45 min., Bake: 18 min.**

ANILLOS

MAKES 1 DOZEN

These airy, jelly-filled breads are probably the closest thing we know to baked doughnuts.

- 1 (¼-ounce) envelope active dry yeast
- 1 cup warm water (100° to 110°)
- ½ cup sugar, divided
- 5 cups bread flour
- 2 large eggs
- 6 tablespoons shortening
- ¼ teaspoon salt
- ¾ cup strawberry preserves
- 1 cup powdered sugar
- ⅓ cup water

STIR together yeast, 1 cup warm water, and 2 tablespoons sugar in a 2-cup liquid measuring cup; let stand 5 minutes. **STIR** together remaining 6 tablespoons sugar, flour, and next 3 ingredients in bowl of a heavy-duty electric stand mixer. Add yeast mixture, and beat at medium speed with mixer, using dough hook attachment, 6 minutes.

DIVIDE dough into 12 equal portions; shape into balls, and place on 2 lightly greased baking sheets (6 balls per baking sheet). Flatten to 4-inch-wide circles with hand; press thumb in center of each circle to make an indentation (about the size of a quarter). Spoon 1 tablespoon preserves in each indentation.

COVER and let stand in a warm place (85°), free from drafts, 20 minutes (dough will not double in bulk).

BAKE at 375° for 13 to 15 minutes or until golden brown. Cool on baking sheets on wire racks. Stir together powdered sugar and ⅓ cup water; drizzle evenly over breads. **Prep: 20 min., Stand: 25 min., Bake: 15 min.**

MOLLETES

MAKES 1 DOZEN

Molletes get their characteristic scalloped design from a tool called a *dulce* marker (see "Cook's Notes," at right, for ordering information).

1 (¼-ounce) envelope active dry
    yeast
1 cup warm water (100° to 110°)
⅔ cup sugar, divided
5 cups bread flour
½ cup shortening, divided
2 large eggs
¼ teaspoon salt
⅓ cup all-purpose flour

STIR together yeast, 1 cup warm water, and 2 tablespoons sugar in a 2-cup liquid measuring cup, and let stand 5 minutes.

STIR together 6 tablespoons sugar, bread flour, ⅓ cup shortening, eggs, and salt in bowl of a heavy-duty electric stand mixer. Add yeast mixture to flour mixture; beat at medium speed with mixer, using dough hook attachment, 6 minutes.

COMBINE remaining 3 tablespoons sugar and all-purpose flour in a bowl, and cut in remaining 3 tablespoons shortening with a fork until blended to form a paste.

DIVIDE dough into 12 equal portions; shape into balls; place on 2 lightly greased baking sheets (6 balls per baking sheet). Spread 2 teaspoons flour paste on top of each ball. Slightly flatten each ball using a *dulce* marker dipped in flour or a kaiser roll stamp dipped in flour. Cover with wax paper or plastic wrap.

PREHEAT oven to 170° to 200°; turn off oven, leaving oven door open 1 minute.

PLACE dough, covered, in oven; let rise, with oven door closed, 2 hours and 10 minutes or until doubled in bulk. Remove dough; preheat oven to 425°.

BAKE *molletes* at 425° for 8 to 10 minutes or until golden brown. Cool on baking sheets on wire racks. **Stand: 5 min.; Prep: 20 min.; Rise: 2 hrs., 10 min.; Bake: 10 min.**

CHOCOLATE MOLLETES: Stir 2 tablespoons cocoa into paste mixture. Makes 1 dozen.

PINK MOLLETES: Stir 3 drops red liquid food coloring into paste mixture. Makes 1 dozen.

RED MOLLETES: Stir 6 drops red liquid food coloring into paste mixture. Makes 1 dozen.

YELLOW MOLLETES: Stir 6 drops yellow liquid food coloring into paste mixture. Makes 1 dozen.

Cook's Notes

■ These recipes call for bread flour, which contains more hard wheat than all-purpose and cake flours. Bread flour increases a dough's elasticity and ability to rise.

■ If you don't have a heavy-duty electric stand mixer, you can mix the dough by hand. (We do not recommend using a hand mixer.) For testing purposes, we used a KitchenAid stand mixer.

■ *Dulce* markers, used to make the scalloped designs on the *Molletes,* are available by mail order ($9) at Rodriguez Bakery Equipment, 1405 West Barton Street, Harlingen, TX 78550; (956) 421-2387. An alternative tool is a kaiser roll stamp ($8.75), available at The Baker's Catalogue, 1-800-827-6836 or **www.kingarthurflour.com**

Quick Cake

If you have a sweet tooth but you're short on time, this family-favorite cake takes just 45 minutes to prepare, bake, and frost, leaving you plenty of time to savor a sweet slice.

SHORTCUT CARROT CAKE

MAKES 1 (3-LAYER) CAKE

1 (26.5-ounce) package cinnamon
    streusel coffee cake mix
3 large eggs
1¼ cups water
⅓ cup vegetable oil
3 large carrots, finely grated
½ cup chopped pecans,
    toasted
1 cup flaked coconut
2 tablespoons orange juice
Cream Cheese Frosting

GREASE 3 (8-inch) round cakepans. Line with wax paper; grease and flour.

COMBINE cake mix and streusel packet in a mixing bowl, reserving glaze packet.

ADD eggs, 1¼ cups water, and oil; beat at medium speed with an electric mixer 2 minutes.

STIR in carrot, chopped pecans, and coconut. Pour batter evenly into prepared pans.

BAKE at 350° for 18 to 20 minutes. Cool in pans on wire racks 10 minutes. Remove from pans; place on racks.

STIR together reserved glaze and juice; brush evenly over warm cake layers. Cool completely on wire racks.

SPREAD Cream Cheese Frosting between layers and on top and sides of cake. Chill at least 2 hours. **Prep: 15 min., Bake: 20 min., Chill: 2 hrs.**

Cream Cheese Frosting:

MAKES 5 CUPS

1 (8-ounce) package cream cheese,
    softened
1 (3-ounce) package cream cheese,
    softened
¾ cup butter or margarine,
    softened
7 cups powdered sugar
1 tablespoon vanilla extract
3 to 4 tablespoons milk

BEAT cream cheese and butter at medium speed with an electric mixer until fluffy; gradually add powdered sugar, beating well. Stir in vanilla.

ADD milk, 1 tablespoon at a time, until frosting reaches desired consistency. **Prep: 10 min.**

Splashed With Juicy Flavor

Squeeze tangy juice and juice concentrates into these recipes.

You don't need expensive marinades and designer sauces to perk up blah recipes. Just reach into your fridge or freezer for fruit juices and juice concentrates. Lime juice, for example, enlivens Zesty Rice-and-Bean Salad. Lemon juice does the same for Blackberry-Lemon Sorbet, while white grape juice adds to the sweet and hot flavors of Herb-Mustard Vinaigrette. These low-fat flavor boosters aren't just for drinking anymore.

HERB-MUSTARD VINAIGRETTE

MAKES ABOUT 1 CUP

- 1 (4-ounce) jar pear baby food
- 3 tablespoons frozen white grape juice concentrate, thawed
- 3 tablespoons white wine vinegar
- 1 teaspoon Dijon mustard
- ¼ teaspoon hot sauce
- 2 teaspoons chopped fresh tarragon
- 2 teaspoons chopped fresh basil
- ¼ teaspoon salt
- 1 tablespoon olive oil

WHISK together first 8 ingredients; gradually add oil, whisking until blended. **Prep: 10 min.**

PERSIS SCHLOSSER
DENVER, COLORADO

Per 2 tablespoons: Calories 57 (46% from fat); Fat 2.9g (sat 0.4g, mono 2g, poly 0.3g); Protein 0.2g; Carb 8.3g; Fiber 0.9g; Chol 0mg; Iron 0.2mg; Sodium 145mg; Calc 7.4mg

SWEET-AND-SOUR SHRIMP WITH ONION AND RED PEPPER

MAKES 4 SERVINGS

Jasmine rice gives this dish a savory aroma. You can substitute long-grain and wild rice if you don't have jasmine rice on hand.

- 1 pound unpeeled, medium-size fresh shrimp
- 1 tablespoon dry sherry
- 6 teaspoons cornstarch, divided
- 3 teaspoons vegetable oil, divided
- 4 thin slices fresh ginger
- 4 green onions, cut into 1-inch pieces
- 2 garlic cloves, minced
- 1 small red bell pepper, cut into thin strips
- 1 (6-ounce) can unsweetened pineapple juice
- 1 tablespoon cider vinegar
- 1 tablespoon lite soy sauce
- 1 tablespoon frozen orange juice concentrate, thawed
- 2 tablespoons water
- 2 cups hot cooked jasmine rice

PEEL shrimp, and devein, if desired. **WHISK** together sherry and 2 teaspoons cornstarch in a medium bowl; add shrimp, coating well. Chill 30 minutes, turning occasionally.
HEAT 2 teaspoons vegetable oil in a large nonstick skillet or wok at medium-high 2 minutes. Add ginger and next 3 ingredients; cook 1 minute or until tender. **REMOVE** vegetables from skillet; discard ginger. Remove shrimp from marinade, discarding marinade.

HEAT remaining 1 teaspoon vegetable oil in skillet; add shrimp, and cook, stirring often, 2 minutes or until shrimp turn pink. Return vegetables to skillet; stir in pineapple juice and next 3 ingredients. **STIR** together 2 tablespoons water and remaining 4 teaspoons cornstarch; add to shrimp mixture. Bring to a boil; cook, stirring constantly, 1 minute or until thickened. Serve over rice. **Prep: 40 min., Chill: 30 min., Cook: 6 min.**

PERSIS SCHLOSSER
DENVER, COLORADO

Per serving: Calories 333 (11% from fat); Fat 4.2g (sat 0.5g, mono 2.2g, poly 1.3g); Protein 18.3g; Carb 53g; Fiber 2g; Chol 135mg*; Iron 2.8mg; Sodium 309mg; Calc 44mg

*Most of the cholesterol comes from shrimp. But they're also low in saturated fat, which makes them a nutritious, heart-healthy choice.

ZESTY RICE-AND-BEAN SALAD

MAKES 4 CUPS

Enjoy this fiber- and flavor-packed salad for lunch. Use instant brown rice to shorten your prep time.

- 2 tablespoons olive oil
- 1 garlic clove, minced
- ½ teaspoon ground red pepper
- ½ teaspoon grated lime rind
- ¼ cup fresh lime juice
- ¼ teaspoon salt
- 2 cups cooked brown rice
- 1 (15-ounce) can black beans, rinsed and drained
- 1 (15-ounce) can kidney beans, rinsed and drained
- 4 green onions, chopped
- ¼ cup chopped fresh cilantro
- ¼ cup chopped fresh mint
- ¼ cup crumbled feta cheese

WHISK together first 6 ingredients in a large bowl; add rice and next 5 ingredients, tossing to coat. Sprinkle with feta cheese. Cover and chill 1 hour, if desired. **Prep: 20 min.**

LISA HELM
MONTICELLO, FLORIDA

Per 1-cup serving: Calories 352 (28% from fat); Fat 11g (sat 2.6g, mono 6.1g, poly 1.6g); Protein 13g; Carb 51g; Fiber 13g; Chol 8.3mg; Iron 2.4mg; Sodium 473mg; Calc 96mg

ORANGE-GLAZED ROASTED CHICKEN WITH WILD RICE

MAKES 8 SERVINGS

While the chicken bakes, prepare the vegetable-rice mixture.

    1 large shallot, minced
    Vegetable cooking spray
    1 (12-ounce) can frozen orange juice
        concentrate, thawed
    1½ cups water
    2 tablespoons honey
    ¾ teaspoon salt, divided
    ¼ teaspoon ground
        marjoram
    2 teaspoons rubbed sage,
        divided
    ¾ teaspoon pepper, divided
    1 (5½-pound) whole chicken
    2 (6-ounce) packages long-grain and
        wild rice mix
    1 medium onion,
        chopped
    2 celery ribs, chopped
    1 fennel bulb, chopped
    2 garlic cloves, minced
    ½ cup sweetened dried cranberries,
        chopped

SAUTÉ shallot in skillet coated with cooking spray over medium-high heat 3 minutes or until tender. Add juice concentrate, 1½ cups water, honey, ½ teaspoon salt, marjoram, 1 teaspoon sage, and ½ teaspoon pepper, whisking until blended.
PLACE chicken, breast side up, on a rack in an aluminum foil-lined roasting pan coated with cooking spray. Sprinkle with remaining ¼ teaspoon salt; drizzle with juice mixture.
BAKE at 350° for 2 hours and 15 minutes or until a meat thermometer inserted into chicken thigh registers 180°, basting every 30 minutes. Shield after 30 minutes, if necessary.
COOK rice according to package directions, omitting fat.
COOK onion, celery, and fennel in a large nonstick skillet coated with cooking spray over medium-high heat 5 to 7 minutes. Add garlic, and sauté 2 minutes.
STIR together onion mixture, rice, dried cranberries, remaining 1 teaspoon sage, and remaining ¼ teaspoon pepper.

Cover and keep warm. Serve with chicken and any remaining sauce in pan. **Prep: 25 min.; Bake: 2 hrs., 15 min.**

JONATHAN GOLDMAN
SAN ANTONIO, TEXAS

Per serving: Calories 496 (17% from fat); Fat 9.6g (sat 2.4g, mono 3.3g, poly 2g); Protein 39g; Carb 63g; Fiber 3.5g; Chol 99mg; Iron 3.4mg; Sodium 809mg*; Calc 77mg

*Reduce sodium by 218 milligrams per serving by omitting salt.

BLACKBERRY-LEMON SORBET

MAKES 14 CUPS

This tart, refreshing dessert is a terrific source of calcium.

    10 cups fresh blackberries*
    2¼ cups sugar
    1 teaspoon grated lemon rind
    ¼ cup fresh lemon juice
    4 cups nonfat buttermilk

BRING first 4 ingredients to a boil in a saucepan, stirring constantly; reduce heat, and simmer 15 minutes. Cool.
PROCESS blackberry mixture, in batches, in a blender or food processor until smooth, stopping to scrape down sides.
POUR blackberry puree through a fine wire-mesh strainer into a bowl, pressing pulp with back of a wooden spoon. Discard pulp, and stir in buttermilk. Freeze 8 hours.
PROCESS frozen blackberry mixture, in batches, until smooth. Freeze 5 hours.
Prep: 40 min., Cook: 20 min., Freeze: 13 hrs.

*Substitute 5 (14-ounce) packages frozen blackberries, thawed, if desired.

NOTE: Recipe may be halved.

Per 1-cup serving: Calories 207 (4% from fat); Fat 1g (sat 0.4g, mono 0.2g, poly 0.3g); Protein 3g; Carb 49g; Fiber 5.5g; Chol 2.4mg; Iron 0.6mg; Sodium 74mg; Calc 115mg

Bayou Favorite

No Creole or Cajun recipe is complete without the blessing of the "holy trinity"—celery, onion, and bell pepper, that is. This time-honored blend gives our luxurious Crawfish Étouffée a little lagniappe, or something extra.

CRAWFISH ÉTOUFFÉE

MAKES 4 TO 6 SERVINGS

    ¼ cup butter or margarine
    1 medium onion, chopped
    2 celery ribs, chopped
    1 medium-size green bell pepper,
        chopped
    4 garlic cloves, minced
    1 large shallot, chopped
    ¼ cup all-purpose flour
    1 teaspoon salt
    ½ to 1 teaspoon ground red pepper
    1 (14-ounce) can chicken broth
    ¼ cup chopped fresh parsley
    ¼ cup chopped fresh chives
    2 pounds cooked, peeled crawfish
        tails*
    Hot cooked rice
    Garnishes: chopped fresh chives,
        ground red pepper

MELT butter in a large Dutch oven over medium-high heat. Add onion and next 4 ingredients; sauté 5 minutes or until tender.
ADD flour, salt, and red pepper; cook, stirring constantly, until caramel colored (about 10 minutes). Add next 3 ingredients; cook, stirring constantly, 5 minutes or until thick and bubbly.
STIR in crawfish; cook 5 minutes or until thoroughly heated. Serve with rice. Garnish, if desired. **Prep: 35 min., Cook: 30 min.**

*Substitute 2 pounds frozen cooked crawfish tails, thawed and drained, for fresh crawfish, if desired.

Supper Clubs Simplified

Delicious recipes and hardworking tips from our readers will make your special gathering a cinch.

Menu 1

Casual Southwestern Hospitality

Serves 10 to 12

Balsamic Strawberry Salsa   Tortilla chips

Texas White Sangría

Bacon-Mandarin Salad

Chicken With Polenta

Mocha Cake

Awhile back, we asked readers to tell us about their supper clubs. The response was overwhelming. In only a short time, it was crystal clear that whether it's Bixby, Oklahoma, or Staunton, Virginia, supper clubs are alive and well all over our region.

We did find, however, that not all clubs follow the same rules—some prefer to meet during the week, while others find weekends more relaxing. Some create themes for dinners, while others don't.

Readers agree that you don't need a large home or a lavishly appointed kitchen to host a supper club. If you can't comfortably fit a large group in your dining room, plan a more casual menu, and eat in the living room or backyard. If your kitchen is small, prepare most of the food in advance.

In addition to tips, readers also sent some of their favorite recipes, which we feature in our two menus—one centered around chicken, the other focused on beef. Mix-and-match the recipes to suit your style and comfort level in the kitchen.

Regardless of how you and your friends decide to structure the supper club, you'll find it's a great opportunity to meet new people and build lasting friendships. An atmosphere of food and fun elevates the everyday dining experience to something truly special.

BALSAMIC STRAWBERRY SALSA

MAKES 6 CUPS

For make-ahead convenience, prepare this recipe the morning of the party.

> 6 tablespoons olive oil
> 2 tablespoons white balsamic vinegar
> ½ teaspoon salt
> 1 pint fresh strawberries, coarsely chopped
> 8 green onions, chopped
> 2 pints cherry tomatoes, chopped
> ½ cup chopped fresh cilantro

WHISK together first 3 ingredients in a large bowl; add strawberries and remaining ingredients, tossing to coat. **CHILL** at least 1 hour. Serve with tortilla chips. **Prep: 15 min., Chill: 1 hr.**

MELISSA WEBB
SEWANEE, TENNESSEE

TEXAS WHITE SANGRÍA

MAKES 10 TO 12 SERVINGS

Fresh mint and cinnamon infuse this fruity, refreshing cooler.

> 1⅓ cups water
> ½ cup sugar
> 4 (3-inch) cinnamon sticks
> 1 cup fresh mint leaves, divided
> 1 (750-milliliter) bottle dry white wine
> 2 lemons, sliced
> 2 oranges, sliced
> 2 peaches, peeled and sliced
> 2 cups club soda, chilled

BRING first 3 ingredients and ½ cup mint leaves to a boil in a saucepan over medium heat.
REDUCE heat, and simmer 5 minutes. Remove from heat, and cool.
COVER and let stand 8 hours, if desired. Remove cinnamon sticks and mint leaves with a slotted spoon.
COMBINE sugar mixture, remaining ½ cup mint leaves, wine, and next 3 ingredients in a pitcher; chill overnight, if desired. Stir in club soda before serving. Serve over ice. **Prep: 15 min.**

BROAD OAKS SUPPER CLUB
HOUSTON, TEXAS

BACON-MANDARIN SALAD

MAKES 12 SERVINGS

Wash the lettuces the night before. Wrap in a damp paper towel, and chill in zip-top plastic bags; cook the bacon, and toast the almonds too. Assemble and dress right before serving. *(pictured on page 78)*

- ½ cup olive oil
- ¼ cup red wine vinegar
- ¼ cup sugar
- 1 tablespoon chopped fresh basil
- ⅛ teaspoon hot sauce
- 2 (15-ounce) cans mandarin oranges, drained and chilled*
- 1 head Red Leaf lettuce, torn
- 1 head romaine lettuce, torn
- 1 (16-ounce) package bacon, cooked and crumbled
- 1 (4-ounce) package sliced almonds, toasted

WHISK together first 5 ingredients in a large bowl, blending well.

ADD oranges and lettuces, tossing gently to coat.

SPRINKLE with crumbled bacon and sliced almonds. Serve immediately. **Prep: 15 min., Cook: 18 min.**

*Substitute fresh orange segments for canned mandarin oranges, if desired.

CARLA MCFARLAND
CLEVELAND, TENNESSEE

CHICKEN WITH POLENTA

MAKES 10 SERVINGS

To prepare this recipe ahead, grill the chicken, cut into strips, and chill. Make the polenta just before serving, and reheat the chicken in the microwave. *(pictured on page 78)*

- 5 cups chicken broth, divided
- 1⅓ cups yellow cornmeal*
- ¾ cup half-and-half
- 1 cup grated Parmesan cheese
- 8 to 10 skinned and boned chicken breast halves
- 1 teaspoon salt, divided
- ¼ teaspoon ground black pepper
- 2 red bell peppers, diced
- 1 large Vidalia onion, diced
- 1 tablespoon olive oil
- 3 cups fresh corn kernels (about 4 ears)
- ¾ cup dry white wine
- ½ cup orange juice
- ⅛ to ¼ teaspoon ground red pepper
- Garnish: chopped fresh chives

BRING 4½ cups chicken broth to a boil in a 3-quart saucepan over medium heat. Gradually whisk in cornmeal. Reduce heat to low, and simmer, stirring often, 30 minutes. Remove from heat; stir in half-and-half and cheese.

SPRINKLE chicken with ½ teaspoon salt and black pepper.

GRILL chicken, uncovered, over medium-high heat (350° to 400°) 7 minutes on each side or until done. Cool to touch, and cut into thin strips; set aside.

SAUTÉ bell pepper and onion in hot oil in a large nonstick skillet over medium heat 7 minutes or until tender. Add corn; sauté 4 minutes. Stir in wine; simmer 5 minutes. Stir in juice, remaining ½ cup broth, remaining ½ teaspoon salt, and ground red pepper; simmer 10 minutes or until slightly thickened. Serve over polenta and chicken strips. Garnish, if desired. **Prep: 30 min.; Cook: 1 hr., 10 min.**

*Substitute 1 cup regular grits, if desired. Bring 4 cups chicken broth to a boil, and stir in grits. Cover, reduce heat, and simmer 5 minutes. Remove from heat; stir in half-and-half and cheese.

JUDITH WHICHARD
GRIMESLAND, NORTH CAROLINA

MOCHA CAKE

MAKES 1 (10-INCH) CAKE

Cake mix is the secret to this extraeasy and ultrarich dessert. A splash of coffee liqueur and a sprinkling of almond toffee bits enrich this crowd-pleasing cake.

- 2 cups sour cream
- 2 large eggs
- 1 (18.25-ounce) package chocolate cake mix
- ½ cup coffee liqueur
- ¼ cup vegetable oil
- 1 (12-ounce) package semisweet chocolate morsels
- ½ cup crushed almond toffee bits (optional)
- Powdered sugar
- 1 pint whipping cream
- ¼ cup powdered sugar

STIR together first 5 ingredients in a large bowl; blend well. Stir in morsels and, if desired, toffee bits. Pour batter into a greased and floured 10-inch Bundt pan.

BAKE at 350° for 50 to 55 minutes or until a wooden pick inserted in center comes out clean.

COOL in pan on a wire rack 10 to 15 minutes; remove from pan, and cool completely on wire rack. Sprinkle with powdered sugar.

BEAT whipping cream at medium speed with an electric mixer until foamy; gradually add ¼ cup powdered sugar, beating until soft peaks form. Serve with cake. **Prep: 25 min., Bake: 55 min., Cool: 15 min.**

NOTE: For testing purposes only, we used Kahlúa coffee liqueur and Heath Bits 'O Brickle Almond Toffee Bits.

THE SUPPER CLUB
WILMINGTON, NORTH CAROLINA

BAKED VIDALIA ONION DIP

MAKES 6 CUPS

2 tablespoons butter or margarine
3 large Vidalia onions, coarsely
    chopped
2 cups (8 ounces) shredded Swiss
    cheese
2 cups mayonnaise
1 (8-ounce) can sliced water
    chestnuts, drained and chopped
¼ cup dry white wine
1 garlic clove, minced
½ teaspoon hot sauce

MELT butter in a large skillet over medium-high heat; add onion, and sauté 10 minutes or until tender.
STIR together shredded Swiss cheese and next 5 ingredients; stir in onion, blending well. Spoon mixture into a lightly greased 2-quart baking dish.
BAKE at 375° for 25 minutes, and let stand 10 minutes. Serve with tortilla chips or crackers. **Prep: 15 min., Bake: 25 min., Stand: 10 min.**

TO LIGHTEN: Substitute vegetable cooking spray for butter; substitute reduced-fat Swiss cheese and light mayonnaise.

LE BON TEMPS SUPPER CLUB
TUSCUMBIA, ALABAMA

CHOCOLATE MARTINIS

MAKES 10 TO 12 SERVINGS

2 to 2½ cups vodka, chilled
1¼ cups chocolate liqueur
¼ cup raspberry liqueur
¼ cup half-and-half (optional)
Chocolate liqueur or syrup
Sweetened cocoa

STIR together vodka, liqueurs, and, if desired, half-and-half in a large pitcher; chill at least 1 hour.
FILL martini glasses with ice. Let stand 5 minutes; discard ice.
DIP rims of chilled glasses in chocolate liqueur; dip in cocoa, coating rims.
POUR vodka mixture into glasses. Serve immediately. **Prep: 15 min., Stand: 5 min., Chill: 1 hr.**

NOTE: For testing purposes only, we used Godiva Liqueur for chocolate liqueur, Chambord for raspberry liqueur, and Ghirardelli Sweet Ground Chocolate and Cocoa for sweetened cocoa.

INDIVIDUAL CHOCOLATE MARTINI: Combine ¼ cup vodka, 2 tablespoons chocolate liqueur, 1½ teaspoons raspberry liqueur, 6 ice cubes, and, if desired, a dash of half-and-half in a martini shaker. Cover with lid, and shake until thoroughly chilled. Remove lid, and strain into a chilled martini glass. Serve immediately. Makes 1 serving.

JULIE THOMAS
CHARLOTTESVILLE, VIRGINIA

ITALIAN POT ROAST

MAKES 6 TO 8 SERVINGS

To make ahead, chill baked roast overnight. Cut into thin slices, and place in a 13- x 9-inch baking dish. Top with gravy. Bake at 350° for 30 minutes or until thoroughly heated.

1 (4½-pound) rib-eye roast, trimmed*
2 tablespoons vegetable oil
1 (15-ounce) can tomato sauce
½ cup red wine
2 large tomatoes, chopped
1 medium onion, minced
4 garlic cloves, minced
1 tablespoon salt
1 tablespoon pepper
2 teaspoons chopped fresh or
    1 teaspoon dried basil
2 teaspoons chopped fresh or
    1 teaspoon dried oregano
1 (16-ounce) package red potatoes,
    cut into wedges
½ teaspoon salt
¼ teaspoon pepper
3 tablespoons all-purpose flour
1 cup beef broth or water
Garnish: chopped fresh parsley

COOK roast in hot oil in a large Dutch oven over medium-high heat 5 to 6 minutes or until browned on all sides.
COMBINE tomato sauce and next 8 ingredients; pour over roast in Dutch oven.
BAKE, covered, at 325° for 3 hours or until roast is tender. Remove roast; keep warm. Reserve drippings in Dutch oven.
PLACE potato wedges in a lightly greased 15- x 10-inch jellyroll pan. Bake at 450° for 30 minutes. Sprinkle with ½ teaspoon salt and ¼ teaspoon pepper.
SKIM fat from drippings in Dutch oven. Whisk together flour and beef broth until smooth; add to drippings. Cook mixture, stirring constantly, over low heat 8 minutes or until thickened.
CUT roast into thin slices. Arrange roast and potatoes on a serving platter. Garnish, if desired. Serve with tomato gravy. **Prep: 35 min.; Cook: 3 hrs., 38 min.**

*Substitute 1 (4½-pound) boneless beef rump roast, trimmed, if desired. Bake, covered, at 325° for 2 hours and 20 minutes or until tender.

THE GOURMET CLUB
LEVELLAND, TEXAS

Roasted Zucchini

MAKES 12 SERVINGS

If you don't have sesame oil, it's fine to use olive oil instead.

    4 pounds baby zucchini,
        sliced
    ¼ cup sesame oil, divided
    1 (12-ounce) jar roasted red bell
        peppers, drained and coarsely
        chopped
    ½ cup coarsely chopped walnuts
    ½ teaspoon ground ginger or
        1 teaspoon minced fresh
        ginger
    2 garlic cloves, minced
    ¼ teaspoon dried crushed red
        pepper
    ¼ cup chicken broth
    ¼ cup soy sauce
    ½ to 1 teaspoon sugar

ARRANGE zucchini in an aluminum foil-lined jellyroll pan; drizzle with 2 tablespoons sesame oil.

BAKE at 475° for 30 minutes, turning zucchini once.

SAUTÉ bell pepper and next 4 ingredients in remaining 2 tablespoons hot sesame oil in a large skillet over medium-high heat 2 minutes.

REDUCE heat to medium. Stir in chicken broth, soy sauce, and sugar; cook until thoroughly heated. Serve over zucchini. **Prep: 10 min., Bake: 30 min., Cook: 4 min.**

THE FRIDAY NIGHT GROUP
LEXINGTON, KENTUCKY

Coco Loco Custard

MAKES 8 SERVINGS

This island-inspired dessert makes a beautiful presentation on a single plate or in individual custard cups.

    1½ cups sugar, divided
    ½ cup water
    3 large eggs
    2 egg yolks
    2½ cups warm milk
    ½ cup sweetened flaked coconut,
        toasted
    2 tablespoons dark rum
    1 tablespoon vanilla extract
    Garnish: toasted flaked coconut

COMBINE 1 cup sugar and ½ cup water in a 9-inch cakepan, and cook over low heat 10 minutes or until sugar caramelizes, tipping pan to cover bottom evenly.

WHISK together eggs, yolks, and remaining ½ cup sugar until blended. Gradually add milk, whisking constantly; stir in coconut, rum, and vanilla.

POUR mixture into prepared pan. Cover with foil; place on a jellyroll pan. Add hot water to jellyroll pan to a depth of ¼ to ½ inch.

BAKE at 325° for 1 hour and 10 minutes or until a knife inserted in center comes out clean.

REMOVE from water, and uncover; cool in cakepan on a wire rack. Cover and chill 3 hours.

RUN a knife around edge of custard to loosen; invert onto a serving plate. Garnish, if desired. **Prep: 30 min.; Bake: 1 hr., 10 min.; Chill: 3 hrs.**

NOTE: Substitute 8 (4-ounce) custard cups for cakepan, if desired. Caramelize sugar in heavy saucepan instead of cakepan.

MILL GLEN-WITHMERE SUPPER CLUB
DUNWOODY, GEORGIA

Supper Club Strategies

Many of you responded to our survey and offered excellent suggestions for successful supper clubs. Here's a sampling.

Getting a Club Up and Running

"When we relocated to Florida, I decided to host a kickoff breakfast with a few neighbors. My advice: Center your initial planning meeting around a theme and menu ideas, dietary restrictions, monthly schedules, and general guidelines. The schedule and dish assignments made organizing the dinners on a monthly basis easier and left little room for confusion."

CHERYL HOWLIN
FAIRWAY HILLS SUPPER CLUB
LAKE MARY, FLORIDA

"While most supper clubs are all-adult events, consider inviting children to a meeting. We let them plan the menu, and each of the children gets to prepare his or her dish."

LYNN GARDNER
MEMPHIS, TENNESSEE

To Keep It Going, Keep It Interesting

"Capture memorable supper club moments by starting a scrapbook or even a recipe collection. We published a cookbook celebrating 38 years of dining together."

THE SUPPER CLUB
DALLAS, TEXAS

"I remember a supper club where grits casserole was served as part of a Southern theme. The host filled canvas bags with uncooked grits for each guest and tied the bags with rope. Place cards containing the casserole recipe were then attached to the rope and placed at each table setting. Guests left with not only a better appreciation for Southern cuisine but also a great recipe."

ANNEMARIE CARNEY
PROVIDENCE, RHODE ISLAND

Better Beef for Less

These thrifty main dishes offer not only great value but also family-pleasing flavor.

For everyday meals, look to economical cuts of meat for flavorful options. Ground beef, flank steak, and rump roast all make perfect choices for family-style entrées. Not only are they affordable, but they're versatile too. Watch for sales on these cuts at your supermarket, and purchase extra to freeze for later.

MINI MEXICAN MEAT LOAVES

MAKES 6 SERVINGS

- 1½ pounds ground beef
- ¾ cup mild picante sauce
- 1 (4.5-ounce) can chopped green chiles, drained
- ½ cup finely crushed corn chips
- 1 medium onion, chopped
- 1 large egg, lightly beaten
- 1½ teaspoons ground cumin
- 1 teaspoon salt
- Picante sauce
- 1 cup (4 ounces) shredded Monterey Jack or sharp Cheddar cheese
- Garnishes: sour cream, fresh cilantro sprigs

COMBINE first 8 ingredients; shape into 6 loaves. Place on a lightly greased rack in a broiler pan. Chill 2 hours, if desired.
BAKE at 375° for 40 minutes or until done. Spoon desired amount of picante sauce over loaves, and sprinkle with cheese. Garnish, if desired. **Prep: 20 min., Bake: 40 min.**

JANICE M. FRANCE
DEPAUW, INDIANA

SOY-GINGER FLANK STEAK

MAKES 6 SERVINGS

- ½ cup soy sauce
- 2 tablespoons sesame seeds
- 3 tablespoons honey
- 3 tablespoons vegetable oil
- 2 green onions, sliced
- 1 garlic clove, minced
- 1 teaspoon grated fresh ginger
- 1 (2-pound) flank steak, trimmed

COMBINE first 7 ingredients in a shallow dish or large heavy-duty zip-top plastic bag; add flank steak. Cover or seal, and chill 8 hours, turning occasionally.
REMOVE flank steak from marinade, discarding marinade.
GRILL, covered with grill lid, over medium-high heat (350° to 400°) 7 minutes on each side or to desired degree of doneness. Let stand 5 minutes; cut diagonally across grain into thin slices. **Prep: 10 min., Chill: 8 hrs., Grill: 14 min., Stand: 5 min.**

LISA MCDANIEL
BURLINGTON, NORTH CAROLINA

POT ROAST WITH MUSHROOM GRAVY

MAKES 8 TO 10 SERVINGS

Substitute less-expensive chuck roast for rump roast, if desired.

- 1 (3½-pound) boneless beef rump roast, trimmed
- 2 large garlic cloves, thinly sliced
- 1 teaspoon salt
- 1 teaspoon garlic salt
- 1 teaspoon pepper
- ¼ cup all-purpose flour
- 3 tablespoons vegetable oil
- 2 cups brewed coffee
- 1 (10¾-ounce) can cream of mushroom soup
- 1 tablespoon Worcestershire sauce
- 1 large onion, sliced
- 3 tablespoons cornstarch
- 3 tablespoons water

CUT slits in roast, using a sharp knife; push a garlic slice into each slit. Sprinkle roast with salts and pepper; lightly dredge in flour, patting off excess flour.
BROWN roast on all sides in hot oil over medium-high heat in a large Dutch oven. Stir together coffee, soup, and Worcestershire sauce; pour over roast.
TOP with onion. Reduce heat, cover, and simmer 3 hours and 40 minutes or until tender. Transfer roast to a serving platter, reserving drippings in Dutch oven; keep roast warm.
COMBINE cornstarch and 3 tablespoons water; stir into drippings. Bring mixture to a boil, and cook, stirring constantly, 1 minute or until thickened. Pour gravy over roast. **Prep: 25 min.; Cook: 3 hrs., 40 min.**

JEAN VOAN
SHEPHERD, TEXAS

Beef Made Simple

Many cheaper cuts come from the chuck (front) or round (hind) area, both of which tend to be tough. Chuck roasts include shoulder, seven-bone, and chuck eye, while round roasts include eye of round, boneless rump, and top or bottom round. Slow, moist-heat cooking tenderizes them.

New Chicken Classics

Enjoy making and serving these delicious entrées that are easy to prepare and a pleasure to eat.

If you're looking for innovative ways to prepare chicken but don't have a lot of time, these recipes are for you. Cheesy Mexican Chicken is ideal for families. If you're entertaining friends, try Chicken With Fresh Herbs and Vegetables or Lemon-Basil Chicken. Either way, the folks at your dinner table won't have a clue that all three of these delectable dishes can be made in less than an hour.

CHEESY MEXICAN CHICKEN

MAKES 4 SERVINGS

- 1 teaspoon ground black pepper
- ¼ teaspoon ground red pepper
- ½ teaspoon paprika
- ½ teaspoon garlic powder
- 4 skinned and boned chicken breast halves
- 1 tablespoon butter or margarine
- 1 (4.5-ounce) can chopped green chiles
- 1 cup (4 ounces) shredded Monterey Jack cheese
- Paprika (optional)

COMBINE first 4 ingredients; sprinkle evenly over chicken. Melt butter in a large skillet over medium-high heat. Add chicken, and cook 5 to 6 minutes on each side or until golden brown. Remove from heat; top with chiles and cheese. Cover and let stand 2 to 3 minutes or until cheese melts. Sprinkle with paprika, if desired. **Prep: 10 min., Cook: 12 min., Stand: 3 min.**

SHARON SINKEY
TAMPA, FLORIDA

LEMON-BASIL CHICKEN

MAKES 4 SERVINGS

Lemon basil has a distinct citrus aroma and flavor.

- ½ cup fresh lemon juice
- ½ cup olive oil
- ½ cup chopped fresh lemon basil or basil
- 3 green onions, chopped
- 2 tablespoons white wine vinegar
- ½ teaspoon freshly ground pepper
- 4 (½-inch-thick) skinned and boned chicken breast halves
- 1 tablespoon olive oil
- Hot cooked rice

WHISK together first 6 ingredients in a large bowl, blending well. Add chicken; cover and chill 40 minutes, turning occasionally.

REMOVE chicken from marinade, reserving marinade.

COOK chicken in 1 tablespoon hot oil in a large skillet over medium-high heat 5 minutes on each side or until golden brown.

POUR reserved marinade through a wire-mesh strainer into skillet. Reduce heat to medium-low, cover, and simmer 8 to 10 minutes or until chicken is done. Serve chicken over hot cooked rice. **Prep: 10 min., Chill: 40 min., Cook: 20 min.**

PATSY BELL HOBSON
LIBERTY, MISSOURI

CHICKEN WITH FRESH HERBS AND VEGETABLES

MAKES 4 SERVINGS

Serve over rice or linguine for a one-dish meal. If you don't have fresh herbs, substitute 1 tablespoon dried basil and 1 teaspoon dried oregano.

- ¼ cup fine, dry breadcrumbs
- 6 tablespoons shredded Parmesan cheese, divided
- 4 skinned and boned chicken breast halves
- 2 tablespoons olive oil
- 10 large mushrooms, quartered
- 1 large green bell pepper, thinly sliced
- 3 large tomatoes, coarsely chopped
- 1 large garlic clove, pressed
- ½ teaspoon salt
- ¼ cup chopped fresh basil
- 1 tablespoon chopped fresh oregano

COMBINE breadcrumbs and 4 tablespoons Parmesan cheese, and dredge chicken in mixture.

COOK chicken in hot oil in a large skillet over medium-high heat 4 minutes on each side or until browned. Remove chicken from skillet.

ADD mushrooms and bell pepper to skillet; sauté 3 minutes. Add tomato, garlic, and salt; return chicken to skillet. Cover, reduce heat, and simmer 10 minutes.

STIR in basil, oregano, and remaining 2 tablespoons Parmesan cheese. Serve immediately. **Prep: 10 min., Cook: 21 min.**

SYLVIE SWEENEY
BLUFFTON, SOUTH CAROLINA

Cream Pies Without the Fuss

These lavish desserts are sweet, simple, and satisfying.

Cream pies are the stuff that food memories are made of. Luscious filling nestled in a crumb crust and topped with billowy clouds of whipped cream is a combination a dessert lover won't soon forget.

Jan Moon of our Test Kitchens has created pies with all the cozy qualities of old-fashioned ones but without the fuss. You don't even have to cook the filling (the traditional kind requires carefully cooked egg yolks). Just spoon it into the cooled pie shell.

Jan whipped up three versions of these simple, satisfying desserts: lemon-blueberry, coconut, and orange. Give one—or all—of them a try.

LEMON-BLUEBERRY CREAM PIE

MAKES 1 (9-INCH) PIE

A kiss of lemon adds a bright note to this sweet-and-tangy dessert featuring sweet, juicy blueberries. *(pictured on page 80)*

- 1⅔ cups graham cracker crumbs
- ¼ cup sugar
- ⅓ cup butter or margarine, melted
- 1 (8-ounce) package cream cheese, softened
- 1 (14-ounce) can sweetened condensed milk
- ¼ cup powdered sugar
- 1 (3.4-ounce) package lemon instant pudding mix
- 2 teaspoons grated lemon rind
- ½ cup fresh lemon juice
- 1 pint fresh blueberries
- 2 tablespoons blueberry preserves
- 1 cup whipping cream
- Garnishes: lemon slices, fresh blueberries

STIR together first 3 ingredients; press evenly in bottom and up sides of a 9-inch pieplate.

BAKE piecrust at 350° for 8 minutes; remove piecrust to a wire rack, and cool completely.

BEAT cheese, milk, and powdered sugar at medium speed with an electric mixer until creamy.

ADD pudding mix, rind, and juice; beat until blended. Spread half of lemon mixture into prepared crust.

STIR together blueberries and preserves; spread evenly over lemon mixture.

SPREAD remaining lemon mixture over blueberry mixture; cover and chill 2 hours or until set.

BEAT whipping cream with an electric mixer until soft peaks form, and spread around outer edge of pie, forming a 3-inch border. Garnish, if desired. **Prep: 25 min., Bake: 8 min., Chill: 2 hrs.**

COCONUT CREAM PIE

MAKES 1 (9-INCH) PIE

Look for cream of coconut near the piña colada and margarita mixes.

- 1⅔ cups graham cracker crumbs
- ¼ cup sugar
- ⅓ cup butter or margarine, melted
- 1 (8-ounce) package cream cheese, softened
- 1 cup cream of coconut
- 1 (3.4-ounce) package cheesecake instant pudding mix
- 1 (6-ounce) package frozen sweetened flaked coconut, thawed
- 1 (8-ounce) container frozen whipped topping, thawed
- 1 cup whipping cream
- Garnish: sweetened flaked coconut

STIR together first 3 ingredients; press mixture evenly in bottom and up sides of a 9-inch pieplate.

BAKE at 350° for 8 minutes; remove to a wire rack, and cool completely.

BEAT cheese and cream of coconut at medium speed with an electric mixer until smooth. Add pudding mix, beating until blended.

STIR in coconut; fold in whipped topping. Spread cheese mixture into crust; cover and chill 2 hours or until set.

BEAT whipping cream with an electric mixer until soft peaks form, and spread evenly over top of pie. Garnish, if desired. **Prep: 25 min., Bake: 8 min., Chill: 2 hrs.**

NOTE: For testing purposes only, we used Jell-O Instant Pudding Cheesecake Flavor.

ORANGE DREAM PIE

MAKES 1 (9-INCH) PIE

Orange curd can be found in the jams-and-jellies area of the supermarket. *(pictured on page 80)*

- 1 (7.25-ounce) package butter cookies, crushed
- ¼ cup butter or margarine, melted
- 1 (8-ounce) package cream cheese, softened
- ⅓ cup powdered sugar
- 1 teaspoon vanilla extract
- Orange liquid food coloring (optional)
- 1 (12-ounce) container frozen whipped topping, thawed and divided
- 1 (10-ounce) jar orange curd
- 2 teaspoons grated orange rind
- 2 tablespoons fresh orange juice
- Garnishes: whipped topping, orange rind curls, almond bark curls

STIR together cookie crumbs and butter; press evenly in bottom and up sides of a 9-inch pieplate.

BAKE at 350° for 8 minutes; remove to a wire rack, and cool completely.

BEAT cheese and powdered sugar at medium speed with an electric mixer until smooth. Stir in vanilla and, if desired, food coloring until blended; fold in 2 cups whipped topping. Spread cream cheese mixture evenly into prepared crust.

STIR together curd, rind, juice, and 2 tablespoons whipped topping. Spread evenly over cheese mixture; cover and chill 2 hours or until set. Garnish, if desired. **Prep: 25 min., Bake: 8 min., Chill: 2 hrs.**

NOTE: For testing purposes only, we used Pepperidge Farm Chessmen butter cookies and Dickinson's Orange Curd.

A Reunion in Nashville

Farflung relatives gather and enjoy an eclectic menu.

When the descendants of Kama Oyafuso and Maka Miyasato gathered in Nashville recently, the occasion was truly multicultural. Though the Japanese couple's 12 children were all born and raised in Hawaii, most of them have ended up across the mainland, from California to New Jersey to Virginia.

DATE PINWHEEL COOKIES

MAKES 2½ DOZEN

- 1 (10-ounce) package chopped dates
- ¾ cup sugar, divided
- ½ cup water
- ¼ teaspoon salt, divided
- 1 cup chopped walnuts
- ½ cup butter or margarine, softened
- ½ cup firmly packed brown sugar
- 1 large egg
- ½ teaspoon vanilla extract
- 2 cups all-purpose flour
- ¼ teaspoon baking soda

STIR together dates, ¼ cup sugar, ½ cup water, and ⅛ teaspoon salt in a saucepan; bring mixture to a boil over medium-high heat. Reduce heat; simmer 3 to 5 minutes. Remove from heat; stir in walnuts, and set aside.

BEAT remaining ½ cup sugar, softened butter, and brown sugar at medium speed with an electric mixer until light and fluffy.

ADD egg and vanilla, beating until blended. Gradually add remaining ⅛ teaspoon salt, flour, and baking soda, beating until blended. Cover and chill dough 1 hour.

TURN dough out onto floured wax paper, and roll into an 18- x 12-inch rectangle.

Spread date mixture evenly over dough, leaving a ½-inch border.

ROLL up dough jellyroll fashion, beginning at 1 long side. Wrap in wax paper, and chill 1 hour.

CUT roll into ¼-inch-thick slices; place on lightly greased baking sheets.

BAKE, in batches, at 375° for 12 to 14 minutes or until lightly browned. Cool cookies 2 to 3 minutes on baking sheets, and remove to wire racks to cool completely. **Prep: 20 min., Chill: 2 hrs., Bake: 14 min. per batch, Cool: 3 min.**

SHARON DELAURIER
MEMPHIS, TENNESSEE

CHINESE-STYLE SPARERIBS

MAKES 6 SERVINGS

- 2 pounds pork spareribs, cut into small pieces
- 2 garlic cloves, minced
- 1 teaspoon grated fresh ginger
- 1 tablespoon vegetable oil
- 1 (8-ounce) jar black bean sauce
- ¼ cup teriyaki sauce
- 2 tablespoons chile-garlic sauce

RUB ribs with garlic and ginger.

BROWN ribs in hot oil in a Dutch oven over medium-high heat 4 to 5 minutes on each side.

STIR together sauces. Pour over ribs; reduce heat, and simmer, stirring occasionally, 1 hour. Arrange ribs in a 13- x 9-inch pan. Pour sauce mixture over ribs.

BAKE at 350° for 1 hour. **Prep: 20 min., Cook: 1 hr., Bake: 1 hr.**

NOTE: For testing purposes only, we used Ka-Me Black Bean Sauce.

CAROL LORIA
DUBLIN, NEW HAMPSHIRE

Hot Browns

This Louisville specialty is a delicious piece of Southern history.

Mention "Hot Brown," and folks either look mystified or they immediately call to mind an open-faced turkey sandwich smothered in a delicate cheese sauce and topped with crisp bacon strips. It originated at The Brown Hotel (now The Camberley Brown) in Louisville in 1923.

The hotel's current executive chef, Joe Castro, comes from a big food family; he and brother John Castro, executive chef at Winston's Restaurant and a culinary instructor at Louisville's Sullivan University, often cook together. "A little friendly competition is good," Joe says, "but when it comes to the Hot Brown, we have varying opinions." Joe wouldn't change the original recipe, while John believes ripe tomatoes are key to the flavor of this dish. "The acidity in the tomatoes cuts the rich cheese sauce," John says.

Next time you're in Louisville, make sure to savor a Hot Brown. In the meantime, though, try these versions.

KENTUCKY HOT BROWNS

MAKES 4 SERVINGS

- **8 thick white bread slices**
- **1 pound roasted turkey slices**
- **Cheese Sauce**
- **1 cup shredded Parmesan cheese**
- **8 bacon slices, cooked**
- **2 large tomatoes, sliced and halved**

TRIM crusts from bread slices, and discard. Place bread on a baking sheet, and broil 3 inches from heat until toasted, turning once.
ARRANGE 2 bread slices in each of 4 lightly greased individual baking dishes.

Top bread evenly with turkey. Pour hot Cheese Sauce evenly over turkey, and sprinkle with Parmesan cheese.
BROIL 6 inches from heat 4 minutes or until bubbly and lightly browned; remove from oven. Top evenly with bacon and tomato. Serve immediately. **Prep: 20 min., Broil: 4 min.**

NOTE: A lightly greased 15- x 10-inch jellyroll pan may be substituted for individual baking dishes. Arrange bread slices evenly in bottom of pan. Top evenly with turkey and Cheese Sauce, and sprinkle with Parmesan cheese. Proceed with recipe as directed.

Cheese Sauce:

MAKES ABOUT 4 CUPS

- **½ cup butter or margarine**
- **⅓ cup all-purpose flour**
- **3½ cups milk**
- **½ cup shredded Parmesan cheese**
- **¼ teaspoon salt**
- **¼ teaspoon pepper**

MELT butter in a 3-quart saucepan over medium-high heat. Whisk in flour, and cook, whisking constantly, 1 minute. Gradually whisk in milk.
BRING to a boil, and cook, whisking constantly, 1 to 2 minutes or until thickened. Whisk in cheese, salt, and pepper. Remove from heat. **Prep: 5 min., Cook: 8 min.**

BISCUIT HOT BROWNS: Bake 4 large frozen biscuits according to package directions. Split biscuits in half, and toast. Substitute biscuits for bread, and proceed with recipe as directed.

SOUTHWESTERN HOT BROWNS: Substitute 4 large, thick cornbread squares, split and toasted, for bread slices. Sprinkle 1 (4.5-ounce) can chopped green chiles evenly over turkey before adding Cheese Sauce. Substitute 1 cup (4 ounces) shredded sharp Cheddar cheese for 1 cup shredded Parmesan cheese; sprinkle over sauce. Proceed as directed.

HOT BROWNS WITH FRIED CHEESE GRITS: Prepare 1 cup regular grits according to package directions. Stir in 1 cup (4 ounces) shredded extra-sharp Cheddar cheese until melted. Pour hot cooked grits into a greased 9-inch square pan. Cover and chill 8 hours or until firm. Invert onto a cutting board, and cut into 4 squares. Cut each square into 4 triangles (see below). Fry grits, in batches, in 2 tablespoons hot vegetable oil in a large nonstick skillet over medium-high heat 2 minutes on each side or until golden brown. Remove from pan, and set aside. Cook 2 large diced sweet onions and 1 tablespoon sugar in 2 tablespoons hot oil in skillet over medium-high heat, stirring constantly 20 minutes or until deep golden brown. Arrange 4 grits triangles in a single layer in a lightly greased individual baking dish; top with one-fourth each of turkey, sautéed onion, and Cheese Sauce. Repeat with remaining grits triangles, turkey, onion, and Cheese Sauce. Proceed with recipe as directed.

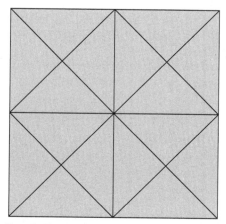

To make Hot Browns With Fried Cheese Grits, cut chilled grits into four squares, and cut each square into four triangles.

World-Class Coleslaw

No summer picnic or cookout would be complete without a bowl of coleslaw. Mounded atop a barbecued-pork sandwich or served alongside crispy catfish, it ranks as a warm-weather favorite any way you serve it.

Few side dishes are more adaptable; there are almost as many variations as there are Southern cooks who make it. Take this Asian-inspired version, for example. The basic foundation of cabbage and carrot gets international flair from crispy ramen noodles and sliced almonds; a tart oil-and-vinegar dressing replaces the traditional mayonnaise base. So take your taste buds on a trip to points east—no passport required.

CRUNCHY CABBAGE SLAW

MAKES 7½ CUPS

- 1 (3-ounce) package ramen noodle soup mix
- ¼ cup sliced almonds
- ⅓ cup canola oil*
- ¼ cup cider vinegar
- 2½ tablespoons sugar
- 1 small green cabbage, shredded
- 1 small carrot, grated
- 3 green onions, sliced

REMOVE flavor packet from soup mix, and reserve. Break ramen noodles into pieces, and place on a lightly greased baking sheet. Add sliced almonds.

BAKE at 350°, stirring occasionally, 5 to 10 minutes or until toasted. Set aside.

WHISK together reserved flavor packet, oil, vinegar, and sugar in a bowl until blended. Chill 1 hour.

TOSS together cabbage, carrot, onions, and dressing. Sprinkle with noodle mixture before serving. **Prep: 30 min., Bake: 10 min., Chill: 1 hr.**

*Substitute ⅓ cup vegetable oil for canola oil, if desired.

DARLENE EVANS
BIRMINGHAM, ALABAMA

Cook's Corner

Looking for ways to bring variety to meals? Check out these products and recipe booklets for inspiration for breakfast, lunch, and dinner.

Breakfast Magic

Make breakfast enchanting with Kellogg's new line of Disney cereals. Mickey's Magix, Buzz Blasts, and Hunny B's will turn breakfast time into story time. These whole-grain cereals are filled with shapes and colors that help kids become part of their favorite character's adventures.

"Potatoes 1-2-3! Trendy Dinner Ideas for America's Favorite Vegetable"

Versatile potatoes give busy cooks a quick start to meal planning and can be prepared in a variety of ways. Whether you buy them whole, precut, frozen, or instant, you have a wealth of easy, family-friendly options for breakfast, lunch, and dinner. To get a copy of this free brochure from the National Potato Promotion Board, send a request to "Potatoes 1-2-3!," 5105 East 41st Avenue, Denver, CO 80216; send an e-mail with your name and street address to **potatobrochure@eagledirect.com**; or visit **www.potatohelp.com**

"Specialty Mushrooms—What a Good Idea"

All mushrooms except for the white button kind—including portobellos, shiitakes, and oysters—are considered specialty varieties. Because most of these mushrooms are cultivated under controlled conditions, they are widely available in supermarkets year-round. This brochure offers buying and storing tips, recipes, and other information. To order your copy of the informational booklet, send a self-addressed, stamped, business-size envelope to "Specialty Mushroom Leaflet," 11875 Dublin Blvd., Suite D262, Dublin, CA 94568; e-mail a request with your name and postal address to **info@mushroomcouncil.com**; or visit **www.mushroomcouncil.com**

Culinary Adventures With Friends

Good food and good company are a classic combination.

A Friendly Feast

Serves 6

Asparagus, Roasted-Beet, and Goat Cheese Salad

Grilled Lamb Chops
With Chipotle and Cilantro Oils

Onion Risotto

Ginger Pound Cake   Ice cream

Cooking for friends is one of Foods Editor Andria Scott Hurst's favorite pastimes. An adventurous and appreciative audience, her friends willingly try whatever ingredients she experiments with or flavors she introduces.

She served this menu at a gathering that proved to be one of her greatest successes. But she still has more recipes and party ideas than she'll ever have time to produce. She just loves dreaming about the possibilities.

ASPARAGUS, ROASTED-BEET, AND GOAT CHEESE SALAD

MAKES 6 SERVINGS

18 small red beets (about 6 pounds)
1 cup olive oil
⅓ cup red wine vinegar
½ teaspoon salt, divided
½ teaspoon freshly ground pepper, divided
60 small fresh asparagus spears
1 (11-ounce) goat cheese log
1 tablespoon chopped fresh chives
Cracked pepper (optional)
Chopped fresh chives (optional)
Gourmet salad greens (optional)

ARRANGE beets in a single layer on a lightly greased baking sheet; bake at 425° for 40 to 45 minutes or until tender, stirring every 15 minutes. Cool beets completely.

WHISK together oil, vinegar, ¼ teaspoon salt, and ¼ teaspoon ground pepper.

PEEL beets, and cut into wedges. Toss together beet wedges, ½ cup vinaigrette, remaining ¼ teaspoon salt, and remaining ¼ teaspoon ground pepper; set aside.

SNAP off tough ends of asparagus, discarding ends; cook in boiling water to cover 1 to 2 minutes or until crisp-tender. Plunge into ice water to stop the cooking process, and drain. Combine asparagus and ½ cup vinaigrette; set aside.

CUT cheese into 6 equal slices. Place 1 cheese slice in a 3-inch round cutter or ring mold; sprinkle with ½ teaspoon chives. Press chives into cheese; remove cutter. Repeat procedure with remaining cheese and 2½ teaspoons chives.

ARRANGE asparagus over cheese. Surround with beets; drizzle with remaining vinaigrette. Sprinkle with cracked pepper and chives, if desired; serve with salad greens, if desired. **Prep: 15 min., Bake: 45 min., Cook: 2 min.**

GRILLED LAMB CHOPS WITH CHIPOTLE AND CILANTRO OILS

MAKES 8 SERVINGS

Andria credits Dallas chef Kent Rathbun for this company-worthy entrée. *(pictured on page 76)*

1 cup loosely packed fresh cilantro leaves
½ cup canola oil
8 garlic cloves
4 shallots
2 jalapeño peppers, seeded
16 (2-inch-thick) loin lamb chops
Hickory wood chips
2 tablespoons kosher salt
2 tablespoons cracked pepper
Chipotle Oil
Cilantro Oil
Garnish: fresh cilantro sprigs

PROCESS first 5 ingredients in a blender or food processor until smooth, stopping to scrape down sides.

PLACE chops in a large shallow dish or heavy-duty zip-top plastic bags. Pour oil mixture evenly over chops. Cover or seal; chill 2 hours, turning occasionally. **SOAK** wood chips in water 30 minutes. Remove chops from marinade, discarding marinade. Sprinkle chops evenly with salt and pepper.

PREPARE a fire by piling charcoal and wood chips in grill. Place food rack on grill. Arrange chops on rack, and grill, covered with grill lid, over high heat (400° to 500°) 6 to 8 minutes on each side or until desired degree of doneness. **DRIZZLE** with Chipotle and Cilantro Oils; garnish, if desired. **Prep: 45 min., Chill: 2 hrs., Soak: 30 min., Grill: 16 min.**

Chipotle Oil:

MAKES ½ CUP

- 2 tablespoons chipotle peppers in adobo sauce
- ½ cup olive oil
- ½ teaspoon kosher salt

PROCESS all ingredients in a blender or food processor until smooth. **Prep: 5 min.**

Cilantro Oil:

MAKES ½ CUP

- ½ cup loosely packed fresh cilantro leaves
- ½ cup olive oil
- 1 tablespoon fresh lime juice
- ½ teaspoon kosher salt

PROCESS all ingredients in a blender or food processor until smooth. **Prep: 5 min.**

KENT RATHBUN
ABACUS RESTAURANT, DALLAS

ONION RISOTTO

MAKES 6 SERVINGS

This creamy dish gets a flavor boost from sweet onions, garlic, and Parmesan cheese. *(pictured on page 76)*

- 3 large sweet onions, chopped
- 2 garlic cloves, pressed
- 1 teaspoon salt
- 2 tablespoons olive oil
- 1 (16-ounce) package Arborio rice
- 8 cups chicken broth, warmed
- 1 cup dry white wine
- ½ cup shredded Parmesan cheese
- 2 tablespoons butter or margarine

SAUTÉ first 3 ingredients in hot oil in a Dutch oven over medium-high heat until tender.

ADD rice; cook, stirring constantly, 2 minutes. Reduce heat to medium; add 1 cup broth.

COOK, stirring often, until liquid is absorbed.

REPEAT procedure with remaining chicken broth, 1 cup at a time. (Cooking time is about 30 minutes.)

ADD wine; cook, stirring gently, until liquid is absorbed. Stir in cheese and butter. Serve immediately. **Prep: 10 min., Cook: 45 min.**

GINGER POUND CAKE

MAKES 1 (10-INCH) CAKE

Crystallized ginger updates a traditional Southern dessert. *(pictured on page 77)*

- ¾ cup milk
- 1 (2.7-ounce) jar crystallized ginger, finely minced
- 2 cups butter or margarine, softened
- 3 cups sugar
- 6 large eggs
- 4 cups all-purpose flour
- 1 teaspoon vanilla extract
- Vanilla ice cream
- Garnish: crystallized ginger

COOK milk and ginger in a saucepan over medium heat until thoroughly heated (do not boil). Remove from heat, and let stand 10 to 15 minutes.

BEAT butter at medium speed with an electric mixer until creamy; gradually add sugar, beating 5 to 7 minutes. Add eggs, 1 at a time, beating after each addition just until yellow disappears.

ADD flour to butter mixture alternately with milk mixture, beginning and ending with flour. Beat at low speed just until blended after each addition. Stir in vanilla. Pour batter into a greased and floured 10-inch tube pan.

BAKE at 325° for 1 hour and 25 minutes or until a wooden pick inserted in center comes out clean. Cool in pan on a wire rack 10 minutes. Remove from pan, and cool completely on wire rack. Serve with ice cream, and garnish, if desired. **Prep: 25 min.; Stand: 15 min.; Bake: 1 hr., 25 min.; Cool: 10 min.**

Pass the Mashed Potatoes

Try a creamy twist on this favorite comfort food.

We've eaten mashed potatoes all our lives, but most of us want them just the way Mama made 'em. Whether hers were lumpy or creamy, that's the way we still like them. A fork, masher, or ricer each gives you different textures, but for the smoothest, creamiest consistency, try an electric mixer.

These may not be quite the same as your mother's, but they got top ratings in our Test Kitchens. You're sure to like them.

CHEESY MASHED POTATOES

MAKES 4 TO 6 SERVINGS

- 2 pounds Yukon gold potatoes, peeled and cubed
- 2 (4-ounce) packages buttery garlic-and-herb spreadable cheese
- ⅔ cup half-and-half
- ¼ cup butter or margarine
- ¼ teaspoon salt
- ¼ teaspoon pepper

BRING potato and water to cover to a boil in a large saucepan; reduce heat, and cook 15 to 20 minutes or until tender.

DRAIN and return potato to saucepan. Cook over medium heat 30 seconds. Remove pan from heat.

ADD cheese and next 4 ingredients; beat at medium speed with an electric mixer until smooth. Spoon into a lightly greased 2½-quart baking dish.

BAKE at 350° for 15 minutes. **Prep: 35 min., Bake: 15 min.**

SHARON WALKER HOWARD
MAYFIELD, KENTUCKY

LEEK MASHED POTATOES

MAKES 6 SERVINGS

- 2 medium leeks
- ¼ cup dry sherry or chicken broth
- 1 tablespoon butter or margarine
- 4 large baking potatoes, peeled and cubed
- 4 cups water
- 1 tablespoon chicken bouillon granules
- 4 garlic cloves, chopped
- ¼ cup butter or margarine, softened
- 3 tablespoons half-and-half
- ¼ teaspoon seasoned salt

REMOVE root, tough outer leaves, and green tops from leeks. Cut leeks in half lengthwise; rinse and drain. Chop leeks.

COOK sherry and 1 tablespoon butter in a large saucepan over medium-high heat until butter melts; add leek, and sauté 5 minutes. Add potato, 4 cups water, bouillon granules, and garlic. Bring to a boil; reduce heat, and cook 15 to 20 minutes or until potatoes are tender. Drain.

COMBINE potato mixture, ¼ cup butter, half-and-half, and salt in a large bowl; mash with a potato masher until smooth. **Prep: 20 min., Cook: 20 min.**

ALEXIS M. EIDSON
SAN ANTONIO, TEXAS

SWIRLED MASHED-POTATO BAKE

MAKES 8 TO 10 SERVINGS

- 2½ pounds Yukon gold potatoes, peeled and cubed
- 2½ pounds sweet potatoes, peeled and cubed
- 1½ cups milk, divided
- 1 (8-ounce) package light cream cheese, divided
- 2 tablespoons butter or margarine, divided
- 2 green onions, finely chopped
- 1½ teaspoons salt, divided
- ¼ teaspoon pepper
- ½ teaspoon dried thyme
- Garnish: chopped green onions

BRING Yukon gold potato and water to cover to a boil in a large Dutch oven.

REDUCE heat, and cook 20 minutes or until tender; drain. Repeat procedure with sweet potato.

BEAT Yukon gold potato at medium speed with an electric mixer until mashed. Add half of milk, half of cheese, and 1 tablespoon butter, beating until smooth.

STIR in green onions, 1 teaspoon salt, and pepper. Spoon into a lightly greased 3-quart oval baking dish.

BEAT sweet potato until mashed; add remaining milk, remaining cheese, and remaining 1 tablespoon butter, beating until smooth. Stir in remaining ½ teaspoon salt and thyme. Spread over Yukon gold potato mixture, and swirl gently with a knife. Cover and chill up to 8 hours, if desired.

BAKE at 350° for 25 to 30 minutes or until thoroughly heated. Garnish, if desired. **Prep: 20 min., Cook: 40 min., Bake: 30 min.**

MARCIA LOOMIS
ST. LOUIS, MISSOURI

Heavenly Stuffed Pitas

Healthy recipes make Doe's Pita Plus one of Charleston's favorite eateries.

For the past 12 years, Doe Cote has served delicious, nutritious fare at one of Charleston, South Carolina's downtown fixtures, Doe's Pita Plus. A transplant from Massachusetts with a love of Middle Eastern food, Doe says she opened the restaurant to fill "a big void" in her adopted hometown. We think she's succeeded brilliantly.

Her Avocado Salad-Hummus Pita pleases vegetarians and meat lovers alike. Fresh Fruit Salad Pita is topped with tangy yogurt and brown sugar. An on-site 900-degree oven bakes the bread in just 45 seconds.

AVOCADO SALAD-HUMMUS PITA

MAKES 8 SERVINGS

The creamy hummus is also great for dipping lightly steamed or blanched veggies, such as sugar snap peas, asparagus, and carrots. It's also a wonderful appetizer served with pita wedges.

- Hummus
- 4 pita bread rounds, halved
- Avocado Salad
- Romaine lettuce leaves
- Tomato slices
- Alfalfa sprouts (optional)

SPREAD ¼ cup of Hummus inside each pita half.
SPOON Avocado Salad evenly into each pita half.
ADD lettuce, tomato, and, if desired, sprouts. Serve sandwiches immediately. **Prep: 10 min.**

Hummus:

MAKES 2 CUPS

- 1 (15-ounce) can chickpeas, rinsed and drained
- 3 garlic cloves, minced
- ⅓ cup tahini*
- ¼ cup fresh lemon juice
- ¼ cup water
- ¾ teaspoon salt

PROCESS chickpeas in a food processor until smooth, stopping to scrape down sides. Add garlic and remaining ingredients; pulse until blended. **Prep: 10 min.**

*Tahini is sesame seed paste, found in the import sections of large supermarkets or in health food stores.

Avocado Salad:

MAKES 2½ CUPS

- 2 large ripe avocados, coarsely chopped
- 4 large radishes, chopped
- 2 celery ribs, chopped
- 2 green onions, chopped
- 2 tablespoons fresh lemon juice
- 2 tablespoons olive oil
- ½ teaspoon salt
- ¼ to ½ teaspoon freshly ground pepper

COMBINE all ingredients. Cover and chill 1 hour. **Prep: 10 min., Chill: 1 hr.**

FRESH FRUIT SALAD PITA

MAKES 24 SERVINGS

Try this for a light lunch and get a head start on your five-a-day requirement of fruits and veggies.

- ⅓ cup fresh orange juice (about 1 orange)
- 2 large oranges, peeled, sectioned, and coarsely chopped
- 2 large apples, coarsely chopped
- 2 cups seedless green grapes
- 1 cantaloupe, cut into 1-inch cubes
- 1 pint fresh strawberries, sliced
- 1 pint fresh blueberries
- 12 pita bread rounds, halved
- 1 (8-ounce) container nonfat vanilla yogurt
- 3 tablespoons brown sugar

COMBINE first 7 ingredients in a bowl.
SPOON ½ cup fruit mixture into each pita half with a slotted spoon.
TOP each evenly with yogurt; sprinkle with brown sugar. Serve immediately. **Prep: 25 min.**

from our kitchen

The subject makes most of us nervous. However, Robert V. Tauxe, chief of the Foodborne and Diarrheal Diseases Branch of the Centers for Disease Control and Prevention (CDC), reports that food-borne illness and deaths could be reduced by as much as 25% by irradiating just half of poultry, ground beef, pork, and processed meats.

It need not scare you. Irradiation is to meats and vegetables what pasteurization is to dairy products: a means of reducing harmful bacteria in foods. When shopping, if you have a choice, choose the irradiated products—you can't see or taste any difference. To read more about it, visit the USDA/FDA Foodborne Illness Education Information Center online at **www.nal.usda.gov/fnic/foodborne**; the CDC's food-irradiation FAQ, **www.cdc.gov/ncidod/dbmd/diseaseinfo/foodirradiation.htm**; or the USDA Food Safety and Inspection Service Irradiation of Raw Meat and Poultry Q&A, **www.fsis.usda.gov/oa/pubs/qa_irrad.htm**

Baking Basics

We know the wonderful story about Mexican bakeries on pages 81-83 makes your mouth water. So now that you're in the mood to bake, here are some tips to ensure a delicious experience.

■ Make sure your ingredients are at room temperature. Bring out eggs and milk just as you're about to start.

■ Select good heavy pans and baking sheets for long-term use. Choose shiny pans, which reflect heat best and produce tender, nicely browned baked goods.

■ To measure all-purpose flour, stir it lightly; then spoon it into a dry measuring cup (don't pack it). Level using the flat edge of a spatula or knife.

■ Place the pan in the center of the oven to be sure your bread bakes evenly. If you are baking more than one batch in the same oven, leave some space around each pan so heat can circulate freely.

Don't Get Foiled

Suzanne Ezell of Atlanta put flank steak and marinade in a metal baking pan and covered it with aluminum foil. "When I checked on the meat, I discovered holes in the foil," Suzanne writes. "I contacted the Reynolds Kitchens, and they explained what happened."

They replied: ". . . In rare occurrences, aluminum foil may react with the food that is being covered and form small pinholes in the foil. This does not affect the safety of the food.

"When aluminum and a dissimilar metal are in contact in the presence of moisture, an electrolytic reaction may occur, causing a breakdown of the aluminum. To avoid this reaction we recommend that aluminum, glass, ceramic, plastic, or paper items be used with foil rather than stainless steel, iron, sterling silver, or silver-plated pieces.

"If the reaction occurred while using an aluminum, glass, ceramic, plastic, or paper container, the reaction was chemical. This may occur when salt, vinegar, highly acidic foods or highly spiced foods come in contact with aluminum foil.

"The product of either of these reactions is a harmless aluminum salt that can be safely consumed."

Our Test Kitchens staff recommends marinating foods in heavy-duty zip-top plastic bags or glass containers.

Beef Demystified

As our story on page 90 demonstrates, beef can be a terrific value if you know what to look for. Let this handy chart be your guide.

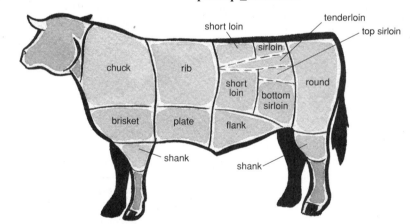

Tips and Tidbits

■ The next time you consider buying one of those whole-grain health bars, check the label—some have as much fat and calories as the average chocolate bar. Weigh the numbers before you snack.

■ Choose honey instead of sugar to sweeten cereals, desserts, and beverages. Different flavors and colors of honey result from the location and the kinds of flowers the bees visited. For example, clover honey is light in color, with a spicy cinnamon aroma and flavor; orange blossom honey has a sweet perfume, clover nectar flavor, and flowery aftertaste; and blueberry honey has a greenish tint, lemony aroma, and fruity flavor. Taste the subtle differences on hot oatmeal or in a cup of hot tea.

Southern Living Favorites

Masters of Entertaining

A beloved Louisiana couple known for hospitality and a South Carolina church secretary who's also a caterer share their recipes and secrets.

While some culinary talents are legendary throughout the South, others share their gifts only with friends, family, and colleagues. Here are three kitchen whizzes we'd like you to know better: Gene and Peggy Dean St. Martin of Shreveport and Debbi Covington of Beaufort, South Carolina. Meet our discoveries—and taste the recipes that have earned them their reputations.

Guess Who's Coming To Dinner?

"There was just no telling who Gene might invite to a party," Peggy Dean says. "We've had local legislators and members of the Louisiana State Medical Society in our home."

Although the St. Martins are not formally trained cooks, Southern foods have been a part of their lives since childhood. In fact, Peggy Dean grew up in Shreveport's Washington-Youree Hotel, managed by her father; as a girl, she spent hours observing the hotel's chef.

Gene is a born-and-raised Cajun from Houma, Louisiana, and, quite rightfully, a true oyster aficionado. A favorite is Oysters Pierre, a recipe that Gene named after himself. "When I was at Tulane medical school, my buddies and I gave each other nicknames. They dubbed me 'Pierre' because of the notoriously wild Cajun stories I loved to tell," Gene says.

The St. Martins' skill in the kitchen is no exaggeration, though. Try their three oyster recipes to see for yourself.

Do Something Nice, and Watch What Happens

Sharing our talents with others can surprisingly nurture more than friendship. It was that kind of sharing that launched a new career for Debbi. "I prepared the food for the 70th birthday party of one of our church members, and the next thing I knew, I was in the catering business," she explains.

After that party in 1997, Debbi's delicacies were in high demand. Now, Catering by Debbi Covington regularly turns out fabulous appetizers that transform any gathering into a festive event. Read on for Debbi's delicious Crab Imperial, Ham-and-Asparagus Cheesecake, and Honey-Mustard Pork Tenderloin With Miniature Buttermilk Biscuits.

Oyster Soup

MAKES ABOUT 11 CUPS

Gene drains and cooks the oysters separately to plump them.

- 4 cups water
- 1 large onion, chopped
- 2 celery ribs, sliced
- 2 garlic cloves, minced
- 2 pints fresh oysters, rinsed and drained
- 2 cups water
- 1 cup butter or margarine
- ½ cup all-purpose flour
- 2 cups milk
- 2 tablespoons chicken bouillon granules
- 2 tablespoons chopped fresh or 1 tablespoon dried parsley
- ¾ teaspoon ground white pepper
- ¾ teaspoon ground black pepper

BRING 4 cups water, onion, celery, and garlic to a boil in a large Dutch oven. Reduce heat, and simmer, stirring occasionally, 35 minutes or just until vegetables are tender.

BRING oysters and 2 cups water to a boil in a 3-quart saucepan, and cook, stirring often, 3 minutes or until edges of oysters begin to curl. Remove oysters, and coarsely chop half; set oysters aside. Pour oyster stock into Dutch oven with vegetables.

MELT butter in a saucepan over medium heat; gradually whisk in flour, and cook, whisking constantly, 2 minutes or until smooth and bubbly. Stir flour mixture into vegetable mixture in Dutch oven, and simmer, stirring occasionally, over medium heat 5 minutes.

STIR in chopped oysters, milk, bouillon granules, and next 3 ingredients; cook, stirring occasionally, over medium heat 8 to 10 minutes or until thickened and bubbly. Stir in remaining whole oysters. **Prep: 25 min., Cook: 55 min.**

Oysters Pierre

MAKES 6 TO 8 SERVINGS

Serve these oysters with crackers.

- 6 green onions, thinly sliced
- 2 garlic cloves, minced
- ⅓ cup vegetable oil
- 2 tablespoons lemon juice
- ½ teaspoon salt
- ½ teaspoon pepper
- 2 pints fresh oysters, undrained

STIR together first 6 ingredients in a medium bowl; cover and chill 2 hours. Stir in oysters and liquid just before serving. **Prep: 10 min., Chill: 2 hrs.**

FRIED BACON-WRAPPED OYSTERS

MAKES 6 TO 8 MAIN-DISH SERVINGS OR
23 APPETIZER SERVINGS

- 1 cup all-purpose flour
- 1 teaspoon salt
- 1 teaspoon pepper
- 2 pints fresh oysters (about 46), rinsed and drained
- 23 bacon slices, cut in half
- Peanut oil

COMBINE first 3 ingredients in a shallow dish. Dredge oysters in flour mixture. Wrap each oyster with a bacon piece, and secure with a wooden pick.

POUR peanut oil to a depth of 1 inch in a deep cast-iron skillet or Dutch oven; heat to 350°.

FRY oysters, in batches, 2½ to 3 minutes or until bacon is cooked. Drain on paper towels. Serve immediately. **Prep: 30 min., Cook: 3 min. per batch**

CRAB IMPERIAL

MAKES 4 TO 6 SERVINGS

- 1 tablespoon butter or margarine
- 1 (2-ounce) jar diced pimiento, drained
- 2 small celery ribs, chopped
- ½ small green bell pepper, chopped
- 1 tablespoon chopped fresh parsley
- 1 teaspoon Old Bay seasoning
- ½ teaspoon prepared mustard
- ⅛ teaspoon ground red pepper
- ⅛ teaspoon hot sauce
- 3 tablespoons mayonnaise
- 1 large egg
- 1 pound fresh lump crabmeat, drained

MELT butter in a large skillet over medium-high heat. Add pimiento, celery, and bell pepper; sauté 3½ minutes or until tender. Remove from heat; stir in parsley and next 4 ingredients.

STIR together mayonnaise and egg in a bowl until blended; stir in pimiento mixture. Fold in crabmeat. Spoon into a lightly greased 1-quart baking dish.

BAKE at 375° for 15 minutes. Serve with assorted crackers. **Prep: 30 min., Bake: 15 min.**

HAM-AND-ASPARAGUS CHEESECAKE

MAKES 1 (9-INCH) CHEESECAKE, ABOUT
24 APPETIZER SERVINGS

- 1 sleeve buttery crackers, crushed
- 6 tablespoons butter or margarine, melted
- 1 (8-ounce) package cream cheese, softened
- 3 large eggs
- 1 (8-ounce) container sour cream
- ¼ cup all-purpose flour
- ¼ teaspoon pepper
- 2 cups (8 ounces) shredded Swiss cheese
- 1¼ cups diced cooked ham
- 2 (10½-ounce) cans asparagus pieces, drained and chopped*
- 4 green onions, minced
- Garnishes: chopped green onions, cooked asparagus tips

STIR together cracker crumbs and melted butter, and press mixture into a 9-inch springform pan. Bake at 350° for 10 minutes; cool on a wire rack. Reduce oven temperature to 300°.

BEAT cream cheese at medium speed with an electric mixer 2 to 3 minutes or until light and fluffy. Add eggs, 1 at a time, beating well after each addition. Add sour cream, flour, and pepper, beating until blended. Stir in Swiss cheese.

POUR one-third of cheese mixture into prepared pan; sprinkle evenly with ham. Pour half of remaining cheese mixture evenly over ham; sprinkle with asparagus and green onions. Top evenly with remaining cheese mixture.

BAKE at 300° for 1 hour or until center of cake is set. Turn off oven, and let cake stand in oven 1 hour with door partially open. Cover and chill, if desired. Garnish, if desired. **Prep: 30 min.; Bake: 1 hr., 10 min.; Stand: 1 hr.**

NOTE: For testing purposes only, we used Keebler Town House crackers.

*Substitute 1 pound fresh asparagus, trimmed, cooked, and cut into 1-inch pieces, for canned asparagus, if desired.

HONEY-MUSTARD PORK TENDERLOIN WITH MINIATURE BUTTERMILK BISCUITS

MAKES ABOUT 20 APPETIZER SERVINGS

- ¾ cup honey
- 6 tablespoons light brown sugar
- 6 tablespoons cider vinegar
- 3 tablespoons Dijon mustard
- 1½ teaspoons paprika
- 4 (¾- to 1-pound) pork tenderloins
- 1 teaspoon salt
- 1 teaspoon pepper
- Miniature Buttermilk Biscuits

STIR together first 5 ingredients until well blended.

PLACE pork in a greased 15- x 10-inch jellyroll pan; sprinkle with salt and pepper. Pour honey mixture over pork.

BAKE at 375° for 20 to 30 minutes or until a meat thermometer inserted into thickest portion of pork registers 160°, basting occasionally. Remove to a wire rack; let stand 10 minutes before slicing.

POUR pan drippings into a 3-quart saucepan, and cook, stirring often, over medium-high heat until slightly reduced and thickened for sauce. Serve pork with split Miniature Buttermilk Biscuits and reduced sauce. **Prep: 15 min., Bake: 30 min., Stand: 10 min.**

Miniature Buttermilk Biscuits:

MAKES ABOUT 5 DOZEN

- 1 cup butter or margarine
- 4 cups self-rising flour
- 1½ cups buttermilk
- ¼ cup butter or margarine, melted

CUT 1 cup butter into flour with a pastry blender or fork until crumbly; add buttermilk, stirring until dry ingredients are moistened.

TURN dough out onto a lightly floured surface; knead 3 to 5 times.

PAT or roll dough to ½-inch thickness, and cut with a 2-inch round cutter. Place on lightly greased baking sheets. Reroll excess dough, and proceed as directed.

BAKE at 425° for 10 to 13 minutes or until golden. Brush with ¼ cup melted butter. **Prep: 25 min., Bake: 13 min.**

Sweetened With Strawberries

We all enjoy these tongue-tingling desserts.

Executive Editor Susan Dosier has always loved a good piece of pound cake. There's just something about its buttery vanilla simplicity, its grass-roots goodness. She admits, however, that this humble dessert takes on a splashy new character when paired with the dynamic strawberry—as in our Cream Cheese Pound Cake With Strawberries and Cream. Accompanied with luscious Strawberry Syrup, it's the ultimate salute to spring.

Another of her family's favorite ways to savor the season's strawberries is in shortcake. Susan's Midwestern husband grew up eating it made with those tender cake cups you buy at the grocery store. But when he came South, she introduced him to our shortcut (see facing page) that calls for frozen biscuits topped with butter, cinnamon, and sugar. He adopted the recipe as his own, quickly mastering the art of whipping cream with precisely the right amount of sugar, then layering it with juicy sugared berries.

For a fancier rendition, try our Party-Perfect Strawberry Shortcakes. This recipe uses sour cream for flavor and enough egg to lend a cakelike (rather than biscuit-style) texture, even though we still knead the dough. After baking, we ensure moistness by spreading the insides of the split shortcakes with a spot of jam. For a cool twist, we've stirred a little chopped mint into the jam. This time of year, strawberries make even the best dishes taste better.

CREAM CHEESE POUND CAKE WITH STRAWBERRIES AND CREAM

MAKES 1 (10-INCH) CAKE

If you don't have cake flour, substitute 1 cup minus 2 tablespoons of sifted all-purpose flour for each cup of cake flour. *(pictured on page 116)*

- **1 (16-ounce) container fresh strawberries, sliced**
- **2 tablespoons sugar**
- **1 cup butter, softened**
- **1 (8-ounce) package cream cheese, softened**
- **2½ cups sugar**
- **6 large eggs**
- **3 cups sifted cake flour**
- **⅛ teaspoon salt**
- **1½ teaspoons vanilla extract**
- **1 cup whipping cream**
- **3 tablespoons sugar**
- **Strawberry Syrup (recipe at right)**
- **Garnish: whole fresh strawberries**

SPRINKLE sliced strawberries with 2 tablespoons sugar; cover and chill until ready to serve.

BEAT butter and cream cheese at medium speed with an electric mixer until creamy; gradually add 2½ cups sugar, beating well.

ADD eggs, l at a time, beating until combined. Stir in flour by hand just until moistened. Stir in salt and vanilla. Pour batter into a greased and floured 10-inch tube pan.

BAKE at 300° for 1 hour and 50 minutes or until a wooden pick inserted in center comes out clean. Cool in pan on a wire rack 10 to 15 minutes; remove from pan, and cool completely on wire rack. Cut into slices.

BEAT whipping cream and 3 tablespoons sugar at high speed with an electric mixer until stiff peaks form. Serve with cake; top with strawberry mixture, and drizzle with Strawberry Syrup. Garnish, if desired. **Prep: 10 min.; Bake: 1 hr., 50 min.**

NOTE: We got great results for this recipe using a hand mixer and then stirring the flour in by hand. High-powered stand mixers can overbeat some pound cakes, giving them a tough texture.

STRAWBERRY SYRUP

MAKES 2¼ CUPS

Drizzle this ruby-hued syrup over waffles or pancakes for a sweet surprise at breakfast. *(pictured on page 116)*

- **1 pint (2 cups) fresh strawberries***
- **2 cups sugar**
- **¼ teaspoon lemon juice**

PROCESS strawberries in a food processor until smooth.

POUR strawberry puree through a wire-mesh strainer into a saucepan, discarding seeds.

STIR in sugar and juice; cook over low heat, stirring until sugar dissolves.

BRING to a boil over medium-high heat; reduce heat, and simmer 5 minutes. Remove from heat; cool. **Prep: 10 min., Cook: 5 min.**

*Substitute 2 cups frozen strawberries, thawed, if desired.

PARTY-PERFECT STRAWBERRY SHORTCAKES

MAKES 16 SERVINGS

These smaller shortcakes are sized to serve on a cake stand. To keep them moist and delicious, we spread strawberry jam onto the bottom cut sides of each shortcake before adding the strawberries and whipped cream.

- 1 (16-ounce) container fresh strawberries, sliced
- ½ cup sugar, divided
- 2½ cups all-purpose flour
- 4 teaspoons baking powder
- ¾ cup butter or margarine, cut into pieces
- 2 large eggs
- 1 cup sour cream
- 1 teaspoon vanilla extract
- 1 cup whipping cream
- 2 tablespoons sugar
- 2 tablespoons strawberry jam
- ¼ teaspoon chopped fresh mint
- Garnishes: fresh mint leaves, strawberry halves

COMBINE sliced strawberries and ¼ cup sugar. Cover strawberry mixture, and set aside.

COMBINE all-purpose flour, baking powder, and ¼ cup sugar; cut in butter with a pastry blender or fork until mixture is crumbly.

WHISK together eggs, sour cream, and vanilla until blended; add to flour mixture, stirring just until dry ingredients are moistened.

TURN dough out onto a lightly floured surface, and knead 6 times. Pat dough into an 8-inch square; cut into 16 (2-inch) squares. Place dough on a lightly greased baking sheet.

BAKE at 425° for 9 to 11 minutes or until golden.

BEAT whipping cream at medium speed with an electric mixer until foamy, and gradually add 2 tablespoons sugar, beating mixture at high speed until stiff peaks form.

REMOVE shortcakes from oven, and split in half horizontally. Combine strawberry jam and chopped mint; spread cut sides of bottom shortcake halves evenly with jam mixture, and top evenly with half of strawberry mixture. Cover mixture evenly with whipped cream; top with remaining strawberry mixture and remaining shortcake halves. Garnish, if desired. Serve immediately. **Prep: 30 min., Bake: 11 min.**

ROUND SHORTCAKES: Pat dough to a ½-inch thickness, and cut with a 3-inch round cutter. Place dough on a lightly greased baking sheet, and proceed with recipe as directed. Makes 12 servings.

Shortcake Shortcut

Here's a fast-fix dessert that is as impressive as it is easy to prepare.

Combine 1 (16-ounce) container fresh strawberries, sliced, and ¼ cup sugar; cover and set aside. Brush 9 large frozen biscuits with 3 tablespoons melted butter. Combine 3 tablespoons sugar and 1 teaspoon ground cinnamon; sprinkle over biscuits. Bake according to package directions. Serve immediately with strawberry mixture and whipped cream, and enjoy with 8 happy friends.

French Toast Stuffed With Flavor

There's something so delicious about waking up to comforting French toast right out of the skillet. You can make it even better by serving thick slices of French bread stuffed with a luscious mixture of orange marmalade, cream cheese, and—for that Southern touch—chopped pecans. Grill until golden, and let the goodness melt in your mouth. Don't forget the syrup!

STUFFED FRENCH TOAST

MAKES 8 SERVINGS

Serve with your favorite syrup.

- ½ (8-ounce) package cream cheese, softened
- ¼ cup chopped dates
- ¼ cup chopped pecans, toasted
- 4 teaspoons orange marmalade
- 2 French bread loaves, cut diagonally into 8 (1-inch-thick) slices
- 4 large eggs
- 1 cup milk
- 1 teaspoon ground cinnamon
- 3 tablespoons butter or margarine
- 2 tablespoons powdered sugar

STIR together first 4 ingredients.

CUT a horizontal pocket into top crust of each bread slice. Spoon about 2 teaspoons cream cheese mixture into each pocket.

WHISK together eggs, milk, and cinnamon; dip stuffed bread slices into mixture, coating all sides.

MELT butter in a large nonstick skillet over medium-high heat. Cook bread slices, in batches, 2 minutes on each side or until golden. Sprinkle with powdered sugar. **Prep: 30 min., Cook: 4 min. per batch**

W. N. COTTRELL II
NEW ORLEANS, LOUISIANA

Taste of the South

So Southern, Soulful, and Delicious

Try some of our region's most treasured dishes.

Southern Sunday Dinner

Serves 4

Our Best Southern Fried Chicken

Simple Turnip Greens   Pepper Sauce

Hearty Black-Eyed Peas   Hot-Water Cornbread

Classic Chess Pie   Southern Sweet Tea

OUR BEST SOUTHERN FRIED CHICKEN

MAKES 4 SERVINGS

Soaking the chicken before frying produces an irresistible crispy crust. *(pictured on page 113)*

- 3 quarts water
- 1 tablespoon salt
- 1 (2- to 2½-pound) broiler-fryer, cut up
- 1 teaspoon salt
- 1 teaspoon pepper
- 1 cup all-purpose flour
- 2 cups vegetable oil
- ¼ cup bacon drippings

COMBINE 3 quarts water and 1 tablespoon salt in a large bowl; add chicken. Cover and chill 8 hours. Drain chicken; rinse with cold water, and pat dry.

COMBINE 1 teaspoon each of salt and pepper; sprinkle half of mixture evenly over chicken. Combine remaining salt-and-pepper mixture and flour in a large heavy-duty zip-top plastic bag. Place 2 pieces of chicken in bag; seal. Shake to coat completely. Remove chicken; repeat procedure with remaining chicken, 2 pieces at a time.

COMBINE oil and drippings in a 12-inch cast-iron skillet or chicken fryer, and heat to 360°. Add chicken, a few pieces at a time, skin side down. Cover and cook 6 minutes; uncover and cook 9 minutes.

TURN chicken; cover and cook 6 minutes. Uncover and cook 5 to 9 minutes, turning pieces during the last 3 minutes for even browning, if necessary. Drain chicken on a paper towel-lined plate placed over a large bowl of hot water. **Prep: 25 min., Chill: 8 hrs., Cook: 30 min.**

NOTE: For best results, keep the oil temperature between 300° to 325° after adding chicken. If desired, substitute 2 cups buttermilk for the saltwater solution.

SIMPLE TURNIP GREENS

MAKES 4 TO 6 SERVINGS

We added sugar during cooking to eliminate bitterness—but some Southerners hotly debate this step. *(pictured on page 113)*

- 1 bunch fresh turnip greens (about 4½ pounds)
- 1 pound salt pork (streak of lean) or smoked pork shoulder
- 3 quarts water
- ¼ teaspoon freshly ground pepper
- 2 teaspoons sugar (optional)

REMOVE and discard stems and discolored spots from turnip greens. Wash greens thoroughly; drain and tear into pieces. Set aside.

SLICE salt pork at ¼-inch intervals, cutting to, but not through, skin.

COMBINE salt pork, 3 quarts water, pepper, and, if desired, sugar in a Dutch oven; bring to a boil. Cover, reduce heat, and simmer 1 hour.

ADD greens; cook, uncovered, 30 to 35 minutes or until tender. Serve with a slotted spoon. **Prep: 1 hr., 30 min.; Cook: 35 min.**

PEPPER SAUCE

MAKES 1½ CUPS

Many Southerners consider this an essential condiment for turnip greens. *(pictured on page 113)*

- ¾ cup cider or white wine vinegar
- 10 long, fresh green chile peppers, washed and trimmed*

BRING vinegar to a boil in a saucepan.

PACK peppers tightly into a hot 12-ounce jar; cover with boiling vinegar. **COVER** at once with a metal lid; screw on band. Store up to 2 weeks. **Prep: 20 min.**

NOTE: For an 8-ounce jar, use 6 peppers and ½ cup vinegar.

*Substitute banana peppers, jalapeño peppers, or other hot peppers, if desired.

HEARTY BLACK-EYED PEAS

MAKES 8 SERVINGS

Canned black-eyed peas doctored with country ham or smoked sausage make a respectable 10-minute substitute. *(pictured on page 113)*

1 (16-ounce) package dried black-eyed peas
4 cups water
1 medium onion, chopped
¾ teaspoon salt
½ teaspoon pepper
1 (1-pound) ham steak, cut into ½-inch cubes, or 1 ham hock

BRING all ingredients to a boil in a Dutch oven. Cover; reduce heat, and simmer 1 hour or until peas are tender. **Prep: 20 min., Cook: 1 hr.**

HOT-WATER CORNBREAD

MAKES 8 CAKES

These hot, crispy golden patties will tempt you to eat more than just one. *(pictured on page 113)*

2 cups white cornmeal
¼ teaspoon baking powder
1¼ teaspoons salt
1 teaspoon sugar
¼ cup half-and-half
1 tablespoon vegetable oil
¾ cup to 1¼ cups boiling water
Vegetable oil
Softened butter

COMBINE first 4 ingredients; stir in half-and-half and 1 tablespoon oil. Gradually

add boiling water; stir until batter is the consistency of grits.

POUR oil to a depth of ½ inch into a heavy skillet; place over medium-high heat. Scoop batter into a ¼-cup measure, and fry in batches 3 minutes on each side or until golden. Drain well. Serve with butter. **Prep: 5 min., Cook: 6 min. per batch**

NOTE: Stone-ground (coarsely ground) cornmeal requires more liquid.

COUNTRY HAM HOT-WATER CORN-BREAD: Stir in 1 to 2 cups finely chopped country ham after adding boiling water.

BACON-CHEDDAR HOT-WATER CORN-BREAD: Stir in 8 slices cooked, crumbled bacon; 1 cup shredded sharp Cheddar cheese; and 4 minced green onions after adding boiling water.

SOUTHWESTERN HOT-WATER CORN-BREAD: Stir in 1 seeded, minced jalapeño pepper; 1 cup shredded Mexican four-cheese blend; 1 cup frozen whole kernel corn, thawed; and ¼ cup minced fresh cilantro after adding boiling water.

BAKED HOT-WATER CORNBREAD: Omit skillet procedure. Pour ⅓ cup vegetable oil into a 15- x 10-inch jellyroll pan. Drop batter onto pan. Bake at 475° for 12 to 15 minutes. Turn; bake 5 more minutes.

CLASSIC CHESS PIE

MAKES 1 (9-INCH) PIE

1 (15-ounce) package refrigerated piecrusts
2 cups sugar
2 tablespoons cornmeal
1 tablespoon all-purpose flour
¼ teaspoon salt
½ cup butter or margarine, melted
¼ cup milk
1 tablespoon white vinegar
½ teaspoon vanilla extract
4 large eggs, lightly beaten

UNFOLD piecrusts; stack on a floured surface. Roll into a 12-inch circle.

FIT piecrust into a 9-inch pieplate according to package directions; fold edges under, and crimp.

LINE piecrust with aluminum foil, and fill crust with pie weights or dried beans. **BAKE** at 425° for 4 to 5 minutes. Remove weights and foil; bake 2 to 3 more minutes or until golden. Cool completely.

STIR together sugar and next 7 ingredients until blended. Add eggs, stirring well. Pour into piecrust.

BAKE at 350° for 50 to 55 minutes, shielding edges of pie with aluminum foil after 10 minutes to prevent excessive browning. Cool pie completely on a wire rack. **Prep: 23 min.; Bake: 1 hr., 3 min.**

COCONUT CHESS PIE: Prepare filling as directed; stir in 1 cup toasted flaked coconut before pouring into piecrust. Bake as directed.

CHOCOLATE-PECAN CHESS PIE: Prepare filling as directed; stir in 3½ tablespoons cocoa and ½ cup toasted pecans before pouring into piecrust. Bake as directed.

LEMON CHESS PIE: Prepare filling as directed; stir in ⅓ cup fresh lemon juice and 2 teaspoons grated lemon rind before pouring into piecrust. Bake as directed.

SOUTHERN SWEET TEA

MAKES 1 GALLON

Add a sprig of mint to this Southern sipper for extra refreshment. *(pictured on page 113)*

6 cups water
4 family-size tea bags
1 cup to 1¾ cups sugar
Lemon slices (optional)

BRING 6 cups water to a boil in a saucepan; add tea bags. Boil 1 minute; remove from heat. Cover; steep 10 minutes. Remove tea bags. Add sugar, stirring until dissolved. Pour into a 1-gallon pitcher; add enough water to fill pitcher. Serve over ice and, if desired, with lemon. **Prep: 2 min., Cook: 5 min., Steep: 10 min.**

Quick & Easy

Our Top Picks for Speedy Meals

These simple recipes deliver fantastic flavor without fuss.

It's 6 p.m., and you're just getting home after a long, hard day. You open the fridge and pantry, appraising each shelf in hope that a delicious meal will miraculously appear on the table in 30 minutes. Sound familiar? Hey, we've all been there.

This sampling of recipes from our "Quick & Easy" column will make your supper deadline doable. Our Sesame-Crusted Turkey Mignons With Creamy Wine Sauce, for example, comes together in a flash.

Save even more time by planning ahead. Look over recipes that appeal to you, make a grocery list, and check off any items you already have. Finally, do whatever you can beforehand.

We're confident that your family and friends will beg for encores of these fast, delicious dishes.

TOMATO-PESTO TART

MAKES 4 MAIN-DISH OR 8 APPETIZER SERVINGS

- 1 (15-ounce) package refrigerated piecrusts
- 2 cups (8 ounces) shredded mozzarella cheese, divided
- 5 plum tomatoes, sliced
- ¼ cup grated Parmesan cheese
- ½ cup mayonnaise
- 2 tablespoons basil pesto
- ½ teaspoon freshly ground pepper
- 3 tablespoons chopped fresh basil

UNFOLD piecrusts; stack on a lightly greased baking sheet, and roll into a 12-inch circle. Brush outer 1 inch of crust with water. Fold edge over, and crimp; prick bottom.

BAKE at 400° for 8 to 10 minutes. Remove from oven.

SPRINKLE with 1 cup mozzarella cheese; cool 15 minutes. Arrange tomato slices over cheese.

STIR together remaining 1 cup mozzarella cheese, Parmesan cheese, and next 3 ingredients; spread over tomato.

BAKE at 375° for 20 to 25 minutes. Sprinkle with basil. **Prep: 15 min., Bake: 35 min.**

MINI TOMATO-PESTO TARTS: Stir together ⅓ cup mayonnaise, ¼ cup shredded mozzarella cheese, 3 tablespoons grated Parmesan cheese, 2 teaspoons basil pesto, and ⅛ teaspoon pepper; stir in 2 chopped plum tomatoes. Spoon filling evenly into 1 (2.1-ounce) package frozen miniature phyllo tart shells. Bake at 375° for 12 minutes. Sprinkle with basil. Makes 15 tarts.

PARMESAN CHEESE BITES

MAKES 32 APPETIZER SERVINGS

- 1 cup all-purpose flour
- ⅓ cup grated Parmesan cheese
- ¼ teaspoon ground red pepper
- ½ cup butter or margarine, cut up
- 2 tablespoons milk

STIR together first 3 ingredients in a medium bowl; cut in butter with a pastry blender or fork until mixture is crumbly (mixture will look very dry). Gently press mixture together with hands, working until blended and smooth (about 2 to 3 minutes).

ROLL into a 10- x 8- x ¼-inch rectangle on a lightly floured surface. Cut lengthwise into 8 strips and crosswise into 4 strips, using a pastry wheel or knife, to form 32 pieces. Place on a lightly greased baking sheet; brush with milk.

BAKE at 350° for 12 to 15 minutes or until lightly browned. **Prep: 10 min., Bake: 15 min.**

NOTE: To make ahead, shape dough into 2 (4-inch-long) logs. Wrap in plastic wrap, and place in an airtight container; freeze dough up to 3 months. When ready to use, thaw dough overnight in refrigerator. Cut into ¼-inch-thick slices, and place rounds on a lightly greased baking sheet. Brush with milk, and bake as directed. Baked bites may be frozen up to 1 month.

WILD RICE-AND-SHRIMP SALAD

MAKES 4 SERVINGS

- 1 (6-ounce) package long-grain and wild rice mix
- 6 cups water
- 1½ pounds unpeeled, medium-size fresh shrimp
- ⅓ cup mayonnaise
- 2½ tablespoons lemon juice
- ¾ teaspoon sugar
- ⅛ teaspoon salt
- 1 teaspoon curry powder
- ⅛ teaspoon ground red pepper
- 1 (14-ounce) can quartered artichoke hearts, drained
- 4 green onions, sliced
- 1 small green bell pepper, chopped
- 1 celery rib, sliced
- 12 ripe olives, sliced (optional)
- Leaf lettuce

COOK rice according to package directions; set aside.

BRING 6 cups water to a boil, and add shrimp; cook 3 to 5 minutes or just until shrimp turn pink. Drain and rinse with cold water.

PEEL shrimp, and devein, if desired; coarsely chop.

STIR together mayonnaise and next 5 ingredients in a large bowl; stir in rice, shrimp, artichokes, next 3 ingredients, and, if desired, olives.

COVER and chill up to 5 hours, if desired. Serve over lettuce. **Prep: 25 min., Cook: 25 min.**

CORN WAFFLES WITH CILANTRO-LIME BUTTER

MAKES 10 (4-INCH) WAFFLES

- 1¾ cups self-rising flour
- ⅓ cup sugar
- ½ teaspoon salt
- 3 large eggs
- ½ cup buttermilk
- ⅓ cup vegetable oil
- 1 cup frozen whole kernel corn, thawed
- Cilantro-Lime Butter

COMBINE first 3 ingredients in a large bowl; make a well in center of mixture.

WHISK together eggs, buttermilk, and vegetable oil; stir in corn. Add corn mixture to dry ingredients, stirring just until moistened.

COOK in a preheated, oiled waffle iron until golden. Serve with Cilantro-Lime Butter, honey, or maple syrup. **Prep: 5 min., Cook: 20 min.**

Cilantro-Lime Butter:

MAKES ½ CUP

Try this on corn or steamed fresh veggies too.

- ½ cup butter, softened
- 1 tablespoon chopped fresh cilantro
- 1 teaspoon grated lime rind
- 1 teaspoon fresh lime juice

STIR together all ingredients until well blended. Cover and chill until ready to serve. **Prep: 5 min.**

SESAME-CRUSTED TURKEY MIGNONS WITH CREAMY WINE SAUCE

MAKES 4 SERVINGS

Turkey mignons come from the tenderloin, the leanest cut; they're available in the meat sections of large supermarkets.

- 1 (2.4-ounce) jar sesame seeds, toasted (½ cup)
- ¼ cup olive oil
- 1 garlic clove, minced
- 1 tablespoon chopped fresh chives
- 1 tablespoon soy sauce
- 2 teaspoons lemon juice
- 1 teaspoon grated fresh ginger
- ½ teaspoon sesame oil
- 2 (11-ounce) packages turkey mignons*
- Creamy Wine Sauce
- Hot cooked spaghetti
- Garnishes: lemon slices, whole chives

STIR together first 8 ingredients; dredge mignons in sesame seed mixture. Place on a lightly greased rack in a broiler pan.

BROIL turkey mignons 5½ inches from heat 12 minutes on each side or until done. Serve with Creamy Wine Sauce over hot cooked spaghetti, and garnish, if desired. **Prep: 20 min., Broil: 24 min.**

*Substitute 2 turkey tenderloins, cut in half crosswise, for turkey mignons, if desired.

Creamy Wine Sauce:

MAKES ABOUT ¾ CUP

- 1 cup Chablis or other white wine*
- 2 teaspoons lemon juice
- ¼ cup whipping cream
- 2 tablespoons soy sauce
- ⅓ cup butter or margarine

BRING wine and juice to a boil in a saucepan over medium-high heat.

BOIL 6 to 8 minutes or until mixture is reduced by half. Whisk in cream; cook, whisking constantly, 3 to 4 minutes or until thickened. Reduce heat to simmer; whisk in soy sauce and butter until butter melts. **Prep: 5 min., Cook: 15 min.**

*Substitute white grape juice, if desired.

HOT FUDGE ICE-CREAM TOPPING

MAKES 1½ CUPS

- 2 (1-ounce) semisweet chocolate baking squares
- 1 cup evaporated milk
- ¾ cup sugar
- 2 tablespoons butter or margarine
- 1 teaspoon vanilla extract

COOK first 3 ingredients in a saucepan over low heat, stirring constantly, 6 minutes or until chocolate melts and mixture is smooth.

BRING to a boil over medium heat. Boil, stirring constantly, 6 minutes. Remove from heat; stir in butter and vanilla. Serve warm over ice cream. Store in refrigerator up to 3 weeks. **Prep: 5 min., Cook: 12 min.**

Sensational Steak

It's quick, easy, and downright delicious. So splurge on a mouthwatering cookout favorite this weekend.

Southerners love grilling in all its incarnations. Many of us naturally gravitate toward ribs and chicken; others go for hot dogs and burgers. But we're willing to bet that for most of you, there are times when nothing else will do but a big, juicy steak.

So get ready to smell the smoke and hear the sizzle. We guarantee this will taste better than any steak-house fare, and we suggest you tip the cook.

PEPPERED RIB-EYE STEAKS

MAKES 6 SERVINGS

The mixture of black, red, and lemon peppers gives this steak its lively flavor.

    3 teaspoons garlic powder
    3 teaspoons dried thyme
    2 teaspoons ground black pepper
    1½ teaspoons salt
    1½ teaspoons lemon pepper
    1½ teaspoons ground red pepper
    1½ teaspoons dried parsley flakes
    6 (1½-inch-thick) rib-eye steaks
    3 tablespoons olive oil

COMBINE first 7 ingredients. Brush steaks with oil; rub with seasoning mixture. Cover and chill 1 hour.
GRILL steaks, covered with grill lid, over medium-high heat (350° to 400°) 6 to 8 minutes on each side or to desired degree of doneness. **Prep: 5 min., Chill: 1 hr., Grill: 16 min.**

DAWN HOLLOWAY
BIRMINGHAM, ALABAMA

GREEN ONION-AND-BACON MASHED POTATOES

MAKES 6 TO 8 SERVINGS

Cook and crumble bacon ahead of time to make this dish faster. If you're in a hurry, substitute frozen mashed potatoes.

    4 large baking potatoes, peeled and
        cut into 2-inch pieces*
    2 cups (8 ounces) shredded colby-
        Monterey Jack cheese
    6 to 8 bacon slices, cooked and
        crumbled
    4 green onions, chopped
    2 garlic cloves, pressed
    ½ cup sour cream
    ¼ cup butter or margarine,
        softened
    1½ teaspoons salt
    ½ teaspoon pepper

COMBINE potato and water to cover in a large Dutch oven; bring to a boil, and cook 25 minutes or until tender. Drain.
MASH potato with a fork or potato masher; stir in cheese and remaining ingredients. Serve immediately. **Prep: 15 min., Cook: 25 min.**

TO LIGHTEN: Substitute shredded light Mexican cheese blend, reduced-fat bacon, and nonfat sour cream; reduce butter to 2 tablespoons.

*Substitute 1 (22-ounce) package of frozen mashed potatoes, if desired. Prepare potatoes according to package directions; stir in cheese and remaining ingredients.

Steak-Savvy Sides

Buttery Garlic Bread: Melt ½ cup butter or margarine in a skillet over medium-high heat; add 4 garlic cloves, pressed, and ½ teaspoon salt. Sauté 2 minutes. Cut 1 (16-ounce) Italian bread loaf into 8 (1½-inch) slices, and dip into butter mixture, coating both sides. Place on a baking sheet. Stir together 1½ teaspoons Italian seasoning and ¼ cup grated Parmesan cheese; sprinkle on 1 side of each bread slice. Broil 5 inches from heat 4 minutes or until cheese melts. Makes 8 slices. **Prep: 10 min., Broil: 4 min.**

Fresh Mozzarella-Tomato-Basil Salad: Cut ½ pound fresh mozzarella cheese into 12 slices. Slice 2 large tomatoes; sprinkle with ½ teaspoon salt. Alternate tomato and cheese slices on a platter; drizzle with 3 tablespoons olive oil. Cover and chill 4 hours. Just before serving, sprinkle with freshly ground pepper and ½ cup shredded or chopped fresh basil. Makes 6 servings. **Prep: 10 min., Chill: 4 hrs.**

Marinated Grilled Squash: Place 3 medium-size yellow squash and 3 medium zucchini, each sliced diagonally, in a heavy-duty zip-top plastic bag. Whisk together ⅓ cup olive oil; 1 tablespoon lemon juice; 1 garlic clove, pressed; ½ teaspoon marjoram; and ¼ teaspoon each of salt and pepper. Pour over vegetables; chill 1 hour. Remove from marinade, reserving marinade. Arrange in a grill basket. Grill, covered, over medium-high heat (350° to 400°) 20 minutes, turning and brushing occasionally with marinade. Makes 6 servings. **Prep: 13 min., Chill: 1 hr., Grill: 20 min.**

Gadgets We Love

Want to know which culinary tools the *Southern Living* Foods staff can't live without? Read on.

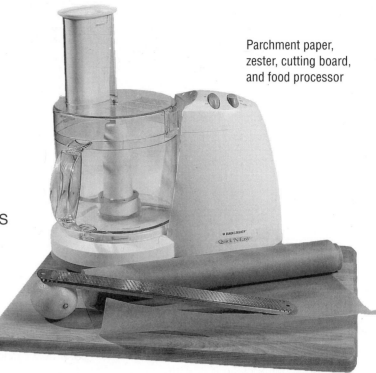

Parchment paper, zester, cutting board, and food processor

People who cook for a living can be pretty particular when it comes to kitchen equipment. Our staff of Foods editors and Test Kitchens chefs is no exception. We asked them to name their favorite tools of the trade. Here are their choices.

A good cutting board: This ranked at the top of the list among our staff. Portable cutting boards usually are made from wood or polyethylene, a soft but rigid plastic. Carefully clean after each use, and store away from heat.

Food processor: "I couldn't live without a good food processor," says Test Kitchens staffer Vanessa McNeil. "It dices, liquifies, grates, slices, and makes life much easier."

Zester: Margaret Monroe Dickey, our Test Kitchens Director, thinks the Microplane Zester is the "greatest gadget." The idea for this grater began when a hardware-store owner's wife realized that a wood planer removed citrus zest with ease. The new stainless steel version is popular with cooks for zesting and grating chocolate. "It's a lot easier to use than other zesters available, and I even use it to grate cheese," Margaret says.

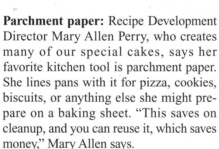

Parchment paper: Recipe Development Director Mary Allen Perry, who creates many of our special cakes, says her favorite kitchen tool is parchment paper. She lines pans with it for pizza, cookies, biscuits, or anything else she might prepare on a baking sheet. "This saves on cleanup, and you can reuse it, which saves money," Mary Allen says.

Immersion blender: Jan Moon of the Test Kitchens favors the Cuisinart Quick Prep handheld blender for its convenience and practicality. "It saves you from preparing a recipe in portions because you can now blend large amounts in the same container," she says. The immersion blender makes it easier to chop ice, mince vegetables, and puree soups—no more precariously pouring hot soup into a blender.

Kitchen tongs: Lyda Jones, our Assistant Test Kitchens Director, finds these indispensable. "This tool makes it easy to turn meats without piercing them and losing their juices," she says. She also uses the tongs for tossing salads, checking pasta for doneness, and arranging food on a plate.

Digital thermometer: Vicki Poellnitz, our Foods Editorial Assistant, thinks a digital thermometer is a must for grilling or roasting meats. Our staff prefers instant-read thermometers because they're more accurate and make a smaller hole in the meat, releasing fewer juices. When you want to test for doneness, insert the thermometer in the center of a piece of meat or roast or into the thickest part of the thigh of a bird. Make sure it doesn't touch the bone, and remove it immediately after reading.

Kitchen scissors: Every kitchen should have at least one pair of scissors for cutting poultry, herbs, fruit, parchment paper, kitchen string, cheesecloth, etc. We especially like the performance of the dishwasher-safe Joyce Chen brand.

Chef's knife: When our Foods staffers were asked to name their all-time favorite kitchen knife, Wüsthof's 8-inch-blade Cook's Knife was the answer. It's made with high-carbon, stain-resistant steel, and the handle is easy to hold. All Wüsthof knives are guaranteed for life.

Test Kitchens Secrets

Our Test Kitchens staff agrees that organization is the
key to efficiency and safety while working in the kitchen.
Here are some of their favorite tips.

■ Read recipes thoroughly
before cooking to make sure you
have all ingredients. It never
hurts to buy extra ones in case
of unexpected mistakes.

■ For easier pouring, coat measuring cups and utensils with
vegetable cooking spray before
measuring corn syrup or honey.

■ Spoon flour into a metal or
plastic dry measuring cup, and
level with a knife for an accurate
measurement.

■ When making a chocolate
cake, dust cakepans with cocoa
powder instead of all-purpose
flour.

■ To open Champagne or
sparkling wine safely, fit the
pocket of a pot holder over the
bottle, give the bottle a firm twist,
hold the cork tightly through the
pot holder, and capture the cork
in the pocket.

■ Freeze bar cookies 10 minutes
so they cut cleanly.

■ Before whipping heavy cream,
chill the bowl and beaters in the
freezer.

■ Ice cakes with an angled spatula (available at kitchen stores or
from cake-decorating suppliers).

■ Prevent cake layers from tear-
ing by chilling them before slicing
or icing.

■ Substitute jarred mango slices
for fresh; look for it in the produce
section of your grocery store.

■ Shred cheese easily by chilling
the grater in the freezer.

■ Add fresh herbs to coals when
grilling for flavorful meats and
vegetables. (Dampen with water
first so they don't burn.)

■ Soften corn tortillas quickly by
coating them with vegetable
cooking spray and sprinkling with
a few drops of water. Place in a
zip-top plastic bag, seal, and
microwave for 10 seconds or until
pliable.

■ Sharpen knives frequently.
More kitchen accidents occur
with dull knives.

■ After grilling, wrap meat in
aluminum foil, and allow it to rest
for 15 minutes. The internal
temperature may climb another
5 to 10 degrees, cooking the
meat further.

■ Place a damp paper towel or
dishtowel under your cutting
board to keep it from sliding.

■ Keep salt from clumping by
adding a few grains of rice.

■ Cool cookies completely before
storing. Put different types in separate containers so they'll keep
their original flavors and textures.

Our Best Southern Fried Chicken, Pepper Sauce, Simple Turnip Greens, page 106;
Southern Sweet Tea, Hot-Water Cornbread, Hearty Black-Eyed Peas, page 107

Beef and Chicken Fajitas, Red Rice, page 119

Frances's Margaritas, page 118

Guacamole, page 118

Tomato Salsa, page 118

Cream Cheese Pound Cake With Strawberries and Cream, page 104

May

Poolside Fiesta

Divide the chores, and multiply the fun.

An Engaging Menu
Serves 8

Frances's Margaritas

Chimayó Cocktails   Assorted beers

Tomato Salsa   Guacamole   Tortilla chips

Beef and Chicken Fajitas

Red Rice   Frijoles

Pralines

Planning an engagement party for 100 guests would be daunting for most of us, but it can be a piece of cake with the help of a few friends. Eight couples hosted this Mexican-themed event for Susan Stroup and Carlos Anderson in Austin. The action took place at Debbi and Mark Blackbird's hillside home, where the group worked (and played) together like a fine-tuned entertaining machine. In no time, the house, the mood, and the food were set.

Susan and Carlos's wedding destination inspired the lively menu. A talented kitchen duo kept beef and chicken fajitas hot and plentiful. For dessert, they served fabulous pralines from La Mexicana, a local bakery.

Take your cues from these savvy hosts. Assign tasks based on the talents of those involved. You'll need teams for decorating, buffet styling, food setup, cooking, and bartending. Everyone serves on the cleanup team—it speeds the work and might be as much fun as the party.

The food and decor can be as casual or elaborate as you like. Whatever your approach, share the chores—and the applause.

FRANCES'S MARGARITAS

MAKES 8 CUPS

This potent potable is bursting with juicy lime flavor. *(pictured on page 115)*

> 2 cups sugar
> 2 cups water
> 2 cups orange liqueur
> 2 cups tequila
> 2 cups fresh lime juice
> Margarita salt
> Garnish: lime wedges

BRING sugar and water to a boil over medium heat; cook, stirring constantly, 1 to 2 minutes or until sugar dissolves. Remove from heat; cool. Stir together sugar mixture, liqueur, tequila, and juice; cover and chill at least 30 minutes. **DIP** glass rims in water; dip rims in salt. Serve margaritas over crushed ice. Garnish, if desired. **Prep: 5 min., Chill: 30 min.**

NOTE: For testing purposes only, we used Cointreau for orange liqueur. For frozen margaritas, freeze mixture 8 hours; let stand 5 minutes before serving.

FRANCES ECHOLS
AUSTIN, TEXAS

CHIMAYÓ COCKTAILS

MAKES 3 CUPS

> 1½ cups apple juice
> ¾ cup crème de cassis (black currant liqueur)
> ¾ cup tequila
> ¼ cup fresh lime juice

STIR together all ingredients. Serve over ice. **Prep: 5 min.**

MARK BLACKBIRD
AUSTIN, TEXAS

TOMATO SALSA

MAKES 1¾ CUPS

Be sure to seed the peppers if you prefer a milder salsa. *(pictured on page 115)*

> 12 large plum tomatoes
> 1 small red onion
> 2 banana peppers
> ⅓ cup chopped fresh cilantro
> 1 teaspoon grated lime rind
> 2 tablespoons fresh lime juice
> ¼ teaspoon salt
> Garnish: fresh cilantro sprigs

CHOP first 3 ingredients; stir together tomato mixture and next 4 ingredients. Cover and chill salsa at least 1 hour. Garnish, if desired. **Prep: 30 min., Chill: 1 hr.**

GUACAMOLE

MAKES 4 CUPS

A splash of fresh lime juice and a sprinkling of fresh cilantro add a bright note to this thick and chunky dip. *(pictured on page 115)*

> 6 ripe avocados, peeled
> ⅓ cup fresh lime juice
> 2 large tomatoes, chopped
> 3 to 4 garlic cloves, minced
> 1 tablespoon chopped fresh cilantro
> ½ teaspoon salt
> ¼ teaspoon pepper
> Garnishes: chopped red and yellow bell peppers

PLACE avocados in a bowl; mash, leaving some small pieces. Stir in juice until blended.

STIR in tomato and next 4 ingredients. Cover tightly with plastic wrap; chill 30 minutes. Garnish, if desired. **Prep: 10 min., Chill: 30 min.**

BEEF AND CHICKEN FAJITAS

MAKES 8 TO 10 SERVINGS

Chipotle seasoning contributes a smoky essence to the flavorful fillings for the fajitas. *(pictured on page 114)*

> 2 tablespoons chili powder
> 2 teaspoons ground cumin
> 1 teaspoon brown sugar
> 1 teaspoon pepper
> ¼ teaspoon salt
> ¼ teaspoon garlic powder
> ¼ teaspoon chipotle seasoning (optional)
> 1 cup Italian dressing
> 6 skinned and boned chicken breast halves
> 4 pounds flank steak
> 20 (8-inch) flour tortillas, warmed
> Toppings: sour cream, shredded lettuce, chopped tomato, shredded Cheddar cheese

COMBINE first 6 ingredients and, if desired, chipotle seasoning.

STIR together chili powder mixture and dressing. Pour half of marinade in a shallow dish or large heavy-duty zip-top plastic bag; add chicken. Cover or seal.

POUR remaining marinade in a separate shallow dish or large heavy-duty zip-top plastic bag; add beef. Cover or seal; chill chicken and beef 2 hours.

REMOVE chicken and beef from marinade, discarding marinade.

GRILL, covered with grill lid, over medium heat (300° to 350°) about 15 minutes on each side or until chicken is done and beef is to desired degree of doneness.

CUT chicken and beef into strips. Serve in warmed flour tortillas with desired toppings. **Prep: 20 min., Chill: 2 hrs., Grill: 30 min.**

RED RICE

MAKES 6 TO 8 SERVINGS

Onion, garlic, and green chiles give rice a Tex-Mex flair. *(pictured on page 114)*

> 1 small onion, chopped
> 2 to 3 garlic cloves, chopped
> 1 teaspoon olive oil
> 1 cup uncooked long-grain rice
> 2 cups chicken broth or water
> 1 teaspoon salt
> ¼ teaspoon pepper
> 1 (4.5-ounce) can chopped green chiles
> 3 tablespoons tomato paste
> ¼ cup chopped fresh parsley

SAUTÉ onion and garlic in hot oil in a large saucepan over medium-high heat 3 minutes or until onion is tender.

STIR in rice and next 3 ingredients; bring to a boil. Cover, reduce heat, and cook 20 minutes.

REMOVE from heat; stir in green chiles, tomato paste, and parsley. **Prep: 10 min., Cook: 23 min.**

FRIJOLES

MAKES 6 TO 8 SERVINGS

> 4 (19.75-ounce) cans pinto beans
> 3 tablespoons bacon drippings or vegetable oil
> 1 medium onion, chopped
> 3 to 4 garlic cloves, chopped
> ¼ to ½ teaspoon salt
> Toppings: shredded cheese, tortilla strips

DRAIN pinto beans, reserving liquid. Set beans and reserved liquid aside.

SAUTÉ onion in hot drippings in skillet over medium heat 5 minutes or until golden. Add garlic and salt; sauté 1 minute.

ADD beans to skillet, 1 cup at a time, and cook, mashing constantly, over medium heat about 24 minutes or until desired consistency; add reserved bean liquid, if necessary. Serve with desired toppings. **Prep: 20 min., Cook: 30 min.**

The Light Side of Comfort Food

Many of us crave beefy, cheesy dishes. If they're merely an occasional indulgence for you because of calories, fat, and cholesterol, feel free to dig into this hearty, comforting recipe. We've trimmed calories and fat from a reader's original submission by using extra-lean ground beef and reduced-fat shredded cheese, but we've added extra tomatoes. We're sure this robust entrée will become a weeknight favorite at your house.

CHEESEBURGER MACARONI

MAKES 8 CUPS

> 8 ounces uncooked small elbow macaroni
> 1 pound extra-lean ground beef
> 1 medium onion, chopped
> Vegetable cooking spray
> 2 (14½-ounce) cans Italian stewed tomatoes, undrained
> ¼ cup ketchup
> 1 teaspoon ground red pepper
> ½ teaspoon salt
> 1 cup (4 ounces) reduced-fat shredded Cheddar cheese

COOK elbow macaroni according to package directions, omitting salt and fat; drain.

COOK beef and onion in a large nonstick skillet coated with cooking spray over medium-high heat until beef crumbles and is no longer pink. Drain well; pat with paper towels. Return beef mixture to skillet.

STIR in stewed tomatoes and next 3 ingredients; cook until thoroughly heated. Stir in cooked macaroni. Sprinkle with shredded Cheddar cheese, and serve immediately. **Prep: 30 min., Cook: 15 min.**

CHRIS BRYANT
JOHNSON CITY, TENNESSEE

Per 1 cup: Calories 243 (20% from fat); Fat 5.4g (sat 2.2g, mono 2g, poly 0.4g); Protein 17g; Carb 32g; Fiber 2.9g; Chol 18mg; Iron 2.5mg; Sodium 699mg; Calc 90mg

Spinach Makes the Salad

Mix good-for-you greens with these mighty-fine fixings.

Spinach Pointers

- Spinach, available year-round, is at its peak during spring and fall because it grows best in cooler weather.
- There are three main varieties of spinach: flat leaf, semi-savoyed (crinkled), and heavily savoyed. The more crinkly the leaves, the more dirt and grit they trap.
- Wash bunched spinach thoroughly in a sink or large container by swishing and immersing in cold water. Let stand for a few minutes to allow dirt to sink to bottom. Repeat twice.
- Trapped moisture in plastic bags can cause spinach to spoil quickly. After washing, dry well using a salad spinner or by blotting with paper towels. To keep spinach fresh longer, wrap in dry paper towels, and store in a zip-top plastic bag. Use within two to four days.
- Because spinach is mostly water, it wilts to a fraction of its original size when cooked. One pound of fresh spinach yields about ¾ to 1 cup cooked.
- It's fine to buy spinach prewashed in sealed plastic bags (re-rinse with fresh water, and pat or spin dry, if desired). Delicate baby spinach, also available prewashed, is ideal for salads.

As the temperature rises, we start craving all things cool. Fresh spinach salads with tempting toppings couldn't be more refreshing and flavorful during this time of year. With this oh-so-good green popping up in gardens (and farmers markets) across the South, now's just the right time to fill up big bowls with it, accompanied by bold toppings such as Creole Croutons and Sweet Parsley Dressing.

You probably already know that spinach is a good source of iron. What you may not know is that it also contains oxalic acid, a substance that makes the mineral difficult to absorb. To counteract this effect, pair spinach with vitamin C-rich foods such as citrus fruit, tomato, bell pepper, and broccoli. Or enjoy it alongside lean meat, which is a great source of easily absorbed iron.

These three creative recipes will satisfy your taste for something cool, hearty, and nutritious.

SPINACH SALAD WITH SWEET PARSLEY DRESSING

MAKES 6 SERVINGS

- 1 (10-ounce) package fresh baby spinach
- 8 bacon slices, cooked and crumbled
- ½ cup shredded Jarlsberg cheese
- ½ cup chopped walnuts, toasted
- Sweet Parsley Dressing

PLACE first 4 ingredients in a large bowl, and toss. Drizzle with Sweet Parsley Dressing, tossing gently to coat. **Prep: 20 min.**

Sweet Parsley Dressing:

MAKES ABOUT 1 CUP

- ½ cup sugar
- ½ cup white vinegar
- 2 tablespoons vegetable oil
- 1 green onion, thinly sliced
- 1 tablespoon chopped fresh parsley
- 1 teaspoon Worcestershire sauce
- 1 teaspoon prepared mustard
- ¼ teaspoon freshly ground pepper

WHISK together all ingredients; chill mixture 20 minutes. **Prep: 10 min., Chill: 20 min.**

ANN HENLEY PERRY
RALEIGH, NORTH CAROLINA

SPINACH SALAD WITH APRICOT VINAIGRETTE

MAKES 6 SERVINGS

Sweet dried fruit, toasted pecans, and tangy goat cheese complement baby spinach in this colorful salad.

- 1 (10-ounce) package fresh baby spinach
- 1 pint grape tomatoes, halved
- 1 small purple onion, thinly sliced
- ½ cup chopped dried apricots
- 1 (4-ounce) package crumbled goat cheese
- 1 ripe avocado, peeled and diced
- ½ cup chopped pecans, toasted
- Apricot Vinaigrette

PLACE first 7 ingredients in a large bowl, tossing gently. Drizzle with Apricot Vinaigrette, tossing gently to coat. **Prep: 10 min.**

Apricot Vinaigrette:

MAKES ½ CUP

- ⅓ cup vegetable oil
- 2 tablespoons white wine vinegar
- 2 tablespoons orange juice
- 2 tablespoons apricot jam
- ½ teaspoon salt
- ½ teaspoon ground coriander
- ½ teaspoon freshly ground pepper

WHISK together all ingredients in a small bowl. **Prep: 5 min.**

Spinach Salad With Zesty Blue Cheese Dressing

MAKES 4 TO 6 SERVINGS

¼ cup white vinegar
2 teaspoons Dijon mustard
1 garlic clove, minced
½ teaspoon freshly ground pepper
⅔ cup olive oil
1 (4-ounce) package crumbled
    blue cheese
1 (10-ounce) package fresh spinach
½ (8-ounce) package sliced fresh
    mushrooms
1 cup grape or cherry tomatoes,
    halved
½ small purple onion, thinly sliced
Creole Croutons

WHISK together first 4 ingredients; gradually whisk in oil. Add cheese, and stir gently.

COMBINE spinach and next 3 ingredients; drizzle with dressing, tossing to coat. Sprinkle with Creole Croutons. Serve immediately. **Prep: 15 min.**

Creole Croutons:

MAKES ABOUT 8 CUPS

5 (1-inch-thick) white bread slices,
    cubed
¼ cup freshly grated Parmesan
    cheese
¼ cup butter or margarine, melted
½ tablespoon Creole seasoning

COMBINE all ingredients in a large zip-top plastic bag; seal bag, and shake to coat.

ARRANGE seasoned bread cubes in an even layer on an aluminum foil-lined baking sheet.

BAKE at 300° for 30 minutes or until croutons are crisp and golden. **Prep: 10 min., Bake: 30 min.**

Begin With Barbecue

Take a break from the deli-chicken-and-sides routine. Once you taste these dishes, you'll bypass the grocery store and head for the nearest 'cue joint.

Brunswick Stew-Cornbread Pie

MAKES 6 TO 8 SERVINGS

1 pound shredded barbecued pork
1 (16-ounce) package frozen vegetable
    gumbo mixture
1 (8½-ounce) can baby lima beans,
    drained
1 (8¼-ounce) can cream-style corn
1½ cups chicken broth
1 cup chopped cooked chicken
½ cup ketchup
½ cup barbecue sauce
1½ cups self-rising white cornmeal
1¼ cups buttermilk
⅓ cup all-purpose flour
1 large egg, lightly beaten
1 tablespoon vegetable oil

BRING first 8 ingredients to a boil in a Dutch oven over medium heat; reduce heat, and simmer 15 minutes, stirring occasionally. Pour into a lightly greased 13- x 9-inch baking dish.

STIR together cornmeal and next 4 ingredients; spread evenly over stew mixture, leaving a ½-inch border.

BAKE at 375° for 30 to 35 minutes or until cornbread is done. **Prep: 25 min., Bake: 35 min.**

Barbecue Spaghetti

MAKES 4 SERVINGS

MELT 3 tablespoons butter in a 3-quart saucepan over medium heat; add 1 small onion, chopped, and sauté until tender. Add 1 pound shredded barbecued pork and 3½ cups barbecue sauce; cook 10 minutes or until thoroughly heated. Serve over 12 ounces hot cooked spaghetti. **Prep: 10 min., Cook: 18 min.**

Black Bean Soup

MAKES 8 CUPS

1 small onion, chopped
2 tablespoons olive oil
2 garlic cloves, chopped
3 cups chicken broth
3 (15-ounce) cans black beans, rinsed
    and drained
1 (10½-ounce) can diced tomatoes
    and green chiles
1 pound shredded barbecued beef
2 tablespoons red wine vinegar
Toppings: sour cream, shredded
    Monterey Jack cheese, chopped
    fresh cilantro

SAUTÉ onion in hot oil in a Dutch oven over medium heat 5 minutes or until tender; stir in garlic, and sauté 1 minute. Stir in broth, beans, and tomatoes and green chiles; reduce heat, and simmer, stirring often, 15 minutes.

PROCESS 1 cup bean mixture in a food processor until smooth. Return puree to Dutch oven; add beef, and simmer 10 minutes. Stir in vinegar. Serve with desired toppings. **Prep: 10 min., Cook: 31 min.**

ROSIE MELLIS
GARDNER, MASSACHUSETTS

Barbecue Quesadillas

MAKES 4 SERVINGS

DIVIDE ½ pound shredded barbecued pork evenly among 8 (6-inch) flour tortillas; sprinkle each with 2 tablespoons shredded Mexican four-cheese blend or Monterey Jack cheese. Fold in half. Cook in a nonstick skillet over medium heat 3 minutes on each side or until tortillas are crisp and cheese melts. Serve with salsa and guacamole. **Prep: 5 min., Cook: 12 min.**

Barbecue Sundae

MAKES 4 SERVINGS

DIVIDE 2 cups warm baked beans evenly among 4 small bowls, mugs, or glass jars; top each portion of beans with ½ cup coleslaw and ¼ pound hot shredded barbecued pork. Serve sundae with a dill pickle wedge, if desired. **Prep: 10 min.**

Grill Once, Enjoy All Week

Toss veggies on the fire this weekend to get a head start on next week's suppers.

Grilled vegetables always make great side dishes, and we'd like to show you new ways to use them. These recipes use items found in most kitchens—garlic, olive oil, and citrus juices—along with spices and herbs. To save time, plan your menu ahead using some of these recipes, and then load the grill with all the vegetables you will need for the week. Some of these vegetables will require longer cooking times than others, so keep an eye on them, and remove them when done. Store in plastic bags in the refrigerator until ready to use. Experiment for yourself: Include a few grilled, pureed tomatillos in a favorite vegetable soup, or add a little whipping cream to grilled, pureed red peppers for a steak sauce. Let your imagination guide you to some inventive dishes, and when you come up with a winner, please share your recipe with us.

GRILLED PORTOBELLO MUSHROOMS AND ASPARAGUS

MAKES 6 SERVINGS

> 4 portobello mushroom caps
> 2 tablespoons Rosemary Oil
> 1 pound fresh asparagus

REMOVE brown gills from undersides of portobello mushroom caps using a spoon, discarding gills. Brush mushrooms with 1 tablespoon Rosemary Oil. Snap off tough ends of asparagus; brush with remaining 1 tablespoon Rosemary Oil.
GRILL mushrooms, covered with grill lid, over high heat (400° to 500°) 5 minutes on each side. Cut mushrooms into strips. Grill asparagus, covered with grill lid, over high heat 2 minutes on each side. **Prep: 5 min., Grill: 14 min.**

Rosemary Oil:

MAKES ⅓ CUP

> ⅓ cup olive oil
> 2 fresh rosemary sprigs
> 1 teaspoon pepper

BRING all ingredients to a boil over high heat, and cook, stirring occasionally, 3 minutes. Remove from heat; cool. Discard rosemary sprigs. **Prep: 5 min., Cook: 3 min.**

NOTE: Use remaining Rosemary Oil in the vinaigrette for Grilled Mushroom-Asparagus Salad.

GRILLED MUSHROOM-ASPARAGUS SALAD: Whisk together ¼ cup balsamic vinegar; 3 tablespoons Rosemary Oil; 1 garlic clove, pressed; 1 teaspoon chopped fresh rosemary; and ½ teaspoon salt, and set dressing aside. Spread 1 cup (about 8 ounces) goat cheese on 1 side of 12 French baguette slices, toasted, and sprinkle each portion with ⅛ teaspoon black pepper. Prepare 1 recipe Grilled Portobello Mushrooms and Asparagus, slicing mushrooms rather than cutting into strips. Arrange 6 cups gourmet salad greens, sliced mushrooms, and asparagus on a large serving platter, and drizzle with dressing. Serve with goat cheese toast; garnish with fresh rosemary sprigs, if desired. Makes 6 servings. **Prep: 20 min.**

THREE-PEPPER GRILL

MAKES 6 SERVINGS

> 4 large tomatoes
> 1 medium eggplant
> 1 large red bell pepper
> 1 large green bell pepper
> 1 large yellow bell pepper
> ¼ cup olive oil
> 1 tablespoon fresh thyme leaves
> 3 tablespoons lemon juice
> 2 garlic cloves, pressed
> ½ teaspoon salt

CUT tomatoes in half; peel eggplant, and cut into cubes. Cut bell peppers into 2-inch pieces. Combine vegetables, oil, and remaining ingredients in a large heavy-duty zip-top plastic bag; seal and chill 2 to 4 hours. Remove vegetables, reserving marinade. Grill eggplant and bell pepper, in batches, in a grill wok, covered with grill lid, over high heat (400° to 500°), stirring occasionally, 10 minutes or until tender. Place bell pepper and eggplant in a large bowl. Grill tomato, cut sides up, covered with grill lid, over high heat 4 to 5 minutes. Coarsely chop tomato; toss with bell pepper mixture. Drizzle with reserved marinade, tossing to coat. **Prep: 25 min., Chill: 4 hrs., Grill: 25 min.**

THREE PEPPER-SAUSAGE PASTA: Grill 1½ pounds Italian sausage, covered with grill lid, over high heat (400° to 500°) 8 minutes on each side. Cut into 2-inch pieces; toss with 1 recipe Three-Pepper Grill, and serve over 12 ounces hot cooked linguine. Sprinkle with shredded Parmesan cheese. Makes 6 servings. **Prep: 10 min., Grill: 16 min.**

GRILLED CORN AND SQUASH

MAKES 6 TO 8 SERVINGS

> 4 ears fresh corn
> 4 medium-size yellow squash
> ½ medium-size sweet onion
> Vegetable cooking spray
> 3 poblano chile peppers
> 1 garlic clove, pressed
> 2 tablespoons chopped fresh basil
> 1 tablespoon chopped fresh oregano
> ½ teaspoon salt
> ½ teaspoon ground cumin

REMOVE husks from corn; cut squash in half lengthwise, and cut onion into ¼-inch-thick slices. Coat corn, squash, and onion with cooking spray, and set aside.

GRILL chile peppers, covered with grill lid, over medium-high heat (350° to 400°) 5 minutes on each side.

GRILL corn and onion, covered with grill lid, over medium-high heat 4 minutes on each side.

GRILL squash, cut sides down, covered with grill lid, over medium-high heat 5 minutes. Turn squash, and grill 2 more minutes.

CUT corn kernels from cob. Chop vegetables, discarding chile pepper seeds, and place corn kernels and vegetables in a large bowl. Toss with remaining ingredients. **Prep: 25 min., Grill: 25 min.**

GRILLED CORN-AND-SQUASH QUESA-DILLAS: Spoon 1 recipe Grilled Corn and Squash evenly on half of 12 (8-inch) flour tortillas, and sprinkle each portion with 2 cups (8 ounces) shredded Monterey Jack cheese. Fold tortillas over filling. Cook in batches on a hot, lightly greased griddle or nonstick skillet 2 to 3 minutes on each side or until lightly browned. Serve quesadillas immediately. Makes 12 servings. **Prep: 5 min., Cook: 6 min. per batch**

Tomatillo Salsa

MAKES ABOUT 5 CUPS

This fresh mixture is great for eating with tortilla chips as well as flavoring grilled meat and poultry. Jalapeño pepper and fresh cilantro add extra zing to this flavor-packed salsa.

- **10 fresh tomatillos, husks removed**
- **3 medium tomatoes**
- **1 jalapeño pepper**
- **½ medium-size purple onion, sliced**
- **½ cup chopped fresh cilantro**
- **1 garlic clove**
- **2 tablespoons lime juice**
- **¾ teaspoon salt**
- **½ teaspoon pepper**
- **½ teaspoon ground cumin**

GRILL first 4 ingredients, covered with grill lid, over high heat (400° to 500°) 3 to 4 minutes on each side or until tomatoes look blistered and onion is tender. Cool 10 minutes. Discard jalapeño seeds, if desired.

PULSE grilled tomatillo mixture and remaining ingredients in a blender or food processor 6 times or until mixture is coarsely chopped, stopping to scrape down sides.

COVER salsa, and chill at least 2 hours. Serve with tortilla chips. **Prep: 20 min., Grill: 8 min., Chill: 2 hrs.**

GRILLED CHICKEN WITH TOMATILLO SALSA: Combine 6 skinned and boned chicken breast halves and 2 cups Tomatillo Salsa in a shallow dish or large heavy-duty zip-top plastic bag. Cover or seal, and chill 2 hours. Remove chicken, discarding marinade. Grill, covered with grill lid, on high heat (400° to 500°) 8 minutes on each side. Slice chicken, and serve over hot cooked rice with additional Tomatillo Salsa. Makes 6 servings. **Prep: 10 min., Chill: 2 hrs., Grill: 16 min.**

Living Light

Creamy and Delicious

Mention cheese, sour cream, and the like, and most folks' thoughts immediately go to foods that have an indulgent quality. Predictably, these ingredients are often associated with high fat and cholesterol.

Well, get ready to sample scrumptious, healthy dishes loaded with great taste. We took advantage of widely available low-fat dairy products to create recipes with fantastic flavor. We guarantee that you'll find these easy selections, from a home-style casserole to a tantalizing dessert, completely irresistible. Silky texture and satisfying flavor don't have to equal a diet disaster when you cook with low-fat dairy products.

Mini Lemon Cheesecakes with Raspberry Sauce

MAKES 6 SERVINGS

This tart dessert makes a sweet, pretty finale to your meal. It also contains respectable amounts of fiber and calcium.

- **Vegetable cooking spray**
- **9 gingersnaps, crushed**
- **1½ (8-ounce) packages ⅓-less-fat cream cheese**
- **⅔ cup sugar**
- **1 tablespoon cornstarch**
- **1 large egg**
- **¼ cup egg substitute**
- **1 tablespoon grated lemon rind**
- **1 teaspoon vanilla extract**
- **Raspberry Sauce**

COAT 6 (4-ounce) individual baking dishes with cooking spray; sprinkle evenly with cookie crumbs.

BEAT cream cheese at medium speed with an electric mixer until smooth.

COMBINE sugar and cornstarch; add to cream cheese, beating until blended. Add egg and egg substitute, beating until blended. Stir in rind and vanilla. Spoon mixture evenly into prepared dishes. Place dishes in a 13- x 9-inch pan, and add boiling water to a depth of 1 inch.

BAKE at 325° for 30 to 35 minutes or until set. Remove baking dishes from pan; cool completely on wire racks. Cover and chill up to 8 hours, if desired. Serve with Raspberry Sauce. **Prep: 30 min., Bake: 35 min.**

Per serving: Calories 354 (34% from fat); Fat 13.5g (sat 7g, mono 3.4g, poly 0.8g); Protein 9.2g; Carb 50g; Fiber 4g; Chol 67mg; Iron 1.9mg; Sodium 231mg; Calc 90mg

Raspberry Sauce:

MAKES ABOUT 1½ CUPS

- **¼ cup sugar**
- **2 tablespoons water**
- **2 (6-ounce) containers fresh raspberries**

BRING sugar and 2 tablespoons water to a boil in a small heavy saucepan. Boil 1 minute. Remove mixture from heat; gently stir in raspberries. Serve sauce over cheesecakes. **Prep: 10 min.**

PAT BAILEY
BIRMINGHAM, ALABAMA

CREAMY BEEF STROGANOFF

MAKES 6 SERVINGS

1 (8-ounce) package egg noodles
1½ pounds sirloin steak, cut into
    thin strips
2 teaspoons olive oil
Vegetable cooking spray
1 large sweet onion, diced
1 (8-ounce) package sliced fresh
    mushrooms
2 tablespoons all-purpose flour
1 (14.25-ounce) can low-sodium
    fat-free beef broth
3 tablespoons tomato paste
3 tablespoons dry sherry
½ teaspoon salt
½ teaspoon pepper
¼ teaspoon dried tarragon
1 (8-ounce) container fat-free
    sour cream
2 tablespoons chopped fresh
    parsley

COOK noodles according to package directions, omitting salt and fat.

COOK beef, in 2 batches, in hot oil in a large nonstick skillet coated with cooking spray over medium-high heat 3 to 4 minutes or just until browned. Remove from skillet, and set aside.

ADD onion to skillet, and sauté over medium-high heat 2 minutes. Add mushrooms, and sauté 3 minutes. Sprinkle with flour, and stir until blended. Add beef broth and tomato paste, and cook, stirring constantly, 2 to 3 minutes or until thickened.

RETURN beef to skillet; add sherry and next 3 ingredients. Reduce heat to low; simmer 5 minutes. Remove from heat; stir in sour cream. Sprinkle with parsley. Serve over hot cooked noodles. **Prep: 30 min., Cook: 31 min.**

Per serving: Calories 391 (24% from fat); Fat 10.3g (sat 3.5g, mono 4.5g, poly 0.8g); Protein 36g; Carb 37g; Fiber 2.5g; Chol 111mg; Iron 5mg; Sodium 311mg; Calc 84mg

SHRIMP RISOTTO

MAKES 5 (1-CUP) SERVINGS

¾ pound unpeeled, medium-size
    fresh shrimp
1 (32-ounce) box low-sodium
    fat-free chicken broth
1 small onion, diced
1 tablespoon olive oil
1 garlic clove, minced
1½ cups uncooked Arborio rice
⅔ cup dry white wine (at room
    temperature)
1 (8-ounce) package sliced fresh
    mushrooms
⅔ cup fresh sugar snap peas
¼ teaspoon salt
½ teaspoon freshly ground
    pepper
½ cup shredded Parmesan cheese

PEEL shrimp, and devein, if desired; set shrimp aside.

BRING chicken broth to a boil in a small saucepan. Reduce heat to low, and simmer.

SAUTÉ onion in hot oil in a saucepan over medium-high heat 7 minutes or until tender. Add minced garlic, and sauté 1 minute. Add rice, and sauté 2 minutes. Reduce heat to medium.

ADD wine and 1 cup hot broth to saucepan. Cook, stirring constantly, until liquid is absorbed. Repeat procedure with remaining hot broth, ½ cup at a time. (Cooking time is 25 minutes.) When adding last ½ cup broth, stir in mushrooms and peas. Cook, stirring constantly, 10 minutes.

ADD shrimp, and cook, stirring constantly, 5 minutes or just until shrimp turn pink. Remove from heat; stir in salt and pepper. Sprinkle with cheese. **Prep: 30 min., Cook: 50 min.**

Per serving: Calories 351 (13% from fat); Fat 4.8g (sat 1.4g, mono 2.3g, poly 0.5g); Protein 18g; Carb 54g; Fiber 2.7g; Chol 85mg; Iron 4.3mg; Sodium 627mg; Calc 70mg

CHICKEN, ORZO, AND SPINACH CASSEROLE

MAKES 8 SERVINGS

Orzo is a rice-shaped pasta.

4 skinned and boned chicken
    breast halves
⅔ cup uncooked orzo
1 (8-ounce) package sliced fresh
    mushrooms
Vegetable cooking spray
1 (10-ounce) package chopped
    frozen spinach, thawed and
    well drained
1 (10½-ounce) can fat-free cream
    of mushroom soup, undiluted
½ cup reduced-fat mayonnaise
2 teaspoons lemon juice
½ teaspoon seasoned pepper
¾ cup (6 ounces) shredded
    reduced-fat Monterey Jack
    cheese
¼ cup Italian-seasoned breadcrumbs

BOIL chicken and water to cover in a large Dutch oven 12 minutes or until done. Remove chicken, reserving broth. Chop chicken, and set aside.

COOK pasta in reserved broth according to package directions, omitting salt and fat.

SAUTÉ mushrooms until tender in a large nonstick skillet coated with cooking spray.

REMOVE from heat. Stir in chicken, pasta, spinach, and next 4 ingredients. Spoon mixture into a 13- x 9-inch baking dish coated with cooking spray. Sprinkle with cheese and breadcrumbs. **BAKE** at 350° for 30 minutes or until thoroughly heated. **Prep: 25 min., Cook: 12 min., Bake: 30 min.**

Per serving: Calories 323 (31% from fat); Fat 11g (sat 3.9g, mono 0.4g, poly 0.4g); Protein 36g; Carb 18g; Fiber 1.5g; Chol 85mg; Iron 2.3mg; Sodium 664mg; Calc 242mg

Serve a New Pasta Tonight

These entrées are easy, delicious, and, best of all, different.

Looking for something to shake up your supper lineup? Here are some dishes with unique seasonings.

SPICY CHICKEN PASTA

MAKES 4 SERVINGS

3 celery ribs, chopped
2 garlic cloves, minced
1 medium onion, chopped
½ green bell pepper, chopped
½ yellow bell pepper, chopped
3 tablespoons olive oil
1 pound skinned and boned chicken
   breast halves, cubed
1 (16-ounce) jar salsa
1 tablespoon dried parsley flakes
½ teaspoon salt
¼ teaspoon hot sauce
8 ounces penne, cooked

SAUTÉ first 5 ingredients in hot oil in a large saucepan over medium-high heat 3 to 4 minutes or until crisp-tender. Add chicken, and cook, stirring often, 3 to 4 minutes or until done. Stir in salsa; bring to a boil. Reduce heat, and simmer, stirring often, 2 minutes or until thickened. Stir in parsley, salt, and hot sauce. Serve over pasta. **Prep: 10 min., Cook: 10 min.**

ELLIE WELLS
LAKELAND, FLORIDA

NOODLES WITH SPRING VEGETABLES

MAKES 4 SERVINGS

1 (12-ounce) package whole wheat
   fettuccine or linguine, uncooked
1 pound fresh asparagus
½ cup rice vinegar
¼ cup peanut oil
3 tablespoons sesame oil
1 medium cucumber
1 pound small broccoli florets
1 large carrot, grated
1 (8-ounce) can sliced water
   chestnuts, drained
5 large radishes, sliced (optional)
½ teaspoon salt
¼ teaspoon pepper

COOK noodles in boiling salted water 6 to 8 minutes; remove noodles with a slotted spoon, reserving boiling water. Rinse noodles; drain and set aside.
SNAP off tough ends of asparagus; cut into ½-inch pieces. Add asparagus to boiling water, and cook 3 minutes; drain. Plunge into ice water to stop the cooking process; drain and set aside.
WHISK together vinegar and oils. Pour over noodles, and toss.
CUT cucumber in half lengthwise; remove seeds, and cut cucumber into thin slices. Add cucumber, asparagus, broccoli, and remaining 5 ingredients to noodle mixture, tossing well. **Prep: 25 min., Cook: 11 min.**

NOTE: For testing purposes only, we used Sugar Busters! 100% Whole Wheat Fettuccine.

JACKIE OGLESBY
FORT WORTH, TEXAS

HOT RED CURRY SHRIMP

MAKES 4 SERVINGS

The unusual ingredients in this dish offer a refreshing change of pace. You can also substitute chicken for the shrimp.

1 dried whole red chile pepper
¼ cup boiling water
1 pound unpeeled, medium-size
   fresh shrimp
2¼ cups chicken broth
1 (14-ounce) can coconut milk
1 tablespoon hot curry paste
1 tablespoon fish sauce
2 (4.9-ounce) packages toasted Israeli
   couscous
1 tablespoon lime juice
3 tablespoons chopped fresh cilantro

PLACE chile pepper in ¼ cup boiling water; let stand 30 minutes. Drain, cool, and chop.
PEEL shrimp, and devein, if desired.
COOK chile pepper, broth, and next 3 ingredients in a saucepan over low heat, stirring often, 8 minutes. Add shrimp, and cook, stirring often, 2 to 3 minutes or until shrimp turn pink.
REMOVE seasoning packets from couscous, and reserve for another use. Stir couscous into broth mixture; remove from heat, cover, and let stand 15 minutes. Stir in juice; sprinkle with cilantro. **Prep: 10 min., Cook: 11 min., Stand: 45 min.**

NOTE: For testing purposes only, we used Patak's Original Hot Curry Paste and Marrakesh Express CousCous Grande Toasted Onion, which are available at Asian markets or in the Asian-food sections of larger supermarkets.

FRAN POINTER
KANSAS CITY, MISSOURI

Sweet on Onions

Enjoy the gentle side of a strong vegetable.

Sweet onions are marvels. These mild giants offer wonderful flavor without the bite. Even raw, they're easy on the palate, unlike their eye-watering cousins. Some folks even enjoy eating them like apples.

Vidalias, Walla Wallas, 1015s, and Mauis are all similar, and they work nicely in any dish that requires some punch. And because they're available much of the year, you can savor their flavor regularly.

PICKLED ONION AND CUCUMBER

MAKES 2 GALLONS

This makes a crisp, cooling addition to a warm-weather meal.

- 5 pounds sweet onions, thinly sliced and separated into rings
- 8 medium cucumbers, thinly sliced
- 1 gallon white vinegar (5% acidity)
- 2 teaspoons pepper
- 1 teaspoon salt

STIR together all ingredients in a large bowl; cover and chill 24 hours. Store in refrigerator up to 2 weeks. **Prep: 25 min., Chill: 24 hrs.**

ONION PUDDINGS

MAKES 6 SERVINGS

- ¼ cup butter or margarine
- 3 medium-size sweet onions, diced
- 1 cup half-and-half
- 4 large eggs
- 1 teaspoon salt
- ½ teaspoon freshly ground pepper

MELT butter in a large skillet over medium heat; add diced onion, and cook, stirring occasionally, 30 minutes or until caramel colored. Remove mixture from heat.

PROCESS onion, half-and-half, and remaining ingredients in a food processor or blender until smooth, stopping to scrape down sides.

POUR into 6 lightly greased 6-ounce custard cups. Cover cups with aluminum foil, and place in a 13- x 9-inch pan. Add hot water to pan to a depth of ½ inch.

BAKE at 350° for 45 minutes or until a knife inserted in center comes out clean. Remove from hot-water bath, and cool slightly; invert onto individual plates. **Prep: 35 min., Bake: 45 min.**

STEAK-AND-ONION SANDWICHES

MAKES 8 SANDWICHES

- 1 large yellow onion, coarsely chopped
- 2 large garlic cloves, coarsely chopped
- ½ cup lemon juice
- 2 tablespoons canola oil
- ½ teaspoon salt
- 1½ teaspoons freshly ground pepper
- 2 (1¼-pound) flank steaks
- 1 cup light mayonnaise
- ¼ cup salsa, drained
- 12 light rye bread slices
- 2 avocados, peeled and thinly sliced

PULSE onion and garlic in a food processor until finely chopped. Add juice and next 3 ingredients; pulse 2 times or until blended.

PLACE steaks in a large shallow dish or heavy-duty zip-top plastic bag, and pour onion mixture over steaks. Cover or seal bag, and chill 1 hour, turning occasionally.

REMOVE steaks from marinade, discarding marinade.

GRILL, covered with grill lid, over medium-high heat (350° to 400°) 5 minutes on each side or to desired degree of doneness. Cut across grain into thin slices.

STIR together mayonnaise and salsa; spread evenly on 1 side of each bread slice. Arrange steak evenly on half of bread slices; top with avocado slices and remaining bread slices. **Prep: 15 min., Chill: 1 hr., Grill: 10 min.**

LILANN TAYLOR
SAVANNAH, GEORGIA

Chicken Thighs Done Right

Taste why they deserve newfound respect—try these outstanding recipes.

Before you buy that next package of chicken breasts for dinner, consider using thighs instead. They offer more flavor than chicken breasts—with the same benefits of convenience and versatility—but at remarkably lower prices.

Best of all, the deep, assertive flavor of dark meat complements bold seasonings. Experiment with your favorite marinades or herb and spice blends, but do try our recipes. We think they'll convince you that chicken thighs are a cut above the rest.

HONEY-PECAN CHICKEN THIGHS

MAKES 4 SERVINGS

- ½ teaspoon salt
- ½ teaspoon ground black pepper
- ½ teaspoon ground red pepper
- ½ teaspoon dried thyme
- 8 skinned and boned chicken thighs
- ¾ cup honey, divided
- ¾ cup Dijon mustard, divided
- 2 garlic cloves, minced
- 1 cup finely chopped pecans
- ½ teaspoon curry powder
- Garnish: Italian parsley sprigs

COMBINE first 4 ingredients; sprinkle evenly over chicken in a shallow dish.
STIR together ½ cup honey, ½ cup mustard, and garlic; pour over chicken. Cover and chill 2 hours.
REMOVE chicken from marinade, discarding marinade. Dredge chicken in pecans; place on a lightly greased rack in an aluminum foil-lined broiler pan.

BAKE at 375° for 40 minutes or until chicken is done.
STIR together remaining ¼ cup honey, remaining ¼ cup mustard, and curry powder; serve sauce with chicken. Garnish, if desired. **Prep: 25 min., Chill: 2 hrs., Bake: 40 min.**

HERB-ROASTED CHICKEN THIGHS

MAKES 4 SERVINGS

- ⅓ cup dry white wine
- 2 tablespoons chopped fresh chives
- 1 tablespoon chopped fresh parsley
- 1 garlic clove, minced
- 2 tablespoons fresh lemon juice
- 2 tablespoons olive oil
- 2 teaspoons Greek seasoning or herbes de Provence
- ½ teaspoon salt
- ½ teaspoon pepper
- 8 skinned and boned chicken thighs

COMBINE first 9 ingredients in a shallow dish or large heavy-duty zip-top plastic bag; add chicken. Cover or seal, and chill 4 hours.
REMOVE chicken from marinade, discarding marinade. Place chicken on a lightly greased rack in an aluminum foil-lined broiler pan.
BAKE at 400° for 25 minutes or until chicken is done. **Prep: 15 min., Chill: 4 hrs., Bake: 25 min.**

SUE HESS
BARNHART, MISSOURI

ZESTY CHICKEN STEW

MAKES 10 CUPS

- ¾ teaspoon dried oregano
- ¾ teaspoon dried basil
- ¾ teaspoon salt
- ¾ teaspoon pepper
- 8 skinned and boned chicken thighs
- ¼ cup all-purpose flour
- 3 tablespoons olive oil, divided
- 1 large onion, chopped
- 1 cup dry white wine*
- 3 cups low-sodium chicken broth
- 3 medium-size red potatoes, peeled and diced
- 3 medium tomatoes or 6 plum tomatoes, peeled, seeded, and chopped
- 2 large carrots, sliced
- 1 bay leaf
- 3 tablespoons chopped fresh cilantro
- Hot cooked couscous

COMBINE oregano, basil, salt, and pepper, and sprinkle seasoning mixture evenly over chicken. Lightly dredge chicken in flour, shaking to remove excess.
BROWN 4 chicken thighs in 1 tablespoon hot oil in a Dutch oven over medium-high heat 3 to 4 minutes on each side. Remove chicken thighs, and set aside. Repeat procedure with remaining 4 chicken thighs and 1 tablespoon hot oil.
SAUTÉ onion in remaining 1 tablespoon hot oil in Dutch oven 3 minutes or until lightly browned. Stir in wine, and cook 2 to 3 minutes.
RETURN chicken to Dutch oven; add chicken broth and next 4 ingredients. Partially cover, reduce heat, and simmer, stirring occasionally, 45 minutes. Stir in cilantro; remove and discard bay leaf. Serve over couscous. **Prep: 45 min.; Cook: 1 hr., 10 min.**

*Substitute 1 cup chicken broth for dry white wine, if desired.

JANET M. MARTINEAU
BALTIMORE, MARYLAND

The World's Easiest Cakes

These delectable dump-and-stir desserts are as simple to make as their name implies.

These versatile delights, especially Apple-Blueberry Crunch or Cherry-Pineapple Dump Cake, can be made with almost any canned fruit and any flavor of cake mix. Add butter and your choice of chopped nuts to create your own version. (See facing page for a few of our suggestions.) You'll be ready to enjoy an old-fashioned dessert no matter where you choose to serve it. Just don't forget the ice cream—homemade or from the store.

APPLE-BLUEBERRY CRUNCH

MAKES 8 TO 10 SERVINGS

- 1 (21-ounce) can apple pie filling
- 1 (14-ounce) package frozen blueberries
- 1 cup sugar, divided
- 1 (18.25-ounce) package white cake mix
- ½ cup butter or margarine, melted
- 1 cup chopped walnuts, toasted
- Ice cream or whipped topping

SPREAD apple pie filling in a lightly greased 13- x 9-inch pan.
TOSS together frozen blueberries and ¾ cup sugar, and spoon over apple pie filling. Sprinkle cake mix evenly over fruit, and drizzle with melted butter. Sprinkle with chopped walnuts and remaining ¼ cup sugar.
BAKE at 350° for 45 to 50 minutes or until golden and bubbly. Serve with ice cream. **Prep: 10 min., Bake: 50 min.**

BARBARA SHERRER
BAY CITY, TEXAS

CHERRY-PINEAPPLE DUMP CAKE

MAKES 8 TO 10 SERVINGS

- 1 (20-ounce) can crushed pineapple, undrained
- 1 (21-ounce) can cherry pie filling
- 1 (18.25-ounce) package yellow cake mix
- ¾ cup butter or margarine, melted
- ½ cup chopped pecans, toasted
- Ice cream or whipped topping

SPREAD crushed pineapple in a lightly greased 13- x 9-inch pan. Top pineapple with cherry pie filling; sprinkle cake mix evenly over fruit. Drizzle with melted butter, and sprinkle with chopped pecans.
BAKE at 350° for 50 to 60 minutes or until golden and bubbly. Serve with ice cream. **Prep: 10 min., Bake: 1 hr.**

WILEY R. BEALES
ELIZABETH CITY, NORTH CAROLINA

BLACK FOREST CRISP

MAKES 8 TO 10 SERVINGS

- 1 (21-ounce) can cherry pie filling
- 1 (8¼-ounce) can crushed pineapple, undrained
- ½ cup slivered almonds, toasted
- 1 cup semisweet chocolate morsels
- 1 cup sweetened flaked coconut
- 1 (18.25-ounce) package devil's food cake mix
- ½ cup butter or margarine, cut up
- Ice cream or whipped topping

LAYER cherry pie filling, crushed pineapple, slivered almonds, chocolate morsels, and coconut in a lightly greased 13- x 9-inch baking dish. Sprinkle cake mix over layers, and dot evenly with butter.
BAKE at 350° for 45 to 50 minutes or until golden. Serve with ice cream. **Prep: 15 min., Bake: 50 min.**

DEBORAH CROY
BELTON, MISSOURI

TROPICAL DUMP CAKE

MAKES 8 TO 10 SERVINGS

Sweet pineapple and toasty pecans make this dessert a family favorite.

- 2 (20-ounce) cans crushed pineapple, undrained
- 1 (18.25-ounce) package white cake mix
- ½ cup butter or margarine, cut up
- 2 cups pecans, toasted
- Ice cream or whipped topping

DRAIN 1 can crushed pineapple; spread both cans of pineapple in a lightly greased 13- x 9-inch pan. Sprinkle cake mix over fruit. Dot evenly with butter; sprinkle with pecans.
BAKE at 350° for 45 to 50 minutes or until golden and bubbly. Serve with ice cream. **Prep: 10 min., Bake: 50 min.**

LOREE JEAN POWELL
GLOUCESTER, VIRGINIA

GERMAN CHOCOLATE SNACK CAKE

MAKES 18 SQUARES

This dessert requires a little more effort than the others, but it's worth it.

- 1 (18.25-ounce) package German chocolate cake mix
- 4 large eggs, divided
- ½ cup chopped pecans, toasted
- ½ cup butter or margarine, melted
- 1 (16-ounce) package powdered sugar
- 1 (8-ounce) package cream cheese, softened
- Ice cream or whipped topping

STIR together cake mix, 1 egg, pecans, and butter; press mixture into a lightly greased 13- x 9-inch pan.

BEAT powdered sugar, cream cheese, and remaining 3 eggs at medium speed with an electric mixer until creamy. Spoon powdered sugar mixture over batter in pan.

BAKE at 300° for 1 hour. Cool and cut into 2½- to 3-inch squares. Serve with ice cream. **Prep: 15 min., Bake: 1 hr.**

PATRICIA BEAM
FALLSTON, NORTH CAROLINA

Get Creative With Dump Cakes

Mix-and-match these ingredients according to the proportions used in our recipes for a wide variety of combinations. Or use this list to brainstorm even more sweet possibilities.

Frozen fruit: blueberries, raspberries, sliced strawberries

Canned pie fillings: apple, cherry, peach, blueberry, strawberry

Cake mixes: yellow, white, chocolate, spice, strawberry

Toasted nuts (chopped or slivered): pecans, walnuts, peanuts, almonds

Toppings: milk chocolate morsels, semisweet chocolate morsels, white chocolate morsels, sweetened flaked coconut, cinnamon chips

Crave Carrots

Will Rogers once said, "Some guy invented vitamin A out of a carrot. I'll bet he can't invent a good meal out of one." If you feel the same, we've gathered reader recipes that are sure to change your mind about these flavorful orange roots.

GLAZED CARROTS AND PARSNIPS

MAKES 6 SERVINGS

½ pound carrots (about 4)
½ pound parsnips (about 6)
2 tablespoons dried currants (optional)
2 tablespoons butter
2 tablespoons whole-grain mustard
2 tablespoons honey
¼ teaspoon salt
1 tablespoon chopped fresh parsley

CUT carrots and parsnips into 2- x ¼-inch strips. Cook carrot and parsnip in boiling water to cover in a large saucepan 10 to 12 minutes or until tender, adding currants, if desired, before the last 2 minutes; drain.

MELT butter in saucepan over medium heat; stir in mustard, honey, and salt until blended. Stir in carrot mixture, and cook until thoroughly heated. Sprinkle with chopped parsley. **Prep: 20 min., Cook: 15 min.**

SUE CONANT
CLEVELAND HEIGHTS, OHIO

SCALLOPED CARROTS

MAKES 6 SERVINGS

4 cups sliced carrot (about 11)
4 bacon slices, chopped
1 medium onion, chopped
1 (10¾-ounce) can cream of mushroom soup, undiluted
1 cup (4 ounces) shredded sharp Cheddar cheese
½ teaspoon pepper
2 cups herb-seasoned stuffing mix
¼ cup butter or margarine, melted

COOK carrot in boiling water to cover in a large saucepan 10 to 12 minutes or until tender. Drain and set aside.

COOK bacon in a large saucepan until crisp; remove bacon, and drain on paper towels, reserving 2 tablespoons drippings in pan.

SAUTÉ chopped onion in hot drippings 5 minutes or until tender. Stir in bacon, soup, Cheddar cheese, and pepper until cheese melts; stir in carrot. Spoon mixture into a lightly greased 11- x 7-inch baking dish.

STIR together stuffing mix and butter; spoon evenly over carrot mixture.

BAKE at 350° for 25 minutes. **Prep: 30 min., Cook: 12 min., Bake: 25 min.**

EILEEN R. MACUTCHAN
CLEARWATER, FLORIDA

CARROT-AND-DILL SALAD

MAKES 6 TO 8 SERVINGS

Brighten up your table with this "dill-icious" and easy-to-make salad.

2 (10-ounce) packages French-cut cooking carrots*
⅓ cup olive oil
¼ cup red wine vinegar
2 tablespoons lemon juice
2 tablespoons chopped fresh or 2 teaspoons dried dill
1 shallot, minced
1 garlic clove, minced
1 teaspoon salt
½ teaspoon pepper
Garnish: fresh dill sprig

COOK carrot in boiling water to cover in a medium saucepan 10 to 12 minutes or until tender. Plunge carrot into ice water to stop the cooking process, and drain.

WHISK together oil and next 7 ingredients in a medium bowl. Add carrot, and toss gently to coat. Cover and chill 2 hours. Garnish, if desired. **Prep: 20 min., Cook: 12 min., Chill: 2 hrs.**

*Substitute 2 pounds carrots, cut into 2- x ¼-inch strips, if desired.

DOROTHY J. CALLAWAY
COOLIDGE, GEORGIA

Sensational Spring Brunch

For easy, elegant entertaining, plan a brunch.

Serve our fabulous selections together as a menu for Mother's Day or any other celebration, or combine them with some of your favorite breakfast items. If you want to serve something sophisticated, try rich Ham and Eggs Mornay. Or if you prefer something sweet, try Make-Ahead French Toast With Strawberry Sauce. This, along with Gazpacho and Cucumber-Salmon Sandwiches With Dill, can be prepared in advance so you'll have plenty of time to enjoy the occasion.

Mother's Day Brunch

Serves 6

Gazpacho

Ham and Eggs Mornay

Cucumber-Salmon Sandwiches With Dill

Make-Ahead French Toast With Strawberry Sauce

Mimosas   Bloody Marys

GAZPACHO

MAKES 3 QUARTS

This refreshing soup makes the most of garden-fresh, ripe tomatoes. A jar of roasted red bell peppers contributes flavor and eases preparation.

- 2 large ripe tomatoes, chopped
- 2 yellow onions, chopped
- 2 medium cucumbers, peeled, seeded, and chopped
- 2 garlic cloves, minced
- 1 (7-ounce) jar roasted red bell peppers, drained
- ½ cup chopped fresh cilantro
- 1 (46-ounce) can tomato juice
- ¼ cup lime juice
- ¼ cup red wine vinegar
- 2 tablespoons olive oil
- 1½ teaspoons salt
- ½ teaspoon pepper
- 2 teaspoons hot sauce
- Sour cream (optional)
- Ground red pepper (optional)

PROCESS first 6 ingredients in a food processor until smooth, stopping to scrape down sides.

STIR together vegetable puree, tomato juice, and next 6 ingredients. Cover and chill at least 4 hours. Top gazpacho with sour cream, if desired, and sprinkle with ground red pepper, if desired. **Prep: 20 min., Chill: 4 hrs.**

ODESSA FELLS
BIRMINGHAM, ALABAMA

HAM AND EGGS MORNAY

MAKES 6 SERVINGS

Mornay sauce sounds fancy, but it's simply a white sauce fortified with cheese. Egg yolks add further richness.

- 1 (10-ounce) package frozen puff pastry shells
- 6 tablespoons butter or margarine, divided
- 3 tablespoons all-purpose flour
- 2 cups milk
- 2 egg yolks
- ¼ cup grated Parmesan cheese
- ¼ cup (1 ounce) shredded Swiss cheese
- 1½ cups diced cooked ham
- ¼ teaspoon salt
- ¼ teaspoon pepper
- 2 teaspoons white vinegar
- 6 large eggs
- ½ teaspoon paprika
- 3 tablespoons chopped fresh parsley

PREPARE puff pastry shells according to package directions; remove tops, and reserve.

MELT 3 tablespoons butter in a heavy saucepan over low heat, and whisk in flour until smooth. Cook butter mixture, whisking constantly, 1 minute. Gradually add milk; cook over medium heat, whisking constantly, until mixture is thickened and bubbly.

BEAT 2 egg yolks until thick and pale. Gradually whisk one-fourth of hot milk mixture into yolks; add to remaining hot milk mixture, whisking constantly. Add remaining 3 tablespoons butter; cook, whisking constantly, 2 to 3 minutes or until thickened. Add cheeses, stirring until melted. Remove from heat; stir in ham, salt, and pepper.

BRING 1½ inches water and 2 teaspoons vinegar to a boil in a large skillet, and reduce heat to maintain a light simmer. Gently break eggs, 1 at a time, into water. Simmer 5 to 7 minutes or until done. Remove eggs with a slotted spoon, trimming edges, if desired.

SPOON about 2 tablespoons sauce into each pastry shell, and top each with a poached egg. Spoon remaining sauce over eggs, and sprinkle with paprika and parsley. Replace pastry tops. **Prep: 15 min., Cook: 30 min.**

MICROWAVE POACHED EGGS: Place 2 tablespoons water in each of 6 (6-ounce) custard cups; add ¼ teaspoon vinegar to each. Microwave at HIGH 3 to 4 minutes or until water is boiling. Break 1 egg into each cup, and lightly pierce egg yolk with a wooden pick. Cover custard cups with heavy-duty plastic wrap, folding back a small portion of plastic wrap to allow steam to escape, and space cups evenly on a microwave-safe platter. Microwave eggs at MEDIUM-HIGH (70% power) for 3 to 3½ minutes or until most of egg white is opaque. Let stand 2 to 3 minutes. Serve as directed.

CUCUMBER-SALMON SANDWICHES WITH DILL

MAKES 24 SANDWICHES

> 1 (8-ounce) package cream cheese, softened
> 1 small cucumber, seeded, peeled, and diced
> 2 teaspoons chopped fresh dill
> 1 teaspoon fresh lemon juice
> ¼ teaspoon salt
> ⅛ to ¼ teaspoon ground red pepper
> 12 miniature bagels, split*
> 6 ounces smoked salmon, thinly sliced

PROCESS cream cheese and next 5 ingredients in a food processor until combined, stopping to scrape down sides. Cover cream cheese mixture, and chill 1 hour.

PLACE split bagels on a lightly greased baking sheet.

BAKE at 350° for 10 minutes or until bagels are toasted.

SPREAD cucumber mixture on cut side of each bagel half, and top each portion with smoked salmon. **Prep: 25 min., Chill: 1 hr., Bake: 10 min.**

*Substitute 24 miniature rye bread slices for bagels, if desired.

WENDY GOLDSTEIN
ROCKVILLE, MARYLAND

MAKE-AHEAD FRENCH TOAST WITH STRAWBERRY SAUCE

MAKES 10 SERVINGS

Challah bread is a rich egg bread with a light, airy texture.

> 1 (16-ounce) challah bread loaf, cubed*
> 1 (8-ounce) package cream cheese, cut into pieces
> 6 large eggs
> 4 cups half-and-half
> ½ cup butter or margarine, melted
> ¼ cup maple syrup
> 2 cups fresh strawberries, sliced
> 1 (10-ounce) jar strawberry preserves

ARRANGE half of challah bread in a lightly greased 13- x 9-inch pan. Sprinkle with cheese pieces, and top with remaining bread.

WHISK together eggs and next 3 ingredients; pour over bread mixture, pressing bread cubes to absorb egg mixture. Cover and chill 8 hours.

BAKE, covered, at 350° for 25 minutes. Uncover and bake 20 more minutes.

HEAT sliced strawberries and strawberry preserves in a saucepan over low heat, and serve over toast. **Prep: 25 min., Chill: 8 hrs., Bake: 45 min.**

*Substitute French bread, if desired.

TO LIGHTEN: Substitute 1 (8-ounce) package ⅓-less-fat cream cheese for cream cheese, 1½ cups egg substitute for eggs, and 4 cups fat-free milk for half-and-half.

SANDY LOMBARDO
MAPLE GLEN, PENNSYLVANIA

Irresistible Onion Rings

Ask folks where to find the best onion rings, and you'll get almost as many answers as there are places that serve the crispy golden gems.

If you can't make it to your favorite eatery before a craving hits, try our wonderful recipe—one of the best in our archives. A crisp-tender interior is surrounded by slightly sweet, crunchy batter. Once you taste 'em, you might even revise your opinion about which rings are the best.

BUTTERMILK BATTER-FRIED ONION RINGS

MAKES 4 SERVINGS

These are best served the moment they come out of the fryer.

> 2 large onions
> 1 cup all-purpose flour
> 2 cups buttermilk
> 1 tablespoon sugar
> 1 teaspoon baking powder
> ½ teaspoon salt
> Peanut oil

CUT onions into ½-inch slices, and separate into rings. Set aside.

WHISK together flour and next 4 ingredients until smooth.

POUR oil to a depth of 2 inches into a Dutch oven; heat to 375°.

DIP onion rings in batter, coating well. Fry a few rings at a time until golden. Drain on paper towels. Serve immediately. **Prep: 20 min., Cook: 10 min.**

from our kitchen

Grill Safely

Before you fire up the gas grill this month, make sure it's accident proof. Nowadays all gas cylinders are required to include an overfill-protection device, which shuts off the flow of gas into a cylinder at a safe 80% full capacity. (Cylinders that are filled more than 80% can release gas when heated, creating a fire hazard.)

A safe cylinder is equipped with a triangular knob—if the knob on yours is round or star shaped, it does not have the safety shutoff device. You can't refill a cylinder without it. Fortunately, you can exchange an outdated cylinder for a properly equipped one. For more information contact Blue Rhino Corporation, **www.bluerhino.com**; The National Propane Gas Association, **www.npga.org**; or the federal Consumer Product Safety Commission, **www.cpsc.gov**

Is It Still Good?

If homemade holiday food gifts linger on your shelves, make sure they're still safe to use. First, check the tags for instructions.

Dry mixes packed in sealed glass containers (soups, salad dressings, and beverages) are perfectly safe several months after they're assembled. The same mixes packed in plastic containers and bags should be fine too. Nuts get stale quickly, so check them if they're included in cake, cookie, and brownie mixes. Taste one to see if there's an odd or rancid flavor.

Jams and jellies are safe if the seals on the jars have not been broken. Once opened, these tasty condiments should be kept in the refrigerator. Discard any items you question.

If you're planning to make your own food gifts, be sure to include a "use by" date on the card, along with any storage information.

Spinach Savvy

Read Assistant Foods Editor Joy Zacharia's story on spinach (pages 120-121) to renew your love for this dark green vegetable. Our recipes will make you want to keep plenty of the popular leafy green on hand.

To prepare fresh spinach for the freezer, clean the leaves, and remove the stems; blanch two minutes in boiling water; drain and cool. Pack into airtight freezer containers or heavy-duty zip-top plastic bags. (Date and label before freezing.) Spinach will keep this way for about six months.

Here are some quick nutrition facts for 1 cup of raw spinach: 6.6 calories, 0.86 grams of protein, 1 gram of carbohydrate, 0.10 grams of fat, and 0.81 grams of fiber. It's also an excellent source of vitamin A and a good source of folate, vitamin C, beta-carotene, and lutein. The latter three nutrients are believed to reduce the incidence of macular degeneration, an eye disease that causes blindness.

Wait To Wash

With all the talk these days about food safety, we are very careful about washing produce when we bring it home. However, this hastens the spoilage of some foods. Protect your investment by storing the following fruits and vegetables unwashed: cherries, grapes, strawberries, green beans, mushrooms, and apples. The first five will stay fresh in the refrigerator for three to seven days; apples will keep considerably longer. Wash what you need just before using it.

Tips and Tidbits

■ Lots of recipes feature roasted bell peppers. Because the raw product can be expensive, you should take advantage of the times when it's on sale. Buy as many peppers as you can; then roast and freeze. Cook them directly over the flames on your gas cooktop or under the broiler, turning until blackened all over. Then drop them into a zip-top plastic bag to cool. The charred skins will slide off easily under running water. Seed the peppers, and pack in airtight freezer bags. Store frozen for about six months.

■ To remove excess fat from browned ground meat, transfer it from the skillet to a strainer or colander, drain on paper towels, and pat dry. This step removes fat, not flavor. You may choose to move all the meat to one side of the skillet, tilt the pan in the opposite direction, and pour off the drippings.

■ Fragrant fresh mint is good for so much more than juleps and iced tea. It brightens the flavors of tossed salads and fruit salsas as well; tomato sauce and dried beans also benefit from a leaf or two in the mix. No matter how you use it, this bracing herb perks up your recipes. (Nibble the mint garnish on your dessert plate for fresh after-dinner breath.)

■ At the end of a gathering, freeze any leftover wine in ice trays. (If you don't use it right away, wine loses its flavor.) Drop the cubes in an airtight freezer bag, and use to flavor soups and sauces, or to chill lemonade or tea.

June

Take the Party Outside

When the weather's inviting, host a gathering in the garden. Our do-ahead menu makes it easy.

Summer Garden Party

Serves 10 to 12

Lemon Flank Steak Skewers With
Lemon Dipping Sauce

Chilled Shrimp With Rémoulade Sauce

Balsamic Marinated Olives   Crusty bread

Spicy Jack Cheese Crisps

Creamy Citrus Tartlets   Mint Bellinis

You don't need excuses to bring a circle of friends together for an outdoor celebration.

We've selected a variety of foods for everyone's taste, from colorful Balsamic Marinated Olives to Chilled Shrimp With Rémoulade Sauce, which is always a crowd pleaser. Even if you're a beginning cook, you'll find the ingredient lists short and the techniques easy. It's okay to mix-and-match these recipes with some of your favorites. Choose your menu early, and set a work schedule that's doable. (See our make-ahead schedule on facing page.)

With your detailed planning, you'll have time to relax and be as fresh as a bouquet of hydrangeas when your guests arrive.

LEMON FLANK STEAK SKEWERS

MAKES 12 TO 16 APPETIZER SERVINGS

For easy slicing, freeze meat for 10 minutes first.

⅔ cup olive oil
4 teaspoons lemon zest
½ cup fresh lemon juice
2 teaspoons salt
½ teaspoon dried crushed red pepper
4 (2-pound) flank steaks, cut diagonally into ¼-inch slices
50 (12-inch) wooden skewers
Lemon Dipping Sauce
Garnish: Italian parsley

COMBINE first 5 ingredients in a shallow dish or heavy-duty zip-top plastic bag; add steak. Cover or seal, and chill 8 hours, turning occasionally.
PLACE skewers in water to cover, and let soak 10 minutes.
REMOVE steak from marinade, discarding marinade.
THREAD each steak slice onto 1 skewer.

GRILL skewers, covered with grill lid, over medium-high heat (350° to 400°) 4 to 5 minutes on each side or to desired degree of doneness. Serve with Lemon Dipping Sauce. Garnish, if desired. **Prep: 30 min., Chill: 8 hrs., Soak: 10 min., Grill: 10 min.**

Lemon Dipping Sauce:

MAKES 4½ CUPS

One medium lemon yields 2 to 3 tablespoons lemon juice and 1½ to 2 teaspoons lemon zest.

2 (16-ounce) containers light sour cream
2 tablespoons prepared horseradish
2 teaspoons lemon zest
6 tablespoons fresh lemon juice
1 teaspoon salt
Garnish: lemon zest

COMBINE first 5 ingredients; cover and chill at least 1 hour. Garnish, if desired. **Prep: 5 min., Chill: 1 hr.**

CHILLED SHRIMP WITH RÉMOULADE SAUCE

MAKES 4 POUNDS

In a hurry? Substitute 2 (2-pound) packages frozen cooked, peeled, and deveined large shrimp for fresh shrimp.

4 pounds unpeeled, large fresh shrimp, cooked
Rémoulade Sauce
Lemon wedges

PEEL shrimp, and devein, if desired.
SERVE shrimp with Rémoulade Sauce and lemon wedges. **Prep: 10 min.**

Rémoulade Sauce:

MAKES 1 CUP

¾ cup light mayonnaise
2 tablespoons chopped fresh parsley
2 tablespoons Creole mustard
1 tablespoon lemon juice
1 garlic clove, pressed
1 teaspoon paprika
¼ teaspoon salt

COMBINE all ingredients; cover and chill at least 1 hour. **Prep: 10 min., Chill: 1 hr.**

BALSAMIC MARINATED OLIVES

MAKES 6 CUPS

This make-ahead recipe can easily be halved.

> 2 (8-ounce) jars ripe olives,
>   drained
> 2 (7-ounce) jars kalamata olives,
>   drained
> 2 (7-ounce) jars pimiento-stuffed
>   olives, drained
> ½ cup olive oil
> ½ cup balsamic vinegar
> 1 tablespoon Italian seasoning

COMBINE all ingredients; cover and chill at least 8 hours. Let stand 30 minutes at room temperature before serving. **Prep: 10 min., Chill: 8 hrs., Stand: 30 min.**

SPICY JACK CHEESE CRISPS

MAKES 8 DOZEN

> ½ cup butter, softened
> 2 (8-ounce) blocks Monterey Jack
>   cheese with peppers, shredded
> 2 cups all-purpose flour
> 96 pecan halves

BEAT softened butter and Monterey Jack cheese at medium speed with an electric mixer until blended; add flour, beating until blended.

DIVIDE dough into 3 equal portions; shape each portion into a 6-inch log. Cover and chill at least 8 hours.

CUT each log into 32 (⅛-inch) slices, and place on ungreased baking sheets. Gently press 1 pecan half into center of each wafer.

BAKE, in batches, at 350° for 8 to 10 minutes. Remove crisps to wire racks to cool. Store in an airtight container. **Prep: 30 min., Chill: 8 hrs., Bake: 10 min. per batch**

Get It Done With Organization

Two weeks ahead:

- Send out invitations. (Plan a one-week lead time if using printed invitations. After choosing them, ask the printer for the envelopes so you can address them while waiting on the inserts.)
- Choose the color scheme; start collecting serving pieces and linens.
- Prepare and freeze dough logs for the Spicy Jack Cheese Crisps.
- Make and refrigerate Balsamic Marinated Olives.

One week ahead:

- Shop for pantry staples and beverages.
- Order flowers and greenery.

Three days ahead:

- Shop for perishable/refrigerated items.
- Order fresh shrimp.
- Prepare Mint Bellinis except for adding champagne or sparkling water; chill.
- Thaw dough logs in the refrigerator, and bake Spicy Jack Cheese Crisps as directed. Store in an airtight container at room temperature.

One to two days ahead:

- Make Lemon Dipping Sauce and Rémoulade Sauce; cover and chill.
- Purchase extra bags of ice for shrimp and Mint Bellinis. (If space is limited, ask neighbors if they can help with storage.)

One day ahead:

- Cook and peel shrimp. Store in a large zip-top plastic bag, and set over a pan of ice in refrigerator.
- Slice lemons for garnishes (crosswise slices for Mint Bellinis, wedges for shrimp). Wrap in a damp paper towel, and chill in a zip-top plastic bag.
- Bake tart shells for Creamy Citrus Tartlets. Store at room temperature in an airtight container or tin.
- Combine ingredients for Lemon Flank Steak Skewers, and marinate overnight in refrigerator.
- Chill bottles of champagne or sparkling water for the Mint Bellinis.
- Arrange serving pieces on the table. Write down recipe names on sticky notes, and attach them to each serving piece.

Party day:

- Grill Lemon Flank Steak Skewers, and chill (allow to come to room temperature before serving). Or grill just before guests arrive.
- Drain Balsamic Marinated Olives.
- Slice breads to accompany dishes.
- Make tartlet fillings.

CREAMY CITRUS TARTLETS

MAKES 30 TARTLETS

Look for orange and lemon curds on the grocery aisle with the jams and jellies.

 2 (2.1-ounce) packages frozen mini
 phyllo pastry shells
 1 cup whipping cream, divided
 ⅓ cup orange curd*
 ½ teaspoon almond extract, divided
 ⅓ cup lemon curd*
 Garnish: fresh mint leaves

BAKE pastry shells according to package directions; cool completely.
BEAT ½ cup whipping cream, orange curd, and ¼ teaspoon almond extract at medium speed with an electric mixer until thickened and soft peaks form. Spoon mixture evenly into half of pastry shells.
BEAT lemon curd, remaining ½ cup cream, and remaining ¼ teaspoon extract at medium speed with an electric mixer until thickened and soft peaks form. Spoon into remaining shells. Chill tartlets 1 hour. Garnish, if desired. **Prep: 30 min., Chill: 1 hr.**

*Substitute strawberry curd, if desired.

NOTE: For testing purposes only, we used Dickinson's Orange Curd and Lemon Curd.

MINT BELLINIS

MAKES 9½ CUPS

 4 (12-ounce) cans peach nectar
 2 cups sugar
 1 lemon, halved
 ¼ cup firmly packed fresh mint leaves
 1 (750-milliliter) bottle champagne or
 2½ cups sparkling water
 Garnish: lemon slices

BRING first 4 ingredients to a boil, and cook 20 minutes. Cool. Remove and discard lemon and mint; store mixture in an airtight container in refrigerator until ready to serve. Stir in champagne before serving. Serve over ice; garnish, if desired. **Prep: 10 min., Cook: 20 min.**

Tempting Tenderloins

These delectable, low-fat cuts of beef, pork, or turkey star in menus both simple and fancy.

There are so many reasons to appreciate tenderloin. Carved from an area where there's little fat surrounding or running through the meat, this succulent selection is leaner than many other choices. It's rather pricey, but the nutritional bonus and great flavor make it worth the cost. Remember to keep cooking time relatively short—you don't want to dry out this prize delicacy. Read on for some irresistible recipes and savvy shopping tips.

BEEF TENDERLOIN IN WINE SAUCE

MAKES 6 TO 8 SERVINGS

 1 (3-pound) beef tenderloin
 ½ teaspoon salt
 ½ teaspoon pepper
 ½ cup butter or margarine
 1 onion, thinly sliced
 1 garlic clove, minced
 1 (8-ounce) package sliced fresh
 mushrooms
 ½ cup dry red wine
 1½ teaspoons Worcestershire
 sauce
 1 teaspoon Italian seasoning
 1 teaspoon hot sauce
 1 cup beef broth
 1 teaspoon all-purpose flour

SPRINKLE beef evenly with salt and pepper. Place in an aluminum foil-lined roasting pan.
BAKE at 450° for 15 minutes.
MELT butter in a medium saucepan over medium heat. Add onion, garlic, and mushrooms; sauté 7 minutes. Stir in wine and next 3 ingredients. Whisk together beef broth and all-purpose flour, and stir into wine mixture. Reduce heat, and simmer, stirring occasionally, 10 minutes or until onion is tender.
REMOVE beef from oven, and top with sauce. Bake beef 18 more minutes or to desired degree of doneness, basting once. Transfer beef to a serving platter, reserving sauce in pan. Let beef stand 10 minutes before slicing. Serve with sauce. **Prep: 20 min., Bake: 33 min., Cook: 20 min., Stand: 10 min.**

JANIE BAUR
SPRING, TEXAS

PORK MEDAILLONS WITH BLACKBERRY SAUCE

MAKES 6 SERVINGS

 2 (1-pound) pork tenderloins
 1 teaspoon salt
 1 teaspoon coarsely ground black
 pepper
 1 teaspoon coarsely ground
 allspice
 ¼ cup butter or margarine,
 divided
 ½ cup diced shallots (about
 3 large)
 ⅔ cup dry white wine
 3 tablespoons seedless blackberry
 fruit spread
 Garnishes: fresh blackberries, fresh
 thyme sprigs

SPRINKLE pork evenly with salt, black pepper, and allspice. Cover and chill 30 minutes.

Let's Talk Tenderloin

These cuts are available at most large supermarkets, and you can save a lot if you catch them on sale. Here's a quick guide to each.

Beef

At about $13 to $20 a pound, this is a special-occasion purchase. Sometimes you can find a great deal on the whole tenderloin; also known as the short loin, it can vary between 3 and 6 pounds. Ask the butcher to cut it into two or more tenderloins or steaks (also known as filets mignons).

If you've got a nice dinner planned or just want to stock up, call the meat department at your local supermarket to find the best price. (Whole tenderloins are often as low as $8 a pound.) This cut takes well to broiling, grilling, or sautéing. Savory rubs and simple marinades lend vibrant flavor without a lot of work.

Pork

This long, narrow cut usually comes in packages of two weighing between 3 and 4 pounds; some markets sell it individually packaged. It generally costs about $6 a pound and $3 on sale.

Pork tenderloin is a terrific choice for busy folks because it cooks quickly and pairs well with sweet or savory flavors. Serve roasted or grilled, and then sliced.

Turkey

Sold whole or in medaillons (slices) for $4 to $5 a pound, this is an occasional addition to weeknight menus as well as fancier ones. Some grocers carry turkey mignons (the most tender cut) wrapped in bacon.

Much like pork, turkey tenderloins are versatile because of their mild flavor and ease of preparation. Cut into strips for a quick stir-fry or into cubes for kabobs. For a fabulous weeknight entrée, try Turkey Tenderloin Scaloppine (recipe at right). It calls for medaillons that are flattened with a mallet for superfast cooking.

GRILL pork, covered with grill lid, over medium-high heat (350° to 400°) 20 minutes or until a meat thermometer inserted into thickest portion registers 160°, turning pork once. Remove from grill, and let stand 10 minutes.

MELT 2 tablespoons butter in a small saucepan over medium-high heat while pork stands. Add shallots, and sauté 5 minutes or until tender. Add wine; cook 13 minutes or until liquid is reduced by half. Reduce heat to low; whisk in fruit spread and remaining

2 tablespoons butter. Cook 2 minutes or until slightly thickened.

CUT pork tenderloin into ¼-inch-thick slices. Drizzle blackberry sauce over pork. Garnish, if desired. **Prep: 15 min., Chill: 30 min., Grill: 20 min., Stand: 10 min., Cook: 20 min.**

NOTE: For testing purposes only, we used Polaner All Fruit for blackberry fruit spread.

KATHY HUNT
DALLAS, TEXAS

TURKEY TENDERLOIN SCALOPPINE

MAKES 4 SERVINGS

This impressive entrée is special enough to serve to guests, and its quick cooking time and relatively low cost allow it to double as a great weeknight dish. *(pictured on page 149)*

> 1½ pounds turkey breast tenderloins
> ⅓ cup all-purpose flour
> ½ teaspoon salt
> ½ teaspoon pepper
> 3 tablespoons butter, divided
> 1 tablespoon olive oil
> ½ cup dry white wine
> 3 tablespoons lemon juice
> 2 tablespoons chopped fresh Italian parsley
> 2 garlic cloves, minced
> 2 tablespoons capers
> Garnishes: lemon wedges, fresh Italian parsley

CUT turkey into ½-inch-thick slices. Place between 2 sheets of heavy-duty plastic wrap; flatten to ⅛-inch-thickness, using a meat mallet or rolling pin.

COMBINE flour, salt, and pepper, and dredge turkey in mixture.

MELT 2 tablespoons butter with oil in a large skillet over medium-high heat. Add turkey; cook, in batches, 1½ minutes on each side or until golden. Remove from skillet, and keep warm.

ADD remaining 1 tablespoon butter, wine, and juice to skillet, stirring to loosen bits from bottom of skillet. Cook 2 minutes or just until thoroughly heated.

STIR in parsley, garlic, and capers, and spoon over turkey. Garnish, if desired. Serve immediately. **Prep: 15 min., Cook: 15 min.**

NOTE: Serve over hot cooked angel hair pasta, if desired.

Potato Salad, Plain and Simple

When *Southern Living* Editor John Floyd told the Foods staff to get down to potato salad basics, he meant it: "No celery, onion, or pickle," he insisted. We could keep the hard-cooked eggs, even though some people consider them heresy. A recipe with only potato and mayo would be, well, no potato salad at all in our book.

Because John wanted readers to know that potato salad "is as easy as boiling eggs and potatoes and mixing them with mayonnaise," Senior Writer Donna Florio found herself on a mission. She asked co-workers, family, and strangers which ingredients they considered essential.

Opinions were strong—and strongly divided. She delved through old cookbooks and queried food researchers. She found a wide array of tastes, along with some unusual ingredients.

With all these considerations, finding one combination that would please many people offered quite a challenge.

Then Donna remembered the wonderfully simple and delicious version her niece Michele Fipps makes. She "married into" the recipe when she joined the Fipps family of Johns Island, South Carolina. "Most of my husband's surviving sisters make this the same way," Michele told Donna. "The recipe came from their mother, who called it 'poor man's salad.' We have it at every family gathering. I always make it right before we leave home, because we like it warm or at room temperature."

Recipe Development Director Mary Allen Perry came up with some variations for those of you who just can't do without a little celery, onion, or pickle. It's all a matter of what you consider the basics. Give this recipe a try, and let us know what you think.

FIPPS FAMILY POTATO SALAD

MAKES 8 TO 10 SERVINGS

Michele uses Duke's Mayonnaise and grates the eggs on the largest holes of a cheese grater.

    4 pounds baking potatoes (8 large)
    3 hard-cooked eggs, grated
    1 cup mayonnaise
    1 tablespoon spicy brown mustard
    1½ teaspoons salt
    ¾ teaspoon pepper

COOK potatoes in boiling water to cover 40 minutes or until tender; drain and cool. Peel potatoes, and cut into 1-inch cubes.
STIR together potato and egg.
STIR together mayonnaise and next 3 ingredients; gently stir into potato mixture. Serve immediately, or cover and chill, if desired. **Prep: 20 min., Cook: 40 min.**

RED POTATO SALAD: Substitute 4 pounds red potatoes (8 large red potatoes) for baking potatoes.

POTATO SALAD WITH SWEET PICKLE: Add ⅓ cup sweet salad cube pickles to potato mixture.

POTATO SALAD WITH ONION AND CELERY: Add 2 celery ribs, diced, and ½ small sweet onion, diced, to potato mixture.

LIGHT POTATO SALAD: Substitute 1 cup low-fat mayonnaise.

MICHELE FIPPS
JOHNS ISLAND, SOUTH CAROLINA

New Ideas for Fresh Beets

Beets are a most surprising vegetable. If you give them a try, you'll be amazed at their earthy flavor and versatility. Available year-round, they're most abundant March through July.

GLAZED ORANGE BEETS

MAKES 3 TO 4 SERVINGS

    2½ cups water
    2½ cups orange juice
    4 medium beets, peeled and cut into thin strips
    3 tablespoons butter or margarine
    2 tablespoons brown sugar
    ½ teaspoon salt
    ¼ teaspoon ground nutmeg

BRING 2½ cups water and orange juice to a boil over high heat. Add beet strips, and cook 20 minutes or until tender. Drain beets.
MELT butter in a saucepan over medium heat; add brown sugar, salt, and nutmeg, stirring until blended. Pour mixture over beet strips. **Prep: 25 min., Cook: 35 min.**

MARLYS WARD
MANKATO, MINNESOTA

PICKLED BEETS

MAKES 5 QUARTS

    3½ pounds small fresh beets
    3 medium onions, halved and sliced
    20 whole cloves
    4 (3-inch) cinnamon sticks
    4 cups white vinegar (5% acidity)
    2 cups sugar
    3 tablespoons salt

CUT tops from beets, leaving a 1-inch stem. Cook beets in boiling water to cover 30 minutes or until tender. Drain, reserving 3 cups liquid.
PACK beets and sliced onion into hot jars; set aside.
PLACE whole cloves on a 6-inch square of cheesecloth; tie with cheesecloth string.
BRING 3 cups reserved beet liquid, spice bag, cinnamon sticks, and remaining ingredients to a boil in a Dutch oven. Remove and discard spice bag and cinnamon sticks. Pour hot mixture into jars, filling to within ½ inch from top. Remove air bubbles, and wipe jar rims. Cover at once with metal lids; screw on bands.
PROCESS in boiling-water bath 10 minutes. **Prep: 35 min.; Cook: 30 min., Process: 10 min.**

ETHEL WHALEN
LEXINGTON, KENTUCKY

Pretty Pasta Salads

Welcome these cool creations to your table.

Have you ever tasted a dish that you liked so much you had to have the recipe for it? We guarantee friends and family will be smitten with these selections. Shrimp Pasta Salad With Green Goddess Dressing and Greek Pasta Salad are ideal for entertaining. Cheese Tortellini Pasta Salad is delectable weeknight fare.

SHRIMP PASTA SALAD WITH GREEN GODDESS DRESSING

MAKES 6 TO 8 SERVINGS

Our taste testers gave this rave reviews.

- 3 cups water
- 1 pound unpeeled, medium-size fresh shrimp
- 1 (8-ounce) package small shell pasta, cooked, rinsed, and drained
- 2 teaspoons champagne or white wine vinegar
- ⅛ teaspoon salt
- ⅛ teaspoon pepper
- 1 small head Green Leaf lettuce, separated into leaves
- 2 medium tomatoes, cut into wedges
- 1 yellow bell pepper, cut into strips
- Green Goddess Dressing

BRING 3 cups water to a boil, and add shrimp; cook 3 to 5 minutes or just until shrimp turn pink. Drain and rinse with cold water.

PEEL shrimp, and devein, if desired.

TOSS together pasta, vinegar, salt, and pepper. Line a large platter with lettuce leaves; spoon pasta in center, and top with shrimp. Arrange tomato and bell pepper around pasta. Serve salad with Green Goddess Dressing. **Prep: 30 min., Cook: 5 min.**

Green Goddess Dressing:

MAKES ABOUT 1⅓ CUPS

- 1⅓ cups mayonnaise
- ½ cup fresh parsley leaves
- 2 tablespoons chopped fresh chives
- 2 teaspoons champagne or white wine vinegar
- 1 teaspoon anchovy paste
- 1 teaspoon grated lemon rind
- 2 tablespoons fresh lemon juice
- ¼ teaspoon pepper

PROCESS all ingredients in a food processor until smooth, stopping to scrape down sides. Cover and chill. **Prep: 10 min.**

CHEESE TORTELLINI PASTA SALAD

MAKES 4 TO 6 SERVINGS

- ¼ cup balsamic vinegar
- 2 tablespoons chopped dried tomatoes
- 1½ tablespoons chopped fresh or dried rosemary
- 1 tablespoon sugar
- ¼ teaspoon salt
- ¼ teaspoon pepper
- ½ cup olive oil
- 2 (9-ounce) packages refrigerated cheese-filled tortellini, cooked, rinsed, and drained
- 1 pint grape tomatoes, cut in half
- 3 tablespoons minced red onion

PROCESS first 6 ingredients in a food processor; stop to scrape down sides. With processor running, pour oil in a slow, steady stream through food chute.

TOSS together tortellini, tomato halves, onion, and dressing in a large bowl. Cover and chill 2 hours. **Prep: 20 min., Chill: 2 hrs.**

GREEK PASTA SALAD

MAKES 4 SERVINGS

To save time, chill the pasta and beans together.

- 1 (8-ounce) package rotini, cooked
- 2 tablespoons olive oil
- ½ pound fresh green beans, trimmed and cut into bite-size pieces
- 1 head romaine lettuce, torn
- 2 celery ribs, sliced
- 2 tablespoons finely chopped red onion
- 4 ounces crumbled feta cheese
- 8 kalamata olives, pitted
- 2 large tomatoes, cut into wedges
- Greek Dressing

TOSS together pasta and oil; cover and chill 30 minutes to 1 hour.

COOK beans in boiling salted water to cover 4 minutes. Drain and chill 30 minutes to 1 hour.

LAYER lettuce, pasta, beans, and celery on a serving platter, and sprinkle with red onion, cheese, and olives. Arrange tomato wedges around salad; drizzle with ½ cup Greek Dressing, and serve immediately. Serve with remaining dressing. **Prep: 20 min., Cook: 4 min., Chill: 1 hr.**

Greek Dressing:

MAKES ¾ CUP

- ½ cup olive oil
- ¼ cup fresh lemon juice
- 2 tablespoons water
- 2 garlic cloves, pressed
- 1½ teaspoons chopped fresh basil
- ¾ teaspoon garlic salt
- ¼ teaspoon pepper

WHISK together all ingredients until blended. **Prep: 5 min.**

LINDA DAVIS
LANTANA, FLORIDA

Southern Fish and Chips

Crunchy, golden fillets and crispy, addictive chips make a perfect summer supper.

Fried fish and potatoes is a traditional British favorite, but making it with catfish gives it a Southern twist. We came up with three terrific variations. The first features a batter of flour, baking powder, ground red pepper, and dark beer. This creates a delicately crisp, nongreasy coating. Potato-Crusted Catfish and Chips uses potato flakes, cornmeal, and butter, producing delicious results. Southern-Fried Catfish and Chips relies on cornbread mix and buttermilk to make fillets extra crunchy.

BATTERED CATFISH AND CHIPS

MAKES 4 SERVINGS

- 4 large baking potatoes
- 2 cups all-purpose flour
- 1 tablespoon baking powder
- 1 teaspoon kosher salt
- ¼ teaspoon ground red pepper
- 1 (12-ounce) bottle dark beer
- Vegetable oil
- 1¼ teaspoons salt, divided
- ¾ teaspoon ground black pepper, divided
- 4 (6-ounce) catfish fillets
- Malt vinegar

CUT potatoes into paper-thin slices. Combine potato and water to cover in a large bowl; set aside.

COMBINE flour and next 3 ingredients. Add beer, whisking until smooth. Cover and chill 1 hour, if desired.

DRAIN potato well. Pour oil to a depth of 1½ inches into a heavy skillet; heat to 375°. Fry potato, in 4 batches, 2 to 3 minutes or until golden. Drain on paper towels; sprinkle with 1 teaspoon salt and ½ teaspoon black pepper. Keep warm.

SPRINKLE fish with remaining ¼ teaspoon each salt and black pepper. Dip fish in batter; carefully add to skillet, and fry, 2 fillets at a time, 1½ to 2 minutes on each side or until golden. Serve with chips and malt vinegar. **Prep: 15 min., Fry: 20 min.**

SOUTHERN-FRIED CATFISH AND CHIPS

MAKES 6 SERVINGS

- Peanut or vegetable oil
- 4 large baking potatoes, peeled and cut into thin strips
- 2½ cups yellow cornbread mix
- 1 tablespoon garlic powder
- 2 tablespoons dried thyme
- 6 (6-ounce) catfish fillets
- 1 cup buttermilk
- 1 tablespoon salt
- 2 teaspoons ground black pepper
- 2 teaspoons ground red pepper

POUR oil to a depth of 4 inches into a large Dutch oven, and heat to 375°. Fry potato strips, in 4 batches, 2 to 3 minutes or until golden. Drain on paper towels; keep warm.

COMBINE cornbread mix, garlic powder, and thyme in a shallow dish. Dip fish in buttermilk. Sprinkle with salt and peppers; dredge in dry mixture.

HEAT oil in Dutch oven to 400°; add fish, and fry 2 fillets at a time 2 to 3 minutes or until fillets float. Drain on paper towels; serve with chips. **Prep: 15 min., Fry: 21 min.**

POTATO-CRUSTED CATFISH AND CHIPS

MAKES 4 SERVINGS

- Vegetable oil
- 3 large baking potatoes, peeled and cut into thin strips
- 1¼ teaspoons salt, divided
- 4 (6-ounce) catfish fillets
- ¼ teaspoon pepper
- 1 cup yellow cornmeal
- 1 cup instant potato flakes
- ¼ cup butter or margarine, melted

POUR oil to a depth of 4 inches into a large Dutch oven, and heat to 375°. Fry potato strips, in 4 batches, 2 to 3 minutes or until golden. Drain on paper towels, and sprinkle with 1 teaspoon salt. Keep strips warm.

SPRINKLE fish evenly with remaining ¼ teaspoon salt and pepper. Combine cornmeal and instant potato flakes. Dip fish in melted butter, and dredge in cornmeal mixture.

HEAT oil in Dutch oven to 400°; add fish, and fry, 2 fillets at a time, 2 to 3 minutes or until fillets float. Drain on paper towels; serve with chips. **Prep: 15 min., Fry: 18 min.**

A Versatile Staple

There's no mistaking the South's long-standing love of cornbread. It's usually enjoyed hot from the oven and slathered with butter. However, in those rare instances when a fresh plateful isn't wiped clean, you can put leftover cornbread to work in surprisingly tasty ways. We think the following recipes will make you stand up and take notice.

Cornbread doesn't have to maintain its role as a side, either; we've given it a starring role in these two dishes. They can be palate-pleasing starters or light entrées. We've provided our Basic Cornbread recipe, but you can, of course, substitute your family's favorite recipe.

BASIC CORNBREAD

MAKES 6 SERVINGS

You can freeze this bread in a heavy-duty zip-top plastic bag up to one month. Thaw it in the refrigerator.

⅓ cup butter
2 cups self-rising white cornmeal
¾ cup all-purpose flour
1 tablespoon sugar
2¼ cups buttermilk
2 large eggs

PLACE butter in a 10-inch cast-iron skillet, and heat in a 425° oven 5 minutes or until melted.
COMBINE cornmeal, flour, and sugar in a large bowl.
STIR together buttermilk and eggs. Add to dry ingredients; stir just until moistened. Pour over melted butter in skillet.
BAKE at 425° for 25 minutes or until golden. Prep: 10 min., Bake: 25 min.

NOTE: For testing purposes only, we used White Lily Self-Rising White Cornmeal.

OPEN-FACED SHRIMP-CORNBREAD SANDWICHES

MAKES 6 ENTRÉE SERVINGS OR
12 APPETIZER SERVINGS

6 cups water
2 pounds unpeeled, medium-size fresh shrimp*
¾ cup mayonnaise**
½ small red onion, chopped
2 celery ribs, finely chopped
2 tablespoons chopped fresh chives
1 tablespoon chopped fresh tarragon
1 tablespoon lemon juice
½ teaspoon salt
1 teaspoon pepper
6 (4- x 2-inch) cornbread wedges, split
2 tablespoons butter or margarine, melted
1 head Bibb lettuce
3 plum tomatoes, sliced

BRING 6 cups water to a boil, and add shrimp; cook 3 to 5 minutes or just until shrimp turn pink. Drain and rinse in cold water.
PEEL shrimp; devein, if desired. Chop.
STIR together mayonnaise and next 7 ingredients in a large bowl; add shrimp. Cover and chill until ready to serve.
BRUSH cut sides of cornbread slices evenly with melted butter; place on a baking sheet.
BROIL 5 inches from heat 3 minutes or until toasted.
LAYER each cornbread slice with lettuce and tomato, and top with shrimp mixture. Prep: 30 min., Cook: 5 min., Broil: 3 min.

*Substitute medium-size frozen cooked shrimp, thawed, if desired.

**Substitute light mayonnaise for regular mayonnaise, if desired.

BRIAN LIPSON
LOS ANGELES, CALIFORNIA

LAYERED CORNBREAD-AND-TURKEY SALAD

MAKES 6 TO 8 SERVINGS

1 (15-ounce) bottle roasted garlic dressing
½ cup buttermilk
1 head romaine lettuce, shredded
1½ cups chopped smoked turkey (about ½ pound)
8 ounces crumbled feta cheese
1 (12-ounce) jar roasted red bell peppers, drained and chopped
2 cups cornbread, crumbled
8 bacon slices, cooked and crumbled
5 green onions, chopped

STIR together dressing and buttermilk, blending well.
LAYER a 3-quart glass bowl with half each of lettuce and next 6 ingredients; top with half of dressing. Repeat layers with remaining ingredients and dressing. Cover and chill 2 hours. Prep: 25 min., Chill: 2 hrs.

NOTE: For testing purposes only, we used T. Marzetti's Roasted Garlic Dressing.

JAKE BAGLEY
ORLANDO, FLORIDA

Spicy Blue Crabs

Blue crabs are among the South's great culinary treasures. This month, Atlantic and Gulf Coast waters teem with these delicious oceanic gems; now's the time to take advantage of their abundance. Hard-shell blue crabs are traditionally steamed; this simple recipe draws out the meat's natural sweetness.

STEAMED BLUE CRABS

MAKES 1 DOZEN

¼ cup plus 2 tablespoons coarse grain salt
¼ cup plus 2 tablespoons Old Bay seasoning
3 tablespoons ground red pepper
3 tablespoons pickling spice
2 tablespoons celery seeds
1 tablespoon dried crushed red pepper (optional)
White vinegar
12 live hard-shell crabs
Lemon Butter

COMBINE first 6 ingredients. Combine equal portions of water and vinegar to a depth of 1 inch in a stockpot; bring to a boil. Place a rack in stockpot over boiling liquid; arrange half of crabs on rack. Sprinkle with half of seasoning mixture.
COVER tightly with lid, and cook 20 to 25 minutes or until crabs turn bright red. Rinse with cold water, and drain well. Repeat with remaining crabs and seasoning mixture. Serve hot or cold with Lemon Butter. Prep: 10 min., Cook: 1 hr.

Lemon Butter:
MAKES 1¼ CUPS

1 cup butter
½ cup lemon juice

MELT butter in a saucepan over low heat. Skim foam off melted butter. Pour off clear butter, discarding solids. Add juice to clarified butter, stirring well. Chill; reheat before serving. Prep: 5 min.

Great Grilling

Try our chicken and vegetable selections cooked outdoors for a tasty meal with no fuss.

Grilling is a favorite way to cook during the summer. It doesn't heat up the house, it brings out the best in food, and afterward there's minimal cleanup. You can grill like the experts by following the tips in our "Chicken Pointers" box below.

Chicken Pointers

■ Place chicken quarters on grill with bony sides down. The bones act as heat conductors.

■ Cook until internal temperature reaches 180° for whole chicken, 170° for bone-in parts, and 160° for boneless parts. Juices should run clear when grilled chicken is pierced with a fork.

■ Discard marinade in which uncooked chicken has sat; never use it on cooked meat.

■ Do not leave cooked chicken at room temperature for more than two hours.

■ Do not place cooked chicken on a plate where uncooked poultry has sat.

MARINATED CHICKEN QUARTERS

MAKES 4 SERVINGS

Bone-in breast halves can be used in place of the chicken quarters.

   ½ cup butter or margarine, melted
   ½ cup lemon juice
   1 tablespoon paprika
   1 tablespoon dried oregano
   1 teaspoon garlic salt
   1 teaspoon dried or 1 tablespoon chopped fresh cilantro
   1 teaspoon ground cumin
   1 (2½-pound) whole chicken, quartered
   ½ teaspoon salt
   ½ teaspoon pepper

COMBINE first 7 ingredients; reserve ½ cup butter mixture.
SPRINKLE chicken evenly with salt and pepper. Place in shallow dishes or heavy-duty zip-top plastic bags; pour remaining butter mixture evenly over chicken.
COVER or seal, and chill, along with reserved butter mixture, 8 hours.
REMOVE chicken from marinade, discarding marinade.
GRILL, covered with grill lid, over medium-high heat (350° to 400°) 40 to 45 minutes or until done, basting often with reserved butter mixture and turning once. Prep: 15 min., Chill: 8 hrs., Grill: 45 min.

GAYLE MILLICAN
ROWLETT, TEXAS

LIME-GRILLED CHICKEN

MAKES 4 SERVINGS

   ⅓ cup lime juice
   1 tablespoon peanut oil
   1½ teaspoons soy sauce
   1 garlic clove, minced
   1 bay leaf
   4 skinned and boned chicken breast halves

COMBINE first 5 ingredients in a shallow dish or heavy-duty zip-top plastic bag; add chicken. Cover or seal, and chill 1 hour.
REMOVE chicken from marinade, discarding marinade.
GRILL, covered with grill lid, over medium-high heat (350° to 400°) 4 minutes on each side or until done. Prep: 10 min., Chill: 1 hr., Grill: 8 min.

LAURIE TIEMAN
NEW BRAUNFELS, TEXAS

EASY VEGETABLE KABOBS

MAKES 4 SERVINGS

   8 small mushroom caps
   2 small zucchini, cut into 8 slices
   1 medium-size yellow bell pepper, cut into ½- to ¾-inch pieces
   1 small red onion, cut into 1½-inch pieces
   ½ cup butter or margarine, melted
   1 tablespoon chopped fresh basil
   1 teaspoon garlic powder

THREAD vegetables evenly onto 12-inch metal skewers.
STIR together melted butter, basil, and garlic powder; reserve ¼ cup butter mixture, and set aside.
COAT food rack with cooking spray; place on grill. Place vegetables on rack.
GRILL, covered with grill lid, over medium-high heat (350° to 400°) 20 to 25 minutes or until vegetables are tender, turning and basting with remaining butter mixture every 5 minutes. Serve with reserved butter mixture. Prep: 20 min., Grill: 25 min.

DEBRA SCHNEIDER
MARIETTA, GEORGIA

Speedy Southwestern Fare

South-of-the-border recipes have never been so fast—and so good.

If you enjoy Tex-Mex flavors, you must give these quick, delicious recipes a try. Whether you're planning a party or a weeknight dinner, you'll love preparing and serving these simple selections.

EASY ENCHILADA CASSEROLE

MAKES 8 SERVINGS

1 medium onion, chopped
2 tablespoons vegetable oil
1 (19-ounce) can enchilada sauce
1 (16-ounce) can black beans, rinsed
  and drained
1 (14½-ounce) can diced tomatoes
  with jalapeños
1 (11-ounce) can Mexican-style corn,
  drained
1 teaspoon fajita seasoning or chili
  powder
1 teaspoon ground cumin
1 (10-ounce) package 6-inch corn
  tortillas
3 cups chopped cooked chicken*
3 cups (12 ounces) shredded Mexican
  four-cheese blend

SAUTÉ onion in hot oil in a large skillet over medium-high heat until tender. Stir in next 6 ingredients. Reduce heat to low, and cook, stirring often, 5 minutes or until thoroughly heated.
SPOON one-third of sauce mixture into a lightly greased 13- x 9-inch baking dish. Layer with one-third of tortillas, half of chopped chicken, and 1 cup cheese. Repeat layers with one-third each of sauce mixture and tortillas, remaining chicken, and 1 cup cheese. Top with remaining tortillas, sauce mixture, and 1 cup cheese.
BAKE at 350° for 15 to 20 minutes or until golden and bubbly. **Prep: 15 min., Bake: 20 min.**

*Substitute 2 pounds lean ground beef, cooked, if desired.

CANDI GANDLER
BIRMINGHAM, ALABAMA

CINNAMON-CHOCOLATE CHIP ICE-CREAM BALLS

MAKES 6 SERVINGS

1½ cups cinnamon-sugar whole
  wheat-and-rice cereal, crushed
½ cup semisweet chocolate mini-
  morsels
1 cup finely chopped pecans
  (optional)
½ gallon vanilla ice cream
Caramel syrup

COMBINE crushed cereal, morsels, and, if desired, pecans in a large bowl.
SCOOP out ice cream, and shape into 6 (3-inch) balls.
ROLL balls in cereal mixture, coating evenly. Place in a 9-inch square pan; freeze 2 hours or until firm. Drizzle with caramel syrup before serving. **Prep: 25 min., Freeze: 2 hrs.**

NOTE: For testing purposes only, we used Cinnamon Toast Crunch cereal.

QUICK QUESADILLAS

MAKES 6 APPETIZER SERVINGS

For easier flipping, place one tortilla in the skillet, top with fillings, and fold in half. Cook as directed, and cut into triangles.

6 (6-inch) flour tortillas
¾ cup (3 ounces) shredded Monterey
  Jack cheese
¾ cup (3 ounces) shredded Cheddar
  cheese
1 (4-ounce) can chopped green chiles,
  undrained
3 medium plum tomatoes, chopped
Vegetable cooking spray
Sour cream
Salsa

PLACE 1 flour tortilla in a small lightly greased nonstick skillet. Sprinkle with 2 tablespoons each of shredded cheeses. Spread with 1 tablespoon chiles; sprinkle with 3 tablespoons tomatoes. Top with 1 tortilla; coat with cooking spray.
COOK quesadillas over low heat 2 to 3 minutes on each side or until golden. Remove from skillet; keep warm.
REPEAT procedure with remaining tortillas, cheeses, chiles, and tomatoes. Cut each quesadilla into 6 triangles. Serve with sour cream and salsa. **Prep: 10 min., Cook: 18 min.**

SHARON SYLVESTER
TULSA, OKLAHOMA

BLUE MARGARITAS

MAKES ABOUT 5 CUPS

For an even coating around the rim of each glass, dip first in lime juice and then salt.

1 (10-ounce) can frozen margarita mix
¾ cup tequila
¼ cup blue curaçao liqueur
2 tablespoons lime juice

COMBINE all ingredients in a blender. Fill with ice to 5-cup level, and process until smooth. Serve immediately. **Prep: 5 min.**

LISA GOLDSTEIN
BRENTWOOD, TENNESSEE

Real Food, Healthfully

Cathryn Matthes shares her love of cooking (and eating) with guests of the Hilton Head Health Institute in Hilton Head, South Carolina. As executive chef, she whips up inviting, nutritious recipes.

Cathryn packs her cooking classes and demonstrations with user-friendly tips. She challenges her audiences to experiment with new foods to avoid boredom. As one of the guests says, "Cathryn creates magic with healthy food."

PORK CHOPS WITH WARM PINEAPPLE SALSA

MAKES 6 SERVINGS

Enjoy with a side of thinly sliced green beans and fluffy couscous or brown rice.

    6 (6-ounce) lean boneless pork chops
    Caribbean Spice Rub
    Vegetable cooking spray
    Warm Pineapple Salsa

RUB pork evenly with Caribbean Spice Rub. Place on a broiler rack coated with cooking spray; place rack in broiler pan.
BROIL 5 inches from heat 5 minutes on each side or until done. Serve with Warm Pineapple Salsa. **Prep: 5 min., Broil: 10 min.**

Caribbean Spice Rub:

MAKES ⅓ CUP

    2 tablespoons ground allspice
    1 tablespoon ground ginger
    1 tablespoon dried thyme, crushed
    1 tablespoon garlic powder
    1 tablespoon onion powder
    2 teaspoons salt
    ½ teaspoon freshly ground black
       pepper
    ⅛ teaspoon ground red pepper

COMBINE all ingredients. Store in an airtight container. **Prep: 5 min.**

Warm Pineapple Salsa:

MAKES 6 TO 8 SERVINGS

    2 shallots, finely chopped
    1 jalapeño pepper, minced
    1½ teaspoons grated fresh
       ginger
    Vegetable cooking spray
    1¼ cups fresh orange juice
    1 pineapple, peeled and chopped
    1 tablespoon chopped fresh mint
    1 tablespoon chopped fresh basil
    ½ teaspoon curry powder

SAUTÉ first 3 ingredients in a skillet coated with cooking spray over high heat 2 minutes. Add juice, and cook 5 minutes or until mixture is reduced by half. Stir in pineapple and remaining ingredients; reduce heat to low, and cook until thoroughly heated. **Prep: 10 min., Cook: 10 min.**

Per serving: Calories 318 (34% from fat); Fat 12g (sat 4g, mono 4.9g, poly 1.2g); Protein 32g; Carb 21g; Fiber 2.5g; Chol 91mg; Iron 2.6mg; Sodium 858mg; Calc 59mg

ROASTED RED PEPPER-DILL DRESSING

MAKES 2¼ CUPS

    4 large red bell peppers
    4 medium shallots, minced
    1 teaspoon olive oil
    1½ teaspoons dried dill
    ½ cup vegetable broth
    ½ cup rice vinegar
    1 teaspoon honey
    1 teaspoon salt
    ½ teaspoon pepper

BAKE bell peppers on an aluminum foil-lined baking sheet at 500° for 20 minutes or until bell peppers look blistered, turning once. Place bell peppers in a zip-top plastic bag; seal and let stand 10 minutes to loosen skins. Peel bell peppers; remove and discard seeds.
SAUTÉ shallots in hot oil in a skillet over medium-high heat until softened. Remove from heat; stir in dill.
PROCESS peppers, shallot mixture, broth, and remaining ingredients in a blender until smooth. **Prep: 20 min., Bake: 20 min., Stand: 10 min.**

Per ¼ cup: Calories 24 (20% from fat); Fat 0.6g (sat 0.1g, mono 0.4g, poly 0.1g); Protein 0.7g; Carb 4.6g; Fiber 0.5g; Chol 0mg; Iron 0.4mg; Sodium 434mg; Calc 10.3mg

CREAMY MISO-GINGER DRESSING

MAKES 1 CUP

Serve this fragrant mixture over salad greens or broiled fish.

    4 ounces low-fat silken tofu
    2 tablespoons light miso*
    1 green onion, chopped
    2 teaspoons grated fresh ginger
    ⅓ cup fresh orange juice
    1 teaspoon lite soy sauce
    1 teaspoon brown sugar
    1 teaspoon dark sesame oil

PROCESS all ingredients in a blender or food processor until mixture is smooth. Cover and chill until ready to serve. **Prep: 10 min.**

*Miso is fermented soybean paste, an ingredient commonly used in Japanese cooking. It comes in a variety of flavors and colors and has the consistency of peanut butter. Look for it in the Asian-food sections of large supermarkets, in Asian food stores, or in health food stores.

Per 2 tablespoons: Calories 26 (32% from fat); Fat 0.9g (sat 0.1g, mono 0.1g, poly 0.2g); Protein 1.5g; Carb 3g; Fiber 0.3g; Chol 0mg; Iron 0.2mg; Sodium 220mg; Calc 7mg

COUNTRY CHICKEN-AND-BUTTERMILK SOUP

MAKES 8½ CUPS

    4 skinned and boned chicken breast
       halves (about 1½ pounds)
    5 cups low-sodium fat-free chicken
       broth
    1 tablespoon butter or margarine
    2 medium-size red potatoes, cut into
       wedges
    1 celery rib, chopped
    ¼ large white onion, coarsely
       chopped
    ½ carrot, peeled and chopped
    ½ cup fresh or frozen green peas
    ½ cup fresh or frozen corn kernels
    1 tablespoon chopped fresh parsley
    2 cups nonfat buttermilk
    ½ cup all-purpose flour
    ½ teaspoon salt
    ½ to 1 teaspoon dried crushed red
       pepper
    1 teaspoon Worcestershire sauce

BRING chicken and broth to a boil in a large saucepan, and cook 5 to 7 minutes or until done. Drain, reserving 4 cups broth. Let chicken cool, and chop.

MELT butter in a Dutch oven; add potato wedges and next 3 ingredients, and sauté 3 to 4 minutes or until onion is tender. Add reserved broth, and simmer 30 minutes or until potato is tender. Add chicken, peas, corn, and parsley.

STIR together buttermilk and flour until smooth; add to potato mixture, and cook, stirring constantly, 5 minutes. Stir in salt, red pepper, and Worcestershire sauce. **Prep: 30 min., Cook: 46 min.**

Per 1 cup: Calories 204 (14% from fat); Fat 3.1g (sat 1.5g, mono 0.8g, poly 0.4g); Protein 25g; Carb 20g; Fiber 2g; Chol 52mg; Iron 1.5mg; Sodium 652mg; Calc 91mg

Snacks Make a Splash

It's that time of year when entertaining gets laid-back and is often near a refreshing pool, lake, river, or ocean. Add these flavorful, easy-to-prepare appetizers to your outdoor menu.

SANTA FE SEEDS

MAKES 2 CUPS

Reader Roxanne Chan takes a spicy approach with this recipe. "I use crushed red pepper and chili powder, but you can adjust the heat according to your taste," she says. We gave it a big thumbs-up.

- ½ teaspoon ground cumin
- ½ teaspoon chili powder
- ¼ teaspoon dried crushed red pepper
- 2 tablespoons olive oil
- 2 tablespoons sugar
- 1 tablespoon honey
- 1 cup pumpkin seeds
- 1 cup sunflower seeds

STIR together first 3 ingredients in hot oil in a medium-size nonstick skillet over medium-high heat 30 seconds. Stir in sugar and honey, stirring until sugar dissolves.

ADD seeds; cook, stirring constantly, 8 minutes or until toasted. Spread on lightly greased aluminum foil-lined baking sheets; separate seeds, if necessary. Cool. Store in an airtight container. **Prep: 5 min., Cook: 10 min.**

ROXANNE CHAN
ALBANY, CALIFORNIA

CHEESY BACON PUFFS

MAKES ABOUT 5 DOZEN

- 1½ cups water
- ½ cup butter or margarine
- 1½ cups all-purpose flour
- ½ teaspoon salt
- ¼ teaspoon ground black pepper
- ⅛ teaspoon ground red pepper
- ⅛ teaspoon garlic powder
- 6 large eggs
- 2 cups (8 ounces) shredded sharp Cheddar cheese
- 8 bacon slices, cooked and crumbled
- ½ cup chopped fresh chives*

COMBINE 1½ cups water and butter in a heavy saucepan; bring to a boil.

COMBINE flour and next 4 ingredients in a bowl, and mix well. Add flour mixture to pan, and cook, beating with a wooden spoon, 5 minutes or until mixture leaves sides of pan and forms a smooth ball. Remove mixture from heat, and cool 5 minutes.

ADD eggs, 1 at a time, beating well after each addition. Beat in cheese, bacon, and chives.

DROP by rounded teaspoonfuls 2 inches apart onto lightly greased baking sheets.

BAKE at 400° for 20 to 25 minutes or until golden. **Prep: 10 min., Cook: 10 min., Cool: 5 min., Bake: 25 min.**

*Substitute finely chopped green onions for chives, if desired.

BONNIE WARREN
NEW ORLEANS, LOUISIANA

TORTILLA BITES WITH SESAME-SOY DIPPING SAUCE

MAKES 40 APPETIZERS

- 2 (8-ounce) containers roasted-garlic cream cheese, softened
- 10 (6-inch) flour tortillas
- 3 cups cold cooked long-grain rice
- ¼ (10-ounce) package shredded carrot (about 1 medium carrot)
- 1 medium cucumber, peeled, seeded, and cut into thin strips
- 3 medium avocados, thinly sliced
- 2 cups fresh spinach, shredded
- ½ cup sesame seeds, toasted
- 1 pound fresh lump crabmeat, drained*
- Sesame-Soy Dipping Sauce

SPREAD cream cheese evenly over 1 side of each tortilla; top one half of each tortilla evenly with cooked rice and next 6 ingredients. Roll up tortillas tightly, and cut each tortilla crosswise into 4 slices. Serve immediately, or chill. Serve with Sesame-Soy Dipping Sauce. **Prep: 20 min.**

*Substitute canned crabmeat, tuna, or chopped cooked chicken for fresh lump crabmeat, if desired.

SHARYN L. HILL
ORGAN, NEW MEXICO

Sesame-Soy Dipping Sauce:

MAKES ABOUT ¼ CUP

- ¼ cup soy sauce
- ½ teaspoon dried crushed red pepper
- ¼ teaspoon ground ginger
- 1 tablespoon sesame oil

WHISK together first 3 ingredients in a bowl. Gradually whisk in oil. Cover and chill until ready to serve. **Prep: 5 min.**

Scrumptious Strawberry Pies

Savor the season's bounty
with these irresistible desserts.

Homemade pies deserve only the very best fruit. Visit a "U-pick" farm to select your own strawberries, or head to the supermarket to get these ruby jewels at the peak of ripeness.

Reader Kay Wilkerson of Greenville, North Carolina, fondly recalls serving Strawberry-Mascarpone Tart for the first time to her supper club during the spring, when beautiful berries were available. She declares, "This recipe turned out perfectly and is the prettiest dessert I've ever made."

STRAWBERRY-MASCARPONE TART

MAKES 1 (9-INCH) TART

Plan ahead when preparing this recipe—the steps are easy, but the components require chilling separately. Kay Wilkerson also suggests using a good-quality balsamic vinegar when making Marinated Strawberries With Balsamic-Strawberry Syrup.

- ½ cup plus 2 tablespoons unsalted butter, softened
- ⅓ cup granulated sugar
- 2 tablespoons milk
- 1 egg yolk
- 1½ cups all-purpose flour
- 1 tablespoon powdered sugar
- ⅛ teaspoon salt
- Mascarpone Filling
- Marinated Strawberries
- Balsamic-Strawberry Syrup

BEAT butter at medium-high speed with an electric mixer until creamy; gradually add ⅓ cup sugar, beating well. Add milk and egg yolk, beating until blended.

COMBINE flour, powdered sugar, and salt. Add to butter mixture, beating at low speed just until a dough forms.
SHAPE dough into a thick disk; wrap in plastic wrap, and chill 2 hours.
ROLL dough to ¼-inch thickness on a lightly floured surface. Carefully press dough into bottom and 2 inches up sides of a lightly greased 9-inch springform pan; trim off excess dough along edges. Freeze 10 minutes.
LINE dough with aluminum foil, and fill with pie weights or dried beans.
BAKE at 400° for 6 minutes. Remove pie weights and foil, and bake 6 to 10 more minutes or until firm. (Do not brown.) Cool on a wire rack. Gently run a knife around edge of pan, and release sides.
SPREAD Mascarpone Filling in tart shell; arrange Marinated Strawberries over tart. Cut tart into slices, and drizzle with Balsamic-Strawberry Syrup. Serve immediately. **Prep: 20 min., Chill: 2 hrs., Freeze: 10 min., Bake: 16 min.**

Mascarpone Filling:

MAKES ABOUT 2½ CUPS

- 1 (16-ounce) package mascarpone cheese*
- ¼ cup whipping cream
- ⅓ cup sugar
- 1 tablespoon vanilla extract
- ½ teaspoon grated orange rind

STIR together all ingredients just until smooth. **Prep: 5 min.**

*Substitute 2 (8-ounce) packages cream cheese, softened; ⅓ cup sour cream; and ¼ cup whipping cream, beaten until blended, if desired.

Marinated Strawberries With Balsamic-Strawberry Syrup:

MAKES ¼ CUP

- 3 pints fresh strawberries, sliced
- ½ cup balsamic vinegar
- 3 tablespoons sugar

TOSS together all ingredients until sugar dissolves. Cover strawberry mixture, and chill 2 hours, gently stirring occasionally.
POUR strawberry mixture through a fine wire-mesh strainer into a saucepan, reserving strawberries for tart.
BRING strawberry liquid to a boil over medium-high heat, and cook, stirring constantly, 2 minutes or until liquid is reduced to a syrup. Remove strawberry liquid from heat, and cool. **Prep: 5 min., Chill: 2 hrs., Cook: 2 min.**

KAY WILKERSON
GREENVILLE, NORTH CAROLINA

EASY STRAWBERRY PIE

MAKES 1 (9-INCH) PIE

This simple, delicious dessert is reminiscent of a familiar classic served at a well-known national restaurant chain.

- 1 cup sugar
- 1 cup water
- 3 tablespoons cornstarch
- ¼ cup strawberry gelatin
- 4 cups fresh strawberries, halved
- 1 baked (9-inch) pastry shell
- Sweetened whipped cream or frozen whipped topping, thawed (optional)

BRING first 3 ingredients to a boil in a saucepan over medium heat, and cook, stirring constantly, 1 minute or until thickened. Stir in strawberry gelatin until dissolved. Remove from heat; chill 2 hours.
ARRANGE strawberries in pastry shell, and pour gelatin mixture over strawberries. Cover and chill 2 hours. Uncover and, if desired, serve pie with whipped cream. **Prep: 30 min., Cook: 8 min., Chill: 4 hrs.**

THELMA CLARK
CLARKSVILLE, ARKANSAS

Fried Strawberry Pies

MAKES 18 PIES

Freeze the pies before frying to prevent the crusts from disintegrating in the hot oil. Hide one for yourself before they all get away.

- **2 cups fresh strawberries, mashed**
- **¾ cup granulated sugar**
- **¼ cup cornstarch**
- **1 (15-ounce) package refrigerated piecrusts**
- **Vegetable oil**
- **Powdered sugar**

COMBINE first 3 ingredients in a saucepan. Bring strawberry mixture to a boil over medium heat. Cook, stirring constantly, 1 minute or until thickened. Cool completely.

ROLL 1 piecrust to press out fold lines; cut into 9 circles with a 3-inch round cutter. Roll circles to 3½-inch diameter; moisten edges with water. Spoon 2 teaspoons strawberry mixture in the center of each circle; fold over, pressing edges to seal. Repeat with remaining piecrust and strawberry mixture.

PLACE pies in a single layer on a baking sheet, and freeze at least 1 hour.

POUR oil to a depth of 1 inch into a large heavy skillet; heat to 350°. Fry pies, in batches, 1 minute on each side or until golden. Drain on paper towels; sprinkle with powdered sugar. **Prep: 30 min., Cook: 6 min., Freeze: 1 hr., Fry: 2 min. per batch**

MARJORIE HENSON
BENTON, KENTUCKY

Double-Stuffed Vegetables

These recipes highlight fresh, flavor-packed produce.

Spinach-and-Basil Stuffed Eggplant

MAKES 4 SERVINGS

- **1 large eggplant**
- **1 large egg**
- **2 tablespoons milk**
- **¾ cup Italian-seasoned breadcrumbs**
- **2 tablespoons olive oil**
- **1 large egg, lightly beaten**
- **1 (15-ounce) container ricotta cheese**
- **1 (6-ounce) package fresh baby spinach, shredded**
- **1 cup (4 ounces) shredded mozzarella cheese**
- **½ cup (2 ounces) shredded Parmesan cheese**
- **½ cup chopped fresh basil**
- **½ teaspoon seasoned pepper**
- **¼ teaspoon salt**
- **1 (26-ounce) jar marinara sauce**

CUT eggplant lengthwise into 8 slices.

WHISK together 1 egg and milk until smooth. Dip eggplant in egg mixture; dredge in breadcrumbs.

COOK eggplant, in batches, in hot oil in a skillet over medium-high heat 2 minutes on each side or until golden.

COMBINE remaining egg and next 7 ingredients; spread over each eggplant slice. Roll up eggplant; secure with a wooden pick, if necessary.

SPOON half of marinara sauce into a lightly greased 11- x 7-inch baking dish. Arrange eggplant rolls, seam sides down, over sauce; top with remaining sauce.

BAKE, loosely covered, at 350° for 45 to 50 minutes. Uncover; let stand 10 to 15 minutes. **Prep: 30 min., Cook: 4 min. per batch, Bake: 50 min., Stand: 15 min.**

YVONNE EVANS
TUSCALOOSA, ALABAMA

Stuffed Peppers With Chicken and Corn

MAKES 8 SERVINGS

- **4 large red bell peppers**
- **1 (12-ounce) package frozen corn soufflé, thawed**
- **3 cups chopped cooked chicken**
- **1 cup fresh corn kernels**
- **¾ cup soft breadcrumbs**
- **1 (4.5-ounce) can chopped green chiles, drained**
- **½ medium-size sweet onion, finely chopped**
- **1 tablespoon taco seasoning**
- **2 cups (8 ounces) shredded Monterey Jack cheese with peppers, divided**
- **Garnish: chopped fresh cilantro**

CUT peppers in half lengthwise, leaving stems intact; remove seeds. Place cut sides down on a lightly greased baking sheet. Broil 6 inches from heat 4 to 5 minutes or until peppers begin to blister.

COMBINE corn soufflé and next 6 ingredients; stir in 1 cup cheese.

TURN peppers cut sides up; spoon corn mixture evenly into peppers.

BAKE at 375° for 25 minutes. Top evenly with remaining 1 cup cheese; bake 5 to 10 minutes or until cheese melts. Garnish, if desired. **Prep: 25 min., Broil: 5 min., Bake: 35 min.**

NOTE: For testing purposes only, we used Stouffer's Corn Soufflé.

KEITH MCNEIL
FLOWER MOUND, TEXAS

from our kitchen

You'll enjoy hosting a bridal shower, anniversary lunch, or company dinner when you have everything you need right at hand. Turn a cabinet—or a closet, if you can spare one—into your party pantry.

In addition to china, linens, and glassware, you'll want to collect spools of ribbon for decorating, colorful paper to make your own invitations and place cards, and assorted candles.

Add to your party stockpile on a regular basis. Pick up unusual serving pieces at flea markets. Check out department store clearance sales to find flatware, glasses, and linens at drastically reduced prices. You can mix-and-match china with several silver patterns for a unique and eclectic table setting.

Here's a way for you and your friends to expand your collections without spending a dime: Invite everyone to bring two serving dishes, glasses, trays, or accessories to a swap session. Everyone goes home with something new.

Food Pages

We highly recommend adding *Hints & Pinches*, by essayist, novelist, and Mobile native Eugene Walter, to your cookbook collection. Seasoned with the author's lifetime of food experiences from 1921 to 1998, it makes delicious reading whether you like to cook or not.

Here's a sample: "The best Southern breakfast of all," he writes, "consists of scrambled eggs to which a little fresh cream has been added, and a nice pinch of dried dill, with spicy pork sausage patties and sliced fresh pineapple cooked in the skillet with the sausage. Hot grits, naturally."

Here's one of the author's tips for perking up your recipes: "Try adding some grated lemon peel to your next beef stew, your next sparerib sauce, to your gumbo, your shrimp cocktail." He also suggests, "Cinnamon toast is a classic, but try tucking dabs of sugar and cinnamon inside biscuits before baking them."

Order *Hints & Pinches* from Hill Street Press, 191 East Broad Street, Suite 209, Athens, GA 30601-2848; 1-800-295-0365 or **www.hillstreetpress.com**. The 402-page softbound book will stir up some of your taste memories and may inspire you to create new ones.

Name That Meat

Wonderful foods and taste experiences are waiting to be tried, but sometimes they appear on menus without explanations. When you find these items listed, here's what they mean.

Carnitas ("little meats") are inexpensive cuts of pork simmered until tender, shredded, and browned. It's a pork alternative for tacos, enchiladas, and the like.

Barbacoa is shredded, pit-roasted beef seasoned with chipotle peppers, cumin, cloves, and garlic.

Bresaola is thinly sliced, air-dried beef filet. It looks like prosciutto and is served with lemon and olive oil as an antipasto.

Churrascos are flaming skewers of beef served tableside at Latin (usually Brazilian) restaurants.

Tips and Tidbits

■ One package of chicken breasts may contain pieces of several different weights and thicknesses. Our Test Kitchens staff suggests cutting them into strips or cubes before cooking to make them uniform—for speed and tenderness. If you're serving the breasts whole, pound the thick ones for more even cooking. Some of us like flash-frozen boneless, skinless breasts (in the large plastic bags) for consistency of size and flavor.

■ Fresh apricots and cherries are in season right now. Remember, these fruits don't store well, so buy only what you and your family will consume in a couple of days.

■ Walter Taliaferro of Winston-Salem, North Carolina, recycles fabric softener sheets for sparkling-clean kitchen surfaces. "I stack and sew several sheets together in the middle," Walter writes. "Spray glass shelves and doors, and polish them with the homemade cleaning cloth for spotless, streak-free results. It works great on faucets and other chrome items, too."

Turkey Tenderloin Scaloppine, page 137

Front-Porch Fried Catfish, page 166;
Barbecue Beans, Creamy Coleslaw, page 167

Crab-and-Scallop Cakes, page 165

Sweet Corn Soup With Crab, page 159

Macadamia-Mango Chicken, page 162; Peanut-Noodle Salad, page 163;
Fruit Punch, page 162; Tropical Fruit Salad, page 163

Peanut-Noodle Salad, page 163

Tropical Fruit Salad, page 163

Fruit Punch, page 162

Teacakes, page 161; Sweet-Tart Lemonade, page 160

Fig-and-Raspberry Cobbler, page 160

Summertime Peach Ice Cream, page 158

July

From Orchard to Table

This time of year, peaches take the lead in an array of fabulous recipes.

After the last school bell of the year rang, Assistant Foods Editor Cybil Brown would head to Fort Valley, Georgia, to spend the summer with her grandparents. Once she arrived at their home in Peach County, she couldn't wait to take that first bite into a sweet, juicy peach.

Cybil admits a fierce loyalty to Georgia peaches, but she's been known to swoon over those grown elsewhere in the South too. She's even come to love newer types, such as the white-fleshed Charity Belle.

If you're like Cybil, you might be tempted to start snacking on a purchase of locally grown goodness before you get it home from the farm or market. Just be sure to save some for our delicious dishes.

PEACH MELBA SHAKE

MAKES 4½ CUPS

The original peach Melba dessert was created for Australian opera singer Dame Nellie Melba. It consists of a poached peach half topped with vanilla ice cream, raspberry sauce, whipped cream, and sliced almonds.

    2 cups peeled, sliced fresh peaches
        (about 2 medium-size ripe peaches)
    2 cups vanilla ice cream
    ¾ cup milk
    3 tablespoons sugar
    ¼ teaspoon almond extract
    ½ cup fresh raspberries*
    ½ cup sugar

PROCESS first 5 ingredients in a food processor or blender until smooth, stopping to scrape down sides. Pour mixture into glasses.

PROCESS raspberries and ½ cup sugar until smooth; swirl evenly into shakes. Serve immediately. **Prep: 15 min.**

*Substitute ½ cup fresh strawberries, if desired.

SUMMERTIME PEACH ICE CREAM

MAKES 2 QUARTS

Soft, ripe fruit lends the smoothest texture and most pronounced flavor. *(pictured on page 156)*

    4 cups peeled, diced fresh peaches
        (about 8 small ripe peaches)
    1 cup sugar
    1 (12-ounce) can evaporated milk
    1 (3.75-ounce) package vanilla instant
        pudding mix
    1 (14-ounce) can sweetened
        condensed milk
    4 cups half-and-half

COMBINE peaches and sugar, and let stand 1 hour.

PROCESS peach mixture in a food processor until smooth, stopping to scrape down sides.

STIR together evaporated milk and pudding mix in a large bowl; stir in peach puree, sweetened condensed milk, and half-and-half.

POUR mixture into freezer container of a 4-quart hand-turned or electric freezer; freeze according to manufacturer's instructions. Spoon into an airtight container, and freeze until firm. **Prep: 30 min., Stand: 1 hr., Freeze: 30 min.**

CAROL S. NOBLE
BURGAW, NORTH CAROLINA

PEACH-CARAMEL CHEESECAKE

MAKES 12 TO 15 SERVINGS

    2 cups crushed shortbread cookies
        (about 28 cookies)
    3 tablespoons butter or margarine,
        melted
    4 (8-ounce) packages cream cheese,
        softened
    ¾ cup sugar
    4 large eggs
    1 teaspoon vanilla extract
    ¼ teaspoon almond extract (optional)
    1 (5-ounce) jar caramel topping
    3 tablespoons whipping cream
    ½ cup chopped fresh peaches (about
        1 small ripe peach)
    5 cups thinly sliced fresh peaches
        (about 5 medium-size ripe peaches)
    1 (12-ounce) jar peach preserves

COMBINE cookie crumbs and butter; press into bottom and up sides of a greased 10-inch springform pan.

BAKE at 350° for 8 minutes or until lightly browned. Cool on a wire rack.

BEAT cream cheese at high speed with an electric mixer until creamy, and gradually add sugar, beating well. Add eggs, 1 at a time, beating after each addition. Stir in vanilla extract and, if desired, almond extract. Pour mixture into prepared crust.

STIR together caramel topping and cream in a large glass bowl, and microwave at HIGH 1 to 2 minutes, stirring once. Stir in chopped peaches.

ADD peach mixture to cream cheese mixture, swirling gently.

BAKE at 325° for 50 minutes or until cheesecake is almost set. Turn off oven, and let cheesecake stand in oven, with door partially open, 30 minutes. Remove from oven, and cool on a wire rack. Cover and chill at least 8 hours. Release sides of pan; arrange sliced peaches over cheesecake.

MICROWAVE peach preserves in a glass bowl at HIGH 1 to 2 minutes or until melted, stirring once. Pour preserves through a wire-mesh strainer into a bowl, and brush over sliced peaches. **Prep: 25 min., Bake: 58 min., Stand: 30 min., Chill: 8 hrs., Cook: 2 min.**

GRILLED BALSAMIC-GLAZED PEACHES

MAKES 6 SERVINGS

Serve this simple side with grilled chicken, beef, or fish.

½ cup balsamic vinegar
3 tablespoons brown sugar
1 teaspoon cracked pepper
⅛ teaspoon salt
6 firm, ripe peaches, halved
¼ cup vegetable oil

COMBINE first 4 ingredients in a saucepan. Bring to a boil; reduce heat, and simmer 2 to 3 minutes.

PLACE peaches in a shallow dish. Pour vinegar mixture over peaches, tossing gently to coat. Let stand 10 minutes.

REMOVE peaches from vinegar mixture, reserving 2 tablespoons mixture. Set aside remaining vinegar mixture.

WHISK together reserved 2 tablespoons vinegar mixture and oil, blending well. Set vinaigrette aside.

PLACE peach halves, cut sides down, on a lightly greased grill rack. Grill, covered with grill lid, over medium heat (300° to 350°) 5 minutes on each side or until firm and golden, basting with remaining vinegar mixture. Serve peaches with vinaigrette. **Prep: 15 min., Cook: 3 min., Stand: 10 min., Grill: 10 min.**

HONEYED PORK TENDERLOIN WITH AVOCADO-PEACH SALSA

MAKES 4 SERVINGS

½ cup soy sauce
1 tablespoon sesame oil
2 teaspoons teriyaki sauce
2 garlic cloves, minced
1 teaspoon ground ginger
1 (1-pound) pork tenderloin
¼ cup honey
2 tablespoons brown sugar
4½ tablespoons sesame seeds
Avocado-Peach Salsa

COMBINE first 5 ingredients in a large shallow dish or heavy-duty zip-top plastic bag; add pork. Cover or seal, and chill 6 to 8 hours.

REMOVE pork from marinade, discarding marinade.

STIR together honey and brown sugar. Brush pork with honey mixture, and sprinkle with sesame seeds. Place on a lightly greased rack in a roasting pan.

BAKE at 400° for 25 to 30 minutes or until meat thermometer inserted into thickest portion registers 160°. Cut pork into slices; serve with Avocado-Peach Salsa. **Prep: 15 min., Chill: 8 hrs., Bake: 30 min.**

Avocado-Peach Salsa:

MAKES 2¾ CUPS

1 cup peeled, diced fresh peaches (about 2 small ripe peaches)
1 large tomato, diced
½ cup diced avocado (about 1 small avocado)
1 tablespoon minced red onion
1 tablespoon lime juice
1 teaspoon olive oil
¼ teaspoon salt
¼ teaspoon ground red pepper
¼ cup diced jícama (optional)

COMBINE first 8 ingredients and, if desired, jícama in a large bowl; cover and chill until ready to serve. **Prep: 10 min.**

ZITA WILENSKY
NORTH MIAMI, FLORIDA

Savor Sweet Corn

Summer's gift of sweet corn excites all the senses. The moist green shucks fill your hands with cool, rough texture, while the aroma of kernels just cut from the cob offers a fragrant scent of the season.

Buy corn from a farmers market when you can. Get it right off the truck, early in the morning; that way, you'll know it's fresh. If you have just a few ears, keep them in their husks in the refrigerator until you're ready to cook them. To store, dip unshucked ears in cold water, seal them in an airtight zip-top plastic bag, and refrigerate up to five days.

SWEET CORN SOUP WITH CRAB

MAKES 10½ CUPS

Tom Noelke, chef/owner of Gulf Coast Grill in Macon, Georgia, simmers corncobs with chicken broth for a wonderful depth of flavor. *(pictured on page 151)*

⅓ cup diced salt pork
2 tablespoons butter or margarine
¼ cup white cornmeal
2 celery ribs, diced
1 medium onion, diced
1 red bell pepper, diced
1 jalapeño pepper, diced
3 cups fresh sweet corn kernels (about 6 ears)
4¾ cups chicken broth
2 corncobs
1 pound fresh lump crabmeat, drained
1 cup whipping cream
¼ cup chopped fresh cilantro
½ teaspoon salt
¼ teaspoon ground white pepper
Garnish: fresh cilantro sprigs

BROWN salt pork in a Dutch oven over medium heat; remove pork, and reserve for another use.

ADD butter to pork drippings in Dutch oven over medium heat; whisk in cornmeal, and cook, whisking constantly, 1 minute. Add celery and next 4 ingredients; sauté 2 minutes.

ADD broth and corncobs. Bring to a boil; reduce heat, and simmer 30 minutes. Remove and discard corncobs. Stir in crabmeat and next 4 ingredients; cook until thoroughly heated. Garnish, if desired. **Prep: 25 min., Cook: 45 min.**

TOM NOELKE
GULF COAST GRILL
MACON, GEORGIA

Creamy Fried Confetti Corn

MAKES 6 TO 8 SERVINGS

- 8 bacon slices, chopped
- 4 cups fresh sweet corn kernels (about 8 ears)
- 1 medium-size white onion, chopped
- ⅓ cup chopped red bell pepper
- ⅓ cup chopped green bell pepper
- 1 (8-ounce) package cream cheese, cubed
- ½ cup half-and-half
- 1 teaspoon sugar
- 1 teaspoon salt
- 1 teaspoon pepper

COOK chopped bacon in a large skillet until crisp; remove bacon, and drain on paper towels, reserving 2 tablespoons drippings in skillet. Set bacon aside.

SAUTÉ corn, onion, and bell peppers in hot drippings in skillet over medium-high heat 6 minutes or until tender. Add cream cheese and half-and-half, stirring until cream cheese melts. Stir in sugar, salt, and pepper. Top with bacon. **Prep: 15 min., Cook: 22 min.**

LAURIE MCINTYRE
HOUSTON, TEXAS

Fresh Figs

The season for figs is upon us. Among lovers of this fruit, treasured for its honeylike sweetness and succulent texture, the buzz is unmistakable. Here's why: Figs don't last long off the tree—they must be picked during peak ripeness. (Selections such as the rosy-fleshed Brown Turkey and purple-skinned Celeste are grown widely in the South.) Once they're harvested, the race is on. These gems are so perishable, they're rarely available for more than a few days at farmers markets. The best way to get your fill: Grow your own, or make friends with someone who does.

When not eaten out of hand, figs most often show up in sweet treats such as our Fig-and-Raspberry Cobbler. However, we also found them an ideal match for thin slices of salty country ham and Gorgonzola cheese.

Baked Fig Bites

MAKES 28 BITES

- 14 small fresh figs, stemmed and halved
- 10 ounces Gorgonzola cheese, crumbled*
- 1 teaspoon finely chopped fresh rosemary
- ½ teaspoon pepper
- ¼ pound thinly sliced country ham, cut in half lengthwise
- Garnish: fresh rosemary sprigs

TOP each fig half evenly with Gorgonzola cheese, and sprinkle evenly with rosemary and pepper. Wrap ham around each fig, securing with wooden picks; place rolls, seam sides down, on an aluminum foil-lined baking sheet.

BAKE at 350° for 10 minutes or until cheese melts. Garnish, if desired. **Prep: 25 min., Bake: 10 min.**

*Substitute 10 ounces crumbled blue cheese for Gorgonzola cheese, if desired.

MILES EUSTIS
ARDEN, NORTH CAROLINA

Fig-and-Raspberry Cobbler

MAKES 6 TO 8 SERVINGS

Fresh ginger and cinnamon spice this sweet, juicy cobbler. *(pictured on page 155)*

- 2 pounds fresh figs, stemmed and cut into fourths
- 2 pounds fresh raspberries
- 1 cup granulated sugar
- ½ cup firmly packed brown sugar
- 2 tablespoons all-purpose flour
- 2 teaspoons grated fresh ginger
- 1 teaspoon grated lemon rind
- 2 (3-inch) cinnamon sticks
- 1 (15-ounce) package refrigerated piecrusts

COMBINE half of figs, half of raspberries, and next 6 ingredients in a saucepan, and cook, stirring occasionally, over low heat 40 minutes or until fig mixture is thickened. Stir in remaining figs and raspberries, and remove from heat. Remove and discard cinnamon sticks.

SPOON half of fig mixture into a lightly greased 2-quart baking dish, reserving other half.

ROLL each piecrust into a 12-inch circle. Cut 1 piecrust into 1-inch strips; set aside. Place remaining piecrust on top of fig mixture in baking dish.

BAKE at 475° for 12 minutes.

SPOON remaining fig mixture over baked crust; arrange reserved strips in a lattice design over filling.

BAKE 14 minutes or until golden. **Prep: 25 min., Cook: 40 min., Bake: 26 min.**

Taste of the South

Tea Cakes and Lemonade

When Creative Development Director Valerie Fraser was 10, she spent many Saturdays at the family farm of her friend, Sarah. On a glorious summer day, only one thing could coax them indoors: tea cakes fresh from the oven. The heavenly treats would be baked for them by Sarah's grandmother, Miss Lillian.

A friend of Valerie's recently shared a recipe that came close to Miss Lillian's tea cakes, and, for good measure, she threw in instructions for making homemade lemonade.

So this Saturday, find yourself a cool patch of shade, pour a glass of lemonade, and settle back with a tea cake or two.

Sweet-Tart Lemonade

MAKES 7 CUPS

Enjoy this simple summer sipper anytime. *(pictured on page 154)*

- 3 cups cold water
- 2 cups Sugar Syrup
- 1¾ to 2 cups fresh lemon juice

STIR together all ingredients until well blended; serve over ice. **Prep: 20 min.**

Sugar Syrup:
MAKES 2 CUPS

- 2 cups sugar
- 1 cup water
- ¼ teaspoon fresh lemon juice

STIR together all ingredients in a small saucepan. Bring to a boil over medium heat, stirring often. Reduce heat; simmer 1 minute or until sugar dissolves. Remove from heat; cool. **Prep: 5 min., Cook: 5 min.**

TEA CAKES

MAKES 3 DOZEN

These classic cookies remind Valerie of those baked by her best friend's grandmother, Miss Lillian. *(pictured on page 154)*

- 1 cup butter, softened
- 2 cups sugar
- 3 large eggs
- 1 teaspoon vanilla extract
- 3½ cups all-purpose flour
- 1 teaspoon baking soda
- ½ teaspoon salt

BEAT butter at medium speed with an electric mixer until creamy; gradually add sugar, beating well. Add eggs, 1 at a time, beating until blended after each addition. Add vanilla, beating until blended.

COMBINE flour, soda, and salt; gradually add flour mixture to butter mixture, beating at low speed until blended after each addition.

DIVIDE dough in half; wrap each portion in plastic wrap, and chill 1 hour.

ROLL half of dough to ¼-inch thickness on a floured surface. Cut out with a 2½-inch round cutter; place 1 inch apart on parchment paper-lined baking sheets.

BAKE at 350° for 10 to 12 minutes or until edges begin to brown; let stand on baking sheets 5 minutes.

REMOVE to wire racks to cool. Repeat procedure with remaining dough. **Prep: 20 min., Chill: 1 hr., Bake: 12 min., Stand: 5 min.**

Pasta in 30 Minutes

What is it about summertime that makes people crave pasta? Whatever the reason, we've got the recipes. For a taste of the sea, try Speedy Scampi. Peppery Pasta Primavera combines linguine with fresh vegetables and herbs. If you don't usually have time to make homemade macaroni and cheese, you'll love the quick variation contributed by *Southern Living* Assistant Copy Chief Paula Hughes.

CHEESY PASTA BAKE

MAKES 8 SERVINGS

- 2 tablespoons butter or margarine
- ¼ cup all-purpose flour
- 3 cups milk
- 4 cups (16 ounces) shredded extra-sharp Cheddar cheese
- ¾ cup shredded Parmesan cheese, divided
- ¾ teaspoon salt
- 1 teaspoon freshly ground black pepper
- ½ teaspoon ground red pepper
- 16 ounces rotini or penne pasta, cooked

MELT butter in a Dutch oven over medium heat; whisk in flour until smooth. Gradually whisk in milk, and cook, whisking constantly, 3 minutes or until thickened.

ADD Cheddar cheese, ¼ cup Parmesan cheese, salt, black pepper, and red pepper, whisking until cheese melts. Add pasta, tossing to coat.

POUR mixture into a lightly greased 13- x 9-inch baking dish. Sprinkle with remaining ½ cup Parmesan cheese.

BAKE at 350° for 5 minutes or until cheese melts. **Prep: 10 min., Cook: 5 min., Bake: 5 min.**

PAULA HUGHES
BIRMINGHAM, ALABAMA

PEPPERY PASTA PRIMAVERA

MAKES 10 SERVINGS

If you want to make this dish less spicy, use only ¼ teaspoon crushed red pepper and two shallots.

- 1½ cups fresh broccoli florets
- 1 tomato, coarsely chopped
- 4 shallots, chopped (about ½ cup)
- 2 garlic cloves, pressed
- 1 teaspoon dried crushed red pepper
- 2 tablespoons olive oil
- 12 ounces linguine, cooked
- 1 cup crumbled goat cheese
- ½ cup whipping cream
- ½ teaspoon salt
- 3 tablespoons chopped fresh basil

SAUTÉ first 5 ingredients in hot oil in a large skillet over medium-high heat 4 to 5 minutes or until broccoli and shallots are tender.

COMBINE broccoli mixture, hot pasta, cheese, cream, and salt, tossing gently to coat. Sprinkle with basil. **Prep: 15 min., Cook: 5 min.**

SPEEDY SCAMPI

MAKES 4 SERVINGS

- ⅓ cup butter or margarine
- 2 green onions, sliced
- 4 large garlic cloves, minced
- 1 tablespoon grated lemon rind
- ½ cup fresh lemon juice
- ½ teaspoon salt
- 1¾ pounds large fresh shrimp, peeled and deveined
- ½ cup chopped fresh parsley
- ½ teaspoon hot sauce
- 12 ounces angel hair pasta, cooked

MELT butter in a large skillet over medium-high heat; add green onions, minced garlic, lemon rind, lemon juice, and salt; cook garlic mixture 2 to 3 minutes or until bubbly.

REDUCE heat to medium; add shrimp, and cook, stirring constantly, 5 minutes or just until shrimp turn pink. Stir in parsley and hot sauce. Toss with hot pasta. **Prep: 10 min., Cook: 8 min.**

SHERYL DAVIDSON
MERIDIAN, MISSISSIPPI

summer suppers®

This summer, sample all the diverse flavors of our region—without leaving the comfort of your home.

Plan a Poolside Luau

Luau Menu

Serves 6

Fruit Punch

Macadamia-Mango Chicken

Peanut-Noodle Salad   Tropical Fruit Salad

Frozen Coffee Cooler   Banana-Coconut Ice Cream

Head poolside with an island-themed party full of tropical selections. We used an array of ingredients, such as coconut, pineapple, and macadamia nuts, in these delicious recipes. All of them can be made ahead, so all you have to do the day of the party is put on your sunglasses and grill the chicken.

FRUIT PUNCH

MAKES 12 CUPS

This recipe tastes just as good without the rum.
(pictured on pages 152-153)

> **3 cups cranberry juice cocktail**
> **2 cups pineapple juice**
> **2 cups orange juice**
> **1 (1-liter) bottle ginger ale, chilled**
> **¾ to 1 cup light rum**
> **Garnish: 1 star fruit, cut into ¼-inch slices**

COMBINE first 3 ingredients in a large bowl; cover and chill up to 8 hours, if desired. Stir ginger ale and rum into juice mixture just before serving. Serve over ice; garnish, if desired. **Prep: 5 min.**

KAY LEWIS
BIRMINGHAM, ALABAMA

MACADAMIA-MANGO CHICKEN

MAKES 6 SERVINGS

You'll love the colorful Mango Salsa served with beef, fish, shrimp, or tortilla chips, too.
(pictured on page 152)

> **½ cup soy sauce**
> **2 garlic cloves, minced**
> **1 tablespoon brown sugar**
> **1 tablespoon olive oil**
> **1 teaspoon grated fresh ginger**
> **6 skinned and boned chicken breast halves**
> **Mustard Sauce**
> **3 tablespoons macadamia nuts, chopped**
> **Mango Salsa**

COMBINE first 5 ingredients in a shallow dish or heavy-duty zip-top plastic bag; add chicken. Cover or seal, and chill 1 hour, turning once. Remove chicken from marinade, discarding marinade.
GRILL, covered with lid, over medium-high heat (350° to 400°) 6 minutes on each side or until done. Drizzle chicken with Mustard Sauce; sprinkle evenly with nuts. Serve with Mango Salsa. **Prep: 15 min., Chill: 1 hr., Grill: 12 min.**

Mustard Sauce:

MAKES ⅔ CUP

> **½ cup Dijon mustard**
> **2 tablespoons light brown sugar**
> **2 tablespoons pineapple juice**
> **⅛ to ¼ teaspoon ground red pepper**

STIR together all ingredients; cover and chill sauce up to 8 hours, if desired. **Prep: 5 min.**

summer suppers

Mango Salsa:

MAKES 2 CUPS

2 ripe mangoes (about 1 pound),
    peeled and diced*
1 medium-size red bell pepper, diced
1 jalapeño pepper, seeded and diced
3 tablespoons chopped fresh cilantro
2 tablespoons chopped fresh mint
1 small red onion, chopped
2 tablespoons honey
1 tablespoon fresh lime juice
¼ teaspoon ground red pepper
¼ teaspoon salt

STIR together all ingredients; cover and chill at least 2 hours. **Prep: 25 min., Chill: 2 hrs.**

*Substitute 1 (26-ounce) jar refrigerated mango slices, if desired.

PEANUT-NOODLE SALAD

MAKES 6 TO 8 SERVINGS

Coconut milk, rice wine vinegar, and crushed red pepper create a palate-pleasing combination in this salad. *(pictured on pages 152-153)*

2 large cucumbers
1 cup soy sauce
½ cup coconut milk
½ cup rice wine vinegar
½ cup chunky peanut butter
4 garlic cloves, minced
1 teaspoon sesame oil
½ to 1 teaspoon dried crushed red
    pepper
½ teaspoon salt
1 (16-ounce) package soba noodles or
    angel hair pasta, cooked
1 (8-ounce) package shredded fresh
    carrot
6 green onions, cut diagonally into
    1½-inch pieces

PEEL cucumbers; cut in half lengthwise, removing and discarding seeds. Cut halves into half-moon-shaped slices. **WHISK** together soy sauce and next 7 ingredients; add cucumber, pasta, carrot, and onions, tossing to coat. Cover and chill 8 hours, if desired. **Prep: 25 min.**

TROPICAL FRUIT SALAD

MAKES 6 TO 8 SERVINGS

This island-inspired recipe received our highest rating. *(pictured on pages 152-153)*

2 (20-ounce) cans sliced pineapple,
    undrained
3 tablespoons honey
½ cup fresh lime juice
1 teaspoon grated orange rind
1 teaspoon grated lime rind
6 medium oranges, peeled and
    sliced
4 kiwifruit, peeled, halved, and
    sliced
2 papayas, peeled and cubed*
Garnishes: ½ cup sweetened flaked
    coconut, fresh mint leaves

DRAIN pineapple, reserving ½ cup juice. Cut pineapple into cubes.
STIR together reserved juice, honey, and next 3 ingredients in a large bowl; add pineapple and remaining fruit, tossing gently to coat. Cover and chill 8 hours. Garnish, if desired. **Prep: 30 min., Chill: 8 hrs.**

*Substitute 2 mangoes, peeled and cubed, if desired.

Game Plan

The day before:
■ Prepare the Mustard Sauce and the Mango Salsa for Macadamia-Mango Chicken, and chill.
■ Prepare Peanut-Noodle Salad, and chill.
■ Prepare Tropical Fruit Salad, and chill.
■ Prepare Banana-Coconut Ice Cream, and freeze.
■ Prepare Fruit Punch, and chill.

The day of the party:
■ Prepare Frozen Coffee Cooler.
■ Marinate and grill chicken.

FROZEN COFFEE COOLER

MAKES ABOUT 8 CUPS

6 cups ice cubes
4 cups brewed coffee, cooled
1 cup coffee liqueur
¾ cup sugar
1 teaspoon ground cinnamon
1 cup half-and-half or milk
Garnishes: whipped cream, ground
    cinnamon

PROCESS half of first 5 ingredients in a blender until smooth. Pour coffee mixture into a large pitcher. Repeat with remaining half of first 5 ingredients, and pour into pitcher. Stir half-and-half into coffee mixture, and garnish, if desired. Serve immediately. **Prep: 10 min.**

NOTE: For testing purposes only, we used Kahlúa for coffee liqueur.

BANANA-COCONUT ICE CREAM

MAKES 2½ QUARTS

Use very ripe bananas for the richest flavor.

- **2 cups sweetened flaked coconut**
- **1 cup sugar**
- **6 egg yolks**
- **4 cups milk**
- **2 cups half-and-half**
- **1 (15-ounce) can cream of coconut**
- **2 teaspoons vanilla extract**
- **3 ripe bananas, mashed**
- **Garnish: toasted sweetened flaked coconut**

BAKE coconut in a shallow pan at 350°, stirring occasionally, 10 minutes or until toasted.

WHISK together sugar, egg yolks, and milk in a heavy saucepan over medium heat; cook, whisking constantly, 20 minutes or until mixture thickens and will coat a spoon. (Do not boil.)

REMOVE from heat; whisk in toasted coconut, half-and-half, cream of coconut, and vanilla. Fold in banana. Cover and chill 3 hours.

POUR mixture into freezer container of a 1-gallon hand-turned or electric ice-cream freezer. Freeze according to manufacturer's instructions.

PACK freezer with additional ice and rock salt, and let stand 1 hour before serving. Garnish, if desired. **Prep: 20 min., Bake: 10 min., Cook: 20 min., Chill: 3 hrs., Freeze: 30 min., Stand: 1 hr.**

NOTE: For testing purposes only, we used Coco López Cream of Coconut.

Welcome to the Porch

Join us for coastal views and gracious entertaining.

Poolside Supper

Serves 6 to 8

Nutty Fruit-and-Cheese Spread   Pistachio Twists

Tuna Amandine   Crab-and-Scallop Cakes   Spinach-Stuffed Squash

Honey-Baked Tomatoes   Fig Cake

When Pat Mowry throws a party, you can bet that no matter how lovely the decor and food inside her home, guests will always end up outside. The following recipes offer a delicious taste of her wonderful hospitality.

NUTTY FRUIT-AND-CHEESE SPREAD

MAKES 4 CUPS

- **1 cup boiling water**
- **¼ cup chopped dried apricots**
- **4 cups (16 ounces) shredded Monterey Jack cheese**
- **1 (8-ounce) package cream cheese, softened**
- **½ teaspoon seasoned salt**
- **⅓ cup milk**
- **⅓ cup golden raisins**
- **¼ cup chopped dates**
- **¾ cup chopped walnuts, toasted**

POUR 1 cup boiling water over apricots; let stand 30 minutes. Drain well.

COMBINE cheeses, salt, and milk in a bowl; beat at medium speed with an electric mixer until smooth. Stir in apricots, raisins, dates, and walnuts.

LINE a 1-quart mold with plastic wrap. Spoon cheese mixture into mold, pressing firmly; cover and chill at least 3 hours. Unmold onto serving dish, and remove plastic wrap. Let stand at room temperature 30 minutes before serving. **Prep: 15 min., Stand: 1 hr., Chill: 3 hrs.**

PISTACHIO TWISTS

MAKES 10 TWISTS

- **½ (17¼-ounce) package frozen puff pastry sheets, thawed**
- **2 tablespoons butter or margarine, melted**
- **¼ cup finely chopped pistachio nuts**
- **1 teaspoon ground red pepper or paprika**
- **2 tablespoons grated Parmesan cheese**

UNFOLD puff pastry sheet on a lightly floured surface, and roll to a 12-inch square, trimming edges with a knife.

BRUSH 1 side of pastry with 1 tablespoon melted butter; sprinkle with nuts and ground red pepper. Fold dough in half, pressing to seal. Brush with remaining 1 tablespoon melted butter; sprinkle with cheese. Cut diagonally lengthwise into ½-inch strips. Twist strips, forming a spiral shape; place 1 inch apart on a baking sheet. Bake at 450° for 10 minutes or until golden. Cool on wire racks. **Prep: 10 min., Bake: 10 min.**

TUNA AMANDINE

MAKES 15 SERVINGS

- 2 (0.25-ounce) envelopes unflavored gelatin
- ½ cup cold water
- 1 cup boiling water
- 2 (8-ounce) packages cream cheese, softened
- 2 tablespoons lemon juice
- 1 tablespoon curry powder
- ¾ teaspoon salt
- ¼ teaspoon garlic powder
- 3 finely chopped green onions
- 1 (2-ounce) jar diced pimiento, drained
- 2 (6-ounce) cans solid white tuna in spring water, drained and flaked*
- 1¼ cups sliced almonds, lightly toasted and divided

SPRINKLE gelatin over ½ cup cold water in a large bowl; stir and let stand 1 minute. Add 1 cup boiling water, and stir until gelatin dissolves. Add cream cheese; beat at low speed with an electric mixer until blended. Add lemon juice and next 3 ingredients, beating just until blended. Stir onions, pimiento, tuna, and ½ cup almonds into cheese mixture. Spoon into a shallow serving dish or a 1-quart mold lined with plastic wrap; cover and chill 3 hours. If molded, unmold onto serving dish; remove plastic wrap. Press remaining ¾ cup almonds into tuna mixture in a decorative pattern. Serve with crackers. **Prep: 20 min., Stand: 1 min., Chill: 3 hrs.**

*Substitute 1½ (10-ounce) cans chopped chicken, if desired.

CRAB-AND-SCALLOP CAKES

MAKES 8 SERVINGS

Colorful sauces enliven these golden, crispy cakes. *(pictured on page 151)*

- 1 pound bay scallops, drained
- ⅓ cup whipping cream
- 1 large egg
- 1 teaspoon Old Bay seasoning
- ½ teaspoon salt
- ¼ teaspoon pepper
- 6 green onions, thinly sliced
- 3 medium tomatoes, peeled, seeded, and diced
- 2 pounds fresh lump crabmeat, drained
- 2 tablespoons butter or margarine
- Red Pepper Sauce
- Yellow Pepper Sauce
- Garnishes: parsley sprigs, lemon wedges

PROCESS scallops in a food processor until chopped. Add cream and next 4 ingredients; process until combined, stopping to scrape down sides.

COMBINE scallop mixture, onions, and tomato; gently fold in crabmeat. Cover and chill at least 2 hours. Shape mixture into 8 patties (about ⅓ cup each).

MELT butter in a skillet over medium-high heat; add cakes, and cook, in batches, 3 to 4 minutes on each side or until golden. Serve with sauces; garnish, if desired. **Prep: 30 min., Chill: 2 hrs., Cook: 8 min. per batch**

Red Pepper Sauce:

MAKES 1 CUP

- 2 large red bell peppers, chopped
- 1 cup whipping cream
- ¼ teaspoon salt

COMBINE all ingredients in a saucepan over medium heat; cover and simmer 30 minutes. Process mixture in a blender or food processor until smooth. Pour through a wire-mesh strainer into a bowl. Serve warm. **Prep: 10 min., Cook: 30 min.**

YELLOW PEPPER SAUCE: Substitute 2 yellow bell peppers for red bell peppers.

SPINACH-STUFFED SQUASH

MAKES 6 TO 8 SERVINGS

- 4 large yellow squash
- 1½ teaspoons salt, divided
- ¼ cup butter or margarine, melted and divided
- ½ cup grated Parmesan cheese, divided
- ¼ teaspoon pepper
- 1 small onion, chopped
- 2 (10-ounce) packages frozen chopped spinach, cooked and well drained
- 1 cup sour cream
- 2 teaspoons red wine vinegar
- ¼ cup fine, dry breadcrumbs
- 1 tablespoon cold butter or margarine, cut up

COMBINE squash, ½ teaspoon salt, and water to cover in a Dutch oven. Bring to a boil, and cook 10 minutes or until tender. Cool.

CUT squash in half lengthwise, and remove seeds. Drizzle cut sides of squash evenly with 2 tablespoons melted butter; sprinkle evenly with 2 tablespoons cheese, ½ teaspoon salt, and pepper.

POUR remaining 2 tablespoons melted butter in a large skillet over medium-high heat, and add onion; sauté 4 minutes or until tender. Stir in cooked spinach, sour cream, red wine vinegar, and remaining ½ teaspoon salt. Spoon spinach mixture evenly into squash halves. Place squash in a 13- x 9-inch baking dish. Sprinkle with breadcrumbs and remaining 6 tablespoons cheese, and dot with cold butter.

BAKE at 350° for 15 minutes or until thoroughly heated. **Prep: 15 min., Cook: 14 min., Bake: 15 min.**

HONEY-BAKED TOMATOES

MAKES 8 SERVINGS

Prepare and bake the tomatoes an hour before; keep warm in a 200° oven.

- 8 medium-size ripe tomatoes, cut into 1-inch slices
- 4 teaspoons honey
- 2 white bread slices
- 1 tablespoon dried tarragon
- 1½ teaspoons salt
- 2 teaspoons freshly ground pepper
- 4 teaspoons butter

PLACE tomato slices in a single layer in a lightly greased aluminum foil-lined 15- x 10-inch jellyroll pan. Drizzle with honey, spreading honey into hollows.

PROCESS bread in a food processor or blender until finely chopped.

STIR together breadcrumbs and next 3 ingredients; sprinkle evenly over tomato slices. Dot with butter.

BAKE at 350° for 30 minutes or until tomato skins begin to wrinkle.

BROIL 5 inches from heat 5 minutes or until tops are golden. Serve warm. **Prep: 10 min., Bake: 30 min., Broil: 5 min.**

FIG CAKE

MAKES 16 SERVINGS

Make and freeze the cake up to two weeks in advance; add the glaze the day of the party.

- 2 cups all-purpose flour
- 1½ cups sugar
- 1 teaspoon salt
- 1 teaspoon baking soda
- 1 teaspoon ground cloves
- 1 teaspoon ground nutmeg
- 1 teaspoon ground cinnamon
- 3 large eggs, lightly beaten
- 1 cup vegetable oil
- 1 cup buttermilk
- 1 teaspoon vanilla extract
- 1 cup chopped fresh figs or fig preserves
- 1 cup chopped pecans (optional), toasted
- Buttermilk Glaze

STIR together first 7 ingredients; stir in egg, oil, and buttermilk, blending well. Stir in vanilla. Fold in figs and, if desired, pecans. Pour into a greased and floured 13- x 9-inch pan.

BAKE at 325° for 35 minutes or until a wooden pick inserted in center comes out clean. Pierce top of cake several times with a wooden pick; drizzle Buttermilk Glaze over cake. **Prep: 20 min., Bake: 35 min.**

Buttermilk Glaze:

MAKES ABOUT 1½ CUPS

- 1 cup sugar
- ½ cup butter or margarine
- ½ cup buttermilk
- 1 tablespoon light corn syrup
- 1 teaspoon vanilla extract

BRING all ingredients to a boil in a small saucepan, and cook 3 minutes. **Prep: 10 min., Cook: 3 min.**

Catfish for Dinner

Southerners have long had a love affair with hot, crisp fried catfish. Ours is rolled in cornmeal and fried to crunchy perfection. Add an icy-cold summertime beverage, such as sweet tea or beer, and the company of a few good friends to complete a laid-back outdoor meal.

Summer Fish Fry

Serves 10

Front-Porch Fried Catfish

Barbecue Beans

Creamy Coleslaw

FRONT-PORCH FRIED CATFISH

MAKES 10 SERVINGS

Frying becomes second nature if you follow a few guidelines. First, select an oil, such as peanut oil, with a high smoke point. Next, use a deep-fat thermometer to maintain an accurate temperature. When the oil is hot enough, the cooking process seals the outside of the fish to lock in flavor and moisture. Fry in batches to prevent the oil temperature from dropping too low. *(pictured on page 150)*

- 1 cup all-purpose flour
- 1 tablespoon salt
- 2 teaspoons ground black pepper
- 2 teaspoons ground red pepper
- 2½ cups cornmeal mix
- 1 tablespoon garlic powder
- 2 tablespoons dried thyme
- 10 (6- to 8-ounce) farm-raised catfish fillets, cut into strips
- 1 cup buttermilk
- Peanut oil

COMBINE first 4 ingredients in a large shallow dish.

COMBINE 2½ cups cornmeal mix, garlic powder, and thyme in a heavy-duty zip-top plastic bag.

DREDGE catfish fillets in flour mixture, and dip in buttermilk, allowing excess to drip off. Place catfish fillets in cornmeal mixture; seal bag, and shake to coat.

POUR oil to a depth of 1½ inches into a large cast-iron or other heavy skillet; heat to 360°.

FRY catfish fillets, in batches, 3 minutes or until golden. Drain on paper towels, and serve immediately. **Prep: 10 min., Fry: 3 min. per batch**

BARBECUE BEANS

MAKES 10 SERVINGS

When we ran this recipe in 1994, it called for 10 pieces of bacon. It's still good that way, but you can use half the bacon or use turkey bacon and still get great results. *(pictured on page 150)*

½ medium onion, chopped
½ pound ground beef (optional)
10 bacon slices, cooked and crumbled
⅔ cup firmly packed brown sugar
¾ cup barbecue sauce
1 (15-ounce) can kidney beans, rinsed and drained
1 (15-ounce) can butter beans, rinsed and drained
1 (15-ounce) can pork and beans, undrained
2 tablespoons molasses
2 teaspoons Dijon mustard
½ teaspoon salt
½ teaspoon pepper
½ teaspoon chili powder

COOK onion and, if desired, ground beef in a Dutch oven, stirring until meat crumbles and is no longer pink; drain. Stir in bacon and remaining ingredients; spoon into a lightly greased 2½-quart baking dish. Chill 8 hours, if desired. **BAKE** bean mixture at 350° for 1 hour, stirring once. **Prep: 25 min., Bake: 1 hr.**

CREAMY COLESLAW

MAKES 5 CUPS

Dill pickle juice gives a flavor boost to this cool, tangy slaw. *(pictured on page 150)*

1 (16-ounce) jar coleslaw dressing
½ cup dill pickle juice
½ teaspoon celery seeds
2 (16-ounce) packages coleslaw mix

STIR together dressing, pickle juice, and celery seeds in a large bowl; add coleslaw mix, tossing to coat. Cover and chill at least 1 hour. **Prep: 5 min., Chill: 1 hr.**

NOTE: For testing purposes only, we used Marzetti Original Slaw Dressing.

You'll Love This Menu

Y ou don't have to trot the globe to discover the magic of Middle Eastern food. Bringing these fresh, earthy flavors to your table isn't difficult, thanks to an increasing number of ethnic-food stores and the greater availability of certain ingredients in local markets.

Mediterranean Menu
Serves 8

Grilled Lamb Patties

Persian Rice Pilaf

Marinated Cucumber-Tomato Salad

GRILLED LAMB PATTIES

MAKES 8 SERVINGS

2 pounds lean ground lamb
1 large onion, chopped
½ cup chopped fresh cilantro
⅓ cup chopped fresh parsley
¼ cup chopped fresh mint
1 teaspoon ground allspice
1½ teaspoons ground cumin
2 teaspoons salt
1 teaspoon pepper

COMBINE all ingredients in a bowl. Process lamb mixture, in batches, in a food processor until well combined, stopping to scrape down sides. Cover; chill at least 30 minutes. Shape lamb mixture into 16 (4- to 5-inch) patties. **GRILL,** covered with grill lid, over medium-high heat (350° to 400°) 5 to 7 minutes on each side or until meat is no longer pink. **Prep: 25 min., Chill: 30 min., Grill: 14 min.**

PERSIAN RICE PILAF

MAKES 6 CUPS

Real basmati rice has a distinctive nutty flavor and fragrant aroma. If you can't find it, try American-grown Texmati, which is a cross between long-grain and basmati rices, or substitute the regular long-grain kind.

2 tablespoons butter or margarine
1 small onion, chopped
½ cup slivered almonds
1½ cups uncooked basmati rice
½ cup golden raisins
1½ teaspoons ground turmeric
¼ teaspoon ground cinnamon
½ teaspoon salt
3 cups chicken broth

MELT butter in a skillet over medium-high heat; add onion and almonds, and sauté 7 minutes or until onion is tender and almonds are golden. Stir in rice and next 4 ingredients; sauté 2 minutes. Add broth, and bring to a boil; cover, reduce heat, and simmer 20 to 25 minutes or until rice is tender. **Prep: 10 min., Cook: 35 min.**

MARINATED CUCUMBER-TOMATO SALAD

MAKES 8 SERVINGS

½ cup white vinegar
¼ cup olive oil
¼ cup sugar
2 tablespoons chopped fresh mint
1½ teaspoons salt
¼ teaspoon pepper
3 medium cucumbers, peeled and cut into ¼-inch slices
3 medium tomatoes, cut into wedges
1 medium-size red onion, thinly sliced

WHISK together first 6 ingredients in a large bowl. Add cucumber slices, tomato wedges, and onion slices, tossing gently to coat. Cover vegetable mixture, and chill at least 2 hours. Serve with a slotted spoon. **Prep: 20 min., Chill: 2 hrs.**

LA JUAN COWARD
JASPER, TEXAS

Southwestern Sampler

These dishes combine vibrant colors
with mouthwatering taste.

Soup in the summer? We thought it was a crazy idea too—until we spoke with Mary Treviño, founder of El Mirador, a landmark San Antonio restaurant.

"I learned to love soups because of my mother," Mary says. "She was from Guanajuato, Mexico, and didn't have much money, so she had to be creative. Soups were a great way to make dinner out of whatever you had on hand." She particularly enjoys *caldo xochitl* (KAHL-doh SO-cheel), a spicy, broth-based chicken-and-vegetable soup, because it's a complete meal that isn't heavy.

Mary shared this and some other specialties with us. We're delighted to share them with you.

CREAMY GUACAMOLE

MAKES 2½ CUPS, ABOUT 10 SERVINGS

  4 ripe avocados
  ¼ cup chopped sweet onion
  ¼ cup chopped fresh cilantro
  1 small garlic clove, minced
  3 tablespoons fresh lemon juice
  2 tablespoons half-and-half
  ¾ teaspoon salt
  Garnish: avocado wedges

CUT avocados in half. Scoop pulp into a bowl; mash with a potato masher or fork just until chunky. Stir in next 6 ingredients. Garnish, if desired. **Prep: 15 min.**

PICO DE GALLO

MAKES 4 CUPS

The name of this popular tomato-based condiment means "rooster's beak" in English; when you dip tortilla chips into it, your thumb and forefinger loosely resemble a pecking chicken.

  3 large tomatoes, chopped
  ½ cup chopped sweet onion
  1 to 2 jalapeño peppers, seeded and
    minced
  ¼ cup chopped fresh cilantro
  3 tablespoons lime juice
  1 teaspoon salt
  ½ teaspoon freshly ground pepper

STIR together all ingredients; serve with tortilla chips. **Prep: 15 min.**

LIME SOUP

MAKES 4 QUARTS

The combination of cinnamon and lime creates a perfect flavor match.

  3 whole cloves
  1 to 2 teaspoons dried oregano
  1 (3-inch) cinnamon stick
  4 (32-ounce) containers chicken
    broth
  ½ to ⅔ cup fresh lime juice
  ½ teaspoon salt
  Toppings: diced cooked chicken,
    diced avocado, lime slices, fried
    tortilla strips, shredded Monterey
    Jack cheese

COOK first 3 ingredients in a large stockpot over medium-high heat 2 to 3 minutes, stirring constantly. Add broth, lime juice, and salt. Bring to a boil; reduce heat, and simmer 1 to 2 minutes. Remove and discard cloves and cinnamon stick. Serve soup with desired toppings. **Prep: 10 min., Cook: 15 min.**

SPICY CHICKEN-VEGETABLE SOUP

MAKES 3 QUARTS

  2½ quarts water
  1 (2½- to 3-pound) whole chicken
  3 bay leaves
  1 tablespoon salt
  1 tablespoon ground cumin
  1 teaspoon pepper
  1 fresh basil sprig
  4 whole cloves
  4 garlic cloves
  1 tablespoon dried oregano
  2 zucchini, chopped
  2 carrots, sliced
  1 large green bell pepper, chopped
  1 medium onion, chopped
  1 (15½-ounce) can chickpeas,
    rinsed and drained
  Tomato Rice
  Toppings: chopped fresh cilantro,
    chopped green onions, minced
    jalapeño pepper, coarsely
    chopped tomato, chopped
    avocado

COMBINE first 7 ingredients in a large stockpot; bring to a boil, skimming surface to remove excess foam.
PROCESS cloves, garlic, and oregano in a food processor until finely chopped.
ADD garlic mixture to broth, and cook, stirring occasionally, 35 minutes or until chicken is done. Remove chicken from broth, and cool. Skim fat from broth, and set broth aside.
SKIN and bone chicken; shred chicken, and set aside.
ADD zucchini and next 4 ingredients to broth; bring to a boil, and cook 5 minutes. Add chicken. Serve with Tomato Rice and desired toppings. **Prep: 30 min., Cook: 40 min.**

Tomato Rice:

MAKES 1½ CUPS

    ¾ cup long-grain rice
    1 teaspoon lemon juice
    1 cup hot water
    2 tablespoons olive oil
    2 tomatoes, chopped
    1 medium-size green bell pepper,
        chopped
    1 large garlic clove, minced
    1 tablespoon chicken base*
    1 cup hot water
    1 teaspoon ground cumin
    ½ teaspoon salt
    ½ teaspoon pepper

SOAK rice in lemon juice and 1 cup hot water 5 minutes; drain.
SAUTÉ rice in hot oil in a large saucepan over medium-high heat 10 minutes or until golden. Stir in tomato, bell pepper, and garlic.
STIR together chicken base and remaining ingredients; stir into rice mixture. Cover, reduce heat, and simmer 15 minutes or until liquid evaporates (do not uncover while rice is cooking). **Prep: 10 min., Soak: 5 min., Cook: 25 min.**

*Chicken base, a highly concentrated paste made from chicken stock, may be found with broth and bouillon in the supermarket.

Make These Ahead for Company

Enjoy the aroma of fresh herbs and seasonings as you prepare a Greek-style meal. The large Greek communities across the South have given us a cuisine we've come to cherish with its bright flavors, which include garlic, lemon, oregano, and mint.

We offer a tasty seafood wrap and a cool, creamy fruit salad, both of which received high ratings in our Test Kitchens.

GRILLED-SHRIMP GYROS WITH HERBED YOGURT SPREAD

MAKES 4 SERVINGS

    1½ pounds unpeeled, medium-size
        fresh shrimp
    2 tablespoons Greek seasoning
    2 tablespoons olive oil
    6 (12-inch) wooden skewers
    4 (8-inch) pita rounds or gyro rounds
    Herbed Yogurt Spread
    ½ cup crumbled feta cheese
    1 large tomato, chopped
    1 cucumber, thinly sliced

PEEL shrimp, and devein, if desired.
COMBINE seasoning and olive oil in a heavy-duty zip-top plastic bag; add shrimp. Seal and chill 30 minutes.
SOAK skewers in water 30 minutes while shrimp marinates; thread shrimp onto skewers.
GRILL, covered with grill lid, over medium heat (300° to 350°) about 5 minutes on each side or just until shrimp turn pink.
WRAP each pita round in a damp cloth; microwave at HIGH 10 to 15 seconds or until soft. Spread 1 side of each pita round with Herbed Yogurt Spread. Top evenly with shrimp, cheese, tomato, and cucumber; roll up. **Prep: 25 min., Chill: 30 min., Soak: 30 min., Grill: 10 min.**

Herbed Yogurt Spread:

MAKES ABOUT ½ CUP

    ½ cup plain low-fat yogurt
    1 garlic clove, minced
    1 tablespoon chopped fresh or
        ¾ teaspoon dried oregano
    1 teaspoon chopped fresh mint
    2 teaspoons lemon juice
    ¼ teaspoon pepper

WHISK together all ingredients; cover and chill until ready to serve or up to 8 hours. **Prep: 5 min.**

MIXED FRUIT WITH SOUR CREAM SAUCE

MAKES 4 SERVINGS

    ⅓ cup granulated sugar
    1 cup water
    6 fresh mint leaves
    1 (8-ounce) can pineapple chunks in
        juice, drained
    1 banana, sliced
    1 Granny Smith apple, chopped
    1 cup seedless green grapes
    1 cup sliced strawberries
    Sour Cream Sauce

BRING first 3 ingredients to a boil in a small saucepan, and cook, stirring constantly, 4 to 5 minutes or until sugar mixture reaches a syrup consistency. Discard mint leaves, and cool sugar syrup completely.
COMBINE pineapple, banana, apple, grapes, and strawberries in a large bowl. Pour syrup over fruit mixture; toss gently. Cover and chill at least 1 hour. Serve with Sour Cream Sauce. **Prep: 15 min., Cook: 5 min., Chill: 1 hr.**

Sour Cream Sauce:

MAKES ABOUT 1¾ CUPS

    ⅓ cup butter or margarine, softened
    1 cup powdered sugar
    ½ cup sour cream
    ½ teaspoon lemon juice
    ¼ teaspoon vanilla extract

BEAT butter and powdered sugar at medium speed with an electric mixer until smooth. Add sour cream, lemon juice, and vanilla, beating until mixture is creamy. Cover and chill until ready to serve or up to 8 hours. **Prep: 10 min.**

CONNIE MOORE
MEDWAY, OHIO

No-Fuss Italian

Like down-home Southern cooking,
Tuscan cuisine will satisfy the whole family.

Tuscan cooking, like Southern cooking, is typically simple, hearty food. Both cuisines make use of fresh herbs and other garden delights.

Reader Deborah Mazzotta Prum of Charlottesville, Virginia, and a descendant of Italian immigrants, still has relatives in the old country. "Various family members [in the States], such as my father and son, will visit and bring back recipes," she says. One example is her Tuscan Fennel Salad. "My relatives in Tuscany use blood oranges; I like to make it whenever I come across some nice sweet oranges." Anise Biscuits With Balsamic Strawberries is our twist on a biscotti recipe handed down from her maternal grandmother.

BISTECCA

MAKES 4 SERVINGS

This recipe uses thinly pounded steaks seasoned with traditional Italian flavors.

  4 (1-inch-thick) chuck-eye steaks
  ½ teaspoon salt
  ¼ teaspoon pepper
  ½ cup olive oil
  ¼ cup balsamic vinegar
  2 to 3 garlic cloves, chopped
  1 to 2 teaspoons chopped fresh
    thyme

PLACE steaks between 2 sheets of heavy-duty plastic wrap; flatten to ½-inch thickness, using a meat mallet or rolling pin.
SPRINKLE chuck-eye steaks evenly with salt and pepper.
COMBINE oil and next 3 ingredients in a large shallow dish or heavy-duty zip-top plastic bag; add steaks. Cover or seal; chill 1 to 2 hours.
REMOVE steaks from marinade, discarding marinade.
GRILL steaks, covered with grill lid, over medium-high heat (350° to 400°) 6 minutes on each side or until done. **Prep: 15 min., Chill: 2 hrs., Grill: 12 min.**

DEBORAH MAZZOTTA PRUM
CHARLOTTESVILLE, VIRGINIA

TUSCAN FENNEL SALAD

MAKES 4 TO 6 SERVINGS

Fennel is a sweet anise-flavored bulb that tastes great raw or cooked.

  2 fennel bulbs
  ⅔ cup extra-virgin olive oil
  ⅓ cup balsamic vinegar
  2 tablespoons sugar
  ¾ teaspoon salt
  ½ teaspoon pepper
  6 navel oranges, peeled and
    sectioned
  9 medium carrots, sliced
  4 celery ribs, chopped
  ½ cup chopped walnuts,
    toasted
  Lettuce

TRIM and discard fennel bases, and trim stalks from bulbs. Cut bulbs lengthwise into fourths; cut into very thin slices.
WHISK together olive oil and next 4 ingredients in a large bowl. Add sliced fennel, orange sections, and next 3 ingredients, tossing gently to coat. Serve over lettuce. **Prep: 25 min.**

DEBORAH MAZZOTTA PRUM
CHARLOTTESVILLE, VIRGINIA

ANISE BISCUITS WITH BALSAMIC STRAWBERRIES

MAKES ABOUT 16 BISCUITS

You can also dip these into a cup of dark-roasted coffee.

  ½ cup butter, softened
  ¾ cup sugar
  3 large eggs
  2¼ cups all-purpose flour
  1 tablespoon baking powder
  ⅛ teaspoon salt
  ¼ cup milk
  ¾ teaspoon anise extract
  Balsamic Strawberries
  Garnish: whipped cream

BEAT butter at medium speed with an electric mixer until creamy; gradually add sugar, beating until blended. Add eggs, 1 at a time, beating well after each addition.
COMBINE flour, baking powder, and salt; add to butter mixture alternately with milk, beginning and ending with flour mixture. Beat at low speed just until blended after each addition. Stir in extract. Spoon batter into a lightly greased 13- x 9-inch pan.
BAKE at 350° for 22 minutes; cool 10 minutes. Cut biscuits with a 2½-inch round or square cutter. Cool completely on wire racks. Split biscuits, and serve with Balsamic Strawberries. Garnish, if desired. **Prep: 20 min., Bake: 22 min., Cool: 10 min.**

DEBORAH MAZZOTTA PRUM
CHARLOTTESVILLE, VIRGINIA

Balsamic Strawberries:
MAKES ABOUT 2 CUPS

  1 (16-ounce) container fresh
    strawberries, sliced
  ½ cup sugar
  3 tablespoons balsamic vinegar

COMBINE all ingredients; let stand 1 hour at room temperature. **Prep: 5 min., Stand: 1 hr.**

Let's Do Lunch

For more than 30 years, Test Kitchens staffer Mary Allen Perry's great-aunt, Agatha, hosted the annual luncheon for the ladies of the Mount Wedelia Garden Club. The menu was classic tearoom fare. Aunt Agatha had a gift for growing roses and doubling recipes without a hitch. Her luncheons were admirable affairs, and yours can be too. Just use these tried-and-true recipes.

Ladies Luncheon

Serves 8

Chicken Tetrazzini

Miniature Date Muffins

Mocha Charlottes

Mint tea

CHICKEN TETRAZZINI

MAKES 8 SERVINGS

- ½ cup butter or margarine
- ½ medium-size sweet onion, diced
- ½ cup all-purpose flour
- 4 cups milk
- ½ cup dry white wine
- 2 tablespoons chicken bouillon granules
- 1 teaspoon seasoned pepper
- 1½ cups freshly grated Parmesan cheese, divided
- 4 cups diced cooked chicken
- 12 ounces vermicelli, cooked
- 1 (6-ounce) jar sliced mushrooms, drained
- 1 cup soft breadcrumbs
- 2 tablespoons butter or margarine, melted

MELT ½ cup butter in a Dutch oven over medium-high heat; add diced onion, and sauté 5 minutes or until tender.

WHISK in flour until smooth, and cook, whisking constantly, 1 minute. Gradually add milk and wine; cook, whisking constantly, 5 to 6 minutes or until mixture is thickened.

ADD bouillon granules, seasoned pepper, and 1 cup cheese. Cook, whisking constantly, 1 minute or until bouillon granules dissolve and cheese melts. Remove from heat. Stir in chicken, pasta, and mushrooms. Spoon into a lightly greased 13- x 9-inch baking dish.

BAKE chicken mixture, covered, at 350° for 20 minutes.

STIR together remaining ½ cup cheese, breadcrumbs, and 2 tablespoons melted butter, and sprinkle evenly over casserole. Bake casserole 10 to 15 more minutes. **Prep: 30 min., Cook: 12 min., Bake: 35 min.**

MINIATURE DATE MUFFINS

MAKES 4 DOZEN

- 1 (1-pound, 6-ounce) package date quick bread-and-muffin mix
- 1 tablespoon grated orange rind
- 1 large egg, lightly beaten
- 1 cup fresh orange juice
- ½ cup butter or margarine, melted

STIR together all ingredients; spoon evenly into lightly greased miniature muffin pans.

BAKE, in batches, at 400° for 10 to 12 minutes or until golden. Remove muffins from pans immediately, and cool on wire racks. **Prep: 5 min., Bake: 12 min. per batch**

MOCHA CHARLOTTES

MAKES 8 SERVINGS

For a quick version of this dessert, line pretty cups with ladyfingers, fill with chocolate ice cream, and top with whipped cream.

- 1 envelope unflavored gelatin
- ¼ cup cold water
- ½ cup granulated sugar
- 2 large eggs
- 1 cup milk
- ⅓ cup semisweet chocolate morsels
- 1½ teaspoons instant coffee granules
- 2 teaspoons vanilla extract
- 1½ cups whipping cream, divided
- 2 (3-ounce) packages ladyfingers, split
- 3 tablespoons powdered sugar
- Garnish: 8 (3-inch) cinnamon sticks

SPRINKLE gelatin over ¼ cup cold water; stir and let stand 1 minute. Set gelatin mixture aside.

BEAT granulated sugar and eggs at medium speed with an electric mixer 2 to 3 minutes or until thick and pale.

HEAT milk in a large saucepan over low heat. Gradually add about one-fourth of milk to egg mixture; add to remaining hot milk, stirring constantly. Cook over low heat, stirring mixture constantly, 4 to 5 minutes or until mixture coats a spoon. Remove from heat; stir in gelatin mixture until gelatin dissolves.

WHISK in chocolate morsels, coffee granules, and vanilla until coffee granules dissolve and chocolate melts.

POUR mixture into a metal bowl; place bowl over ice, and let stand, stirring often, 6 to 8 minutes or until cold and slightly thickened.

BEAT 1 cup whipping cream at high speed with an electric mixer until soft peaks form, and gradually fold into coffee mixture.

LINE each of 8 teacups with 6 ladyfinger halves, placing rounded sides of ladyfingers against edge of each cup. Spoon custard into cups; cover and chill 8 hours.

BEAT remaining ½ cup whipping cream and powdered sugar until soft peaks form. Top custards with whipped cream; garnish, if desired. **Prep: 20 min., Stand: 9 min., Cook: 5 min., Chill: 8 hrs.**

Bring Home the Farmers Market

Let fresh produce inspire your next gathering.

Summer is peak season for casual entertaining and going to the local farmers market or roadside stand. This year, combine both for a get-together that'll rejuvenate body and spirit with farm-fresh fruits and vegetables. Most of these delicious recipes can be prepared in advance, requiring little more than last-minute assembly or reheating.

TOMATO PIE

MAKES 6 SERVINGS

  2 cups baking mix
  ⅔ cup buttermilk or milk
  1¼ cups grated Parmesan cheese,
      divided
  2 large tomatoes, seeded and
      thinly sliced
  2 tablespoons all-purpose flour
  1 small sweet onion, minced and
      divided
  ½ cup chopped fresh basil,
      divided
  ½ teaspoon salt, divided
  ½ teaspoon pepper, divided
  ¾ cup creamy mustard-mayonnaise
      blend

STIR together baking mix and buttermilk in a medium bowl just until blended; pat into bottom and up sides of a lightly greased 9-inch pieplate.
BAKE at 400° for 7 minutes. Remove from oven, and sprinkle with ¼ cup cheese.
TOSS tomato slices with flour; arrange 1 layer of tomato slices over cheese. Sprinkle evenly with half of onion, basil,

salt, and pepper. Repeat procedure with remaining tomato slices, onion, basil, salt, and pepper.
STIR together remaining 1 cup cheese and mustard-mayonnaise blend, and spread over top of pie.
BAKE at 400° for 24 minutes or until lightly browned. Let stand 10 minutes before serving. **Prep: 15 min., Bake: 31 min., Stand: 10 min.**

NOTE: For testing purposes only, we used Dijonnaise for creamy mustard-mayonnaise blend and Bisquick for baking mix.

VALERIE G. STUTSMAN
NORFOLK, VIRGINIA

CUCUMBER-AND-YOGURT DIPPING SAUCE

MAKES 3 CUPS

This is based on the classic Greek dip *tzatziki*.

  1 (16-ounce) container plain yogurt
  1 large cucumber, peeled, seeded, and
      diced
  2 to 3 garlic cloves, minced
  ¼ cup minced sweet onion
  1 tablespoon olive oil
  2 to 3 teaspoons lemon juice
  1 tablespoon fresh or 1 teaspoon
      dried dill
  ½ teaspoon salt
  ¼ teaspoon pepper
  Garnish: fresh dill sprigs

LINE a mesh strainer with a paper coffee filter or paper towel. Spoon yogurt into

filter, and place strainer over a bowl. Cover with plastic wrap; chill 4 hours.
SPOON yogurt into a bowl, discarding strained liquid.
STIR in diced cucumber and next 7 ingredients. Cover and chill yogurt mixture until ready to serve. Garnish, if desired. Serve with pita chips and fresh vegetables. **Prep: 15 min., Chill: 4 hrs.**

NOTE: The sauce may also be served as a spread for tomato or roast beef sandwiches.

GEORGE GEORGIADIS
ORLANDO, FLORIDA

GREEN BEANS WITH BASIL VINAIGRETTE

MAKES 4 TO 6 SERVINGS

  2 pounds fresh green beans,
      trimmed
  3 tablespoons red wine vinegar
  2 tablespoons fresh basil
  1 teaspoon Dijon mustard
  1 teaspoon sugar
  1 teaspoon salt
  ½ teaspoon pepper
  ½ cup olive oil
  1 red bell pepper, cut into thin
      strips
  1 small red onion, thinly
      sliced
  ½ cup toasted pecans or walnuts,
      chopped

COOK green beans in boiling water to cover 8 minutes or until crisp-tender; drain. Plunge into ice water to stop the cooking process; drain.
PROCESS vinegar and next 5 ingredients in a blender until smooth. With blender running, pour oil through top opening in a slow, steady stream, and process until smooth.
COMBINE beans, bell pepper strips, and onion. Pour vinaigrette over vegetables, tossing gently to coat. Sprinkle with pecans. Serve chilled or at room temperature. **Prep: 10 min., Cook: 8 min.**

MARIE RIZZIO
TRAVERSE CITY, MICHIGAN

Pointers for Picking Produce

■ Do a little digging when you're searching for beans. The smallest, most tender ones usually fall to the bottom of the bin. Also, look for fresh pods that snap rather than bend.

■ Check the bottoms of berry cartons for juice stains (nature's expiration date).

■ Select melons that are about the same size, and then pick the heaviest. The extra weight indicates a more flavorful melon.

GRILLED-TUNA SANDWICHES

MAKES 4 SANDWICHES

    4 (½-inch-thick) tuna steaks (about
        1 pound)
    2 tablespoons olive oil, divided
    ½ teaspoon salt
    ½ teaspoon pepper
    8 slices sourdough bread
    ¼ teaspoon ground red pepper
        (optional)
    ¼ cup finely chopped green
        onions
    ¼ cup mayonnaise
    2 tablespoons fresh lime juice
    2 teaspoons prepared horseradish
    1 large tomato, thinly sliced
    1 ripe avocado, sliced

RUB tuna with 1 tablespoon olive oil, and sprinkle salt and pepper evenly on both sides of tuna.

GRILL, covered with grill lid, over medium-high heat (350° to 400°) 5 minutes on each side or until tuna reaches desired degree of doneness.

BRUSH bread slices with remaining 1 tablespoon olive oil, and grill 1 minute on each side or until golden.

FLAKE tuna; combine with ground red pepper, if desired, and next 4 ingredients. Spread tuna mixture evenly on 1 side each of 4 bread slices; top with tomato and avocado slices. Cover with remaining 4 bread slices. **Prep: 10 min., Grill: 10 min.**

NOTE: The tuna steaks may be broiled, if desired.

The Flavors of Friendship

As Assistant Foods Editor Joy Zacharia slipped off her shoes at the back door of Penpit "Penny" Koommoo's Hampton, Georgia, home, the aromas of steamed rice, sizzling meat, and chopped fresh herbs greeted her. Luckily for Joy, Penny, a friend and former colleague, invited her over for a hands-on Thai cooking class in Penny's kitchen. Joy talked Penny into letting us showcase her best recipes in our cookbook. They'll show you what Thai home cooking is all about.

CHICKEN SKEWERS WITH PEANUT SAUCE

MAKES 2 TO 4 SERVINGS

Lemongrass is an essential herb in Thai cooking. It tastes like fresh citrus; has long, gray-green leaves; and looks like a stiff green onion.

    1 pound skinned and boned chicken
        breast halves
    1 (14-ounce) can lite coconut milk
    2 tablespoons sugar
    1 tablespoon chopped lemongrass*
    1 tablespoon curry powder
    1 tablespoon fish sauce**
    2 teaspoons grated lime rind
    2 teaspoons ground coriander
    1 teaspoon salt
    ½ teaspoon ground red pepper
    16 (8-inch) bamboo skewers
    Peanut Sauce
    Garnish: cucumber slices

CUT chicken into ½-inch strips. Place in a shallow dish or heavy-duty zip-top plastic bag.

STIR together coconut milk and next 8 ingredients, and pour over chicken. Cover or seal, and chill 2 hours.

SOAK bamboo skewers in water 1 hour while chicken marinates. Thread 2 to 3 chicken pieces onto each skewer.

GRILL, covered with grill lid, over medium-high heat (350° to 400°) 2 to 3 minutes on each side or until done. Serve with Peanut Sauce; garnish, if desired. **Prep: 15 min., Soak: 1 hr., Chill: 2 hrs., Grill: 6 min.**

*Substitute 2 teaspoons grated lemon rind, if desired.

**Fish sauce may be found in the Asian section of larger grocery stores or at Asian markets.

Peanut Sauce:

MAKES 1½ CUPS

    ¾ cup lite coconut milk
    ⅓ cup crunchy peanut butter
    2 tablespoons fresh lemon juice
    1 tablespoon soy sauce
    1 tablespoon brown sugar
    1 garlic clove
    1 teaspoon chopped fresh ginger
    ¼ teaspoon ground red pepper
    ¼ cup milk
    1 teaspoon grated lemon rind

COOK first 8 ingredients in a small saucepan over medium heat, stirring often, 15 minutes or until thickened.

PROCESS mixture in a food processor or blender until smooth. Return to pan; whisk in milk and lemon rind. **Prep: 15 min., Cook: 15 min.**

Fried Noodles With Shrimp

MAKES 4 TO 6 SERVINGS

1½ pounds unpeeled, large fresh
    shrimp
1 (8-ounce) package Thai
    rice noodles*
2 garlic cloves, minced
¼ cup vegetable oil
2 large eggs, lightly beaten
2 tablespoons sugar
2 tablespoons fish sauce
2 tablespoons Asian garlic-chili
    sauce
2 green onions, chopped
2 to 3 tablespoons chopped
    peanuts
¼ cup chopped fresh cilantro
Lime wedges (optional)

PEEL shrimp, and devein, if desired; set aside.

COOK noodles in boiling water 3 to 4 minutes; drain.

SAUTÉ minced garlic cloves in hot vegetable oil in a large nonstick skillet over medium heat 2 minutes. Add shrimp; cook 2 minutes or just until shrimp turn pink. Add beaten egg to shrimp mixture in skillet. Cook shrimp mixture over medium heat, without stirring, until egg begins to set. Stir until cooked, breaking up egg.

ADD sugar, fish sauce, and garlic-chili sauce, stirring until blended. Add noodles, and cook 1 minute or until thoroughly heated. Sprinkle with onions, peanuts, and cilantro. Squeeze lime wedges over noodles, if desired. **Prep: 15 min., Cook: 10 min.**

*Thai rice noodles may be found in the Asian section of larger grocery stores or at Asian markets.

Spicy Beef Salad

MAKES 4 TO 6 SERVINGS

1 large tomato, cut into thin wedges
1 large sweet onion, cut in half and
    thinly sliced
1 cucumber, diced
2 green onions, chopped
1 pound flank steak
1½ teaspoons salt, divided
2 teaspoons ground coriander,
    divided
2 small fresh Thai peppers or
    serrano peppers
1 stalk lemongrass, coarsely
    chopped*
2 garlic cloves
1 tablespoon chopped fresh ginger
2 tablespoons fresh lemon juice
1 tablespoon rice wine vinegar
¼ cup fish sauce
1 tablespoon vegetable oil
1 teaspoon sugar
Mixed salad greens
Garnish: sliced green onions

COMBINE first 4 ingredients; set aside.

RUB steak with ½ teaspoon salt and 1 teaspoon coriander.

PROCESS remaining 1 teaspoon salt, remaining 1 teaspoon coriander, and next 9 ingredients in a food processor or blender until smooth. Cover and chill dressing 1 hour.

GRILL steak, covered with grill lid, over medium-high heat (350° to 400°) 6 minutes on each side or to desired degree of doneness. Let stand 5 minutes. Thinly slice steak.

PLACE steak and vegetable mixture in a large bowl, and drizzle with dressing, tossing to coat. Serve over salad greens; garnish, if desired. **Prep: 15 min.; Chill: 1 hr.; Grill: 12 min., Stand: 5 min.**

*Substitute 2 teaspoons grated lemon rind, if desired.

Thai Iced Tea

MAKES 7 CUPS

6 cups water
1 cup Thai tea leaves*
4 cardamom pods, crushed
1 whole clove, crushed
¼ teaspoon ground cinnamon
1 cup sugar
1 cup half-and-half**
Garnish: lime-peel rose

BRING 6 cups water to a boil. Stir in tea leaves and next 3 ingredients, and cover. Remove mixture from heat, and steep 5 minutes.

POUR tea through a fine wire-mesh strainer into a large pitcher, discarding tea leaves. Add sugar, stirring until dissolved, and cool. Cover and chill tea 2 hours.

SERVE tea in a glass over crushed ice. Top each with 3 to 4 tablespoons half-and-half; garnish, if desired. **Prep: 5 min., Cook: 10 min., Steep: 5 min., Chill: 2 hrs.**

*Thai tea may be found in the Asian section of larger grocery stores or at Asian markets.

**Substitute fat-free half-and-half for regular half-and-half, if desired.

Fun in the Kitchen

Kelsey Corbin, 12, who lives near Kansas City, Missouri, has been cooking for seven years. Her mom, Laurie, instilled in her a love of all things culinary at an unusually early age. In fact, Kelsey started helping Laurie bake cookies as a toddler.

During the summer Kelsey likes to whip up tasty treats, such as the ones she shared here, for her best pals. "You get pretty hungry riding your bike all day," she explains.

CHEESY STUFFED POTATOES

MAKES 8 SERVINGS

- 4 large baking potatoes
- 1 (3-ounce) package cream cheese, softened
- ¾ cup sour cream
- ½ (1-ounce) envelope Ranch-style dressing mix
- 2 tablespoons butter or margarine
- ½ cup (2 ounces) shredded Swiss cheese
- ½ cup (2 ounces) shredded Cheddar cheese
- ½ teaspoon salt
- ½ teaspoon pepper
- Toppings: sour cream, crumbled cooked bacon, chopped green onions

PLACE potatoes in a lightly greased aluminum foil-lined 15- x 10-inch jelly-roll pan. Bake at 400° for 1 hour or until tender; cool 30 minutes.

CUT each potato in half lengthwise; carefully scoop out pulp into a large bowl, leaving a ¼-inch-thick shell.

BEAT pulp and next 8 ingredients at medium speed with an electric mixer until blended; spoon into shells.

BAKE at 350° for 20 minutes. Serve with desired toppings. **Prep: 15 min.; Bake: 1 hr., 20 min.; Cool: 30 min.**

EASY CHICKEN CORDON BLEU

MAKES 6 SERVINGS

- ½ teaspoon salt
- ¼ teaspoon pepper
- 6 skinned and boned chicken breast halves
- 1 (5.5-ounce) box seasoned croutons, crushed
- ⅓ cup shredded Parmesan cheese
- 2 egg whites
- 2 tablespoons water
- 12 thinly sliced smoked ham slices
- 6 Swiss cheese slices
- Honey mustard dressing (optional)

SPRINKLE salt and pepper evenly over chicken; set aside.

COMBINE seasoned crouton crumbs and Parmesan cheese in a large zip-top plastic bag. Whisk together egg whites and 2 tablespoons water in a shallow bowl.

DIP chicken in egg white mixture, and drain. Place 1 breast half in bag; seal and shake to coat. Remove chicken to a lightly greased aluminum foil-lined baking sheet, and repeat with remaining chicken.

BAKE at 450° for 20 minutes or until chicken is done. Top each breast half with 2 ham slices and 1 Swiss cheese slice. Bake 5 more minutes or until cheese melts. Serve with honey mustard dressing, if desired. **Prep: 20 min., Bake: 25 min.**

MANDARIN SALAD ORIENTAL

MAKES 8 SERVINGS

- 1 (3-ounce) package Oriental-flavored ramen noodle soup mix
- ½ cup sliced almonds
- 5 tablespoons sugar, divided
- ½ cup vegetable oil
- 3 tablespoons white vinegar
- 1 tablespoon chopped fresh parsley
- ½ teaspoon salt
- ¼ teaspoon pepper
- ⅛ teaspoon hot sauce
- ½ head iceberg lettuce, torn
- ½ head romaine lettuce, torn
- 5 celery ribs, chopped
- 2 green onions, chopped
- 1 (11-ounce) can mandarin oranges, drained

REMOVE flavor packet from soup mix, and set aside. Crumble noodles.

BAKE noodles in a shallow pan at 350° for 10 minutes or until toasted, stirring after 5 minutes. Remove from oven, and cool.

COOK sliced almonds and 3 tablespoons sugar in a small nonstick skillet over medium-low heat, stirring constantly, 5 to 6 minutes or until sugar is dissolved and almonds are evenly coated. Remove almond mixture from heat, and set aside.

WHISK together reserved flavor packet, remaining 2 tablespoons sugar, oil, and next 5 ingredients.

TOSS together lettuces, celery, and onions in a bowl. Drizzle with dressing; toss. Add noodles, almond mixture, and oranges; toss. Serve immediately. **Prep: 25 min., Bake: 10 min., Cook: 6 min.**

MIXED-BERRY ANGEL CAKES WITH ALMOND SUGAR

MAKES 32 CUPCAKES

- 1 (8-ounce) package fresh strawberries (about 1 cup), sliced
- 1 pint fresh blueberries (about 1 cup)
- 1 (6-ounce) package fresh raspberries (about 1 cup)
- ⅔ cup sugar
- ¾ teaspoon almond extract
- 1 (1-pound) package angel food cake mix
- Frozen whipped topping, thawed

TOSS together berries in a large bowl. Stir together sugar and extract, and sprinkle over berries, tossing to coat. Cover and chill 1 hour.

PREPARE cake mix according to package directions.

PLACE paper baking cups in muffin pans; spoon batter into cups, filling two-thirds full.

BAKE, 1 muffin pan at a time, at 350° for 15 minutes or until lightly browned. Remove cupcakes from pans to wire racks; cool.

CUT cupcakes in half horizontally; spoon 1 tablespoon berry mixture on bottom halves, and cover with tops. Spoon 1 tablespoon berry mixture on top halves, and dollop with whipped topping. Serve immediately. **Prep: 25 min., Chill: 1 hr., Bake: 15 min. per batch**

Sweet Celebration

These luscious delights are a party on a plate.

Each year Assistant Foods Editor Cynthia Briscoe's family finds plenty of reasons to gather with friends. No matter what the season, the time is always perfect for dessert. Cynthia and her mom endure the challenge of brainstorming an array of recipe ideas, but it's those traditional treats that are the mainstays on their menu, pleasing friends year after year.

Surprise the special people in your life with these superb sweets at your next gathering. You can make all four, or serve them on their own. Then watch the smiles begin.

STRAWBERRY CHEESECAKE

MAKES 12 SERVINGS

1¾ cups graham cracker crumbs
½ cup butter or margarine, melted
¼ cup chopped pecans
½ teaspoon ground cinnamon
2 (8-ounce) packages cream cheese, softened
1 (16-ounce) container sour cream
2 large eggs
1 cup sugar
¼ teaspoon salt
2 teaspoons grated lemon rind
2 teaspoons vanilla extract
½ teaspoon almond extract
⅓ cup red currant jelly
1 teaspoon water
2 cups halved fresh strawberries

COMBINE first 4 ingredients, stirring well; press into bottom and 1 inch up sides of a 9-inch springform pan.
BEAT cheese and next 7 ingredients at medium speed with an electric mixer until smooth. Pour into crust.
BAKE at 375° for 1 hour or until center of cheesecake is set. Cool on a wire rack; cover and chill 8 hours.

STIR together jelly and 1 teaspoon water in a small saucepan. Cook over low heat until jelly melts; cool slightly. Arrange strawberries over cheesecake; brush with jelly mixture. **Prep: 25 min., Bake: 1 hr., Chill: 8 hrs.**

CHOCOLATE-PECAN PIE

MAKES 1 (9-INCH) PIE

½ (15-ounce) package refrigerated piecrusts
1½ cups chopped pecans
1 cup (6 ounces) semisweet chocolate morsels
½ cup granulated sugar
½ cup firmly packed brown sugar
1 cup dark corn syrup
¼ cup bourbon*
4 large eggs
2 teaspoons cornmeal
½ teaspoon salt
¼ cup butter or margarine, melted
2 teaspoons vanilla extract

FIT piecrust into a 9-inch pieplate according to package directions; fold edges under, and crimp.
SPRINKLE chopped pecans and chocolate morsels evenly onto piecrust; set aside.
COMBINE sugars, corn syrup, and bourbon in a large saucepan; bring to a boil over medium heat. Cook 3 minutes, stirring constantly.
WHISK together eggs and remaining ingredients. Gradually stir about one-fourth hot mixture into egg mixture; add to remaining hot mixture, stirring constantly. Pour filling into piecrust.
BAKE at 325° for 55 minutes; cool. **Prep: 15 min., Cook: 3 min., Bake: 55 min.**

*Substitute ¼ cup water for the bourbon, if desired.

MOCHA-CHOCOLATE SHORTBREAD SQUARES

MAKES 25 SQUARES

1¼ cups all-purpose flour
½ cup powdered sugar
2 teaspoons instant coffee granules
⅔ cup butter or margarine, softened
½ teaspoon vanilla extract
1 cup (6 ounces) semisweet chocolate morsels
Chocolate morsels, melted (optional)

COMBINE first 3 ingredients; add butter and vanilla, and beat at low speed with an electric mixer until blended. Stir in 1 cup chocolate morsels.
PRESS dough into an ungreased 9-inch square pan; prick dough with a fork.
BAKE at 325° for 20 minutes or until lightly browned. Cut into small squares while warm. Drizzle with melted chocolate, if desired. **Prep: 15 min., Bake: 20 min.**

CLEAR-THE-CUPBOARD COOKIES

MAKES 4½ DOZEN

1 cup shortening
1 cup granulated sugar
1 cup firmly packed brown sugar
2 large eggs
2 cups all-purpose flour
1 cup uncooked regular oats
1 teaspoon baking soda
1 teaspoon baking powder
1 teaspoon salt
1 cup flaked coconut
1 cup crisp rice cereal
1 teaspoon vanilla extract
1 cup chopped pecans, toasted (optional)

BEAT shortening at medium speed with an electric mixer until fluffy, and add sugars, beating well. Add eggs, beating until blended.
COMBINE flour and next 4 ingredients; gradually add to sugar mixture, beating until blended. Stir in coconut, cereal, vanilla, and, if desired, pecans. Drop by tablespoonfuls onto baking sheets.
BAKE, in batches, at 350° for 10 minutes or until lightly golden. Remove to wire racks to cool. **Prep: 20 min., Bake: 10 min. per batch**

Packed With Blueberries

Assistant Foods Editor Joy Zacharia's friend, Donna Leaf, sees a lot of Joy during blueberry season. They head out the door, wicker baskets in tow, to gather sun-ripened blueberries from the bushes in Donna's backyard. A few hours later, Joy heads home with purple fingers and a basketful of gorgeous fruit. (Don't worry—Joy makes sure that Donna gets a blueberry treat the next day.)

If you can't pick your own, visit your favorite farmers market or grocery store soon. Now's the time to enjoy the tastiest and most affordable berries. You'll definitely want to add these fabulous dishes to your culinary repertoire.

CHICKEN-BLUEBERRY SALAD

MAKES 4 SERVINGS

- 3 tablespoons olive oil
- ½ cup rice wine vinegar
- 2 teaspoons minced fresh ginger
- 1 garlic clove, minced
- ¼ teaspoon salt
- ½ teaspoon pepper
- 3 skinned and boned chicken breast halves
- 1 celery rib, chopped
- ½ cup sweet onion, diced
- ½ cup red bell pepper, chopped
- 1 cup shredded carrot
- 4 cups torn mixed salad greens
- 1 cup fresh blueberries

WHISK together first 6 ingredients. Reserve half of mixture, and chill.

PLACE chicken in a shallow dish or heavy-duty zip-top plastic bag; pour remaining mixture over chicken. Cover or seal, and chill at least 1 hour.

REMOVE chicken from marinade; discard marinade. Grill, covered with grill lid, over medium-high heat (350° to 400°) 6 minutes on each side or until done. Cut into thin slices.

COMBINE celery and next 3 ingredients; add reserved dressing, tossing to coat.

PLACE chicken over greens. Top with celery mixture; sprinkle with berries. **Prep: 20 min., Chill: 1 hr., Grill: 12 min.**

Per serving: Calories 183 (23% from fat); Fat 4.8g (sat 0.8g, mono 2.8g, poly 0.7g); Protein 21g; Carb 14g; Fiber 3.3g; Chol 49mg; Iron 1.2mg; Sodium 127mg; Calc 48mg

BLUEBERRY-CINNAMON MUFFINS

MAKES 15 MUFFINS

To prevent berries from bleeding, toss them in flour, and then gently fold them into batter.

- ¼ cup regular oats
- 2 tablespoons brown sugar
- 1 teaspoon ground cinnamon, divided
- ¼ cup butter, softened
- 1 cup granulated sugar
- ½ cup egg substitute
- 1 teaspoon vanilla extract
- 2 cups all-purpose flour
- 1 teaspoon baking soda
- ½ teaspoon baking powder
- ½ teaspoon salt
- 1¼ cups fat-free buttermilk
- 1 cup fresh blueberries
- Vegetable cooking spray

STIR together oats, brown sugar, and ½ teaspoon cinnamon; set aside.

BEAT butter and granulated sugar at medium speed with an electric mixer until fluffy. Add egg substitute, beating until blended. Stir in vanilla.

COMBINE flour, baking soda, baking powder, salt, and remaining ½ teaspoon cinnamon; add to butter mixture alternately with buttermilk, ending with flour mixture. Gently stir in blueberries.

SPOON batter into muffin pans coated with cooking spray, filling two-thirds full. Sprinkle batter evenly with oat mixture.

BAKE at 350° for 15 to 20 minutes or until tops are golden. Cool muffins in pans 5 minutes; remove from pans, and cool on wire racks. **Prep: 25 min., Bake: 20 min., Cool: 5 min.**

BETH SHROAT
ATLANTA, GEORGIA

Per muffin: Calories 174 (21% from fat); Fat 4g (sat 2g, mono 1.1g, poly 0.4g); Protein 3.7g; Carb 31g; Fiber 0.9g; Chol 9mg; Iron 1.1mg; Sodium 249mg; Calc 39mg

Enjoy the Flavor of Prime Rib

When it comes to beef, it's hard to beat prime rib. And when cooked on a smoker, the results redefine delicious. In fact, this recipe received our highest rating.

SMOKED PRIME RIB

MAKES 8 TO 10 SERVINGS

- Hickory wood chunks
- 4 garlic cloves, minced
- 1 tablespoon salt
- 2 tablespoons coarsely ground pepper
- 1 tablespoon dried rosemary
- 1 teaspoon dried thyme
- 1 (6-pound) beef rib roast
- 1½ cups dry red wine
- 1½ cups red wine vinegar
- ½ cup olive oil

SOAK wood chunks in water 1 hour.

COMBINE minced garlic and next 4 ingredients, and rub garlic mixture evenly over beef roast.

STIR together dry red wine, red wine vinegar, and olive oil; set wine mixture aside.

PREPARE charcoal fire in smoker; let burn 15 to 20 minutes.

DRAIN wood chunks, and place on coals. Place water pan in smoker, and add water to just below fill line. Place beef roast in center on lower food rack. Gradually pour wine mixture over beef roast.

COOK beef roast, covered, 6 hours or until a meat thermometer inserted into thickest portion of beef roast registers 145° (medium rare), adding more water to depth of fill line, if necessary. Remove beef roast from smoker, and let stand 15 minutes before slicing. **Prep: 25 min., Soak: 1 hr., Smoke: 6 hrs., Stand: 15 min.**

from our kitchen

Peach Primer

Cybil Brown's story "From Orchard to Table" (pages 158-159) brought back bushels of sweet memories for Foods Editor Andria Scott Hurst. Her mom's relentless search for a specific peach required many trips to the farmers market. She always wanted small clingstones for pickling, large freestones for pies, and juicy white-fleshed peaches for eating out of hand.

When you go to the market or stop at the stands on the side of the highway, talk to the vendor about how you plan to use the peaches to enjoy a particular kind at its best.

A bushel of peaches weighs about 48 to 50 pounds. Depending on their size, 1 pound equals three or four medium peaches, or 2 to 3 cups sliced.

If you've never experienced white-fleshed peaches (such as the Belle of Georgia and the Charity Belle), look for them this season. They're Andria's absolute favorites for intense flavor and aroma. Plus, they're so juicy you may need to eat them over the sink. Enjoy these, or any peaches, at room temperature for the fullest flavor.

If you can't find white-fleshed peaches in your market, ask the produce manager at your grocery store to order some. For mail order, call Durbin Farms toll free at 1-877-818-0202 or Stewart & Jasper Orchards at (209) 862-9600, and have them delivered to your door.

what's for supper this summer?

Our Summer Suppers special section is sure to give you great ideas for adding variety to meals. Many of these recipes are geared toward entertaining, but others lend themselves well to easy weeknight dinners. Here's a menu we've put together; as a reminder, we've placed a "What's for Supper?" logo next to each recipe within the section.

Family-Pleasing Menu

Serves 6 to 8

Fruit Punch
(nonalcoholic version, page 162)

Chicken Tetrazzini (page 171) or
Easy Chicken Cordon Bleu (page 175)

Honey-Baked Tomatoes (page 166)

Tossed green salad

Mixed-Berry Angel Cakes With
Almond Sugar (page 175)

Grate Corn

Pull out that box grater to do a terrific job of cutting corn off the cob. Remove the husks and silk, and wash the corn well. Position the grater on its side in a large baking dish. Slide one ear horizontally down the large grater holes, bring it back to the top of the grater, and turn the cob slightly to grate the next rows of kernels. Grate each ear twice so you won't miss any of the sweet juices. You'll get a smooth, even texture that's perfect for tamales or creamed corn. (To put these kernels to use, see pages 159-160.)

Sterling Replacements

If you're missing pieces of silver flatware or want to add place settings and serving pieces, The Silver Queen can help. Get a head start on your holiday planning with their fine china and crystal too. The company's bridal registry is a convenient way to shop, and their experts will help you identify patterns. Call 1-800-262-3134 to order the 60-page catalog, or visit **www.silverqueen.com**

Tips and Tidbits

- Nora Henshaw of Okemah, Oklahoma, suggests sprinkling freshly cut peaches, pears, bananas, and apples with pineapple juice instead of lemon juice to prevent the fruit from browning. This not only works well but also perks up flavors.
- *Southern Living* Senior Writer Donna Florio shapes hamburgers on a baking sheet, places them in the freezer for an hour, and then stores the frozen ground beef patties in a zip-top plastic freezer bag.
- Mary Pappas of Richmond says, "When you have leftover phyllo dough, don't throw it out. Make phyllo flakes, and use them like breadcrumbs. Brush the sheets with butter, bake them until golden, and cool. Crush baked phyllo into small crumbs using a rolling pin, and store in an airtight glass jar. Use in stuffed mushrooms or as a breading for baked chicken."
- Ginger Laxton of Columbia, Tennessee, makes wonderful gift baskets for her friends. She wraps selected items in a basket with cellophane, ties on a pretty bow, and adds a note that says, "Bread—so this house will never go hungry; salt—so life will always have flavor; wine—so life will be full of joy and happiness forever."

You can give these baskets to honor a hostess or to greet new neighbors.

August

Down-Home Reunion

This guy really knows how to cook. Here's a taste of the food he grew up on.

Down-Home Menu

Serves 6

Mama's Fried Chicken

Barbecue Eggplant

Stuffed Summer Squash

Chocolate-Zucchini Cake   Peach Iced Tea

Thanks to hard work, an unbeatable personality, and the popularity of his nationally televised cooking shows, Curtis Aikens has become a celebrity. Luckily, fame hasn't gone to his head. Curtis greets you with a warm hug, genuine Southern charm, and an enthusiasm for life that's downright infectious. You feel like you've known him forever.

These winning attributes, combined with his undeniable talent in the kitchen, landed Curtis a spot on the Food Network in 1993. Curtis still owns a place in his hometown of Conyers, Georgia. He and his family gather there several times a year to enjoy the kinds of home-cooked meals he so fondly remembers from his childhood.

Strong roots are what distinguish Curtis from his colleagues on the Food Network. "Growing up, the three most important things were church, family, and food," he remembers. At an early age, Curtis recognized the importance of having family around the dinner table. "I'm so blessed with the parents I have," he says. "They taught us to keep our chins high and treat people the way we'd want to be treated. No matter who you are or where you come from, food is our common bond. It's that social interaction and breaking of bread that makes preparing and eating food so much fun."

To his credit, Curtis has never lost sight of his Southern upbringing and the tremendous influence both his immediate and extended families have had on his career. "My mom is probably my biggest culinary influence, followed closely by both of my grandmas," Curtis says. "Of course, I loved to spend time with my granddaddy Curtis, who grew the best collards in the world. He also grew onions and hung them to dry, and he smoked hams. Through my grandparents, I had the privilege of seeing where all the food came from, so I had a much better appreciation for tastes, flavors, and tradition."

Today, when the Aikens family gets together for one of their signature homecoming meals, there's no mistaking their bond. We certainly hope you and your family will enjoy these scrumptious specialties too.

MAMA'S FRIED CHICKEN

MAKES 4 TO 6 SERVINGS

- 1 (3- to 4-pound) whole chicken, cut into pieces
- 1 teaspoon salt
- 1 teaspoon pepper
- 2 cups buttermilk
- Self-rising flour
- Vegetable oil

SPRINKLE chicken pieces with salt and pepper. Place chicken in a shallow dish or zip-top plastic bag, and add 2 cups buttermilk.

COVER or seal, and chill at least 2 hours. Remove chicken from buttermilk, discarding buttermilk. Dredge chicken in flour.

POUR oil to a depth of 1½ inches into a deep skillet or Dutch oven; heat to 360°. Add chicken, a few pieces at a time; cover and cook 6 minutes. Uncover chicken, and cook 9 minutes. Turn chicken; cover and cook 6 minutes. Uncover and cook 5 to 9 minutes, turning chicken the last 3 minutes for even browning, if necessary. Drain on paper towels. **Prep: 30 min., Chill: 2 hrs., Fry: 30 min. per batch**

BARBECUE EGGPLANT

MAKES 6 SERVINGS

- 1 large eggplant, peeled and cut into ¼-inch slices
- 2¼ teaspoons salt, divided
- ¼ teaspoon pepper
- 2 tablespoons olive oil
- ⅓ cup barbecue sauce

SPRINKLE eggplant slices with 2 teaspoons salt; let stand 1 hour. Rinse eggplant well, and pat dry. Sprinkle eggplant with remaining ¼ teaspoon salt and pepper; drizzle with oil. Let stand 15 minutes.

PLACE eggplant on a rack in a broiler pan. Broil 5 inches from heat 10 minutes on each side, basting with barbecue sauce the last 3 minutes. **Prep: 10 min.; Stand: 1 hr., 15 min.; Broil: 20 min.**

NOTE: For testing purposes only, we used K.C. Masterpiece for barbecue sauce.

STUFFED SUMMER SQUASH

MAKES 8 SERVINGS

- ¼ cup butter or margarine
- 2 celery ribs, diced
- ½ medium onion, diced
- 2 cups crumbled cornbread
- 1 cup Italian-seasoned croutons
- 4 to 5 saltine crackers, crumbled
- 1 cup chicken broth
- 1 large egg
- ½ teaspoon dried sage
- ¼ teaspoon pepper
- 1¼ teaspoons salt, divided
- 8 to 10 yellow squash, halved and seeded

MELT butter in a skillet over medium-high heat. Add celery and onion; sauté 5 to 6 minutes or until tender.

COMBINE cornbread, croutons, and crackers in a large bowl; stir in onion mixture, broth, next 3 ingredients, and ¼ teaspoon salt.

MICROWAVE squash halves on HIGH 5 to 7 minutes or until tender.

SPRINKLE squash halves with remaining 1 teaspoon salt; place in a 13- x 9-inch baking dish. Spoon ¼ cup stuffing in each squash half.

BAKE at 375° for 30 minutes or until stuffing is lightly browned. **Prep: 15 min., Cook: 13 min., Bake: 30 min.**

CHOCOLATE-ZUCCHINI CAKE

MAKES 8 TO 10 SERVINGS

No one will guess the surprise ingredient in this moist, chocolaty cake. *(pictured on pages 190-191)*

- 3 cups all-purpose flour
- 1½ teaspoons baking powder
- 1 teaspoon baking soda
- 1 teaspoon salt
- 4 large eggs
- 3 cups granulated sugar
- 3 (1-ounce) unsweetened chocolate baking squares, melted
- 1½ cups vegetable oil
- 3 cups grated zucchini (about 5)
- 1 cup pecans, chopped
- Powdered sugar

COMBINE first 4 ingredients.

BEAT eggs at medium speed with an electric mixer. Gradually add granulated sugar; beat until blended. Add chocolate and oil; beat until blended. Gradually add flour mixture; beat at low speed until blended. Fold in zucchini and pecans. Pour batter into a well-greased and floured Bundt pan.

BAKE at 350° for 1 hour and 15 minutes or until a wooden pick inserted in center comes out clean. Cool in pan 15 minutes. Remove from pan; cool completely on a wire rack. Sprinkle with powdered sugar before serving. **Prep: 15 min.; Bake: 1 hr., 15 min.; Cool: 15 min.**

PEACH ICED TEA

MAKES ABOUT ¾ GALLON

- 3 (11.5-ounce) cans peach nectar
- 2 quarts brewed tea
- 1 cup sugar
- ¼ cup fresh lemon juice

STIR together all ingredients; cover and chill until ready to serve. **Prep: 5 min.**

Taste of the South

A Slice That Impresses

"Where There's Coke, There's Hospitality." Coca-Cola came up with that slogan in 1948, but reader Anne Kracke knows the sentiment holds just as true today whenever she serves her fabulous Coca-Cola Cake. This Southern-to-the-core dessert has been a tradition in her family ever since she began making it for each of her four children's birthdays. Although her kids are now grown, she continues to offer this cake at dinner parties, church gatherings, and picnics.

We love this cake because it's simple to prepare, easy to slice, and convenient to freeze. We guarantee you'll enjoy it, but don't count on leftovers.

COCA-COLA CAKE

MAKES 12 SERVINGS

Don't make the frosting ahead—you need to pour it over the cake shortly after baking.

- 1 cup Coca-Cola
- ½ cup buttermilk
- 1 cup butter or margarine, softened
- 1¾ cups sugar
- 2 large eggs, lightly beaten
- 2 teaspoons vanilla extract
- 2 cups all-purpose flour
- ¼ cup cocoa
- 1 teaspoon baking soda
- 1½ cups miniature marshmallows
- Coca-Cola Frosting
- Garnish: ¾ cup chopped pecans, toasted

COMBINE Coca-Cola and buttermilk; set aside.

BEAT butter at low speed with an electric mixer until creamy. Gradually add sugar; beat until blended. Add egg and vanilla; beat at low speed until blended.

COMBINE flour, cocoa, and soda. Add to butter mixture alternately with cola mixture; begin and end with flour mixture. Beat at low speed just until blended.

STIR in marshmallows. Pour batter into a greased and floured 13- x 9-inch pan.

BAKE at 350° for 30 to 35 minutes. Remove from oven; cool 10 minutes. Pour Coca-Cola Frosting over warm cake; garnish, if desired. **Prep: 8 min., Bake: 35 min., Cool: 10 min.**

Coca-Cola Frosting:

MAKES 2¼ CUPS

- ½ cup butter or margarine
- ⅓ cup Coca-Cola
- 3 tablespoons unsweetened cocoa
- 1 (16-ounce) package powdered sugar
- 1 tablespoon vanilla extract

BRING first 3 ingredients to a boil in a large saucepan over medium heat, stirring until butter melts. Remove from heat; whisk in sugar and vanilla. **Prep: 5 min., Cook: 5 min.**

ANNE KRACKE
BIRMINGHAM, ALABAMA

Sample Summer's Best

Getting your vegetables is as easy as pie.

If you're looking for new ways to cook the season's prized produce, try these easy-to-make pies. Serve them in place of the usual salad or vegetable side dish along with a simple entrée of grilled chicken or fish. We think you'll be impressed with how effortless and delicious these pies are. Be prepared for the oohs and aahs sure to come your way when you serve them.

MAQUE CHOUX PIES

MAKES 6 TO 8 SERVINGS

Maque choux is a classic Cajun vegetable dish similar to succotash. *(pictured on page 189)*

> 4 ears fresh corn, husked
> ¼ cup butter or margarine
> 1 small red bell pepper, chopped
> 1 small green bell pepper, chopped
> 1 small onion, diced
> 2 tablespoons all-purpose flour
> 2 tablespoons sugar
> ½ teaspoon salt
> ¼ teaspoon pepper
> ½ cup whipping cream
> 1 (17¼-ounce) package frozen puff pastry sheets, thawed
> 1 egg yolk, lightly beaten
> 2 tablespoons water
> Tomato-Basil Sauce

CUT corn kernels from cobs, scraping to remove milk.
MELT butter in a large skillet over medium-high heat; add corn, bell peppers, and onion; sauté 8 minutes or until corn is almost tender. Stir in flour, sugar, salt, and pepper. Gradually add cream, and cook, stirring constantly, 5 minutes or until slightly thickened. Cover and chill 30 minutes.
ROLL puff pastry to an 11½- x 10½-inch rectangle on a lightly floured surface; cut into 32 circles with a 3¼-inch round cutter.
SPOON 2 tablespoons corn mixture in center of each pastry circle; fold circles in half, and crimp edges with a fork to seal. Place on an ungreased baking sheet.
STIR together egg yolk and 2 tablespoons water; brush over pastry.
BAKE at 450° for 10 to 15 minutes or until pastry is golden. Serve pies with Tomato-Basil Sauce. **Prep: 40 min., Cook: 13 min., Chill: 30 min., Bake: 15 min.**

STEVE ROONEY
ALPHARETTA, GEORGIA

Tomato-Basil Sauce:

MAKES ⅔ CUP

Test Kitchens Director Lyda Jones developed this zippy accompaniment.

> 1 shallot, minced
> 1 garlic clove, minced
> 1 tablespoon olive oil
> 3 medium tomatoes, peeled, seeded, and chopped
> 2 tablespoons minced fresh basil
> ¼ teaspoon salt
> ¼ teaspoon pepper

SAUTÉ shallot and garlic in hot oil in a saucepan over low heat 1 minute. Add tomato, and simmer 15 minutes. Stir in remaining ingredients, and cook 2 minutes. Cool.
PROCESS tomato mixture in a food processor until smooth, stopping to scrape down sides. **Prep: 10 min., Cook: 18 min.**

SUMMER GARDEN PIE

MAKES 4 TO 6 SERVINGS

We salted the tomato slices and let them stand for 30 minutes to draw out any excess moisture that could make the pie soggy. *(pictured on page 189)*

> 3 large tomatoes, peeled, seeded, and sliced
> 1 teaspoon salt, divided
> ½ (15-ounce) package refrigerated piecrusts
> 4 bacon slices
> 3 medium-size sweet onions, halved and thinly sliced
> 1 cup (4 ounces) shredded sharp Cheddar cheese
> 1 cup mayonnaise
> ¼ teaspoon pepper
> ⅓ cup grated Parmesan cheese
> 2 tablespoons fine, dry breadcrumbs

PLACE tomato slices on paper towels, and sprinkle with ½ teaspoon salt; let stand 30 minutes.
UNFOLD piecrust, and fit into a 9-inch deep-dish pieplate. Fold edges of piecrust under, and crimp. Line with aluminum foil, and fill with pie weights or dried beans.
BAKE at 425° for 10 to 12 minutes or until lightly browned. Remove pie weights and foil.
COOK bacon in a large skillet until crisp; remove bacon, and drain on paper towels, reserving 1 teaspoon drippings in skillet. Crumble bacon, and set aside.
SAUTÉ onion in hot drippings in skillet over medium-high heat 8 to 10 minutes or until tender. Spoon onion over prepared piecrust, and top with tomato slices.
STIR together Cheddar cheese, mayonnaise, pepper, and remaining ½ teaspoon salt. Spread mixture over tomato slices. Combine Parmesan cheese and breadcrumbs; sprinkle over top.
BAKE at 350° for 30 minutes or until golden. Let stand 5 minutes before serving. Sprinkle with bacon. **Prep: 40 min., Cook: 20 min., Bake: 42 min., Stand: 35 min.**

PENNY L. COOPER
SOUTH SHORE, KENTUCKY

ITALIAN SQUASH PIE

MAKES 6 SERVINGS

A thin layer of Dijon mustard on the crust seals it and prevents the pie from becoming soggy.

1 (8-ounce) can refrigerated crescent rolls
2 teaspoons Dijon mustard
¼ cup butter or margarine
1½ pounds yellow squash (about 4 cups), thinly sliced*
1 medium onion, chopped
1 garlic clove, pressed
¼ cup chopped fresh parsley
1 tablespoon chopped fresh or ½ teaspoon dried basil
2 teaspoons chopped fresh or ½ teaspoon dried oregano
2 teaspoons chopped fresh or ½ teaspoon dried thyme
½ teaspoon salt
½ teaspoon pepper
2 large eggs
¼ cup milk
2 cups (8 ounces) shredded mozzarella cheese
Garnishes: fresh oregano sprigs, sliced yellow squash

UNROLL crescent rolls; press dough on bottom and up sides of a 10-inch tart pan, pressing to seal perforations.

BAKE at 375° for 6 minutes or until lightly browned. Gently press crust down with a wooden spoon. Spread crust with mustard, and set aside.

MELT butter in a large skillet over medium-high heat. Add 1½ pounds sliced squash, onion, and garlic; sauté mixture 7 minutes or until tender. Remove from heat, and stir in parsley and next 5 ingredients.

WHISK together eggs and milk in a large bowl; stir in cheese and vegetable mixture. Pour over crust.

BAKE at 375° for 20 to 25 minutes or until a knife inserted in center comes out clean. Garnish, if desired. **Prep: 20 min., Cook: 7 min., Bake: 31 min.**

*Substitute 1½ pounds zucchini for yellow squash, if desired.

BLANCHE A. BRACKIN
SHALIMAR, FLORIDA

ASPARAGUS SQUARES

MAKES 3 DOZEN

2 (8-ounce) cans refrigerated crescent rolls
3 tablespoons butter or margarine
1 Vidalia onion, chopped
2 garlic cloves, minced
1 pound fresh asparagus
¼ teaspoon pepper
1 cup (4 ounces) shredded mozzarella cheese
1 cup (4 ounces) shredded Swiss cheese

UNROLL crescent rolls, and press dough into an ungreased 15- x 10-inch jellyroll pan, pressing to seal perforations.

BAKE on lower oven rack at 375° for 6 to 8 minutes or until lightly browned.

MELT butter in a skillet over medium-high heat; add onion, and sauté 5 minutes. Add minced garlic; sauté 2 minutes.

SNAP off tough ends of asparagus. Cut asparagus into 1-inch pieces, and reserve tips.

ADD asparagus pieces to skillet; sauté 4 to 6 minutes or until crisp-tender. Add pepper and asparagus tips; sauté 1 to 2 minutes or until tender.

SPOON asparagus mixture onto prepared crust; sprinkle with cheeses.

BAKE asparagus mixture on lower oven rack at 375° for 6 to 8 minutes or until cheese melts. Cut into squares. **Prep: 20 min., Cook: 15 min., Bake: 16 min.**

ELLIE WELLS
LAKELAND, FLORIDA

VIDALIA ONION PIE WITH MUSHROOMS

MAKES 4 TO 6 SERVINGS

1 large Vidalia onion, halved and thinly sliced
2 cups sliced shiitake mushrooms
1 tablespoon olive oil
4 large eggs
1 cup whipping cream
1 tablespoon chopped fresh thyme
1½ teaspoons salt
1 teaspoon pepper
⅛ teaspoon ground nutmeg
1 frozen (9-inch) deep-dish pastry shell, thawed

SAUTÉ onion and mushrooms in hot oil in a large skillet over medium heat 15 minutes or until tender.

STIR together eggs and next 5 ingredients in a large bowl; stir in onion mixture. Spoon mixture into pastry shell, and place on a baking sheet.

BAKE on lower oven rack at 350° for 45 minutes or until done. **Prep: 10 min., Cook: 15 min., Bake: 45 min.**

MARK HAMRICK
DILLSBORO, NORTH CAROLINA

Get a Kick Out of Green

These enticing recipes highlight the delicious results when green tomatoes and tomatillos are prepared together. You'll definitely want to try both of these yummy selections.

GREEN BARBECUE SAUCE

MAKES 3 CUPS

Serve over grilled chicken, fish, or shrimp.

2½ pounds green tomatoes, coarsely chopped
1½ pounds tomatillos, husked and coarsely chopped
2 garlic cloves, pressed
½ to 1 cup sugar
1 cup white vinegar
1 large sweet onion, coarsely chopped (about 1½ cups)
1 tablespoon dry mustard
½ teaspoon dried crushed red pepper
1 teaspoon salt

COOK all ingredients in a stockpot over medium-low heat 2 hours or until tomatoes and tomatillos are tender. Cool.

PROCESS green tomato mixture, in batches, in a food processor or blender until smooth. **Prep: 15 min., Cook: 2 hrs.**

NOTE: Sauce may be stored in refrigerator up to 1 week.

FRIED GREEN TOMATO STACKS

MAKES 6 SERVINGS

For bacon drippings, fry three to four bacon slices in a skillet until crisp; remove bacon from skillet, and reserve bacon for another use.

- 3 tomatillos, husked
- 2 tablespoons bacon drippings
- 1 garlic clove, pressed
- 1½ teaspoons salt, divided
- 1 teaspoon pepper, divided
- ½ teaspoon paprika
- ¼ cup thinly sliced fresh basil
- 1½ cups self-rising yellow cornmeal
- 4 large green tomatoes, cut into 18 (¼-inch) slices
- 1 cup buttermilk
- Peanut oil
- 1 (8-ounce) package cream cheese, softened
- 1 (4-ounce) package goat cheese, softened
- ⅓ cup milk
- 1 teaspoon sugar
- Garnish: fresh basil leaves

BRING tomatillos and water to cover to a boil in a small saucepan; reduce heat, and simmer 10 minutes. Drain tomatillos, and cool.

PROCESS tomatillos, bacon drippings, garlic, ½ teaspoon salt, ½ teaspoon pepper, and paprika in a food processor or blender until smooth; stir in basil. Cover and chill until ready to serve.

STIR together cornmeal, ¾ teaspoon salt, and remaining ½ teaspoon pepper. Dip tomato slices in buttermilk; dredge in cornmeal mixture.

POUR oil to a depth of ½ inch into a skillet; heat to 375°. Fry tomato slices, in batches, in hot oil 1 to 2 minutes on each side; drain on a wire rack over paper towels. Keep warm.

COMBINE cream cheese, next 3 ingredients, and remaining ¼ teaspoon salt. Place 1 fried tomato slice on each of 6 salad plates; top each evenly with half of cream cheese mixture. Top each with 1 fried tomato slice and remaining cream cheese mixture. Top with remaining 6 fried tomato slices; drizzle with tomatillo dressing. Garnish, if desired. **Prep: 15 min., Cook: 10 min., Fry: 4 min. per batch**

Perfect Po'boys

This New Orleans institution, which is also a favorite at seafood restaurants along the Gulf Coast, is rich with history and some of the best flavors of the region. It's a loaf of warm, fresh French bread piled high with fried shrimp, plump fried oysters, or a variety of other savory fillings.

A 1929 New Orleans streetcar strike inspired the owners of Martin Brothers restaurant to start making these sandwiches for the struggling workers, or "poor boys." In no time, po'boys were in demand. We invite you to take a bite.

DRESSED OYSTER PO'BOYS

MAKES 4 SANDWICHES

- 1¼ cups self-rising cornmeal
- 2 tablespoons Creole seasoning
- 2 (12-ounce) containers fresh Select oysters, drained
- Peanut or vegetable oil
- 1 cup mayonnaise, divided
- 2 tablespoons white vinegar
- 2 tablespoons Dijon mustard
- 1 (10-ounce) package finely shredded cabbage
- 2 tablespoons ketchup
- 1 tablespoon prepared horseradish
- 1 teaspoon Creole seasoning
- ¾ teaspoon paprika
- 4 French bread rolls, split and toasted

COMBINE cornmeal and Creole seasoning; dredge oysters in mixture.

POUR oil to a depth of 2 inches into a Dutch oven; heat to 375°. Fry oysters, in 3 batches, 2 to 3 minutes or until golden. Drain on wire racks.

STIR together ½ cup mayonnaise, vinegar, and mustard. Stir in cabbage; set slaw aside.

STIR together remaining ½ cup mayonnaise, ketchup, and next 3 ingredients.

SPREAD cut sides of rolls with mayonnaise mixture. Place oysters and slaw on bottom halves of rolls; cover with roll tops. **Prep: 30 min., Fry: 3 min. per batch**

SHRIMP PO'BOYS

MAKES 4 SANDWICHES

Southern Living photographer Beth Dreiling recalls, "I went through college eating these." *(pictured on page 192)*

- 2 pounds unpeeled, large fresh shrimp
- 1¼ cups all-purpose flour
- ½ teaspoon salt
- ½ teaspoon pepper
- ½ cup milk
- 1 large egg
- Peanut oil
- ⅓ cup butter
- 1 teaspoon minced garlic
- 4 French bread rolls, split
- Rémoulade Sauce
- 1 cup shredded lettuce

PEEL shrimp, and devein, if desired.

COMBINE flour, salt, and pepper. Stir together milk and egg until smooth. Toss shrimp in milk mixture; dredge in flour mixture.

POUR oil to a depth of 2 inches into a Dutch oven; heat to 375°. Fry shrimp, in batches, 1 to 2 minutes or until golden; drain on wire racks.

MELT butter; add garlic. Spread cut sides of rolls evenly with butter mixture; place on a large baking sheet.

BAKE at 450° for 8 minutes. Spread cut sides of rolls evenly with Rémoulade Sauce. Place shrimp and lettuce on bottom halves of rolls; cover with roll tops. **Prep: 32 min., Fry: 2 min. per batch, Bake: 8 min.**

Rémoulade Sauce:

MAKES 1½ CUPS

- 1 cup mayonnaise
- 3 green onions, sliced
- 2 tablespoons Creole mustard
- 1 tablespoon chopped fresh parsley
- 1 teaspoon minced garlic
- 1 teaspoon prepared horseradish

STIR together all ingredients; cover and chill until ready to serve. **Prep: 5 min.**

BETH DREILING
BIRMINGHAM, ALABAMA

Beat-the-Heat Beverages

Refreshing drinks rival a dip in the pool as a way to cool off.

Settle into a real or an imaginary beach chair, and sip these fruity frozen concoctions. Several can be prepared ahead, so when temperatures across the South soar, just grab some out of the freezer, finish the last recipe step, and enjoy.

SOUTHERN BREEZE

MAKES 12 SERVINGS

The raspberry ice cubes can be made in advance and stored in heavy-duty zip-top plastic bags in the freezer until ready to serve.

- **1 cup sugar**
- **1 (0.22-ounce) envelope unsweetened blue raspberry lemonade mix**
- **7 cups water**
- **1 (6-ounce) can frozen lemonade concentrate, thawed**
- **1 (46-ounce) can unsweetened pineapple juice, chilled**
- **1 (2-liter) bottle ginger ale, chilled**

STIR together first 4 ingredients in a 2-quart pitcher; pour evenly into 5 ice cube trays, and freeze at least 8 hours.
COMBINE pineapple juice and ginger ale; serve over raspberry ice cubes. **Prep: 10 min., Freeze: 8 hrs.**

NOTE: For testing purposes only, we used Kool-Aid Island Twists Ice Blue Raspberry Lemonade Unsweetened Soft Drink Mix.

DONNA EVANS
BIRMINGHAM, ALABAMA

WATERMELON MARGARITAS

MAKES 5 CUPS

- **Lime juice**
- **Sugar**
- **⅓ cup tequila**
- **2 cups crushed ice**
- **2 cups seeded, chopped watermelon**
- **¼ cup sugar**
- **¼ cup lime juice (about 1½ limes)**
- **1 tablespoon vodka**
- **1 tablespoon orange liqueur**

COAT rims of cocktail glasses with lime juice; dip in sugar.
PROCESS next 7 ingredients in a blender until slushy. Pour into prepared glasses. **Prep: 10 min.**

NOTE: To make ahead, place mixture into a large heavy-duty zip-top plastic bag; seal and freeze up to 1 month. Let stand about 30 minutes before serving.

MARY PAPPAS
RICHMOND, VIRGINIA

STRAWBERRY SLUSH

MAKES ABOUT 11 CUPS

- **2 (10-ounce) cans frozen strawberry daiquiri mix concentrate, thawed and divided**
- **1 cup water, divided**
- **Ice cubes**
- **3 cups lemon-lime soft drink, chilled**

COMBINE 1 can daiquiri mix, ½ cup water, and enough ice cubes to reach 4-cup level in blender container; process until smooth. Pour into a 3-quart container; set aside.
REPEAT procedure with remaining 1 can daiquiri mix, remaining ½ cup water, and enough ice cubes to reach 4-cup level in blender container; process until smooth. Add to first batch in 3-quart container; cover and freeze 8 hours or until firm.
REMOVE from freezer; let stand 15 minutes or until slush can be broken into pieces. Add lemon-lime soft drink, stirring until smooth. **Prep: 10 min., Freeze: 8 hrs., Stand: 15 min.**

NOTE: To make ahead, place each blended batch of strawberry daiquiri mixture into a large heavy-duty zip-top plastic bag; seal and freeze. When ready to use, proceed with recipe as directed, using 1½ cups lemon-lime soft drink per batch.

FRUIT PARFAIT SLUSHY

MAKES ABOUT 1 GALLON

- **¾ cup sugar**
- **1¼ cups water**
- **1 (20-ounce) can crushed pineapple in juice**
- **1 (10-ounce) package frozen strawberries**
- **1 (12-ounce) can frozen pink lemonade concentrate, thawed**
- **1 (6-ounce) can frozen orange juice concentrate without pulp, thawed**
- **2 (1-liter) bottles lime-flavored sparkling water**

HEAT sugar and 1¼ cups water in a saucepan over medium heat 5 minutes or until sugar dissolves and reaches a syrup consistency.
PROCESS crushed pineapple, frozen strawberries, lemonade concentrate, and orange juice concentrate, in batches, in a blender until smooth. Stir in sugar syrup, and freeze at least 8 hours.
REMOVE from freezer, and let stand 30 minutes or until mixture can be broken into pieces. Stir in sparkling water, and serve immediately. **Prep: 10 min., Cook: 5 min., Freeze: 8 hrs., Stand: 30 min.**

RENEE HEISER
SARASOTA, FLORIDA

Start With Pasta

Pasta is one of the most versatile foods around. Southerners love it chilled in macaroni salad, a covered-dish dinner standard; we've included some twists on that basic idea, such as Tortellini Salad. Except for chilling, baking, and standing times, all of these recipes can be assembled in 30 minutes or less. Just right for the time-pressed pasta lovers among us.

ELLIE'S LASAGNA

MAKES 6 SERVINGS

Reader Donald Ruffle remembers his mother, Ellie, making this simple dish every Christmas Eve. His wife, Betty, now makes it year-round.

- 12 lasagna noodles
- 1 (15-ounce) container ricotta cheese
- 1 teaspoon pressed garlic
- 1 pound ground beef
- 2 (26-ounce) jars spaghetti sauce
- 4 cups (16 ounces) shredded Italian three-cheese blend

COOK lasagna noodles according to package directions; drain and set aside.
STIR together ricotta cheese and garlic; set aside.
COOK beef in a large skillet, stirring until it crumbles and is no longer pink; drain. Stir in sauce.
LAYER one-third each of lasagna noodles, ricotta cheese mixture, shredded cheese, and beef mixture in a lightly greased 13- x 9-inch baking dish. Repeat layers twice.
BAKE at 375° for 35 to 40 minutes. Let stand 5 to 10 minutes before serving. Prep: 30 min., Bake: 40 min., Stand: 10 min.

NOTE: For testing purposes only, we used Classico di Napoli Tomato & Basil Pasta Sauce.

BETTY RUFFLE
ELLICOTT CITY, MARYLAND

SESAME NOODLE SALAD

MAKES 4 SERVINGS

This simple side can become a main dish if you add meat or vegetable stir-ins. Try finely diced fresh tomato, squash, and green pepper; chopped cooked chicken; leftover grilled shrimp or flank steak; or fried tofu cubes.

- 1 (8-ounce) package linguine
- ¼ cup rice vinegar
- ¼ cup soy sauce
- ¼ cup dark sesame oil
- 1 teaspoon sugar
- 5 green onions, sliced
- Toasted sesame seeds (optional)

COOK linguine according to package directions; drain and rinse linguine with cold water.
STIR together vinegar and next 3 ingredients in a large bowl. Stir in linguine and onions; sprinkle with sesame seeds, if desired. Serve immediately. Prep: 20 min.

LINDA L. SHERRILL
RESTON, VIRGINIA

TORTELLINI SALAD

MAKES 6 SERVINGS

- 2 (9-ounce) packages refrigerated cheese tortellini
- 1 (14-ounce) can quartered artichoke hearts, drained
- 1 cup Caesar salad dressing
- 3 ounces salami, sliced
- 1 (2¼-ounce) can sliced ripe olives, drained
- 4 green onions, chopped
- Garnish: whole green onions

COOK cheese tortellini according to package directions; drain and rinse with cold water.
TOSS together tortellini and next 5 ingredients; garnish, if desired. Serve immediately. Prep: 20 min.

MARILYN STARKS
BATON ROUGE, LOUISIANA

ZESTY CHICKEN-PASTA SALAD

MAKES 4 SERVINGS

- 1 (8-ounce) package elbow macaroni
- 1 (13-ounce) bottle peppercorn-Ranch dressing
- 2½ cups chopped cooked chicken
- 1 (9-ounce) package frozen sweet peas, thawed
- 1 (2¼-ounce) can sliced ripe olives, drained
- 1 pint cherry tomatoes, halved
- Salt to taste

COOK elbow macaroni according to package directions; drain and rinse with cold water.
STIR together macaroni and remaining ingredients; cover and chill at least 1 hour. Prep: 20 min., Chill: 1 hr.

DONNA JOHNSON
HAMPSTEAD, MARYLAND

Starry Night Nibbles

Grab your sleeping bag and flashlight. A roomy backyard is ideal for young campers to sleep out amid the glow of lightning bugs and sounds of nature. But the experience wouldn't be complete without bite-size nibbles. These recipes received enthusiastic nods from our little tasters. (If the dark skies get scary, cozy up with man's best friend. He'll oversee the troops until dawn and won't let the bedbugs bite.)

WIENIE ROLLUPS

MAKES 32 ROLLUPS

- 2 (8-ounce) cans refrigerated crescent rolls
- 1 (8-ounce) block Cheddar cheese
- 1 (16-ounce) package cocktail franks
- ½ cup warm barbecue sauce

UNROLL crescent rolls (do not separate), and cut into 32 (1-inch-wide) strips.

CUT block of cheese lengthwise to make 2 rectangular blocks; slice each block into 16 slices.

PLACE 1 cocktail frank and 1 cheese slice on each dough strip, and roll up tightly, pinching seams to seal.

PLACE rollups on an aluminum foil-lined baking sheet; bake at 375° for 12 to 15 minutes or until golden. Serve immediately with barbecue sauce. **Prep: 15 min., Bake: 15 min.**

NOTE: For testing purposes only, we used Bryan Cocktail Smokies for cocktail franks.

COURTNEY SNOW
WYLIE, TEXAS

HONEY-NUT SNACK MIX

MAKES 7 CUPS

    4 cups toasted oat bran cereal
    2 cups uncooked quick-cooking oats
    1 cup chopped pecans
    ¼ teaspoon salt
    1½ teaspoons ground cinnamon
    ½ cup butter or margarine
    ½ cup firmly packed brown
       sugar
    ½ cup honey
    1 cup sweetened dried cranberries or
       raisins

COMBINE first 5 ingredients in a large bowl; set aside.

STIR together butter, brown sugar, and honey in a small saucepan over low heat, stirring until butter melts and sugar dissolves.

POUR butter mixture over cereal mixture, stirring to coat. Spread in a single layer on an aluminum foil-lined 15- x 10-inch jellyroll pan.

BAKE at 325° for 20 minutes, stirring once. Stir in cranberries, and bake 5 more minutes. Spread immediately on wax paper; cool. Store snack mix in an airtight container. **Prep: 10 min., Bake: 25 min.**

NOTE: For testing purposes only, we used Quaker Oat Bran for toasted oat bran cereal.

SARAH ROBERTS
WATAUGA, TENNESSEE

BANANA-CHOCOLATE CUPCAKES

MAKES 1½ DOZEN

These treats are delicious with or without the vanilla frosting.

    ¼ cup butter or margarine, softened
    1½ cups sugar
    2 large eggs
    3 small bananas, mashed (about
       1 cup)
    1 teaspoon vanilla extract
    2 cups all-purpose flour
    1½ teaspoons baking soda
    ⅛ teaspoon salt
    ⅓ cup buttermilk
    1 cup (6 ounces) semisweet chocolate
       morsels
    Vegetable cooking spray
    1 (16-ounce) container ready-to-
       spread vanilla frosting (optional)

BEAT butter at medium speed with an electric mixer until creamy; gradually add sugar, beating well. Add eggs, banana, and vanilla, beating until blended.

STIR together flour, soda, and salt. Add flour mixture to banana mixture alternately with buttermilk, beginning and ending with flour mixture; beat at low speed until blended after each addition. Stir in morsels.

PLACE paper baking cups in muffin pans, and coat with cooking spray; spoon batter into pans, filling cups two-thirds full.

BAKE at 350° for 17 minutes. Remove cupcakes from pans immediately, and cool on wire racks. Spread with frosting, if desired. **Prep: 30 min., Bake: 17 min.**

LISA MENCI
AIKEN, SOUTH CAROLINA

Great Grilled Pork

The next time you want to wow your friends, give this dish a try. You'll be glad you did.

GRILLED PORK TENDERLOIN

MAKES 8 TO 10 SERVINGS

    1 garlic bulb
    2 tablespoons extra-virgin olive oil
    1 teaspoon salt
    ½ teaspoon pepper
    4 (¾- to 1-pound) pork tenderloins
    2 cups dry red wine, divided
    1 tablespoon butter or margarine
    12 dried tomatoes, cut into strips
    12 kalamata olives, pitted and halved
    4 fresh mushrooms, sliced
    2 fresh rosemary sprigs
    1 (14-ounce) can beef broth

CUT off pointed end of garlic bulb; place garlic on a piece of aluminum foil. Fold foil to seal. Bake at 400° for 30 minutes; cool. Squeeze pulp from garlic cloves.

STIR together 1 tablespoon garlic pulp, oil, salt, and pepper; rub over pork. Place in a large heavy-duty zip-top plastic bag; pour ½ cup wine over pork. Seal and chill 2 hours, turning once.

MELT butter in a skillet over medium heat. Add next 3 ingredients; sauté 4 to 5 minutes. Add remaining 1½ cups wine and rosemary; cook over medium-high heat 20 minutes. Add broth; cook 20 minutes. Discard rosemary. Stir in remaining garlic pulp; cook 2 minutes. Remove from heat. Remove pork from marinade, discarding marinade.

GRILL, covered with grill lid, over medium-high heat (350° to 400°) about 20 minutes, turning once, or until meat thermometer inserted into thickest portion registers 160°. Remove from heat; let stand 5 minutes. Cut into ½-inch-thick slices. Top with tomato mixture; serve immediately. **Prep: 20 min., Bake: 30 min., Chill: 2 hrs., Cook: 47 min., Grill: 20 min., Stand: 5 min.**

CHARLES WITT
JACKSON, MISSISSIPPI

Ground Beef to the Rescue

Your family's summer activities are soon to be replaced by back-to-school shopping, soccer practice, and car pools. While you've still got some breathing room, cook and freeze several batches of Savory Meat Base to get a jump-start on weeknight meals. Dolores Long of Abingdon, Virginia, who shared this recipe with us, says she raised all four of her children on it.

SAVORY MEAT BASE

MAKES 8 CUPS

- **3 pounds lean ground beef**
- **2 large onions, chopped**
- **1 large green bell pepper, chopped**
- **1 teaspoon bottled minced garlic**
- **1 (26-ounce) jar marinara sauce**
- **1 teaspoon salt**
- **½ teaspoon pepper**

COOK first 4 ingredients in a Dutch oven over medium-high heat; stir until meat crumbles and is no longer pink. Drain mixture; return to Dutch oven.
STIR in marinara sauce, salt, and pepper; cover and simmer, stirring occasionally, 15 minutes. Cool 10 minutes. Spoon about 4 cups mixture into each of 2 heavy-duty zip-top plastic bags; seal and freeze until ready to use. **Prep: 20 min., Cook: 15 min., Cool: 10 min.**

SPAGHETTI WITH MEAT SAUCE: Heat 1 package (4 cups) Savory Meat Base, thawed, in a Dutch oven over medium heat. Stir in 1 (14½-ounce) can diced tomatoes with Italian herbs, 1 (8-ounce) can tomato sauce, 1 teaspoon dried Italian seasoning, and ½ teaspoon dried basil. Cover, reduce heat, and simmer 20 minutes. Serve over 12 ounces hot cooked spaghetti with a tossed green salad and garlic bread. Makes 6 servings.

SLOPPY JOES: Heat 1 package (4 cups) Savory Meat Base, thawed, in a Dutch oven over medium heat. Stir in 2 teaspoons chili powder and 1 teaspoon brown sugar. Cover and simmer, stirring occasionally, 15 to 20 minutes. Serve on hamburger buns with potato chips and fresh fruit. Makes 6 servings.

EASY BEEF AND MACARONI: Heat 1 package (4 cups) Savory Meat Base, thawed, in a Dutch oven over medium heat. Stir in 1 (14½-ounce) can diced tomatoes, 2 teaspoons chili powder, 2 teaspoons paprika, and 1 bay leaf. Cover, reduce heat, and simmer 15 minutes. Discard bay leaf. Stir in 4 cups hot cooked elbow macaroni; cook 5 minutes. Top with sour cream and sliced green onions. Makes 6 servings.

DOLORES LONG
ABINGDON, VIRGINIA

TACO SALAD

MAKES 6 SERVINGS

- **1 package (4 cups) Savory Meat Base, thawed**
- **2 teaspoons chili powder**
- **½ teaspoon salt**
- **¼ teaspoon dried oregano**
- **¼ teaspoon ground cumin**
- **1 (6.5-ounce) package taco salad shells**
- **Shredded iceberg lettuce**
- **Toppings: shredded Mexican four-cheese blend, chopped tomato, sour cream, salsa, sliced ripe olives, sliced jalapeño pepper**

HEAT Savory Meat Base in a Dutch oven over medium heat. Stir in chili powder and next 3 ingredients; cover, reduce heat, and simmer 15 minutes.
BAKE 6 taco salad shells according to package directions, reserving remaining shells for another use.
FILL each shell with lettuce, and top evenly with meat mixture. Serve with desired toppings. **Prep: 20 min., Cook: 15 min., Bake: 7 min.**

NOTE: For testing purposes only, we used Old El Paso Taco Salad Shells.

GREEN CHILE ENCHILADAS

MAKES 6 SERVINGS

Here's another great use of ground beef.

- **1 pound lean ground beef**
- **½ teaspoon garlic powder**
- **1 (8-ounce) block colby-Jack cheese blend, shredded**
- **1 large onion, chopped**
- **1 (10¾-ounce) can cream of chicken soup**
- **1 (5-ounce) can evaporated milk**
- **1 (8-ounce) loaf pasteurized prepared cheese product, cubed**
- **1 (0.4-ounce) envelope Ranch dip mix**
- **1 (4-ounce) can chopped green chiles**
- **1 (2-ounce) jar diced pimiento, drained**
- **Water**
- **12 (8-inch) corn tortillas**

COOK beef and garlic powder in a skillet, stirring until meat crumbles and is no longer pink. Remove from heat; drain. Stir in shredded cheese and onion; set aside.
HEAT next 3 ingredients in a saucepan over medium heat; stir until melted. Stir in dip mix, chiles, and pimiento.
POUR water to a depth of 1 inch into a skillet; heat over medium-high heat. Dip tortillas, 1 at a time, into hot water, using tongs; soak 2 to 3 seconds. Spoon about ⅓ cup meat mixture onto 1 side of each tortilla; roll up tightly, and place in a lightly greased 13- x 9-inch baking dish. Top with cheese sauce.
BAKE, covered, at 350° for 30 minutes. Uncover and bake 10 more minutes. **Prep: 30 min., Bake: 40 min.**

VIVIAN M. PRINE
PELL CITY, ALABAMA

Summer Garden Pie, page 182

Maque Choux Pies, page 182

Chocolate-Zucchini Cake, page 181

Shrimp Po' Boys, page 184

Living Light

Savory, Meaty Dishes

Full of high-quality protein and easy-to-absorb iron, meat is a delicious, versatile, and nutritious dinnertime choice. The following recipes take lower fat cuts of beef and lamb and infuse them with vibrant flavors. When supper's ready, rest assured that you can dig in without guilt.

SMART AND SAUCY ROSEMARY-CHERRY LAMB CHOPS

MAKES 4 SERVINGS

- ½ teaspoon salt
- ½ teaspoon white pepper
- 2 garlic cloves, pressed
- 2 teaspoons grated fresh ginger
- 1¼ pounds bone-in lamb loin chops (2 inches thick)
- Vegetable cooking spray
- Rosemary-Cherry Sauce

COMBINE first 4 ingredients; rub over chops. Cover and chill up to 8 hours.
SPRAY chops evenly on both sides with cooking spray.
GRILL, covered with grill lid, over medium-high heat (350° to 400°) 8 to 10 minutes on each side or to desired degree of doneness (140° to 150° for medium). Serve with Rosemary-Cherry Sauce. **Prep: 8 min., Chill: 8 hrs., Grill: 20 min.**

Cooking Chart: Bone-In Lamb Loin Chops

Rare: 8 minutes per side
Medium rare: 10 minutes per side
Medium: 12 minutes per side
Medium well: 14 minutes per side

Rosemary-Cherry Sauce:

MAKES ¾ CUP

- ¼ cup chopped onion
- 1 teaspoon olive oil
- 1 garlic clove, minced
- ½ teaspoon grated fresh ginger
- ½ cup fat-free chicken broth
- ½ cup cherry fruit spread*
- 1 tablespoon balsamic vinegar
- 2 teaspoons cornstarch
- 1 tablespoon chopped fresh rosemary
- ¼ teaspoon salt
- ½ teaspoon pepper

COOK onion in hot olive oil in a small saucepan over medium heat 5 minutes or until onion is tender.
ADD garlic and ginger; cook 1 minute. Whisk in broth and fruit spread; bring to a boil.
WHISK together vinegar and remaining ingredients, and whisk into boiling onion mixture.
COOK, whisking constantly, 1 to 2 minutes or until sauce is thickened. Serve immediately. **Prep: 10 min., Cook: 8 min.**

NOTE: If sauce is too thick, add a little extra chicken broth, and cook, covered, over low heat until thoroughly heated, stirring often.

*For testing purposes only, we used Polaner All Fruit for cherry fruit spread. Seedless raspberry or blackberry jam may be substituted.

Recipe adapted from *Grill Power* (QVC Publishing, 2000) by Holly Rudin-Braschi, M.A., ACSM.

Per serving: Calories 251 (27% from fat); Fat 7.5g (sat 2.5g, mono 3.3g, poly 0.7g); Protein 20g; Carb 25g; Fiber 0.4g; Chol 63mg; Iron 1.7mg; Sodium 557mg; Calc 22mg

CILANTRO-GARLIC SIRLOIN WITH ZESTY CORN SALSA

MAKES 8 SERVINGS

- 1 cup (1 bunch) fresh cilantro, packed
- 2 garlic cloves
- 1 tablespoon grated lime rind
- 3 tablespoons fresh lime juice
- ½ teaspoon salt
- ½ teaspoon ground cumin
- ¼ to ½ teaspoon ground red pepper
- 2 pounds top sirloin steak (1¼ inches thick)
- Zesty Corn Salsa
- Garnish: fresh cilantro sprig

PROCESS first 7 ingredients in a food processor or blender until blended, and rub cilantro mixture over sirloin steak. Chill 2 hours.
GRILL, covered with grill lid, over medium-high heat (350° to 400°) 10 to 12 minutes on each side or to desired degree of doneness. Let steak stand 10 minutes.
CUT steak diagonally across the grain into thin strips. Serve with Zesty Corn Salsa; garnish, if desired. **Prep: 15 min., Chill: 2 hrs., Grill: 24 min., Stand: 10 min.**

Zesty Corn Salsa:

MAKES 2 CUPS (ABOUT 8 SERVINGS)

- 6 ears fresh corn, husked
- 2 teaspoons olive oil
- ½ teaspoon grated lime rind
- ¼ cup fresh lime juice
- 1 small jalapeño pepper, minced
- ¼ teaspoon salt
- ¼ teaspoon ground cumin

GRILL corn, covered with grill lid, over medium-high heat (350° to 400°) 10 minutes on each side or until browned on all sides. Remove from grill; cool.
CUT corn from cob into a bowl; stir in oil and remaining ingredients. **Prep: 15 min., Grill: 20 min.**

LISA ZACHARIA
TALLAHASSEE, FLORIDA

Per serving: Calories 232 (30% from fat); Fat 7.9g (sat 2.6g, mono 3.6g, poly 0.7g); Protein 27.7g; Carb 13g; Fiber 2g; Chol 75mg; Iron 3.4mg; Sodium 285mg; Calc 25mg

from our kitchen

Is It Red Snapper?

A discussion in a restaurant made us curious about fish labeled "red snapper." There's a whole category of great-tasting fish called snapper, and there are some differences among species. When you buy small (2- to 3-pound) whole red snapper at a seafood market, there's a good chance it's vermilion snapper. While these two types of seafood look very similar, this small fish has a darker, finer flesh; richer taste; and softer texture than true red snapper. The latter is large (generally 5 pounds and up) and seldom found whole. If you must have the real thing, look for big, red-skinned, firm-fleshed fillets. You'll find the freshest fish at seafood markets. Get to know the staff, and tell them what you like. They'll help you get the best selections.

Southern Style on the Cheap

Whether we're entertaining guests or simply having dinner with family, we Southerners like to do it with flair. We've learned, too, that elegant decor doesn't have to be expensive. To substitute creativity for cash at your next gathering, adorn the table with fresh flowers from your yard instead of buying costly floral arrangements. If your garden isn't in bloom, display a combination of greenery and candles.

Kitchen Mathematician

Here's a tool that takes the guesswork out of food preparation. KitchenCalc can scale your favorite recipe up or down to serve any number of guests. It calculates portion sizes and converts measurements. The built-in timer counts forward and backward and keeps elapsed time. Get the handheld model for $24.95 or the countertop version for $39.95. For more information call 1-800-854-8075, or visit **www.kitchencalc.com**

Drink Your Yogurt

Assistant Foods Editor Cynthia Ann Briscoe is a fan of Stonyfield Farm's new Drinkable Lowfat Yogurt. The 10-ounce beverage is portable, convenient, and available in four delicious flavors: Peach, Raspberry, Strawberry, and Tropical Fruit. Keep some on hand for breakfast on the go or a nutritious, refreshing afternoon snack. You'll find this new product next to the regular yogurt in your supermarket's dairy case.

Get Rid of the Red

New Cascade Plastic Booster brightens discolored plastic containers. It gets rid of the stains left by spaghetti sauce, chili, etc.; it's also a good way to freshen the interior of your dishwasher. Squeeze ¼ cup into the prewash cup (the one without a closable lid); then fill the main dispenser cup with your favorite detergent, load the washer, and let it run on the normal setting (including drying cycle). The product is available in 6.8-ounce tubes for about $3.

Road Food

Pass up burgers and fries on your next road trip, and pack your own lunch. You can enjoy healthy sandwiches, fruit, and beverages at a fraction of the cost. Here are our travel tips.
- Pita bread makes great sandwiches that don't get smashed.
- Choose easy-to-pack snacks, such as nuts and pretzels, in family-size bags. You'll save money and have less trash in the car.
- Crackers, spreads, dips, and cheeses are also terrific between-meal treats.
- Let the kids help pack the cooler. Store it in the backseat of the car instead of the trunk. It'll stay cool and be within easy reach.
- Stop, stretch, and eat in a shady spot at a rest area.

Tips and Tidbits

- Sherri Brown of Brooksville, Florida, gets creative with quick dessert toppings. "I melt the kids' favorite candy bars to pour over ice cream or cake."

- To keep the meringue on your favorite pie from weeping, Vie Warshaw of our Test Kitchens staff suggests substituting powdered sugar for granulated sugar in the recipe. Be sure to seal the meringue all the way around the edge of the crust.

- Prevent stuffed mushrooms and cherry tomatoes from sliding around the serving platter by anchoring them with cream cheese. Pipe or spoon dots of softened cheese on the plate; then gently press the appetizers onto the cheese. Guests can pass around trays of these delicious bites without accidents.

September

Pears Ripe for the Harvest

This seasonal fruit is more versatile than you think. Enjoy it in salads, entrées, and desserts.

Pear trees are a familiar sight in backyards throughout the South. Perhaps you even have memories of watching the snowy white blossoms turn into fruit that was either eaten fresh from the tree or cooked up in sweet preserves.

But pears aren't just for snacking or canning anymore. They make an elegant addition to main dishes and, of course, desserts. You can also serve pears with a fine port and a bold blue cheese (such as Gorgonzola) to end a special meal.

CARAMEL-GLAZED PEAR CAKE

MAKES 12 SERVINGS

Crunchy pecans and a creamy brown sugar glaze give this cake a decidedly Southern touch. *(pictured on pages 226-227)*

> 4 ripe Bartlett pears, peeled and diced (about 3 cups)
> 1 tablespoon sugar
> 3 large eggs
> 2 cups sugar
> 1¼ cups vegetable oil
> 3 cups all-purpose flour
> 1 teaspoon salt
> 1 teaspoon baking soda
> 1½ cups pecans, coarsely chopped
> 2 teaspoons vanilla extract
> Caramel Glaze

TOSS together pears and 1 tablespoon sugar; let stand 5 minutes.
BEAT eggs, 2 cups sugar, and oil at medium speed with an electric mixer until blended.
COMBINE flour, salt, and baking soda, and add to egg mixture, beating at low speed until blended. Fold in pears, chopped pecans, and vanilla. Pour batter into a greased and floured 10-inch Bundt pan.
BAKE at 350° for 1 hour or until a wooden pick inserted in center of cake comes out clean. Remove from pan, and drizzle Caramel Glaze over warm cake. **Prep: 25 min., Stand: 5 min., Bake: 1 hr.**

Caramel Glaze:

MAKES 1½ CUPS

> 1 cup firmly packed brown sugar
> ½ cup butter
> ¼ cup evaporated milk

STIR together brown sugar, butter, and evaporated milk in a small saucepan over medium heat; bring to a boil, and cook, stirring constantly, 2½ minutes or until sugar dissolves. **Cook: 8 min.**

CAROL S. NOBLE
BURGAW, NORTH CAROLINA

PEAR-CRANBERRY COMPOTE

MAKES 6 SERVINGS

Complement the smoky flavors of baked ham, grilled chicken, or pork tenderloin with this sweet, tangy side dish. *(pictured on page 227)*

> 1 (12-ounce) tub whole cranberry-orange sauce
> ¼ cup sugar
> 2 tablespoons fresh lemon juice
> ¼ teaspoon ground cinnamon
> ¼ teaspoon ground ginger
> 8 ripe Seckel pears, peeled
> Garnish: orange rind strips

BRING first 5 ingredients to a boil in a medium saucepan over high heat, stirring constantly. Remove from heat.
ARRANGE pears in a lightly greased deep 8-inch round baking dish; pour cranberry mixture over pears.
BAKE at 350° for 1 hour. Garnish, if desired. **Prep: 10 min., Cook: 5 min., Bake: 1 hr.**

NOTE: For testing purposes only, we used Ocean Spray Cran-Fruit Cranberry-Orange Sauce. To save time, boil sauce as directed; reduce heat to low, and add pears. Cover and simmer 20 to 25 minutes or until tender.

MRS. WADE HARMON
GREENVILLE, NORTH CAROLINA

FRESH PEAR SALAD WITH ASIAN SESAME DRESSING

MAKES 6 SERVINGS

Sweet slices of Red Bartlett pears add layers of taste, color, and texture to this salad. *(pictured on page 226)*

> 2 cups shredded red cabbage
> 2 cups shredded romaine lettuce
> 3 Red Bartlett pears, sliced
> 2 medium carrots, shredded (about 1 cup)
> 1 green onion, chopped
> Asian Sesame Dressing
> 2 teaspoons sesame seeds, toasted (optional)

TOSS together first 5 ingredients in a large bowl, and drizzle with Asian Sesame Dressing, tossing gently to coat. Sprinkle with sesame seeds, if desired. Serve immediately. **Prep: 15 min.**

Asian Sesame Dressing:

MAKES ½ CUP

> ¼ cup vegetable oil
> 2 tablespoons white wine vinegar
> 1 tablespoon soy sauce
> 2 teaspoons sugar
> ½ teaspoon sesame oil
> ¼ teaspoon dried crushed red pepper

WHISK together all ingredients. **Prep: 5 min.**

ADELYNE SMITH
DUNNVILLE, KENTUCKY

BEEF TENDERLOIN WITH PAN-ROASTED PEARS

MAKES 4 SERVINGS

This recipe works best with a regular (not non-stick) skillet.

4 (6-ounce) beef tenderloin fillets
½ teaspoon salt
½ teaspoon pepper
2 tablespoons butter or margarine
2 tablespoons olive oil
3 Bartlett pears, peeled and halved
1 cup Madeira wine
1 garlic clove, pressed
¼ teaspoon dried thyme
4 ounces blue cheese

SPRINKLE fillets with salt and pepper.
MELT butter with oil in a large skillet over medium-high heat; add fillets, and cook 5 minutes on each side or to desired degree of doneness. Remove fillets, and keep warm.
ADD pear halves to skillet; cook over medium heat 5 minutes on each side or until browned. Add wine, garlic, and thyme; cook 5 minutes or until pear halves are tender. Remove pear halves from skillet, reserving wine mixture in skillet.
COOK wine mixture in skillet over high heat 7 to 8 minutes or until mixture is reduced by half.
STUFF each pear half evenly with blue cheese. Serve with fillets, and drizzle with sauce. **Prep: 15 min., Cook: 33 min.**

GEORGANA MCNEIL
HOUSTON, TEXAS

CHEDDAR-PEAR PIE

MAKES 6 SERVINGS

5 medium-size ripe pears, peeled and chopped
⅓ cup sugar
2 tablespoons butter
¼ teaspoon vanilla extract
1 (9-inch) frozen unbaked pie shell
½ cup (2 ounces) shredded sharp Cheddar cheese
½ cup all-purpose flour
¼ cup sugar
¼ teaspoon salt
¼ cup butter, melted

COMBINE pears and ⅓ cup sugar in a 3½-quart saucepan. Cook, stirring often, over medium-low heat 12 to 14 minutes or until pears are tender. Remove from heat. (Drain excess liquid, if necessary.)
PROCESS pears in a blender until smooth; stir in 2 tablespoons butter and vanilla. Set aside.
LINE pie shell with aluminum foil; fill with pie weights or dried beans.
BAKE on lowest oven rack at 425° for 10 minutes. Remove weights and foil; bake 4 more minutes.
COMBINE cheese and next 3 ingredients. Stir in ¼ cup melted butter.
SPOON pear mixture into prepared piecrust; sprinkle with cheese mixture. Cover edges with aluminum foil.
BAKE at 425° for 25 minutes. **Prep: 25 min., Cook: 14 min., Bake: 39 min.**

Simple Sides

If your tried-and-true side dishes have escaped your recipe files, now is the time to reclaim some favorites. Green Bean Casserole, with a crusty topping of breadcrumbs and butter, is a sure bet. Crunchy Marinated Carrots has just enough sugar to be pleasantly sweet.

CRUNCHY MARINATED CARROTS

MAKES 4 SERVINGS

4 carrots, peeled and cut into 3-inch sticks
1½ tablespoons cider vinegar
1½ tablespoons vegetable oil
1 small garlic clove, minced
¼ to ½ teaspoon salt
¼ teaspoon sugar
Chopped fresh parsley (optional)

COMBINE first 6 ingredients; cover and chill 8 hours. Drain. Sprinkle carrots with parsley, if desired. **Prep: 10 min., Chill: 8 hrs.**

BRITTANY KOLLMAN
TULSA, OKLAHOMA

GREEN BEAN CASSEROLE

MAKES 4 SERVINGS

¼ cup butter or margarine, divided
1 (8-ounce) package sliced fresh mushrooms
2 tablespoons all-purpose flour
2 cups milk
1 pound fresh green beans, trimmed
¼ teaspoon salt
¼ teaspoon pepper
¼ cup Italian-seasoned breadcrumbs
2 tablespoons butter or margarine, melted

MELT 2 tablespoons butter in a large saucepan over medium heat; add sliced mushrooms, and sauté 10 minutes. Whisk in flour and 2 tablespoons butter until smooth.
GRADUALLY add milk; cook, whisking constantly, 10 minutes or until thickened. Add green beans, salt, and pepper. Pour into a lightly greased 2-quart baking dish.
STIR together breadcrumbs and 2 tablespoons melted butter; sprinkle over green bean mixture.
BAKE casserole at 350° for 20 minutes or until bubbly. **Prep: 20 min., Cook: 25 min., Bake: 20 min.**

POTATOES AU GRATIN

MAKES 8 SERVINGS

4 large baking potatoes
1 large sweet onion, chopped
1 (8-ounce) loaf pasteurized prepared cheese product, diced
1 teaspoon salt
¾ teaspoon pepper
1 cup whipping cream

COOK potatoes in boiling water to cover 25 to 30 minutes. Let cool slightly; peel and slice.
LAYER half of potatoes, half of onion, and half of cheese in a lightly greased 13- x 9-inch baking dish. Sprinkle with half of salt and pepper. Repeat layers. Drizzle with cream.
BAKE at 350° for 1 hour or until golden. **Prep: 20 min., Cook: 30 min., Bake: 1 hr.**

MISSY JUSTICE
WHARTON, TEXAS

Potluck Suppers

Tired of taking the same old covered dish? Jazz up
your next event with these delectable recipes.

Getting invited to a potluck is always
fun. If you're pondering what to
take, look no further. Whether you need a
cool and creamy appetizer or a hot, hearty
entrée, we've got great ideas.

Goat Cheese Spread—a great opener—
is packed with flavorful ingredients and
takes only 30 minutes to make. Turkey
Pot Pie With Cranberry-Pecan Crusts features turkey tenderloins, caramelized
onions, and fresh spinach for the perfect
sweet/savory combination.

All these dishes received high ratings
in our Test Kitchens and can be made
ahead of time. We know you'll be thrilled
to prepare and share them at your next
get-together.

Have Food, Will Travel

■ Wrap casseroles with aluminum
foil; cover with newspaper or
towels to keep food warm longer.
■ Use lightweight, sealable serving
containers. Shallow ones provide
ample surface area to keep food
cold and make packing easier.
■ Pack perishable foods in a
cooler. Avoid messes by using ice
sealed in plastic bags or frozen
gel packs.
■ Bring dishes in reusable disposable containers that the hostess
can throw away or keep.
■ To keep dairy products, meats,
fish, shellfish, poultry, cream pies,
creamy salads, and custards at 40
degrees or below, chill before
placing in the cooler.

GOAT CHEESE SPREAD

MAKES 12 TO 16 APPETIZER SERVINGS

To garnish, cut one dried tomato into slivers.
Gently press fresh oregano sprigs and tomato
slivers in a decorative pattern over the top of the
cheese after it's inverted.

> 2 (8-ounce) packages cream cheese,
>   softened
> 8 ounces goat cheese
> 2 garlic cloves, minced
> 4 teaspoons chopped fresh or
>   1¼ teaspoons dried oregano
> ⅛ teaspoon freshly ground pepper
> ¼ cup basil pesto
> ½ cup dried tomatoes in oil, drained
>   and chopped
> Garnishes: dried tomato slivers, fresh
>   oregano sprigs
> French bread slices or crackers

PROCESS first 5 ingredients in a food
processor until smooth. Spread one-
third of cheese mixture in a plastic wrap-
lined 8- x 4-inch loafpan. Top with
pesto; spread one-third cheese mixture
over pesto. Sprinkle with dried tomatoes; top with remaining cheese mixture.
Cover and chill 8 hours.
INVERT spread onto a serving plate, discarding plastic wrap. Garnish, if desired.
Serve with French bread slices or crackers. **Prep: 30 min., Chill: 8 hrs.**

PETER HALFERTY
CORPUS CHRISTI, TEXAS

TURKEY POT PIE WITH CRANBERRY-PECAN CRUSTS

MAKES 10 TO 12 SERVINGS

If making the crusts ahead, store them separately, and place on pie before serving so they
stay firm.

> 3 tablespoons butter, divided
> 2 large sweet onions, diced
> ½ cup all-purpose flour
> 1 teaspoon salt
> 1 teaspoon pepper
> 4 (12-ounce) turkey tenderloins,
>   cut into 1½-inch cubes
> 2 tablespoons vegetable oil
> 1½ cups chicken broth
> 1 cup milk
> 1 (10-ounce) package fresh
>   spinach, torn
> Cranberry-Pecan Crusts

MELT 1 tablespoon butter in a large skillet over medium-high heat; add onion,
and sauté 15 minutes or until caramel
colored. Place onion in a bowl, and set
aside.
COMBINE flour, salt, and pepper; dredge
turkey in flour mixture.
MELT remaining 2 tablespoons butter
with oil in skillet over medium-high
heat; add turkey, and brown on all sides.
Gradually stir in chicken broth and milk.
Bring to a boil, and cook, stirring constantly, 1 minute or until thickened. Stir
in onion. Add spinach, stirring just until
wilted. Pour turkey mixture into a lightly
greased 13- x 9-inch baking dish.
BAKE, covered, at 350° for 30 minutes.
Remove from oven, and arrange desired
amount of Cranberry-Pecan Crusts over
pie before serving. Serve with any
remaining Cranberry-Pecan Crusts on the
side. **Prep: 15 min., Cook: 25 min., Bake: 30 min.**

Cranberry-Pecan Crusts:

MAKES 3 TO 4 DOZEN

Reroll any leftover scraps of dough, and repeat
the procedure.

> 1 (15-ounce) package refrigerated
>   piecrusts
> ½ cup finely chopped pecans, toasted
> ½ cup finely chopped dried
>   cranberries

UNFOLD each piecrust, and press out fold lines. Sprinkle 1 piecrust with pecans and cranberries; top with remaining piecrust. Roll into a 14-inch circle, sealing together piecrusts. Cut into desired shapes with a 2- to 3-inch cutter. Place pastry shapes on a lightly greased baking sheet.

BAKE at 425° for 8 to 10 minutes or until golden. **Prep: 15 min., Bake: 10 min.**

SPAGHETTI-AND-SPINACH CASSEROLE

MAKES 8 TO 10 SERVINGS

To make ahead, bake as directed, cover, and freeze. Thaw overnight in the refrigerator. Bake, covered, at 350° for 30 minutes; uncover and bake 10 more minutes.

1½ pounds ground beef
2 garlic cloves, minced
½ teaspoon salt
½ teaspoon pepper
1 (26-ounce) jar spaghetti sauce
1 teaspoon Italian seasoning
1 (10-ounce) package frozen chopped
　　spinach, thawed and drained
2 cups (8 ounces) shredded Monterey
　　Jack cheese
1½ cups sour cream
1 large egg, lightly beaten
1 teaspoon garlic salt
8 ounces wide egg noodles, cooked
1½ cups (6 ounces) shredded
　　Parmesan cheese

COOK first 4 ingredients in a large non-stick skillet over medium heat, stirring until beef crumbles and is no longer pink. Drain and return to skillet. Stir in spaghetti sauce and Italian seasoning.

COMBINE spinach and next 4 ingredients. Fold in noodles, and spoon mixture into a lightly greased 13- x 9-inch baking dish. Sprinkle with half of Parmesan cheese; top with beef mixture and remaining Parmesan cheese.

BAKE at 350° for 30 minutes or until bubbly and golden. **Prep: 20 min., Bake: 30 min.**

SUSANNE PETTIT
MEMPHIS, TENNESSEE

Potluck Pointers

Here are some tips to help make hosting a potluck easy and fun.

Planning and More

■ Decide which type of food you want ahead of time. Be as specific as possible when assigning dishes; communicate which kinds you want and how many people you'll serve.

■ Monitor the menu by selecting dishes with a variety of tastes and textures. (Go for opposites: crunchy/smooth, spicy/mild, soft/firm.)

■ Plan a menu that can be served at room temperature if you're worried about having to keep items warm. If not, foods that should be kept hot or cold should not enter the "danger zone" (temperatures between 40 and 140 degrees) for more than two hours. Use small platters, and replenish as needed.

■ Stack mix-and-match plates and napkins to add a colorful element to your buffet table.

■ Place food on pedestals for visual appeal; fill vertical space with flowers or breadsticks.

■ Enhance the serving table with one or more centerpieces. Use votives or lanterns to avoid open flames from candlesticks.

Creative Containers

■ Look for unique plates and serving dishes at local outlets or discount stores. For example, you can place a cake on a terra-cotta plate or put a salad in a similar pot.

■ Serve cookies or brownies in decorative gift bags.

■ Line a basket with a bandanna or colorful tea towels to hold croissants, rolls, or muffins.

■ Use a decorative ice bucket for cold foods such as potato salad or coleslaw. Fill with ice, and place a bowl or container of your chilled side dish in the bucket. Then serve from on top of the ice.

■ Collect containers suitable for instant flower arranging. Simple vases or bottles will work, as well as planters, galvanized buckets, or hurricane lanterns.

RAGIN' CAJUN CASSEROLE

MAKES 4 SERVINGS

1 pound unpeeled, medium-size fresh
　　shrimp
8 ounces low-fat smoked sausage, cut
　　into ¼-inch slices
1 small onion, diced
1 celery rib, diced
1 large green bell pepper, cut into thin
　　strips
2 garlic cloves, minced
1 (14½-ounce) can diced tomatoes
　　with garlic, basil, and oregano
1 (14-ounce) can fat-free
　　chicken broth
1¾ teaspoons Creole seasoning
⅛ to ½ teaspoon ground red pepper
¾ cup uncooked long-grain rice

PEEL shrimp, and devein, if desired; set aside.

SAUTÉ smoked sausage in a large non-stick skillet over medium-high heat 3 to 4 minutes or until browned. Add onion and next 3 ingredients; sauté 2 to 3 minutes.

ADD tomatoes and next 3 ingredients. Bring to a boil, and stir in rice; cover, reduce heat to low, and simmer 15 to 20 minutes or until liquid is absorbed. Stir in shrimp; cook 3 to 5 minutes or just until shrimp turn pink. **Prep: 15 min., Cook: 32 min.**

AMY HALL
TULLAHOMA, TENNESSEE

A Chicken Menu Made Easy

Looking for a fun, fresh, simple meal for company?
Try this one with a Mediterranean accent.

Mediterranean Menu

Serves 4

Stuffed Chicken Breasts With White Bean Puree

Tabbouleh Couscous

Easy Herb Focaccia

Lemon Ice

Pinot Grigio

These winning recipes from our Test Kitchens transform basic ingredients from the pantry and garden into a Mediterranean-style treat. Couscous and feta cheese, available at larger supermarkets, make it authentic. Our menu for four is short on preparation time; to make it even easier, assemble the cool Lemon Ice a day ahead.

If you'd like to serve wine with your meal, a crisp white, such as Pinot Grigio, would make an excellent choice.

STUFFED CHICKEN BREASTS WITH WHITE BEAN PUREE

MAKES 4 SERVINGS

Pounding the chicken helps it cook faster.

- 4 skinned and boned chicken breast halves
- 1 (4-ounce) package crumbled feta cheese
- ¼ cup chopped kalamata olives
- 1 tablespoon capers
- 1 teaspoon paprika
- 2 tablespoons olive oil
- 2 (16-ounce) cans navy beans, rinsed and drained
- 2 to 4 garlic cloves
- ½ teaspoon salt
- ½ teaspoon pepper
- 1 tablespoon lemon juice

PLACE each chicken breast between 2 sheets of heavy-duty plastic wrap; flatten to ¼-inch thickness, using a meat mallet or rolling pin.

COMBINE cheese, olives, and capers; spread over chicken. Roll up, starting at a short side; secure with wooden picks. Sprinkle with paprika.

BROWN chicken in hot oil in a skillet over medium-high heat. Cover, reduce heat, and cook 20 minutes or until chicken is done.

PROCESS beans and next 4 ingredients in a food processor until smooth, stopping to scrape down sides.

POUR into a small saucepan; cook over medium heat, stirring often, until heated. Serve with chicken. **Prep: 25 min., Cook: 35 min.**

TABBOULEH COUSCOUS

MAKES 4 SERVINGS

The fresh flavors of parsley, mint, and lemon season this quick side dish.

- 1 (14½-ounce) can chicken broth
- ¼ cup fresh lemon juice
- 1½ cups uncooked couscous
- 10 plum tomatoes, seeded and chopped
- 4 green onions, diced
- 1 cup minced fresh Italian parsley
- 1 cup minced fresh mint
- ½ cup frozen whole kernel corn, thawed
- 2 garlic cloves, pressed
- 1 tablespoon grated lemon rind
- ⅓ cup olive oil
- ¼ cup fresh lemon juice
- 1 teaspoon salt

BRING chicken broth and ¼ cup lemon juice to a boil in a large saucepan; stir in couscous. Cover, remove from heat, and let stand 5 minutes. Fluff with a fork, and cool.

STIR in chopped tomato and remaining ingredients. **Prep: 30 min., Stand: 5 min.**

EASY HERB FOCACCIA

MAKES 8 SERVINGS

Brush leftover slices with olive oil, and toast on a baking sheet. Top with chopped tomato, fresh basil, and crumbled feta or goat cheese for a great appetizer or snack.

- 1 (10-ounce) can refrigerated pizza dough
- 2 tablespoons olive oil
- ½ teaspoon kosher salt
- 1 teaspoon freshly ground pepper
- 1 teaspoon dried oregano
- 1 teaspoon dried basil
- ½ teaspoon dried thyme

SHAPE dough into a ball, and pat into a 10-inch circle onto a baking sheet. Press handle of a wooden spoon into dough to make indentations at 1-inch intervals. Drizzle with oil; sprinkle with salt and remaining ingredients.
BAKE at 375° for 12 to 14 minutes or until lightly browned. **Prep: 10 min., Bake: 14 min.**

LEMON ICE

MAKES 4 CUPS

Putting the mixture in the blender twice gives it a great texture. This refreshing recipe is a must-try for sweltering summer days.

- 1 (12-ounce) can frozen lemonade concentrate, thawed
- 3 cups ice cubes
- 1 cup water
- ⅓ cup sugar

PROCESS all ingredients in a food processor or blender until smooth. Pour mixture into a 13- x 9-inch pan, and freeze 45 minutes.
PROCESS partially frozen mixture in a food processor or blender until smooth. Return to pan; freeze 8 hours. Scrape with a fork before serving. **Prep: 15 min.; Freeze: 8 hrs., 45 min.**

Taste of the South

Barbecue Shrimp

Spicy, buttery, and decidedly hands-on, this dish is a New Orleans classic.

The ingredients are things you might have on hand, and the dish requires very little cooking skill. Because everything is assembled a couple of hours ahead and then baked at the last minute, New Orleans Barbecue Shrimp is great casual company fare. You just place the shrimp in a large baking dish or pan, pour the sauce over them, chill for a couple of hours, and bake. The results are spicy, simple, and divine.

Cook's Notes

- Use heads-on shrimp if you can get them.
- Always cook the shrimp in the sauce. "Some people make the sauce separately and pour it over the baked shrimp later," Bob DeFelice, owner of New Orleans' Pascal's Manale Restaurant & Bar, says. "It's just not the same."
- Offer plenty of napkins, paper towels, or, if you have them, bibs. (If you don't like getting your hands dirty when you eat, this isn't the dish for you.)
- Leftover shrimp keep well in the refrigerator for a day or two. Be careful not to overcook them when reheating. You can also peel them, put them back in the sauce, and serve them over pasta.

NEW ORLEANS BARBECUE SHRIMP

MAKES 6 TO 8 SERVINGS

Serve with a green salad and corn on the cob for a complete meal.

- 4 pounds unpeeled, large fresh shrimp or 6 pounds shrimp with heads on
- ½ cup butter
- ½ cup olive oil
- ¼ cup chili sauce
- ¼ cup Worcestershire sauce
- 2 lemons, sliced
- 4 garlic cloves, chopped
- 2 tablespoons Creole seasoning
- 2 tablespoons lemon juice
- 1 tablespoon chopped parsley
- 1 teaspoon paprika
- 1 teaspoon dried oregano
- 1 teaspoon ground red pepper
- ½ teaspoon hot sauce
- French bread

SPREAD shrimp in a shallow, aluminum foil-lined broiler pan.
COMBINE butter and next 12 ingredients in a saucepan over low heat, stirring until butter melts; pour over shrimp. Cover and chill 2 hours, turning shrimp every 30 minutes.
BAKE, uncovered, at 400° for 20 minutes, turning shrimp once. Serve with bread. **Prep: 5 min., Chill: 2 hrs., Bake: 20 min.**

Full of Beans

Fabulous flavor and great versatility are just a couple of reasons to love legumes.

Remember when you ate beans only if your mom or grandma fixed them? That was probably because they take so long to cook. Today, they're no longer as time-consuming. Canned varieties let you enjoy beans in salsas, burgers, pasta dishes, and much more.

Beans aren't just delicious; they're also full of protein, soluble fiber, folic acid, and iron. So stir up good nutrition with these tasty dishes.

SMOKY THREE-BEAN SALSA

MAKES 12 SERVINGS

1 (15.8-ounce) can black-eyed peas, rinsed and drained
1 (15-ounce) can black beans, rinsed and drained
1 (16-ounce) can navy beans, rinsed and drained
1 small sweet onion, finely chopped (about ½ cup)
1 green bell pepper, finely chopped
2 small garlic cloves, minced
1 (14½-ounce) can diced tomatoes, undrained
½ cup chopped fresh cilantro
1 chipotle pepper in adobo sauce, minced*
¼ cup fresh lime juice
¼ teaspoon salt

COMBINE all ingredients in a large bowl; cover and chill at least 2 hours. Prep: 15 min., Chill: 2 hrs.

*Chipotle peppers in adobo sauce may be found in the Mexican section of supermarkets or at Mexican grocery stores; substitute 1 small jalapeño pepper, seeded and minced, if desired.

SHARON BRADBERRY
TALLAHASSEE, FLORIDA

Per ½ cup: Calories 60 (2% from fat); Fat 0.1g (sat 0g, mono 0.1g, poly 0.02g); Protein 4g; Carb 13g; Fiber 3.8g; Chol 0mg; Iron 1.1mg; Sodium 276mg; Calc 37mg

PASTA WITH BEANS AND GREENS

MAKES 6 SERVINGS

This delicious and colorful main-dish recipe boasts generous amounts of protein, fiber, complex carbohydrates, iron, and calcium.

8 ounces uncooked bow tie pasta
1 large onion, chopped
1 (6-ounce) package portobello mushroom caps, halved and sliced*
2 teaspoons olive oil
4 cups chopped fresh kale or spinach (about 6 ounces)
1 cup reduced-sodium chicken broth
2 garlic cloves, minced
½ teaspoon salt
½ teaspoon pepper
1 (15-ounce) can great Northern beans, rinsed and drained
¼ cup (1 ounce) shredded Parmesan cheese

COOK pasta according to package directions, omitting salt and fat; drain. Place pasta in a large bowl; set aside.

SAUTÉ onion and mushrooms in hot oil in a large skillet over medium heat 5 minutes. Add kale and next 4 ingredients; cook, stirring often, 15 minutes or until kale is tender. Add beans, and cook 1 minute.

ADD bean mixture to pasta; toss gently. Sprinkle with cheese. Prep: 20 min., Cook: 32 min.

*Substitute 1 (8-ounce) package sliced fresh mushrooms, if desired.

Per serving: Calories 224 (13% from fat); Fat 3.4g (sat 0.9g, mono 1.6g, poly 0.6g); Protein 10.8g; Carb 40.5g; Fiber 5.4g; Chol 2.4mg; Iron 2.8mg; Sodium 434mg; Calc 136mg

BEAN BURGERS WITH ADOBO MAYONNAISE

MAKES 8 SERVINGS

These hearty, well-seasoned sandwiches, enhanced with a creamy, savory spread, will win you over. (pictured on page 228)

1 small onion, chopped
1 carrot, grated
2 garlic cloves, minced
1 jalapeño pepper, seeded and minced
2 teaspoons olive oil
1 (15-ounce) can black beans, rinsed and drained
1 (15-ounce) can pinto beans, rinsed and drained
½ cup salsa
2 tablespoons self-rising cornmeal mix
½ teaspoon salt
½ teaspoon dried oregano
½ teaspoon ground cumin
Vegetable cooking spray
Adobo Mayonnaise
8 whole-grain buns
Lettuce
Tomato slices
Salsa

SAUTÉ first 4 ingredients in hot olive oil in a large nonstick skillet over medium-high heat 8 minutes or until onion is tender.

MASH black beans and pinto beans in a large bowl; stir in onion mixture, salsa, and next 4 ingredients. Cover and chill 30 minutes.

SHAPE mixture into 8 patties. Place on an aluminum foil-lined baking sheet coated with cooking spray. Coat patties evenly with cooking spray. Chill 30 minutes.

BAKE at 400° for 15 minutes or until browned and thoroughly heated.

SPREAD Adobo Mayonnaise on bottom halves of buns. Top with lettuce, tomato, patties, salsa, and top halves of buns. **Prep: 20 min., Cook: 8 min., Chill: 1 hr., Bake: 15 min.**

SHARON BRADBERRY
TALLAHASSEE, FLORIDA

Adobo Mayonnaise:

MAKES ⅓ CUP

⅓ cup light mayonnaise
1 teaspoon adobo sauce*

STIR together both ingredients; cover and chill until ready to serve.

*Adobo sauce is the thick liquid that comes with canned chipotle peppers. Look for them in the Mexican section of supermarkets or at Mexican grocery stores.

Per sandwich: Calories 250 (28% from fat); Fat 7.9g (sat 1.4g, mono 2.2g, poly 1.1g); Protein 8.8g; Carb 37g; Fiber 6.4g; Chol 3.5mg; Iron 3.5mg; Sodium 659mg; Calc 87mg

Fast Facts on Beans

■ Soaking dried beans softens and rehydrates them, reducing cooking time. It also dissolves some of the gas-causing substances, making beans more digestible. (Discard soaking water before cooking.)
■ One pound dried packaged beans equals 2 cups dried or 6 cups cooked. Use 10 cups hot water for every 2 cups beans.
■ Most beans triple their size when rehydrated, so start with a large enough pot.
■ To ensure thorough cooking, add acidic ingredients, such as tomatoes, vinegar, or citrus juices, when beans are almost tender. If you add them too soon, the beans won't soften.
■ Cooked beans may be stored in the refrigerator for four to five days or frozen in heavy-duty zip-top plastic bags or sealable plastic containers for up to six months.

Incredible Egg Salads

Assistant Foods Editor Cybil Brown confesses that egg salad didn't top her list of favorite foods until she tried reader Hilda Marshall's updated version of this classic spread. Hilda's touches of smoky bacon, fresh chives, and onion won Cybil's vote at our taste-testing table.

As with potato salad, the basic combination of eggs and mayonnaise gives you the freedom to pare down or embellish however you see fit. (Smoked Salmon-and-Egg Salad, for example, offers an unexpectedly fancy rendition.) And here's an excellent tip: If your favorite egg salad recipe seems a little wet, stir in 2 tablespoons of instant potato flakes. That worked great when we experimented with our sweet pickle version inspired by Hilda's recipe.

SMOKED SALMON-AND-EGG SALAD

MAKES ABOUT 2 CUPS

This is also good on bite-size rounds of dark pumpernickel bread.

¼ cup mayonnaise*
¼ cup sour cream*
1 teaspoon lemon juice
⅛ teaspoon salt
¼ teaspoon pepper
6 large hard-cooked eggs, chopped
1 (4-ounce) package smoked salmon, finely chopped
2 celery ribs, finely chopped
½ cup red onion, minced
1 tablespoon minced fresh dill
1 teaspoon to 2 teaspoons capers, chopped (optional)
Toasted miniature bagels or crackers

STIR together first 5 ingredients in a large bowl; gently fold in eggs and next 5 ingredients. Serve with bagels or crackers. **Prep: 15 min.**

*Substitute light mayonnaise and light sour cream, if desired.

EGG SALAD CLUB SANDWICHES

MAKES 4 SERVINGS

Substitute fresh arugula for the spinach if you prefer its spicy bite. For a checkerboard effect, you can use both white and wheat breads. If you want to serve only the salad, just omit the bread, spinach, and ⅓ cup mayonnaise.

⅔ cup mayonnaise, divided
4 large hard-cooked eggs, chopped
1 celery rib, diced
4 bacon slices, cooked and crumbled
¼ cup chopped fresh chives
1 tablespoon minced sweet onion
¼ teaspoon seasoned salt
½ teaspoon freshly ground pepper
12 very thin white or wheat sandwich bread slices, lightly toasted
1 cup firmly packed fresh spinach
Garnish: whole fresh chives

STIR together ⅓ cup mayonnaise and next 7 ingredients.
SPREAD remaining ⅓ cup mayonnaise evenly over 1 side of each bread slice. Spread 4 bread slices, mayonnaise side up, evenly with half of egg salad. Top evenly with half of spinach and 4 bread slices.
REPEAT procedure with remaining egg salad, spinach, and bread slices. Cut each sandwich into quarters; garnish, if desired. **Prep: 25 min.**

SWEET-PICKLE EGG SALAD CLUB: Omit bacon and chives. Add 2 tablespoons instant potato flakes and 1 tablespoon sweet pickle relish; proceed with recipe as directed.

SHRIMP-EGG SALAD CLUB: Omit bacon. Add ⅔ cup finely chopped boiled shrimp, ½ teaspoon grated lemon rind, and ¼ teaspoon ground red pepper. Proceed with recipe as directed.

HILDA MARSHALL
CULPEPER, VIRGINIA

A Fresh Look at Southern Classics

Time-honored regional foods benefit from a new perspective.

Foods Editor Scott Jones has come up with ways to give contemporary twists to such Southern staples as grits, creamed corn, and pork chops. For instance, when you make grits ahead and then cool them on a baking sheet, they can be cut into any number of interesting shapes, reheated under the broiler, and stacked for a striking presentation. Make these updated favorites for your next dinner.

STUFFED PORK CHOPS

MAKES 6 SERVINGS

Stuffed with fontina cheese, chopped Granny Smith apples, and herbs, these pork chops become something spectacular without losing their homey appeal. (pictured on page 225)

> 6 bacon slices
> 2 Granny Smith apples, peeled and diced
> 2 shallots, finely chopped
> 1 tablespoon chopped fresh ginger
> 1 tablespoon chopped fresh sage
> 1 cup cubed fontina cheese
> 6 (1½-inch-thick) center-cut pork loin chops
> 1⅛ teaspoons salt
> 1¼ teaspoons pepper
> 2 tablespoons olive oil

COOK bacon in a large skillet until crisp; remove bacon, and drain on paper towels, reserving 2 tablespoons drippings in skillet. Crumble bacon; set aside.

SAUTÉ apples, shallots, and ginger in hot drippings 5 minutes or until tender. Remove from heat; stir in sage.

STIR together apple mixture, bacon, and cheese. Cut a horizontal slit through thickest portion of each pork chop, cutting to, but not through, other side to form a pocket. Sprinkle both sides and pocket of each pork chop with salt and pepper. Spoon apple mixture evenly into pockets; secure with wooden picks.

COOK chops, in 2 batches, in hot olive oil in a large skillet over medium-high heat 1 to 2 minutes on each side or until golden. Place in a lightly greased roasting pan or large shallow baking dish.

BAKE at 425° for 25 to 30 minutes or until done. **Prep: 30 min., Cook: 20 min., Bake: 30 min.**

STACKABLE GRITS

MAKES 6 SERVINGS

A Southern standby gets a new look in this impressive dish. (pictured on page 225)

> ½ large Vidalia onion, diced
> 2 garlic cloves, minced
> 2 tablespoons olive oil
> 1 (14½-ounce) can chicken broth
> 1 cup half-and-half
> 1 cup uncooked quick-cooking grits
> 1½ teaspoons salt
> ½ cup (2 ounces) shredded Cheddar cheese
> ⅛ teaspoon ground red pepper
> ⅛ teaspoon ground nutmeg
> Vegetable cooking spray

SAUTÉ diced onion and minced garlic in hot oil in a 3-quart saucepan over medium-high heat until tender. Add broth and half-and-half; bring to a boil. Gradually stir in grits and salt. Cover, reduce heat, and simmer, stirring occasionally, 10 minutes or until thickened.

ADD cheese, pepper, and nutmeg; stir until cheese melts. Pour grits into a lightly greased 11- x 7-inch baking dish; chill 8 hours.

INVERT grits onto a flat surface; cut into 12 wedges. Spray top and bottom of each wedge with cooking spray; arrange wedges on a baking sheet.

BROIL wedges 6 inches from heat 2 minutes on each side or until golden. **Prep: 10 min., Cook: 15 min., Chill: 8 hrs., Broil: 4 min.**

SKILLET CREAMED CORN

MAKES 4 TO 6 SERVINGS

A sprinkling of smoky bacon enhances this creamy side. (pictured on page 225)

> 6 bacon slices
> ½ Vidalia onion, finely chopped
> 1 garlic clove, finely chopped
> 3 cups fresh corn kernels (about 6 ears)
> ¼ cup all-purpose flour
> 1½ cups half-and-half
> ½ teaspoon salt
> ¼ teaspoon pepper
> 1 tablespoon butter or margarine
> 1 tablespoon chopped fresh basil
> Garnish: fresh basil sprigs

COOK bacon in a large skillet until crisp; remove bacon, and drain on paper towels, reserving 2 tablespoons drippings in skillet. Crumble bacon; set aside.

SAUTÉ onion and garlic in hot drippings 5 minutes or until tender. Stir in corn; cook 5 to 7 minutes or until golden. Remove from heat.

COOK flour in a large clean skillet over medium heat, stirring occasionally, about 5 minutes or until golden. Gradually whisk in half-and-half until smooth. Add corn mixture, salt, and pepper; cook 5 minutes or until thickened. Remove from heat; stir in butter and basil. Sprinkle each serving with bacon, and garnish, if desired. **Prep: 20 min., Cook: 27 min.**

Game-Day Appetizers

Kick off football season with an array of quick bites.

Cheering on your favorite team certainly can make you work up an appetite. Offer plenty of savory snacks and cold drinks, and you're sure to score major points with friends and family who drop by. To take the fun into overtime, buy some hearty hoagie-style sandwiches and brownies for a great spread.

CHILE-CHEESE SPREAD

MAKES 3 CUPS

Make this zesty starter up to three days ahead. Serve leftovers on sandwiches.

    2 (8-ounce) packages light cream
        cheese, softened
    1 cup (4 ounces) shredded Cheddar
        cheese
    3 green onions, finely chopped
    3 chipotle peppers in adobo
        sauce
    1 teaspoon adobo sauce
    ½ teaspoon Creole seasoning
    ½ teaspoon ground cumin
    ½ teaspoon chili powder
    ¼ teaspoon Worcestershire sauce
    ⅛ teaspoon hot sauce
    ⅓ cup pecan pieces, toasted
    Garnishes: green onion curls, pecan
        halves
    Assorted crackers and vegetables

COMBINE first 10 ingredients in a food processor, and pulse 3 times, stopping to scrape down sides. Stir in toasted pecans, and chill 2 hours. Garnish, if desired. Serve with assorted crackers and vegetables. **Prep: 20 min., Chill 2 hrs.**

RUDIE SLAUGHTER
VIENNA, VIRGINIA

OLIVE CROSTINI

MAKES 42 APPETIZERS

    1 (4¼-ounce) can chopped black
        olives, drained
    ½ cup pimiento-stuffed olives,
        chopped
    ½ cup (2 ounces) shredded Parmesan
        cheese
    4 tablespoons butter or margarine,
        softened
    2 garlic cloves, minced
    ¾ cup (3 ounces) shredded Monterey
        Jack cheese
    ¼ cup chopped fresh parsley
    1 (8-ounce) French baguette, cut into
        ¼-inch-thick slices

COMBINE first 7 ingredients.
TOP each bread slice evenly with olive mixture. Arrange on baking sheets.
BROIL, with oven door partially open, 3 to 4 minutes or until topping is bubbly and golden. **Prep: 20 min., Broil: 4 min.**

PAM BINKOWSKI
CULLMAN, ALABAMA

Cheers for Chocolate

Tailgating just got sweeter with M&M's Colorworks candies. You can order premixed team colors or individual ones to combine. To order call 1-888-265-6788, or visit **www.colorworks.com**

GREEN GODDESS "GUACAMOLE" WITH CUMIN CRISPS

MAKES ABOUT 3 CUPS

No one will ever imagine that canned asparagus is the secret to this twist on avocado guacamole. Spread leftovers on turkey sandwiches.

    2 (15-ounce) cans asparagus spears,
        drained
    4 plum tomatoes, seeded and chopped
    2 green onions, chopped
    ¼ cup mayonnaise
    2 garlic cloves, minced
    ½ teaspoon chili powder
    ¼ teaspoon salt
    ¼ teaspoon ground red pepper
    Cumin Crisps

PROCESS asparagus in a food processor until smooth, stopping to scrape down sides. Stir in tomatoes and next 6 ingredients. Cover and chill 30 minutes. Serve with Cumin Crisps. **Prep: 15 min., Chill: 30 min.**

Cumin Crisps:

MAKES 38 CRISPS

You can also use regular pita bread cut into wedges for this recipe.

    6 tablespoons butter or margarine,
        melted
    1 teaspoon ground cumin
    ½ teaspoon lemon pepper
    1 (7-ounce) package mini pita rounds,
        split

STIR together melted butter, cumin, and lemon pepper.
CUT split pitas into wedges, and brush with butter mixture. Arrange wedges on an aluminum foil-lined baking sheet.
BAKE wedges at 375° for 15 minutes or until crisp. **Prep: 10 min., Bake: 15 min.**

NOTE: For testing purposes only, we used Toufayan White Mini Pitettes for mini pita rounds.

LIZ BARCLAY
ANNAPOLIS, MARYLAND

Southern Living Cooking School

The Southern Living *Cooking School invites fun and family into the kitchen with these easy recipes for memorable meals and come-as-you-are gatherings.*

Host a Get-Together

A Simple Fall Picnic

Step out into the backyard to picnic, or head out to tailgate at the football stadium.
Serves 4

Thai Chicken-Avocado Wraps

Sesame Slaw

Orange slices and grapes

Chocolate Brownies

September kicks off three months packed with have-to-do and want-to-do activities. You're back into the school routine in full force, and finding space on the calendar to entertain friends is a struggle. To help, here are two menus and a couple of potluck-supper recipes perfect for casual fall gatherings.

THAI CHICKEN-AVOCADO WRAPS

MAKES 4 SERVINGS

   1 (1½-pound) roasted whole chicken
   ½ cup reduced-fat mayonnaise
   ½ cup chopped fresh basil
   2 tablespoons lime juice
   1 teaspoon Asian garlic-chili sauce
   ⅛ teaspoon salt
   4 (10-inch) flour tortillas
   2 GENUINE CALIFORNIA AVOCADOS, peeled and sliced
   ½ cup chopped cashews
   4 lettuce leaves

REMOVE skin and bones from chicken, and coarsely chop meat.
STIR together chicken, mayonnaise, and next 4 ingredients.
SPREAD chicken mixture evenly down center of 1 side of each tortilla; top evenly with avocado slices, chopped cashews, and lettuce. Roll up; wrap in plastic wrap. Chill 30 minutes or up to 2 hours. **Prep: 20 min., Chill: 30 min.**

SESAME SLAW

MAKES 4 SERVINGS

   ¼ cup SPLENDA Granular
   ¼ cup rice vinegar
   2 tablespoons sesame oil
   2 tablespoons chopped fresh cilantro
   ½ teaspoon salt
   1 medium napa cabbage, sliced
   1 red bell pepper, sliced
   3 green onions, sliced
   Garnish: 2 tablespoons sesame seeds, toasted

STIR together first 5 ingredients in a large bowl. Add cabbage, bell pepper, and onions, tossing to coat. Garnish, if desired. **Prep: 15 min.**

cooking school

Savory Spinach Appetizer Cheesecake

MAKES 20 TO 25 APPETIZER SERVINGS

- 1 (12-ounce) package STOUFFER'S Spinach Soufflé
- 1 cup (4 ounces) shredded Parmesan cheese
- 2 (8-ounce) containers onion-and-chive cream cheese, softened
- 2 (3-ounce) packages goat cheese, softened
- 3 large eggs, lightly beaten
- 1 teaspoon seasoned pepper
- ½ teaspoon dried oregano
- ½ teaspoon dried basil
- ½ teaspoon dried thyme
- 2 garlic cloves, pressed
- Vegetable cooking spray
- ¼ cup Italian-seasoned breadcrumbs
- Toppings: sour cream, toasted pine nuts, shredded Parmesan cheese
- Crackers

THAW spinach soufflé in microwave at MEDIUM (50% power) 6 to 7 minutes. Stir together spinach soufflé, 1 cup Parmesan cheese, and next 8 ingredients.
COAT a 9-inch springform pan with cooking spray. Sprinkle breadcrumbs over bottom of pan. Spoon spinach mixture into pan.
BAKE at 325° for 50 to 55 minutes or just until set. Remove from oven; cool in pan on a wire rack. Cover and chill 8 hours. Serve with desired toppings on crackers. **Prep: 20 min., Bake: 55 min., Chill: 8 hrs.**

Asian Pork Tenderloin With Spicy Sweet Potatoes

MAKES 6 SERVINGS

- 1 tablespoon McCORMICK Gourmet Collection Chinese Five Spice
- 3 tablespoons vegetable oil, divided
- 2 (16-ounce) pork tenderloins
- Spicy Sweet Potatoes
- Garnish: 2 green onions, thinly sliced

STIR together five spice and 1 tablespoon oil. Spread evenly over pork; cover and chill 30 minutes or up to 2 hours.

Dinner on the Deck

Pair a Johannisberg Riesling or Sauvignon Blanc with the appetizer cheesecake. A Chardonnay, rosé, or lightly chilled Pinot Noir will complement the pork entrée.
Serves 6

Savory Spinach Appetizer Cheesecake

Asian Pork Tenderloin With Spicy Sweet Potatoes

Green salad   Crusty sourdough bread

Chocolate Brownies

BROWN pork in remaining 2 tablespoons oil in a skillet over medium-high heat 2 minutes on each side.
BAKE at 425° for 20 to 25 minutes or until a meat thermometer inserted into thickest portion registers 160°. Let tenderloin stand 10 minutes before slicing. Arrange pork slices on a serving platter; arrange Spicy Sweet Potatoes around pork. Garnish, if desired. **Prep: 10 min., Chill: 30 min., Bake: 25 min., Stand: 10 min.**

Spicy Sweet Potatoes:

MAKES 4 TO 6 SERVINGS

- 3 large sweet potatoes, peeled and cut into ½-inch cubes
- 1 cup water
- 1 cup fresh orange juice
- ¼ cup soy sauce
- 2 tablespoons minced McCORMICK Gourmet Collection Crystallized Ginger
- 2 tablespoons rice wine or white wine vinegar
- 1 teaspoon minced garlic
- ½ teaspoon salt
- ½ teaspoon McCORMICK Gourmet Collection Red Crushed Pepper
- 1 tablespoon cornstarch
- 1 tablespoon water

COMBINE cubed sweet potatoes, 1 cup water, and next 7 ingredients in a Dutch oven. Bring mixture to a boil; cover, reduce heat, and simmer 20 to 25 minutes or until sweet potatoes are tender.
STIR together cornstarch and 1 tablespoon water, stirring until smooth; stir into sweet potato mixture. Bring to a

boil over medium heat; boil, stirring constantly, 1 minute or until mixture is slightly thickened. Remove from heat. **Prep: 10 min., Cook: 30 min.**

Chocolate Brownies

MAKES 2 DOZEN

- 1 cup butter or margarine
- 2 cups (12-ounce package) NESTLÉ TOLL HOUSE Semi-Sweet Chocolate Morsels, divided
- 2 cups sugar
- 4 large eggs
- 1 tablespoon vanilla extract*
- 1 cup all-purpose flour, divided
- 1½ cups chopped walnuts, toasted
- ⅛ teaspoon salt

MICROWAVE butter and 1 cup chocolate morsels in a 2-quart glass bowl at HIGH 1½ minutes or until chocolate morsels are melted, stirring mixture twice. Whisk in sugar, eggs, and vanilla.
TOSS together 1 tablespoon flour, walnuts, and remaining 1 cup chocolate morsels. Stir walnut mixture, salt, and remaining flour into chocolate mixture. Spread batter into a lightly greased 13- x 9-inch pan.
BAKE at 350° for 35 to 40 minutes (a wooden pick inserted in center will not come out clean). Cool on a wire rack. **Prep: 15 min., Bake: 40 min.**

*Substitute bourbon for vanilla extract, if desired.

Covered-Dish Winners

Invited to a potluck supper? Stressing over which dish to take? This hearty mac and cheese and rich bread pudding are sure to be a hit.

MACARONI WITH BLUE CHEESE AND WALNUTS

MAKES 6 SERVINGS

- 1 (40-ounce) package STOUFFER'S Family Style Recipes Macaroni & Cheese
- 1 cup (4 ounces) shredded Parmesan cheese
- ½ (4-ounce) package crumbled blue cheese
- 1½ cups soft breadcrumbs
- 1¼ cups chopped walnuts
- 3 tablespoons butter or margarine, melted

THAW macaroni and cheese in microwave at MEDIUM (50% power) 10 to 15 minutes.

STIR together macaroni and cheese, Parmesan cheese, and crumbled blue cheese. Spoon mixture into a lightly greased 11- x 7-inch baking dish. Stir together breadcrumbs, chopped walnuts, and melted butter, and spread evenly over macaroni and cheese mixture.

BAKE at 350° for 30 to 35 minutes or until bubbly, shielding topping with aluminum foil after 25 minutes to prevent excessive browning. **Prep: 15 min., Bake: 35 min.**

PINEAPPLE-APPLE BREAD PUDDING WITH VANILLA-NUTMEG SAUCE

MAKES 8 SERVINGS

- 1 (16-ounce) day-old French bread loaf, cubed
- 2 (12-ounce) cans evaporated milk
- 1 cup water
- 6 large eggs, lightly beaten
- 1 (8-ounce) can crushed pineapple, drained
- 1 large Red Delicious apple, grated
- 1 cup raisins
- 1½ cups sugar
- 5 tablespoons vanilla extract
- ¼ cup butter or margarine, cut up and softened
- 1 REYNOLDS Pot Lux Cookware Pan With Lid (9- x 12½-inch size)
- Vanilla-Nutmeg Sauce

PREHEAT oven to 350° for at least 20 minutes.

COMBINE first 3 ingredients, and stir in eggs, blending well. Stir in crushed pineapple and next 4 ingredients. Stir in butter, blending well. Pour mixture into pan. Place pan in center of a baking sheet.

BAKE, uncovered, at 350° for 45 to 55 minutes or until set and crust is golden. Remove baking sheet with pan from oven, and let stand 2 minutes. Serve with Vanilla-Nutmeg Sauce. **Prep: 35 min., Bake: 55 min., Stand: 2 min.**

Vanilla-Nutmeg Sauce:

MAKES 1½ CUPS

- 3 tablespoons butter or margarine
- 1 tablespoon all-purpose flour
- ½ cup sugar
- 1 cup whipping cream
- 1 tablespoon vanilla extract
- 1 teaspoon ground nutmeg

MELT butter in a small saucepan over medium-low heat; whisk in flour, and cook, whisking constantly, 5 minutes. Stir in sugar and cream; cook, whisking constantly, 3 minutes or until thickened. Stir in vanilla and nutmeg; simmer 5 minutes. **Prep: 2 min., Cook: 13 min.**

Sweet Indulgences

Let us show you how to create baked goods with the help of quality convenience products. You don't need to be a trained pastry chef to bake impressive—and delicious—confections. Read on for guaranteed success.

FUDGE TRUFFLE-PECAN TART

MAKES 8 TO 10 SERVINGS

- ½ cup butter or margarine, softened
- ¾ cup firmly packed light brown sugar
- 3 large eggs
- 2 cups (12-ounce package) NESTLÉ TOLL HOUSE Semi-Sweet Chocolate Morsels, melted
- 2 teaspoons vanilla extract, divided
- ½ cup all-purpose flour
- 1 cup finely chopped pecans
- 2 teaspoons instant coffee granules
- Chocolate Tart Shell
- 1 cup whipping cream
- 2 tablespoons granulated sugar
- Garnish: shaved chocolate

BEAT butter and brown sugar at medium speed with an electric mixer until blended; add eggs, beating well. Stir in melted chocolate, 1 teaspoon vanilla, and next 3 ingredients. Pour into Chocolate Tart Shell.

BAKE at 375° for 20 minutes. Cool on a wire rack 30 minutes.

BEAT cream at high speed until foamy; gradually add granulated sugar, beating until soft peaks form. Stir in remaining 1 teaspoon vanilla. Dollop cream around tart; garnish, if desired. **Prep: 20 min., Bake: 20 min., Cool: 30 min.**

CHOCOLATE TART SHELL: Combine 1¼ cups chocolate graham cracker crumbs and ⅓ cup melted butter; press into the bottom of a 10-inch tart pan. Bake at 350° for 6 minutes; cool on a wire rack. **Prep: 5 min., Bake: 6 min.**

cooking school

APPLE-ALMOND BAKE

MAKES 6 SERVINGS

- 2 (12-ounce) packages STOUFFER'S Harvest Apples
- 6 tablespoons butter or margarine
- 20 shortbread cookies, crushed
- ½ cup sliced almonds
- ¼ cup granulated sugar
- 1 teaspoon ground cinnamon, divided
- ¼ teaspoon ground nutmeg
- 2 tablespoons brown sugar
- Vanilla ice cream
- Garnishes: toasted almond slices, ground cinnamon

THAW apples in microwave at MEDIUM (50% power) 6 to 7 minutes; let stand 2 minutes.

MELT butter in a skillet over medium heat; add cookie crumbs and almonds. Cook, stirring constantly, 2 to 3 minutes. Remove from heat, and stir in granulated sugar, ½ teaspoon cinnamon, and nutmeg.

COMBINE brown sugar and remaining ½ teaspoon cinnamon; sprinkle in a 1½-quart baking dish. Layer with half each of apples and cookie crumb mixture; repeat layers.

BAKE at 375° for 25 to 30 minutes. Serve warm with vanilla ice cream; garnish, if desired. **Prep: 5 min., Thaw: 7 min., Stand: 2 min., Cook: 3 min., Bake: 30 min.**

CAFFE LATTE SLUSH

MAKES 5 CUPS

- ½ cup EQUAL Spoonful
- 2 cups hot brewed coffee or espresso
- 2 cups fat-free milk or fat-free half-and-half, divided

COMBINE no-calorie sweetener and coffee in a large bowl, stirring until sweetener dissolves; stir in 1 cup milk. Cover and freeze 8 hours.

THAW slightly in refrigerator; add remaining 1 cup milk. Break into pieces with a fork; beat at medium speed with an electric mixer until smooth. Serve immediately. **Prep: 15 min., Freeze: 8 hrs.**

STRAWBERRY CHEESECAKE

MAKES 12 SERVINGS

Don't worry if your cheesecake cracks on the top; the layer of slightly sweetened sour cream and strawberries will hide any flaws.

- 4 (8-ounce) packages light cream cheese, softened
- ¾ cup plus 2 tablespoons SPLENDA Granular
- 2 tablespoons lemon juice
- 3 large eggs
- ⅔ cup light sour cream, divided
- Wafer Crust
- 1 teaspoon SPLENDA Granular
- 1 quart fresh strawberries, sliced
- 1 tablespoon SPLENDA Granular
- 1 tablespoon water

BEAT cream cheese at medium speed with an electric mixer until smooth; add ¾ cup plus 2 tablespoons no-calorie sweetener and lemon juice, beating until blended. Add eggs, 1 at a time, beating just until blended. Add ⅓ cup sour cream, beating just until blended. Pour cheesecake batter into Wafer Crust.

ADD water to an 8-inch square pan to depth of 1 inch, and place on lower rack in oven.

BAKE cheesecake on rack in middle of oven at 350° for 45 minutes. Turn off oven, and let cheesecake stand in oven 30 minutes. Cool on a wire rack. Cover and chill 8 hours.

STIR together remaining ⅓ cup sour cream and 1 teaspoon no-calorie sweetener; spread over cheesecake. Toss together strawberries, 1 tablespoon no-calorie sweetener, and 1 tablespoon water; spoon evenly over sour cream mixture. **Prep: 15 min., Bake: 45 min., Stand: 30 min., Chill: 8 hrs.**

WAFER CRUST: Stir together 1¼ cups low-fat graham cracker crumbs; 3 tablespoons SPLENDA Granular; and ¼ cup light margarine, melted. Press evenly into bottom of a lightly greased 9-inch springform pan. **Prep: 5 min.**

HARVEST SPICE CAKE WITH CREAM CHEESE FROSTING

MAKES 10 TO 12 SERVINGS

- 1 cup butter or margarine, softened
- 1 cup granulated sugar
- 1 cup firmly packed light brown sugar
- 2 large eggs
- 2 cups all-purpose flour
- 1 teaspoon baking soda
- 1½ teaspoons McCORMICK Gourmet Collection Saigon Cinnamon
- ½ teaspoon McCORMICK Gourmet Collection Ground Nutmeg
- 1 cup buttermilk
- 1 teaspoon vanilla extract
- 1 cup chopped mixed dried fruit
- 1 cup chopped pecans
- Cream Cheese Frosting

BEAT butter at medium speed with an electric mixer until creamy; gradually add sugars, beating well. Add eggs, 1 at a time, beating until blended after each addition.

COMBINE flour and next 3 ingredients; add to butter mixture alternately with buttermilk, beginning and ending with flour mixture. Beat at low speed until blended after each addition. Stir in vanilla, dried fruit, and pecans. Pour into 3 greased and floured 9-inch cakepans.

BAKE at 350° for 20 to 22 minutes or until a wooden pick inserted in center comes out clean. Cool in pans on wire racks 10 minutes; remove from pans, and cool on wire racks.

SPREAD Cream Cheese Frosting between layers and on top and sides of cake. Store in refrigerator. **Prep: 20 min., Bake: 22 min., Cool: 10 min.**

CREAM CHEESE FROSTING: Beat 1 (8-ounce) package softened cream cheese and ½ cup softened butter until creamy. Gradually add 1 (16-ounce) package powdered sugar and 1½ teaspoons vanilla extract; beat until light and fluffy. Makes 3 cups. **Prep: 5 min.**

Make Supper Easy

Whether it's a salad, entrée, or dessert, one-dish recipes are a bonus for everyone. First, we looked at family favorites such as King Ranch chicken (a recipe said to have come from the famous ranch in Texas) and Black Forest cake. Then we streamlined them using convenience products and items commonly found in your refrigerator and pantry. So call on these mouthwatering, no-fuss choices to solve your weeknight dining dilemmas. Cleanup is effortless, so you're out of the kitchen in no time.

BLACK FOREST PUDDING CAKE

MAKES ABOUT 12 SERVINGS

2 (21-ounce) cans cherry pie filling
2 cups (12-ounce package) NESTLÉ TOLL HOUSE Semi-Sweet Chocolate Morsels, divided
1 cup chopped pecans, toasted and divided
1 (18.25-ounce) package chocolate cake mix
¾ cup butter or margarine, melted

SPREAD cherry pie filling in a lightly greased 13- x 9-inch pan.
SPRINKLE pie filling evenly with 1 cup chocolate morsels and ½ cup chopped pecans, and sprinkle chocolate cake mix evenly over pecans.
SPRINKLE remaining 1 cup chocolate morsels and remaining ½ cup chopped pecans over cake mix. Drizzle with melted butter.
BAKE at 350° for 50 to 55 minutes or until bubbly. **Prep: 5 min., Bake: 55 min.**

AVOCADO-BREAD SALAD

MAKES 4 TO 6 SERVINGS

2 tablespoons chopped fresh parsley
1 garlic clove, pressed
2 tablespoons vegetable oil
1¼ teaspoons salt, divided
3 cups (½-inch) French bread cubes
⅓ cup mayonnaise
2 tablespoons Dijon mustard
1 tablespoon fresh lime juice
½ teaspoon sugar
4 plum tomatoes, chopped
2 large GENUINE CALIFORNIA AVOCADOS, peeled and chopped
¼ cup chopped red onion

STIR together first 3 ingredients and ¼ teaspoon salt in a medium bowl. Add bread cubes; toss gently. Arrange bread cubes in an even layer in a 15- x 10-inch jellyroll pan.
BAKE bread cubes at 350° for 15 minutes or until lightly toasted.
STIR together mayonnaise, next 3 ingredients, and remaining 1 teaspoon salt until blended.
ADD bread cubes, tomato, avocado, and onion; toss gently. Serve immediately. **Prep: 25 min., Bake: 15 min.**

CHILE PEPPER PORK CHOPS

MAKES 6 SERVINGS

3 plum tomatoes, chopped
½ small onion, chopped
2 tablespoons chopped fresh cilantro
1 garlic clove, minced
2½ teaspoons McCORMICK Gourmet Collection Chipotle Chile Pepper, divided
¾ teaspoon salt, divided
3 tablespoons fresh lime juice, divided
6 (1-inch-thick) boneless pork loin chops

STIR together first 4 ingredients, ½ teaspoon chipotle chile pepper, ¼ teaspoon salt, and 2 tablespoons lime juice; cover and chill 30 minutes.
COMBINE remaining 2 teaspoons chipotle chile pepper and remaining

½ teaspoon salt; rub evenly over pork chops. Sprinkle with remaining 1 tablespoon lime juice.
GRILL pork chops, covered with grill lid, over medium-high heat (350° to 400°) 6 to 7 minutes on each side or until done. Serve immediately with chilled tomato mixture. **Prep: 25 min., Chill: 30 min., Grill: 14 min.**

NOTE: Pork chops may also be cooked on the stovetop in 1 tablespoon olive oil in a large nonstick skillet over medium-high heat 6 to 7 minutes on each side or until done.

KING RANCH CASSEROLE

MAKES 6 TO 8 SERVINGS

2 tablespoons butter or margarine
1 medium onion, chopped
1 green bell pepper, chopped
1 red bell pepper, chopped
3 cups chopped cooked chicken
1 (10¾-ounce) can cream of chicken soup
1 (10¾-ounce) can cream of mushroom soup
1 (10-ounce) can diced tomatoes and green chiles
1 teaspoon chili powder
1 teaspoon ground cumin
2 cups tortilla chips, crushed
1 REYNOLDS Pot Lux Cookware Pan With Lid (9- x 12½-inch size)
2 cups (8 ounces) shredded Cheddar cheese
Garnish: chopped fresh cilantro

PREHEAT oven to 325° for at least 20 minutes.
MELT butter in a medium skillet over medium-high heat. Add chopped onion and bell peppers; sauté 8 minutes or until tender.
STIR in chicken and next 5 ingredients; cook, stirring occasionally, 2 minutes.
PLACE half of crushed tortilla chips in pan. Layer with half each of chicken mixture and shredded Cheddar cheese. Repeat layers, ending with cheese.

BAKE, uncovered, at 325° for 45 minutes or until mixture is thoroughly heated. Garnish, if desired. **Prep: 25 min., Cook: 10 min., Bake: 45 min.**

MARINATED VEGETABLE SALAD

MAKES 8 CUPS

- ¼ cup EQUAL Spoonful
- ¾ cup cider vinegar
- ½ cup vegetable oil
- 1 medium-size green bell pepper, chopped
- 1 medium onion, chopped
- 3 celery ribs, sliced
- 1 (15-ounce) can small sweet peas, rinsed and drained
- 1 (14½-ounce) can French-cut green beans, rinsed and drained
- 1 (11-ounce) can white shoepeg corn, drained
- 1 (7-ounce) jar diced pimiento, undrained
- ½ teaspoon salt
- ¼ teaspoon pepper

BRING first 3 ingredients to a boil in a small saucepan over medium heat, and cook, stirring often, 5 minutes or until no-calorie sweetener dissolves. Remove from heat, and cool 30 minutes.

STIR together bell pepper and next 8 ingredients in a large bowl; gently stir in dressing. Cover and chill up to 8 hours. Serve with a slotted spoon. **Prep: 15 min., Cook: 8 min., Cool: 30 min., Chill: 8 hrs.**

Brunch Anytime

These doable recipes are crowd pleasers around the clock.

Why go to a restaurant for brunch when you can make these easy dishes for an enjoyable at-home meal? Plum Preserves Coffee Cake and Mixed Fruit Grand make just-right accompaniments. Avocado-and-Black Bean Frittata and Southwestern Corn Muffins showcase the popular flavors of Tex-Mex cuisine.

Whichever combination of recipes you choose, we guarantee they will get your day off to a great start.

Cook's Notes

For make-ahead convenience, we've provided the following freezing instructions for Plum Preserves Coffee Cake and Southwestern Corn Muffins.

■ Place a layer of heavy-duty aluminum foil directly on top of baked Plum Preserves Coffee Cake. Attach Pot Lux Cookware Lid, and freeze up to one month. To thaw coffee cake, let stand at room temperature.

■ Place Southwestern Corn Muffins in an airtight container or heavy-duty zip-top plastic bags, and freeze up to three months. To thaw muffins, let stand at room temperature.

PLUM PRESERVES COFFEE CAKE

MAKES 6 TO 8 SERVINGS

- ½ cup firmly packed light brown sugar
- ½ teaspoon ground cinnamon
- 2 (12-ounce) cans refrigerated buttermilk biscuits
- ¼ cup butter or margarine, melted
- 1 REYNOLDS Pot Lux Cookware Pan With Lid (8- x 8-inch size)
- 1 (12-ounce) jar plum preserves
- ½ cup powdered sugar
- 2 teaspoons milk

PREHEAT oven to 350° for at least 20 minutes.

STIR together brown sugar and cinnamon in a shallow dish.

SEPARATE 1 can biscuits; flatten each biscuit. Dip in butter; dredge in brown sugar mixture. Arrange in an even layer in pan. Spread plum preserves evenly over biscuits in pan.

SEPARATE remaining 1 can biscuits; flatten biscuits. Dip in butter; dredge in remaining brown sugar mixture. Arrange in an even layer over plum preserves.

PLACE pan in center of a baking sheet.

BAKE, uncovered, at 350° for 40 to 45 minutes, loosely shielding top with aluminum foil the last 20 minutes to prevent excessive browning. Remove baking sheet with pan; cool on a wire rack 15 minutes. Stir together powdered sugar and milk until blended. Drizzle over coffee cake. **Prep: 20 min., Bake: 45 min., Cool: 15 min.**

Avocado-and-Black Bean Frittata

MAKES 6 SERVINGS

This hearty brunch dish is an authentic beginning to a border-style meal. *(pictured on page 228)*

1 medium onion, chopped
1 tablespoon vegetable oil
2 large GENUINE CALIFORNIA
    AVOCADOS, peeled and
    chopped
1 (15-ounce) can black beans,
    rinsed and drained
10 large eggs
½ cup sour cream
½ teaspoon salt
¼ teaspoon pepper
¼ teaspoon ground cumin
1 cup (4 ounces) shredded Cheddar
    cheese
Toppings: GENUINE CALIFORNIA
    AVOCADO slices, plum tomato
    slices, sour cream
Chunky salsa (optional)

SAUTÉ chopped onion in hot vegetable oil in a 12-inch ovenproof skillet over medium-high heat 3 to 4 minutes or until tender.
REMOVE from heat; sprinkle top evenly with chopped avocado and beans.
WHISK together eggs and next 4 ingredients; pour over avocado mixture in skillet.
BAKE at 350° for 25 minutes; sprinkle top evenly with cheese, and bake 5 more minutes.
REMOVE from oven, and let stand 5 minutes before serving. Serve with desired toppings and, if desired, with salsa. **Prep: 15 min., Cook: 4 min., Bake: 30 min., Stand: 5 min.**

Southwestern Corn Muffins

MAKES 1 DOZEN

¼ cup butter or margarine
¼ cup chopped onion
1 (11-ounce) can yellow corn with red
    and green peppers, drained
1 cup self-rising yellow cornmeal
1 cup all-purpose flour
1 cup (4 ounces) shredded Cheddar
    cheese
¼ cup SPLENDA Granular
½ teaspoon baking powder
½ teaspoon salt
1¼ cups nonfat buttermilk
1 large egg, lightly beaten

MELT butter in a skillet over medium-high heat; add chopped onion, and sauté 3 minutes or until onion is tender.
STIR together onion, corn, cornmeal, and remaining ingredients in a bowl, stirring just until dry ingredients are moistened. Spoon batter evenly into 12 lightly greased muffin cups. Bake at 375° for 18 to 20 minutes or until a wooden pick inserted in center comes out clean. Remove from pans; cool on a wire rack. **Prep: 10 min., Cook: 3 min., Bake: 20 min.**

Mixed Fruit Grand

MAKES 6 TO 8 SERVINGS

1 (6-ounce) jar orange marmalade
¼ cup EQUAL Spoonful
¼ cup orange liqueur
4 large oranges, peeled and sectioned
1 pineapple, peeled, cored, and cut
    into 1-inch pieces
1 quart strawberries, halved

COOK orange marmalade and no-calorie sweetener in a small saucepan over medium heat 5 minutes or until sweetener dissolves, stirring often. Cool slightly.
STIR together marmalade mixture, liqueur, orange sections, pineapple, and strawberry halves. Cover; chill at least 4 hours. **Prep: 25 min., Cook: 5 min., Chill: 4 hrs.**

Grill Sirloin Tonight

If your family loves steak, then try hearty top sirloin. It's a versatile, affordable cut that tastes great either grilled or broiled; you can serve it whole, thinly sliced, or cubed for kabobs. The delicious, easy-to-make recipe featured here gets a flavor boost from a seasoned marinade that uses red pepper flakes for a touch of heat. What's more, you can do the preparation the night before and be ready to grill when you get home.

Peppery Grilled Sirloin

MAKES 4 SERVINGS

This steak is great sliced and served in warm flour tortillas with your choice of toppings.

¼ cup olive oil
4½ tablespoons fresh lime juice
    (1 to 2 limes)
3 tablespoons soy sauce
1 teaspoon sugar
1 teaspoon garlic powder
1 teaspoon ground ginger
½ teaspoon dried crushed red pepper
    flakes
4 (¾-inch-thick) top sirloin
    steaks
½ teaspoon salt

COMBINE first 7 ingredients in a shallow dish or heavy-duty zip-top plastic bag; add steaks. Cover or seal; chill at least 2½ hours, turning occasionally.
REMOVE steaks, reserving marinade for basting. Sprinkle steaks with salt.
GRILL, covered with grill lid, over medium-high heat (350° to 400°), basting often with reserved marinade, 7 minutes on each side or to desired degree of doneness. Discard any excess marinade. **Prep: 15 min., Chill: 2½ hrs., Grill: 14 min.**

CHARLOTTE BRYANT
GREENSBURG, KENTUCKY

Last Tomatoes of Summer

Get them before they're gone, and put them to delicious use in these recipes.

Don't leave those end-of-season tomatoes hanging; use their ripe perfection to enhance these flavorful dishes. Their sweet-acidic taste, combined with other ingredients, is hard to beat. We sampled a variety of these juicy gems, from whole red tomatoes to small cherry ones, in our Test Kitchens. Toss them with pasta, stuff them with cornbread and bacon, or simply enjoy them as an appetizer on toasted bread, sprinkled with a dash of salt and coarsely ground black pepper. You'll savor the taste memory until next summer.

CORNBREAD-STUFFED TOMATOES

MAKES 4 SERVINGS

Remove tomato pulp from the shells easily with a grapefruit spoon.

    4 ripe tomatoes
    2 cups crumbled cornbread
    ½ cup mayonnaise
    4 to 6 bacon slices, cooked and
        crumbled
    3 to 4 green onions, chopped
    Salt and pepper to taste

REMOVE tomato cores; scoop out pulp, and place in a bowl, leaving shells intact. Stir together tomato pulp, cornbread, and remaining ingredients. Spoon mixture into tomato shells. **Prep: 15 min.**

MARILYN SWINEFORD
HOWE, TEXAS

FRESH TOMATO SAUCE WITH LINGUINE

MAKES 6 SERVINGS

Use a wide-blade vegetable peeler to shave the Parmesan cheese that garnishes this garden-fresh dish.

    1 (16-ounce) package linguine
    3 garlic cloves, thinly sliced
    ½ teaspoon dried crushed red
        pepper
    3 tablespoons olive oil
    4 cups cherry or grape tomatoes,
        halved
    ½ cup fresh basil leaves, coarsely
        chopped
    2 tablespoons chopped fresh
        parsley
    2 tablespoons red wine vinegar
    ½ to 1 teaspoon salt
    Garnishes: shaved Parmesan cheese,
        fresh basil sprig

COOK linguine according to package directions; drain.
SAUTÉ garlic and red pepper in hot oil in a large skillet over low heat. Add tomatoes and next 4 ingredients, and cook 3 to 5 minutes.
TOSS together pasta and tomato mixture; garnish, if desired. **Prep: 20 min., Cook: 10 min.**

TOMATO-BLUE CHEESE CRACKERS

MAKES ABOUT 18 APPETIZER SERVINGS

Plum, or Italian, tomatoes are egg-shaped and available year-round.

    3 ounces crumbled blue cheese,
        softened
    2 (3-ounce) packages cream cheese,
        softened
    1 teaspoon salt marinade-and-
        seasoning mix
    Assorted crackers
    3 ripe plum tomatoes, sliced

STIR together first 3 ingredients; cover mixture, and chill up to 1 week, if desired. Spread over crackers; top each with a tomato slice. **Prep: 10 min.**

NOTE: For testing purposes only, we used Jane's Original Krazy Mixed-Up Salt Marinade & Seasoning (a blend of salt, spices, onion, and garlic).

JOANNE MARINER
SNOW HILL, MARYLAND

ROASTED PEPPER-TOMATO BRUSCHETTA

MAKES 2 DOZEN

Seeding the tomatoes will enhance the appearance of these appetizers.

    1 (7-ounce) jar roasted red bell
        peppers, drained and chopped
    6 ripe tomatoes, seeded and diced
    3 tablespoons shredded Parmesan
        cheese
    2 tablespoons chopped fresh basil
    1 garlic clove, minced
    ½ teaspoon coarse-grained sea salt or
        kosher salt
    ¼ teaspoon freshly ground pepper
    24 French bread slices, toasted

COMBINE first 7 ingredients; spoon 1 heaping tablespoon over each toasted bread slice. **Prep: 15 min.**

GAIL GUNDERSEN
TAMPA, FLORIDA

Cozy Up to Warm Desserts

As summer gives way to the cool promise of fall, treat yourself to the comfort of these delectable sweets. They couldn't be easier to make.

With fall just around the corner, it's time to start enjoying warm, down-home desserts again. Don't be surprised to find yourself nestled up, savoring every bite of these heavenly, fruit-filled treats.

In several recipes, we replaced homemade crusts, doughs, and batters with supermarket convenience products. We used canned refrigerated crescent rolls, for example, to speed up the prep time of Cinnamon-Apple Rolls—the hardest part was waiting for them to bake.

MIXED-BERRY COBBLER

MAKES 12 SERVINGS

You could also top this tangy dessert with a scoop of vanilla ice cream.

> **1 (15-ounce) package refrigerated piecrusts**
> **1 tablespoon sugar**
> **1½ cups sugar**
> **2 (16-ounce) packages frozen blueberries**
> **1 (16-ounce) package frozen cherries**
> **1 cup fresh or frozen cranberries***
> **3 tablespoons all-purpose flour**
> **¼ teaspoon salt**
> **¼ cup cold butter or margarine, cut up**
> **Garnish: whipped topping**

UNFOLD 1 piecrust, and press out fold lines; cut pastry into 1-inch strips, and place on a baking sheet. Unfold remaining piecrust; press out fold lines, and cut into ½-inch strips. Sprinkle evenly with 1 tablespoon sugar, and place on a baking sheet.

BAKE pastry strips at 425° for 7 to 8 minutes or until golden.

STIR together 1½ cups sugar and next 5 ingredients. Spoon half of berry mixture into a lightly greased 13- x 9-inch baking dish, and top evenly with 1-inch baked pastry strips. Spoon remaining berry mixture into baking dish; dot with butter.

BAKE at 400° for 30 to 35 minutes or until bubbly. Top with ½-inch baked pastry strips. Garnish, if desired. **Prep: 25 min., Bake: 43 min.**

*Substitute 1 Granny Smith apple, peeled and chopped, if desired.

SPICED PINEAPPLE UPSIDE-DOWN CAKE

MAKES 12 SERVINGS

> **1 cup butter or margarine, softened and divided**
> **1½ cups firmly packed brown sugar**
> **1 (20-ounce) can pineapple slices, drained**
> **12 maraschino cherries**
> **1 cup chopped pecans**
> **2 cups granulated sugar**
> **3 large eggs**
> **1½ teaspoons vanilla extract**
> **3 cups all-purpose flour**
> **2½ teaspoons baking powder**
> **1 teaspoon baking soda**
> **1 teaspoon salt**
> **1 teaspoon ground cinnamon**
> **1 teaspoon ground nutmeg**
> **1½ cups buttermilk**

MELT ¾ cup butter in a saucepan, and add brown sugar, stirring until sugar dissolves.

SPREAD sugar mixture into a 13- x 9-inch pan. Arrange pineapple slices in a single layer in pan, placing a maraschino cherry in center of each pineapple slice. Sprinkle with chopped pecans, and set aside.

BEAT remaining ¼ cup butter and 2 cups granulated sugar at medium-high speed with an electric mixer until smooth; add eggs, 1 at a time, beating until blended after each addition. Beat in vanilla.

COMBINE flour, baking powder, baking soda, salt, cinnamon, and nutmeg; add to butter mixture alternately with buttermilk, beginning and ending with flour mixture. Beat at low speed just until blended after each addition. Pour batter over pineapple.

BAKE at 350° for 50 minutes or until a wooden pick inserted in center comes out clean. Invert immediately onto a serving platter. **Prep: 10 min., Bake: 50 min.**

ELLIE WELLS
LAKELAND, FLORIDA

HONEYED APPLE-CRANBERRY FRIED PIES

MAKES 1½ DOZEN

If you don't want to fry these irresistible pies, you can bake them instead. Place them on lightly greased baking sheets, and bake at 425° for 12 minutes or until golden and crispy.

> **2 Granny Smith apples, peeled and chopped**
> **1 cup fresh cranberries***
> **½ cup sugar**
> **2 tablespoons honey**
> **⅛ teaspoon salt**
> **¾ teaspoon ground cinnamon, divided**
> **1 (15-ounce) package refrigerated piecrusts**
> **Vegetable oil**
> **1 tablespoon sugar**

COOK first 5 ingredients and ½ teaspoon cinnamon in a large saucepan over medium heat 5 minutes; reduce heat to medium-low, and cook, stirring occasionally, 20 minutes or until apples are tender. Cool completely, and drain.

ROLL piecrusts to 12-inch circles; cut each crust into 9 (4-inch) circles.

SPOON 1 level tablespoon fruit mixture onto half of each pastry circle. Moisten edges with water; fold dough over fruit mixture, pressing edges to seal. Crimp edges with a fork dipped in flour.

POUR oil to a depth of ¼ inch into a large heavy skillet; heat to 350°. Fry pies, in batches, 2 minutes on each side. Combine 1 tablespoon sugar and remaining ¼ teaspoon cinnamon, and sprinkle over hot pies. **Prep: 25 min., Cook: 25 min., Fry: 4 min. per batch**

*Substitute thawed frozen cranberries or dried cranberries, if desired.

LYNN AIGNER
WOODSBORO, TEXAS

CINNAMON-APPLE ROLLS

MAKES 8 SERVINGS

- ¼ cup butter or margarine
- ¼ cup granulated sugar
- ¼ cup water
- 2 (8-ounce) cans refrigerated crescent rolls
- 2 (12-ounce) packages frozen escalloped apples, thawed
- ½ cup chopped pecans, toasted
- ½ cup firmly packed light brown sugar
- 2 tablespoons all-purpose flour
- ½ teaspoon ground cinnamon

MELT butter in a 13- x 9-inch baking dish; set aside.

STIR together granulated sugar and ¼ cup water in a saucepan over medium heat, and stir until sugar dissolves.

ROLL each can crescent roll dough to a 10- x 14-inch rectangle.

COMBINE apples and next 4 ingredients; spread evenly over each rectangle. Roll up dough, jellyroll fashion, pressing seams to seal; cut each roll into 16 (¾-inch) slices, and place in prepared baking dish. Drizzle with sugar syrup.

BAKE at 400° for 20 to 25 minutes. Serve immediately. **Prep: 15 min., Cook: 5 min., Bake: 25 min.**

NOTE: For testing purposes only, we used Stouffer's Escalloped Apples.

Chicken in the Oven

It goes without saying that work doesn't end when you leave the office. How do you juggle cooking with everything else that demands your time?

Let us help you multitask. We offer distinctively delicious chicken dishes—spicy Tex-Mex rollups and an easy comfort food casserole—along with fast sides. Each entrée bakes while you catch up on other projects (or take a breather to watch some Brady Bunch reruns).

SOUTHWESTERN CHICKEN BUNDLES

MAKES 4 SERVINGS

Donna Ehinger calls this "Chicken Cordon Green;" it's her spin on chicken cordon bleu.

- 4 skinned and boned chicken breast halves
- 1 (5.25-ounce) can whole green chiles, drained
- 4 (1-ounce) slices Monterey Jack cheese with peppers
- 1 large egg
- 2 tablespoons water
- 1 cup finely crushed tortilla chips
- Salsa
- Garnish: lime wedge

PLACE chicken between 2 sheets of heavy-duty plastic wrap, and flatten to ⅛-inch thickness, using a meat mallet or rolling pin. Top each chicken breast with 1 green chile and 1 cheese slice; roll up, securing with wooden picks.

WHISK together egg and 2 tablespoons water in a shallow bowl. Dip chicken rolls in egg mixture; dredge in crushed chips. Place rolls in a lightly greased 13- x 9-inch pan.

BAKE at 375° for 30 to 35 minutes. Let stand 5 minutes before slicing. Serve with salsa; garnish, if desired. **Prep: 20 min., Bake: 35 min., Stand: 5 min.**

TANGY SLAW: Whisk together ¼ cup fresh lime juice (about 2 large limes), ¼ cup olive oil, and 1 (0.06-ounce) envelope zesty Italian dressing mix in a large bowl. Add 2 (11.5-ounce) packages shredded coleslaw mix and ⅓ cup chopped fresh cilantro, tossing to coat. Cover and chill at least 2 hours. Makes 4 servings. **Prep: 10 min., Chill: 2 hrs.**

DONNA L. EHINGER
GREENSBORO, NORTH CAROLINA

HERBED CHICKEN-AND-RICE BAKE

MAKES 4 SERVINGS

- 1 (4-pound) whole chicken, cut up
- 2 tablespoons butter or margarine
- 1 (8-ounce) package sliced fresh mushrooms
- 1 medium-size green bell pepper, chopped
- 2½ cups chicken broth
- 1 (6.5-ounce) package quick-cooking wild rice mix
- ½ teaspoon dried thyme
- 1 (10¾-ounce) can cream of mushroom soup
- 1 (8-ounce) can sliced water chestnuts, drained

PLACE chicken in a lightly greased 13- x 9-inch roasting pan.

BAKE at 425° for 20 minutes. Remove chicken, discarding drippings in pan. Reduce oven temperature to 350°.

MELT butter in a large skillet over medium heat. Add sliced mushrooms and chopped bell pepper; sauté 5 minutes or until tender. Stir in chicken broth, rice mix, and thyme; cook 5 minutes. Stir in cream of mushroom soup and water chestnuts. Pour mixture into roasting pan; top with chicken.

BAKE at 350° for 45 minutes. **Prep: 20 min.; Cook: 10 min.; Bake: 1 hr., 5 min.**

LEMON PEPPER STEAMED BROCCOLI: Cut 1½ pounds fresh broccoli into spears. Cook in boiling water to cover 8 minutes or until crisp-tender; drain. Toss with 2 tablespoons olive oil and ½ teaspoon lemon pepper. Serve immediately. Makes 4 to 6 servings. **Prep: 5 min., Cook: 8 min.**

from our kitchen

(See pages 196-197 for some mouthwatering pear recipes.)

Pick the Right Pear

Pears are at their peak right now. Whatever your preference, there's a variety to fit your needs. (See pages 196-197 for some mouthwatering pear recipes.)

■ Bartlett is thin-skinned, juicy when very ripe, and highly versatile.

■ Anjou, a slightly sweet variety, is best eaten fresh or poached. It's not a good candidate for pies or canning.

■ Comice is probably the juiciest of all pears when ripe. It's excellent for eating out of hand and in salads. However, it doesn't hold up well when cooked.

■ Bosc has a firm texture and nutty aroma. These characteristics make this pear great for poaching, pies, muffins, and preserves. It's terrific eaten firm and crisp or ripened to a mellow, juicy state.

■ Seckel is a small, very sweet pear with dense flesh. It's not recommended for pies because of its size, but it does make great jams and preserves.

■ Forelle is similar to Seckel in size, texture, and flavor. It's better for pies than Seckel but not quite as good for canning.

Don't neglect those hard, rough-skinned varieties on trees and at farmers markets around our region. They make the best marmalades, preserves, and pies because of their firm, grainy texture. Before eating out of hand, ripen them completely in brown paper bags.

Keep pears at room temperature up to a week; store ripe ones in the refrigerator two to three days. Remember to peel very ripe pears before cooking because the skin will become bitter and tough.

Add this buttery fruit to your list for a great party; wine and cheese are its natural partners. The Pear Bureau Northwest offers a Pear Cheese Wine selector that makes pairing a breeze. Simply line up your favorite pear in the window to see its recommended accompaniments. To get this handy device, send $1 to Hood River Country Fruit Loop, 2665 Reed Road, Hood River, OR 97031.

Fry Right

At a recent gathering, crisp catfish sparked lots of questions about oil and frying. We love perfectly fried foods—chicken, shrimp, green tomatoes—and we want you to be comfortable cooking them. Here are a few tips to take the guesswork out of the process.

■ The best oils for frying are corn, peanut, canola, and safflower. These have high smoke points, which means they can be heated to high temperatures without burning.

■ If you haven't used an oil in a while, always taste or smell it to be sure it's still good. Discard any oil that has an off odor or taste.

■ Although good for sautéing, olive oil isn't the best candidate for frying.

■ Solid vegetable shortening and vegetable oil can be used interchangeably for frying.

■ Fry large quantities of food in batches to ensure even cooking. Overcrowding will lower the oil's temperature, causing food to absorb excess grease.

■ Generally, oil can be strained and then reused to fry the same type of food. For instance, you can use the same oil to cook French fries up to three times. (Note: Hot oil absorbs flavors and transfers them to whatever you're cooking.) Refrigerate strained oil in an airtight container up to three months.

Newfangled Foil

Aluminum foil, among the most indispensable kitchen items, is better than ever thanks to Reynolds. Release Non-Stick Aluminum Foil won't stick to the food you're cooking, storing, freezing, or transporting. One side is coated with a nonstick surface; just place the food on this side, and proceed as usual. The foil won't lift the skin from your poultry or the icing from your cake. It makes oven frying easy because there's no need for vegetable cooking spray, and the crisp edges stay on the food—not on the foil. Find this new product at supermarkets in a 35-square-foot roll for about $2.50.

Tips and Tidbits

■ Rebecca Kracke Gordon of our Test Kitchens staff always makes perfect whipped cream. Her secret is Whip it, a stabilizer by Oetker. She sprinkles one packet of powder into cold whipping cream and beats until peaks form; the finished mixture stays stiff for hours without separating. Look for it at larger supermarkets near the gelatin and canned fruit.

■ Plan ahead and serve perfectly crisp cheese straws. Underbake them slightly; cool and freeze in an airtight container. Reheat on a baking sheet for just-baked flavor and texture. This method is great for large parties.

■ To clean stuck-on food from the inside of your blender, pour in warm water and a drop of dishwashing liquid. Cover with the lid, and pulse a few times.

■ Executive Editor Susan Dosier's formula for perfect rice is as easy as one-two-three. One cup long-grain rice plus 2 cups water equals 3 cups cooked rice—just enough for a family of four. Bring water to a boil; add rice, and cook, covered, over medium heat for 20 minutes.

October

Celebrate Goodwill & Great Food

Visit Amory, Mississippi, as it comes together for a worthy cause and a chance to brag on the South.

Down-to-earth stars shine bright in this tiny Mississippi town, thanks to native son and Hollywood agent Sam Haskell. He established the Mary Kirkpatrick Haskell Scholarship Foundation in 1991 in honor of his mother, the town's first school nurse-practitioner. Designed to provide financial assistance for deserving college-bound seniors at Amory and Monroe County High Schools, the foundation's primary fund-raiser is the biennial Stars Over Mississippi concert.

Showcasing the South, One Plate at a Time

Amory's 7,000 residents roll out the red carpet for their special guests. Before it's over, the stars from film, television, and music will attend everything from a catfish fry to an elegant dinner for more than 800. What's more, everything is prepared by local volunteers. Coordinating all this is caterer Steve Stockton, food-service administrator for Amory Schools.

Steve uses his own recipes, along with a few from friends and family, to create a delicious menu for the Gala dinner (we've picked a few of Steve's favorite dishes for this story). As for the Catfish Fry, that's the bailiwick of Stephina and Doug Fowlkes, owners of The Friendship House restaurant in nearby Aberdeen. Stephina, Doug, and their staff have dazzled the stars with their famous catfish—both fried and baked. Their recipe for Cajun-Baked Catfish received our stamp of approval, too, and we're happy to share it with you.

Friends for Life

One of the most unusual aspects of the weekend is that many of the stars stay with local families. Some even become close friends. Such is the case with Amory resident Wanda Wright and Emmy- and Golden Globe-winning performer Debbie Allen, who first met eight years ago. Over a heaping plate of Wanda's light-as-air Old Southern Biscuits, the two women formed a lasting bond.

A Community Comes Together

"The volunteerism is what's so incredible about this event," Sam says as he reflects upon the 10-year history of the Stars Over Mississippi concerts.

We hope, through these wonderful recipes, you and your family are blessed by a little bit of Amory's small-town charm.

OLD SOUTHERN BISCUITS

MAKES 1 DOZEN

- ¼ cup vegetable shortening
- 2 cups self-rising flour
- 1 cup buttermilk
- Melted butter (optional)

CUT shortening into flour with a pastry blender or fork until crumbly. Add buttermilk, stirring the mixture just until moistened.

PAT dough to ½-inch thickness; cut with a 2-inch round cutter. Place on a lightly greased baking sheet.

BAKE at 425° for 14 minutes or until golden. Brush the hot biscuits with melted butter, if desired. **Prep: 10 min., Bake: 14 min.**

WANDA D. WRIGHT
AMORY, MISSISSIPPI

CAJUN-BAKED CATFISH

MAKES 4 SERVINGS

For a twist, the Fowlkeses recommend substituting 1 tablespoon lemon pepper for 1 tablespoon Cajun seasoning.

- 2 cups cornmeal
- 2 teaspoons salt
- 1 tablespoon pepper
- 8 (3- to 4-ounce) catfish fillets
- 2 tablespoons Cajun seasoning
- 1 to 2 teaspoons seasoned salt
- ¼ cup butter or margarine, melted
- Garnish: lemon wedges

COMBINE first 3 ingredients. Dredge catfish fillets in cornmeal mixture; place fillets, skin sides down, on a greased baking sheet.

COMBINE Cajun seasoning and seasoned salt; sprinkle over fillets. Drizzle with butter.

BAKE at 400° for 30 minutes or until golden and fish flakes with a fork. Garnish, if desired. **Prep: 10 min., Bake: 30 min.**

DOUG AND STEPHINA FOWLKES
THE FRIENDSHIP HOUSE
ABERDEEN, MISSISSIPPI

PORK ROAST WITH JEZEBEL SAUCE

MAKES 6 TO 8 SERVINGS

- 6 tablespoons hot sauce
- 6 tablespoons Worcestershire sauce
- 2 tablespoons garlic salt
- 2 tablespoons pepper
- 1 (3- to 4-pound) boneless pork loin
- Jezebel Sauce
- Garnishes: paprika, fresh parsley sprigs, cracked black pepper

STIR together hot sauce and Worcestershire sauce; set aside.

COMBINE garlic salt and pepper.

PLACE pork in a lightly greased roasting pan. Brush all sides of pork with sauce mixture; sprinkle with garlic salt mixture.

BAKE at 325° for 2 hours or until a meat thermometer inserted into thickest portion registers 160°, shielding with aluminum foil the last 30 minutes. Let stand, covered, 15 minutes. Cut into slices. Serve with Jezebel Sauce; garnish if desired. **Prep: 15 min., Bake: 2 hrs., Stand: 15 min.**

Jezebel Sauce:

MAKES 3½ CUPS

Prepare in advance, and chill up to eight hours. Store leftover sauce in the refrigerator.

- 1 (18-ounce) jar apple jelly
- 1 (18-ounce) jar apricot-pineapple preserves
- ¼ cup dry mustard
- 2 tablespoons pepper
- 3 tablespoons prepared horseradish

STIR together all ingredients; serve with pork. **Prep: 5 min.**

ELIZABETH SAYLORS
AMORY, MISSISSIPPI

BACON-CHEESE CUPS

MAKES 10 SERVINGS

Fill the two unused cups with water to keep bottoms from burning.

- 2 (3-ounce) packages cream cheese, softened
- 1 large egg
- 2 tablespoons milk
- ½ cup (2 ounces) shredded Swiss cheese
- 1 green onion, chopped
- 1 (10-ounce) package refrigerated flaky biscuits
- 5 bacon slices, cooked, crumbled, and divided

BEAT first 3 ingredients at medium speed with an electric mixer until combined. Stir in shredded Swiss cheese and chopped green onion.

SEPARATE biscuits, and pat into 5-inch circles. Press circles into greased 3½-inch muffin cups, leaving a ¼-inch border at top of each cup. Sprinkle evenly with half of bacon; top with 2 tablespoons cream cheese mixture.

BAKE at 375° for 22 minutes or until set. Remove from oven, and sprinkle with remaining bacon, gently pressing into filling. **Prep: 20 min., Bake: 22 min.**

STEVE STOCKTON
AMORY, MISSISSIPPI

Giving Back, Every Day

"The scholarship helped me realize my dream," reflects Leigh Abney Stanford from her desk at Amory Middle School. "Ever since I was a little girl, I played school," Leigh remembers. The winner of the prestigious Mary Kirkpatrick Haskell Scholarship Foundation award in 1996, Leigh has fond memories of the Haskell family. "I was a little girl, but I remember Sam from when he taught swimming lessons at the city pool, and his mom was my nurse in elementary school," she says.

Financial aid in hand and college in her sights, Leigh was encouraged by family and friends to pursue a degree in medicine. Deep down, though, she wanted to teach. Leigh enrolled in the premed program at Mississippi State University, but after a year she transferred to Mississippi University for Women and decided to major in education.

After graduating, she headed back to Amory to fulfill her student-teaching requirements. "I was a little nervous at first," Leigh says of returning to the very school she had attended only a few years before. "Most of the teachers taught me coming up through school." With her degree complete, Leigh decided to call Amory home for good. "I want to raise my family here. I want my kids to grow up being Amory Panthers," she says. And what has the scholarship meant to Leigh? "It's enabled me to do something I love and help others at the same time. Every day I impress upon my students the importance of an education. I make sure they know that with hard work, they, too, can reach their dreams."

PHYLLO POTATOES

MAKES 15 SERVINGS

Leftover phyllo sheets can be refrozen.

- 6 bacon slices, chopped
- 1 medium-size yellow onion, diced
- 5 green onions, finely chopped
- 2 garlic cloves, minced
- 6 large baking potatoes, baked*
- 1 (8-ounce) container sour cream
- ½ cup butter or margarine, melted
- 1 teaspoon salt
- ¼ teaspoon pepper
- 1½ teaspoons soy sauce
- 10 frozen phyllo pastry sheets, thawed
- ½ cup butter or margarine, melted
- Garnishes: chopped green onions, green onion curls

COOK bacon in a large skillet until crisp; remove bacon, and drain on paper towels, reserving 2 tablespoons drippings in skillet. Set bacon aside.

SAUTÉ yellow and green onions in hot drippings in skillet over medium-high heat 5 minutes or until tender. Add garlic; sauté 1 minute.

SCOOP out potato pulp, and place in a large bowl. Add sour cream, and mash with a potato masher. Stir in onion mixture, ½ cup butter, bacon, salt, pepper, and soy sauce.

BRUSH thawed phyllo sheets with ½ cup melted butter. Arrange 5 sheets on bottom of a lightly greased 11- x 15-inch jellyroll pan. Spread with potato mixture; top with remaining 5 phyllo sheets.

BAKE at 350° for 25 to 30 minutes or until golden. Cut into squares before serving; garnish, if desired. **Prep: 35 min., Cook: 10 min., Bake: 30 min.**

*Substitute 1 (22-ounce) package frozen mashed potatoes for baked potato pulp, if desired. Cook according to package directions.

STEVE STOCKTON
AMORY, MISSISSIPPI

APRICOT TORTE

MAKES 12 SERVINGS

- 3 cups all-purpose flour
- 1 cup butter, softened
- ¾ cup sugar
- ⅛ teaspoon salt
- 1 large egg
- 2 cups sour cream
- 1½ cups powdered sugar
- 1 cup chopped pecans, toasted
- 1 teaspoon vanilla extract
- 1 (8-ounce) jar apricot preserves
- Powdered sugar (optional)
- Whipped cream (optional)

PULSE first 4 ingredients in a food processor 7 or 8 times or until mixture is crumbly. Add egg, and pulse 4 or 5 times until dough forms. Divide dough into 7 equal portions, shaping each portion into a ball.

ROLL each ball into a 9-inch circle on inverted greased 9-inch cakepans covered with parchment paper.

BAKE, in batches, at 350° for 10 to 12 minutes or until golden. Cool on pans.

BEAT sour cream and next 3 ingredients at medium speed with an electric mixer until combined; cover and chill.

PROCESS preserves in a food processor until smooth.

SPREAD 6 cookie layers alternately with about 3 tablespoons sour cream mixture and 3 tablespoons apricot preserves; stack. Top with remaining cookie layer; chill 8 hours. Sprinkle top with powdered sugar, if desired; pipe whipped cream around outer edge, if desired. **Prep: 25 min., Bake: 12 min. per batch, Chill: 8 hrs.**

STEVE STOCKTON
AMORY, MISSISSIPPI

Cozy Beverages for Chilly Days

Snuggle up to these tasty treats that include a hot chocolate inspired by a favorite candy, the chocolate-covered cherry. Look to the Mocha Cappuccino for our Test Kitchens' clever method of frothing milk without an espresso machine—they shake the milk in a jar! Hang on to these recipes for the holidays, and enjoy the compliments they bring.

CHERRY CORDIAL HOT CHOCOLATE

MAKES ABOUT 8½ CUPS

- 5½ cups milk
- 1½ cups half-and-half
- 1½ cups chocolate syrup
- ½ cup maraschino cherry juice, divided
- 1¾ cups whipping cream
- 1 tablespoon powdered sugar
- Maraschino cherries with stems (optional)

HEAT first 3 ingredients and 7 tablespoons cherry juice in a Dutch oven over medium-low heat, stirring often.

BEAT whipping cream at medium speed with an electric mixer until foamy; gradually add powdered sugar and remaining cherry juice, beating until soft peaks form. Serve with hot chocolate; top each serving with a cherry, if desired. **Prep: 10 min., Cook: 10 min.**

MOCHA CAPPUCCINO

MAKES 4 SERVINGS

- ½ cup sugar
- ⅓ cup cocoa
- 2½ cups strong brewed coffee
- ¼ cup coffee liqueur
- 1 teaspoon vanilla extract
- 2 cups milk

STIR together first 5 ingredients in a saucepan; cook, whisking constantly, over medium heat, 5 minutes or until thoroughly heated.

MICROWAVE milk in a 2-cup glass measuring cup at HIGH 2 minutes, or until thoroughly heated. Pour one-third of hot milk in a heat-proof jar; seal with lid. Shake until frothy. Repeat twice with remaining milk.

POUR coffee into 4 mugs; top with frothed milk. Serve immediately. **Prep: 10 min., Cook: 7 min.**

NOTE: For testing purposes only, we used Kahlúa coffee liqueur.

APRICOT-APPLE CIDER SIPPER

MAKES ABOUT 21 CUPS

- 1 gallon apple cider
- 1 (11.5-ounce) can apricot nectar
- 2 cups sugar
- 2 cups orange juice
- ¾ cup lemon juice
- 4 (3-inch) cinnamon sticks
- 2 teaspoons ground allspice
- 1 teaspoon ground cloves
- ½ teaspoon ground nutmeg

BRING all ingredients to a boil in a Dutch oven; reduce heat, and simmer 10 minutes. Remove cinnamon sticks. Serve hot. **Prep: 10 min., Cook: 15 min.**

APPLE CIDER SIPPER: Omit nectar. Makes 19 cups.

MILDRED BICKLEY
BRISTOL, VIRGINIA

A Passion for Sweet Potatoes

These golden delights are at their best in the fall.

In Courtney Taylor's world, sweet potatoes reign as one of the South's most flavorful and versatile crops. "They're pretty much everything you can ask of a food," says the Madison, Mississippi, newspaper columnist and co-author of *The Southern Cook's Handbook*. Courtney feels that sweet potatoes in season offer better flavor and texture, and she prefers small specimens, especially the Vardaman variety from Mississippi. While she uses them in everything from soup to dessert, she also admires them in their most basic form. "A baked sweet potato is one of my favorite lunches in the fall," Courtney says. "With a pat of butter, salt, and pepper, you don't need anything else."

SWEET POTATO SOUP

MAKES 12 (8-OUNCE) SERVINGS

In a hurry? Caramelize the onions on top of the stove. Cook 1 pound chopped onions in 1 tablespoon butter and 1 tablespoon oil in a heavy skillet over medium heat 12 to 15 minutes, stirring often, until tender.

- **4 large sweet potatoes**
- **1 to 2 cups Oven-Browned Onions, divided**
- **8 cups fat-free chicken broth, divided**
- **½ teaspoon salt**
- **½ teaspoon pepper**
- **¼ teaspoon ground nutmeg**

BAKE sweet potatoes at 425° for 1 hour, or until very soft. Cool 20 minutes; scoop out the pulp (about 4 cups).

PROCESS sweet potato pulp, half of Oven-Browned Onions, and 4 cups chicken broth in a food processor until mixture is smooth.

POUR sweet potato mixture into a Dutch oven; add remaining chicken broth, salt, pepper, and nutmeg. Bring to a boil; reduce heat to medium, and simmer, stirring occasionally, 20 minutes. Serve soup with remaining Oven-Browned Onions. **Prep: 20 min., Bake: 1 hr., Cool: 20 min, Cook: 25 min.**

Oven-Browned Onions:

MAKES ABOUT 6 CUPS

CHOP 2 pounds onions; place in a lightly greased roasting pan. Bake at 200° for 6 hours or until the onions are evenly browned, stirring occasionally. Cool. Serve immediately, or freeze in ½-cup portions in heavy-duty zip-top bags. **Prep: 20 min., Bake: 6 hrs.**

SWEET POTATO CAKE WITH CITRUS FILLING

MAKES 12 SERVINGS

- **2 cups sugar**
- **1½ cups canola oil**
- **4 large eggs, separated**
- **½ cup hot water**
- **2 cups cake flour**
- **1 tablespoon baking powder**
- **¼ teaspoon salt**
- **1¼ teaspoons ground cinnamon**
- **½ teaspoon ground nutmeg**
- **½ teaspoon ground cloves**
- **½ teaspoon ground ginger**
- **1 large sweet potato, peeled and grated (1½ cups)**
- **1 cup finely chopped pecans, toasted**
- **1 teaspoon vanilla extract**
- **Citrus Filling**
- **Orange Glaze**

BEAT sugar and oil at low speed in a large bowl with an electric mixer until smooth. Add egg yolks, one at a time, beating well after each addition. Stir in hot water.

STIR together flour and next 6 ingredients; add to sugar mixture, stirring just until blended. Stir in sweet potato, pecans, and vanilla.

BEAT egg whites at high speed with an electric mixer until soft peaks form, and fold into batter. Pour batter evenly into 3 lightly greased and floured 8-inch cake pans.

BAKE at 350° for 25 to 30 minutes or until a wooden pick inserted in center comes out clean. Cool in pans on wire racks 10 minutes; remove from pans, and cool on wire racks.

SPREAD 1 cup Citrus Filling between each cake layer. Pour Orange Glaze over cake, letting it run down sides. **Prep: 20 min., Bake: 30 min., Cool: 10 min.**

Citrus Filling:

MAKES APPROXIMATELY 2 CUPS

- **3 egg yolks, lightly beaten**
- **½ cup sugar**
- **⅓ cup water**
- **2 tablespoons all-purpose flour**
- **½ teaspoon grated lemon or orange rind**
- **6 tablespoons fresh orange juice**
- **2½ tablespoons fresh lemon juice**
- **Pinch of salt**

COOK all ingredients in a small saucepan over medium-low heat, stirring constantly, 11 minutes or until thickened. Cool. Cover and chill 30 minutes. **Prep: 10 min., Cook: 11 min., Chill: 30 min.**

Orange Glaze:

MAKES ¾ CUP

- **1¾ cups powdered sugar**
- **3 tablespoons fresh orange juice***
- **1 teaspoon vanilla extract**

STIR together all ingredients until smooth, adding more juice if mixture is too thick. **Prep: 5 min.**

*Substitute tangerine juice, if desired.

Fun With Friendly Ghosts

There's no trick to these treats. Let our recipes and ideas spark your party.

Assistant Foods Editor Kate Nicholson loves to recall her childhood memories of Halloween. For her, it was never about scary things—it was about the magic of whimsical costumes, carved pumpkins, neighborhood laughter, and the essence of fall. Many years have passed since she's been trick-or-treating, but she still gets just as excited.

Start a new tradition at your house this year, and invite family and friends for a festive gathering. We've assembled easy recipes and ideas that are sure to delight your costume-clad guests. We're betting you'll create many memories of your own.

PUMPKIN CHEESE BALL

MAKES 16 APPETIZER SERVINGS

- 2 (8-ounce) blocks extra-sharp Cheddar cheese, shredded
- 1 (8-ounce) package cream cheese, softened
- 1 (8-ounce) container chive-and-onion cream cheese
- 2 teaspoons paprika
- ½ teaspoon ground red pepper
- 1 broccoli stalk
- Red and green apple wedges

COMBINE first 5 ingredients in a medium bowl until blended. Cover and chill 4 hours or until mixture is firm enough to be shaped.

SHAPE mixture into a ball to resemble a pumpkin. Smooth entire outer surface with a frosting spatula or table knife. Make vertical grooves in ball, if desired, using fingertips.

CUT florets from broccoli stalk, and reserve for another use. Cut stalk to resemble a pumpkin stem, and press into top of cheese ball. Serve cheese ball with apple wedges. **Prep: 30 min., Chill: 4 hrs.**

NOTE: To make ahead, wrap cheese ball in plastic wrap without stalk, and store in refrigerator up to 2 days. Attach stalk before serving.

MONSTER EYES

MAKES ABOUT 6 DOZEN

Children will love these sausage balls that stare back at them.

- 3 cups all-purpose baking mix
- 1 pound ground hot or mild pork sausage
- 1 (10-ounce) block extra-sharp Cheddar cheese, shredded
- 72 small pimiento-stuffed olives

COMBINE first 3 ingredients in a large bowl until blended.

SHAPE sausage mixture into 1-inch balls, and place on lightly greased baking sheets. Press 1 olive deeply in the center of each ball.

BAKE at 400° for 20 minutes or until lightly browned. **Prep: 30 min., Bake: 20 min. per batch**

NOTE: For testing purposes only, we used Cracker Barrel Extra-Sharp Cheddar Cheese.

DEVILED GREEN GOBLIN EGGS

MAKES 1 DOZEN

For a festive look, serve in decorative Halloween cupcake liners.

- 6 cups hot water
- 1 (0.3-ounce) bottle yellow liquid food coloring
- ½ (0.3-ounce) bottle blue liquid food coloring
- ½ (0.3-ounce) bottle green liquid food coloring
- 2 tablespoons cider vinegar
- 12 large unpeeled hard-cooked eggs, with shells cracked (see box below)
- ½ cup instant potato flakes
- ½ cup mayonnaise
- ½ cup sour cream
- ¼ cup minced fresh chives
- ½ teaspoon salt
- ½ teaspoon seasoned pepper

STIR together first 5 ingredients in a large bowl; add eggs, and let stand 1 hour. Remove and drain on paper towels. Peel eggs to reveal pattern on whites.

CUT eggs in half lengthwise; carefully remove yolks. Mash yolks; stir in potato flakes and next 5 ingredients until blended.

SPOON the yolk mixture evenly into egg white halves. Attach 2 halves, gently pressing together stuffed sides. **Prep: 30 min., Stand: 1 hr.**

Helpful Egg Tips

- Gently tap warm eggs on kitchen counter immediately after cooking, cracking evenly over entire shell. Food coloring will seep into the cracks, forming a pattern on the whites that can be seen after peeling.

- Attach egg halves with stuffed sides facing each other so that yolk mixture is sandwiched between white.

WIENER WORMS: Cut bun-length hot dogs lengthwise into quarters. Place on grill rack crosswise, and grill uncovered to desired degree of doneness. They'll curl into "worms" on their own as they cook. Serve alone or in buns with mustard and ketchup. In addition to red, offer colored ketchups such as green and purple.

Peanut Brittle

You can make this sweet crunch of a candy on the cooktop or in the microwave.

Southerners love peanuts. There are many ways to eat these nutty bites, but they are perhaps at their best in peanut brittle. These recipes will surprise you with their ease and remind you why you fell for peanuts in the first place. Betsy Owens, executive director of Virginia Carolina Peanut Promotions, sums up their robust flavor best: "It's like the aroma of brewing coffee and sizzling bacon. They taste and smell so good, there's no turning back."

CLASSIC PEANUT BRITTLE

MAKES 1 POUND

1 cup sugar

½ cup light corn syrup

⅛ teaspoon salt

1 cup dry-roasted or shelled raw peanuts

2 tablespoons butter

1 teaspoon baking soda

2 teaspoons vanilla extract

COMBINE first 3 ingredients in a large glass bowl. Microwave at HIGH 5 minutes, add peanuts, and microwave 2 more minutes with 1,000-watt microwave. Microwave 4 more minutes if using a 700-watt microwave. Stir in butter and remaining ingredients.

POUR into a buttered 15- x 10-inch jellyroll pan; shake pan to spread thinly. Cool until firm, and break into pieces. Store in an airtight container. **Prep: 15 min.**

COOKTOP BRITTLE: Cook first 3 ingredients in a medium-size heavy saucepan over medium heat, stirring constantly, until mixture starts to boil. Boil without stirring 5 minutes or until a candy thermometer reaches 310°. Add peanuts, and cook 2 to 3 more minutes or to 280°. (Mixture should be golden brown.) Remove from heat, and stir in butter and remaining ingredients. Pour mixture onto a metal surface or into a shallow pan. Allow to stand 5 minutes or until hardened. Break into pieces. **Prep: 5 min., Cook: 8 min., Stand: 5 min.**

PECAN BRITTLE: Substitute 1 cup chopped pecans for peanuts.

CHOCOLATE-DIPPED PEANUT BRITTLE: Prepare peanut brittle as directed. Melt 2 (2-ounce) chocolate bark coating squares; dip peanut brittle pieces into melted chocolate. Place on wax paper, and let harden.

POPCORN PEANUT BRITTLE: Prepare brittle as directed. Stir in 1 cup popped popcorn before pouring into pan.

KATIE MOON
BIRMINGHAM, ALABAMA

Cook's Notes

Choose a sunny, dry day to make this candy. It's sensitive to humidity. Store it in an airtight tin to keep the candy crisp and crunchy, not sticky to the touch.

Satisfying Breads

Cooler weather calls for food that's satisfying and substantial. It's the season to try versatile vegetable, fruit, and nut breads. These need little gilding served hot from the oven. Bake one of the sweeter breads for a delicious anytime treat, or pair the savory bread with a salad for a mouthwatering autumn supper.

BLACK-EYED PEA BREAD

MAKES 12 SERVINGS

> 1 (32-ounce) package frozen bread dough loaves
> 1 (16-ounce) package ground pork sausage
> 1 (3.5-ounce) package pepperoni slices, chopped
> 1 small onion, chopped
> 1 (15.8-ounce) can black-eyed peas, rinsed and drained
> 1 cup (4 ounces) shredded sharp Cheddar cheese
> 1 cup (4 ounces) shredded mozzarella cheese
> 3 egg yolks, lightly beaten

THAW bread dough loaves in refrigerator 8 hours.

COOK sausage, pepperoni, and onion in a large skillet, stirring until sausage crumbles and is no longer pink. Drain well. Cool slightly, and stir in black-eyed peas, Cheddar cheese, and mozzarella cheese.

ROLL each loaf of thawed bread dough into a 12- x 5-inch rectangle on a lightly floured surface. Brush with egg yolks. Spread each loaf evenly with sausage mixture.

ROLL UP, starting with a long side; pinch ends to seal. Place, seam side down, on a lightly greased baking sheet. Brush with remaining egg yolks.

BAKE at 350° for 30 minutes; cover loosely with aluminum foil, and bake 10 more minutes. **Thaw: 8 hrs., Prep: 25 min., Bake: 40 min.**

JEAN VOAN
SHEPHERD, TEXAS

BROWN SUGAR BISCUIT BREAD

MAKES 8 SERVINGS

> Vegetable cooking spray
> 1 cup chopped pecans, divided
> 1 cup firmly packed brown sugar
> 1 teaspoon ground cinnamon
> ½ cup butter
> ¼ cup orange juice
> 3 (7.5-ounce) cans refrigerated biscuits, cut into quarters

SPRAY a 10-inch Bundt pan evenly with cooking spray. Sprinkle bottom evenly with ⅓ cup pecans.

MICROWAVE brown sugar, cinnamon, butter, and orange juice in a 1-quart glass bowl at HIGH 2 minutes or until thoroughly heated, stirring once. Dip half of biscuits in sugar mixture; arrange evenly in pan. Sprinkle with remaining pecans. Dip remaining biscuits in sugar mixture; arrange in pan.

BAKE at 350° for 25 to 30 minutes or until done. Cool in pan about 2 minutes. Invert pan onto plate, and serve warm. **Prep: 10 min., Bake: 30 min., Cool: 2 min.**

LINDA T. BRIGGS
SOMERSET, KENTUCKY

PUMPKIN-PECAN BREAD

MAKES 16 SERVINGS

> 3 cups sugar
> 1 cup vegetable oil
> 4 large eggs
> 1 (15-ounce) can pumpkin
> 3½ cups all-purpose flour
> 2 teaspoons baking soda
> 2 teaspoons salt
> 1 teaspoon ground cinnamon
> 1 teaspoon ground allspice
> 1 teaspoon ground nutmeg
> ½ teaspoon ground cloves
> ⅔ cup water
> 1 to 1½ cups chopped pecans, toasted

BEAT first 11 ingredients at low speed with an electric mixer 3 minutes or until blended. Add ⅔ cup water, beating until blended. Stir in pecans. Pour batter into 2 greased and floured 9- x 5-inch loafpans.

BAKE at 350° for 1 hour and 15 minutes or until a wooden pick inserted in center comes out clean. Cool in pans on a wire rack 10 minutes; remove from pans, and cool completely on wire rack. **Prep: 12 min.; Bake: 1 hr., 15 min.; Cool: 10 min.**

NOTE: Bread may be frozen for up to 3 months.

ROBERT K. DYE
VERNON, TEXAS

One Great Shortbread

Here, tasty coconut gives simple shortbread a tropical twist.

COCONUT SHORTBREAD

MAKES 2 DOZEN

> 4 cups sweetened flaked coconut
> 2 cups all-purpose flour
> 1 cup sugar
> ¼ teaspoon salt
> 1 cup butter, softened
> 1½ teaspoons vanilla extract
> 1 cup (6 ounces) semisweet chocolate morsels, melted (optional)

BEAT first 6 ingredients at medium speed with an electric mixer until dry ingredients are moistened. Press evenly into 2 lightly greased 9-inch tart pans or cakepans. Bake at 350° for 25 minutes or until lightly browned. Let stand 5 minutes. Cut each into 12 wedges. Place wedges on a large ungreased baking sheet; bake 5 more minutes or until crisp. Remove to wire racks to cool. Trim coconut from edges of shortbread; drizzle with melted chocolate, if desired. **Prep: 15 min., Bake: 30 min., Stand: 5 min.**

TO MAKE AHEAD: Place baked and cooled shortbread between layers of wax paper in an airtight container, and freeze up to 1 month, if desired. Bring to room temperature; drizzle with melted chocolate, if desired, before serving.

LOUISE BODZIONY
GLADSTONE, MISSOURI

Stuffed Pork Chops, Skillet Creamed Corn, Stackable Grits, page 204

Caramel-Glazed Pear Cake, page 196

Fresh Pear Salad With Asian Sesame Dressing, page 196

Pear-Cranberry Compote, page 196

Caramel-Glazed Pear Cake, page 196

Avocado-and-Black Bean Frittata, page 212

Bean Burgers With Adobo Mayonnaise, page 202

Stir-and-Drop Cookies

Bake a batch the easy way.

The kids are home from school, the cookie jar is empty, and you need to produce a sweet snack now. Fear not. These recipes offer speed and flavor from just a few ingredients. There's no creaming of butter and sugar, then adding eggs one at a time. Simply put all the ingredients in a large bowl, stir well, and then drop onto baking sheets. The recipes are so easy, even the kids can do it—although they may need Mom's or Dad's muscle for stirring. Your family will call it fun, and you'll call it child's play.

CRISPY PRALINE COOKIES

MAKES ABOUT 2 DOZEN

Let the butter sit at room temperature for several hours, or soften it in the microwave at HIGH for 10 to 20 seconds (do not melt).

1 cup all-purpose flour
1 cup firmly packed dark brown sugar
1 large egg
1 cup chopped pecans
½ cup butter, softened
1 teaspoon vanilla extract

STIR together all ingredients in a large bowl, blending well. Drop by tablespoonfuls onto ungreased baking sheets. **BAKE** at 350° for 13 to 15 minutes. Cool on baking sheets 1 minute; remove cookies to wire racks to cool completely. **Prep: 10 min., Bake: 15 min. per batch, Cool: 1 min.**

CRISPY PRALINE-CHOCOLATE CHIP COOKIES: Add 1 cup semisweet chocolate morsels; bake as directed.

JULIA PENNINGTON
FORT WORTH, TEXAS

SOFT COCONUT MACAROONS

MAKES 2½ TO 3 DOZEN

Using clear vanilla extract will keep the macaroons pearly white, but regular vanilla will work fine.

4 egg whites
2⅔ cups sweetened flaked coconut
⅔ cup sugar
¼ cup all-purpose flour
½ teaspoon clear vanilla extract
¼ teaspoon salt
¼ to ½ teaspoon almond extract

STIR together all ingredients in a large bowl, blending well. Drop by teaspoonfuls onto lightly greased baking sheets. **BAKE** at 325° for 18 to 20 minutes. Remove to wire racks to cool. **Prep: 10 min., Bake: 20 min. per batch**

PATRICIA A. ODAM
GREENVILLE, CALIFORNIA

Cook's Notes

■ Make cleanup quick by lining baking sheets with parchment paper. This versatile tool is perfectly sized for baking sheets, comes in rolls, and can be reused. If it's not available in a large supermarket in your area, ask the manager to order it for you.
■ If you don't have wire cooling racks, line your counter with a towel, and top it with wax paper. Allow cookies to cool there after removing from pan.

QUICK PEANUT BUTTER COOKIES

MAKES 2½ TO 3 DOZEN

1½ cups powdered sugar
1 cup creamy peanut butter
1 large egg
1 teaspoon vanilla extract

STIR together all ingredients in a large bowl, blending well.
ROLL cookie dough into ¾-inch balls, and place on lightly greased or parchment paper-lined baking sheets. Lightly press cookies with a fork.
BAKE at 325° for 10 minutes. Let cool 2 minutes on baking sheets; remove to wire racks to cool completely. **Prep: 10 min., Bake: 10 min. per batch, Cool: 2 min.**

LAURA MORRIS
BUNNELL, FLORIDA

CREAM CHEESE COOKIES

MAKES 4½ TO 5 DOZEN

Use the smallest holes of a grater to grate lemon rind; be careful not to get the bitter white flesh that's underneath the yellow skin.

1 cup butter, softened
1 (8-ounce) package cream cheese, softened
2 cups sugar
2 cups all-purpose flour
2 teaspoons grated lemon rind
1 teaspoon vanilla extract

STIR together butter and cream cheese in a large bowl until smooth; stir in sugar and remaining ingredients. Drop by teaspoonfuls onto ungreased baking sheets. Bake at 350° for 13 to 15 minutes or until light brown. Remove to wire racks to cool. **Prep: 5 min., Bake: 15 min. per batch**

NOTE: For easier stirring, allow cream cheese to soften at room temperature for 30 minutes, or unwrap and microwave at HIGH 15 to 20 seconds.

CREAM CHEESE-CHOCOLATE CHIP COOKIES: Omit lemon rind, and add 1 cup semisweet chocolate morsels. Bake as directed.

BARBARA SHERRER
BAY CITY, TEXAS

Casual Weeknight Supper

These hearty recipes warm both body and soul.

Casual Supper

Serves 4

Tomato-Basil Bisque

Apple-Spinach Salad

Italian BLT Sandwiches

Ginger-Oatmeal Sorghum Cookies

Add variety to your weekly menu by elevating a basic soup-and-sandwich meal to the next level. Fresh basil and tangy buttermilk in our Tomato-Basil Bisque impart a wonderful garden-fresh taste to ordinary tomato soup, and it's ready in less than 15 minutes. Staples, such as canned soup, bottled salad dressing, and Parmesan cheese, are the keys to this high-flavor, low-stress meal.

TOMATO-BASIL BISQUE

MAKES ABOUT 7 CUPS

2 (10¾-ounce) cans tomato soup, undiluted
1 (14½-ounce) can diced tomatoes
2½ cups buttermilk
2 tablespoons chopped fresh basil
¼ teaspoon freshly ground pepper
Garnish: shredded fresh basil

COOK first 5 ingredients in a 3-quart saucepan over medium heat, stirring often, 6 to 8 minutes or until thoroughly heated. Garnish, if desired; serve immediately, or serve chilled. **Prep: 5 min., Cook: 8 min.**

APPLE-SPINACH SALAD

MAKES 4 SERVINGS

1 (6-ounce) package fresh baby spinach
2 small Granny Smith apples, chopped
½ cup cashews
¼ cup golden raisins
¼ cup sugar
¼ cup apple cider vinegar
¼ cup vegetable oil
¼ teaspoon garlic salt
¼ teaspoon celery salt

COMBINE first 4 ingredients in a bowl. **WHISK** together sugar and next 4 ingredients until blended. Serve dressing with salad. **Prep: 10 min.**

NOTE: You can chill dressing up to 1 day; whisk well before serving.

ITALIAN BLT SANDWICHES

MAKES 4 SERVINGS

½ (16-ounce) Italian bread loaf
¼ cup Italian dressing
⅓ cup shredded Parmesan cheese
½ cup mayonnaise
½ cup mustard
½ pound thinly sliced Genoa salami
½ pound thinly sliced mortadella or bologna
4 (1-ounce) provolone cheese slices
Romaine lettuce leaves
3 plum tomatoes, sliced
8 bacon slices, cooked and cut in half
Garnish: pimiento-stuffed olives

CUT bread diagonally into 8 slices; arrange on a baking sheet. Brush slices evenly with Italian dressing, and sprinkle with Parmesan cheese.
BAKE at 375° for 5 to 6 minutes or until lightly toasted.
STIR together mayonnaise and mustard; spread untoasted side of bread evenly with mayonnaise mixture.
LAYER 4 bread slices, mayonnaise mixture side up, with salami and next 5 ingredients. Top with remaining 4 bread slices, mayonnaise side down. Secure with wooden picks. Garnish, if desired.
Prep: 25 min., Bake: 6 min.

GINGER-OATMEAL SORGHUM COOKIES

MAKES 20 COOKIES

4 cups all-purpose flour
1 tablespoon baking soda
1½ teaspoons salt
4 cups quick-cooking oats
1½ cups raisins
1¼ cups sugar
1½ teaspoons ground ginger
1 cup butter or margarine, melted
1 cup sorghum
1 cup chopped walnuts
2 tablespoons hot water
2 large eggs, lightly beaten
1 to 2 tablespoons water
½ cup sugar

COMBINE first 7 ingredients in a large bowl; add butter and next 4 ingredients, stirring until blended.

DIVIDE dough into 20 (2-inch) balls. Place 2 inches apart on lightly greased baking sheets; flatten each ball to ¼-inch thickness. Brush tops with 1 to 2 tablespoons water, and sprinkle evenly with ½ cup sugar.

BAKE at 375° for 10 to 12 minutes or until lightly browned. **Prep: 30 min., Bake: 12 min. per batch**

Perfect Pumpkin Dessert

The sight of golden pumpkins is a sure sign that autumn has arrived. Carved and decorated, they bewitchingly greet trick-or-treaters, but their spooky guises don't stop us from savoring this treat in dishes such as Stuffed Pumpkin With Cranberry-Raisin Bread Pudding. Be sure to purchase a blemish-free, brightly colored pumpkin that's heavy for its size. Look for sweet types such as sugar pumpkins, because the flesh is less stringy, sweeter, and more tender than other types. Enjoy a taste of the season with this update on classic pumpkin pie flavors.

STUFFED PUMPKIN WITH CRANBERRY-RAISIN BREAD PUDDING

MAKES 12 SERVINGS

- 1 (2½- to 3-pound) pumpkin
- 2 tablespoons butter or margarine, melted and divided
- 2 tablespoons sugar, divided
- 2 large eggs
- ½ cup sugar
- ½ cup butter or margarine, melted
- ¾ cup half-and-half
- ¾ cup chopped pecans, toasted
- 1 (16-ounce) raisin bread loaf, cut into 1-inch cubes
- ½ cup fresh cranberries
- Lemon-Vanilla Sauce

CUT off top of pumpkin, reserving lid with stem. Scoop out pumpkin seeds and pulp, and reserve for another use. Brush inside of pumpkin shell with 1 tablespoon melted butter. Sprinkle with 1 tablespoon sugar. Top with lid.

BAKE at 350° for 35 minutes.

BRUSH inside of baked pumpkin shell with 1 tablespoon butter; sprinkle with 1 tablespoon sugar.

STIR together eggs and next 6 ingredients; spoon pudding mixture into a lightly greased 8-inch square pan.

BAKE pumpkin and bread pudding at 350° for 25 minutes. Let pumpkin cool; spoon bread pudding evenly into pumpkin shell. Serve with Lemon-Vanilla Sauce. **Prep: 35 min., Bake: 1 hr.**

NOTE: For individual servings, substitute 12 (½-pound) pumpkins. Scoop out seeds and pulp; sprinkle each pumpkin shell with 1 teaspoon butter and 1 teaspoon sugar, and bake with the bread pudding. (Do not prebake as with the larger pumpkin.) Spoon bread pudding evenly into baked pumpkin shells.

Lemon-Vanilla Sauce:

MAKES 1⅔ CUPS

- 1 vanilla bean, split
- 1 cup water
- ½ cup sugar
- 2 tablespoons cornstarch
- ⅛ teaspoon salt
- 1 tablespoon butter or margarine
- 2 tablespoons grated lemon rind
- ⅓ cup fresh lemon juice

COOK vanilla bean, water, sugar, cornstarch, and salt in a saucepan over medium heat, stirring until smooth and thickened.

STIR in butter and remaining ingredients, and cook until thoroughly heated. Remove vanilla bean. **Prep: 20 min.**

SAMANTHA SMITH
PANAMA CITY, FLORIDA

Lasagna With a Twist

It's hard to resist the lure of lasagna. Layers of melted cheese, rich filling, and chunky tomato sauce blanketing tender noodles deliver warm, tasty comfort. Here we offer a scrumptious Chicken Lasagna Florentine along with equally delicious Artichoke-Red Pepper Rollups. You might be tempted to serve these dishes right from the oven, but letting lasagna stand for 10 or 15 minutes gives it time to firm up and allows for easier slicing.

ARTICHOKE-RED PEPPER ROLLUPS

MAKES 6 SERVINGS

- 2 (26-ounce) jars roasted red pepper pasta sauce, divided
- 1 (15-ounce) container ricotta cheese
- 2 cups (8 ounces) shredded mozzarella cheese
- 1 large egg, lightly beaten
- 6 lasagna noodles, cooked and drained
- 1 (12-ounce) jar roasted red bell peppers, drained and chopped
- ¼ cup chopped fresh oregano
- 1 (14-ounce) can artichoke hearts, drained, chopped, and divided
- Garnishes: shredded Parmesan cheese, chopped fresh oregano

SPREAD half of pasta sauce in a 13- x 9-inch pan.

COMBINE cheeses and egg, stirring well. Spread mixture evenly on 1 side of each noodle; sprinkle with peppers, oregano, and half of artichokes. Roll up, starting at short ends; cut in half. Place, cut side down, in prepared pan.

BAKE, covered, at 350° for 30 minutes; uncover and bake 15 minutes or until thoroughly heated. Heat remaining pasta sauce and artichokes in a saucepan. Serve with rollups. Garnish, if desired. **Prep: 20 min., Bake: 45 min.**

CHICKEN LASAGNA FLORENTINE

MAKES 6 SERVINGS

- 2 cups chopped cooked chicken
- 1 (10¾-ounce) can cream of mushroom soup, undiluted
- 1 (10-ounce) package frozen chopped spinach, thawed and well drained
- 2 cups (8 ounces) shredded Cheddar cheese
- 1 (6-ounce) jar sliced mushrooms, drained
- ¼ teaspoon pepper
- 1 cup sour cream
- 6 lasagna noodles, cooked and drained
- 1 cup grated Parmesan cheese
- ¾ cup to 1 cup chopped pecans

STIR together first 7 ingredients.
ARRANGE 3 noodles in a lightly greased 11- x 7-inch baking dish; top with half of chicken mixture. Repeat layers with remaining noodles and chicken mixture. Sprinkle with Parmesan cheese and pecans.
BAKE, covered, at 350° for 45 minutes; uncover, and bake 15 minutes or until bubbly. Let lasagna stand 15 minutes before serving. **Prep: 25 min., Bake: 1 hr., Stand: 15 min.**

TO MAKE AHEAD: Cover and chill. Let stand at room temperature 30 minutes before baking; proceed as directed.

TO LIGHTEN: Substitute reduced-fat cream of mushroom soup, 2% reduced-fat Cheddar cheese, and reduced-fat sour cream.

CINDY MCRIGHT
GREENVILLE, MISSISSIPPI

Easy Fruit Crisps

Crisps—fruit baked with crumbly toppings—are Southern favorites, especially when made with apples. For this story, however, we left the traditional crisp recipes for another day. How did we fare? Tropical Pineapple Crisp with its white chocolate-and-macadamia nut cookie topping received our highest Test Kitchens rating.

TROPICAL PINEAPPLE CRISP

MAKES 6 SERVINGS

- 1 fresh pineapple, peeled, cored, and cubed (about 4 cups)*
- 2 tablespoons coconut rum**
- ⅓ cup all-purpose flour
- ⅓ cup firmly packed dark brown sugar
- ⅓ cup cold butter or margarine, cut up
- 1 cup crumbled white chocolate-and-macadamia nut cookies
- ½ cup sweetened flaked coconut
- Simple Coconut Ice Cream (optional)

COMBINE pineapple and rum; spoon into a 9-inch baking dish or 6 (5-inch) individual baking dishes.
COMBINE flour and sugar; cut in butter with a pastry blender or fork until mixture is crumbly. Stir in cookie crumbs and coconut; sprinkle over pineapple.
BAKE at 400° for 30 minutes or until golden. Serve with Simple Coconut Ice Cream, if desired. **Prep: 20 min., Bake: 30 min.**

NOTE: For testing purposes only, we used Pepperidge Farm Tahoe White Chocolate Macadamia BIG Cookies.

*Substitute 2 (20-ounce) cans pineapple chunks in juice, drained, if desired.

**Substitute 1 teaspoon coconut extract for coconut rum, if desired.

SIMPLE COCONUT ICE CREAM: Stir together ½ gallon softened vanilla ice cream, 1 (16-ounce) can cream of coconut, and ½ to 1 cup sweetened flaked coconut in a large bowl. Cover and freeze 8 hours or until firm.

PEACH-AND-RASPBERRY CRISP

MAKES 8 SERVINGS

For a total indulgence, top this crisp with vanilla ice cream, and sprinkle with toasted slivered almonds.

- 1 (14-ounce) package frozen raspberries, thawed
- 2 (1-pound, 4-ounce) cans sliced peaches in heavy syrup, drained
- ¼ cup granulated sugar, divided
- 5 tablespoons all-purpose flour, divided
- 2 cups oatmeal cookie crumbs
- ½ cup cold butter or margarine, cut up
- 1 teaspoon cornstarch
- ¼ cup powdered sugar

DRAIN raspberries, reserving juice.
COMBINE peaches, 2 tablespoons sugar, and 1 tablespoon flour; pour into an 11- x 7-inch baking dish, and top with raspberries.
COMBINE cookie crumbs and remaining sugar and flour; cut in butter with a pastry blender or fork until mixture is crumbly. Sprinkle evenly over fruit mixture.
BAKE at 375° for 25 to 30 minutes or until bubbly and golden.
WHISK together reserved raspberry juice, cornstarch, and powdered sugar in a small saucepan over medium-high heat. Bring to a boil, and cook 1 minute. Serve with baked crisp. **Prep: 20 min., Cook: 5 min., Bake: 30 min.**

PEAR CRISP

MAKES 8 SERVINGS

- ½ cup peach preserves
- 5 pears, peeled and thinly sliced (about 3 cups)
- 2 tablespoons cornstarch
- ⅓ cup sugar
- ⅓ cup all-purpose flour
- ¾ teaspoon ground cinnamon
- ¼ teaspoon ground nutmeg
- ⅓ cup cold butter or margarine, cut up
- 1 cup granola with raisins, dates, and almonds

MICROWAVE preserves in a large glass bowl at MEDIUM-HIGH (70% power) for 90 seconds or until melted. Stir in pears and cornstarch. Place in an 11- x 7-inch baking dish.

COMBINE ⅓ cup sugar, flour, cinnamon, and nutmeg; cut in butter with a pastry blender or fork until mixture is crumbly. Stir in granola. Sprinkle over pear mixture.

BAKE at 375° for 30 minutes or until topping is crisp and fruit is tender. Serve immediately, or chill. **Prep: 20 min., Bake: 30 min.**

What's for Supper?

Sensational Sausage

In the South, we're always looking for an excuse to eat sausage. The variety of flavors and seasonings—from mild and sweet to bold and spicy—are sure to suit any taste. If you're searching for healthier options, check out the reduced-fat or turkey varieties. Sausage is also easy on your budget, and it offers a great way to get dinner on the table in minutes without sacrificing flavor. Serve these hearty recipes with crusty French bread, fruit salad, or our easy Corn Salad (see box on page 234), and supper is ready.

Sausage Savvy

■ Raw sausage is usually packaged ground, formed into patties, or made into links. Fully cooked sausage is usually sold in 1-pound links and only needs to be heated before serving.

■ To remove excess fat from sausage without losing flavor, follow these steps. Cook sausage according to package or recipe directions. Remove from pan; drain well, and pat dry with paper towels. Place sausage in a colander, and rinse briefly with hot or boiling water. Drain well, and pat dry with paper towels.

SAUSAGE-AND-BEAN SUPPER

MAKES 4 TO 6 SERVINGS

- 1 pound smoked sausage, cut into ¼-inch slices
- 3 bacon slices, diced
- 1 small sweet onion, diced
- ½ (10-ounce) bag shredded carrot
- 2 celery ribs, chopped
- 1 (19-ounce) can cannellini beans or navy beans, rinsed and drained
- 1 (14-ounce) can chicken broth
- 1 teaspoon dried rosemary
- ½ teaspoon dried thyme
- ½ teaspoon pepper
- Breadcrumb Topping

COOK sausage, bacon, diced onion, shredded carrot, and celery in a large skillet over medium-high heat 10 minutes or until sausage is browned and vegetables are tender.

STIR in beans, chicken broth, rosemary, thyme, and pepper; cook over medium heat 10 minutes or until mixture is hot and bubbly. Sprinkle with Breadcrumb Topping. **Prep: 10 min., Cook: 20 min.**

Breadcrumb Topping:

MAKES ABOUT 1 CUP

- 2 tablespoons butter or margarine
- 1 cup breadcrumbs
- ½ cup grated Parmesan cheese

MELT butter in a small skillet; add breadcrumbs and sauté until lightly browned. Remove from heat, and stir in Parmesan cheese.

WAYNE WRIGHT
SUWANEE, GEORGIA

SAUSAGE AND PEPPERS WITH PARMESAN CHEESE GRITS

MAKES 4 SERVINGS

- 1 (19-ounce) package sweet Italian sausage
- 3 red, yellow, or green bell peppers, cut into strips
- 1 large sweet onion, cut in half and thinly sliced
- 2 garlic cloves, minced
- 1 to 2 teaspoons Italian seasoning
- ½ teaspoon garlic powder
- 1 teaspoon salt
- ½ teaspoon pepper
- Parmesan Cheese Grits

REMOVE sausage casings, and discard. Cook sausage and next 7 ingredients in a large skillet over medium-high heat, stirring until sausage crumbles and is no longer pink and vegetables are tender. Serve over Parmesan Cheese Grits. **Prep: 15 min., Cook: 15 min.**

Parmesan Cheese Grits:

MAKES 4 SERVINGS

- 1 cup quick-cooking grits
- 4 cups water
- ¾ teaspoon salt
- 1 tablespoon butter or margarine
- 1 (5-ounce) package shredded Parmesan cheese

COOK grits according to package directions, using 4 cups water. Stir in salt, butter, and Parmesan cheese. **Prep: 5 min., Cook: 5 min.**

ADELYNE SMITH
DUNNVILLE, KENTUCKY

Start With Frozen Vegetables

From a box or bag, these veggies make creating nutritious side dishes a snap.

If you're seeking ways to add vegetables to your diet, then harvest a few of these recipes. Frozen vegetables provide many nutrients and also offer convenience, affordability, and great flavor. Okra Creole, for example, brims with fresh-from-the-field goodness, while Creamy Baked Corn will satisfy your craving for corn pudding—all without having to slice, shuck, or scrape.

SAUSAGE-APPLE KRAUT DINNER

MAKES 4 SERVINGS

- 1 (16-ounce) package kielbasa sausage, cut into ½-inch pieces
- 1 (32-ounce) jar sauerkraut, drained
- 1 cup apple juice
- 1 to 2 tablespoons brown sugar
- 1 teaspoon caraway seeds
- 2 to 3 medium-size Rome apples, peeled and sliced

BROWN sausage in a large skillet over medium-high heat, stirring occasionally, 8 to 10 minutes or until lightly browned. Drain. Add sauerkraut and next 4 ingredients. Cover, reduce heat, and simmer 10 minutes or until apple is tender, stirring occasionally. **Prep: 10 min., Cook: 20 min.**

BERNADETTE COLVIN
HOUSTON, TEXAS

Cold Facts

- Freezing vegetables helps maintain their flavors and textures. In addition, frozen vegetables often retain more nutrients than those on the produce aisle.
- Frozen foods lose quality more quickly in a refrigerator freezer that is opened more frequently than in a chest or upright freezer.
- Do not refreeze thawed frozen vegetables.
- Purchase packages that are firm—avoid those that are limp, wet, or sweating. Also bypass packages that are stained by their contents or that have ice on the outside—this indicates the vegetables may have been thawed and refrozen.

OKRA CREOLE

MAKES 4 SERVINGS

- 3 bacon slices
- 1 (16-ounce) package frozen sliced okra
- 1 (14.5-ounce) can chopped tomatoes
- 1 cup frozen onion seasoning blend
- 1 cup frozen corn kernels
- ½ cup water
- 1 teaspoon Creole seasoning
- ¼ teaspoon pepper
- Hot cooked rice (optional)

COOK bacon in a Dutch oven until crisp; drain bacon on paper towels, reserving drippings. Crumble and set aside.
COOK okra and next 6 ingredients in hot drippings in Dutch oven over medium-high heat, stirring occasionally, 5 minutes. Reduce heat to low, cover, and simmer 15 minutes or until vegetables are tender. Top with crumbled bacon. Serve over rice, if desired. **Prep: 15 min., Cook: 25 min.**

CREAMY BAKED CORN

MAKES 4 TO 6 SERVINGS

- 2 to 4 bacon slices
- 1 tablespoon butter or margarine
- 2 tablespoons chopped onion
- 2 tablespoons all-purpose flour
- 1 teaspoon salt
- 1 cup sour cream
- 1 (16-ounce) package frozen corn, thawed

COOK bacon in a large skillet until crisp; remove bacon, and drain on paper towels, reserving 1 tablespoon drippings in skillet. Crumble bacon; set aside.

MELT butter in hot drippings over medium heat; add onion, and sauté until tender.

WHISK in flour and salt until smooth and bubbly. Whisk in sour cream until smooth; cook, whisking often, 3 minutes. Stir in corn, and cook until thoroughly heated. Spoon into a lightly greased 8-inch baking dish; top with crumbled bacon.

BAKE at 350° for 15 to 20 minutes or until bubbly. **Prep: 10 min., Cook: 20 min., Bake: 20 min.**

KELLEY MILLER WILSON
CINCINNATI, OHIO

EASY ITALIAN SPINACH

MAKES 4 SERVINGS

- 2 (10-ounce) packages frozen chopped spinach, thawed and drained
- 1 garlic clove, chopped
- 2 tablespoons olive oil
- ½ cup Italian-seasoned breadcrumbs
- ½ cup grated Romano cheese
- ½ teaspoon salt
- ½ teaspoon pepper

SAUTÉ spinach and garlic in hot oil in a nonstick skillet over medium-high heat, 10 to 12 minutes or until thoroughly heated and liquid evaporates. Add breadcrumbs and remaining ingredients, stirring well. Serve immediately. **Prep: 5 min., Cook: 12 min.**

Hint of Horseradish

We think you'll be opening that little jar of prepared horseradish a lot more when you sample these zesty recipes. From a spectacular yet easy Prime Rib With Spicy Horseradish Sauce to simple Chicken-Horseradish Salad, these recipes are sure to add some flair to standard fare.

PRIME RIB WITH SPICY HORSERADISH SAUCE

MAKES 6 TO 8 SERVINGS

During cooking, rock salt's protective covering makes for a juicy and perfectly seasoned beef dish. The salt is brushed off after baking.

- 1 (6-pound) boneless beef rib roast
- 3 garlic cloves, minced
- 2 tablespoons coarsely ground pepper
- 1 tablespoon Worcestershire sauce
- 2 (4-pound) packages rock salt
- ½ cup water
- Spicy Horseradish Sauce

RUB roast on all sides with garlic, pepper, and Worcestershire sauce.

POUR salt to a depth of ½ inch into a disposable aluminum roasting pan; place roast in center of pan. Add remaining salt; sprinkle with ½ cup water.

BAKE at 500° for 12 minutes per pound or until a meat thermometer inserted into thickest portion registers 145° (medium-rare) or to desired degree of doneness. (Be sure to use a meat thermometer for best results.) Let stand 10 minutes. Crack salt with a hammer; remove roast, and brush away salt. Let stand 20 minutes. Serve roast with Spicy Horseradish Sauce. **Prep: 15 min.; Cook: 1 hr., 12 min.; Stand: 30 min.**

Spicy Horseradish Sauce:

MAKES ABOUT 1 CUP

- ⅔ cup reduced-fat sour cream
- 3 tablespoons prepared horseradish
- 2 tablespoons light mayonnaise
- 1 tablespoon white wine vinegar
- 1 teaspoon dry mustard
- ¼ teaspoon salt
- ¼ teaspoon ground red pepper

STIR together all ingredients. Cover and chill 1 hour. Serve with beef, pork, steamed shrimp, as a sandwich spread, on baked potatoes, or as a dip for chips or raw vegetables. **Prep: 5 min., Chill: 1 hr.**

CHICKEN-HORSERADISH SALAD

MAKES 5 (1-CUP) SERVINGS

A large rotisserie chicken from your supermarket makes a great shortcut for this recipe.

- 3 cups chopped cooked chicken (about 4 skinned and boned chicken breast halves)
- ½ cup minced green onions
- 2 celery ribs, chopped
- ½ cup chopped pecans, toasted
- ⅔ cup light mayonnaise
- 2 to 3 tablespoons prepared horseradish
- ½ teaspoon grated lemon rind
- 2 teaspoons fresh lemon juice
- ¼ teaspoon salt
- ½ teaspoon pepper

STIR together all ingredients in a large bowl. Cover and chill at least 2 hours before serving. **Prep: 20 min., Chill: 2 hrs.**

BROCCOLI AND PARSNIPS WITH HORSERADISH

MAKES 6 SERVINGS

If you can't find parsnips, carrots make a terrific substitute.

- 1 pound fresh parsnips, peeled and cut into thin strips
- 1 pound fresh broccoli, cut into florets
- 3 tablespoons butter or margarine
- 2 tablespoons prepared horseradish
- 2 tablespoons fresh lemon juice
- ½ teaspoon salt
- ¼ cup chopped walnuts, toasted

ARRANGE parsnips in a steamer basket over boiling water. Cover and steam 8 minutes. Add broccoli; cover and steam 5 minutes. Place parsnips and broccoli in a large bowl.

MELT butter in a small saucepan over low heat. Cook 5 minutes or until lightly browned. Remove from heat. Stir in horseradish, lemon juice, and salt. Pour sauce over vegetables, tossing to coat. Sprinkle with walnuts. Serve immediately. **Prep: 10 min., Cook: 20 min.**

Tastes Like a Million Bucks

Senior Writer Donna Florio knew from Denise Yennie's cast-iron skillet that she was a Southern cook. The Nashville resident's Chicken Florentine Panini—made with that skillet—won the $1,000,000 Grand Prize in the Pillsbury Bake-Off®. Southerners were well represented, with category winners from Alabama, Florida, Kentucky, and Virginia.

CHICKEN FLORENTINE PANINI

MAKES 4 SERVINGS

- 1 (10-ounce) can refrigerated pizza crust
- 1 (9-ounce) package frozen spinach
- ¼ cup light mayonnaise
- 2 garlic cloves, minced and divided
- 1 medium-size red onion, chopped
- 1 tablespoon olive oil
- 1 tablespoon sugar
- 1 tablespoon balsamic vinegar
- 2 skinned and boned chicken breast halves
- ½ teaspoon dried Italian seasoning
- Vegetable cooking spray
- 4 (4-inch) provolone cheese slices

UNROLL pizza crust, and press into a 15- x 10-inch jellyroll pan.

BAKE at 375° for 10 minutes. Cool.

PREPARE spinach according to package directions. Drain well, pressing between paper towels. Set aside.

STIR together mayonnaise and half of minced garlic in a bowl; cover and chill.

SAUTÉ onion in hot oil in a saucepan over medium-high heat 2 to 3 minutes or until crisp-tender. Add sugar and vinegar. Reduce heat to low; simmer, stirring occasionally, 3 to 5 minutes or until almost all liquid evaporates.

PLACE chicken between 2 sheets of heavy-duty plastic wrap or wax paper; flatten to ¼-inch thickness using a meat mallet or rolling pin. Sprinkle with Italian seasoning and remaining garlic.

BROWN chicken in a large nonstick skillet coated with cooking spray over medium-high heat; cook 8 minutes, turning once.

CUT pizza crust into 4 rectangles. Remove rectangles from pan; spread 1 side of each with 1 tablespoon garlic mayonnaise. Top 2 rectangles evenly with chicken, spinach, onion mixture, and cheese; top with remaining 2 rectangles, mayonnaise sides down.

COOK sandwiches in a cast-iron skillet over medium-high heat. Top with a smaller skillet or press down with spatula to flatten sandwiches slightly, cooking 2 to 3 minutes on each side or until golden brown and cheese melts. Cut each sandwich into fourths. **Prep: 30 min., Bake: 10 min., Cook: 22 min.**

DENISE YENNIE
NASHVILLE, TENNESSEE

CHICKEN-CHEESE ENCHILADAS

MAKES 6 SERVINGS

- ½ cup water, divided
- 1 (1.25-ounce) package taco seasoning
- 1 tablespoon olive oil
- 1 pound skinned and boned chicken breast halves, cut into bite-size pieces
- 1 (16-ounce) jar chunky salsa, divided
- 12 ounces (3 cups) shredded Monterey Jack cheese, divided
- 1 (15-ounce) container ricotta cheese
- 1 (4.5-ounce) can chopped green chiles
- 1 large egg
- ⅓ cup chopped fresh cilantro
- ½ teaspoon salt
- 1 (10.5-ounce) package flour tortillas
- Sour cream
- Garnish: fresh cilantro sprigs

COMBINE ¼ cup water, taco seasoning, and oil in a shallow dish or heavy-duty zip-top plastic bag; mix well. Add chicken pieces; cover or seal and chill 5 minutes or up to 12 hours.

COOK chicken and marinade in a large, hot nonstick skillet over medium-high heat, stirring often, 5 to 10 minutes or until chicken is done.

STIR together ½ cup salsa and remaining ¼ cup water in a 13- x 9-inch baking dish until well blended. Spread evenly in dish.

STIR together 2½ cups Monterey Jack cheese, ricotta cheese, and next 4 ingredients. Spoon ⅓ cup cheese mixture down the center of each tortilla; top with chicken, and roll up. Place tortillas, seam side down, over salsa mixture in dish. Drizzle remaining salsa over enchiladas; sprinkle with remaining ½ cup Monterey Jack cheese.

BAKE at 350° for 20 to 25 minutes or until cheese melts. Top with sour cream; garnish, if desired. **Prep: 15 min., Chill: 5 min., Cook: 10 min., Bake: 25 min.**

BARBIE LEE
TAVERNIER, FLORIDA

Living Light

Try Greek for a Change

Tonight's dinner recipes needn't rely on lots of fat to deliver delicious flavor. We've learned that fish, fluffy grains, and fresh vegetables and herbs are all you need to create delicious and satisfying dishes. Tomatoes, olives, and lemon—popular ingredients in many Southern kitchens—will bring a taste of the Mediterranean to your family's table.

FRESH BEET SALAD

MAKES 4 SERVINGS

To avoid staining your hands, wear disposable latex gloves while peeling and cutting beets.

- 6 medium beets
- 2 tablespoons red wine vinegar
- 1 tablespoon olive oil
- 1 garlic clove, minced
- 2 teaspoons sugar
- ¼ teaspoon salt
- ¼ teaspoon pepper
- 2 tablespoons chopped flat-leaf parsley
- Mixed greens

COVER beets with water, and bring to a boil. Boil 30 minutes or until tender. Drain and cool. Peel beets, and cut into wedges.

WHISK together vinegar, olive oil, minced garlic, sugar, salt, and pepper in a large bowl; add beets, tossing to coat. Sprinkle with parsley; serve over mixed greens. **Prep: 15 min., Cook: 30 min.**

Calories 136 (27% from fat); Fat 4g (sat 0.6g, mono 2.8g, poly 0.5g); Protein 4g; Carb 23.2g; Fiber 6.6g; Chol 0mg; Iron 2.6mg; Sodium 296mg; Calc 83mg

MEDITERRANEAN SWORDFISH

MAKES 4 SERVINGS

Grouper makes a terrific substitute for swordfish, but it will cook more quickly than swordfish. Check to see if it flakes with a fork after 15 to 20 minutes.

1 medium onion, chopped
2 teaspoons olive oil
1 garlic clove, minced
½ teaspoon salt, divided
½ teaspoon pepper, divided
½ cup dry white wine or chicken broth
¼ cup chopped pimiento-stuffed olives
1 tablespoon small capers, drained
4 (8-ounce) swordfish steaks (about ¾ to 1 inch thick)
2 plum tomatoes, seeded and diced
¼ cup chopped fresh parsley

SAUTÉ onion in hot oil in an ovenproof skillet or pan over medium heat 3 minutes or until tender. Add garlic, ¼ teaspoon salt, and ¼ teaspoon pepper; sauté 1 minute. Reduce heat to low; stir in wine, olives, and capers.

SPRINKLE fish evenly with remaining salt and pepper. Place fish over onion mixture.

BAKE, covered, at 400° for 26 minutes or until fish flakes with a fork. Sprinkle with diced tomatoes and parsley. **Prep: 20 min., Cook: 5 min., Bake: 26 min.**

CAROLINE KENNEDY
NEWBORN, GEORGIA

Calories 247 (35% from fat)*; Fat 9.6g (sat 2.2g, mono 4.9g, poly 1.8g); Protein 32g; Carb 5.9g; Fiber 1.5g; Chol 60mg; Iron 1.9mg; Sodium 665mg; Calc 32mg

*Most of the fat is monounsaturated, the type that reduces LDL (bad cholesterol).

LEMON COUSCOUS

MAKES 6 CUPS

If you can boil water, you can make couscous—one of the quickest, easiest side dishes.

2 (5.4-ounce) packages toasted pine nut couscous mix
2 cups fat-free reduced-sodium chicken broth
1 tablespoon grated lemon rind
⅓ cup fresh lemon juice
2 teaspoons butter or margarine
2 tablespoons chopped fresh parsley
⅓ cup diced red bell pepper

REMOVE seasoning packet from couscous package.

COMBINE broth, next 3 ingredients, and seasoning packet in a medium saucepan; bring to a boil over medium-high heat. Stir in couscous; cover, remove from heat, and let stand 10 minutes. Stir in parsley and bell pepper. **Prep: 10 min., Cook: 5 min., Stand: 10 min.**

NOTE: For testing purposes only, we used Near East Toasted Pine Nut Couscous Mix.

Calories 224 (15% from fat); Fat 3.8g (sat 1.3g); Protein 8.2g; Carb 42g; Fiber 2.3g; Chol 3.5mg; Iron 0.7mg; Sodium 674mg; Calc 5mg

Fall Comes to the Table

Earthy autumn colors and bountiful produce inspire us to celebrate the season with delicious dishes from Sherron Goldstein, of Birmingham, a cooking teacher and author of the cookbook *Fresh Fields—A Celebration of Good Food.*

"Cool evenings and subtle seasonal changes call for comfy dishes celebrating fall's harvest," Sherron says. Her Beef Brisket With Fall Vegetables offers that warm comfort, and Sweet Noodle Casserole is a creamy dish so versatile, you can serve it as a side or for dessert.

Walk into Sherron's sleek black-and-stainless steel kitchen, and you'll know why cooks both new and experienced enjoy her classes. Designed for teaching, the large kitchen offers her students the opportunity to learn through doing. Just like her students, you'll love trying her easy-to-make, tasty fall dishes.

BEEF BRISKET WITH FALL VEGETABLES

MAKES 8 TO 10 SERVINGS

1 (5- to 6-pound) beef brisket, trimmed
2 teaspoons salt
1 teaspoon pepper
6 carrots
1 tablespoon vegetable oil
4 parsnips, peeled and sliced
4 celery ribs, sliced
2 large onions, sliced
1 fennel bulb, cut into fourths
1 (2-ounce) package onion soup mix
1½ cups water
1½ cups red wine
1½ cups low-sodium beef broth
½ cup ketchup
2 tablespoons Beau Monde seasoning
1 garlic bulb, pressed
12 fresh thyme sprigs
¾ cup chopped fresh parsley
Garnish: fresh fennel fronds

SPRINKLE beef with salt and pepper. Cut carrots into 2-inch pieces.

COOK beef in hot vegetable oil in a roasting pan over medium-high heat 3 to 4 minutes on each side or until browned. Add carrot, parsnip, celery, onion, and fennel.

STIR together soup mix, 1½ cups water, and next 5 ingredients; pour over beef and vegetables in pan. Sprinkle with thyme and chopped parsley. Bring to a boil; remove from heat, and cover with aluminum foil.

BAKE at 350° for 3½ hours or until tender, basting with juices every 30 minutes. Remove beef from pan, reserving gravy. Cut beef into slices; place beef and vegetables on a large serving platter. Pour gravy through a wire-mesh strainer into a bowl, discarding solids. Drizzle a small amount of gravy over beef on platter; serve brisket with remaining gravy. Garnish, if desired. **Prep: 30 min., Cook: 15 min., Bake: 3½ hrs.**

Sweet Noodle Casserole

MAKES 12 SERVINGS

Also known as noodle kugel (KOO-guhl), this creamy dish makes a unique and delicious side or dessert.

- 1 (12-ounce) package wide egg noodles
- 1 (8-ounce) package cream cheese, softened
- 1 (8-ounce) container sour cream
- 1 cup sugar
- 4 large eggs
- 1 (20-ounce) can crushed pineapple in juice, drained
- ½ cup butter or margarine, melted and divided
- 3 cups frosted flaked cereal, coarsely crushed
- 1½ teaspoons ground cinnamon

COOK pasta according to package directions; drain and set aside.

PROCESS cream cheese and next 3 ingredients in a food processor until smooth. Stir in pineapple.

STIR together pasta, ¼ cup melted butter, and cream cheese mixture; spoon into a lightly greased 13- x 9-inch baking dish.

STIR together cereal, cinnamon, and remaining ¼ cup melted butter; sprinkle over noodle mixture.

BAKE at 350° for 45 to 50 minutes or until set. **Prep: 25 min., Bake: 50 min.**

Fall Breakfast, Southern Style

Quail offers an alternative to the typical morning meal.

Fall Breakfast Menu

Serves 6

Wild Rice Pancakes

Bacon-Wrapped Quail

Shallot Gravy   Spiced Pineapple

O ur readers tell us they enjoy breakfast fare, and we've found just the man to help us put a twist on the traditional. David Larson, chef-in-residence at Labrot & Graham Distillery in Versailles, Kentucky, believes that mornings should be more than bacon and eggs. This meal clearly reflects his Southern roots and family traditions. Give it a try. Both early risers and late sleepers will applaud your culinary efforts. David's menu can also double as a hearty fall dinner.

Wild Rice Pancakes

MAKES 16 TO 18 PANCAKES

Prepare and refrigerate pancakes up to three days in advance, if desired.

- ½ cup all-purpose flour
- 1 tablespoon baking powder
- 1 teaspoon salt
- ⅛ teaspoon ground red pepper
- 1¼ cups milk
- ¼ cup butter or margarine, melted
- 2 large eggs, separated
- 1 cup cooked wild rice
- 3 green onions, chopped
- Garnish: green onion slivers

COMBINE first 4 ingredients in a bowl; add milk and butter, whisking until blended. Stir in egg yolks until blended.

BEAT egg whites at medium speed with an electric mixer until stiff peaks form. Fold egg whites, rice, and green onions into flour mixture.

POUR about ¼ cup batter for each pancake onto a hot, lightly greased griddle. Cook pancakes 2 to 3 minutes or until tops are covered with bubbles and edges look cooked; turn and cook 2 to 3 minutes. Garnish, if desired. **Prep: 15 min., Cook: 6 min. per pancake**

Bacon-Wrapped Quail

MAKES 8 SERVINGS

- 8 quail, dressed
- 1 teaspoon salt
- ½ teaspoon pepper
- 8 bacon slices
- 2 tablespoons butter or margarine, melted

SPRINKLE quail with salt and pepper, and wrap with bacon slices. Place, breast side down, in a roasting pan. Brush with melted butter.

BAKE at 425° for 10 minutes; reduce heat to 325°, and bake, covered, 40 to 45 minutes or until done. Let stand 5 to 10 minutes before serving. **Prep: 15 min., Bake: 55 min., Stand: 10 min.**

Shallot Gravy

MAKES 3 CUPS

- 6 tablespoons butter or margarine, divided
- ½ pound fresh whole mushrooms, quartered
- 3 shallots, finely chopped
- ¼ cup all-purpose flour
- 1½ cups chicken broth
- ⅓ cup whipping cream
- ¼ cup sour cream
- 1 teaspoon salt
- ½ teaspoon pepper
- Garnish: chopped parsley

MELT 2 tablespoons butter in a large saucepan over medium-high heat; add mushrooms and shallots, and sauté 3 to 5 minutes or until tender. Remove from pan.
MELT remaining butter in saucepan over medium-high heat; whisk in flour. Cook, whisking constantly, 1 minute. Whisk in chicken broth until smooth, and cook, whisking constantly, until slightly thickened. Stir in whipping cream and sour cream. Add mushrooms, shallots, salt, and pepper. Cook, stirring constantly, until thoroughly heated. Garnish, if desired. **Prep: 15 min., Cook: 10 min.**

Spiced Pineapple

MAKES 6 SERVINGS

- 1 fresh pineapple, peeled and cored
- 2 tablespoons butter or margarine, melted
- 2 tablespoons bourbon or apple cider
- ¼ cup firmly packed brown sugar
- ½ teaspoon freshly ground pepper

CUT pineapple lengthwise into 4 pieces; cut into ½-inch slices. Place in a lightly greased 13- x 9-inch baking dish. Drizzle with butter and bourbon; sprinkle with brown sugar and pepper. Bake at 350° for 25 to 30 minutes. **Prep: 10 min., Bake: 30 min.**

Mixing Up a Perfect Pound Cake

Perhaps one of the mixer's most important jobs in the Southern kitchen is making a pound cake. So we put one of our favorite recipes, Million Dollar Pound Cake, to the test using a hand mixer, a mid-range stand mixer, and a heavy-duty stand mixer. We got excellent results in all three cakes. The trick is knowing how long to beat and what visual cues to look for in the cake batter. Our recipe takes you through the process, step-by-step.

Million Dollar Pound Cake

MAKES 10 TO 12 SERVINGS

For the best results, preheat your oven to 300° before you begin. We also soften butter at room temperature for 30 minutes.

- 1 pound butter, softened
- 3 cups sugar
- 6 large eggs
- 4 cups all-purpose flour
- ¾ cup milk
- 1 teaspoon almond extract
- 1 teaspoon vanilla extract

BEAT butter at medium speed with an electric mixer until creamy. (The butter will become a lighter yellow color; this is an important step, as the job of the mixer is to incorporate air into the butter so the cake will rise. It will take 1 to 7 minutes, depending on the power of your mixer.) Gradually add sugar, beating at medium speed until light and fluffy. (Again, the times will vary, and butter will turn to a fluffy white.) Add eggs, 1 at a time, beating just until yellow yolk disappears.
ADD flour to butter mixture alternately with milk, beginning and ending with flour. Beat at low speed until blended after each addition. (The batter should be smooth and flour should be well incorporated; to rid batter of lumps, stir gently with a rubber spatula.) Stir in flavorings.

POUR into a greased and floured 10-inch tube pan. (Use vegetable shortening or butter to grease the pan, getting every nook and cranny covered. Sprinkle a light coating of flour over the greased surface.)
BAKE at 300° for 1 hour and 40 minutes or until a long wooden pick inserted in center comes out clean. Cool in pan on a wire rack 10 to 15 minutes. Remove from pan, and cool completely on a wire rack. **Prep: depends on your mixer; Bake: 1 hr., 40 min.; Cool: 15 min.**

NOTE: For testing purposes only, we used White Lily All-Purpose Flour.

Cook's Notes

- If you've never used a heavy-duty stand mixer, such as those made by KitchenAid, here's a tip: Decrease the mixing time. This type of mixer will cream butter in one minute at medium speed; other stand mixers may take as long as seven minutes at high speed (you'll have to stop and scrape the sides, lengthening the time spent). Less-expensive hand mixers (we used a 125-watt one) take two to three minutes at medium speed. Some of our readers like a hand mixer because you can scoot it around the bowl and have more control.
- Mixers come in all price ranges. A KitchenAid heavy-duty stand mixer is the most powerful and has many built-in, trademark features. Their most popular model ranges from $199 to $250. Less powerful stand and hand mixers cover the middle of the spectrum, beginning at $25 to $40 and going upward.
- A lower wattage, less expensive mixer usually needs a little more time to achieve the desired results. As long as you understand the difference, you're guaranteed excellent results, regardless of your mixer's price.

from our kitchen

While Lafayette, Louisiana, is known as a hotbed of Cajun cooking, it may soon be known as the home of Burgundy L. Olivier, the ultimate spinach connoisseur and driver of the "Spinach Mobile." Burgundy's van is a vehicular billboard that encourages people to enjoy spinach.

Her, um, passion for the leafy green began at age 16 when Burgundy tasted her first oysters Rockefeller. Smitten with the spinach-covered oysters, she resolved to keep on trying recipes with spinach. Twenty-eight years and thousands of recipes later, Burgundy has packaged 300 best-of-the-best selections in her cookbook, *I Love Spinach* ($19.95).

Healthful tips explain how to wash and prepare this lutein-rich vegetable, which is also a good source of vitamin C. Besides enjoying fresh spinach, Burgundy gives the nod to frozen and canned varieties, especially if you have the right recipes. She says frozen, chopped spinach is often better if it's re-chopped after defrosting. Her secret to eliminating excess moisture is to place the spinach in a stainless steel potato ricer (a tool similar to a garlic press) and squeeze out the water by pressing down on the handle.

For more great tips and to purchase Burgundy's cookbook, visit **www.ilovespinach.com**

The Secret's Out

It's here, it's fantastic, and every cook will want one. *Secrets From the Southern Living® Test Kitchens* is an easy-to-use kitchen companion reference book. This big, beautiful 576-page book has more than 5,000 cooking secrets, more than 300 never-fail recipes, 2,000 dictionary entries, about 300 illustrations, and much more. It's like having the entire *Southern Living* Foods staff within arm's reach at all times.

Secrets From the Southern Living® Test Kitchens is really several books in one—a combination of cooking terms, time-savers, recipe rescues, shopping savvy tips, questions and answers, recipes, and Southernisms arranged A to Z. It's the perfect book for beginning cooks, experienced cooks, and anyone else who enjoys good food and has a hunger for learning more.

To order your copy of *Secrets From the Southern Living® Test Kitchens* ($31.96 plus shipping and handling), call 1-800-765-6400; or you can log on to **www.sltestkitchen.com**

Tropical Fruits

Let us help you get acquainted with some of the types of tropical fruit that supermarket produce sections have available.
- **Longans** look like large rustic grapes, similar to scuppernongs. Inside a leathery skin is sweet transparent white flesh around a black seed.
- **Rainbow Papayas** are tree ripened and some of the best-tasting papayas in the world. While some papayas can be quite bland, this specific variety grown in Kapoho, Hawaii, is very flavorful and sweet.
- **Rambutan,** a red, prickly looking ball, is similar to litchi with a juicy-sweet texture. Peel and remove the inner seed for a taste of Hawaii.

Recipe Instructions

When you make one of our recipes, we want you to enjoy complete success. With this in mind, we've made a few adjustments. Now you'll know at the *beginning* of each recipe how much time is involved and how many servings you'll get. For your convenience, the total time is divided into stages.

Here's how to interpret our recipe language.
- **PREP** is the time required for tossing, processing, slicing, chopping, mixing, beating, and measuring and gathering all ingredients.
- **COOK** means the actual time that any part of the recipe is over heat on the cooktop.
- **BAKE** is the time the recipe spends in the oven.
- **CHILL** refers to the total time the recipe spends in the refrigerator.
- **STAND** time means the total time for a partially completed or completed recipe to stand at room temperature.

As always, we continue to look for ways to simplify techniques that help you make the most of your time in the kitchen.

Tips and Tidbits

- Keep pasta salads creamy by spritzing the pasta with cooking spray. The dressing will cling but not be completely absorbed by thirsty pasta.

- A flat whisk is perfect for stirring cooktop sauces because it reaches into all the corners.

- Take cheese out of the refrigerator the morning of the day of your party for the best texture and flavor.

November

holiday dinners®

Thanksgiving With Family and Friends

Try a new approach to the
traditional holiday meal—take it outside.

A Harvest Menu

Serves 6 to 8

Cream of Curried Peanut Soup

Spinach-and-Cranberry Salad With Warm Chutney Dressing

Sugar-and-Spice Cured Turkey

Crabmeat-and-Oyster Dressing   Cranberry sauce

Marinated Asparagus   Brussels Sprouts With Apples

Baked Sweet-and-Savory Mashed Potatoes   Rolls

Elegant Pumpkin-Walnut Layered Pie

If it's still warm at your house in November, consider having the whole Thanksgiving meal outdoors. The crackle of crisp fall leaves beneath your feet, the warm glow of an autumn sun, and the earthy smell of the air give your celebration a closer connection to the land. Here we offer you a twist on the traditional menu and an easy decorating idea that will let you move your casual feast outside. We used bright-eyed pansies, Indian corn, colorful gourds, and pumpkins in rustic colors to tie together the harvest theme of our meal. If you can't bear to be more than an arm's length from the big game, know that this menu is equally tantalizing in a cozy dining room. (See our "Cook's Notes" on page 244 for make-ahead suggestions.)

CREAM OF CURRIED PEANUT SOUP

MAKES 6 CUPS

> 2 tablespoons butter or margarine
> 1 small onion, minced
> 3 celery ribs, minced
> 1 garlic clove, minced
> 2 tablespoons all-purpose flour
> 2 tablespoons curry powder
> 1/8 to 1/4 teaspoon ground red pepper
> 3 1/2 cups chicken broth
> 1 cup creamy peanut butter
> 2 cups half-and-half
> Garnish: chopped peanuts

MELT butter in a saucepan over medium heat; add onion and celery, and sauté 5 minutes. Add garlic; sauté 2 minutes. Stir in flour, curry powder, and red pepper until smooth; cook, stirring constantly, 1 minute. Add broth; bring to a boil. Reduce heat to low, and simmer 20 minutes.
STIR in peanut butter and half-and-half; cook, stirring constantly, 3 to 4 minutes. Cool slightly. Process mixture, in batches, in a food processor or blender until smooth. Garnish, if desired. Serve immediately. **Prep: 15 min., Cook: 35 min.**

GEORGENE TICKNOR FALCON
ALEXANDRIA, VIRGINIA

SPINACH-AND-CRANBERRY SALAD WITH WARM CHUTNEY DRESSING

MAKES 8 SERVINGS

> 2 tablespoons butter or margarine
> 1 1/2 cups coarsely chopped pecans
> 1 teaspoon salt
> 1 teaspoon freshly ground pepper
> 2 (6-ounce) packages fresh baby spinach
> 6 bacon slices, cooked and crumbled
> 1 cup dried cranberries
> 2 hard-cooked eggs, finely chopped
> Warm Chutney Dressing

MELT butter in a nonstick skillet over medium-high heat; add pecans, and cook, stirring constantly, 2 minutes or until toasted. Remove from heat; add salt and pepper, tossing to coat. Drain pecans on paper towels.
TOSS together pecans, spinach, bacon, and next 2 ingredients. Drizzle with Warm Chutney Dressing, gently tossing to coat. Serve immediately. **Prep: 20 min., Cook: 3 min.**

Warm Chutney Dressing:

MAKES 1 CUP

> 6 tablespoons balsamic vinegar
> 1/3 cup bottled mango chutney
> 2 tablespoons Dijon mustard
> 2 tablespoons honey
> 2 garlic cloves, minced
> 1/4 cup olive oil

COOK first 5 ingredients in a saucepan over medium heat, stirring constantly, 3 minutes. Stir in olive oil, blending well; cook 1 minute. **Prep: 5 min., Cook: 4 min.**

DEVON DELANEY
PRINCETON, NEW JERSEY

SUGAR-AND-SPICE CURED TURKEY

MAKES 8 TO 10 SERVINGS

Marinating the bird in a brown sugar rub keeps the meat flavorful and succulent. *(pictured on page 266)*

- 1 (12-pound) frozen whole turkey, thawed
- ¼ cup firmly packed light brown sugar
- 2 tablespoons kosher or coarse-grain sea salt
- 1 teaspoon onion powder
- ½ teaspoon garlic powder
- ½ teaspoon ground allspice
- ½ teaspoon ground cloves
- ½ teaspoon ground mace
- 1 large onion, quartered
- 2 (14-ounce) cans low-sodium chicken broth
- Additional chicken broth
- 2 tablespoons all-purpose flour
- Garnishes: fresh rosemary sprigs, apple slices, nuts

REMOVE giblets and neck; rinse turkey with cold water. Pat dry. Tie legs together with string; tuck wingtips under. Combine brown sugar and next 6 ingredients. Rub over turkey. Cover with plastic wrap; chill 8 hours.

PLACE turkey on a rack in a roasting pan, breast side up. Arrange onion quarters around turkey. Pour 2 cans chicken broth in pan.

BAKE, loosely covered with foil, at 325° for 1½ hours. Uncover and bake 1½ more hours or until meat thermometer registers 180°. (Cover with foil to prevent excessive browning, if necessary.) Remove onion; discard, reserving pan drippings. Let turkey stand 15 minutes before carving.

COMBINE pan drippings and enough chicken broth to equal 2 cups in a saucepan over medium heat. Whisk in flour, and cook, whisking constantly, 5 minutes or until thickened. Serve with turkey. Garnish, if desired. **Prep: 10 min., Chill: 8 hrs., Bake: 3 hrs., Stand: 15 min., Cook: 5 min.**

JEAN ROCZNIAK
ROCHESTER, MINNESOTA

CRABMEAT-AND-OYSTER DRESSING

MAKES 8 SERVINGS

Offer this seafood- and rice-based dressing for a tasty change of pace. *(pictured on page 266)*

- 1 (6.2-ounce) package long-grain and wild rice mix
- 2⅓ cups water
- 5 tablespoons butter or margarine, divided
- 1 medium onion, chopped
- ½ medium-size green bell pepper, chopped
- 1 cup chopped fresh mushrooms
- 1 pound fresh crabmeat, drained and flaked
- 1 (12-ounce) container fresh oysters, drained
- 1 (10¾-ounce) can cream of celery soup
- 1 cup chopped pecans, toasted
- ½ cup Italian-seasoned breadcrumbs
- 1 green onion, chopped
- ¼ teaspoon salt
- ¼ teaspoon ground black pepper
- ⅛ teaspoon ground red pepper

BRING rice mix, 2⅓ cups water, and 1 tablespoon butter to a boil in a saucepan. Reduce heat to low, cover, and simmer 25 minutes or until rice is tender.

MELT remaining 4 tablespoons butter in a large nonstick skillet over medium heat; add onion, bell pepper, and mushrooms, and sauté 8 minutes or until tender.

STIR in crabmeat and oysters, and cook 4 minutes. Stir in rice, soup, and remaining ingredients; cook, stirring occasionally, 5 to 10 minutes or until thoroughly heated. **Prep: 25 min., Cook: 47 min.**

LUCY T. LEGER
LAFAYETTE, LOUISIANA

MARINATED ASPARAGUS

MAKES 6 TO 8 SERVINGS

- 2 pounds fresh asparagus
- ¾ cup olive oil
- 1 tablespoon sugar
- ½ cup white balsamic vinegar
- 4 garlic cloves, minced
- 1 teaspoon red pepper flakes

SNAP off tough ends of asparagus, and cook asparagus in boiling water to cover 3 minutes or until crisp-tender; drain.

PLUNGE asparagus into ice water to stop the cooking process; drain. Arrange asparagus in a 13- x 9-inch dish.

WHISK together olive oil, sugar, balsamic vinegar, garlic, and red pepper flakes until well blended; pour over asparagus. Cover; chill 8 hours. Drain before serving. **Prep: 15 min., Cook: 3 min., Chill: 8 hrs.**

BRUSSELS SPROUTS WITH APPLES

MAKES 6 TO 8 SERVINGS

Crisp, sweet apples and crunchy water chestnuts complement tender brussels sprouts in this seasonal side dish. *(pictured on page 267)*

- 2¼ pounds fresh brussels sprouts, halved
- 3 tablespoons fresh lemon juice
- 2 teaspoons salt, divided
- ¼ cup butter or margarine, divided
- 1 medium onion, diced
- ¼ cup apple juice
- 1 large Red Delicious apple, diced
- 1 garlic clove, minced
- 1 teaspoon sugar
- 1 (8-ounce) can sliced water chestnuts, drained
- ½ cup golden raisins
- 2 teaspoons grated lemon rind
- ½ teaspoon freshly ground pepper
- ⅛ teaspoon grated nutmeg

BRING brussels sprouts, lemon juice, 1½ teaspoons salt, and water to cover to a boil in a saucepan. Cover, reduce heat, and simmer 5 to 10 minutes or until tender. Drain and keep warm.

MELT 2 tablespoons butter in a large skillet over medium-high heat; add onion, and sauté 15 minutes or until caramel-colored. Add apple juice; cook 2 minutes, stirring to loosen browned particles.

ADD apple, garlic, and sugar; cook, stirring constantly, 5 to 6 minutes or until apple is tender. Add water chestnuts, next 4 ingredients, remaining ½ teaspoon salt, and remaining 2 tablespoons butter; cook, stirring constantly, 3 to 4 minutes. Stir in brussels sprouts. **Prep: 25 min., Cook: 42 min.**

MARY ANN LEE
MARCO ISLAND, FLORIDA

Cook's Notes

One day ahead:
- Stir together spice mixture for Sugar-and-Spice Cured Turkey, and spread over turkey; cover and chill 8 hours.
- Cut brussels sprouts in half, and place in a zip-top plastic bag; seal and chill.
- Prepare long-grain and wild rice mix for Crabmeat-and-Oyster Dressing; cover and chill.
- Assemble Baked Sweet-and-Savory Mashed Potatoes (do not bake); cover and chill.
- Prepare and bake pastry leaves for Elegant Pumpkin-Walnut Layered Pie; store in an airtight container.
- Hard-cook eggs for spinach salad; cover and chill.
- Prepare Marinated Asparagus; cover and chill.

3½ hours before serving:
- Bake turkey; make pan gravy.
- Bake pie; garnish with pastry.
- Prepare ingredients for spinach salad and dressing.

One hour ahead:
- Remove unbaked mashed potatoes from refrigerator, and let stand 30 minutes. (Potatoes can stand up to 1 hour, if needed.)
- Prepare crabmeat dressing.
- Prepare Brussels Sprouts With Apples; cover with aluminum foil to keep warm.

45 minutes ahead:
- Prepare Cream of Curried Peanut Soup.

30 minutes ahead:
- Bake prepared potatoes.

10 minutes ahead:
- Reheat pan gravy for turkey.
- Toss salad and reheat dressing.

BAKED SWEET-AND-SAVORY MASHED POTATOES

MAKES 6 TO 8 SERVINGS

- 3½ pounds baking potatoes, peeled and cut into 1-inch pieces
- 1 tablespoon salt, divided
- 1 (29-ounce) can sweet potatoes in syrup, drained and mashed
- 1 (8-ounce) package ⅓-less-fat cream cheese, softened
- 6 bacon slices, cooked and crumbled
- ¾ cup light sour cream
- ⅔ cup chicken broth
- ½ teaspoon pepper
- Garnish: crumbled cooked bacon

BRING potatoes, 1 teaspoon salt, and water to cover to a boil in a Dutch oven; cook 30 minutes or until tender. Drain. Return potatoes to pan. Add sweet potatoes and cream cheese; mash until smooth. Stir in bacon, next 3 ingredients, and remaining salt. Spoon into a lightly greased 11- x 7-inch baking dish. Bake, uncovered, at 350° for 20 minutes. Garnish, if desired. **Prep: 20 min., Cook: 30 min., Bake: 20 min.**

JEANNE STEADMAN
HUNTSVILLE, ALABAMA

ELEGANT PUMPKIN-WALNUT LAYERED PIE

MAKES 10 SERVINGS

A pecan pie-like filling nestles beneath the creamy pumpkin topping. *(pictured on pages 1 and 267)*

- 1 (15-ounce) package refrigerated piecrusts
- 1 large egg, lightly beaten
- 1¼ cups firmly packed light brown sugar, divided
- 1 cup walnuts, chopped and toasted
- 3 tablespoons butter, melted
- ¼ teaspoon vanilla extract
- 1 (16-ounce) can pumpkin
- 1 (8-ounce) package cream cheese, softened
- 2 large eggs
- 2 tablespoons all-purpose flour
- 1 teaspoon ground cinnamon
- ½ teaspoon ground ginger
- ½ teaspoon ground allspice
- ½ teaspoon ground nutmeg
- Whipped cream (optional)

ROLL 1 piecrust to press out fold lines; cut out leaves with a leaf-shaped cutter. Brush leaves with lightly beaten egg, and place on a baking sheet; set aside.
FIT remaining piecrust into a 9-inch pieplate according to package directions; fold edges under, and crimp.
BAKE leaves at 350° for 10 to 12 minutes or until golden. Bake piecrust for 6 minutes or until lightly browned. Remove leaves and piecrust from oven, and let cool. Increase oven temperature to 425°.
COMBINE ½ cup brown sugar, chopped walnuts, butter, and vanilla; spread on the bottom of baked piecrust.
BEAT pumpkin, cream cheese, 2 eggs, and remaining ¾ cup brown sugar at medium speed with an electric mixer. Add flour, cinnamon, ginger, allspice, and nutmeg, beating until blended. Spoon mixture over walnut mixture.
BAKE at 425° for 15 minutes. Reduce temperature to 350°, and bake 30 more minutes or until pie is set. Remove pie to a wire rack; cool. Arrange leaves on top of pie. Serve warm or chilled with whipped cream, if desired. **Prep: 20 min., Bake: 57 min.**

GLORIA BRADLEY
NAPERVILLE, ILLINOIS

A Season for Coconut

If you like coconut, we have a tasty surprise for you. Just in time for the holiday season, we've assembled a few of our highest-rated recipes that use coconut. They offer something for everybody and almost every occasion.

Choose from an appetizer, dessert, and side dish that use sweetened flaked coconut—a holiday pantry staple. The best part? All can be prepared in less than 30 minutes. Although there are other types of packaged coconut, such as shredded and grated, we prefer to use flaked because of its size and texture. These no-fuss recipes combine traditional uses with new looks.

COCONUT SHRIMP WITH MUSTARD SAUCE

MAKES 10 TO 12 APPETIZER SERVINGS

1½ pounds unpeeled, jumbo fresh
    shrimp
2 cups all-purpose baking mix, divided
1 cup beer
½ teaspoon salt
⅛ to ¼ teaspoon ground red pepper
3 cups sweetened flaked coconut
Vegetable oil
Mustard Sauce

PEEL shrimp, leaving tails intact; devein, if desired. Set aside.

STIR together 1 cup baking mix and 1 cup beer until smooth.

STIR together remaining 1 cup baking mix, salt, and ground red pepper. Dredge shrimp in dry mixture, and dip in beer mixture, allowing excess coating to drip. Gently roll shrimp in flaked coconut.

POUR vegetable oil to a depth of 3 inches into a Dutch oven or heavy saucepan, and heat to 350°. Cook shrimp, in batches, 1 to 2 minutes or until golden; remove shrimp, and drain on paper towels. Serve immediately with Mustard Sauce. **Prep: 20 min., Cook: 2 min. per batch**

Mustard Sauce:

MAKES ⅔ CUP

½ cup Dijon mustard
2 tablespoons light brown sugar
2 tablespoons beer
⅛ to ¼ teaspoon ground red pepper

STIR together all ingredients. **Prep: 5 min.**

Know Your Coconut

■ Shredded coconut is the type with the largest pieces, followed in descending order by flaked and grated.
■ Store unused frozen coconut in a heavy-duty zip-top plastic bag for up to six months. (Do not refreeze thawed frozen coconut.)

TOASTED COCONUT COOKIES

MAKES 4 DOZEN

¼ cup butter or margarine, softened
¼ cup shortening
1 cup sugar
1 large egg
½ teaspoon coconut extract
1½ cups all-purpose flour
1 teaspoon baking powder
½ teaspoon baking soda
½ teaspoon salt
1 cup sweetened flaked coconut
½ cup crispy rice cereal
½ cup uncooked regular oats

BEAT softened butter and shortening at medium speed with an electric mixer until fluffy; gradually add sugar, beating until blended. Add egg and coconut extract, beating well.

COMBINE flour, baking powder, soda, and salt; gradually add to butter mixture, beating well after each addition. Stir in coconut, cereal, and oats.

DROP dough by heaping teaspoonfuls onto lightly greased baking sheets.

BAKE at 325° for 12 to 14 minutes or until golden. Let cool slightly on baking sheets, and remove to wire racks to cool completely. **Prep: 10 min., Bake: 14 min. per batch**

KELLI GOLDSTEIN
MARIETTA, GEORGIA

GINGERED AMBROSIA

MAKES 6 TO 8 SERVINGS

6 large navel oranges
2 (20-ounce) cans pineapple chunks, drained
⅔ cup sweetened flaked coconut
¼ cup fresh mint leaves, cut into strips
2½ tablespoons fresh lime juice
1½ tablespoons grated fresh ginger
Garnish: fresh mint sprigs

PEEL and section oranges over a bowl, reserving juice. Combine orange sections, juice, pineapple, and next 4 ingredients; gently toss. Cover and chill until ready to serve. Garnish, if desired. **Prep: 10 min.**

Making the Most of Leftovers

Ever wonder what to do with all that extra ham, roast beef, and turkey left from holiday feasts? These wonderful reader recipes make terrific use of extra meat and poultry, and they're sure to add a little pizzazz to your next get-together. However, don't limit yourself to these suggested fillings; the recipes also work great with steak, chicken, and lamb.

MEXICAN TURKEY TURNOVERS

MAKES 16 TURNOVERS

1 medium onion, diced
½ red or green bell pepper, diced
2 tablespoons vegetable oil
2 cups chopped cooked turkey
1 (8-ounce) can tomato sauce
½ (1.25-ounce) package taco seasoning mix
1 (16-ounce) can refrigerated jumbo biscuits, split
1 cup (4 ounces) shredded colby-Jack cheese blend
6 green onions, chopped
Toppings: sour cream, salsa

SAUTÉ onion and bell pepper in hot oil over medium-high heat 5 minutes or until onion is tender. Stir in chopped turkey, tomato sauce, and taco seasoning mix. Remove mixture from heat; let cool.

ROLL each biscuit half into a 6-inch circle. Spoon about 2 tablespoons turkey mixture, 1 tablespoon cheese, and 2 teaspoons green onions on 1 side of each circle; fold in half, sealing edges with a fork. Place on a lightly greased baking sheet.

BAKE at 400° for 15 minutes or until golden. Serve with sour cream and salsa. **Prep: 45 min., Cook: 5 min., Bake: 15 min.**

NOTE: For testing purposes only, we used Pillsbury Grands! Biscuits.

MARY SHIVERS
ADA, OKLAHOMA

Quick Fiesta Quesadillas

MAKES 6 APPETIZER SERVINGS

1½ cups diced cooked ham
3 plum tomatoes, seeded and chopped
1 cup crumbled goat cheese
½ medium-size red onion, diced
¼ cup chopped fresh cilantro
¼ cup lime juice
¼ cup (2 ounces) cream cheese, softened
1 (4.5-ounce) can chopped green chiles, drained
6 (8-inch) flour tortillas

COMBINE first 8 ingredients. Spread 1 side of each tortilla with about ½ cup mixture; fold tortillas in half.
COOK tortillas in a nonstick skillet coated with cooking spray, in batches, over medium-high heat 1 minute on each side or until golden brown. Serve immediately. **Prep: 25 min., Cook: 12 min.**

DOLORES VACCARO
PUEBLO, COLORADO

Roast Beef Slices

MAKES 8 TO 10 APPETIZER SERVINGS

2 cups chopped or shredded cooked roast beef
½ cup mayonnaise
2 tablespoons prepared horseradish
2 to 3 jalapeño peppers, seeded and diced
1 tablespoon chopped fresh chives
¼ teaspoon pepper
⅛ teaspoon salt
1 (16-ounce) Italian bread loaf, cut in half lengthwise
1 (12-ounce) jar roasted red bell peppers, drained and chopped
2 cups (8 ounces) shredded Monterey Jack cheese with peppers
¼ cup chopped fresh parsley

COMBINE first 7 ingredients; spread evenly over cut sides of each bread half. Top with bell peppers; sprinkle with cheese. Place on a baking sheet.
BAKE at 450° for 8 to 10 minutes. Sprinkle with parsley. Cut into slices; serve immediately. **Prep: 10 min., Bake: 10 min.**

MARGARET PACHE
MESA, ARIZONA

Our Best Omelets & Hash Browns

Wake up to a hearty breakfast.

After taking an informal survey at our morning coffeepot, Assistant Foods Editor Joy Zacharia learned that folks are very particular about what they like in their omelets. Favorites range from just ham and American cheese to everything-but-the-kitchen-sink combinations—with plenty of preferences in between. Hash browns, however, are a different story. Most people polled prefer the shredded, crisp-on-the-outside, tender-on-the-inside type with lots of salt and pepper.

Here, Lyda Jones, our Test Kitchens Director and breakfast connoisseur (she's the former breakfast cook at Charleston's Hominy Grill), shares her expertise on making perfect omelets and hash browns. Lyda knows some people are nervous about flipping omelets. She says you can cook without flipping and still get good results—see "Omelet 101" on page 247. Whichever way you choose, we think you're going to flip over this selection worthy of any brunch or supper.

Ham-and-Cheese Omelet

MAKES 2 OMELETS

Havarti, a creamy, buttery-flavored cheese, is a nice update to this traditional omelet.

6 large eggs
2 tablespoons chopped fresh chives
¼ teaspoon salt
¼ teaspoon pepper
Vegetable cooking spray
2 teaspoons butter or margarine, divided
1 cup chopped smoked ham
½ cup shredded Havarti cheese
1 cup (4 ounces) shredded Swiss cheese

WHISK together first 4 ingredients.
MELT 1 teaspoon butter in a small non-stick skillet coated with cooking spray over medium-high heat, rotating pan to coat bottom evenly.
ADD half of egg mixture to skillet. As egg mixture starts to cook, gently lift edges of omelet with a spatula, and tilt pan so uncooked portion flows underneath. Cook 3 minutes or until almost set. Flip omelet over.
SPRINKLE 1 side of omelet with half each of ham and cheeses. Fold in half. Cook 1 to 2 minutes or until cheese melts. To make next omelet, repeat with remaining 1 teaspoon butter, egg mixture, ham, and cheeses. Serve immediately. **Prep: 5 min., Cook: 10 min. per omelet**

Open-Faced Bacon-and-Potato Omelet

MAKES 4 TO 6 SERVINGS

4 bacon slices, chopped
2 cups frozen Southern-style cubed hash browns, thawed
4 green onions, thinly sliced
2 teaspoons butter or margarine
1 large tomato, seeded and chopped
2 tablespoons chopped fresh Italian parsley
6 large eggs
½ teaspoon salt
¼ teaspoon pepper
4 drops hot sauce (optional)
1 cup shredded sharp Cheddar cheese

COOK bacon in a large ovenproof non-stick skillet over medium heat until crisp; remove bacon and drain on paper towels, reserving 1 tablespoon drippings in skillet. Set bacon aside.

COOK hash browns in hot drippings over medium heat 10 minutes or until hash browns are tender, stirring occasionally. Stir in green onions; cook 5 minutes or until tender.

ADD butter to skillet, stirring until melted. Add tomato, and cook over medium-high heat 3 to 4 minutes. Sprinkle with bacon and parsley.

WHISK together eggs, salt, pepper, and, if desired, hot sauce. Pour over hash brown mixture. Gently lift edges of omelet, and tilt pan so uncooked portion flows underneath. Cook over medium heat until omelet begins to set. Sprinkle with cheese.

BROIL 5½ inches from heat 5 minutes or until top is set and cheese melts. Slide out of skillet onto platter. Cut into wedges, and serve immediately. **Prep: 25 min., Cook: 25 min., Broil: 5 min.**

Omelet 101

1. Melt butter in a nonstick skillet coated with vegetable cooking spray, rotating pan to coat evenly. Add half of egg mixture per omelet. Adding the egg mixture to a hot, buttered skillet makes for easy flipping and a buttery flavor.

2. As egg mixture starts to cook, gently lift edges of omelet, and tilt pan so uncooked portion flows underneath. At this point, you may flip omelet over. (Here's where that well-buttered nonstick skillet is a must.) Or, to cook without flipping, continue lifting edges and tilting pan until no uncooked portion remains.

3. Sprinkle toppings over one-half of omelet.

4. Using a spatula, fold plain side over toppings. Slide onto a warm plate. Use a heat-resistant spatula; it will last longer, and plastic won't end up in your food.

SPANISH OMELET WITH FRESH AVOCADO SALSA

MAKES 2 OMELETS

1 cup chopped chorizo sausage
    (about 4 ounces)*
1 small sweet onion, chopped
½ small green bell pepper, chopped
1 garlic clove, minced
6 large eggs
¼ teaspoon salt
¼ teaspoon pepper
Vegetable cooking spray
2 teaspoons butter or margarine,
    divided
1 (3-ounce) package goat cheese,
    crumbled
Fresh Avocado Salsa
Garnishes: sour cream, freshly ground
    pepper

COOK first 4 ingredients in a small non-stick skillet over medium-high heat 10 minutes or until vegetables are tender. Remove chorizo mixture from skillet, and set aside. Wipe skillet clean.

WHISK together eggs, salt, and ¼ teaspoon pepper.

MELT 1 teaspoon butter in skillet coated with cooking spray over medium-high heat, rotating pan to coat bottom evenly. Add half of egg mixture. As egg mixture starts to cook, gently lift edges of omelet with a spatula, and tilt pan so uncooked portion flows underneath. Cook 3 minutes or until almost set. Flip omelet over.

SPRINKLE 1 side of omelet with half each of chorizo mixture and goat cheese. Fold in half. To make next omelet, repeat with remaining 1 teaspoon butter, egg mixture, chorizo mixture, and cheese. Top with Fresh Avocado Salsa; garnish, if desired. **Prep: 15 min., Cook: 10 min. per omelet**

*Substitute spicy smoked sausage for chorizo, if desired.

Fresh Avocado Salsa:

MAKES ABOUT 2 CUPS

4 plum tomatoes, chopped
1 small avocado, chopped
1 small sweet onion, chopped
1 small jalapeño pepper, seeded and
    minced
¼ cup chopped fresh cilantro
2 tablespoons fresh lime juice
½ teaspoon salt

COMBINE all ingredients gently. Cover and chill until ready to serve. **Prep: 10 min.**

NOTE: For best results, serve salsa within 4 hours.

"Eggstra" Know-How

■ Eggs are economical, convenient, easy to prepare, and nutritious. One egg supplies 10% of our daily protein requirement. They're also a terrific source of vitamins A, D, and B12.

■ Egg substitute, such as Egg Beaters, may be used successfully in the place of whole eggs (¼ cup egg substitute equals one egg).

■ Leftovers of vegetables, beef, chicken, or pork make great fillings for omelets. Chop ingredients into bite-size pieces. Heat in the microwave; sprinkle over egg mixture.

■ We used frozen shredded hash browns to shorten prep time for these recipes. Substitute two very large baking potatoes, shredded, for one (16-ounce) package frozen shredded hash browns, if desired.

CREAMY VEGGIE OMELET

MAKES 2 OMELETS

    6 large eggs
    ¼ teaspoon salt
    ¼ teaspoon pepper
    2 teaspoons butter or margarine
    Vegetable cooking spray
    ½ small red bell pepper, chopped
    ½ small green bell pepper, chopped
    1 cup sliced fresh mushrooms
    1 cup chopped fresh broccoli
    ¼ teaspoon salt
    ¼ teaspoon pepper
    2 teaspoons butter or margarine,
      divided
    3 tablespoons soft cream cheese with
      chive and onion
    3 tablespoons crumbled feta cheese*

WHISK together eggs, ¼ teaspoon salt, and ¼ teaspoon pepper; set aside.

MELT 2 teaspoons butter in a small, heavy nonstick skillet coated with cooking spray over medium-high heat, rotating pan to coat bottom evenly. Add red bell pepper and next 5 ingredients. Cook, stirring often, 10 minutes or until peppers are tender. Remove mixture from skillet; set aside. Wipe skillet clean.

COAT skillet with cooking spray; add 1 teaspoon butter to skillet, and melt over medium-high heat. Add half of egg mixture. As egg mixture starts to cook, gently lift edges of omelet with a spatula, and tilt pan so uncooked portion flows underneath. Flip omelet over.

SPRINKLE 1 side of omelet with half of red bell pepper mixture. Dollop with half of cream cheese; sprinkle with half of feta cheese. Fold in half. Cook 2 minutes or until cheese melts. To make next omelet, repeat with remaining butter, egg mixture, vegetable mixture, and cheeses. Serve immediately. **Prep: 20 min., Cook: 10 min. per omelet**

NOTE: For testing purposes only, we used Philadelphia Soft Cream Cheese with Chive & Onion.

*Substitute ¼ cup shredded Swiss cheese, if desired.

SMOTHERED-COVERED HASH BROWNS

MAKES 8 SERVINGS

Pressing down firmly on hash browns with a spatula will help keep them from falling apart.

    1 medium onion, diced
    3 tablespoons vegetable oil, divided
    1 (16-ounce) package frozen shredded
      hash browns, thawed
    1 teaspoon salt
    ½ teaspoon pepper
    8 American cheese slices

SAUTÉ onion in 1 tablespoon hot vegetable oil over medium heat 8 minutes or until tender.

STIR together onion, hash browns, salt, and pepper in a large bowl.

HEAT 1 tablespoon oil in a large nonstick skillet over medium-high heat. Drop hash brown mixture into 3½-inch rounds. Cook, in batches, 5 minutes on each side, or until lightly browned, adding remaining oil as necessary. Press down with a spatula to flatten; top each round with a cheese slice. Cook 5 minutes. **Prep: 10 min., Cook: 30 min.**

SWEET POTATO HASH BROWNS

MAKES 8 SERVINGS

    2 teaspoons butter or margarine
    3 tablespoons vegetable oil, divided
    1 medium onion, diced
    1 tablespoon brown sugar
    1 medium baking potato, peeled and
      shredded
    1 medium-size sweet potato, peeled
      and shredded
    1 teaspoon salt
    ½ teaspoon pepper
    4 bacon slices, cooked and crumbled
    ½ cup chopped pecans, toasted

MELT butter and 1 tablespoon oil in a nonstick skillet over medium heat. Add onion; sauté 15 minutes or until golden. Add brown sugar, and cook 5 minutes, stirring often.

COMBINE onion mixture, potato, salt, and pepper.

HEAT 1 tablespoon vegetable oil in a nonstick skillet over medium-high heat. Drop potato mixture into 3½-inch rounds; cook, in batches, 5 minutes on each side or until golden, adding remaining oil as necessary. Press down with a spatula to flatten; top with bacon and pecans. **Prep: 25 min., Cook: 30 min.**

CHEESY SWEET POTATO HASH BROWNS: Omit onion, brown sugar, bacon, and pecans. Top hash browns evenly with 4 ounces thinly sliced Jarlsberg or Monterey Jack cheese during the last 5 minutes.

ROSEMARY-GARLIC HASH BROWNS: Omit onion, brown sugar, bacon, and pecans. Add 1 tablespoon chopped fresh rosemary and 1 teaspoon chopped garlic to potato mixture. Cook as directed.

Taste of the South

Cornbread Dressing

Making your first cornbread dressing is a rite of passage, something you just want to be able to do so your mama can feel good about your upbringing.

The ingredients you use say something about you. Cooks from coastal areas are likely to stir in seafood. Sausage is added in many locales. And you can argue over whether cornbread, biscuits, or store-bought stuffing mix works best as a base. At first Creative Development Director Valerie Fraser found all those special twists intimidating, but eventually, she decided to find a classic recipe, put aside her fear of excessive sage, and give it a try. She picked one with a cornbread base.

The recipe looks a little soupy when you mix it, but the end result is wonderfully moist. If you like yours a little drier, cut down on the chicken broth. And if you, like Valerie's mother, are "anti sage" (she prefers poultry seasoning), you can reduce or omit it. However, if you've based your judgment on the dried variety, try fresh sage before omitting it. It gives the dressing a more delicate flavor.

CORNBREAD DRESSING

MAKES 16 TO 18 SERVINGS

To boost the flavor, boil inexpensive cuts of turkey, such as wings, and substitute the resulting broth for part of the chicken broth. *(pictured on page 263)*

1 cup butter or margarine, divided
3 cups white cornmeal
1 cup all-purpose flour
2 tablespoons sugar
2 teaspoons baking powder
1½ teaspoons salt
1 teaspoon baking soda
7 large eggs, divided
3 cups buttermilk
3 cups soft breadcrumbs
2 medium onions, diced (2 cups)
1 large bunch celery, diced (3 cups)
½ cup finely chopped fresh sage*
6 (10½-ounce) cans condensed
    chicken broth, undiluted
1 tablespoon pepper

PLACE ½ cup butter in a 13- x 9-inch pan; heat in oven at 425° for 4 minutes.
COMBINE cornmeal and next 5 ingredients; whisk in 3 eggs and buttermilk.
POUR hot butter into batter, stirring until blended. Pour batter into pan. Bake at 425° for 30 minutes or until golden brown. Cool. Crumble cornbread into a large bowl; stir in breadcrumbs, and set aside.
MELT remaining ½ cup butter in a skillet over medium heat; add onion and celery, and sauté until tender. Stir in sage; sauté 1 minute. Stir vegetables, remaining 4 eggs, chicken broth, and pepper into cornbread mixture; pour into 1 lightly greased 13- x 9-inch baking dish and 1 lightly greased 8-inch square baking dish. Cover and chill 8 hours.
BAKE, uncovered, at 375° for 35 to 40 minutes or until golden brown. **Prep: 30 min.; Cook: 5 min.; Chill: 8 hrs.; Bake: 1 hr., 14 min.**

*Substitute 1 tablespoon dried rubbed sage for fresh sage, if desired.

ANDOUILLE SAUSAGE, APPLE, AND PECAN DRESSING: Brown ¾ pound diced andouille sausage in a skillet over medium heat; drain. Add sausage; 2 Granny Smith apples, chopped; and 2 cups chopped toasted pecans. Proceed as directed, baking 40 to 45 minutes.

Perfecting Pecan Pie

We had quite a few discussions around our tasting table trying to choose a grand pecan pie recipe. Each of us had a special way to serve it—whether warm, cold, with or without ice cream or whipped cream. Believe us when we say we tasted a lot of pecan pies. Test Kitchens staffer James Schend prepared every version. In the end, we decided it all comes down to the pie you had growing up. We hope you and your family will enjoy these recipes.

MYSTERY PECAN PIE

MAKES 8 SERVINGS

Taste pecan pie and cheesecake together in this recipe, and the only mystery will be "Where'd it all go?"

1 (15-ounce) package refrigerated
    piecrusts
1 (8-ounce) package cream cheese,
    softened
4 large eggs, divided
¾ cup sugar, divided
2 teaspoons vanilla extract,
    divided
¼ teaspoon salt
1 cup chopped pecans
1 cup light corn syrup

UNFOLD and stack 2 piecrusts; gently roll or press together. Fit into a 9-inch pieplate according to package directions; fold edges under, and crimp.
BEAT cream cheese, 1 egg, ½ cup sugar, 1 teaspoon vanilla, and salt at medium speed with an electric mixer until smooth. Pour into piecrust. Sprinkle with pecans.
STIR together corn syrup, remaining 3 eggs, remaining ¼ cup sugar, and remaining 1 teaspoon vanilla; pour mixture over pecans.
BAKE at 350° for 50 to 55 minutes or until set. **Prep: 15 min., Bake: 55 min.**

GRETCHEN EICKHORST
ST. CHARLES, MISSOURI

MOM'S PECAN PIE

MAKES 8 SERVINGS

1 (15-ounce) package refrigerated
    piecrusts
3 large eggs
1 cup sugar
¾ cup light corn syrup
2 tablespoons butter or margarine,
    melted
2 teaspoons vanilla extract
¼ teaspoon salt
1½ cups pecan halves*

UNFOLD and stack 2 piecrusts; gently roll or press together. Fit into a 9-inch pieplate according to package directions; fold edges under, and crimp.
STIR together eggs and next 5 ingredients; stir in pecans.
POUR filling into piecrust. Bake at 350° for 55 minutes or until set. Serve warm or cold. **Prep: 10 min., Bake: 55 min.**

*Substitute chopped pecans, a less expensive choice, for the pecan halves, if desired.

LINDA SCHEND
KENOSHA, WISCONSIN

Picture-Perfect Pie

To prevent the filling from seeping under the crust, our recipes call for using two crusts and stacking them. Here's how.

1. Unfold one piecrust and press out fold lines.

2. Unfold second crust and stack on top, turning so that fold lines do not match. Press edges to seal.

3. Roll crust out to an approximate 12-inch circle. Fit into a 9-inch pieplate. Trim dough to about ½ inch from edge of pieplate, fold under, and flute or crimp as desired.

holiday dinners®

Join us as we celebrate the season with friends, food, and fellowship.

Supper Club Celebration

Supper Club Menu
Serves 8

Gin-Marinated Pheasant

Point Clear Potatoes

Green Beans With Zucchini

Poinsettia Punch (double recipe)

New kitchen appliances inspired husbands of this Memphis supper club to give the gift of cooking classes to their wives. The women had so much fun, they later sent their husbands to the same classes. The men loved it, and now they do most of the cooking when the group meets.

On this night, the lively bunch gathers at the home of Debbie and Michael Folk. Ginger Owings's Poinsettia Punch kicks the party into high gear, and Dudley Schaefer and John Phillips's pheasant entrée is fantastic. (The recipe also works well with Cornish hens.) Point Clear Potatoes are super-easy, and green beans get a new attitude with zucchini and crumbled bacon.

GIN-MARINATED PHEASANT

MAKES 8 SERVINGS

¾ cup gin
¾ cup vermouth
1 bay leaf
1 teaspoon ground pepper
1 teaspoon minced garlic
4 pheasants, dressed*
½ teaspoon salt
2 tablespoons olive oil
1 cup red wine
½ cup orange-flavored dried plums, chopped
1 (10-ounce) can chicken broth
2 tablespoons butter

COMBINE first 5 ingredients in a large heavy-duty zip-top plastic bag, reserving ½ cup of the mixture. Place pheasants in the remaining mixture in the plastic bag. Seal and chill at least 30 minutes.

REMOVE pheasants from marinade, discarding marinade in bag. Sprinkle with salt; brown on all sides in hot oil in a large roasting pan over medium-high heat.

BAKE at 400° for 40 to 50 minutes. Remove from roasting pan; keep warm.

BRING reserved marinade to a boil in roasting pan over high heat, stirring to loosen browned particles. Stir in red wine, and cook 4 to 5 minutes or until liquid is reduced by half. Pour mixture through a fine wire-mesh strainer in a medium saucepan, discarding solids. Add dried plums and broth, and simmer 5 minutes; remove from heat, and stir in butter until melted.

CUT pheasants into quarters; place on serving platter. Drizzle with sauce and serve. **Prep: 20 min., Chill: 30 min., Bake: 50 min., Cook: 10 min.**

*Eight (1- to 1½-pound) Cornish hens make a delicious substitution for the pheasants.

INSPIRED BY DUDLEY SCHAEFER
AND JOHN PHILLIPS
MEMPHIS, TENNESSEE

POINT CLEAR POTATOES

MAKES 8 SERVINGS

1 (30-ounce) package frozen hash brown potatoes, thawed
1 tablespoon chopped fresh rosemary
½ teaspoon salt
½ teaspoon pepper
1 tablespoon butter or margarine
1 tablespoon olive oil

TOSS together first 4 ingredients.
MELT half of butter in half of oil in a large skillet over medium-high heat. Press half of potato mixture into bottom of skillet. Cook 5 to 7 minutes or until edges brown. Remove from skillet, and place on a lightly greased baking sheet. Repeat with remaining potato mixture, butter, and oil.
BAKE at 400° for 10 to 15 minutes or until crisp and golden. Cut into wedges to serve. **Prep: 10 min., Cook: 14 min., Bake: 15 min.**

KIM BLANKENSHIP
MEMPHIS, TENNESSEE

GREEN BEANS WITH ZUCCHINI

MAKES 8 SERVINGS

2 pounds fresh green beans, trimmed and cut into 1½-inch pieces
¼ cup butter or margarine
1 small onion, diced
2 medium zucchini, sliced
6 bacon slices, cooked and crumbled
¾ teaspoon salt
½ teaspoon pepper

COOK green beans in boiling salted water to cover, in a large Dutch oven, 10 to 15 minutes or until crisp-tender. Drain.
MELT butter in a large skillet over medium-high heat; add onion, and sauté 5 minutes or until tender.
ADD sliced zucchini, and sauté 3 to 4 minutes or until tender. Stir in beans, crumbled bacon, salt, and pepper, and cook 2 to 3 minutes or until thoroughly heated. Serve immediately. **Prep: 20 min., Cook: 28 min.**

GINGER OWINGS
MEMPHIS, TENNESSEE

POINSETTIA PUNCH

MAKES 4 SERVINGS

Chill the Champagne and juice in the refrigerator before the party, then mix the punch right before serving.

1 (750-milliliter) bottle Champagne, chilled
3 cups cranberry-apple juice, chilled
¼ cup thawed frozen white grape juice concentrate
¼ cup orange liqueur

STIR together all ingredients in a 2-quart pitcher.
SERVE in Champagne flutes. (Decorate serving tray with fresh cranberries, if desired.) **Prep: 10 min.**

NOTE: For testing purposes only, we used Korbel Chardonnay Champagne for Champagne and Grand Marnier for orange liqueur.

GINGER OWINGS
MEMPHIS, TENNESSEE

A Gathering of Food and Friendship

On Yorkshire Place in Lumberton, North Carolina, the neighbors open their homes to people of all ages, walks of life, and religious affiliations. The four households that live on this cul-de-sac hold a joint open house in early December.

"It's a really great thing to look out my window and see crowds of people visiting in our yards," says organizer Linda Metzger. "There are young married couples and grandparents all having fun together. Among the four families, we invite about 250 guests."

Linda says keeping the event simple is key to its success. "We try to make it fun, so everyone serves what they are comfortable making." The recipes are easy and delicious—we've included several from current and former neighbors.

The gathering offers great rewards other than the opportunity to sample good food, Linda says. "So often when you have a party, you invite only your friends. When all the houses get together, it incorporates four families and four differing groups of people. It creates a wonderful sense of community."

CHEDDAR-CHILI CHEESECAKE

MAKES 18 TO 20 APPETIZER SERVINGS

¼ cup fine, dry breadcrumbs
¼ cup (1 ounce) shredded sharp Cheddar cheese
3 (8-ounce) packages cream cheese, softened
12 thin slices cooked ham, diced
1 (10-ounce) block sharp Cheddar cheese, shredded
5 green onions, chopped
3 large eggs
2 small jalapeño peppers, minced
1 garlic clove, minced
1 cup sour cream
2 tablespoons milk
Crackers

STIR together breadcrumbs and ¼ cup shredded Cheddar cheese; sprinkle on the bottom of a buttered 9-inch springform pan.
BEAT cream cheese at medium speed with an electric mixer; add half of ham, shredded cheese, and next 6 ingredients, beating at low speed until well blended. Pour half of cheese mixture into prepared pan, and top with remaining ham. Pour remaining cheese mixture over ham.
BAKE at 325° for 1 hour or until center is set. Let stand 30 minutes. Gently run a knife around the edge of cheesecake, and release sides. Serve slightly warm or at room temperature with crackers. **Prep: 25 min., Bake: 1 hr., Stand: 30 min.**

KRISTIN AUSTIN SMITH
FLORENCE, SOUTH CAROLINA

OLIVE TEA SANDWICHES

MAKES 18 SANDWICHES

1 (7.5-ounce) jar pimiento-stuffed
   olives, drained and chopped
½ small onion, diced
2 hard-cooked eggs, chopped
1 cup toasted pecans, chopped
1 cup reduced-fat mayonnaise
36 thin white bread slices

STIR together first 5 ingredients. Cover and chill 1 hour.
SPREAD olive mixture on 1 side of 18 bread slices; top with remaining bread slices. Trim crusts from sandwiches; cut each into triangles, or cut with decorative cookie cutters. **Prep: 40 min., Chill: 1 hr.**

NOTE: For testing purposes only, we used Pepperidge Farm Very Thin White Bread Slices.

LINDA METZGER
LUMBERTON, NORTH CAROLINA

GINGERBREAD BOYS

MAKES ABOUT 6 DOZEN

You can freeze these cookies for several months in airtight containers.

1 cup butter, softened
1 cup sugar
½ teaspoon salt
1 cup molasses
2 tablespoons white vinegar
1 large egg
5 cups all-purpose flour
1½ teaspoons baking soda
1 tablespoon ground ginger
1 teaspoon ground cinnamon
1 teaspoon ground cloves

BEAT butter at medium speed with an electric mixer until creamy; gradually add sugar and salt, beating well. Add molasses, vinegar, and egg, beating at low speed just until blended.
COMBINE flour and next 4 ingredients; add to butter mixture, beating at low speed until blended. Cover and chill dough 8 hours.

DIVIDE dough into fourths. Roll each portion to a ⅛-inch thickness on a floured surface. Cut dough with a 3-inch gingerbread-boy cookie cutter. Place on lightly greased or parchment paper-lined baking sheets.
BAKE at 375° for 8 minutes. Cool on pans 1 minute (this allows cookies to easily lift off the pan); place on wire racks to cool. Decorate as desired. **Prep: 30 min., Chill: 8 hrs., Bake: 8 min. per batch, Cool: 1 min. per batch**

LINDA METZGER
LUMBERTON, NORTH CAROLINA

LAYERED BROWNIES

MAKES 48 (1-INCH) SQUARES

The Vanilla Cream Topping and Brownie Glaze add extra layers of texture and sweetness to this recipe that Cyndy's sister-in-law, Betsy Tusai, gave her. *(pictured on page 268)*

4 (1-ounce) unsweetened chocolate
   baking squares
1 cup butter or margarine
2 cups sugar
4 large eggs, lightly
   beaten
1 cup all-purpose flour
1 cup chopped pecans,
   toasted
Vanilla Cream Topping
Brownie Glaze

MICROWAVE chocolate and butter in a 2-quart glass bowl at HIGH 1½ minutes or until melted, stirring twice. Add sugar and eggs, stirring until blended. Stir in flour and chopped pecans. Pour into a lightly greased, aluminum foil-lined 13-x 9-inch pan.
BAKE at 350° for 20 to 23 minutes. Cool on a wire rack 1 hour.
SPREAD cooled brownies with Vanilla Cream Topping; chill 45 minutes.
POUR Brownie Glaze over Vanilla Cream Topping, and spread evenly. Chill 1 hour. Let stand at room temperature 15 minutes; cut into 1-inch squares. **Prep: 25 min.; Bake: 23 min.; Cool: 1 hr.; Chill: 1 hr., 45 min.; Stand: 15 min.**

Vanilla Cream Topping:
MAKES 1½ CUPS

1 cup butter, melted
1 (16-ounce) package powdered sugar
¼ cup half-and-half
2 teaspoons vanilla extract

STIR together all ingredients in a bowl until smooth. **Prep: 5 min.**

Brownie Glaze:
MAKES ½ CUP

4 (1-ounce) semisweet chocolate
   baking squares
¼ cup butter

MICROWAVE chocolate squares and butter in a 1-quart glass bowl at HIGH 1½ minutes or until melted, stirring twice. **Prep: 5 min.**

CYNDY INMAN
LUMBERTON, NORTH CAROLINA

A Cookie-and-Tree Tradition

Come Thanksgiving, a Blue Ridge, Virginia, home will be transformed by 28 theme trees, yards and yards of greenery, Christmas art, decorative displays of ornaments, and even drapes befitting the season. There also will be 3,000 cookies of 20 different kinds carefully displayed and served near the appropriate trees.

"We never imagined it would turn into this," Andrew Cochran says with a laugh. "We started very small, 10 years ago, with three theme trees. Our friends enjoyed it so much, we kept growing." The two begin serious planning and brainstorming in the summer, but Christmas is on their minds year-round. "We never stop," Art Tatman says. They make regular buying trips to holiday and gift shops around the country, and they collect decorations during other travels. Family and friends even contribute ornaments from their international travels.

They begin the two-month, carefully organized decorating process in early October. "We have a day-by-day schedule," Andrew says. Undecorating and packing everything takes about a month.

They share their delightful surroundings and baked goods during their open houses, which host about 250 people over the course of four nights. Their scrumptious, tried-and-true cookie recipes have been lovingly selected through the years, and all received high ratings from our Test Kitchens. Best of all, you don't have to decorate 28 trees to share them.

GRANDMOM LUCY'S ORANGE CRISPIES

MAKES 5 DOZEN

Andrew got the recipe for these family favorites from his grandmother, Lucy Cochran.

- 1 cup sugar
- 1 cup shortening
- 1 large egg
- 1½ teaspoons orange extract
- 1½ cups all-purpose flour
- 1 teaspoon salt

BEAT 1 cup sugar and 1 cup shortening at low speed with an electric mixer until creamy. Add egg and orange extract, beating until blended. Gradually add flour and salt, beating dough until light and fluffy after each addition.

DROP mixture by rounded teaspoonfuls, 2 inches apart, onto ungreased baking sheets.

BAKE at 375° for 10 minutes or just until edges begin to brown; remove to wire racks to cool. **Prep: 15 min., Bake: 10 min. per batch**

VICTORIAN CHRISTMAS TEA CAKES

MAKES ABOUT 6 DOZEN

Art and Andrew got the recipe for these deliciously different cookies from a woman they know from Wales. You can cook them the traditional way—on a griddle—or bake them. They're wonderful with a cup of tea.

- 1 cup butter, softened
- 1½ cups granulated sugar
- 2 large eggs
- ¼ cup milk
- 4 cups all-purpose flour
- ½ teaspoon salt
- ¼ teaspoon baking soda
- 2 teaspoons baking powder
- 1 teaspoon ground cinnamon
- 1 teaspoon ground nutmeg
- 1 cup currants
- Powdered sugar

BEAT butter and 1½ cups granulated sugar at low speed with an electric mixer until creamy. Add eggs, 1 at a time, beating until blended after each addition. Add milk, beating until blended.

ADD flour and next 6 ingredients, beating until blended. Cover and chill dough 8 hours.

DIVIDE dough into fourths. Roll 1 portion to ¼-inch thickness on a lightly floured surface. Cut dough with a 1½-inch round cookie cutter or very small glass. Repeat procedure with remaining portions.

COOK, in batches, on a hot, lightly greased electric griddle or lightly greased skillet over low heat, 2 to 3 minutes on each side or until golden.

REMOVE to wire racks, and sprinkle warm tea cakes with powdered sugar. Cool slightly and serve, or cool completely and store in wax paper-lined airtight containers. **Prep: 1 hr., Chill: 8 hrs., Cook: 6 min. per batch**

NOTE: Tea cakes may also be baked on lightly greased baking sheets at 350° for 10 minutes or until cookies are golden.

ROYAL RASPBERRY TEA CAKES

MAKES 2½ DOZEN

- 1 cup butter, softened
- ½ cup powdered sugar
- 2 teaspoons vanilla extract
- 2 cups all-purpose flour
- ¼ teaspoon salt
- ¾ cup seedless raspberry preserves

BEAT butter and sugar at low speed with an electric mixer until creamy. Add vanilla, beating until blended.

COMBINE flour and salt in a small bowl; gradually add to butter mixture, beating just until blended after each addition.

SHAPE dough into 1-inch balls; place 2 inches apart on lightly greased baking sheets. Press thumb or end of a wooden spoon into each ball, forming an indentation; fill with raspberry preserves.

BAKE at 325° for 15 to 20 minutes or just until edges begin to brown. Remove to wire racks to cool. **Prep: 25 min., Bake: 20 min. per batch**

MAGIC COOKIE BARS

MAKES 30 BARS

- ½ cup butter, melted
- 2 cups graham cracker crumbs
- 1 (14½-ounce) can sweetened condensed milk
- 1 cup semisweet chocolate morsels
- 1 cup butterscotch morsels
- 1 (7-ounce) package sweetened flaked coconut
- 1 cup chopped walnuts

STIR together melted butter and graham cracker crumbs, and press into bottom of a 13- x 9-inch pan.

POUR sweetened condensed milk over crumbs; sprinkle evenly with chocolate and butterscotch morsels, coconut, and walnuts. Gently press mixture to a uniform thickness with a fork.

BAKE at 350° for 25 to 30 minutes or until coconut is lightly browned. Cool 45 minutes on a wire rack. Cut into 1½- x 2½-inch bars. **Prep: 10 min., Bake: 30 min., Cool: 45 min.**

CRAN-BEAR-Y BREAD COOKIES

MAKES 6½ DOZEN

This dough becomes soft and sticky as it reaches room temperature, so work with one portion at a time; chill remaining dough until ready to use.

- ½ cup shortening
- ½ cup butter, softened
- 2½ cups sugar, divided
- 2 large eggs
- 3 cups all-purpose flour
- 2 tablespoons grated orange rind
- 1 teaspoon baking powder
- 1 teaspoon salt
- 1 teaspoon cream of tartar
- 1½ cups chopped walnuts
- 1½ cups chopped fresh cranberries
- ¼ cup fresh orange juice
- 1 cup fresh cranberries

BEAT ½ cup shortening and ½ cup butter at low speed with an electric mixer until fluffy; add 1½ cups sugar, beating until blended. Add eggs, 1 at a time, beating until blended after each addition.

STIR together flour and next 6 ingredients; add flour mixture to butter mixture, beating at medium speed until blended. Add ¼ cup orange juice, beating until blended. Cover and chill dough 8 hours.

SHAPE dough into 1-inch balls; roll balls in remaining 1 cup sugar. (Dampen hands with water if dough is sticky.)

PLACE on lightly greased baking sheets. Press 1 fresh cranberry into top of each cookie ball.

BAKE at 350° for 10 to 12 minutes or just until edges begin to brown. Cool on baking sheets 1 minute. Remove to wire racks to cool. **Prep: 35 min., Chill: 8 hrs., Bake: 12 min. per batch, Cool: 1 min. per batch**

Five Friends, One Fabulous Christmas Dinner

Progressive Dinner Party

Serves 8

Marinated Shrimp   Cranberry-Apple Salad*

Garlic-and-Rosemary Beef Tenderloin

Green Beans With Roquefort Cheese and Walnuts*

*Double recipe to serve eight.

True friends are special indeed. And for the women who call themselves "The Fabulous Five," there's no better time to celebrate their particular bond than the holidays. For 15 years, these Texans have managed to meet around the supper table each month—regardless of the circumstances.

This began back in 1987 when Phyllis Jones, Stephanie McKee, Jan Tonroy, and Debbie Rubin met through a women's professional organization in Lubbock. They soon discovered they had similar professional interests, and they also loved to cook. This prompted the women to meet each month for supper. At the second gathering, Debbie invited her former college roommate, Diane Earl, and "The Fabulous Five" was born.

Though gatherings are usually billed as girls' nights out, husbands and children are included for their annual Christmas progressive dinner. The group was kind enough to share a few of their holiday favorites. We hope you enjoy!

MARINATED SHRIMP

MAKES 8 TO 10 SERVINGS

- 2 pounds unpeeled, medium-size fresh shrimp
- 6 cups salted water
- ½ cup sugar
- 1½ cups white vinegar
- 1 cup vegetable oil
- ¼ cup capers, undrained
- ½ to 1 teaspoon salt
- 1½ teaspoons celery salt
- 1 medium white or red onion, sliced and separated into rings

PEEL shrimp, leaving tails on. Devein, if desired. Bring 6 cups salted water to a boil; add shrimp, and cook 3 minutes or just until shrimp turn pink. Drain and rinse with cold water. Chill.

COMBINE sugar and next 5 ingredients in a shallow dish; add shrimp alternately with onion. Cover and chill at least 6 hours, turning often.

DRAIN, and discard marinade before serving. **Prep: 20 min., Cook: 3 min., Chill: 6 hrs.**

CRANBERRY-APPLE SALAD

MAKES 4 SERVINGS

2 tablespoons fresh lime juice
2 teaspoons Dijon mustard
½ cup olive oil
2 large Granny Smith apples, coarsely
   chopped
1 cup walnuts, chopped
¼ cup sliced green onions
3 tablespoons sugar
1½ cups dried cranberries
1 head romaine lettuce, torn

WHISK together lime juice and mustard. Gradually whisk in oil.

PLACE apples, walnuts, and green onions in a bowl. Pour dressing over apple mixture; toss to coat. Cover and chill 2 hours.

SPRINKLE sugar over cranberries, and toss to coat. Add to apple mixture, and toss. Line a serving platter with lettuce; top with salad. **Prep: 15 min., Chill: 2 hrs.**

GARLIC-AND-ROSEMARY BEEF TENDERLOIN

MAKES 8 TO 10 SERVINGS

½ cup soy sauce
½ cup olive oil
¼ cup balsamic or red wine vinegar
8 garlic cloves, minced
4 teaspoons dried rosemary
1 (5-pound) beef tenderloin, trimmed
1 tablespoon pepper

COMBINE first 5 ingredients in a large shallow dish or heavy-duty zip-top plastic bag; add beef. Cover or seal, and chill at least 8 hours, turning occasionally.

REMOVE beef from marinade, discarding marinade. Place in a roasting pan; sprinkle evenly with pepper, and let stand 30 minutes.

BAKE at 500° for 15 minutes or until lightly browned. Lower temperature to 375°; bake 20 more minutes or to desired degree of doneness. Let tenderloin stand 10 minutes before slicing. **Prep: 10 min., Chill: 8 hrs., Bake: 35 min., Stand: 40 min.**

GREEN BEANS WITH ROQUEFORT CHEESE AND WALNUTS

MAKES 4 SERVINGS

1 pound fresh green beans, trimmed
4 thick bacon slices, cut into ¼-inch
   pieces
4 ounces Roquefort cheese, crumbled
1 cup walnuts, toasted
¼ teaspoon salt
¼ teaspoon freshly ground pepper

PLACE green beans in boiling water to cover in a large saucepan, and simmer 3 minutes or until crisp-tender. Drain; rinse with cold water and drain. Set aside.

COOK bacon pieces in a large skillet over medium heat 5 to 7 minutes or until crisp; remove bacon with a slotted spoon, and drain on paper towels, reserving drippings in skillet.

SAUTÉ green beans in hot drippings in skillet 2 minutes or until heated. Sprinkle with cheese, and cook, stirring constantly, 30 seconds or just until cheese begins to melt. Sprinkle evenly with walnuts, salt, pepper, and bacon; serve immediately. **Prep: 10 min., Cook: 12 min.**

Helping a Friend in Need

When Debbie Rubin was diagnosed with breast cancer, the other members of the group decided to do something special for her. The ladies culled their recipes and published the cookbook *Always Enough Thyme.* They dedicated it to Debbie, and a portion of the proceeds went to the Susan G. Komen Breast Cancer Foundation. For more information call (817) 441-5032.

It's All in Good Taste

When Sue Thompson talks about the Taste Fair, it's hard not to get excited. The event, which is usually held the Friday before Thanksgiving, originally started 15 years ago as a small church fund-raiser. Today, it includes more than 1,000 visitors. The Ladies Ministry of Woodlawn United Pentecostal Church in Columbia, Mississippi, begins planning this affair a year in advance. Here Sue shares some favorite dishes that have graced their tables in the past.

BLUEGRASS SALAD

MAKES 6 TO 8 SERVINGS

Sweet cranberries mingle with creamy blue cheese and crunchy walnuts in this inventive salad. *(pictured on page 264)*

½ cup vegetable oil
¼ cup rice vinegar
1 tablespoon balsamic vinegar
2 tablespoons sugar
1 teaspoon butter or margarine
¾ cup walnuts
2 heads romaine lettuce,
   torn
2 pears, chopped
1 cup asparagus tips*
½ cup crumbled blue cheese
½ cup dried cranberries

WHISK together first 4 ingredients. Cover and chill at least 1 hour.

MELT butter in a skillet over medium heat; add walnuts, and sauté 5 minutes or until lightly browned. Remove walnuts with a slotted spoon.

TOSS together lettuce, pears, asparagus, and toasted walnuts. Sprinkle with cheese and cranberries; drizzle with dressing. **Prep: 15 min., Chill: 1 hr., Cook: 5 min.**

*Substitute 1 cup broccoli florets or 1 cup snow peas, if desired.

CRUNCHY CATFISH

MAKES 4 SERVINGS

> 1 large egg, lightly beaten
> 3 tablespoons Dijon mustard
> 1 tablespoon milk
> ¼ teaspoon pepper
> 4 (4-ounce) fresh catfish fillets*
> ¼ cup all-purpose flour
> 1 cup pretzels, coarsely chopped
> ¼ cup vegetable oil
> Lemon slices (optional)

WHISK together first 4 ingredients. Dredge fish in flour, dip in mustard mixture, and coat with pretzels.

COOK fish, in batches, in hot oil over medium heat 3 to 4 minutes on each side or until golden and fish flakes with a fork. Serve with lemon slices, if desired. **Prep: 20 min., Cook: 8 min. per batch**

*Substitute 4 (4-ounce) frozen catfish fillets, thawed, if desired.

ROSEMARY CHEESE WITH FIG PRESERVES

MAKES 2 CUPS

Get your celebration off to a tasty start with this sweet-and-savory spread. *(pictured on page 264)*

> 1 (8-ounce) package cream cheese, softened
> 1 (3-ounce) log goat cheese, softened
> 1 tablespoon chopped fresh rosemary
> 2 teaspoons honey
> 1 teaspoon coarsely ground pepper
> ¾ cup fig preserves
> Garnish: fresh rosemary sprigs

PROCESS first 5 ingredients in a food processor until smooth, stopping to scrape down sides. Spoon mixture into a lightly greased 1½-cup mold lined with plastic wrap. Cover; chill 2 hours.

INVERT chilled mixture onto a serving dish, and discard plastic wrap. Spoon preserves over cheese. Garnish, if desired. Serve with crackers. **Prep: 10 min., Chill: 2 hrs.**

CHOCOLATE ITALIAN CAKE

MAKES 10 TO 12 SERVINGS

> 5 large eggs, separated
> ½ cup butter, softened
> ½ cup shortening
> 2 cups sugar
> 2¼ cups all-purpose flour
> ¼ cup unsweetened cocoa
> 1 teaspoon baking soda
> 1 cup buttermilk
> 1 cup sweetened flaked coconut
> ⅔ cup finely chopped pecans
> 2 teaspoons vanilla extract
> Chocolate-Cream Cheese Frosting
> Garnish: pecan halves

BEAT egg whites at high speed with an electric mixer until stiff peaks form, and set aside.

BEAT butter and shortening until creamy; gradually add sugar, beating well. Add egg yolks, 1 at a time, beating until blended after each addition.

COMBINE flour, cocoa, and baking soda; add to butter mixture alternately with buttermilk, beginning and ending with flour mixture. Beat at low speed until blended after each addition. Stir in coconut, chopped pecans, and vanilla. Fold in egg whites. Pour batter into 3 greased and floured 8-inch round cakepans.

BAKE at 325° for 25 to 30 minutes or until a wooden pick inserted in center comes out clean. Cool in pans 10 minutes. Remove to wire racks; cool completely.

SPREAD Chocolate-Cream Cheese Frosting between layers and on top and sides of cake. Garnish, if desired. **Prep: 30 min., Bake: 30 min., Cool: 10 min.**

Chocolate-Cream Cheese Frosting:

MAKES 4 CUPS

> 1 (8-ounce) package cream cheese, softened
> ½ cup butter, softened
> 2 teaspoons vanilla extract
> ¼ teaspoon ground cinnamon
> 1 (16-ounce) package powdered sugar
> ¼ cup unsweetened cocoa
> ¼ cup buttermilk
> ⅔ cup finely chopped pecans

BEAT first 4 ingredients at medium speed with an electric mixer until creamy.

COMBINE powdered sugar and cocoa; gradually add to butter mixture alternately with buttermilk, beginning and ending with powdered sugar mixture. Beat at low speed until blended after each addition. Stir in pecans. **Prep: 10 min.**

Salads for the Season

Add a little sparkle to your table this season with these colorful and creamy congealed salads. Made with simple ingredients, they really are more like dessert than salad; maybe that's why we love them so much. We think these recipes add the perfect trimming to any menu and bring a touch of nostalgia from Christmas past.

APRICOT CONGEALED SALAD

MAKES 12 SERVINGS

> 2 (11.5-ounce) cans apricot nectar
> 2 (3-ounce) packages apricot-flavored gelatin
> 1 (15¼-ounce) can apricots, drained and chopped
> 1½ cups buttermilk
> ½ cup apricot preserves
> 1 (8-ounce) container frozen whipped topping, thawed

BRING apricot nectar to a boil in a medium saucepan. Remove from heat; add gelatin, stirring until gelatin dissolves. Cool.

STIR in apricots, buttermilk, and preserves. Fold in whipped topping, and spoon into a lightly greased 9-cup mold. Cover and chill 6 hours or until mixture is firm. **Prep: 15 min., Cook: 5 min., Chill: 6 hrs.**

Tips for Unmolding Congealed Salads

- Lightly spray the inside of your mold with vegetable cooking spray before filling.
- Be sure the salad is firm before unmolding.
- Loosen edges of mold using a small knife.
- Dip bottom of mold in warm water for 15 seconds before unmolding.
- Moisten serving platter with a little water before inverting mold to help gelatin adhere to surface. Invert and gently shake to loosen mold.
- If mold sticks, return to warm water for five more seconds, and try again.

CHRISTMAS RIBBON SALAD

MAKES 12 SERVINGS

We took one of our favorite congealed salads and added cream cheese to make a pretty pink layer.

- 2 (16-ounce) cans pitted dark sweet cherries
- 2 (3-ounce) packages cherry-flavored gelatin
- 1 envelope unflavored gelatin
- 2 cups boiling water
- ⅓ cup sugar
- ½ cup port or sweet red wine
- ¼ cup lemon juice
- 1 (8-ounce) package cream cheese, softened
- ½ cup pecans, chopped and toasted
- Garnishes: whipped cream, fresh cranberries

DRAIN cherries, reserving 1 cup juice. Chop cherries.

STIR together gelatins and 2 cups boiling water until dissolved. Stir in reserved juice, sugar, port, and lemon juice. Stir in cherries.

POUR half of gelatin mixture into a lightly greased 10-cup ring mold or Bundt cake pan. Chill 2 hours or until almost set.

STIR together remaining gelatin mixture, cream cheese, and pecans, blending well. Pour over slightly set gelatin mixture in mold. Cover; chill 6 hours or until firm. Garnish, if desired. **Prep: 20 min., Chill: 8 hrs.**

LIME CONGEALED SALAD

MAKES 8 SERVINGS

- 1 cup milk
- 16 large marshmallows
- 1 (3-ounce) package lime-flavored gelatin*
- 1 (3-ounce) package cream cheese, softened
- 1 (15½-ounce) can crushed pineapple, drained
- ½ cup pecans, chopped and toasted
- 1 cup whipping cream

HEAT milk and marshmallows in a medium saucepan over low heat, stirring until marshmallows melt. Add gelatin, stirring until dissolved.

COMBINE cream cheese, pineapple, and pecans. Stir into gelatin mixture until blended. Let cool completely.

BEAT whipping cream at medium speed with an electric mixer until stiff peaks form. Fold whipped cream into cream cheese mixture, and spoon into a lightly greased 8-cup mold or an 11- x 7-inch baking dish. Chill 6 hours or until firm. **Prep: 15 min., Cook: 5 min., Chill: 6 hrs.**

*Substitute any flavor gelatin, if desired.

MRS. W. W. BRAGG
MCMINNVILLE, TENNESSEE

True Southern Hospitality

Talk to Jane Nackashi, or "Nana," and she'll say, "You're never too old to ask questions." Although she's been cooking for many, many years, Nana says she's still learning about food. Nana, daughter Betty Trad, and granddaughter Denise Trad Wartan share a common denominator—a tremendous love for family, dear friends, traditions, and delicious food.

Betty says what she loves most about the South is the slower, friendlier way of life. "Southerners are a nurturing people who enjoy sharing good food," she says. This Southern family has a special talent for making folks feel right at home with their warm, welcoming ways and fabulous recipes. Friends new and old often request (and sometimes beg) Nana to make specialties from her homeland of Iraq. Treasured dishes include Roasted Leg of Lamb With Port, Buttery Rice With Vermicelli, homemade Tangy Yogurt, and others that we're happy to share with you here.

Thanks to Nana's devotion to family, tradition, and love of cooking, future generations such as great-granddaughters Nora and Madeline will also learn to prepare these tasty, holiday-worthy recipes.

TURKISH-STYLE COFFEE

MAKES 8 CUPS

This strong-flavored coffee gets a fragrant lift from cardamom.

- ¾ cup ground dark roast coffee
- 1 tablespoon ground cardamom
- 8 cups water
- ¾ cup sugar

COMBINE coffee and cardamom in a coffee filter; brew with 8 cups water in a coffeemaker. Stir in sugar; serve immediately. **Prep: 10 min.**

ROASTED LEG OF LAMB WITH PORT

MAKES 8 SERVINGS

- 1 (6-pound) boneless leg of lamb, trimmed
- 6 garlic cloves, pressed
- 1 teaspoon salt
- ½ teaspoon pepper
- ½ teaspoon ground cardamom
- ½ teaspoon ground allspice
- 1 tablespoon vegetable oil
- 1 cup port wine
- 2 cups water
- 1 tablespoon cider vinegar
- 6 (3-inch) cinnamon sticks
- 1 tablespoon whole allspice
- 1 tablespoon all-purpose flour

CUT slits evenly over lamb roast; insert garlic into slits.

COMBINE salt and next 3 ingredients; rub over roast.

COOK roast in hot oil in a Dutch oven over high heat 5 minutes on each side or until browned. Place in a roasting pan; add wine, 2 cups water, and next 3 ingredients.

BAKE at 375° for 1 hour and 15 minutes or until a meat thermometer inserted into thickest portion of roast registers 145°. Let stand 10 minutes before slicing. Reserve pan drippings; remove and discard cinnamon and allspice.

WHISK together pan drippings and flour in a saucepan; cook, whisking constantly, over medium-high heat 7 minutes or until thickened. Spoon over roast. **Prep: 25 min.; Cook: 17 min.; Bake: 1 hr., 15 min.; Stand: 10 min.**

CREAMY CUCUMBER SALAD

MAKES 6 SERVINGS

- 1 cup Tangy Yogurt (see recipe at right) or plain yogurt
- 2 garlic cloves, minced
- 1 tablespoon dried mint
- 1 tablespoon dried parsley
- ½ teaspoon salt
- ¼ teaspoon pepper
- 4 cucumbers, peeled, seeded, and thinly sliced
- Garnish: fresh mint sprig

STIR together first 6 ingredients. Add cucumbers, and toss. Garnish, if desired. **Prep: 10 min.**

BUTTERY RICE WITH VERMICELLI

MAKES 8 SERVINGS

Soaking and scrubbing the rice creates fluffy, nonsticky rice.

- 2 cups uncooked long-grain rice
- ¼ cup butter or margarine
- 2 ounces (about ½ cup) uncooked vermicelli, broken into 2-inch pieces
- 3 cups fat-free chicken broth
- ½ teaspoon salt
- ½ teaspoon pepper
- Almond-Raisin Butter

COMBINE rice and water to cover in a large bowl. Scrub rice with hands; drain. Repeat procedure 4 times or until water is no longer cloudy. Soak rice in water to cover 3 hours; drain.

MELT butter in a 4-quart saucepan over medium-high heat; add pasta, and sauté 5 minutes or until golden.

ADD rice; cook, stirring constantly, 1 minute. Stir in broth, salt, and pepper; bring to a boil. Cover, reduce heat, and simmer 20 minutes. Spoon into a serving dish. Drizzle with Almond-Raisin Butter. **Prep: 10 min., Soak: 3 hrs., Cook: 27 min.**

Almond-Raisin Butter:

MAKES ¾ CUP

- 1 tablespoon butter
- ¼ cup sliced almonds or pine nuts
- ½ cup golden raisins

MELT 1 tablespoon butter in a skillet over medium-high heat. Add almonds; cook, stirring constantly, 5 minutes or until lightly browned. Stir in raisins; remove from heat. **Prep: 5 min., Cook: 5 min.**

TANGY YOGURT

MAKES 4 CUPS

Sample this super-easy homemade yogurt called Leban over baked potatoes, in dips, or alongside spicy, savory meat dishes.

- 1 quart whole milk
- 1 (5-ounce) can evaporated milk
- ½ (8-ounce) container plain yogurt

COOK whole milk in a saucepan over medium heat 10 minutes or just until it begins to boil and candy thermometer registers 190°. (Do not bring to a full boil.) Stir in evaporated milk; remove from heat. Let stand until a candy thermometer registers 150°.

WHISK in yogurt until smooth; cool 10 minutes. Cover and let stand 8 hours. Chill. **Prep: 5 min., Cook: 10 min., Cool: 10 min., Stand: 8 hrs.**

CHEWY ALMOND COOKIES

MAKES 2 DOZEN

These chewy cookies start with a slightly oily dough. Don't worry; they'll bake to just the right texture. Form them into festive shapes by hand before baking.

- 3¾ cups slivered almonds
- 2 egg whites
- ½ cup sugar
- ½ teaspoon ground cardamom
- 1 tablespoon rose water*

PROCESS almonds in a food processor 9 minutes or until a paste forms, stopping to scrape down sides.

BEAT egg whites at medium speed with an electric mixer until stiff peaks form.

COMBINE almond paste, sugar, and cardamom in a bowl, mixing with hands until blended. Add egg whites; knead by hand until smooth and doughlike consistency.

DIP fingers in rose water, and shape dough into 1-inch balls (about 1 tablespoon dough for each cookie). Slightly flatten with thumb, and pinch sides to form star- and diamond-shaped cookies.

Place cookies on an aluminum foil-lined baking sheet.

BAKE on middle rack of oven at 325° for 15 to 20 minutes or until bottoms are lightly browned. Remove cookies immediately to wire racks; cool. **Prep: 25 min., Bake: 20 min. per batch**

*Rose water can be found in Middle-Eastern markets or in health food stores. Substitute water, if desired.

The Easiest Bread

Bread baking came as naturally to Assistant Foods Editor Joy Zacharia as in-line skating on Mount Everest until Rebecca Gordon, one of our Test Kitchens dough divas, came to her rescue. Rebecca assured Joy that her pumpernickel bread recipe would turn Joy into a bread-baking queen. She was right. Not only was it the easiest bread Joy's ever made, but it's also one of the most delicious our Foods staff has ever tasted.

PUMPERNICKEL BREAD

MAKES 1 LOAF

You'll need a heavy-duty electric stand mixer such as a KitchenAid to prepare this dough, but after that's done, the rest is simple.

- **1¾ cups warm water (100° to 110°)**
- **1 (¼-ounce) envelope active dry yeast**
- **2 tablespoons sugar**
- **2 tablespoons instant coffee granules**
- **¼ cup molasses**
- **4½ cups bread flour**
- **1 cup rye flour**
- **2 teaspoons salt**
- **Vegetable cooking spray**
- **2 tablespoons butter or margarine, melted**

PREHEAT oven to 200°. Stir together first 3 ingredients in the mixing bowl of a heavy-duty electric stand mixer. Let stand 5 minutes.

ADD coffee and next 4 ingredients to yeast mixture. Beat at low speed with dough hook attachment for 1 minute or until soft dough comes together. Beat at medium speed 4 minutes. (Dough will be slightly sticky.)

TURN dough out onto a lightly floured surface; shape dough into a 9- x 5-inch oval loaf. Place on a parchment paper-lined baking sheet; coat lightly with cooking spray, and cover loosely with plastic wrap. Turn oven off, and place loaf in oven. Let rise 30 minutes or until loaf is doubled in bulk. Remove loaf from oven. Remove and discard plastic wrap. Preheat oven to 375°.

BAKE bread for 30 to 35 minutes. Remove from oven; brush with melted butter. Cool on a wire rack. **Prep: 20 min., Stand: 5 min., Rise: 30 min., Bake: 35 min.**

GERMAN-STYLE PUMPERNICKEL ROLLS (MAKES 25 ROLLS): Pat dough into a 10-inch square (½ inch thick). Cut into 2-inch squares. Roll into 1½-inch balls, and place on a parchment paper-lined baking sheet. Proceed with recipe as directed. Bake at 375° for 10 to 12 minutes or until lightly browned.

GERMAN-STYLE PUMPERNICKEL ROLLS WITH CARAWAY: Follow instructions for German-Style Pumpernickel Rolls, adding 1 tablespoon caraway seeds. Proceed with recipe as directed.

WALNUT-RAISIN PUMPERNICKEL BOULE (MAKES 1 LOAF): Add ¾ cup raisins (or golden raisins) and 1 cup coarsely chopped toasted walnuts to dough before mixing. Shape dough into a ball, and gently flatten into a 7-inch circle. Cut 3 slits in dough (¼ to ½ inch deep) with a sharp paring knife just before baking, if desired. Whisk together 1 egg white and 3 tablespoons water in a small bowl; brush loaf with egg mixture. Bake at 375° for 38 minutes or until a wooden pick inserted in center comes out clean. Omit brushing with melted butter.

SOUR-RYE PUMPERNICKEL BREAD: Reduce water to 1 cup. Add 2 tablespoons browning-and-seasoning sauce and 1 cup Sour Starter to dough; mix with dough hook attachment at medium-high speed with a heavy-duty stand mixer 5 minutes. Proceed with recipe as directed.

NOTE: For testing purposes only, we used Kitchen Bouquet sauce.

Sour Starter:

MAKES ABOUT 12 CUPS

This gives the bold bread a subtle tangy flavor.

- **3½ cups bread flour**
- **1 cup rye flour**
- **8 cups water**
- **1 (¼-ounce) envelope active dry yeast**

WHISK together all ingredients in a large bowl. Cover tightly with plastic wrap. Store at room temperature. You may use after 1 day at room temperature.

ADD 1 cup warm water, 1 cup bread flour, and ½ cup rye flour every other day. Discard remaining Sour Starter if you don't intend to use it after a few days. **Prep: 5 min.**

NOTE: Sourdough starters may be stored at room temperature indefinitely, as long as you "feed" the starter with water and flour. In fact, some sourdough starters are more than 20 years old.

Soups for Show-and-Tell

Showing off the presents that you bought can be as much fun as shopping for them, and wrapping them with friends is the bow on top. For the easiest entertaining ever, put on a pot of one of these soups tonight and serve with biscuits or cornbread. You can do much of the preparation a day or two ahead, freeing your time before the party to get your gift wrapping supplies ready. To continue the festive theme on your tabletop, set out colorful mugs and bowls, and use gift wrap and bows as table decor.

Now go call your friends and invite them over for a party that celebrates the season with great food, show-and-tell, and gift wrapping.

CARROT-AND-LEEK SOUP

MAKES 8 SERVINGS

> 4 large leeks, cleaned and sliced
> 1 small onion, chopped
> 3 garlic cloves, chopped
> 1 tablespoon olive oil
> 3 (1-pound) packages baby carrots
> 2 (32-ounce) containers chicken broth
> ½ teaspoon salt
> ¼ teaspoon pepper
> ¼ teaspoon dried thyme
> 1 cup half-and-half

REMOVE and discard green tops from leeks; cut white portions into slices, and set aside.
SAUTÉ chopped onion and chopped garlic in hot olive oil in a large Dutch oven over medium heat just until tender. Do not brown.
STIR in leeks, carrots, and next 3 ingredients. Bring to a boil. Reduce heat and simmer, stirring occasionally, 25 minutes or until vegetables are tender.

STIR in thyme. Remove from heat, and let cool 10 minutes.
PROCESS carrot mixture, in 2 or 3 batches, in a food processor or with a hand emulsion blender until smooth.
RETURN carrot mixture to Dutch oven, and add half-and-half. Heat over low heat until warm. **Prep: 15 min., Cook: 35 min., Cool: 10 min.**

LAURA HURST
ATLANTA, GEORGIA

WHITE CHRISTMAS CHILI

MAKES 6 TO 8 SERVINGS

Try this chicken-and-white bean version of the beef-and-red bean classic for a variation on a winter favorite. *(pictured on page 265)*

> 4 skinned and boned chicken breast halves
> 5 cups water
> 1 large onion, chopped and divided
> 2 tablespoons butter or margarine
> 2 celery ribs, chopped (about ⅓ cup)
> 3 (16-ounce) cans great Northern beans, rinsed, drained, and divided
> 3 (4.5-ounce) cans chopped green chiles
> 1 cup canned chicken broth
> 1 teaspoon ground cumin
> 1 bay leaf
> 1 teaspoon salt
> ⅛ teaspoon ground red pepper
> 1 tablespoon chopped fresh cilantro
> Toppings: tortilla chips, shredded colby-Jack cheese, salsa, sour cream

PLACE chicken, 5 cups water, and half of onion in a large Dutch oven over medium-high heat, and cook 15 to 18 minutes or until chicken is tender. Remove chicken, reserving broth in Dutch oven. Cut chicken into bite-size pieces; set aside.
MELT butter in a skillet; add celery and remaining onion, and sauté until tender. Stir chicken, celery mixture, 2 cans beans, and next 6 ingredients into broth in Dutch oven, and bring to a boil. Reduce heat to medium-low, and cook 1

hour, stirring frequently, until thickened. Process remaining 1 can beans in a blender until smooth, stopping to scrape down sides. Stir bean puree into chili.
REMOVE and discard bay leaf; stir in cilantro just before serving with desired toppings. **Prep: 10 min.; Cook: 1 hr., 30 min.**

CHEESE-GARLIC BISCUITS

MAKES 2 DOZEN

> 4 cups all-purpose baking mix
> 1⅓ cups milk
> 1 cup (4 ounces) shredded Cheddar cheese
> ½ cup butter or margarine, melted
> 1 tablespoon minced fresh parsley
> 1 teaspoon garlic powder

STIR together baking mix, milk, and shredded Cheddar cheese until a soft dough forms.
DROP by heaping tablespoonfuls onto a lightly greased baking sheet.
BAKE at 450° for 6 to 8 minutes or until golden.
STIR together melted butter, minced parsley, and garlic powder; brush over warm biscuits. **Prep: 10 min., Bake: 8 min.**

SUPER-MOIST CORNBREAD

MAKES 6 TO 8 SERVINGS

> 2 cups self-rising cornmeal
> 2 cups buttermilk
> 1 large egg
> 1 tablespoon sugar
> ⅓ cup butter

STIR together first 4 ingredients in a large bowl.
MELT butter in an 8-inch cast-iron skillet in a 425° oven 5 minutes. Tilt skillet to coat evenly with butter.
POUR cornbread batter into buttered skillet.
BAKE at 425° for 25 minutes or until golden. Remove cornbread immediately from skillet, and let cool. **Prep: 5 min., Bake: 25 min.**

Citrus Batida, page 274

Winter Fruit-and-Cucumber Salad, page 274

Slow-Roasted Pork, page 274; Caribbean Rice and Peas, page 275

Dijon Rack of Lamb, page 276

Cornbread Dressing, page 249

Bluegrass Salad, page 255

Rosemary Cheese With Fig Preserves,
page 256

White Christmas Chili, page 260

Holiday Ham Sandwiches, page 286

Sugar-and-Spice Cured Turkey,
Crabmeat-and-Oyster Dressing, page 243

Brussels Sprouts With Apples, page 243

Elegant Pumpkin-Walnut Layered Pie, page 244

Layered Brownies, page 252

Celebrate With Tradition

Rosalie Gaziano and her husband, Dom, share an Italian ancestry, so food as well as love has always been an integral part of the lifestyle in their Charleston, West Virginia, home.

Rosalie offers this delicious, hearty menu, which is great for a busy weeknight any time of the year.

A Taste of Italy

Serves 6 to 8

Caponata alla Siciliana

Hearty Chicken Cacciatore

Caesar Salad

CAPONATA ALLA SICILIANA

MAKES 8 SERVINGS

This sweet-and-tart eggplant appetizer can be frozen for up to three months.

- 2 medium eggplants, cut into 1-inch cubes
- ¼ cup olive oil
- 2 medium onions, sliced
- 2 tablespoons olive oil
- 1 (14½-ounce) can diced tomatoes, undrained
- 1 cup diced celery (about 3 ribs)
- ½ cup pimiento-stuffed olives
- 1 (2½-ounce) can sliced ripe olives, drained
- 2 tablespoons capers, drained
- 1 tablespoon pine nuts
- ½ cup red wine vinegar
- 3 tablespoons sugar
- ½ teaspoon salt
- ¼ teaspoon pepper
- Pita chips or toasted bread rounds

SAUTÉ eggplants in ¼ cup hot oil in a Dutch oven over medium-high heat for 10 minutes or until tender and slightly brown. Remove eggplant, and set aside.
SAUTÉ onions in 2 tablespoons olive oil in Dutch oven over medium heat 5 minutes or until golden. Add tomatoes and celery; simmer, stirring occasionally, 15 minutes or until celery is tender. Stir in olives, capers, and pine nuts. Return eggplant to Dutch oven.
STIR red wine vinegar, sugar, salt, and pepper into eggplant mixture. Cover and simmer, stirring occasionally, 30 minutes. Cool. Cover and chill 8 hours. Remove from refrigerator 30 minutes before serving. Serve with pita chips or toasted bread rounds. **Prep: 20 min., Cook: 1 hr., Chill: 8 hrs., Stand: 30 min.**

HEARTY CHICKEN CACCIATORE

MAKES 6 TO 8 SERVINGS

- 1 (3½-pound) package chicken pieces
- 1½ teaspoons salt, divided
- ½ teaspoon pepper, divided
- 1 tablespoon olive oil
- 1 medium onion, chopped
- 1 garlic clove, minced
- 1 (28-ounce) can diced tomatoes
- 1 (6-ounce) can tomato paste
- ½ cup chicken broth
- 1 green bell pepper, sliced
- 1 teaspoon dried oregano
- 1 teaspoon dried basil
- 2 (8-ounce) packages sliced fresh mushrooms
- 1 cup dry red wine
- 1 (16-ounce) package linguine, cooked

SPRINKLE chicken with ½ teaspoon salt and ¼ teaspoon pepper.
BROWN chicken pieces in hot oil in a large skillet over medium-high heat; remove chicken, and set aside.
ADD onion to skillet; sauté 5 minutes over medium heat, or until transparent.
ADD minced garlic; sauté 1 minute. Stir in tomatoes, tomato paste, and chicken broth. Add bell pepper, oregano, basil, and remaining salt and pepper.
RETURN chicken to skillet; cover and simmer over medium-low heat 45 minutes or until chicken is tender. Add mushrooms and wine; cook, uncovered, 40 minutes. Serve with hot cooked linguine. **Prep: 25 min.; Cook: 1 hr., 35 min.**

CAESAR SALAD

MAKES 8 SERVINGS

- 1 head romaine lettuce, torn
- ½ head iceberg lettuce, torn
- ¼ cup egg substitute
- 3 tablespoons olive oil
- 1 garlic clove, minced
- 1 tablespoon lemon juice
- ½ to 1 teaspoon salt
- ½ teaspoon coarsely ground pepper
- ½ teaspoon Dijon mustard
- 1 (2-ounce) can anchovy fillets, drained (optional)
- 1 cup croutons
- ¼ cup (1 ounce) shredded Parmesan cheese

PLACE lettuces in a large bowl.
PROCESS egg substitute, next 6 ingredients, and, if desired, anchovies in a blender. Drizzle dressing over lettuce, tossing well. Sprinkle with croutons and Parmesan cheese. **Prep: 15 min.**

SPICED AFTER-DINNER COFFEE

MAKES 8 SERVINGS

"The door is always open at our house, with one more person coming through," Rosalie says. This coffee is a great way to welcome them.

- 8 cups brewed dark roast coffee
- 1 cup sugar
- 2 teaspoons whole cloves (about 38)
- 5 (3-inch) cinnamon sticks
- ⅔ cup amaretto liqueur
- Whipped cream
- Orange rind strips

HEAT first 4 ingredients in a saucepan over low heat 10 minutes. (Do not boil.) Stir in amaretto. Remove and discard cloves and cinnamon. Pour into mugs; serve with whipped cream and orange rind strips. Place a strip of orange rind on rim of each cup, if desired. **Prep: 5 min., Cook: 10 min.**

AMARETTI COOKIES

MAKES 50 COOKIES

- 1 pound slivered almonds
- 2 cups powdered sugar
- 2 teaspoons vanilla extract
- 2 egg whites

PROCESS almonds in 2 batches in a food processor or blender until finely ground. Combine ground almonds, powdered sugar, and vanilla in a medium bowl, using hands to mix. Stir in egg whites. (Dough will be sticky.) Drop by teaspoonfuls onto lightly greased baking sheets.
BAKE at 350° for 15 to 20 minutes or until lightly browned. **Prep: 20 min., Bake: 20 min. per batch**

Turkey Two Ways

Chuck Behnke of Peachtree City, Georgia, prepares an outstanding Hickory-Smoked Bourbon Turkey. "The sweetness of maple syrup combined with bourbon offers a subtle but smoky flavor," Chuck says. For a deliciously different flavor, try Citrus-Rosemary Turkey Breast. It's perfect for a smaller family.

CITRUS-ROSEMARY TURKEY BREAST

MAKES 8 SERVINGS

- 3 tablespoons butter, softened and divided
- 3 garlic cloves, minced
- 1 (6-pound) bone-in turkey breast
- 1 teaspoon salt
- 1 teaspoon pepper
- 1 large orange, sliced
- 1 large lemon, sliced
- 4 fresh rosemary sprigs
- 4 fresh sage leaves
- 1 teaspoon seasoned pepper
- 1 onion, quartered
- 2 cups chicken broth

STIR together 2 tablespoons butter and garlic. Loosen skin from turkey without detaching it; sprinkle salt and pepper under skin. Rub 2 tablespoons garlic mixture over meat. Place fruit slices, rosemary, and sage under skin; replace skin.
RUB remaining 1 tablespoon butter over skin; sprinkle with 1 teaspoon seasoned pepper. Place turkey breast on a lightly greased rack in a broiler pan. Add onion and chicken broth.
BAKE at 350° for 1 hour and 30 minutes, basting every 30 minutes. Shield with foil, and bake 1 more hour or until a meat thermometer inserted into thickest breast portion registers 170°. Let stand 10 minutes before slicing. Serve with pan juices. **Prep: 20 min.; Bake: 2 hrs., 30 min.; Stand: 10 min.**

HICKORY-SMOKED BOURBON TURKEY

MAKES 12 TO 14 SERVINGS

We gave this recipe our highest rating.

- 1 (11-pound) frozen whole turkey, thawed
- 2 cups maple syrup
- 1 cup bourbon
- 1 tablespoon pickling spice
- Hickory wood chunks
- 1 large carrot, scraped
- 1 celery rib
- 1 medium onion, peeled and halved
- 1 lemon
- 1 tablespoon salt
- 2 teaspoons pepper

REMOVE giblets and neck from turkey; reserve for other uses, if desired. Rinse turkey thoroughly with cold water, and pat dry.
ADD water to a large stockpot, filling half full; stir in maple syrup, bourbon, and pickling spice. Add turkey and, if needed, additional water to cover. Cover and chill turkey 2 days.
SOAK hickory wood chunks in fresh water at least 30 minutes. Prepare charcoal fire in smoker; let fire burn 20 to 30 minutes.
REMOVE turkey from water, discarding water mixture; pat dry. Cut carrot and celery in half crosswise. Stuff cavity with carrot, celery, and onion. Pierce lemon with a fork; place in neck cavity.
COMBINE salt and pepper; rub mixture over turkey. Fold wings under, and tie legs together with string, if desired.
DRAIN wood chunks, and place on coals. Place water pan in smoker, and add water to depth of fill line. Place turkey in center of lower food rack; cover with smoker lid.
COOK 6 hours or until a meat thermometer inserted into thickest portion of turkey thigh registers 180°, adding additional water, charcoal, and wood chunks as needed. Remove from smoker, and let stand 15 minutes before slicing. Garnish, if desired. **Prep: 30 min., Chill: 48 hrs., Soak: 30 min., Cook: 6 hrs., Stand: 15 min.**

Sustaining a Southern Heritage

This transplanted Texan explores her cultural and culinary roots during the holidays.

Soul Food Supper

Serves 4 to 6

Down-Home Chicken and Onions

Hoppin' John   Fried Cabbage

Chocolate Quad

When Monique Wells followed her dream of living in Paris, France, the last thing the Houston native thought she'd miss was home, let alone the food of her childhood. However, after having "wallowed in the wealth of French cuisine for several months," Monique had a revealing experience.

Ten years later, she clearly remembers that defining day. "I woke up one morning and realized that I didn't want a croissant for breakfast. What I wanted was grits. In that moment my mind was flooded with memories of food from home, such as fresh biscuits and cane syrup," she says.

Monique decided to turn her longing for home into an opportunity to connect with others. She was one of the first members of a group of African-American women in France called SISTERS. Started as a vehicle to discuss life in Paris from shared perspectives, the meetings inevitably turned to reminiscences of food. She began to work on a collection of recipes, and in 2000, Monique published *Food for the Soul,* a collection of Southern, largely soul food, recipes.

Monique realizes that our Southernness is always connected to the foods we ate as a child—good or bad. "Fortunately, mine are great memories," says Monique with a smile. "Food and family are the essence of life. As long as one takes meals with one's family, the two are irrevocably intertwined."

DOWN-HOME CHICKEN AND ONIONS

MAKES 4 TO 6 SERVINGS

- 2½ **pounds chicken legs, wings, and thighs**
- 1 **teaspoon salt**
- 1 **teaspoon pepper**
- 1 **teaspoon seasoned salt (optional)**
- 3 **tablespoons butter or margarine**
- 2 **large onions, halved and sliced**
- ½ **cup water**
- **Hot cooked rice**

SPRINKLE chicken evenly with salt, pepper, and, if desired, seasoned salt.

MELT butter in a large skillet over medium heat. Add chicken pieces, and cook 5 minutes on each side or until browned. Remove chicken; keep warm.

ADD onions to skillet, and sauté 10 minutes or until tender. Return chicken to skillet; stir in ½ cup water, cover, and simmer, stirring occasionally, 30 minutes or until sauce thickens and chicken is done. Serve over hot cooked rice. **Prep: 10 min., Cook: 50 min.**

HOPPIN' JOHN

MAKES 8 TO 10 SERVINGS

- 1 **(16-ounce) package dried black-eyed peas**
- 2 **large ham hocks (about ¾ pound)**
- 2 **tablespoons bacon drippings**
- 4 **cups water**
- 1 **large onion, cut into wedges**
- 1 **teaspoon salt**
- 1 **teaspoon black pepper**
- ½ **to 1 teaspoon dried crushed red pepper**
- ½ **teaspoon dried thyme**
- 2 **bay leaves**
- 1 **teaspoon minced garlic**
- 1 **chicken bouillon cube**
- **Hot cooked white rice**

BRING dried black-eyed peas and water to cover to a boil in a Dutch oven; remove from heat, and let stand 1 hour. Drain.

REMOVE skin from ham hocks. Chop meat from ham hocks, reserving bones. Sauté meat in hot bacon drippings in a large skillet over medium-high heat 3 minutes or until slightly browned.

COMBINE peas, meat, bones, 4 cups water, and next 8 ingredients in Dutch oven. Bring to a boil; reduce heat and simmer, gently stirring occasionally, 1 to 1½ hours or until peas are tender. Remove and discard bones and bay leaves. Serve over rice. **Prep: 20 min.; Stand: 1 hr.; Cook: 1 hr., 35 min.**

The Festive Flavor of Chestnuts

They're good for more than roasting over an open fire—their delicate sweetness and hearty texture add the perfect touch to these holiday recipes from Delaware growers.

FRIED CABBAGE

MAKES 4 TO 6 SERVINGS

4 bacon slices
1 large cabbage, coarsely chopped
1 teaspoon salt
1 teaspoon pepper

COOK bacon in a large skillet 10 minutes or until crisp. Remove bacon, and drain on paper towels, reserving 1 tablespoon drippings in skillet. Crumble bacon.
ADD cabbage to hot drippings in skillet; sprinkle with salt and pepper. Sauté cabbage over medium-high heat 10 to 12 minutes or until tender. Sprinkle with bacon. **Prep: 10 min., Cook: 22 min.**

CHOCOLATE QUAD

MAKES 12 TO 15 SERVINGS

½ cup butter or margarine, cut up
1 cup all-purpose flour
1 cup chopped pecans
1 (8-ounce) package cream cheese, softened
½ cup powdered sugar
1 (12-ounce) container frozen whipped topping, thawed and divided
3 (3.5-ounce) packages chocolate instant pudding mix
3 cups milk

CUT butter into flour with a pastry blender or fork until mixture resembles coarse meal. Stir in pecans. Press mixture onto bottom of a 13- x 9-inch pan.
BAKE at 350° for 15 minutes or until lightly browned. Cool.
BEAT cream cheese, powdered sugar, and 1 cup whipped topping at medium speed with an electric mixer until smooth. Spread mixture over prepared crust.
WHISK together pudding mix and milk 2 minutes or until smooth. Spread over cream cheese mixture. Chill 10 minutes. Spread remaining whipped topping over pudding mixture. Cover and chill at least 1 hour. Cut into squares. **Prep: 20 min.; Bake: 15 min.; Chill: 1 hr., 10 min.**

C hestnuts were once a staple on holiday tables throughout the Upper South. But that changed about 80 years ago, when a blight destroyed most of the nation's chestnut trees.

Nancy Petitt and her husband, Gary, are part of only a handful of commercial chestnut growers in the South. "In the South we tend to grow a Chinese variety, which is a little sweeter and easier to peel than European types," says Nancy.

There are a number of ways to prepare chestnuts, but roasting, which makes for a rich and creamy texture, is perhaps the best-known method. These delicious recipes are a few of Nancy and Gary's favorites. We hope you and your family enjoy them too.

BRAISED CHESTNUTS

MAKES 4 SERVINGS (ABOUT 2 CUPS)

2 tablespoons butter or margarine
1 medium onion, finely chopped
1 cup dry red wine or port
3 cups chicken broth
1 pound whole chestnuts, shelled (about 2½ to 3 cups nut meat)
1 tablespoon chopped fresh thyme
⅛ teaspoon salt
¼ teaspoon pepper

MELT butter in a Dutch oven over medium heat; add onion, and sauté 10 minutes or until tender and slightly browned. Add wine, and bring to a boil; cook, stirring occasionally, 1 minute.
ADD broth and remaining ingredients; reduce heat to medium-low, cover, and simmer 1 hour or until chestnuts are tender and liquid is almost absorbed. **Prep: 45 min.; Cook: 1 hr., 15 min.**

CHESTNUT SOUP

MAKES 10 CUPS

1 leek
3 tablespoons butter or margarine, divided
2 Macintosh apples, peeled and chopped
2 celery ribs, chopped
1 small onion, thinly sliced
1 bay leaf
1 thyme sprig
1 teaspoon salt
⅛ teaspoon ground nutmeg
2 (32-ounce) containers chicken broth
¾ pound whole chestnuts, shelled (about 2 cups nut meat)
1 cup whipping cream or half-and-half
2 tablespoons all-purpose flour
Toppings: sour cream, grated fresh nutmeg (optional)

REMOVE root, tough outer leaves, and tops from leek, leaving 2 inches of dark leaves. Cut into quarters lengthwise. Thinly slice leek; rinse well, and drain.
MELT 1 tablespoon butter in a medium saucepan over medium heat. Add leek, apples, celery, and onion; sauté 5 minutes. Add bay leaf and next 3 ingredients; sauté 8 to 12 minutes or until apples and vegetables are tender.
STIR in chicken broth and chestnuts. Bring to a boil; reduce heat, and simmer 1 hour or until chestnuts are tender. Stir in cream. Discard bay leaf.
PROCESS leek mixture, in batches, in a food processor or blender until smooth. Return mixture to saucepan.
MELT remaining 2 tablespoons butter in a small skillet. Stir in flour until smooth; cook, stirring constantly, 2 to 3 minutes. Add flour mixture to pureed mixture. Bring to a boil; reduce heat, and simmer 3 to 5 minutes or until thickened. Serve warm. Top with sour cream and grated fresh nutmeg, if desired. **Prep: 45 min.; Cook: 1 hr., 25 min.**

Cook's Notes

Use this handy information when cooking with or purchasing chestnuts.

- 1 pound fresh, unpeeled chestnuts yields about 3 cups of nut meat.
- 1 pound dried (which are always peeled) equals about 3 pounds fresh, unpeeled. Dried chestnuts are reconstituted in liquid.
- Store fresh chestnuts in a plastic bag in the freezer or in the crisper of the refrigerator.

For more information or to order chestnuts, call (302) 659-1731, or visit the Petitts' Web site **www.delmarvelouschestnuts. com** or **www.buychestnuts.com**

How to Prepare a Chestnut

Here are Nancy and Gary's tips to make peeling chestnuts easier.

- Cut an "X" on the flat side of the nut using a serrated knife, making sure you cut all the way through the shell. This keeps the shell from bursting.

Roasting

- *Fireplace*—Use a long-handled chestnut roasting pan or a fireplace popcorn basket. Allow enough room for the chestnuts to roast on all sides. Hold the pan just above the flame, and shake as if you are making popcorn. Cook about 15 minutes or until the outside shells are black. Remove nuts from pan, and allow to cool before peeling.
- *Oven*—Place nuts in a single layer in an ovenproof baking dish. Bake at 325° for about 20 minutes. Remove nuts from pan, and allow to cool before peeling.
- *Cooktop*—Place nuts in a single layer in a large, heavy skillet (preferably cast iron). Cook over medium-high heat, shaking the pan occasionally, for 15 minutes or until shells darken. Remove nuts from pan, and cool before peeling.

Boiling

- Combine chestnuts and lightly salted water to cover in a large saucepan; bring to a boil over medium heat. Drain immediately, and allow to cool before peeling.

Microwave

- Place chestnuts around the outer edge of a paper plate, and cook at HIGH in 15-second intervals until shells are soft. Cool before peeling.

CHOCOLATE-CHESTNUT PASTRIES

MAKES 8 SERVINGS

- 1 (10-ounce) package frozen puff pastry shells, thawed
- ½ pound whole chestnuts, shelled (about 1⅓ cups nut meat)
- 1 cup sugar
- 1 cup milk
- 1 (4-ounce) semisweet chocolate baking bar, coarsely chopped
- 2 tablespoons rum or brandy
- 1¼ cups whipping cream
- Garnishes: chocolate shavings, chocolate syrup

PREPARE pastry shells according to package directions; set aside.
BRING chestnuts, sugar, and milk to a boil in a small saucepan, stirring until sugar dissolves; reduce heat, and simmer 30 minutes or until chestnuts are tender and mixture thickens.
MICROWAVE chocolate in a glass bowl at HIGH 30 seconds to 1 minute or until melted, stirring once.
REMOVE chestnut mixture from heat. Stir in melted chocolate and rum.
PROCESS chestnut mixture, in batches, in a food processor until smooth, stopping to scrape down sides. Cool mixture completely.
BEAT cream at medium speed with an electric mixer until soft peaks form. Gently fold whipped cream into chestnut mixture. (Mixture will be soft.) Cover and chill at least 1 hour.
SPOON mixture into prepared pastry shells. Garnish, if desired. **Prep: 40 min., Cook: 31 min., Chill: 1 hr.**

Go Casual on Christmas Eve

Serve Caribbean- and African-inspired dishes before Santa arrives this year.

Casual Christmas Eve Supper

Serves 6 to 8

Citrus Batida

Slow-Roasted Pork

Winter Fruit-and-Cucumber Salad

Rutabaga-Carrot Mash   Caribbean Rice and Peas

Sweet Potato Crème Brûlée

Treat your family and your close friends to dishes with Caribbean and African flavors. Ordinary ingredients such as pork, rice, and citrus fruit are seasoned with pantry staples and easy-to-find ingredients such as chili powder, allspice, and coconut milk. Chef Marvin Woods of Hollywood Prime in Hollywood, Florida, contributed several of his wonderful recipes for this holiday menu, which is great for a laid-back Christmas Eve gathering. Each recipe is perfect to serve buffet style and easy to eat with a fork while balancing a plate on your lap. So fill your plate, find a comfy chair, and be joyful.

CITRUS BATIDA

MAKES 5 CUPS

Let guests man the blender for this festive beverage. Premeasure ingredients into one-batch containers, and chill. When you're ready for another round, all you have to do is pour it into the blender, and push the button. (*pictured on page 261*)

  2 cups orange juice
  2 cups Ruby Red grapefruit juice
  ⅔ cup fresh lemon juice
  ¾ cup superfine sugar
  1 cup rum

PROCESS all ingredients in a blender until frothy. Serve over ice. **Prep: 5 min.**

SLOW-ROASTED PORK

MAKES 8 SERVINGS

Serve shredded pork over Caribbean Rice and Peas. (*pictured on page 261*)

  1 medium onion, finely chopped
  4 garlic cloves, peeled and crushed
  ½ cup fresh orange juice
  ½ cup fresh grapefruit juice
  ⅓ cup fresh lemon juice
  2 tablespoons brown sugar
  3 bay leaves, crumbled
  2 teaspoons salt
  2 teaspoons chili powder
  1 teaspoon ground allspice
  1 teaspoon ground pepper
  1 (5- to 6-pound) Boston butt pork
      roast or pork shoulder
  1 tablespoon vegetable oil
  Garnishes: lemon slices, grated lemon
      rind, parsley sprigs

COMBINE first 11 ingredients in a bowl. Add pork roast, turning to coat with marinade. Cover; chill at least 4 hours. Remove roast from marinade, reserving marinade. Brown all sides of roast in hot oil in a Dutch oven. Add reserved marinade. **BAKE,** covered, at 275° for 6 to 7 hours or until meat can be shredded. Garnish, if desired. **Prep: 15 min., Chill: 4 hrs., Cook: 7 hrs.**

MARVIN WOODS
HOLLYWOOD, FLORIDA

WINTER FRUIT-AND-CUCUMBER SALAD

MAKES 6 TO 8 SERVINGS

Sweet orange and tangy grapefruit brighten this colorful salad. (*pictured on page 261*)

  1 or 2 bunches Red Leaf lettuce, torn
  2 medium navel oranges, peeled and
      sectioned
  1 medium Ruby Red grapefruit, peeled
      and sectioned
  1 seedless cucumber, scored and
      sliced
  1 small red onion, thinly sliced
  1 green onion, thinly sliced
  Basil Vinaigrette

holiday dinners

TOSS first 6 ingredients in a large bowl; serve with Basil Vinaigrette. **Prep: 15 min.**

Basil Vinaigrette:
MAKES ABOUT ¾ CUP

- ½ cup olive oil
- ¼ cup red wine vinegar
- 2 tablespoons fresh lemon juice
- 1 tablespoon sugar
- ¾ teaspoon dried basil leaves or
    1 tablespoon chopped fresh basil
- ½ teaspoon salt

WHISK together all ingredients in a bowl until blended. Cover and chill at least 30 minutes. **Prep: 5 min., Chill: 30 min.**

NORA HENSHAW
OKEMAH, OKLAHOMA

RUTABAGA-CARROT MASH

MAKES 8 TO 10 SERVINGS

Marvin's specialty is Caribbean cooking, but this recipe respects his Carolina roots. Rutabagas look similar to turnips, but they're actually in the cabbage family. Choose ones that are heavy for their size and firm to the touch.

- 2 medium rutabagas, peeled and chopped
- 4 carrots, peeled and chopped (about 2 cups)
- 1 sweet onion, peeled and quartered
- ½ cup butter or margarine
- 1 (10-ounce) can chicken broth
- 1 teaspoon salt
- ½ teaspoon pepper

COOK rutabagas in boiling water to cover in a Dutch oven over medium heat 20 minutes. Add carrots and onion; continue boiling 20 minutes or until vegetables are tender. Drain and place into food processor fitted with a metal blade. Add butter and remaining ingredients; process until smooth. Serve immediately. **Prep: 15 min., Cook: 40 min.**

MARVIN WOODS
HOLLYWOOD, FLORIDA

CARIBBEAN RICE AND PEAS

MAKES 8 TO 10 SERVINGS

Pigeon peas, nicknamed no-eyed peas, are of African origin. They're yellow-gray in color and about the size of green peas. *(pictured on page 261)*

- 1 small onion, finely chopped
- 2 garlic cloves, pressed
- 1 tablespoon olive oil
- 2 cups basmati rice
- 2½ cups water
- 1 (10-ounce) can chicken broth
- ½ cup unsweetened coconut milk
- 1 (15-ounce) can pigeon peas, rinsed and drained*
- 1 tablespoon chopped fresh parsley
- 2 teaspoons grated lemon rind
- 1 teaspoon salt
- Garnish: fresh parsley sprigs

SAUTÉ onion and garlic in hot oil in a Dutch oven over medium-high heat 1 to 2 minutes or until translucent.
ADD rice and next 3 ingredients; bring to a boil. Cover, reduce heat, and simmer 25 minutes or until liquid is absorbed and rice is tender. Stir in peas, parsley, lemon rind, and salt. Garnish, if desired. **Prep: 10 min., Cook: 30 min.**

*Substitute 1 (15-ounce) can field peas, if desired.

MARVIN WOODS
HOLLYWOOD, FLORIDA

SWEET POTATO CRÈME BRÛLÉE

MAKES 8 TO 10 SERVINGS

A French dessert gets a Southern accent in this sinful dessert.

- 2 medium sweet potatoes, baked, skinned, and mashed
- ¼ cup firmly packed brown sugar
- 1 tablespoon fresh lemon juice
- 1 quart whipping cream
- 1 cup granulated sugar
- 8 large egg yolks
- 1 tablespoon vanilla extract
- ⅓ cup firmly packed brown sugar
- Garnish: chopped toasted pecans

COMBINE mashed sweet potatoes, ¼ cup brown sugar, and lemon juice; spoon potato mixture into a buttered 10-inch quiche dish to form a ¼-inch-thick layer.
STIR together cream, 1 cup sugar, egg yolks, and vanilla in a medium saucepan. Cook mixture over low heat, stirring constantly, about 5 minutes or until hot.
POUR over sweet potato mixture in prepared dish. Place dish in a shallow baking pan. Add hot water to pan to a depth of 1 inch.
BAKE at 325° for 1 hour or until a knife inserted in center comes out almost clean. Remove from water. Cool on a wire rack. Cover and chill at least 8 hours.
SPRINKLE custard with ⅓ cup brown sugar; place custard on jellyroll pan. Broil 5½ inches from heat about 2 minutes or until sugar melts. Let stand 5 minutes to allow sugar to harden before serving. Garnish, if desired. **Prep: 20 min., Cook: 5 min., Bake: 1 hr., Chill: 8 hrs., Broil: 2 min., Stand: 5 min.**

MARVIN WOODS
HOLLYWOOD, FLORIDA

All Hands in the Kitchen

This cook spices up relationships while he serves dinner.

Cooking With Friends

Serves 6 to 8

Dijon Rack of Lamb   Cranberry Relish

Gratin Potatoes   Braised Red Cabbage

Chocolate Mousse

When people cook together, they form special bonds. Laughter and fun become part of the menu amid the chopping, peeling, stirring, and tasting. Whether you're planning an intimate dinner for two or a large gathering, be sure to do what this cook does: Bring all hands in the kitchen.

Jacques Haeringer, chef and author of *Two for Tonight*, feels the preparation of food is an act of love. "Most of our memorable moments are celebrated with festive meals," says Jacques. "The pleasures of fine food and wine are essential parts of a passionate life." As chef de cuisine at L'Auberge Chez François, a nationally acclaimed restaurant in Great Falls, Virginia, Jacques shares his passion with all the guests.

"To ignite your passionate life, include your loved ones when you cook; you'll bring more to the table," says Jacques. He suggests planning ahead so everyone will be prepared.

Here are some of Jacques's favorite recipes. Enjoy them with those you love.

DIJON RACK OF LAMB

MAKES 8 SERVINGS

This impressive entrée requires only six ingredients. *(pictured on page 262)*

> 2 (8-rib) lamb rib roasts (2 to 2½ pounds each), trimmed
> 1 teaspoon salt
> 3 teaspoons pepper
> 3 tablespoons olive oil
> 3 tablespoons Dijon mustard
> 1 cup fresh herb focaccia breadcrumbs*

RUB lamb evenly with salt and pepper. COOK lamb in hot oil in a skillet over high heat 3 minutes on each side or until browned. Place, fat side up, on a rack in a broiler pan. Bake at 425° for 20 minutes or until a meat thermometer inserted into the thickest portion registers 145°.
REMOVE lamb from oven, leaving oven on. Cover lamb loosely with aluminum foil, and let stand 10 minutes or until meat thermometer registers 150°.

BRUSH lamb with mustard; cover with breadcrumbs. Return lamb to oven, and bake 4 to 5 minutes or until golden. Cut into chops, and serve. **Prep: 10 min., Cook: 6 min., Bake: 25 min., Stand: 10 min.**

*Substitute 1 cup fresh French breadcrumbs, if desired. Focaccia is a flat Italian bread that can be found in the bakery section of grocery stores.

NOTE: Jacques prefers to cook the lamb until a meat thermometer inserted into the thickest portion registers 135°.

CRANBERRY RELISH

MAKES 3 CUPS

Fresh citrus enlivens this tradtitional condiment. *(pictured on page 1)*

> 1 medium-size orange
> ½ lemon
> 1 pound fresh cranberries
> 1 cup sugar

CUT orange and lemon into quarters, removing white membrane down center of pulp. Process the orange and lemon in a food processor until finely chopped. ADD cranberries and sugar; process until coarsely chopped and well combined.
POUR cranberry mixture into a bowl; cover and chill at least 30 minutes. **Prep: 15 min., Chill: 30 min.**

GRATIN POTATOES

MAKES 8 SERVINGS

> 3 large baking potatoes, peeled and thinly sliced
> 1 quart whipping cream
> 2 garlic cloves, minced
> 2 teaspoons salt
> 1½ teaspoons pepper

LAYER potato slices in a buttered 13- x 9-inch baking dish. Stir together cream and remaining ingredients; pour mixture over potatoes.

BAKE at 400° for 50 minutes or until potatoes are tender and mixture is golden. Let stand 15 minutes before serving. **Prep: 20 min., Bake: 50 min., Stand: 15 min.**

BRAISED RED CABBAGE

MAKES 6 SERVINGS

1 medium-size red cabbage, thinly sliced
¼ cup red wine vinegar
1 teaspoon salt
½ teaspoon pepper
4 bacon slices, diced
1 large onion, thinly sliced
2 apples, peeled and sliced
¾ cup red wine
¼ cup sugar
¼ teaspoon minced garlic

TOSS together first 4 ingredients in a large bowl.

COOK bacon in a large Dutch oven over medium-high heat 10 minutes or until crisp. Add onion; sauté 5 minutes or until tender. Stir in cabbage mixture, apples, red wine, sugar, and garlic. Cover, reduce heat to medium; simmer 30 to 35 minutes. **Prep: 20 min., Cook: 50 min.**

CHOCOLATE MOUSSE

MAKES 6 TO 8 SERVINGS

1 (12-ounce) package semisweet chocolate morsels
2½ cups whipping cream, divided
1 teaspoon vanilla extract
1 tablespoon rum
Garnishes: whipped cream, grated chocolate

MICROWAVE chocolate morsels and ½ cup cream in a small glass bowl at HIGH 1½ minutes or until melted, stirring twice. Stir in vanilla and rum, blending well. Cool 5 minutes.

BEAT remaining 2 cups cream at medium speed with an electric mixer until soft peaks form; fold cream into chocolate mixture. Cover and chill 2 hours.

PIPE or spoon into a large serving bowl or dessert dishes. Garnish with additional whipped cream and grated chocolate, if desired. **Prep: 10 min., Cool: 5 min., Chill: 2 hrs.**

Fun Food Your Kids Will Love

These flavor combinations received high marks from our Foods staff, but the final approval came from our young tasters, Hill and Emma Grace Jones.

Children's Christmas Party

Serves 8

Green Elf Biscuits and Ham
Rudolph's Apple Salad
Granny's Christmas Cookies

GREEN ELF BISCUITS AND HAM

MAKES 28 (2-INCH) BISCUITS

Spinach soufflé adds color and nutrition to these cheesy biscuits.

1 (12-ounce) package frozen spinach soufflé, thawed
2¾ cups all-purpose baking mix
1 (3-ounce) package shredded Parmesan cheese
¼ teaspoon ground red pepper
¼ cup butter, softened
1 tablespoon spicy brown mustard
1 pound thinly sliced baked ham

STIR together first 4 ingredients with a fork just until dry ingredients are moistened.

TURN dough out onto a lightly floured surface; knead 8 to 10 times. Pat or roll dough to a ½-inch thickness; cut with a 2-inch round cutter. Place at least ½ inch apart on lightly greased baking sheets.

BAKE biscuits at 425° for 10 minutes or until golden. Cool completely on wire racks.

STIR together ¼ cup butter and 1 tablespoon mustard. Split biscuits, and spread cut sides evenly with butter mixture; fill biscuits evenly with thinly sliced ham. **Prep: 25 min., Bake: 10 min.**

NITA MORRISSETTE
VESTAVIA HILLS, ALABAMA

RUDOLPH'S APPLE SALAD

MAKES 8 SERVINGS

Serve this salad in a waffle ice-cream bowl.

2 large Red Delicious apples, coarsely chopped
1 large Granny Smith apple, coarsely chopped
1 celery rib, diced
1½ cups miniature marshmallows
¼ cup mayonnaise
½ cup low-fat lemon yogurt
2 cups granola

STIR together first 6 ingredients.

SPOON mixture evenly into 8 individual serving dishes, and sprinkle evenly with granola just before serving. **Prep: 15 min.**

CHERYL GEPP
ATLANTA, GEORGIA

GRANNY'S CHRISTMAS COOKIES

MAKES 2½ DOZEN

- 1 pound butter, softened
- 1 cup sugar
- 2 large eggs
- 2 egg yolks
- 4½ cups sifted all-purpose flour
- 2 teaspoons vanilla extract
- 1 (8-ounce) package candied cherries, cut in half

BEAT butter at medium speed with an electric mixer until creamy. Gradually add sugar, beating well. Add eggs and egg yolks, 1 at a time, beating until blended.

ADD flour to butter mixture gradually, beating at low speed just until blended. Add 2 teaspoons vanilla, beating just until blended.

DROP by rounded teaspoonfuls onto lightly greased baking sheets. Press a candied cherry half in center of each cookie.

BAKE at 350° for 20 minutes or until golden brown. Remove cookies to wire racks, and let cool. **Prep: 30 min., Bake 20 min. per batch**

ANN BOSTICK
TEMPLE, TEXAS

Sharing Their Legacy

Meet Shirley Schmidt, Julia Ann Caruso, Pat Dickinson, Myrt Haas, and Bobbye Ruth Maggio, who have raised 25 children and nurtured each other through 42 years of joy and sorrow. Inspired by the movie, they call themselves "The Steel Magnolias."

"We wear pins that are a cluster of three pewter magnolias made by a local artist," says Shirley. "We've dubbed our daughters and daughters-in-law 'The Buds' and pinned them with a single pewter magnolia."

Last Christmas they celebrated at Shirley's Pass Christian, Mississippi, home. Here are two of their favorite dishes.

PESTO TORTE

MAKES 12 TO 14 APPETIZER SERVINGS

- Vegetable cooking spray
- 2 (4-ounce) packages provolone cheese slices (8 slices)
- 1 (8-ounce) package shredded mozzarella cheese
- 1 (8-ounce) package cream cheese, softened
- 1 (3-ounce) package cream cheese, softened
- 1 (8-ounce) jar dried tomatoes in oil, undrained
- 1 (7.5-ounce) jar pesto in olive oil
- ¼ cup mayonnaise
- 2 tablespoons unsalted butter
- ¼ teaspoon garlic powder
- ¼ teaspoon pepper
- Assorted crackers

LINE the bottom of a 9- x 5-inch loafpan with plastic wrap, allowing 5 to 6 inches to hang over edges; coat plastic wrap with cooking spray. Line bottom and sides of pan with provolone cheese slices.

PROCESS mozzarella cheese and next 8 ingredients in a food processor or blender until smooth, stopping to scrape down sides.

SPOON cheese mixture into prepared pan, pressing with spatula. Fold plastic wrap over torte; chill 12 hours.

INVERT chilled torte onto a serving dish; discard plastic wrap. Serve torte with assorted crackers. **Prep: 20 min, Chill: 12 hrs.**

MYRT HAAS
BAY ST. LOUIS, MISSISSIPPI

PORK LOIN WITH RAISIN SAUCE

MAKES 10 TO 12 SERVINGS

Serve this tender and juicy pork with or without the distinctive Raisin Sauce. *(pictured on page 1)*

- 1 (5-pound) boneless pork loin roast
- 5 garlic cloves, thinly sliced
- ½ teaspoon salt
- ¼ teaspoon pepper
- 2 tablespoons vegetable oil
- Raisin Sauce

CUT slits in pork, using a sharp knife; push garlic slices into each slit. Rub pork evenly with salt and pepper. Brown on all sides in hot vegetable oil in a large skillet over medium heat. Place pork in a large lightly greased roasting pan.

BAKE at 325° for 1 hour and 45 minutes or until a meat thermometer inserted into thickest portion of pork registers 155°. Let stand 10 minutes before serving. Slice and serve with Raisin Sauce. **Prep: 10 min.; Bake: 1 hr., 45 min.; Stand: 10 min.**

Raisin Sauce:

MAKES 1½ CUPS

- ½ cup firmly packed light brown sugar
- ¼ cup water
- ½ cup golden raisins
- 2 tablespoons white vinegar
- 1 tablespoon butter
- ¾ teaspoon Worcestershire sauce
- ¼ teaspoon salt
- ⅛ teaspoon pepper
- ⅛ teaspoon ground cloves
- ⅛ teaspoon ground mace
- ½ cup jellied cranberry sauce

STIR together all ingredients in a small saucepan; cook over low heat, stirring until cranberry sauce melts. Serve

Cream Cheese Makes These Appetizers

Start with this tried-and-true ingredient
for easy, yet impressive, recipes.

It's the time of year when entertaining becomes top priority. As you consider appetizers, look to these recipes that pair cream cheese with a variety of unique ingredients. The results are worthy of any elegant soiree. With such impressive tastes and presentations, folks won't guess that these appetizers began with humble blocks of cream cheese.

CHUTNEY-GLAZED CHEESE PÂTÉ

MAKES ABOUT 8 TO 10 APPETIZER SERVINGS

Shred your own Cheddar rather than buying preshredded; it's stickier and blends better with the cream cheese.

- **1 (8-ounce) block sharp Cheddar cheese, shredded**
- **1 (8-ounce) package cream cheese, softened**
- **3 tablespoons dry sherry**
- **½ teaspoon curry powder**
- **¼ teaspoon salt**
- **1 (9-ounce) jar mango chutney**
- **3 green onions, sliced**
- **Garnishes: cucumber peel, fresh cranberries**

STIR together first 5 ingredients in a large bowl until blended. Spread mixture evenly into a 4-cup shallow serving dish. Cover and chill 8 hours.

SPREAD chutney evenly over top of pâté; sprinkle with green onions. Garnish, if desired. **Prep: 15 min., Chill: 8 hrs.**

CHUTNEY-AND-BLUE CHEESE PÂTÉ: Substitute 1 (3-ounce) package cream cheese and 1 (4-ounce) package blue cheese for sharp Cheddar cheese. Proceed with recipe as directed, substituting cranberry chutney for mango chutney, if desired. Leftovers are great on roast beef sandwiches or burgers.

GENNI HAMBLETON
WINNETKA, ILLINOIS

SPICY MONTEREY JACK CHEESE LOGS

MAKES ABOUT 12 APPETIZER SERVINGS

Wrapped in fun paper, these savory spreads make great holiday gifts.

- **1 (10-ounce) block extra-sharp Cheddar cheese, shredded**
- **1 (8-ounce) block Monterey Jack cheese with peppers, shredded**
- **1 (8-ounce) package cream cheese, softened**
- **1 teaspoon Worcestershire sauce**
- **¼ teaspoon ground red pepper**
- **1 cup chopped walnuts or pecans, toasted**
- **½ cup chopped fresh parsley**

STIR together first 5 ingredients in a large bowl until blended. Divide cheese mixture into 2 equal portions; shape each portion into an 8-inch log.
COMBINE walnuts and parsley. Roll cheese logs evenly in walnut mixture; cover and chill 8 hours. **Prep: 20 min., Chill: 8 hrs.**

NOTE: For testing purposes only, we used Cracker Barrel Extra-Sharp Cheddar. To make ahead, wrap each log in heavy-duty plastic wrap, and freeze. Thaw in refrigerator overnight.

PORT WINE CHEESE LOGS: Substitute 1 (8-ounce) wedge or block Cheddar cheese with port wine for Monterey Jack cheese with peppers. Proceed with recipe as directed. Port wine Cheddar cheese can be found in the deli section of your grocery store.

CHARLES FLOURNOY
DALLAS, TEXAS

How to Make Holly Leaves and Cranberry Garnish

- Cut thin layers of dark cucumber peel, including a layer of the lighter colored interior flesh, into 1½- to 2-inch-long oval leaf shapes, using a sharp paring knife. Score the lighter side of the leaf shapes with the dull side of the knife blade to form the veins of a leaf. (The darker color of the cucumber skin will show through the lighter colored flesh.)

- Arrange leaves and fresh cranberries to resemble Christmas holly.

New Year's Feast for Eight

Chef Vagn Nielsen raises the bar on make-ahead menus with this easy, elegant dinner.

New Year's Eve Menu

Serves 8

Champagne Shooters

Shrimp Martinis With Napa Cabbage Slaw

Grilled Pork Chops With Garlic Mashed Potatoes

Vegetables With Arugula Broth

One of the most stressful aspects of hosting a sit-down dinner party is getting dishes on the table at just the right time. All too often we end up serving hot food cold, letting cold food warm to room temperature, or burning an ill-attended loaf of garlic bread. Sound familiar? Well, we've got just the menu to reduce your party stress.

Chef Vagn Nielsen of Proof of the Pudding, one of Atlanta's premier caterers, shares a simple yet elegant dinner for eight. Thanks to creativity and preparedness, dinner parties at the Nielsens' go off without a hitch. "You can't cook dinner for 5,000, like we do in the catering business, without making most of the food ahead of time," Vagn says. We asked him and his wife, Lotte (also with Proof), to share some of their valuable tips and ideas for low-stress dinners.

It may be hard to imagine your guests enjoying Shrimp Martinis With Napa Cabbage Slaw and a glass of wine in your clean kitchen right at the planned dinnertime, but here are the menu and the tools to get you there.

CHAMPAGNE SHOOTERS

MAKES 8 SERVINGS

Try this easy and refreshing palate cleanser between bold-flavored courses.

- 1 pint lemon or lime sorbet, slightly softened
- 1 (750 ml) bottle sparkling wine*

SPOON mini-scoops of sorbet into 8 cordial glasses (petite after-dinner drink stemware). Cover and freeze until ready to serve. Fill glasses with sparkling wine just before serving. **Prep: 10 min.**

*Substitute alcohol-free sparkling wine, if desired.

SHRIMP MARTINIS WITH NAPA CABBAGE SLAW

MAKES 8 SERVINGS

- 24 unpeeled, large fresh shrimp (about 1½ pounds)
- 2 large eggs, lightly beaten
- 1 cup soft breadcrumbs
- 1 cup sweetened flaked coconut, toasted
- 4 cups vegetable oil
- Napa Cabbage Slaw
- Garnish: lime wedges

PEEL shrimp, leaving tails on; devein, if desired.

DIP shrimp in egg. Stir together breadcrumbs and coconut; dredge shrimp in mixture.

POUR oil into a Dutch oven; heat to 375°. Fry shrimp, in batches, over medium-high heat 2 minutes or until golden. Drain on paper towels.

SPOON Napa Cabbage Slaw evenly into 8 martini glasses. Top each with 3 fried shrimp. Garnish, if desired. **Prep: 30 min., Fry: 2 min. per batch**

Napa Cabbage Slaw:

MAKES 3 CUPS

- ½ cup mayonnaise
- 2 tablespoons lite soy sauce
- 1 tablespoon dark sesame oil
- 4 cups shredded napa cabbage
- 1 large carrot, shredded
- 1 red bell pepper, cut into very thin strips
- 2 tablespoons sesame seeds, toasted

WHISK together first 3 ingredients in a large bowl. Add cabbage, carrot, and red bell pepper, tossing to coat. Sprinkle with sesame seeds. **Prep: 25 min.**

holiday dinners

GRILLED PORK CHOPS WITH GARLIC MASHED POTATOES

MAKES 8 SERVINGS

- ¼ cup olive oil
- 1 tablespoon salt
- 1 tablespoon chopped fresh or dried rosemary
- 1 tablespoon chopped fresh thyme
- 2 tablespoons chopped fresh oregano
- 1 tablespoon coarsely ground pepper
- 8 (12-ounce) bone-in pork loin chops*
- Garlic Mashed Potatoes
- Garnish: fresh thyme sprigs

STIR together first 6 ingredients. Rub evenly over both sides of pork chops.

GRILL, covered with grill lid, over medium-high heat (350° to 400°) 12 minutes or until a meat thermometer inserted into thickest portion registers 160°, turning once. Serve with Garlic Mashed Potatoes. Garnish, if desired. **Prep: 10 min., Grill: 12 min.**

NOTE: To make ahead, slightly undercook chops, and proceed as directed with timeline.

*Substitute 8 (12-ounce) bone-in veal chops, if desired.

Garlic Mashed Potatoes:

MAKES 8 SERVINGS

- 8 baking potatoes, peeled and quartered (about 4 pounds)
- 1¾ teaspoons salt, divided
- ½ cup butter, softened
- ¾ cup half-and-half
- 3 large garlic cloves, pressed
- ½ teaspoon ground white pepper
- ¼ cup chopped fresh parsley

BRING potatoes, 1 teaspoon salt, and water to cover to a boil in a Dutch oven or stockpot; cover, reduce heat, and simmer 30 minutes or until tender. Drain.

BEAT potatoes, remaining ¾ teaspoon salt, butter, half-and-half, garlic, and white pepper at medium speed with an electric mixer until smooth. Stir in parsley. **Prep: 20 min., Cook: 30 min.**

Party Timeline

1 day ahead:
- Shred and cut vegetables for Napa Cabbage Slaw (store red bell pepper strips separately). Toast sesame seeds.
- Cut up vegetables for Vegetables With Arugula Broth. Store carrots and turnips in one zip-top plastic bag, broccoli and asparagus in another.
- Prepare olive oil mixture for Grilled Pork Chops. Rub over chops; cover and chill.

Morning of party:
- Cook and mash potatoes (do not add remaining ingredients). Cover and chill.
- Cook carrots, turnips, broccoli, and asparagus. Cover and chill.
- Scoop sorbet for Champagne Shooters into serving glasses, and freeze.

2 hours before dinner:
- Prepare and fry shrimp for Shrimp Martinis; let stand until ready to assemble.

- Assemble Napa Cabbage Slaw. Cover and chill.

1 hour before dinner:
- Grill pork or veal chops, undercooking slightly. Cover and set aside.
- Assemble Garlic Mashed Potatoes; cover and let stand.

20 minutes before dinner:
- Reheat mashed potatoes in a Dutch oven over medium-low heat (add more half-and-half, if needed). Keep warm.
- Prepare Shrimp Martinis.

Dinnertime:
- Serve Shrimp Martinis With Napa Cabbage Slaw and Champagne Shooters.
- Reheat vegetables in a large skillet; prepare Arugula Broth.
- Reheat pork chops in a large skillet over medium heat until thoroughly heated.
- Serve the main dish.

VEGETABLES WITH ARUGULA BROTH

MAKES 8 SERVINGS

The arugula broth is a slightly thickened, glossy sauce.

- 1 (1-pound) package baby carrots
- 1 pound turnips, peeled and cut into 1-inch cubes
- 6 cups chicken broth, divided
- 1 pound fresh broccoli, cut into florets
- 1 pound asparagus, trimmed and cut into 1-inch pieces
- 2 teaspoons cornstarch
- ¼ teaspoon freshly ground pepper
- 1 (0.75-ounce) package arugula*

COMBINE carrots and turnips in a Dutch oven. Add 4 cups broth. Bring to a boil; cook 10 minutes. Add broccoli and asparagus; cook 5 minutes. Drain.

WHISK together remaining 2 cups broth and cornstarch. Cook in a large skillet over medium-high heat 5 minutes or until slightly thickened. Stir in pepper. Add arugula; cook just until arugula wilts. Drizzle over cooked vegetables. **Prep: 10 min., Cook: 20 min.**

*Substitute 2 cups chopped fresh spinach, if desired.

Feast Without the Fuss

Dinner's a cinch with our delicious, easygoing recipes.

With the holidays in full swing, we want to ensure that planning dinner is the least of your worries. Our simple and satisfying menu works equally well for a Sunday supper or a holiday dinner party. Let our helpful Cook's Notes make preparation worry free.

Easy Holiday Dinner

Serves 6

Honey-Roasted Pork

Carrot-Pecan Casserole

Lemon-Scented Sugar Snap Peas

HONEY-ROASTED PORK

MAKES 8 SERVINGS

A tangy-sweet glaze enhances the tender pork.

  1 (2- to 3-pound) boneless pork loin
    roast
  ¼ cup honey
  2 tablespoons Dijon mustard
  2 tablespoons mixed or black
    peppercorns, crushed
  ½ teaspoon dried thyme
  ½ teaspoon salt
  Garnish: watercress sprigs

PLACE roast on a lightly greased rack in a shallow, aluminum foil-lined roasting pan.
COMBINE honey and next 4 ingredients; brush half of mixture over roast.
BAKE at 325° for 1 hour; brush with remaining honey mixture. Bake 30 more minutes or until a meat thermometer inserted in thickest portion of roast registers 155°. Cover lightly with foil; let stand 10 minutes before slicing. Garnish, if desired. **Prep: 10 min.; Bake: 1 hr., 30 min.; Stand: 10 min.**

CARROT-PECAN CASSEROLE

MAKES 6 TO 8 SERVINGS

Strewn with toasty pecans, this dish is a nice alternative to sweet potatoes. *(pictured on page 1)*

  3 pounds baby carrots, sliced
  ⅔ cup sugar
  ½ cup butter or margarine, softened
  ½ cup chopped pecans, toasted
  ¼ cup milk
  2 large eggs, lightly beaten
  3 tablespoons all-purpose flour
  1 tablespoon grated orange rind
  1 teaspoon vanilla extract
  ¼ teaspoon ground nutmeg

COOK carrot in boiling water to cover in a saucepan 25 minutes or until tender; drain, let cool slightly, and process in food processor until smooth.
TRANSFER carrot to bowl; stir in sugar and remaining ingredients. Spoon into a lightly greased 11- x 7-inch baking dish. Cover; chill 8 hours, if desired.
BAKE casserole, uncovered, at 350° for 40 minutes. **Prep: 15 min., Cook: 25 min., Bake: 40 min.**

LEMON-SCENTED SUGAR SNAP PEAS

MAKES 4 TO 6 SERVINGS

This can be doubled to serve eight.

  2 pounds fresh sugar snap peas
  2 tablespoons butter or margarine
  2 garlic cloves, minced
  2 teaspoons grated lemon rind
  1 tablespoon fresh lemon juice
  ¾ teaspoon salt
  ½ teaspoon freshly ground pepper

COOK peas in boiling salted water to cover 5 minutes or until crisp-tender. Drain and plunge into ice water to stop the cooking process; drain.
MELT butter in a medium skillet over medium-high heat; add peas, and sauté 3 minutes. Add garlic and remaining ingredients. Sauté 2 minutes or until thoroughly heated. **Prep: 15 min., Cook: 10 min.**

Cook's Notes

1 day ahead:
■ Assemble Carrot-Pecan Casserole (do not bake), and refrigerate.
■ Blanch sugar snap peas for Lemon-Scented Sugar Snap Peas. Wrap in paper towels, and place in a zip-top plastic bag; refrigerate.
■ Stir together honey, Dijon mustard, peppercorns, dried thyme, and salt for Honey-Roasted Pork; cover and refrigerate.

2 hours ahead:
■ Assemble Honey-Roasted Pork, and bake as directed. Let roast stand 10 minutes before slicing.

1 hour ahead:
■ Let Carrot-Pecan Casserole stand at room temperature 20 minutes. Bake as directed.

15 minutes ahead:
■ Sauté Lemon-Scented Sugar Snap Peas.

Simple Sides

Add pizzazz to everyday vegetables with these creative touches. Glazes, sauces, and a quick sauté with fresh ingredients take carrots, green beans, and beets to new heights. The simple flavors and common ingredients allow them to pair easily with a variety of family favorites.

WINTER BEETS

MAKES 8 SERVINGS

For a festive look, spoon beets over a bed of gourmet mixed greens.

- ½ cup sugar
- 2 tablespoons all-purpose flour
- ½ cup white vinegar
- ¼ cup water
- ⅛ teaspoon salt
- 2 tablespoons butter or margarine
- 2 (15-ounce) cans sliced beets, drained

COMBINE sugar and flour in a heavy saucepan; whisk in vinegar and ¼ cup water. Bring to a boil over medium heat, and boil, whisking constantly, 1 minute or until thickened. Remove from heat; stir in salt and butter.

STIR beets into sugar mixture, and cook over low heat 5 minutes or until thoroughly heated, stirring often. Serve immediately. Or let cool, and spoon beet mixture into an airtight container; chill 8 hours. **Prep: 5 min., Cook: 8 min.**

CLAIRIECE HUMPHREY
CHARLOTTESVILLE, VIRGINIA

GLAZED CARROTS WITH BACON AND ONION

MAKES 4 SERVINGS

- 1 (1-pound) package baby carrots
- 3 bacon slices
- 1 small onion, chopped
- 3 tablespoons brown sugar
- ¼ teaspoon pepper

COOK carrots in boiling water to cover in a large saucepan 15 minutes or until carrots are tender; drain.

COOK bacon in a medium skillet until crisp; remove bacon, and drain on paper towels, reserving 1 tablespoon drippings in skillet. Crumble bacon; set aside.

SAUTÉ onion in reserved drippings over medium-high heat 3 minutes or until tender. Stir in brown sugar, pepper, and carrots. Cook, stirring often, 5 minutes or until carrots are glazed and thoroughly heated.

TRANSFER carrots to a serving dish, and sprinkle with crumbled bacon. **Prep: 5 min., Cook: 30 min.**

CODIE ALLEN
ABILENE, TEXAS

GINGERED GREEN BEANS

MAKES 6 SERVINGS

Look for fresh ginger in the specialty produce section of your grocery store.

- 3 cups water
- 1 extra-large ham-flavor bouillon cube
- 1 pound fresh green beans, trimmed
- 2 tablespoons butter or margarine
- 1 small sweet onion, diced
- 2 garlic cloves, minced
- 2 tablespoons peeled and minced fresh ginger
- ½ teaspoon salt
- ½ teaspoon seasoned pepper
- ¼ cup finely chopped pecans, toasted
- Garnish: toasted pecan halves

BRING 3 cups water to a boil in a large saucepan over medium-high heat. Stir in bouillon cube until dissolved. Add green beans, and cook 4 to 6 minutes or until crisp-tender; drain.

MELT butter in a large nonstick skillet over medium-high heat. Add onion, garlic, and ginger; sauté 2 minutes. Add beans, salt, and pepper; sauté 1 minute or until heated. Transfer to a serving dish; sprinkle with chopped pecans. Garnish, if desired. **Prep: 10 min., Cook: 10 min.**

NOTE: For testing purposes only, we used Knorr bouillon cubes.

CAROL NOBLE
BURGAW, NORTH CAROLINA

Hearty Potatoes

These potatoes make a great side dish or meatless main dish any time of the year.

STUFFED POTATOES

MAKES 8 SERVINGS

- 4 large baking potatoes (about 2½ pounds)
- 1 (8-ounce) container cream-style cottage cheese
- 1 (8-ounce) container sour cream
- 2 tablespoons shredded Parmesan cheese
- 1 to 2 tablespoons freeze-dried chives
- ½ teaspoon salt
- 1½ cups (6 ounces) shredded Cheddar cheese, divided
- Paprika (optional)

PIERCE potatoes with a fork, and place on a baking sheet. Bake at 350° for 1 hour and 20 minutes or until done. Cut potatoes in half lengthwise, and scoop out pulp, leaving ¼-inch-thick shells.

MASH pulp in a large bowl; stir in cottage cheese, next 4 ingredients, and 1 cup Cheddar cheese, blending well. Spoon into potato shells, and place on baking sheet.

BAKE at 350° for 15 to 20 minutes. Sprinkle top with remaining ½ cup Cheddar cheese. Bake 10 more minutes. Sprinkle with paprika, if desired. **Prep: 20 min.; Bake: 1 hr., 50 min.**

NOTE: To freeze, wrap unbaked stuffed potatoes in heavy-duty aluminum foil, and place in a heavy-duty zip-top plastic bag. Seal and freeze up to 3 months. Thaw overnight in the refrigerator. Bake foil-wrapped potatoes at 350° for 30 minutes. Remove and discard foil; sprinkle with remaining ½ cup cheese. Bake 10 more minutes.

TEANA COMPEAU
WILKESBORO, NORTH CAROLINA

Lightened Holiday Favorites

Delight in dishes with fantastic flavor but fewer calories.

We picked some special-occasion *Southern Living* recipes and reduced their total calories by using less oil, butter, and whole-fat dairy products. But we didn't compromise their delicious appeal. Some dishes contain more than 30% of their calories from fat, but they're still much lower in total fat, saturated fat, and cholesterol than the original versions.

Folks around our tasting table gave these less weighty versions high marks. We believe you'll find them worthy of any special supper.

CHICKEN CAKES WITH CREOLE SAUCE

MAKES 8 SERVINGS

We reduced the oil and butter in the original recipe, and substituted light mayo for the full-fat version.

- ½ **medium-size red bell pepper, diced**
- **4 green onions, thinly sliced**
- **1 garlic clove, pressed**
- **Vegetable cooking spray**
- **3 cups chopped cooked chicken breast**
- **1 cup soft breadcrumbs**
- **1 large egg, lightly beaten**
- **2 tablespoons light mayonnaise**
- **1 tablespoon Creole mustard**
- **1 teaspoon Creole seasoning**
- **Creole Sauce**

SAUTÉ first 3 ingredients in a nonstick skillet coated with cooking spray 4 minutes or until vegetables are tender. Wipe skillet clean.
STIR together bell pepper mixture, chicken, and next 5 ingredients in a bowl. Shape chicken mixture into 8 (3½-inch) patties. Cover and chill 15 minutes.
COOK patties, in 2 batches, in skillet coated with cooking spray over medium heat 3 minutes on each side or until golden. Serve cakes immediately with Creole Sauce. **Prep: 20 min., Chill: 15 min., Cook: 12 min.**

Calories (including 2 tablespoons Creole Sauce) 123 (48% from fat); Fat 6.6g (sat 1g, mono 0.3g, poly 0.1g); Protein 3.8g; Carb 12.4g; Fiber 1.9g; Chol 33mg; Iron 0.8mg; Sodium 370mg; Calc 55mg

Original recipe (including Creole Sauce): Calories 474 (75% from fat); Fat 40g (sat 8g); Chol 104mg

Creole Sauce:

MAKES ABOUT 1¼ CUPS

This original recipe called for 1 cup mayonnaise. We tastefully substituted ½ cup light mayonnaise and ½ cup yogurt.

- ½ **cup light mayonnaise**
- ½ **cup plain nonfat yogurt**
- **3 green onions, minced**
- **2 garlic cloves, minced**
- **2 tablespoons Creole mustard**
- **1 tablespoon chopped fresh parsley**
- ¼ **teaspoon ground red pepper**

STIR together all ingredients until blended. **Prep: 5 min.**

Per 2 tablespoons: Calories 55 (66% from fat); Fat 4g (sat 0.6g, mono 0g, poly 0g); Protein 1.1g; Carb 3.3g; Fiber 0.6g; Chol 4.4mg; Iron 0.2mg; Sodium 154mg; Calc 34mg

SAVORY SPINACH-GORGONZOLA CUSTARDS

MAKES 6 SERVINGS

Serve these bold, cheesy custards with a big tossed salad dressed in tangy vinaigrette alongside crusty multigrain rolls or bread.

- ½ **cup frozen chopped spinach, thawed**
- **2 large onions, halved and thinly sliced**
- **2 teaspoons olive oil**
- **2 teaspoons brown sugar**
- **Vegetable cooking spray**
- **3 ounces crumbled Gorgonzola cheese***
- ½ **(8-ounce) package fat-free cream cheese, softened**
- **1 large egg**
- **1 cup reduced-fat milk (2%)**
- ½ **cup egg substitute**
- ¼ **teaspoon salt**
- ¼ **teaspoon ground nutmeg**
- ¼ **teaspoon pepper**

DRAIN spinach well, pressing between layers of paper towels. Set aside.
SAUTÉ sliced onions in hot oil in a large nonstick skillet over medium heat 5 minutes.
STIR in brown sugar; cook, stirring occasionally, 20 minutes or until onions are caramel-colored. Reserve ¼ cup onions.
SPOON remaining onions evenly into 6 (6-ounce) custard cups coated with cooking spray; sprinkle evenly with Gorgonzola cheese.
BEAT cream cheese with an electric mixer until smooth. Add egg and next 5 ingredients, beating just until blended. Stir in spinach. Spoon evenly over cheese in custard cups.
PLACE cups in a 13- x 9-inch pan. Add hot water to pan to a depth of 1 inch.
BAKE at 350° for 30 to 40 minutes or until almost set. Remove cups from pan. Let stand 10 minutes; unmold, and top with reserved onions. **Prep: 30 min., Cook: 25 min., Bake: 40 min., Stand: 10 min.**

*Substitute 1 (4-ounce) package crumbled blue cheese, if desired.

Calories 160 (48% from fat); Fat 8.6g (sat 3.9g, mono 2g, poly 0.6g); Protein 11.6g; Carb 9.4g; Fiber 1.3g; Chol 56 mg; Iron 1.1mg; Sodium 422mg; Calc 206mg

Original recipe with half-and-half, more cheese, and oil: Calories 265 (70% from fat); Fat 21g (sat 11g); Chol 159mg

TIRAMISÙ

MAKES 10 SERVINGS

- ½ cup granulated sugar
- 1 cup whipping cream, divided
- 2 cups fat-free milk
- ½ cup egg substitute
- 2 egg yolks
- 1 tablespoon all-purpose flour
- ½ vanilla bean, split
- 1 (8-ounce) package fat-free cream cheese, softened
- 1 (8-ounce) package reduced-fat cream cheese, softened
- ½ cup brewed espresso or dark-roast coffee
- 3 tablespoons Marsala
- 3 (3-ounce) packages ladyfingers
- 3 tablespoons powdered sugar
- 1 tablespoon unsweetened cocoa

STIR together granulated sugar, ½ cup cream, milk, and next 4 ingredients in a heavy saucepan. Cook over medium heat, stirring constantly, 30 minutes or until thickened. Cool completely. Discard vanilla bean. Whisk in cream cheeses.

STIR together espresso and Marsala. Layer one-fourth of ladyfingers in a trifle bowl or large clear bowl; brush with espresso mixture. Top with one-fourth of cream cheese mixture. Repeat 3 times with remaining ladyfingers, coffee mixture, and cheese mixture.

BEAT remaining ½ cup whipping cream at high speed with an electric mixer until foamy; gradually add powdered sugar, beating until soft peaks form. Spoon over cream cheese mixture, and sprinkle with cocoa. Cover and chill 2 hours. **Prep: 15 min., Cook: 30 min., Chill: 2 hrs.**

NOTE: To prepare espresso, stir together ¾ cup hot water and ⅓ cup ground espresso or dark-roast coffee. Let stand 5 minutes; pour through a wire-mesh strainer lined with a coffee filter into a glass measuring cup, discarding coffee grounds. Makes ¾ cup.
This may also be prepared in a 13- x- 9-inch dish, layering ladyfingers and cream cheese mixture. Spread with whipped cream mixture.

Calories 345 (43% from fat); Fat 16.6g (sat 9.5g, mono 4.3g, poly 1.1g); Protein 12.3g; Carb 35g; Fiber 0.4g; Chol 182mg; Iron 1.4 mg; Sodium 325mg; Calc 166mg

Original recipe: Calories 618 (75% from fat); Fat 51g (sat 29g); Chol 314mg

BEEF FILLETS WITH GREEN PEPPERCORN SAUCE

MAKES 4 SERVINGS

We lightened this dish by using a fraction of the butter and substituting fat-free evaporated milk for whipping cream. For 8 (4-ounce) servings, cut steaks diagonally into thin slices; divide over 8 plates. Drizzle evenly with sauce.

- 4 (8-ounce) beef tenderloin fillets
- ½ teaspoon salt
- ½ teaspoon pepper
- 1 teaspoon butter or margarine
- 1 teaspoon olive oil
- 2 cups Marsala
- 1 cup fat-free, low-sodium chicken broth
- 20 green peppercorns
- 1 (5-ounce) can fat-free evaporated milk
- ¼ teaspoon Dijon mustard
- Garnish: Italian parsley sprigs

SPRINKLE beef fillets evenly with salt and pepper.

MELT butter with olive oil in a large non-stick skillet over medium-high heat. Add fillets, and cook 6 minutes on each side or to desired degree of doneness. Remove fillets from skillet; keep warm.

ADD wine, broth, and peppercorns to skillet; cook 20 minutes or until liquid is reduced by half. Stir in evaporated milk and mustard, and cook, over low heat, 5 to 7 minutes or until slightly thickened.

RETURN fillets to skillet, and serve warm. Garnish, if desired. **Prep: 15 min., Cook: 40 min.**

NOTE: Green peppercorns are immature, tender peppercorns jarred in brine. They can be found near capers in the pickled food section of the supermarket.

Calories 446 (39% from fat); Fat 19g (sat 7.3g, mono 7.5g, poly 0.8g); Protein 51g; Carb 7.5g; Fiber 0.2g; Chol 146mg; Iron 6.2mg; Sodium 586mg; Calc 128mg

Original recipe: Calories 840 (70% from fat); Fat 65g (sat 36g); Chol 312mg

CARROT-SWEET POTATO PUREE

MAKES 6 SERVINGS

This recipe requires no stove-top cooking; it's all done in the microwave. Our calorie, fat, and cholesterol savings came from using light butter (and less of it) instead of butter, and light sour cream instead of regular.

- 5 carrots, sliced
- ¾ cup water
- 2 tablespoons light butter or light margarine
- 1 (29-ounce) can sweet potatoes, drained
- 1 (16-ounce) can sweet potatoes, drained
- 1 (8-ounce) container light sour cream
- 1 tablespoon sugar
- 1 teaspoon grated lemon rind
- ½ teaspoon ground nutmeg
- ¼ teaspoon salt
- ¼ teaspoon ground black pepper
- ⅛ teaspoon ground red pepper

MICROWAVE carrots and ¾ cup water in a glass bowl at HIGH 8 to 12 minutes or until fork-tender. Drain.

PROCESS carrots and light butter in a food processor until mixture is smooth, stopping to scrape down sides. Add sweet potatoes; process until smooth.

STIR together sweet potato mixture, light sour cream, and remaining ingredients.

SPOON mixture into a 1½-quart glass dish. Microwave at HIGH 4 to 5 minutes or until thoroughly heated. **Prep: 13 min., Cook: 17 min.**

NOTE: To prepare ahead, cover and chill up to 2 days, if desired; let stand at room temperature 30 minutes. Microwave as directed.

Calories 285 (18% from fat); Fat 5.8g (sat 4g, mono 0g, poly 0.3g); Protein 5.6g; Carb 54g; Fiber 7g; Chol 19mg; Iron 1.9mg; Sodium 232mg; Calc 95mg

Original recipe: Calories 363 (37% from fat); Fat 15g (sat 10g); Chol 52mg

Start With a Baked Ham

We love the flavor of home-baked ham, so we began this story with Test Kitchens staffer Jan Moon's Sweet Orange-Glazed Ham. It takes just 10 minutes to prepare a 3½-pound ham for baking. Slice and serve one night for dinner with macaroni and cheese and a vegetable or salad. It makes 12 servings, so there's plenty for dinner and then sandwiches later in the week.

Here we offer an updated ham-and-cheese sandwich: an open-faced ham sandwich topped with Cranberry-and-Apricot Chutney. Use deli ham if you don't have time to bake one. Serve sandwiches with fruit, soup, or baked chips, and you've hit the jackpot on speedy supper solutions.

SWEET ORANGE-GLAZED HAM

MAKES 12 SERVINGS

- 1 (3- to 4-pound) fully cooked boneless ham
- 1 cup firmly packed brown sugar
- ¼ cup prepared mustard
- 5 tablespoons orange juice

SCORE ham in a diamond pattern, if desired. Place ham in an aluminum foil-lined roasting pan.
STIR together brown sugar, mustard, and orange juice; pour over ham.
BAKE at 350° for 1½ to 2 hours or until a meat thermometer inserted into the thickest portion registers 140°, basting ham every 30 minutes with glaze.
REMOVE ham, and let stand 15 minutes before slicing. Serve ham with remaining glaze. **Prep: 10 min., Bake: 2 hrs., Stand: 15 min.**

NOTE: For testing purposes only, we used Hormel Cure 81 Famous Boneless Ham.

HOLIDAY HAM SANDWICHES

MAKES 6 SANDWICHES

These tasty sandwiches feature ham and provolone cheese stacked on cornbread squares and topped with festive Cranberry-and-Apricot Chutney. (pictured on page 265)

- 2 (7-ounce) packages yellow cornbread mix
- ¼ cup mayonnaise
- 12 (1-ounce) provolone cheese slices
- 1 pound sliced Sweet Orange-Glazed Ham (about 6 slices) or deli ham, thinly sliced
- Shredded lettuce (optional)
- Cranberry-and-Apricot Chutney

PREPARE cornbread mix according to package directions; spoon into a lightly greased 13- x 9-inch pan. Bake at 400° for 15 minutes or until golden. Cool.
CUT into 6 squares, and spread 1 side of each with mayonnaise; place on a baking sheet. Top each with 2 cheese slices.
BROIL 5½ inches from heat 5 minutes or until cheese melts. Top evenly with ham and, if desired, lettuce. Top each with 2 tablespoons Cranberry-and-Apricot Chutney. **Prep: 20 min., Bake: 15 min., Broil: 5 min.**

Cranberry-and-Apricot Chutney:

MAKES 3½ CUPS

- 1¼ cups granulated sugar
- ½ cup water
- 1 (12-ounce) package fresh or frozen, thawed cranberries (3 cups)
- ¾ cup chopped dried apricots
- 1 tablespoon brown sugar
- 1 tablespoon peeled and minced fresh ginger
- 1 tablespoon cider vinegar

COOK sugar and ½ cup water in a saucepan over medium-high heat, stirring constantly, until sugar dissolves. Bring mixture to a boil without stirring. Stir in cranberries and remaining ingredients.
REDUCE heat; simmer, stirring occasionally, 10 minutes or until cranberries pop and mixture starts to thicken. Cool. Cover; chill 1 hour. Let stand at room temperature 30 minutes before serving. **Prep: 10 min., Cook: 18 min., Chill: 1 hr., Stand: 30 min.**

BETTY RABE
PLANO, TEXAS

Hearty Pasta Casseroles

Take it easy on yourself by preparing supper all in one dish. You can't go wrong with these meaty pasta bakes, and we've kept prep times to a minimum. Don't let cannelloni shells intimidate you—use our easy stuffing technique.

SMOKED TURKEY TETRAZZINI

MAKES 8 SERVINGS

Assemble this delicious casserole the night before, if desired. Let stand at room temperature 30 minutes before baking.

- 1 (12-ounce) package spinach-and-egg fettuccine
- ¼ cup butter or margarine
- 1 (8-ounce) package sliced fresh mushrooms
- 1 medium-size yellow onion, coarsely chopped
- 3 tablespoons all-purpose flour
- 1½ teaspoons salt
- 1 teaspoon freshly ground pepper
- ¼ teaspoon hot sauce
- 3 cups milk
- 3 cups chopped smoked turkey
- 1 cup white wine
- ½ cup shredded Parmesan cheese

COOK pasta according to package directions; drain.
MELT butter in a large skillet over medium-high heat; add mushrooms and onion, and sauté 7 to 10 minutes or until tender. Gradually stir in flour and next 3 ingredients until smooth; add milk, and cook, stirring constantly, 5 minutes or until thickened. Remove from heat, and stir in turkey and wine.
LAYER a lightly greased 13- x 9-inch baking dish with half each of pasta, turkey mixture, and cheese. Repeat layers with remaining ingredients.
BAKE at 400° for 20 to 25 minutes or until bubbly and golden. **Prep: 10 min., Cook: 15 min., Bake: 25 min.**

MAGGIE ELLWOOD
GRAND RAPIDS, MICHIGAN

CHICKEN CANNELLONI WITH ROASTED RED BELL PEPPER SAUCE

MAKES 6 TO 8 SERVINGS

For quick weeknight solutions, prepare and stuff cannelloni shells. Wrap tightly with wax paper; freeze until ready to serve. Let thaw in the refrigerator. Unwrap and place in a baking dish; top with your favorite supermarket pasta sauce, and bake as directed.

- 1 (8-ounce) package cannelloni or manicotti shells
- 4 cups finely chopped cooked chicken
- 2 (8-ounce) containers chive-and-onion cream cheese
- 1 (10-ounce) package frozen chopped spinach, thawed and well drained
- 1 cup (4 ounces) shredded mozzarella cheese
- ½ cup Italian-seasoned breadcrumbs
- ¾ teaspoon garlic salt
- 1 teaspoon seasoned pepper
- Roasted Red Bell Pepper Sauce
- Garnish: chopped fresh basil or parsley

COOK pasta according to package directions; drain.
STIR together chicken and next 6 ingredients in a bowl.
CUT pasta shells lengthwise through the other side. Spoon about ½ cup chicken mixture into each shell, gently pressing cut sides together. Place, cut sides down, in 2 lightly greased 11- x 7-inch baking dishes. Pour Roasted Red Bell Pepper Sauce evenly over shells.
BAKE, covered, at 350° for 25 to 30 minutes or until thoroughly heated. Garnish, if desired. **Prep: 30 min., Bake: 30 min.**

Roasted Red Bell Pepper Sauce:

MAKES 3½ CUPS

This sauce is also great over your favorite noodles.

- 2 (7-ounce) jars roasted red bell peppers, drained
- 1 (16-ounce) jar creamy Alfredo sauce
- 1 (3-ounce) package shredded Parmesan cheese

PROCESS all ingredients in a blender until smooth, stopping to scrape down sides. **Prep: 5 min.**

NOTE: For testing purposes only, we used Bertolli Five Brothers Creamy Alfredo Sauce.

Have Snacks, Will Travel

Are we there yet?" How often have you heard that road-trip query? Holidays often mean travel, and dealing with car crankiness can be a daunting task. To please kids and grown-ups alike, take along these nonmessy homemade treats. They're just right for folks en route.

WALNUT-DATE BARS

MAKES 16 SQUARES

Wrap these chewy treats in plastic wrap, and place them in a zip-top plastic bag; freeze up to three months, if desired.

- 1 (18.25-ounce) package yellow cake mix
- ⅔ cup firmly packed brown sugar
- 2 large eggs
- ¾ cup butter or margarine, melted
- 2 cups chopped dates, divided
- 2 cups chopped walnuts or pecans, divided

COMBINE cake mix and brown sugar in a mixing bowl. Add eggs and melted butter, beating at medium speed with an electric mixer until blended (batter will be stiff). Spoon half of batter into a lightly greased 13- x 9-inch pan; sprinkle with 1 cup each of dates and walnuts.
STIR remaining 1 cup each of dates and walnuts into remaining batter; spread over mixture in pan.
BAKE at 350° for 30 to 35 minutes or until golden. Run a knife around edge of pan to loosen sides. Let stand 30 minutes before cutting. Cut into bars, and store in an airtight container. **Prep: 20 min., Bake: 35 min., Stand: 30 min.**

PAT ASAY
PHOENIX, ARIZONA

CRISPY PEANUT BUTTER-CHOCOLATE TREATS

MAKES 16 SQUARES

This recipe got our Test Kitchens' highest flavor rating.

- 1½ cups sugar
- 1½ cups light corn syrup
- 1½ cups chunky peanut butter
- 6 cups crisp rice cereal
- 1 (12-ounce) package semisweet chocolate morsels

COOK first 3 ingredients in a large saucepan over medium-low heat, stirring constantly, until blended and mixture begins to bubble. Remove mixture from heat.
COMBINE 6 cups cereal and chocolate morsels in a large bowl. Stir in hot peanut butter mixture until combined. Spread mixture into a plastic wrap-lined 13- x 9-inch pan. Cool completely; cut into squares. **Prep: 15 min., Cook: 5 min.**

SPICY NUT POPCORN

MAKES 8 SERVINGS

- 3 tablespoons butter or margarine
- 1 cup pine nuts or pecans
- ¾ cup slivered almonds
- 1 teaspoon chili powder
- ½ teaspoon salt
- ½ teaspoon grated lime rind
- 1 tablespoon fresh lime juice
- ¼ teaspoon ground cloves
- ¼ teaspoon pepper
- 1 (33.5-ounce) bag low-fat popcorn, popped

MELT butter in a large skillet over medium heat; add pine nuts and next 7 ingredients, and sauté 3 to 4 minutes. Pour warm mixture over popcorn, tossing to coat. **Prep: 10 min., Cook: 4 min.**

NOTE: For testing purposes only, we used Orville Redenbacher's Smart Pop Gourmet Popping Corn.

SPRING DE LEON
LISLE, ILLINOIS

from our kitchen

- Place a meat thermometer in the thickest part of the thigh (being sure not to touch the bone). The turkey is done when the thermometer registers 180°. Breast meat, which has less fat, only needs to come to 170°; remember that temperature if you're doing a turkey breast rather than a whole turkey.
- Don't seal turkey with foil or a roaster lid because it will steam rather than roast. If you choose to use an oven cooking bag, follow instructions on the box for moist, succulent turkey.
- Allow turkey to stand 15 to 20 minutes before carving.

Bring on the Bird—Fresh or Frozen

There's not much difference between a fresh or frozen turkey. Fresh is more convenient if you're pushed for time, but it will cost more per pound than frozen. Fresh turkeys may occasionally have ice crystals (from being refrigerated and transported at very cold temperatures) that will need to thaw. When selecting a turkey, keep in mind that two smaller birds may serve your needs better than one large.

How To Thaw

- Thaw a frozen turkey in the refrigerator in its original wrap. Place it on a tray or pan to catch any drips. Allow two to three days for an 8- to 12-pound turkey; a 12- to 16-pounder will require three to four days.
- To thaw the bird in less time, place the turkey in its unopened bag in a large container, and cover it with cold water. Change the water every 30 minutes to keep it cold (and safe). This will thaw an 8- to 12-pound turkey in four to six hours, while a 12- to 16-pound turkey takes six to nine hours.

How To Prepare

- When the turkey is completely thawed, remove the giblets and the neck from the body cavity (usually in a sack inside the bird).
- Rinse inside and out with cold water.
- Truss the turkey so that it will cook evenly, retain moisture, and have a compact shape. Here's how.

Step 1: Secure the legs. Some turkeys come with a metal clip; if yours doesn't, use cotton twine (ask your butcher for some).

Step 2: Tuck excess skin down between the breast and the legs so the skin won't split as the turkey cooks.

Step 3: Lift the tips of the wings up and over the breast, and tuck them under the turkey; secure excess of the neck flap (use a wooden pick if necessary).

Step 4: Line the roasting pan with foil for easier cleanup.

- Place the turkey on a rack in a shallow roasting pan. If you don't have a roasting pan, use a large foil roasting pan from the supermarket, and place it on a baking sheet for extra support.
- Follow your favorite recipe for seasoning, or try one of the great-tasting recipes on page 270.

How To Store Leftovers

Don't tie up valuable space in the refrigerator with the turkey carcass. Remove the meat from the bones. Place white meat slices and dark meat pieces in separate zip-top plastic bags—ready for sandwiches or other recipes.

For additional information, call the 24-hour Butterball Turkey Talk-Line at 1-800-BUTTERBALL (1-800-288-8372), or visit **www.butterball.com**

Tips and Tidbits

Do as much as possible ahead of time to enjoy a stress-free Thanksgiving feast. These hints will make your meal planning easier.

- Bake, crumble, and store cornbread for dressing in a zip-top plastic bag in the refrigerator up to five days ahead.
- Cranberry sauce and relish can be made two or three days ahead.
- Chop onion, celery, and green bell pepper for dressing up to three days ahead; store in zip-top plastic bags in the refrigerator.
- Don't forget about your microwave oven. Use it to melt chocolate, soften butter, and steam vegetables.

December

Try Our Holiday Favorites

Our Foods staff shares a holiday menu and sure-fire secrets for success. (See "Cook's Notes" on page 292 for helpful hints.) Enjoy this hearty offering of our favorite recipes.

Easy Holiday Menu
Serves 6

Molasses Pork Tenderloin With Red Wine Sauce

Creamy Leek Mashed Potatoes

Broccoli With Pimiento Cheese Sauce

Pepper Jelly-Glazed Carrots

Cranberry Congealed Salad

Two-Seed Bread Knots

Chocolate cake

Pinot noir

All year long, faithful readers send us their best recipes, many of which fill our pages each month with the most delicious Southern food around. In keeping with the holiday spirit, we've decided to give a little something back. We asked several folks from the *Southern Living* Foods staff—Lyda Jones, Rebecca Kracke Gordon, Mary Allen Perry, and Vanessa McNeil of our Test Kitchens, along with Cybil Brown Talley and Susan Dosier of our editorial team—to contribute their favorite holiday recipes. The recipes have been streamlined to make them easy for everyone, from the beginner to the seasoned pro. So enjoy this delicious array of no-fuss dishes that'll add sparkle to your table this season. We offer them with our compliments. Happy holidays.

MOLASSES PORK TENDERLOIN WITH RED WINE SAUCE

MAKES 6 TO 8 SERVINGS

Executive Foods Editor Susan Dosier says Red Wine Sauce adds an extra layer of flavor. She promises, "It's not as tricky as making gravy. If you can boil water, you can make this sauce." *(pictured on page 4)*

1 cup reduced-sodium soy sauce
1¼ cups molasses
¼ cup fresh lemon juice
¼ cup olive oil
3 tablespoons minced fresh ginger
2 large garlic cloves, minced
3 (¾-pound) pork tenderloins
Red Wine Sauce (optional)

COMBINE first 6 ingredients in a shallow dish or heavy-duty zip-top plastic bag; add tenderloins. Cover or seal, and chill 8 hours.

REMOVE tenderloins from marinade, discarding marinade.

GRILL tenderloins, covered with grill lid, over medium-high heat (350° to 400°) 20 minutes or until a meat thermometer inserted into thickest portion registers 160°, turning occasionally. Let stand 10 minutes before slicing. Serve with Red Wine Sauce, if desired. **Prep: 10 min., Chill: 8 hrs., Grill: 20 min., Stand: 10 min.**

NOTE: Tenderloins may be pan-seared in a hot skillet to brown and then baked at 375° for 15 to 20 minutes.

Red Wine Sauce:

MAKES ABOUT 1¼ CUPS

½ small sweet onion, minced
2 tablespoons butter
½ cup dry red wine
1 (14½-ounce) can beef broth
¼ cup water
2 tablespoons cornstarch

SAUTÉ onion in butter in a saucepan over medium-high heat 3 minutes. Add wine; cook 3 minutes. Add beef broth; bring to a boil, and cook 5 minutes.

STIR together ¼ cup water and cornstarch; add to broth mixture, stirring constantly, 1 minute or until mixture thickens. Remove from heat, and serve over tenderloin. **Prep: 5 min., Cook: 12 min.**

CREAMY LEEK MASHED POTATOES

MAKES 6 SERVINGS

Assistant Foods Editor Cybil Brown Talley gives this potato recipe a delightful tang by adding buttermilk.

        4 pounds baking potatoes, peeled
            and quartered
        1½ teaspoons salt, divided
        3 to 4 large leeks
        2 tablespoons butter or
            margarine
        ½ cup butter or margarine
        ½ teaspoon ground white
            pepper
        ½ to ¾ cup milk
        3 tablespoons buttermilk

BRING potatoes, 1 teaspoon salt, and water to cover to a boil in a Dutch oven; boil 20 to 25 minutes or until potatoes are tender. Drain and keep warm.

REMOVE root, tough outer leaves, and tops from leeks, leaving 2 inches of dark leaves. Thinly slice leeks; rinse well, and drain.

MELT 2 tablespoons butter in a large skillet over medium-high heat; add leeks, and sauté 5 minutes. (Do not brown.)

MASH potatoes with a potato masher; stir in remaining ½ teaspoon salt, ½ cup butter, and next 3 ingredients until blended. Stir in leeks. **Prep: 35 min., Cook: 30 min.**

BROCCOLI WITH PIMIENTO CHEESE SAUCE

MAKES 6 TO 8 SERVINGS

"Use any leftover sauce, along with your leftover turkey, to make a delicious open-faced sandwich," recommends Test Kitchens Director Lyda Jones. *(pictured on page 4)*

        2 pounds fresh broccoli, cut into
            spears
        Pimiento Cheese Sauce
        1 cup soft white breadcrumbs
        2 tablespoons butter, melted
        ⅓ cup shredded Parmesan cheese

ARRANGE broccoli in a steamer basket over boiling water. Cover, and steam 5 minutes or until crisp-tender.

ARRANGE broccoli in a lightly greased 11- x 7-inch baking dish. Pour Pimiento Cheese Sauce evenly over broccoli.

COMBINE breadcrumbs, melted butter, and Parmesan cheese; sprinkle evenly over cheese sauce.

BAKE at 375° for 20 minutes or until thoroughly heated. **Prep: 15 min., Cook: 5 min., Bake: 20 min.**

Pimiento Cheese Sauce:

MAKES 3½ CUPS

        ¼ cup butter
        ¼ cup all-purpose flour
        2 cups milk
        ¼ teaspoon salt
        1 teaspoon Worcestershire sauce
        2 cups (8 ounces) shredded sharp
            Cheddar cheese
        1 (4-ounce) jar diced pimiento, drained

MELT butter in a heavy saucepan over medium heat; add flour, stirring until smooth. Cook, stirring constantly, 1 minute.

ADD milk gradually, stirring constantly, until mixture is thickened and bubbly. Stir in salt and remaining ingredients. **Prep: 5 min., Cook: 7 min.**

PEPPER JELLY-GLAZED CARROTS

MAKES 6 SERVINGS

"In Texas, everyone has some type of pepper jelly on hand. It's a great way to add an extra boost of flavor to vegetables and sauces," says Test Kitchens staff member Vanessa McNeil. *(pictured on page 4)*

        1 (2-pound) package baby carrots
        1 (10½-ounce) can condensed chicken
            broth, undiluted
        2 tablespoons butter or margarine
        1 (10½-ounce) jar red pepper jelly

COMBINE carrots and chicken broth in a skillet over medium-high heat. Bring to a boil, and cook, stirring often, 6 to 8 minutes or until carrots are crisp-tender and broth is reduced to ¼ cup.

STIR in butter and pepper jelly, and cook, stirring constantly, 5 minutes or until mixture is thickened and carrots are glazed. **Prep: 5 min., Cook: 14 min.**

Cook's Notes

■ **Molasses Pork Tenderloin With Red Wine Sauce:**
Executive Foods Editor Susan Dosier suggests grilling the meat to free up precious oven and cooktop space. "Have the pork finished about 30 minutes before you're ready to sit down. Wrap it in heavy-duty plastic wrap; then wrap it in foil. This will allow it to rest longer without getting cold. As the meat rests, the flavorful juices are reabsorbed, making for moist slices," she says. Once the Red Wine Sauce is finished, unwrap the pork, and slice it on a clean cutting board.

■ **Broccoli With Pimiento Cheese Sauce:** For smooth, lump-free sauce, Test Kitchens Director Lyda Jones suggests warming milk in the microwave before adding it to the roux.

■ **Cranberry Congealed Salad:**
If you don't have a Bundt pan, don't worry. According to Recipe Development Director Mary Allen Perry, a lightly greased 10-cup ring mold works just fine. "Dip the mold in warm water (be careful not to submerge it) for 15 to 20 seconds, and the salad will release much more easily," she says. Any longer, and the gelatin will begin to melt. Mary Allen also suggests buying bags of cranberries in season and storing them in the freezer so you can enjoy the congealed salad year-round.

CRANBERRY CONGEALED SALAD

MAKES 12 SERVINGS

For a special presentation, Recipe Development Director Mary Allen Perry chills the salad in individual teacups. "This works particularly well for holiday luncheons," she says. Use leftover salad for Frosted Cranberry Congealed Salad Parfaits (see recipe below). *(pictured on page 4)*

1 (12-ounce) package fresh cranberries
½ cup sugar
3 (3-ounce) packages raspberry gelatin
2 cups boiling water
2 cups cranberry juice, chilled
1 (8-ounce) can crushed pineapple, undrained
2 celery ribs, diced (1 cup)
⅔ cup chopped pecans, toasted
Lettuce leaves
Pickled peaches
Fresh mint sprigs
Garnish: chopped pecans, toasted

PROCESS cranberries in a food processor 30 seconds or until coarsely chopped, stopping to scrape down sides.
STIR together cranberries and sugar in a bowl; set aside.
STIR together gelatin and 2 cups boiling water in a large bowl 2 minutes or until gelatin dissolves. Add cranberry juice, and chill 30 minutes or until consistency of unbeaten egg white.
STIR in cranberry mixture, pineapple, celery, and ⅔ cup pecans. Spoon into a lightly greased 10-cup Bundt pan; cover and chill 8 hours or until firm.
UNMOLD onto a lettuce-lined platter. Fill center of ring with pickled peaches and fresh mint sprigs. Garnish, if desired. **Prep: 30 min.; Chill: 8 hrs., 30 min.**

FROSTED CRANBERRY CONGEALED SALAD PARFAITS: Beat 8 ounces softened cream cheese at medium speed with an electric mixer until fluffy. Fold in 8 ounces frozen whipped topping, thawed. Layer parfait glasses evenly with leftover salad and cream cheese mixture.

TWO-SEED BREAD KNOTS

MAKES 20 ROLLS

Test Kitchens professional Rebecca Kracke Gordon serves these delicate rolls with honey butter. *(pictured on page 4)*

1 (¼-ounce) envelope rapid-rise yeast
1 cup warm water (100° to 110°)
3½ cups bread flour
2 tablespoons sugar
1½ teaspoons salt
3 tablespoons olive oil
1 egg yolk
1 tablespoon water
1 tablespoon sesame seeds
1 teaspoon poppy seeds

PREHEAT oven to 200°. Combine yeast and 1 cup warm water in a 1-cup liquid measuring cup; let stand 5 minutes.
COMBINE flour, sugar, and salt in a heavy-duty mixing bowl. Add yeast mixture and oil. Beat at low speed with an electric mixer 1 minute; beat at medium speed 5 minutes.
DIVIDE dough into 20 equal portions. Shape each portion into a 7-inch rope, and shape into a knot. Combine egg yolk and 1 tablespoon water; brush over rolls.
SPRINKLE with seeds; place on parchment paper-lined baking sheets. Turn oven off, and cover rolls loosely with plastic wrap; place in oven, and let rise 15 to 20 minutes or until doubled in bulk. Remove from oven, and preheat oven to 400°. Discard plastic wrap.
BAKE at 400° for 15 to 17 minutes or until golden. **Prep: 30 min., Stand: 5 min., Rise: 20 min., Bake: 17 min.**

NOTE: These rolls are named for their unique shape and a sprinkling of sesame and poppy seeds. To create this distinct look, roll each ball of dough into a 7-inch rope, then form into a knot. A pastry scraper makes cutting and working with dough much easier. Cover dough with plastic wrap or a clean towel to keep dough from drying out.

Christmas Cookies

Cookies are among our favorite holiday treats, and they're great to share as gifts, too.

These traditional Christmas recipes utilize both a refrigerated dough and a nonrefrigerated dough. The Linzer Cookies are decorative sandwiches shaped with a star cookie cutter. Beautiful and buttery, they're perfect for a holiday tea. For families on the go, Lemon Icebox Cookies with four variations are the solution. The easy dough is refrigerated so you can slice and bake cookies when you're ready.

NUTCRACKER SWEETS

MAKES 3½ TO 4 DOZEN

These will remind you of traditional wedding cookies or sand tarts with cherries.

- 1 cup butter, softened
- ¼ cup granulated sugar
- 2 cups all-purpose flour
- 2 cups ground almonds
- ¼ teaspoon almond extract
- ¼ cup maraschino cherries, drained and chopped
- Powdered sugar

BEAT butter and granulated sugar at medium speed with an electric mixer until creamy. Add flour, almonds, and extract, beating at low speed until well blended. Stir in cherries. Shape into 1-inch balls. Place on ungreased baking sheets.

BAKE at 325° for 18 to 22 minutes or until lightly browned. Remove to wire racks; cool 2 minutes. Roll in powdered sugar; cool on wire racks. **Prep: 20 min., Bake: 22 min. per batch, Cool: 2 min.**

TEDDY GRIEGER
OCEANSIDE, CALIFORNIA

LINZER COOKIES

MAKES ABOUT 3 DOZEN

A dough scraper—which can be purchased inexpensively at kitchen stores—makes transferring these star cutouts onto baking sheets a breeze.

- 1¼ cups butter, softened
- 1 cup powdered sugar, sifted
- 2½ cups all-purpose flour
- ½ cup finely chopped pecans, toasted
- ¼ teaspoon salt
- ¼ teaspoon ground cloves
- ¼ teaspoon ground cinnamon
- 1 teaspoon grated lemon rind
- ¼ cup seedless raspberry jam
- Powdered sugar

BEAT butter at medium speed with an electric mixer; gradually add 1 cup powdered sugar, beating until light and fluffy.

COMBINE flour and next 5 ingredients; gradually add to butter mixture, beating just until blended.

DIVIDE dough into 2 equal portions. Cover and chill 1 hour.

ROLL each portion to a ⅛-inch thickness on a lightly floured surface; cut with a 3-inch star-shaped cutter. Cut centers out of half of cookies with a 1½-inch star-shaped cutter. Place all stars on lightly greased baking sheets.

BAKE at 325° for 15 minutes; cool on wire racks. Spread solid cookies with jam; sprinkle remaining stars with powdered sugar. Top each solid cookie with a hollow star. **Prep: 25 min., Chill: 1 hr., Bake: 15 min. per batch**

LEMON ICEBOX COOKIES

MAKES 7 DOZEN

You can freeze these logs of dough up to two months.

- 1 cup butter, softened
- 1 cup granulated sugar
- 1 cup firmly packed light brown sugar
- 2 large eggs
- 1 teaspoon grated lemon rind
- 2 tablespoons fresh lemon juice
- 3½ cups all-purpose flour
- 1 teaspoon baking soda
- ½ teaspoon salt

BEAT butter and sugars at medium speed with an electric mixer until fluffy. Add eggs, 1 at a time, beating well after each addition. Add lemon rind and lemon juice, beating until blended.

COMBINE flour, baking soda, and salt; gradually add to butter mixture, beating just until blended.

DIVIDE dough into 3 equal portions; roll each on wax paper to a 12-inch log. Cover; chill 8 hours. Cut each log into ½-inch slices (about 28 slices); place on lightly greased baking sheets.

BAKE at 350° for 12 to 14 minutes or until edges are lightly browned. Remove to wire racks to cool. Store in an airtight container, or freeze, if desired. **Prep: 20 min., Chill: 8 hrs., Bake: 14 min. per batch**

LEMON-COCONUT COOKIES: Add 1 cup sweetened flaked coconut, toasted; proceed with recipe as directed.

LEMON-ALMOND COOKIES: Add 1 cup sliced almonds, toasted; proceed with recipe as directed.

LEMON-POPPY SEED COOKIES: Add 2 teaspoons poppy seeds; proceed with recipe as directed.

LEMON-PECAN COOKIES: Add 1 cup finely chopped pecans, toasted; proceed with recipe as directed.

Citrus Takes the Cake

Treat your family to one—or all—of these spectacular desserts this season.

Every year it's our pleasure to bring you a special holiday cake. Thanks to our Recipe Development Director, Mary Allen Perry, and Test Kitchens professional Rebecca Kracke Gordon, here's a magnificent trio—Fresh Orange Italian Cream Cake, Orange-Pecan-Spice Pound Cake, and Ambrosia Cheesecake. They're new twists on some of our favorite Southern holiday desserts.

All three received our highest rating. Bake the one that best fits your menu, or serve all three for a dessert buffet.

FRESH ORANGE ITALIAN CREAM CAKE

MAKES 12 TO 16 SERVINGS

You'll need to start this cake a day ahead because the Fresh Orange Curd must chill for 8 hours. *(pictured on cover)*

- ½ cup butter or margarine, softened
- ½ cup shortening
- 2 cups sugar
- 5 large eggs, separated
- 1 tablespoon vanilla extract
- 2 cups all-purpose flour
- 1 teaspoon baking soda
- 1 cup buttermilk
- 1 cup sweetened flaked coconut
- Fresh Orange Curd
- 3 cups Pecan-Cream Cheese Frosting
- ½ cup sweetened flaked coconut, lightly toasted (optional)
- Glazed Pecan Halves (optional)
- Boxwood Garland (optional, see box on page 295)

BEAT butter and shortening at medium speed with an electric mixer until fluffy; gradually add sugar, beating well. Add egg yolks, 1 at a time, beating until blended after each addition. Add vanilla; beat until blended.

COMBINE flour and soda; add to sugar mixture alternately with buttermilk, beginning and ending with flour mixture. Beat at low speed until blended after each addition. Stir in 1 cup coconut.

BEAT egg whites until stiff peaks form; fold into batter. Pour batter into 3 greased and floured 9-inch round cakepans.

BAKE at 350° for 25 minutes or until a wooden pick inserted in center comes out clean. Cool in pans on wire racks 10 minutes; remove from pans, and cool completely on wire racks.

SPREAD ¾ cup chilled Fresh Orange Curd between layers, and spread remaining Fresh Orange Curd on top of cake. (The orange curd layer on top of cake will be very thick.) If desired, loosely cover cake, and chill 8 hours. (Chilling the cake with the curd between the layers helps keep the layers in place and makes it much easier to spread the frosting.)

SPREAD 3 cups Pecan-Cream Cheese Frosting on sides of cake, reserving remaining frosting for another use. Sprinkle ½ cup toasted coconut over top of cake, if desired. Arrange Glazed Pecan Halves around top edge of cake, if desired. Store in refrigerator until ready to serve. Arrange Boxwood Garland around bottom edge of cake before serving, if desired. **Prep: 45 min., Bake: 25 min, Cool: 10 min.**

NOTE: Cake may be frosted with Pecan-Cream Cheese Frosting immediately after adding the Fresh Orange Curd, but the cake layers will not be as steady.

Fresh Orange Curd:

MAKES ABOUT 3 CUPS

You can substitute reconstituted orange juice for fresh; however, squeezing navel oranges only takes about 15 minutes and can make all the difference in this cake's fresh flavor.

- 1 cup sugar
- ¼ cup cornstarch
- 2 cups fresh orange juice (about 4 pounds navel oranges)
- 3 large eggs, lightly beaten
- ¼ cup butter
- 1 tablespoon grated orange rind

COMBINE sugar and cornstarch in a 3-quart saucepan; gradually whisk in fresh orange juice. Whisk in lightly beaten eggs. Bring to a boil (5 to 6 minutes) over medium heat, whisking constantly.

COOK, whisking constantly, 1 to 2 minutes or until a puddinglike thickness. Remove from heat, and whisk in butter and grated orange rind. Cover, placing plastic wrap directly on curd, and chill 8 hours. **Prep: 20 min., Cook: 10 min., Chill: 8 hrs.**

Pecan-Cream Cheese Frosting:

MAKES ABOUT 4 CUPS

Use leftover frosting on cupcakes or cookies, or freeze in an airtight container up to one month.

- 1 (8-ounce) package cream cheese, softened
- ½ cup butter, softened
- 1 tablespoon vanilla extract
- 1 (16-ounce) package powdered sugar
- 1 cup chopped pecans, toasted

BEAT first 3 ingredients at medium speed with an electric mixer until creamy. Gradually add powdered sugar, beating at low speed until blended. Beat at high speed until smooth; stir in pecans. **Prep: 10 min.**

Glazed Pecan Halves:

MAKES 2 CUPS

**2 cups pecan halves
⅓ cup light corn syrup
Vegetable cooking spray**

COMBINE pecan halves and corn syrup, stirring to coat pecans. Line a 15- x 10-inch jellyroll pan with parchment paper or aluminum foil; coat with cooking spray. Arrange pecan halves in an even layer in pan.

BAKE at 350° for 12 minutes; stir gently using a rubber spatula, and bake 8 more minutes. Remove from oven, and stir gently; arrange pecans in an even layer on wax paper, and let cool completely. **Prep: 5 min., Bake: 20 min.**

ORANGE-PECAN-SPICE POUND CAKE

MAKES 10 TO 12 SERVINGS

The chopped pecans form a nice, crisp coating on top of the baked cake.

**2 cups finely chopped pecans,
    toasted and divided
1 pound butter, softened
3 cups sugar
6 large eggs
4 cups all-purpose flour
⅛ teaspoon salt
¾ cup milk
2 tablespoons grated orange rind
2 teaspoons ground cinnamon
1 teaspoon ground nutmeg
1 teaspoon vanilla extract
1 teaspoon lemon extract
1 teaspoon orange extract
½ teaspoon ground cloves
Orange Syrup
Glazed Pecan Halves (optional, recipe
    above)
Boxwood Garland (optional, see box at
    top right)**

SPRINKLE 1¼ cups finely chopped pecans into a generously buttered 10-inch tube pan; shake to evenly coat bottom and sides of pan. (Excess nuts will fall to bottom of pan. Make certain nuts are in an even layer in bottom of pan.) Set aside.

Decorate With Ease

Recipe Development Director Mary Allen Perry designed this decorative garland to be used on all three cakes.

Boxwood Garland
2 dozen small sprigs fresh
    boxwood
3 dozen sour cherry candies*
Glazed Tangerine Segments
Sugared Fruit Ribbons

Just before serving, arrange boxwood sprigs, cherry candies, Glazed Tangerine Segments, and Sugared Fruit Ribbons in a decorative pattern to form a wreath around the outer edges of your holiday cake. *Note:* Boxwood makes a nice garnish but is poisonous if ingested, so be sure to warn guests.

Glazed Tangerine Segments:
Separate a peeled tangerine into individual segments, and brush lightly with corn syrup to create the look of glazed fruit.

Sugared Fruit Ribbons:
Create ribbons from strawberry-flavored chewy fruit rolls by the foot. (They come in 4.5-ounce packages. One roll from the package will provide enough ribbon for the garland.) Unroll fruit roll, and remove paper backing. Using scissors, cut roll in half lengthwise to form 2 narrow ribbons. Brush both sides of each ribbon lightly with water and sprinkle evenly with granulated sugar. Let dry for 15 minutes on a wire rack. Cut into desired lengths, and arrange as desired in the garland.

*Sour cherry candies are available by the pound at Target and other candy outlets. They are also available at some grocery stores in packages. Any round, red candies may be substituted.

BEAT butter at medium speed with an electric mixer until creamy; gradually add sugar, beating well. Add eggs, 1 at a time, beating until blended after each addition.

COMBINE flour and salt; add to butter mixture alternately with milk, beginning and ending with flour mixture. Beat at low speed until blended after each addition. Stir in remaining ¾ cup pecans, orange rind, and next 6 ingredients. Spoon evenly into prepared pan.

BAKE at 300° for 1 hour and 30 to 40 minutes or until a wooden pick inserted in center comes out clean. Cool in pan on a wire rack 20 minutes. Remove cake from pan; invert cake, pecan crust-side-up, onto wire rack.

BRUSH top and sides of cake gently several times with hot Orange Syrup, using a 2-inch-wide pastry brush and allowing the cake to absorb the syrup after each

brushing. (Do not pour syrup over cake.) Let cool completely on wire rack. Arrange Glazed Pecan Halves around top of cake, if desired. Arrange Boxwood Garland around bottom of cake before serving, if desired. **Prep: 25 min.; Bake: 1 hr., 40 min.; Cool: 20 min.**

Orange Syrup:

MAKES 1 CUP

**1 large orange
1 cup sugar**

REMOVE rind from orange with a vegetable peeler, avoiding bitter white pith. Squeeze orange to get ½ cup juice.
COMBINE orange rind, juice, and sugar in a small saucepan. Cook over low heat, stirring until sugar dissolves. Bring to a boil over medium-high heat, and boil 2 minutes. **Prep: 5 min., Cook: 8 min.**

AMBROSIA CHEESECAKE

MAKES 12 SERVINGS

- 1½ cups almond shortbread cookie crumbs (about 12 cookies)
- 3 tablespoons sugar
- 3 tablespoons butter or margarine, melted
- 4 (8-ounce) packages cream cheese, softened
- 3 large eggs
- 1 cup sugar
- 1 (14-ounce) package sweetened flaked coconut
- 2 teaspoons vanilla extract
- 2 cups Fresh Orange Curd (recipe on page 294)
- 1 cup sweetened flaked coconut, lightly toasted (optional)
- Decorated Pastry Strips (optional)
- Garnish: Boxwood garland (see box on page 295)

STIR together first 3 ingredients; press mixture into bottom of a 10-inch spring-form pan.

BAKE at 350° for 8 minutes. Cool.

BEAT cream cheese, eggs, and 1 cup sugar at medium speed with an electric mixer until fluffy. Stir in 14-ounce package coconut and vanilla. Pour into prepared crust.

BAKE at 350° for 1 hour. Cool completely on a wire rack.

COVER and chill 8 hours. Release sides of springform pan, and place cheesecake on a serving platter or cake stand. Spread Fresh Orange Curd evenly over top of cheesecake. Sprinkle 1 cup toasted coconut around outer edge of top, if desired. Arrange Decorated Pastry Strips on sides of cheesecake, if desired. Garnish, if desired. **Prep: 30 min.; Bake: 1 hr., 8 min.; Chill: 8 hrs.**

NOTE: For testing purposes only, we used Keebler Sandies Almond Shortbread cookies.

Decorated Pastry Strips:

MAKES ABOUT 4 DOZEN

- Poster board or sturdy cardboard at least 12 x 2¾ inches
- ½ (15-ounce) package refrigerated piecrusts
- ⅓ cup powdered sugar
- 12 ounces vanilla bark coating, divided

CUT 1 (12- x 2-inch) strip and 1 (12- x ¾-inch) strip from poster board, using a ruler as a guide.

UNFOLD piecrust on a lightly floured surface; gently roll to press out fold lines. Lay the 12- x 2-inch cardboard template horizontally across piecrust; cut piecrust into 5 (2-inch) strips. The bottom cut of each strip will be the top cut of new strip; do not separate strips. Lay the 12- x ¾-inch template vertically across piecrust; cut piecrust into ¾-inch strips. Separate into individual pieces. (There will be about 40 [2- x ¾-inch] pieces.) Arrange pastry pieces on an ungreased baking sheet ¼ inch apart.

BAKE at 425° for 4 to 5 minutes or until golden brown. Remove from oven. Remove half of pastry pieces on baking sheet to wire rack to cool; sprinkle remaining warm pieces evenly with powdered sugar. Let all pastry pieces cool completely.

MICROWAVE half of vanilla coating in a glass bowl at MEDIUM (50% power) 1 minute or until melted, stirring once; spoon into a small zip-top plastic bag, and seal. Snip a small hole in 1 corner of bag; pipe lace design (continuous string of melted coating without touching) on top side of each unsugared pastry piece. Let stand until coating is firm.

REPEAT melting procedure with remaining vanilla coating. Pipe a small amount of melted coating on the back of all pastry pieces; carefully press onto sides of cheesecake, alternating the patterned strips with the powdered sugar strips. (Tip: Press each piece onto cheesecake as it's piped; do not allow coating to harden before pressing onto cheesecake.) **Prep: 30 min., Bake: 5 min.**

Homemade Candy in 30 Minutes

Who doesn't like candy? Whether it's a midday snack, an ending to your meal, or a thoughtful gift for a friend, sweet treats delight your taste buds and boost your spirits.

These scrumptious confections take only 30 minutes or less to prepare.

PEANUT BUTTER FUDGE

MAKES 1¾ POUNDS

- ⅔ cup evaporated milk
- 1⅔ cups sugar
- ½ teaspoon salt
- 1½ cups miniature marshmallows
- 1 (10-ounce) package peanut butter morsels
- ½ cup chopped peanuts
- 1 teaspoon vanilla extract

BRING first 3 ingredients to a boil in a large saucepan; cook over medium heat, stirring constantly, 5 minutes; remove from heat. Add remaining ingredients, stirring until smooth. Pour into a greased 9-inch square pan; cool completely. Cut into squares. **Prep: 5 min., Cook: 5 min.**

SANDRA ENWRIGHT
WINTER PARK, FLORIDA

WHITE CHOCOLATE-PEANUT BUTTER CRUNCH

MAKES 1¾ POUNDS

- 8 (2-ounce) vanilla bark coating squares
- 2 tablespoons creamy peanut butter
- 2 cups miniature marshmallows
- 2 cups crisp rice cereal
- 2 cups dry-roasted peanuts

MICROWAVE coating in a large glass bowl at HIGH 2 minutes or until melted, stirring every 30 seconds. Stir in peanut butter until smooth. Stir in marshmallows, cereal, and peanuts.

DROP by teaspoonfuls onto wax paper. Let stand 15 minutes or until firm. **Prep: 10 min., Cook: 2 min., Stand: 15 min.**

DARK CHOCOLATE BONBONS

MAKES 5 DOZEN

- 6 (1-ounce) semisweet chocolate squares
- 5 tablespoons unsalted butter
- 2 large eggs, lightly beaten
- ½ cup sugar
- ½ cup all-purpose flour
- ½ teaspoon baking powder
- 1 teaspoon vanilla extract
- 1 cup chopped almonds
- Velvet Frosting

MELT chocolate and butter in a heavy saucepan over low heat, stirring until smooth; remove from heat. Add eggs, stirring until blended. Stir in sugar and next 4 ingredients.

LINE miniature muffin pans with miniature baking cups. Spoon chocolate mixture into lightly greased cups, filling about half full.

BAKE at 375° for 8 minutes. Cool in pans 10 minutes. Spread Velvet Frosting over bonbons. Store in refrigerator. Serve chilled. **Prep: 15 min., Bake: 8 min. per batch, Cool: 10 min.**

Velvet Frosting:

MAKES 1 CUP

- ½ cup whipping cream
- ¾ cup sugar
- 1 egg yolk
- 3 (1-ounce) unsweetened chocolate squares
- 2 tablespoons butter, softened
- 2 tablespoons vanilla extract

BRING whipping cream and sugar to a boil in a heavy saucepan, whisking constantly. Add egg yolk, and cook over medium heat, whisking constantly, 6 minutes or until candy thermometer registers 160°. Add chocolate and butter, stirring until smooth. Stir in vanilla. **Prep: 7 min., Cook: 6 min.**

ORANGE-NUT BALLS

MAKES 5 DOZEN

- ½ cup butter or margarine, melted
- 1 (16-ounce) package powdered sugar, sifted
- 1 (6-ounce) can frozen orange juice concentrate, thawed
- 1 (12-ounce) package vanilla wafers, crushed
- 1 cup finely chopped pecans
- 1 (14-ounce) package sweetened flaked coconut

STIR together butter and sugar; stir in orange juice concentrate, vanilla wafers, and pecans. Shape into 1-inch balls, and roll in coconut. Cover and chill at least 1 hour or until firm. Store in refrigerator up to 3 weeks. **Prep: 30 min., Chill: 1 hr.**

PATTI DEMPSEY
GAHANNA, OHIO

Sip on These Desserts

Make sure your guests save room for an after-dinner treat, then serve them one of these heavenly dessert beverages. If you're like our Foods staff, you'll be ready for second servings of these creamy concoctions. Sip on our soothing Mocha-Mint Shake, or try Hot Chocolate Nog for the perfect toddy on a chilly night.

MOCHA-MINT SHAKE

MAKES 4½ CUPS

- 4 cups vanilla ice cream
- 1½ cups milk
- ½ cup peppermint schnapps or
- ¼ teaspoon peppermint extract
- 1 tablespoon instant coffee granules
- 2 tablespoons chocolate syrup

PROCESS all ingredients in a blender until smooth. Serve immediately. **Prep: 5 min.**

EGGNOG-COFFEE PUNCH

MAKES 10 TO 12 SERVINGS

This Southern favorite received our highest marks.

- 1 quart coffee ice cream
- 1 quart vanilla ice cream
- 1 quart eggnog
- 2 cups hot brewed coffee
- ½ cup coffee liqueur or strong brewed coffee
- ½ cup bourbon (optional)
- Frozen whipped topping, thawed
- Ground nutmeg

SCOOP ice cream into a punch bowl. Add eggnog, coffee, liqueur, and, if desired, bourbon, stirring until ice cream slightly melts. Serve in glass mugs. Dollop with whipped topping; sprinkle with nutmeg. Serve immediately. **Prep: 10 min.**

NOTE: For testing purposes only, we used Kahlúa coffee liqueur.

AMANDA HIGHTOWER
MACON, GEORGIA

HOT CHOCOLATE NOG

MAKES 7½ CUPS

It's best to serve this delicious nog immediately, while it's still hot.

- 1 quart eggnog
- 2 cups milk
- ½ cup chocolate syrup
- 1 cup bourbon*
- ¼ teaspoon ground nutmeg
- Miniature marshmallows

HEAT first 3 ingredients in a large saucepan over medium heat, stirring constantly. Remove from heat, and stir in bourbon. Stir in nutmeg. Pour mixture evenly into 8 mugs. Top with marshmallows, and serve immediately. **Prep: 10 min., Cook: 5 min.**

*Substitute 1 cup milk and 1 tablespoon vanilla extract for bourbon, if desired.

BEVERLY MULLINAX
NEW ORLEANS, LOUISIANA

MILK PUNCH

MAKES 6 CUPS

1 cup sugar
½ cup water
1 quart half-and-half
1 cup brandy
1½ teaspoons vanilla extract
Ground nutmeg

BRING sugar and ½ cup water to a boil in a saucepan over medium heat, and cook, stirring constantly, 5 minutes or until syrup consistency. Let cool.
STIR together cooled syrup, half-and-half, brandy, and vanilla. Serve over ice. Sprinkle with nutmeg. **Prep: 10 min., Cook: 8 min.**

LORI COOK
WICHITA FALLS, TEXAS

CREAMY COCONUT SIPPER

MAKES 5 CUPS

2½ cups ice cubes
1 cup half-and-half
½ cup cream of coconut
½ cup crème de cacao
½ cup coffee liqueur
½ cup rum

PROCESS all ingredients in a blender until smooth. Serve immediately. **Prep: 5 min.**

NOTE: For testing purposes only, we used Kahlúa coffee liqueur.

SANDI PICHON
SLIDELL, LOUISIANA

Children in the Kitchen

Looking for gifts your children can make? Youngsters can create these tasty treats with limited preparation time and pantry ingredients.

HOLIDAY TREES

MAKES 12 TREES

Green food coloring paste
8 (2-ounce) vanilla bark coating squares, chopped and melted
12 pointed ice-cream cones
Toppings: green and white sparkling sugars, holiday sprinkles, candy-coated chocolate pieces, gumdrops

STIR paste into melted coating until blended and desired color is achieved. Dip each cone into coating, and immediately sprinkle with green sugar. Press candies into coating, and press 1 gumdrop on the top of each cone. Dry on a wire rack. Pour white sparkling sugar into a clear plastic cup, and add tree; place in a plastic bag, and tie with ribbon, if desired. **Prep: 10 min.**

COLA CANDY

MAKES 2 DOZEN

3½ cups vanilla wafer crumbs
2 cups powdered sugar
1 cup chopped pecans
½ cup cola soft drink*
2 tablespoons butter or margarine, melted
Cola Frosting

STIR together first 5 ingredients; shape mixture into 1-inch balls. Cover and chill at least 30 minutes.
DIP balls in Cola Frosting; chill until ready to serve. **Prep: 15 min., Chill: 30 min.**

Cola Frosting:

MAKES 1½ CUPS

¾ cup powdered sugar
¼ teaspoon vanilla extract
¼ cup butter or margarine, softened
⅓ cup cola soft drink*

STIR together all ingredients. **Prep: 5 min.**

*Substitute your favorite dark soft drink, if desired.

HOLLY HENEGAR
JASPER, TENNESSEE

CHUNKS OF SNOW

MAKES 1½ POUNDS

1 pound vanilla bark coating squares, chopped
1 (3.5-ounce) jar macadamia nuts
1 (6-ounce) package sweetened dried cranberries

MELT coating in a saucepan over low heat, stirring constantly.
REMOVE from heat; stir in nuts and dried cranberries. Spread onto a lightly greased baking sheet. Cool. Break into pieces. **Prep: 5 min., Cook: 5 min.**

CLAIRIECE GILBERT HUMPHREY
CHARLOTTESVILLE, VIRGINIA

MINIATURE PEANUT BUTTER CRACKER BITES

MAKES 3 DOZEN

3 (2-ounce) chocolate bark coating squares
1 tablespoon shortening
3 dozen miniature round peanut butter-filled crackers

COMBINE chocolate coating and shortening in the top of a double boiler. Bring water to a boil in bottom of double boiler; reduce heat, and simmer. Place chocolate and shortening over water, and cook, stirring constantly, until melted.
DIP crackers in chocolate, and place on wax paper. Chill 15 minutes or until chocolate hardens. **Prep: 15 min., Chill: 15 min.**

GAYLE MILLICAN
ROWLETT, TEXAS

CANDY CANE SWIZZLE STICKS

MAKES 12 CANDY CANES

4 (2-ounce) vanilla bark coating squares, chopped and melted
Green food coloring paste
12 large candy canes
Toppings: holiday sprinkles, colored sugars

STIR together melted vanilla coating and desired amount of paste. (We used a wooden pick dipped once in food coloring paste to tint coating.) Dip ends of candy canes 2 to 3 inches into coating; let excess drip off. Sprinkle immediately with desired toppings, and dry on a wire rack. **Prep: 10 min.**

CANDY SHOP PIZZA COOKIES

MAKES 2 (6-INCH) PIZZAS

> 10 tablespoons butter or margarine, softened
> ½ cup granulated sugar
> ½ cup firmly packed light brown sugar
> 1 tablespoon dark brown sugar
> 1 large egg
> ½ teaspoon vanilla extract
> 1½ cups all-purpose flour
> ½ teaspoon baking soda
> ½ teaspoon salt
> 1 cup semisweet chocolate morsels, divided
> 1 cup white chocolate morsels, divided
> ½ cup crunchy peanut butter
> Toppings: holiday sprinkles, candy-coated chocolate pieces, white chocolate pretzels
> White chocolate, melted

BEAT first 4 ingredients at medium speed with an electric mixer until creamy. Beat in egg and vanilla; blend well.

COMBINE flour, soda, and salt; gradually add to butter mixture, beating well after each addition. Stir in ½ cup each of semisweet and white chocolate morsels. Spread dough evenly onto 2 lightly greased 6-inch round pizza pans.

BAKE at 375° for 20 to 25 minutes or until lightly browned. Working quickly, sprinkle crust with remaining semisweet and white chocolate morsels; drop peanut butter by tablespoonfuls onto crust. Let stand 5 minutes or until morsels and peanut butter are softened; gently spread evenly over crust. Decorate with desired toppings; drizzle pizza with melted white chocolate. **Prep: 30 min., Bake: 25 min., Stand: 5 min.**

NOTE: Substitute one lightly greased 12-inch pizza pan, if desired.

VIKKI D. STURM
ROSSVILLE, GEORGIA

Zesty Slow-Cooker Recipes

There may be no better—or easier—way to make dinner than this.

SPICY-SWEET RIBS AND BEANS

MAKES 8 SERVINGS

> 2 (16-ounce) cans pinto beans, drained
> 4 pounds country-style pork ribs, trimmed
> 1 teaspoon garlic powder
> ½ teaspoon salt
> ½ teaspoon pepper
> 1 medium onion, chopped
> 1 (10.5-ounce) jar red jalapeño jelly
> 1 (18-ounce) bottle hickory-flavored barbecue sauce
> 1 teaspoon green hot sauce

PLACE beans in a 5-quart slow cooker; set aside.

CUT ribs apart; sprinkle with garlic powder, salt, and pepper. Place ribs on a broiler pan.

BROIL 5½ inches from heat 18 to 20 minutes or until browned, turning once. Add ribs to slow cooker, and sprinkle with onion.

COMBINE jelly, barbecue sauce, and hot sauce in a saucepan; cook over low heat until jelly melts. Pour over ribs, and stir gently.

COVER and cook at HIGH 5 to 6 hours or at LOW 9 to 10 hours. Remove ribs. Drain bean mixture, reserving sauce. Skim fat from sauce. Arrange ribs over bean mixture; serve with sauce. **Prep: 30 min., Broil: 20 min., Cook: 6 hrs. (HIGH) or 10 hrs. (LOW)**

NOTE: For testing purposes only, we used Kraft Thick 'n' Spicy Hickory Smoke Barbecue Sauce and Tabasco Green Pepper Sauce.

EASY CHILI

MAKES 6 TO 8 SERVINGS

Top this meaty winter favorite with shredded Cheddar cheese and corn chips.

> 1½ pounds lean ground beef
> 1 medium onion, chopped
> 1 small green bell pepper, chopped
> 2 garlic cloves, minced
> 2 (16-ounce) cans red kidney beans, rinsed and drained
> 2 (14½-ounce) cans diced tomatoes
> 2 to 3 tablespoons chili powder
> 1 teaspoon salt
> 1 teaspoon pepper
> 1 teaspoon ground cumin

COOK first 4 ingredients in a large skillet over medium-high heat, stirring until beef crumbles and is no longer pink; drain. Place mixture in a 5-quart slow cooker; stir in beans and remaining ingredients. Cook at HIGH 3 to 4 hours or at LOW 5 to 6 hours. **Prep: 15 min., Cook: 4 hrs. (HIGH) or 6 hrs. (LOW)**

DELLA TAYLOR
JONESBORO, TENNESSEE

SLOW-COOKER BEEF BARBECUE

MAKES 12 SERVINGS

> 4 pounds beef stew meat, cubed
> 2 (8-ounce) cans tomato sauce
> 1 medium onion, chopped
> ½ cup white vinegar
> ¼ cup firmly packed brown sugar
> 2 teaspoons salt
> 1 teaspoon minced garlic
> 1½ teaspoons ground cinnamon (optional)
> ¾ teaspoon ground cloves (optional)
> 12 sandwich buns

PLACE beef in 5-quart slow cooker. Combine tomato sauce, next 5 ingredients, and, if desired, cinnamon and cloves; pour over beef. Cook at LOW 9 hours.

REMOVE beef from slow cooker; shred with two forks. Return beef to slow cooker, and stir into sauce. Serve on buns. **Prep: 15 min., Cook: 9 hrs.**

BETH MARTIN SINE
FAULKNER, MARYLAND

Special Occasion Salads

If you're looking for the perfect salad to accompany that special holiday meal, pick any one of these recipes, and you're in business. In fact, all exude so much color and flavor they might just steal the show. The dressings can be made ahead and chilled for several days. Let those that are olive oil-based stand at room temperature for a while before tossing.

Whichever salad you choose, it will offer a fresh, crisp complement to the other dishes—always a bonus in this season of rich food.

CRANBERRY-STRAWBERRY-JÍCAMA SALAD

MAKES 8 TO 10 SERVINGS

The raw jícama in this salad adds flavor and crunch. Sometimes referred to as the Mexican potato, jícama has a sweet, nutty taste and can be eaten raw or cooked.

- ½ cup olive oil
- ½ cup orange juice
- ¼ cup cranberry-orange relish
- 1 small shallot, peeled and chopped
- 2 tablespoons balsamic vinegar
- ¼ teaspoon ground red pepper
- ¼ teaspoon salt
- ¼ teaspoon freshly ground pepper
- 1 large jícama
- 2 (5-ounce) packages gourmet mixed salad greens
- 2 cups sliced fresh strawberries
- ½ cup sweetened dried cranberries, finely chopped
- 2 large navel oranges, peeled and sectioned (optional)
- Garnish: shaved Pecorino Romano or Parmesan cheese

PROCESS first 8 ingredients in a blender until smooth, stopping to scrape down sides.

CUT jícama into cubes, or if desired, cut into ¼-inch slices, then cut with a 1½-inch star-shaped cutter.
PLACE jícama, salad greens, strawberries, cranberries, and, if desired, orange sections in a large bowl. Drizzle with vinaigrette, and gently toss to coat. Garnish, if desired. **Prep: 30 min.**

NOTE: For testing purposes only, we used Ocean Spray Cran-Fruit Crushed Fruit For Chicken (Cranberry Orange flavor) for the cranberry-orange relish. It comes in a plastic tub with a cardboard sleeve and can be found in the canned fruit section of your grocery store near the cranberry sauces.

GLORIA PLEASANTS
WILLIAMSBURG, VIRGINIA

ITALIAN HOUSE SALAD

MAKES 6 SERVINGS

This salad is the ideal accompaniment with your favorite hot pasta entrée. Add cooked, cubed ham or salami for a main-dish meal or white beans for a meatless main dish.

- ⅓ cup shredded Parmesan cheese
- ⅔ cup vegetable oil
- ⅓ cup red wine vinegar
- 1 teaspoon Italian seasoning
- 1 teaspoon dried parsley
- ¼ teaspoon garlic powder
- ¼ teaspoon pepper
- ⅛ teaspoon salt
- 1 large head Red Leaf lettuce, torn
- 1 (14-ounce) can artichoke heart quarters, drained
- 1 (6-ounce) can pitted ripe olives, drained
- 4 plum tomatoes, coarsely chopped
- 1 small red onion, thinly sliced
- ½ pound provolone cheese, shredded

WHISK together first 8 ingredients.
PLACE lettuce and next 5 ingredients in a large bowl. Drizzle with vinaigrette, and gently toss to coat. **Prep: 20 min.**

MITZI J. ERTHAL
SLIDELL, LOUISIANA

BLUE CHEESE SALAD WITH SPICY PECANS

MAKES 8 SERVINGS

This salad pairs perfectly with fresh raspberries, pear slices, or avocado slices.

- ½ cup olive oil
- 3 tablespoons raspberry vinegar
- 1 shallot, minced
- ¼ teaspoon salt
- ⅛ teaspoon ground white pepper
- 2 large heads Bibb lettuce, torn
- 4 ounces blue cheese, crumbled
- 2 green onions, thinly sliced
- 2 cups Spicy Pecans

WHISK together first 5 ingredients.
PLACE lettuce in a large bowl. Sprinkle with cheese, green onions, and Spicy Pecans. Drizzle with vinaigrette, and gently toss to coat. **Prep: 10 min.**

Spicy Pecans:

MAKES ABOUT 4 CUPS

If the pecans become sticky after storing, reheat on a foil-lined pan. These also are wonderful for snacking.

- ⅓ cup sugar
- ¼ cup butter or margarine
- ¼ cup orange juice
- 1¼ teaspoons salt
- 1¼ teaspoons ground cinnamon
- ¼ to ½ teaspoon ground red pepper
- ¼ teaspoon ground mace
- 1 pound pecan halves (about 4 cups)

STIR together first 7 ingredients in a heavy skillet over medium heat, stirring until butter melts and sugar dissolves. Remove skillet from heat; add nuts, and toss to coat.
PLACE pecan mixture in a single layer in an aluminum foil-lined 15- x 10-inch jellyroll pan.
BAKE at 250° for 1 hour, stirring every 15 minutes. Cool in pan on a wire rack, separating pecans with a fork. Store in an airtight container up to 1 week, or freeze up to 1 month. **Prep: 10 min., Cook: 5 min., Bake: 1 hr.**

FRAN LYONS
MONTGOMERY, ALABAMA

Jamaican Pork Tenderloin With Sauce Caribe, page 320

Aunt Suzi's Brisket, page 321

Bacon 'n' Egg Breakfast Empanadas,
page 324

Pecan Pie Cheesecake, page 318

Pecan-Caramel Crunch Ice Cream,
page 322

Chowder Power

Try these chowders made with ingredients from your pantry and refrigerator. They will provide your family with a quick, hearty meal. All of these recipes can be made ahead and reheated to serve for casual entertaining during the holiday season.

CHICKEN CORN CHOWDER

MAKES 6 SERVINGS

Reader Susan McAllen-Wyatt says this recipe tastes best when served the next day. It can be thinned with milk when reheating, if necessary.

1 tablespoon butter or margarine
1 (8-ounce) package sliced fresh
   mushrooms
1 medium onion, chopped
2 (14½-ounce) cans chicken broth
1 (16-ounce) package frozen shoepeg
   white corn
2 cups cubed cooked chicken breast
1 (10¾-ounce) can cream of chicken
   soup
½ cup uncooked orzo
½ teaspoon dried basil
½ teaspoon dried rosemary or thyme
1 tablespoon sugar
½ teaspoon salt
½ teaspoon pepper
1 cup milk
2 tablespoons all-purpose flour

MELT butter in a large Dutch oven over medium-high heat; add mushrooms and chopped onion, and sauté 5 minutes or until tender.
ADD broth and next 9 ingredients; simmer 10 minutes or until orzo is tender.
STIR together milk and flour in a small bowl; gradually stir into chowder, and simmer 5 minutes. **Prep: 10 min., Cook: 20 min.**

SUSAN MCALLEN-WYATT
HOMEWOOD, ALABAMA

SHOPPING DAY CLAM CHOWDER

MAKES 4 TO 6 SERVINGS

1 (18.5-ounce) can clam chowder
1 (14½-ounce) can chicken broth
1 (10¾-ounce) can cream of celery
   soup
1 medium baking potato, cooked and
   cubed
1 (10-ounce) can chopped clams
1 (5-ounce) can evaporated milk
½ cup half-and-half
3 tablespoons butter or margarine
½ teaspoon pepper
French bread or crackers

COOK first 6 ingredients in a Dutch oven over low heat, stirring often, 8 to 10 minutes or until thoroughly heated. Add half-and-half, butter, and pepper, stirring until butter melts. Serve with French bread or crackers. **Prep: 5 min., Cook: 15 min.**

KIM CHILDERS
CONROE, TEXAS

CHEESE-VEGETABLE CHOWDER

MAKES 6 TO 8 SERVINGS

¼ cup butter or margarine
1 (10-ounce) package frozen peas
¼ cup chopped onion
1 large green bell pepper, chopped
2 medium carrots, chopped
1 medium baking potato, diced
1 (32-ounce) container chicken broth
2 cups milk
⅓ cup all-purpose flour
3 cups (12 ounces) shredded sharp
   Cheddar cheese
¼ teaspoon salt
½ teaspoon pepper

MELT butter in a large Dutch oven over medium heat. Add peas and next 4 ingredients; cover and cook, stirring occasionally, 20 to 25 minutes or until tender. Add broth; bring to a boil.
STIR together milk and flour; gradually stir into chowder, blending well. Cook 1 minute, stirring until thickened.
STIR in cheese. Cook over medium heat, stirring until cheese melts. Add salt and pepper. **Prep: 15 min., Cook: 35 min.**

CHARLOTTE BRYANT
GREENSBURG, KENTUCKY

FIESTA CHOWDER

MAKES 8 TO 10 SERVINGS

The ingredient list may be long, but preparation is fast, and the results are delicious.

3 tablespoons all-purpose flour
1 (1.4-ounce) package fajita
   seasoning, divided
4 skinned and boned chicken breast
   halves, cubed
3 tablespoons vegetable oil
1 medium onion, chopped
1 teaspoon minced garlic
1 (15¼-ounce) can whole kernel corn
   with red and green peppers,
   drained
1 (15-ounce) can black beans, rinsed
   and drained
1 (14½-ounce) can Mexican-style
   stewed tomatoes
1 (4.5-ounce) can chopped green
   chiles
3 cups water
1 cup uncooked instant brown rice
1 (2¼-ounce) can sliced ripe olives
   (optional)
1 (10¾-ounce) can nacho cheese soup
3 tablespoons chopped fresh
   cilantro
1 tablespoon lime juice
Garnish: chopped fresh cilantro

COMBINE flour and 2 tablespoons fajita seasoning in a heavy-duty zip-top plastic bag; add chicken. Seal and shake to coat.
COOK chicken in hot oil in a large Dutch oven over high heat, stirring often, 4 minutes or until browned. Reduce heat to medium-high; add onion and garlic; sauté 5 minutes.
STIR in remaining fajita seasoning, corn, next 5 ingredients, and, if desired, olives.
BRING to a boil; reduce heat to medium-low, cover and simmer 5 minutes.
UNCOVER; stir in cheese soup, 3 tablespoons chopped cilantro, and lime juice. Garnish, if desired. **Prep: 15 min., Cook: 15 min.**

TERESA DRUM
BARTLETT, TENNESSEE

Casual Celebration

Test Kitchens professional Vanessa McNeil shares her family's recipes in a richly satisfying Texas menu. If it's still warm enough to grill, add sizzle with a steak, and savor these simple, fresh side dishes.

Christmas at the Ranch

Serves 4

Sweet-and-Spicy Texas Pecans

Pico de Gallo   Rib-Eye Grill

Lime Sweet Potatoes

Buttery Green Beans

Spicy Brussels Sprouts

Pecan pie   Chocolate cream pie

Test Kitchens professional Vanessa McNeil's family celebrates every Christmas at their Double Mac Ranch in Weimar, Texas. It's casual, mostly spent on the large screened porch that wraps around the house and shelters their Christmas tree and dinner table. Her parents, Vance and Georgana, come from Houston; her brother Keith and his family scoot over from Dallas; and Vanessa and her husband travel from Birmingham.

Vanessa's family loves great food, but they also like to keep it simple; all the recipes can be prepared ahead and have Texas flair. Grilling is a favorite pastime, so Vanessa's Dad cooks rib-eyes on a large grill billowing mesquite smoke. The aroma is as delicious as the food.

When they've savored every bit of the main course and side dishes, they move over to dessert: pecan pie and chocolate cream pie. The best dessert, though, comes as they gather around the burning pit and roast marshmallows for s'mores. Vanessa and her brother have cherished this tradition since they were very young.

As Vanessa sits by the fire, she can close her eyes and feel the cool breeze on her face. Her heart is warm, though, for her family is together for Christmas. Come join them for a piece of pie, and enjoy a big Texas welcome.

SWEET-AND-SPICY TEXAS PECANS

MAKES 2½ CUPS

Make this ahead of time, and store in an airtight tin; reheat in the oven before serving.

- ½ **pound chopped pecans or pecan halves**
- 2 **tablespoons butter or margarine, melted**
- 2 **tablespoons sugar**
- ¼ **teaspoon ground red pepper**

COMBINE pecans and melted butter in an aluminum foil-lined jellyroll pan. **BAKE** at 350° for 5 minutes. **COMBINE** sugar and red pepper; sprinkle half of sugar mixture over pecans. Bake 5 more minutes, stirring once. Remove from oven; toss with remaining sugar mixture. **Prep: 5 min., Bake: 10 min.**

PICO DE GALLO

MAKES 2½ CUPS

- 6 **plum tomatoes, chopped**
- 1 **medium onion, chopped**
- 3 **tablespoons minced fresh cilantro**
- 2 **tablespoons fresh lime juice**
- 1 **garlic clove, minced**
- ½ **teaspoon salt**

COMBINE all ingredients. Cover; chill at least 1 hour. Serve with grilled meats, tortillas, or chips. **Prep: 15 min., Chill: 1 hr.**

RIB-EYE GRILL

MAKES 4 SERVINGS

- 1 **teaspoon salt**
- ½ **teaspoon garlic powder**
- ½ **teaspoon chili powder**
- ½ **teaspoon dried oregano**
- ¼ **teaspoon ground red pepper**
- 4 **(8-ounce) rib-eye steaks**

COMBINE first 5 ingredients, and rub over steaks. Let stand 1 hour. **GRILL,** covered with grill lid, over high heat (400° to 500°) 7 minutes. Turn steaks, and grill 5 more minutes or to desired degree of doneness. **Prep: 10 min., Stand: 1 hr., Grill: 12 min.**

Lime Sweet Potatoes

MAKES 4 SERVINGS

3 large sweet potatoes, peeled and
   cubed
2 tablespoons olive oil
3 tablespoons honey
½ teaspoon grated lime rind
2 tablespoons fresh lime juice

COMBINE potatoes and olive oil, and
spread in an aluminum foil-lined jelly-
roll pan.
BAKE at 350° for 20 minutes.
COMBINE honey, lime rind, and lime
juice. Pour over potatoes; gently toss.
Bake 20 more minutes. Serve warm.
Prep: 20 min., Bake: 40 min.

Buttery Green Beans

MAKES 4 SERVINGS

1 pound fresh green beans
3 tablespoons butter or margarine
½ teaspoon salt

BRING beans and water to cover to a boil
over high heat; cook 2 minutes. Drain
and rinse with cold water; drain.
MELT butter in a large nonstick skillet
over medium heat, and cook 2 minutes
or until butter begins to brown. Add
beans, and cook until thoroughly heated.
Sprinkle with salt. **Prep: 15 min., Cook: 10 min.**

Spicy Brussels Sprouts

MAKES 4 SERVINGS

1 pound brussels sprouts
2 tablespoons butter or margarine
1 small jalapeño pepper, seeded and
   chopped
1 garlic clove, minced
1 tablespoon sugar

CUT each brussels sprout in half, and
slice into shreds.
MELT butter in a large skillet over
medium-high heat. Add jalapeño pepper
and garlic; sauté until tender. Add
sprouts; sauté 2 minutes. Sprinkle with
sugar, and sauté 1 more minute. Serve
immediately. **Prep: 15 min., Cook: 5 min.**

Pork Chops Tonight

The next time you prepare pork chops,
forget about frying. Whether you
decide to grill, bake, or simmer them on
the stove top, choose bone-in or boneless
chops as thick or as thin as you like. Both
kinds are versatile and very flavorful. You
probably have the ingredients for these
recipes on hand, so give a familiar cut of
meat a tasty new attitude.

Cider Pork Chops

MAKES 4 SERVINGS

If you choose a thinner, less expensive chop,
decrease the cooking time. Begin to check for
doneness after 30 minutes.

½ cup all-purpose flour
1 teaspoon salt
¼ teaspoon pepper
4 (1-inch-thick) bone-in pork chops
3 tablespoons butter or margarine,
   divided
4 Granny Smith apples, thinly sliced
1 cup raisins (optional)
1 cup firmly packed dark brown sugar
1 cup apple cider

COMBINE first 3 ingredients in a heavy-
duty zip-top plastic bag; add chops. Seal
and shake to coat. Remove chops, and
set aside.
MELT 2 tablespoons butter in a large skillet; add chops, and cook 5 minutes on
each side or until browned.
GREASE a 13- x 9-inch baking dish with
remaining 1 tablespoon butter. Place
apples in dish; top with raisins, if
desired, and sprinkle with brown sugar.
Arrange chops over brown sugar, and
drizzle with cider.
BAKE at 350° for 1 hour or until pork
chops are done. **Prep: 15 min., Cook: 10 min.,
Bake: 1 hr.**

Grilled Asian Pork Chops

MAKES 6 SERVINGS

Boneless chops also work well in this recipe. If
you splurge on thicker chops, you'll need to
cook them a bit longer.

6 tablespoons soy sauce
6 garlic cloves, minced
1 teaspoon pepper
2 teaspoons dark sesame oil
2 teaspoons fresh lime juice
6 (¼- to ½-inch-thick) bone-in pork
   chops

COMBINE first 5 ingredients in a large
shallow dish or heavy-duty zip-top plastic bag; add chops. Cover or seal, and
chill 4 hours.
REMOVE chops from marinade, discarding marinade.
GRILL chops, covered with grill lid, over
medium-high heat (350° to 400°) 4 minutes on each side or until an instant-read
thermometer inserted into thickest portion registers 160°. **Prep: 10 min., Chill: 4
hrs., Grill: 8 min.**

JUDY LEE
AUSTIN, TEXAS

Italian Pork Chops

MAKES 4 SERVINGS

4 (6-ounce) center-cut pork chops
1 tablespoon vegetable oil
1 (15-ounce) can tomato sauce
½ cup water
1 small onion, sliced
1 teaspoon Italian seasoning
½ teaspoon salt
½ teaspoon pepper
1 (8-ounce) package sliced fresh
   mushrooms
1 green bell pepper, sliced

BROWN chops in hot oil in a large skillet over medium-high heat. Drain and
remove chops from skillet.
ADD tomato sauce and next 7 ingredients
to skillet, stirring to combine. Return chops
to skillet. Bring to a boil; cover, reduce
heat, and simmer 30 minutes or until
chops are tender. **Prep: 10 min., Cook: 40 min.**

NANCY RUSSELL
MORO, ARKANSAS

Lightened-Up Chicken Favorites

Add these fabulous hearty chicken dishes to your recipe collection. These lighter versions of popular *Southern Living* entrées will be a huge hit at your supper table.

Wouldn't it be great if every time you grabbed a package of chicken from the freezer you could expect a delicious, healthy dish without a lot of fuss? Try these superb lighter versions of weeknight-friendly *Southern Living* chicken dishes for wholesome success. They're so richly flavorful, you'd never guess they were light and healthy. One taste, and you'll be a believer.

CHICKEN FINGERS WITH HONEY-HORSERADISH DIP

MAKES 8 SERVINGS

This no-fork-required recipe won our highest rating. We think little and big kids will love it.

16 saltine crackers, finely crushed
¼ cup pecans, toasted and ground
½ teaspoon salt
½ teaspoon pepper
2 teaspoons paprika
4 (6-ounce) skinned and boned chicken breast halves
1 egg white
Vegetable cooking spray
Honey-Horseradish Dip

STIR together first 5 ingredients.
CUT each breast half into 4 strips. Whisk egg white until frothy; dip chicken into egg white; dredge in saltine mixture.

PLACE a rack coated with cooking spray in a broiler pan. Coat chicken strips on each side with cooking spray; arrange on pan.
BAKE at 425° for 18 to 20 minutes or until golden brown. Serve with Honey-Horseradish Dip. **Prep: 25 min., Bake: 20 min.**

Calories 204 (19% from fat); Fat 4.4g (sat 0.7g, mono 2g, poly 1.1g); Protein 23g; Carb 17g; Fiber 1.7g; Chol 50mg; Iron 1.3mg; Sodium 429mg; Calc 61mg

Honey-Horseradish Dip:

MAKES 1 CUP

½ cup plain nonfat yogurt
¼ cup coarse-grained mustard
¼ cup honey
2 tablespoons prepared horseradish

STIR together all ingredients. **Prep: 5 min.**

What's a portion?

For an average 3-pound chicken, a breast half weighs about 7 to 7½ ounces. That leaves about 5 to 6 ounces of trimmed chicken, which makes one generous portion. For more chicken information visit **www.tyson.com**

CHEESY CHICKEN IN PHYLLO

MAKES 4 SERVINGS

This dish is a little time consuming, but the cheesy, flaky outcome is well worth it.

4 (6-ounce) skinned and boned chicken breast halves
¼ teaspoon salt
½ teaspoon pepper
1 (10-ounce) package frozen chopped spinach, thawed
½ medium-size sweet onion, diced
Vegetable cooking spray
½ (8-ounce) package fat-free cream cheese, softened
1 cup (4 ounces) shredded low-fat mozzarella cheese
¼ cup crumbled feta cheese
2 tablespoons egg substitute
1½ teaspoons all-purpose flour
¼ teaspoon ground nutmeg
¼ teaspoon ground cumin
8 frozen phyllo pastry sheets, thawed

PLACE chicken between 2 sheets of heavy-duty plastic wrap, and flatten to ⅛-inch thickness using a meat mallet or rolling pin. Sprinkle evenly with salt and pepper; set aside.
DRAIN spinach well; press between layers of paper towels.
SAUTÉ spinach and onion in a nonstick skillet coated with cooking spray over medium-high heat 3 to 4 minutes or until onion is tender. Remove from heat, and stir in cream cheese until blended. Stir in mozzarella cheese and next 5 ingredients. Spoon spinach mixture evenly on each chicken breast half; roll up, jellyroll fashion.
UNFOLD phyllo on a lightly floured surface. Stack 2 sheets, coating tops lightly with cooking spray between sheets. (Keep remaining sheets covered with plastic wrap.) Place 1 chicken roll on a short side of phyllo stack; gently roll up, folding in long sides. Repeat procedure with remaining phyllo sheets, cooking spray, and remaining chicken. Place a rack coated with cooking spray in a shallow pan; place rolls on top of rack.
BAKE at 425° for 35 to 40 minutes or until chicken is done. **Prep: 30 min., Cook: 4 min., Bake: 40 min.**

Calories 462 (23% from fat); Fat 12g (sat 5.7g, mono 2.3g, poly 1g); Protein 59g; Carb 28g; Fiber 2.6g; Chol 123mg; Iron 4.3mg; Sodium 971mg; Calc 436mg

CREAMY CHICKEN-AND-RICE CASSEROLE

MAKES 8 SERVINGS

We lightened this creamy, hearty dish by using fat-free soup and sour cream instead of regular and by replacing lots of regular Cheddar with a smaller portion of reduced-fat Cheddar. You'll love this terrific source of calcium and iron.

1 (5-ounce) package long-grain and wild rice mix
1 teaspoon salt-free herb-and-spice seasoning
4 (6-ounce) skinned and boned chicken breast halves, cut into small pieces
Vegetable cooking spray
1 small sweet onion, chopped
1 (10¾-ounce) can fat-free cream of mushroom soup
1 (8-ounce) can sliced water chestnuts, drained
1 (8-ounce) container nonfat sour cream
1 (7-ounce) jar roasted red bell peppers, drained and chopped
½ teaspoon pepper
1 cup (4 ounces) shredded reduced-fat sharp Cheddar cheese

COOK rice mix according to package directions, omitting fat.
SPRINKLE seasoning evenly over chicken pieces.
COOK chicken in a large nonstick skillet coated with cooking spray over medium-high heat 10 minutes or until chicken is done, stirring often.
STIR together chicken, rice, onion, and next 5 ingredients in a bowl. Spoon into an 11- x 7-inch baking dish coated with cooking spray. Sprinkle with cheese.
BAKE at 350° for 30 minutes or until bubbly around edges. **Prep: 30 min., Cook: 10 min., Bake: 30 min.**

NOTE: For testing purposes only, we used Mrs. Dash salt-free herb-and-spice seasoning.

Calories 268 (17% from fat); Fat 5g (sat 2.4g, mono 0.8g, poly 0.3g); Protein 28g; Carb 26g; Fiber 1.8g; Chol 59mg; Iron 7mg; Sodium 784mg; Calc 209mg

SPICY GINGER-AND-ORANGE CHICKEN WITH BROCCOLI

MAKES 4 SERVINGS

This colorful dish combines sweet, tart, and salty flavors to create one of the tastiest chicken dinners we've ever tried.

4 (6-ounce) skinned and boned chicken breast halves, cut into thin strips
3 tablespoons lite soy sauce
1 pound fresh broccoli, cut into florets
3 tablespoons cornstarch
Vegetable cooking spray
½ small sweet onion, diced
2 tablespoons minced fresh ginger
1 teaspoon grated orange rind
¼ to ½ teaspoon ground red pepper
1 teaspoon dark sesame oil
2 garlic cloves, minced
½ cup fat-free reduced-sodium chicken broth
¼ cup orange marmalade
2 large oranges, peeled, sectioned, and coarsely chopped

PLACE chicken and soy sauce in a shallow dish or heavy-duty zip-top plastic bag. Cover or seal, and chill 15 minutes.
COOK broccoli in boiling water 3 minutes; drain. Plunge into ice water to stop the cooking process; drain. Set aside.
DRAIN chicken, reserving soy sauce; dredge chicken slices in cornstarch.
BROWN chicken, in batches, in a large nonstick skillet coated with cooking spray over medium-high heat 1 minute on each side or until done. Remove chicken from skillet, reserving drippings in skillet; keep chicken warm.
ADD reserved soy sauce, onion, and next 5 ingredients to reserved drippings in skillet; sauté 2 to 3 minutes or until vegetables are tender.
ADD chicken broth and marmalade, stirring until marmalade is melted. Return chicken to skillet. Bring to a boil; stir in broccoli and chopped orange sections. Serve immediately. **Prep: 30 min., Chill: 15 min., Cook: 15 min.**

Calories 365 (10% from fat); Fat 4g (sat 0.8g, mono 1g, poly 1.2g); Protein 45g; Carb 38g; Fiber 6g; Chol 99mg; Iron 2.6mg; Sodium 666mg; Calc 123mg

Taste of the South

Sweet Potato Casserole

The *Southern Living* Foods staff has diverse opinions on what ingredients make the perfect Sweet Potato Casserole.

In our search to find the perfect Sweet Potato Casserole, we tasted a parade of classic recipes—seven to be exact. Our debates focused on texture, taste, and toppings. We discussed fresh vs. canned sweet potatoes (fresh won hands-down), and whether marshmallows, brown sugar, or pecans belonged on top.

SWEET POTATO CASSEROLE

MAKES 6 TO 8 SERVINGS

4½ pounds sweet potatoes
1 cup sugar
¼ cup milk
½ cup butter, softened
2 large eggs
1 teaspoon vanilla extract
¼ teaspoon salt
1¼ cups cornflakes cereal, crushed
¼ cup chopped pecans
1 tablespoon brown sugar
1 tablespoon butter, melted
1½ cups miniature marshmallows

BAKE sweet potatoes at 400° for about 1 hour or until tender. Let cool to touch; peel and mash potatoes.
BEAT sweet potatoes, sugar, and next 5 ingredients at medium speed with an electric mixer until smooth. Spoon into a greased 11- x 7-inch baking dish. Combine cornflakes cereal and next 3 ingredients in a bowl. Sprinkle diagonally over casserole in rows 2 inches apart.
BAKE at 350° for 30 minutes. Remove from oven; let stand 10 minutes. Sprinkle alternate rows with marshmallows, and bake 10 more minutes. Let stand 10 minutes before serving. **Prep: 20 min.; Bake: 1 hr., 40 min.; Stand: 20 min.**

LORENE BILLUPS
TRUSSVILLE, ALABAMA

Gracious Dinner

Pull out all the stops when you celebrate with this grand menu. Host your next holiday dinner in style with some of our most sumptuous recipes.

Lasting Impressions Dinner

Serves 8

Beef Fillets With Stilton-Portobello Sauce

Sweet Onion Pudding

Roasted Potato Trio

Sautéed green beans

Apple strudel

Entertain friends with an elegant menu that rings in the season with loads of pizzazz. We've chosen three of our very best gourmet recipes to build a sophisticated meal that's guaranteed to make a lasting impression on your guests.

This menu isn't the average flash-in-the-pan dinner. It requires more than a few simple steps. But Test Kitchens professional Jan Moon's silky Sweet Onion Pudding and her herb-infused potato medley combine perfectly with richly sauced beef tenderloin fillets. Their flavors make every step of preparation worthwhile. You'll want to shop for the very best and freshest ingredients that you can find. After all, a final recipe is only as good as its ingredients.

BEEF FILLETS WITH STILTON-PORTOBELLO SAUCE

MAKES 8 SERVINGS

8 (6-ounce) beef tenderloin fillets
1 tablespoon chopped fresh thyme
¾ teaspoon freshly ground pepper
½ cup butter or margarine, divided
2 (6-ounce) packages portobello mushroom caps, sliced
½ cup dry red wine or beef broth
¾ cup sour cream
4½ ounces Stilton or blue cheese, crumbled and divided
Garnish: fresh thyme sprigs

RUB fillets evenly with chopped thyme and pepper.
MELT ¼ cup butter in a large skillet over medium-high heat. Add fillets, and cook 5 to 6 minutes on each side or to desired degree of doneness. Remove from skillet, and keep warm.
MELT remaining ¼ cup butter in skillet. Add sliced mushrooms, and sauté 3 to 4 minutes or until tender. Add wine, and cook 1 to 2 minutes, stirring to loosen particles from bottom of skillet. Stir in sour cream and ¼ cup cheese until melted. Drizzle sauce over fillets; sprinkle with remaining cheese. Garnish, if desired. **Prep: 10 min., Cook: 25 min.**

SWEET ONION PUDDING

MAKES 8 SERVINGS

See our "Cook's Notes" at right for make-ahead suggestions to simplify your party planning.

6 large eggs
2 cups whipping cream
1 (3-ounce) package shredded Parmesan cheese
3 tablespoons all-purpose flour
2 tablespoons sugar
2 teaspoons baking powder
1 teaspoon salt
½ cup butter or margarine
6 medium-size sweet onions, thinly sliced

STIR together first 3 ingredients in a large bowl, blending well.
COMBINE flour and next 3 ingredients, and gradually stir into egg mixture. Set mixture aside.
MELT butter in a large skillet over medium heat; add onions.
COOK, stirring often, 30 to 40 minutes or until caramel colored. Remove pan from heat.
STIR onions into egg mixture, and spoon into a lightly greased 13- x 9-inch baking dish.
BAKE at 350° for 30 minutes or until set. **Prep: 20 min., Cook: 40 min., Bake: 30 min.**

ROASTED POTATO TRIO

MAKES 8 SERVINGS

2½ pounds sweet potatoes
2 pounds red potatoes
1 pound Yukon gold potatoes
¼ cup butter
¼ cup olive oil
⅓ cup chopped fresh rosemary
½ teaspoon salt
½ teaspoon freshly ground pepper

CUT potatoes into ½-inch-thick slices.
COOK butter, oil, and rosemary in a small saucepan over medium heat, stirring until butter melts.
BRUSH ¼ cup butter mixture over 2 baking sheets. Arrange potato slices evenly in a single layer on prepared sheets; brush with remaining butter mixture. Sprinkle with salt and pepper.
BAKE at 450° for 35 minutes or until golden brown. **Prep: 15 min., Bake: 35 min.**

Cook's Notes

1 day ahead:
■ Caramelize onions for Sweet Onion Pudding; cover and chill.

1 hour ahead:
■ Bring caramelized onions to room temperature. Assemble and bake Sweet Onion Pudding.
■ Prepare Roasted Potato Trio. Cover with foil, and keep warm.

30 minutes ahead:
■ Prepare Beef Fillets With Stilton-Portobello Sauce.
■ Sauté green beans.
■ Reheat storebought strudel, if desired.

A Touch of Nutmeg

Use this versatile and aromatic spice in both sweet and savory dishes for flavorful dishes that your family will love.

During the holidays, it's common to add nutmeg to sweet treats, but don't disregard this aromatic spice for use in savory dishes. A sprinkling of freshly grated or ground nutmeg, found in the spice section of your grocery store, can turn everyday fare into tasty dinners. Don't worry—these dishes don't scream nutmeg; its flavor simply enhances the meal.

HOLIDAY CRANBERRY SAUCE

MAKES 3½ CUPS

Orange juice concentrate and apricot preserves give this condiment a sweet citrus twist.

1 cup frozen cranberry juice concentrate, thawed
½ cup sugar
1 (12-ounce) package fresh cranberries
12 dried apricots, chopped
¼ cup apricot preserves or orange marmalade
2 teaspoons grated orange rind
3 tablespoons fresh orange juice
¾ teaspoon ground nutmeg

MICROWAVE cranberry juice concentrate and ½ cup sugar in a large glass bowl at HIGH 2 to 3 minutes or until mixture boils, stirring every minute until sugar dissolves.
ADD cranberries and dried apricots, and microwave at HIGH 7 minutes, stirring every 2 minutes until cranberry skins pop.
STIR in remaining ingredients. Cool. Cover and chill 8 hours. **Prep: 15 min., Chill: 8 hrs.**

NOTE: Sauce may be prepared up to 3 days ahead. Cover and chill until ready to serve.

SHARON WALKER HOWARD
MAYFIELD, KENTUCKY

Nutmeg Success

■ Freshly grated whole nutmeg is more pungent than ground.

■ Whole nutmeg will keep for two years, but replace ground nutmeg every six months.

■ Store nutmeg in an airtight container in a cool, dark, dry place or in the freezer.

■ Clean nutmeg graters and grinders with a toothbrush.

■ Mark the date you purchased the spice with a felt marker on the bottom of the can or jar.

BROCCOLI SUPREME PIZZA

MAKES 4 TO 6 SERVINGS

Create this Florentine-style pizza with leftovers from a broccoli casserole.

- 1 large sweet onion
- 1 tablespoon olive oil
- 1 cup Broccoli Supreme (recipe at right)
- 1 (16-ounce) Italian bread shell
- 1 (6-ounce) package finely shredded Italian cheese blend, divided
- 1 cup chopped cooked chicken
- 4 bacon slices, cooked and crumbled
- 2 tablespoons chopped fresh basil

CUT onion in half; cut into thin slices.
SAUTÉ onion in hot oil in a large skillet over medium-high heat 10 to 12 minutes or until golden.
SPREAD Broccoli Supreme over bread shell. Sprinkle with half of cheese; top with cooked onion, chicken, and bacon.
SPRINKLE with remaining cheese, and top with basil.
BAKE pizza at 425° for 10 to 12 minutes or until cheese melts. **Prep: 20 min., Bake: 12 min.**

NOTE: For testing purposes only, we used Sargento Salad Creations with Parmesan, Mozzarella, and Romano Cheeses.

PORK CHOPS WITH WHITE RICE

MAKES 4 SERVINGS

- 4 (¾-inch-thick) boneless pork chops
- ¼ teaspoon salt
- ¼ teaspoon pepper
- 1 tablespoon all-purpose flour
- 1 tablespoon vegetable oil
- 1 green bell pepper, seeded and thinly sliced
- 1 red bell pepper, seeded and thinly sliced
- 2 green onions, chopped
- 2 tablespoons raisins
- 2 garlic cloves, minced
- 1 tablespoon maple syrup
- ½ cup orange juice
- 1½ teaspoons ground nutmeg
- Hot cooked rice

SPRINKLE pork chops with salt and pepper; dredge in flour.
COOK pork chops in hot oil in a large skillet over medium-high heat 5 minutes on each side. Remove pork from skillet, and keep warm.
SAUTÉ sliced green bell pepper and next 5 ingredients over medium-high heat 5 minutes. Return pork to skillet. Add juice and nutmeg; cook 15 minutes or until pork is tender. Serve over rice. **Prep: 15 min., Cook: 30 min.**

HELEN FARISH
BOULDER, COLORADO

BROCCOLI SUPREME

MAKES 8 SERVINGS

- 2 pounds fresh broccoli
- Crème Fraîche
- ⅔ cup grated Parmesan cheese
- ¼ cup sour cream
- ½ teaspoon salt
- ½ teaspoon ground nutmeg
- ½ teaspoon freshly ground pepper
- 2 tablespoons butter, cut into pieces

REMOVE and discard large leaves and tough ends of stalks from broccoli. Cut away tops, and coarsely chop. Peel and coarsely chop stems.
COOK broccoli in boiling salted water to cover 8 minutes or until crisp-tender, and drain.
PROCESS cooked broccoli and 1 cup Crème Fraîche in a food processor or blender until smooth, stopping to scrape down sides.
STIR together broccoli mixture, cheese, and next 4 ingredients. Pour mixture into a lightly greased 2-quart baking dish. Dot with butter.
BAKE at 350° for 25 minutes or until thoroughly heated. Serve immediately. **Prep: 25 min., Cook: 8 min., Bake: 25 min.**

Crème Fraîche:

MAKES 1 CUP

Make a day ahead, and refrigerate overnight.

- ½ cup whipping cream
- ½ cup sour cream

WHISK together whipping cream and sour cream until blended. Cover and chill at least 4 hours. **Prep: 5 min., Chill: 4 hrs.**

CAROLINE KENNEDY
NEWBORN, GEORGIA

Biscuit Appetizers

These savory quick breads rarely appear on appetizer tables. Until now, that is.

These Southern favorites aren't just for breakfast anymore—they're showing up in lunch and dinner bread baskets at restaurants across the region. Test Kitchens professional Rebecca Gordon turned this Southern staple into extraordinary yet easy hors d'oeuvres.

BLUE CHEESE BISCUITS WITH BEEF AND HORSERADISH-CHIVE CREAM

MAKES 20 APPETIZER SERVINGS

> 2 cups self-rising flour
> 1 (8-ounce) container sour cream
> ½ cup butter, melted
> 1 (4-ounce) package crumbled blue cheese
> 2 (6-ounce) beef tenderloin steaks (about 1½ inches thick)
> ½ teaspoon salt
> ½ teaspoon pepper
> ½ tablespoon vegetable oil
> Horseradish-Chive Cream

STIR together first 4 ingredients just until blended.

TURN dough out onto a lightly floured surface. Pat dough to a ½-inch thickness; cut with a 2-inch round cutter. Place on lightly greased baking sheets.

BAKE at 425° for 12 to 15 minutes or until lightly browned.

SPRINKLE steaks with salt and pepper. Heat oil in a skillet over high heat; add steaks, and cook 8 to 9 minutes on each side or to desired degree of doneness. Remove from pan; let stand 15 minutes.

CUT steak into ¼-inch slices. Split biscuits in half, and top half evenly with beef and Horseradish-Chive Cream. Top with remaining biscuit halves. **Prep: 30 min., Bake: 15 min. per batch, Cook: 18 min., Stand: 15 min.**

Horseradish-Chive Cream:

MAKES 1 CUP

> 1 (8-ounce) container sour cream
> 1 tablespoon prepared horseradish
> 1 tablespoon Dijon mustard
> 1 tablespoon chopped fresh chives

STIR together all ingredients. Cover and chill until ready to serve. **Prep: 5 min.**

CREAM CHEESE-AND-OLIVE BISCUITS WITH TAPENADE

MAKES 30 APPETIZER SERVINGS

> 2¼ cups all-purpose baking mix
> 1 (3-ounce) package cream cheese, softened
> ⅓ cup buttermilk
> ½ cup pimiento-stuffed olives, chopped
> 1 (6-ounce) jar pitted kalamata olives
> 1 tablespoon capers, drained
> 1 garlic clove, pressed
> 1 tablespoon chopped fresh parsley
> 2 tablespoons balsamic vinegar
> 2 tablespoons olive oil
> ¼ teaspoon black pepper
> 1 (3-ounce) log goat cheese*

PULSE first 4 ingredients in a food processor 3 or 4 times or until combined. Turn dough out onto a lightly floured surface. Pat dough to a ½-inch thickness; cut with a 2-inch round cutter. Place on ungreased baking sheets.

BAKE at 425° for 10 minutes.

PULSE kalamata olives and next 6 ingredients in a food processor until combined.

SPLIT biscuits in half, and spread cut sides with goat cheese; top with olive mixture. **Prep: 30 min., Bake: 10 min. per batch**

*Substitute 1 (3-ounce) package cream cheese, if desired.

CREAM CHEESE-AND-OLIVE BISCUITS WITH SUN-DRIED TOMATO SPREAD AND BACON: Omit kalamata olive mixture and goat cheese. Spread biscuit halves with 1 (8-ounce) container sun-dried tomato-basil spreadable cheese. Top with cooked and crumbled bacon.

NOTE: For testing purposes only, we used Alouette spreadable cheese; substitute any flavor, if desired.

SHRIMP-AND-GRITS BISCUITS

MAKES 48 APPETIZER SERVINGS

> 1⅓ cups chicken broth
> ⅛ teaspoon salt
> ⅓ cup quick-cooking grits, uncooked
> 1 tablespoon butter
> ⅛ teaspoon pepper
> ¾ cup milk
> 3 cups all-purpose baking mix
> 1½ pounds large cooked shrimp, peeled and deveined
> 1 (3-ounce) package cream cheese
> 1 green onion, chopped
> ½ teaspoon hot sauce
> ½ teaspoon Old Bay seasoning
> 2 teaspoons lemon juice
> Garnishes: black pepper, barbecue sauce

BRING broth and salt to a boil in a saucepan over medium-high heat; add grits, and cook, stirring often, 5 minutes or until thickened. Add butter and pepper, stirring until butter melts. Remove from heat, and cool 15 to 20 minutes.

WHISK milk into grits; stir in baking mix until a soft dough forms. Turn dough out onto a lightly floured surface. Pat to a ½-inch thickness; cut with a 2-inch round cutter. Place on greased baking sheets.

BAKE at 425° for 10 minutes. Cut 24 shrimp in half lengthwise; set aside.

PROCESS cream cheese, next 4 ingredients, and remaining shrimp in a food processor until smooth, stopping to scrape down sides.

SPLIT biscuits in half, and spread cut sides evenly with shrimp puree; top with remaining shrimp. Garnish, if desired. **Prep: 30 min., Cook: 5 min., Cool: 20 min., Bake: 10 min. per batch**

New Year's Eve Dinner

Enjoy a relaxing, elegant dinner with friends this New Year's Eve.

Easy, Economical New Year's Eve

Serves 4 to 6

Pear-and-Gorgonzola Crostini

Chicken With Artichokes

Yellow rice

Green Beans With Mushrooms and Sage

Chocolate Mousse With Orange Liqueur

What's your ideal New Year's Eve? Ours is eating a delicious meal with a small group of friends—without spending a fortune. If you're searching for an easy menu for six, look no further. These recipes are not only simple to prepare, but they're made with economical ingredients. We've included a shopping list and game plan to help you get dinner on the table while still being able to enjoy the celebration.

PEAR-AND-GORGONZOLA CROSTINI

MAKES 6 SERVINGS

> 1 pear, cut lengthwise into 12 wedges
> 1 teaspoon lemon juice
> 12 (½-inch-thick) French bread slices
> 1 cup crumbled Gorgonzola cheese
> 4 teaspoons milk
> ¼ cup chopped walnuts, toasted
> 4 bacon slices, cooked and crumbled

TOSS together pear slices and lemon juice; set aside.

BROIL bread 5 inches from heat 1 minute on each side or until lightly toasted.

STIR together cheese and milk until smooth; spread evenly on 1 side of each bread slice. Sprinkle each slice with 1 teaspoon walnuts; top with 1 pear slice. Sprinkle with bacon. **Prep: 15 min., Broil: 2 min.**

JULIE DEMATTEO
CLEMENTON, NEW JERSEY

CHICKEN WITH ARTICHOKES

MAKES 6 SERVINGS

> 6 skinned and boned chicken breast halves
> 1 teaspoon paprika
> ½ teaspoon salt
> ½ teaspoon pepper
> 2 tablespoons butter or margarine, divided
> 1 (14-ounce) can artichoke hearts, drained and halved
> 2 green onions, chopped
> ⅔ cup water
> ¼ cup sherry
> 1 tablespoon cornstarch
> 1 teaspoon chicken bouillon granules
> ½ teaspoon dried rosemary

SPRINKLE chicken with paprika, salt, and pepper. Melt 1 tablespoon butter in a large nonstick skillet over medium-high heat; add chicken, and cook 5 minutes on each side or until lightly browned. Remove chicken, and set aside.

MELT remaining 1 tablespoon butter in same skillet over medium heat; add artichoke hearts and green onions, and sauté 1 minute.

STIR together ⅔ cup water and next 4 ingredients; add to artichoke mixture. Return chicken to skillet. Bring to a boil, and cook, stirring constantly, 1 minute. **Prep: 15 min., Cook: 13 min.**

SHERYL DAVIDSON
ATLANTA, GEORGIA

GREEN BEANS WITH MUSHROOMS AND SAGE

MAKES 4 TO 6 SERVINGS

> 1 pound fresh green beans, trimmed and cut into 2-inch pieces
> 2 tablespoons butter or margarine
> 2 tablespoons olive oil
> ½ cup fresh sage leaves, chopped
> ½ (8-ounce) package sliced fresh mushrooms
> 3 garlic cloves, minced
> ½ cup chicken broth
> 2 tablespoons white wine
> 1 teaspoon Worcestershire sauce
> ½ teaspoon salt
> ¼ teaspoon coarsely ground pepper

Game Plan

The day before:
- Prepare Chocolate Mousse With Orange Liqueur, and chill overnight.

New Year's Eve morning:
- Toss pears in lemon juice; cover and chill.
- Cook bacon, and set aside.
- Cut and trim green beans, and chop sage and chocolate.

New Year's Eve afternoon:
- Bring water to a boil, and simmer green beans. Plunge into cold water, and set aside.
- Cook rice according to package directions.
- Slice and toast French bread. Toast walnuts.
- Cook chicken in skillet. While chicken is cooking, sauté sage and mushrooms in another pan.
- Assemble Pear-and-Gorgonzola Crostini. Finish preparing chicken and green beans.

Grocery List

Staples on hand
Paprika
Salt and pepper
Dried rosemary
Olive oil

Produce
½ bunch green onions
1 pound fresh green beans
½ (8-ounce) package sliced fresh mushrooms
½ cup fresh sage leaves
3 garlic cloves
1 pear

General
1 (14-ounce) can artichoke hearts
1 teaspoon chicken bouillon granules
½ cup chicken broth
2 tablespoons white wine
1 teaspoon Worcestershire sauce
¼ cup sherry
1 French bread loaf
¼ cup chopped walnuts
1 (5-ounce) package yellow rice mix
1 (4-ounce) package sweet chocolate baking bars
4 (1-ounce) semisweet chocolate baking squares
¼ cup plus 1 tablespoon orange liqueur
½ cup plus 3 tablespoons powdered sugar
1 tablespoon cornstarch

Dairy
4 tablespoons butter or margarine
1 cup Gorgonzola cheese
4 teaspoons milk
2½ cups whipping cream

Meat
6 skinned and boned chicken breast halves
4 bacon slices

COOK green beans in boiling salted water 10 to 12 minutes or until crisp-tender; drain. Plunge into ice water to stop the cooking process; drain and set aside.

MELT butter with olive oil in a skillet over medium-high heat; add sage, and sauté 1 minute or until crisp and dark green. Remove with a slotted spoon; set aside.

ADD mushrooms and garlic to skillet; sauté 2 minutes or until liquid evaporates. Add green beans, tossing to combine. Stir in chicken broth and next 4 ingredients; cook 5 minutes or until liquid is reduced by half. Stir in sage just before serving. **Prep: 12 min., Cook: 20 min.**

SARA GIBBS
TAYLORSVILLE, KENTUCKY

CHOCOLATE MOUSSE WITH ORANGE LIQUEUR

MAKES 4 CUPS

- 1 (4-ounce) package sweet chocolate baking bars, chopped
- 4 (1-ounce) semisweet chocolate baking squares, chopped
- ¼ cup orange liqueur
- 2 cups whipping cream
- ½ cup powdered sugar
- Orange Whipped Cream

PLACE chocolate and orange liqueur in top of a double boiler. Bring water to a boil in bottom of double boiler; remove from heat. Place chocolate over simmering water, and cook, stirring occasionally, until chocolate melts. Let cool to lukewarm.

BEAT whipping cream at medium speed with an electric mixer until foamy; gradually add powdered sugar, beating until soft peaks form.

FOLD about one-fourth of whipped cream into melted chocolate, working quickly; fold chocolate mixture into remaining whipped cream. Spoon evenly into individual small serving cups. Chill until ready to serve. Dollop with Orange Whipped Cream. **Prep: 20 min.**

Orange Whipped Cream:
MAKES 1¼ CUPS

- ½ cup whipping cream
- 3 tablespoons powdered sugar
- 1 tablespoon orange liqueur

BEAT all ingredients at medium speed with an electric mixer until soft peaks form. Cover and chill until ready to serve. **Prep: 5 min.**

from our kitchen

Bake and Freeze Treats

Do the work ahead of time and enjoy the goodness of homemade baked goods whenever you're ready. Bake cake layers, cool completely, and store in heavy-duty zip-top plastic bags or airtight containers. Freeze up to one month. Thaw completely, uncovered; then frost or decorate as desired. Freeze baked cookies between layers of wax paper in airtight containers.

Frozen cake layers travel well in a tin or heavy plastic container. When you reach your destination, the layers may be ready to frost. Cake is also a wonderful gift to mail. Simply send frozen layers with frosting recipe and instructions for assembly. Our Orange-Pecan-Spice Pound Cake on page 295 is a great choice for mailing as it requires no frosting.

Stocking Stuffers

Give Santa a hint (or a hand) with these gifts for cooks.

Meat tenderizer: Foods Editor Andria Scott Hurst tried this Jaccard product for the first time at a recent seminar and she had to have one. It's a terrific little handheld, manual unit with three rows of stainless steel blades. (Use it on your cutting board to protect countertops.) All you do is gently press the machine over the meat three or four times. Tough, thick cuts of meat become tender and take less time to cook. Use it before you marinate meats for full flavor infusion. This is a great gift for about $39. For more information, call toll free 1-866-478-7373.

Pie/cake server: Among Chantal's new stainless steel serving pieces is a must-have item for bakers: a contemporary-style slicer and server for both pies and cakes. Its sharp, serrated edge makes a clean cut, while the ample spatula lets you lift and serve with ease. The server is available at most kitchen shops

for about $14.99. For more information, contact Chantal at 1-800-365-4354 or **www.chantal.com**

Julienne peeler: This item from Kuhn Rikon costs about $12 but is worth so much more. This little tool is designed to cut decorative julienne strips of fruits, vegetables, and cheese. It makes cutting the tiny, uniform strips as easy as peeling a carrot. Look for this tool at specialty stores and in catalogs. For more information, visit **www.kuhnrikon.com**

Pepper Chef Battery Mill: By William Pounds, this gadget will give you the right grind every time. Operate it manually, or push a button to add freshly ground pepper to any dish. It has a large capacity and is powered by batteries. Pepper Chef may put your old wooden mill to rest. Get one for about $36.99 at any kitchen shop.

Instant Parties

Be the host of some of the best spur-of-the-moment gatherings of the season.
■ Invite folks over for a "come-as-you-are breakfast." Bring out those gourmet coffees you've collected.
■ Turn an evening of gift wrapping into a party with a big pot of chili. Call your friends to join the wrapping, and ask them to bring along their favorite beverages.
■ When you see your neighbors putting up outdoor decorations, invite them over for wine or cider with cheese and fruit.

Tips and Tidbits

■ Make time to record secret family holiday recipes to pass down to the younger generation.

■ For fresher flavor from packaged pesto, drain and discard any standing oil.

■ Delegate Christmas breakfast duties to the teenagers in the house.

■ To keep the kitchen floor splatter free, place sheets of newspaper in front of the stove when frying.

■ Make coupons for home-cooked meals as gifts for friends.

Raisin Hints

It's your choice whether you use dark or golden raisins in recipes. They're the same Thompson seedless grapes. The dark ones are sun-dried, while golden raisins are treated to prevent darkening and then dried with artificial heat. Golden raisins retain a bit more moisture than the dark ones, which makes them appear plumper.

No matter which ones you select, store raisins in an airtight container in your pantry for several months. You may also freeze them up to one year. Keep a ready supply of plump, tasty raisins for baked goods in a glass jar covered with brandy, rum, or liqueur (be sure to drain these before adding to recipes).

Toss raisins in a little flour before adding them to batter; this keeps them evenly distributed through the mix. If your recipe calls for chopped raisins, tuck them in the freezer for a while so they won't be so sticky to work with.

Southern Living 2002 Cook-Off

Cook-Off 2002 Winners

The first-ever *Southern Living* Cook-Off was the result of nearly a year of planning and testing recipes.

In the end, it all boiled down to 15 great recipes and the cooks who created them. We selected the finalists from 40,000 entries submitted in five categories: Taste of the South, Simple and Scrumptious Entrées, One-Dish Wonders, Signature Desserts, and Kids Love It! The finalists received $1,000 each, category winners won $10,000, and the Grand Prize Winner received $100,000. Brand winners—those whose recipes made the best use of a sponsor's product—also received $1,000.

All our work and excitement came together September 26–28 in Orlando at the Gaylord Palms Resort, where the 15 finalists prepared their recipes for final judging.

Finalists prepared their recipes for the judges on Friday. Saturday, the nervous contestants were prepped and primped for their appearances in front of the audience of 1,200.

At 2:00, Al Roker took the stage, introducing the contestants, and asking about the dishes they were preparing. Once each category's demonstrations were completed, he announced the category winner, and gave her a check for $10,000. Finally, the 5 category winners assembled on the stage, where they were joined by *Southern Living* editor, John Floyd, and publisher, Rich Smyth. Drums rolled and excitement mounted as Al tore open the final envelope. Pecan Pie Cheesecake, submitted by Ginnie Prater of Anniston, Alabama, had won the 2002 *Southern Living* Cook-Off.

TASTE OF THE SOUTH

∽ **GRAND PRIZE WINNER** ∾

TASTE OF THE SOUTH
First Prize

PECAN PIE CHEESECAKE

MAKES 16 SERVINGS

Half of a frozen pecan pie is sliced and layered in a graham-cracker crust, covered with cheesecake batter, and baked, resulting in a creative dessert with a wonderful texture. *(pictured on page 304)*

1 (2-pound, 4-ounce) package frozen
    MRS. SMITH'S Special Recipe
    Southern Pecan Pie
2 cups graham cracker crumbs
½ cup DOMINO Granulated
    Sugar
½ cup butter, melted
¼ teaspoon McCORMICK Gourmet
    Collection Saigon Cinnamon
2 (8-ounce) packages PHILADELPHIA
    Cream Cheese, softened
2 large eggs
⅔ cup sour cream
½ cup half-and-half
1 teaspoon vanilla extract
1 cup DOMINO 10-X Confectioners
    Sugar
1 tablespoon all-purpose flour
16 pecan halves

PREHEAT oven to 325°. Thaw pecan pie according to package directions. Cut evenly into 20 thin slices, keeping wedges intact, and set aside. Stir together cracker crumbs and next 3 ingredients, and press mixture onto bottom and 1½ inches up sides of a 10-inch springform pan.

ARRANGE 10 pecan pie wedges in a spoke design in prepared pan, placing 1 cut side of each wedge on crust with narrow end towards center of pan. Reserve remaining pie wedges for another use.

BEAT cream cheese until smooth; add eggs, 1 at a time, beating after each addition. Add sour cream, half-and-half, and vanilla; beat until blended.

FOLD in confectioners sugar and flour. Carefully pour cream cheese mixture evenly over pecan pie wedges in pan, making sure wedges remain in place. Arrange pecan halves evenly around edge of cheesecake.

BAKE at 325° for 50 minutes. Turn off oven, and let cheesecake stand in oven 1 hour. Remove to a wire rack, and let cool completely. Chill at least 8 hours or overnight before serving. **Prep: 15 min., Bake: 50 min., Stand: 1 hr., Chill: 8 hrs.**

GINNIE PRATER
ANNISTON, ALABAMA

MAPLE-CHIPOTLE PORK ON SMOKED GOUDA GRITS WITH SWEET ONION APPLESAUCE

MAKES 6 SERVINGS

- ½ cup barbecue sauce
- ½ cup maple syrup
- 2 chipotle peppers in adobo sauce, seeded and minced
- 1 teaspoon adobo sauce from can
- 2 (1-pound) PORK Tenderloins
- 1 DUPONT TEFLON NON-STICK Jellyroll Pan
- Salt and pepper to taste
- Smoked Gouda Grits
- Sweet Onion Applesauce

PREHEAT oven to 375°. Whisk together first 4 ingredients.

PLACE pork in greased jellyroll pan; sprinkle evenly with salt and pepper. Pour half of chipotle mixture over pork; reserve remaining chipotle mixture.

BAKE at 375° for 20 to 30 minutes or until a meat thermometer inserted into thickest portion registers 160°, basting occasionally with pan drippings. Remove pork to a wire rack, and let stand 10 minutes. Cut into ½-inch-thick slices.

SPOON Smoked Gouda Grits evenly onto 6 serving plates; top with pork slices, and drizzle with remaining chipotle mixture. Dollop Sweet Onion Applesauce around Smoked Gouda Grits. **Prep: 10 min., Bake: 30 min., Stand: 10 min.**

Smoked Gouda Grits:

MAKES 6 TO 8 SERVINGS

- 4 cups low-sodium chicken broth or water
- 3 cups milk
- 2 teaspoons salt
- ½ teaspoon McCORMICK Gourmet Collection Ground White Pepper
- 1¼ cups uncooked regular grits
- 1½ cups (6 ounces) shredded smoked Gouda CHEESE
- 2 to 3 tablespoons unsalted butter

BRING first 4 ingredients to a boil in a medium saucepan; gradually whisk in grits. Cover, reduce heat, and simmer, stirring occasionally, 20 minutes or until thickened. Add cheese and butter, stirring until melted. **Prep: 5 min., Cook: 25 min.**

Sweet Onion Applesauce:

MAKES 1 CUP

- 1 medium-size sweet onion (Vidalia), finely chopped
- 1 tablespoon vegetable oil
- 1 small DUPONT TEFLON NON-STICK Skillet
- 1 tablespoon DOMINO Granulated Sugar
- 1 medium Golden Delicious apple, peeled and chopped
- 1 tablespoon cider vinegar
- 1 cup applesauce
- 1 teaspoon McCORMICK Gourmet Collection Thyme Leaves

SAUTÉ onion in hot oil in skillet over medium-high heat 8 to 10 minutes or until golden. Sprinkle with sugar, and cook, stirring often, 2 minutes. Add apple and vinegar, and cook, stirring often, 3 minutes. Stir in applesauce and thyme leaves. Cover and chill until ready to serve. **Prep: 10 min., Cook: 15 min.**

BOB GADSBY
GREAT FALLS, MONTANA

FRIED LEMON-ROSEMARY CATFISH

MAKES 4 SERVINGS

- 1 large lemon
- ¼ cup milk
- 2 medium eggs, lightly beaten
- 2 tablespoons chopped fresh rosemary
- 2 tablespoons minced fresh garlic
- 4 (4- to 6-ounce) catfish fillets
- 2 cups yellow cornmeal
- ¼ cup extra-virgin olive oil
- 1 large DUPONT TEFLON NON-STICK Skillet
- Garnishes: lemon slices, fresh rosemary sprigs

GRATE lemon rind from lemon, avoiding the bitter white pith, into a large bowl; squeeze lemon juice into bowl. Stir in milk and next 3 ingredients until blended.

RINSE fillets, and pat dry with paper towels. Add fillets to lemon mixture in bowl; cover and chill 1 hour.

PLACE cornmeal on a large plate or in a large shallow dish. Turn fillets in lemon mixture until thoroughly coated; dredge in cornmeal, coating evenly.

COOK fillets in hot oil in skillet over medium-high heat 4 minutes on each side or until browned. Remove fillets from skillet. Garnish, if desired. **Prep: 10 min., Chill: 1 hr., Cook: 8 min.**

CHERISE REMBERT
WOODVILLE, ALABAMA

Judging Notes for Taste of the South

This category asked for new twists on Southern classics. Our Foods staff was especially pleased with the variety of entries in this category. Many entries were based on recipes from our favorite standing column, "Taste of the South." Some of Southerners' favorite dishes were paired with something new. Sometimes, the twist was as simple (and satisfying) as an updated, lemony breading for catfish. The choice of ingredients was what seemed to make entries truly Southern as we received recipes for appetizers, side dishes, casseroles, and desserts.

The grand-prize winner of the contest came from this category. When Ginnie Prater wondered how she could make a cheesecake—her favorite food—more Southern, thoughts of pecans turned her in the right direction.

SIMPLE & SCRUMPTIOUS ENTRÉES

Jamaican Pork Tenderloin With Sauce Caribe

MAKES 6 SERVINGS

Lori Welander loves cooking pork tenderloin because it's a versatile family favorite. "I experimented with a number of McCormick spice blends," she says. "Once I decided on the Jamaican jerk blend, I played with a number of simple sauces to complement the pork. Dark rum and honey-roasted peanuts added a little more Jamaican flair." *(pictured on page 301)*

> 1½ pounds PORK Tenderloin
> 3 tablespoons fresh orange juice
> 1½ tablespoons McCORMICK Gourmet Collection Jamaican Jerk Seasoning
> All Natural PAM Original Cooking Spray
> ½ cup red currant jelly
> ¼ cup Dijon mustard
> 1 (9-inch) CIRCULON Straining Sauté Pan With Pouring Lip
> 1½ tablespoons dark rum or orange juice
> Garnishes: chopped honey-roasted USA PEANUTS, tropical edible flowers

BRUSH pork tenderloin with orange juice, and rub evenly with 1½ tablespoons jerk seasoning.

COAT food rack with cooking spray, and place on grill over medium-high heat (350° to 400°). Place pork on rack, and grill, covered with grill lid, 10 minutes on each side or until a meat thermometer inserted into thickest portion registers 160°. Cut pork diagonally into thin slices, and arrange on a serving platter.

WHISK together jelly and mustard in sauté pan over low heat, and cook, whisking constantly, until thoroughly heated. Remove from heat, and stir in rum. Drizzle sauce over pork; garnish, if desired. Serve with long-grain and wild rice, if desired. **Prep: 10 min., Grill: 20 min.**

LORI WELANDER
RICHMOND, VIRGINIA

Grilled Beef With Mashed Potatoes and Chipotle Cream

MAKES 4 SERVINGS

> 2 to 3 chipotle peppers in adobo sauce
> ½ cup mayonnaise
> ⅓ cup honey
> 1 pound HORMEL Always Tender Peppercorn Beef Filet of Sirloin
> ½ (22-ounce) package frozen mashed potatoes
> Salt and pepper to taste
> Garnish: chopped fresh Italian parsley

REMOVE about half of seeds from peppers, if desired. Puree or mince peppers. Stir together peppers, mayonnaise, and honey until blended.

GRILL beef, covered with grill lid, over medium-high heat (350° to 400°) 8 to 10 minutes, basting with 1 tablespoon chipotle pepper mixture. Turn beef; grill 8 to 10 minutes or until a meat thermometer inserted into thickest portion registers 140°, basting with 1 tablespoon chipotle pepper mixture. Remove to a cutting board; let stand 8 minutes before slicing.

MICROWAVE potatoes according to package directions, stirring in 3 tablespoons chipotle mixture the last 3 minutes of cooking. Stir in salt and pepper to taste. Spoon potatoes in center of a serving platter. Arrange beef slices around potatoes. Drizzle potatoes and beef with remaining chipotle pepper mixture; garnish, if desired. **Prep: 20 min., Grill: 20 min., Stand: 8 min.**

ALEX DESANTIS
BETHLEHEM, PENNSYLVANIA

Peppered Sirloin With Cherry-Merlot Sauce and Gorgonzola

MAKES 4 SERVINGS

> 2 tablespoons unsalted butter
> 1 (1.5-quart) CIRCULON Covered Saucepan
> 1 cup low-sodium beef broth
> 1 cup FETZER Eagle Peak Merlot
> ⅓ cup dried tart cherries
> 2 large garlic cloves, sliced
> 1 large shallot, sliced
> 1 package (about 2 pounds) HORMEL Always Tender Peppercorn Beef Filet of Sirloin
> 2 tablespoons vegetable oil
> 1 (12-inch) CIRCULON Open Clad Skillet
> 2 tablespoons low-sodium beef broth
> 2 tablespoons pure maple syrup
> ½ teaspoon McCORMICK Gourmet Collection Crushed Rosemary
> Salt and pepper to taste
> ½ cup crumbled Gorgonzola CHEESE
> 3 tablespoons chopped fresh parsley

ONE-DISH WONDERS

PREHEAT oven to 325°. Melt butter in saucepan over medium heat. Stir in 1 cup broth and next 4 ingredients. Bring to a boil, and cook, stirring often, 8 minutes or until liquid is reduced to ½ cup. Remove pan from heat, and set aside.

BROWN beef in hot oil in skillet over medium heat 3 to 4 minutes or until browned on all sides.

BAKE beef in skillet at 325° for 32 to 35 minutes or until a meat thermometer inserted into thickest portion registers 155° (medium). Remove beef to a cutting board, reserving juices in pan. Cover loosely with aluminum foil, and let stand 15 minutes before slicing.

ADD cherry mixture, 2 tablespoons broth, maple syrup, and rosemary to skillet. Bring to a boil over medium heat, stirring to loosen browned particles from bottom of skillet. Stir in salt and pepper to taste. Drizzle sauce over sliced beef; sprinkle evenly with cheese and parsley. **Prep: 20 min., Cook: 15 min., Bake: 35 min., Stand: 15 min.**

CAMILLA SAULSBURY
BLOOMINGTON, INDIANA

Judging Notes for Simple & Scrumptious Entrées

In this category, we were searching for those quick recipes that make or break the busy home cook. (Hint: Our category for next year may have a slightly different name, but we'll be looking for those same timesaving ideas.)

Jamaican Pork Tenderloin with Sauce Caribe inspired us because of its simplicity and big flavor. The jerk seasoning made the perfect one-ingredient rub for pork that's been slathered with orange juice. The combination was special enough for company and quick enough for weeknight dining, too.

ONE-DISH WONDERS
First Prize

AUNT SUZI'S BRISKET

MAKES 6 SERVINGS

Maureen Gerber says that when she saw the Cook-Off had a One-Dish Wonder category, "I instantly thought of Aunt Suzi's Brisket. It's a great dish for family and friends. I wanted to share it with others because it's so easy and delicious, and I wanted to make Aunt Suzi famous!" *(pictured on page 302)*

¾ cup firmly packed DOMINO Dark Brown Sugar
¾ cup chili sauce
¾ cup ketchup
½ to ¾ (1.4-ounce) envelope dry onion soup mix
1 (12-ounce) bottle beer
1 (3- to 4-pound) BEEF Brisket
15 small red potatoes
1½ pounds baby carrots

PREHEAT oven to 325°. Stir together first 4 ingredients; gently stir in beer.

PLACE brisket, fat side up, in a large Dutch oven or roasting pan; pierce several times with a fork. Arrange potatoes and carrots evenly around brisket; pour beer mixture over brisket, potatoes, and carrots.

BAKE, covered, at 325° for 3½ hours, basting occasionally with sauce. Remove from oven, and let brisket stand in pan, uncovered, 20 minutes. Remove brisket from pan, and cut into slices. Return slices to pan with potatoes and carrots.

BAKE, covered, 30 minutes or until tender. **Prep: 10 min., Bake: 4 hrs., Stand: 20 min.**

MAUREEN GERBER
STOCKTON, NEW JERSEY

CHILES RELLENOS QUICHE

MAKES 6 SERVINGS

All Natural PAM Original Cooking Spray
2 (4-ounce) cans diced green chiles, drained
2 cups (8 ounces) shredded sharp Cheddar CHEESE
1 cup (4 ounces) shredded Monterey Jack CHEESE With Peppers
2 cups milk
1 cup BISQUICK Original All-Purpose Baking Mix
4 large eggs, lightly beaten
1 cup Ricotta CHEESE

PREHEAT oven to 350°. Coat a 12- x 8- x 2-inch baking dish with cooking spray. Sprinkle green chiles, Cheddar cheese, and Monterey Jack cheese evenly into baking dish.

BEAT milk, baking mix, and eggs at low speed with an electric mixer until smooth. Stir in ricotta cheese; spoon mixture evenly over chiles and cheeses in baking dish.

BAKE, uncovered, at 350° for 45 minutes or until a knife inserted in center comes out clean. Let quiche stand 10 minutes before cutting. **Prep: 10 min., Bake: 45 min., Stand: 10 min.**

DOLORES VACCARO
PUEBLO, COLORADO

SIGNATURE DESSERTS

TORTELLINI ALFREDO WITH PROSCIUTTO AND ARTICHOKE HEARTS

MAKES 4 TO 6 SERVINGS

- 2 (9-ounce) packages refrigerated cheese-filled tortellini
- 1 cup whipping cream
- ½ cup (2 ounces) freshly grated Parmesan CHEESE
- 3 strips prosciutto, chopped
- 3 marinated artichoke hearts, sliced

PREPARE tortellini according to package instructions; drain.

HEAT cream in a large skillet over low heat. Gradually sprinkle in cheese, stirring constantly, until blended. Simmer, stirring occasionally, 15 to 20 minutes.

ADD tortellini, prosciutto, and artichoke hearts; simmer, stirring occasionally, 5 to 10 minutes or until sauce is slightly reduced. Serve immediately. Serve with crusty Italian bread, if desired. **Prep: 10 min., Cook: 30 min.**

NOTE: For testing purposes only, we used Contadina Refrigerated Cheese Tortellini.

DEBBIE ABBOTT
ROCKWALL, TEXAS

Judging Notes for One-Dish Wonders

Aunt Suzi's Brisket was a perfect entry for this category. What's so exciting about a brisket, you ask? This recipe used simple pantry ingredients to create home-run taste. The veggies cooked right along with the meat. Prep was exceptionally easy, and the final, perfectly cooked results couldn't have been better. It was a one-dish meal worth, well, $10,000!

SIGNATURE DESSERTS
First Prize

PECAN-CARAMEL CRUNCH ICE CREAM

MAKES 4 QUARTS

Donna Thomas says she created this recipe when she was trying to make Cookies and Cream ice cream. "I made a gallon a day for 20 days until I got the base right," she says. But she wasn't happy with cookies, and switched to an oatmeal-and-pecan "crunch" to add a contrasting texture, and caramel topping for flavor.
(pictured on page 304)

- ¾ cup quick-cooking oats
- 1 cup chopped pecans
- ¼ cup all-purpose flour
- ¼ cup firmly packed DOMINO Light Brown Sugar
- ¼ cup butter, melted
- 2 cups firmly packed DOMINO Light Brown Sugar
- 3 cups milk
- 1 (12-ounce) can evaporated milk
- ½ teaspoon salt
- 4 egg yolks
- 4 cups whipping cream
- 1 (14-ounce) can sweetened condensed milk
- 2 tablespoons vanilla extract
- 1 (20-ounce) bottle caramel topping

PREHEAT oven to 350°. Stir together first 5 ingredients; spread in a thin layer on a baking sheet. Bake at 350° for 15 minutes. Cool completely. Process in a food processor until finely chopped; set aside.

STIR together 2 cups brown sugar and next 3 ingredients in a large saucepan over low heat; simmer, stirring often, 1 minute. (Do not boil.)

BEAT egg yolks until thick and lemon-colored. Gradually stir 1 cup hot milk mixture into yolks. Add yolk mixture to remaining hot mixture; cook, stirring constantly, over low heat 2 minutes or until

mixture begins to thicken. Remove pan from heat; stir in cream, condensed milk, and vanilla. Cool to room temperature.

POUR mixture into freezer container of a 6-quart hand-turned or electric freezer; freeze according to manufacturer's instructions 5 to 7 minutes or until partially frozen. Layer top of ice cream evenly with oat mixture and caramel topping.

FREEZE, according to manufacturer's instructions, 10 to 15 minutes or until mixture is frozen. If desired, remove from freezer container, and place in another container. Freeze 8 hours or overnight. Let stand 30 minutes before serving. **Prep: 15 min., Bake: 15 min., Cook: 15 min., Freeze: 25 min., Stand: 30 min.**

DONNA THOMAS
DALLAS, TEXAS

NESTLÉ® TOLL HOUSE® MORSELS
Brand Winner

THAT'S INCREDIBLE

MAKES 10 TO 12 SERVINGS

- 1 cup DOMINO Granulated Sugar
- ½ cup all-purpose flour
- ½ cup shortening, melted
- ⅓ cup unsweetened cocoa
- ¼ cup water
- 1 teaspoon vanilla extract
- ½ teaspoon baking powder
- ¼ teaspoon salt
- 2 large eggs, lightly beaten
- 1 cup NESTLÉ TOLL HOUSE Semi-Sweet Chocolate Morsels
- 1 cup mini marshmallows
- ½ cup chopped pecans
- ½ cup NESTLÉ TOLL HOUSE Semi-Sweet Chocolate Mini Morsels
- Chocolate Pudding
- 2 cups whipping cream
- 2 (8-ounce) packages NESTLÉ TOLL HOUSE Semi-Sweet Chocolate Baking Bars, broken into pieces

PREHEAT oven to 350°. Line the bottom of a 10-inch springform pan with parchment paper. Lightly grease and flour paper and sides of pan.

STIR together first 9 ingredients until well blended; fold in chocolate morsels. Pour batter into prepared pan, and spread evenly over bottom.

BAKE on middle rack at 350° for 20 to 25 minutes. Remove from oven, and sprinkle top evenly with marshmallows, pecans, and chocolate mini morsels. Place on a wire rack, and let cool. Pour hot Chocolate Pudding over marshmallow mixture; cover and chill 8 hours or overnight.

HEAT cream in a saucepan; bring to a simmer. Remove pan from heat; add chocolate pieces, stirring until chocolate melts. Let stand 1 hour, stirring occasionally, until spreading consistency. Remove sides from springform pan; spread chocolate mixture evenly on top and sides of cake. **Prep: 25 min., Bake: 25 min., Chill: 8 hrs., Stand: 1 hr.**

Chocolate Pudding:

MAKES 5 CUPS

- 4 cups whipping cream
- 6 tablespoons cornstarch
- 1 cup DOMINO Granulated Sugar
- 1 cup NESTLÉ TOLL HOUSE Semi-Sweet Chocolate Morsels
- 1 teaspoon vanilla extract

STIR together 6 tablespoons cream and cornstarch, stirring until a paste forms. Bring remaining 3½ cups and 2 tablespoons cream to a simmer in a 2-quart saucepan over medium heat. Stir in cornstarch mixture, sugar, chocolate morsels, and vanilla, and cook, stirring constantly, until chocolate melts. Cook mixture, stirring often, 8 minutes or until thick and creamy. **Prep: 15 min., Cook: 10 min.**

CAROLYN JONES
FOLEY, ALABAMA

IRISH CREAM CAKE

MAKES 12 SERVINGS

- ½ cup butter, softened
- ½ cup shortening
- 2 cups DOMINO Granulated Sugar
- 5 large eggs, separated
- 1 tablespoon vanilla extract
- 2 cups all-purpose flour
- 1 teaspoon baking soda
- 1 cup buttermilk
- ½ cup Irish cream liqueur
- Butterscotch Filling
- Cream Cheese Frosting
- ¾ cup chopped pecans, toasted
- 10 toasted pecan halves

PREHEAT oven to 350°. Beat butter and shortening at medium speed with an electric mixer until fluffy; gradually add sugar, beating well. Add egg yolks, 1 at a time, beating until blended. Add vanilla, beating until blended. Combine flour and soda; add to butter mixture alternately with buttermilk, beginning and ending with flour mixture. Beat at low speed until blended after each addition. Beat egg whites until stiff peaks form; fold into batter. Pour into 3 greased and floured 9-inch round cakepans.

BAKE at 350° for 25 minutes or until a wooden pick inserted in center comes out clean. Cool in pans on wire racks 10 minutes; remove and cool completely on wire racks. Brush layers evenly with liqueur. Spread half of Butterscotch Filling between each layer; spread Cream Cheese Frosting on top and sides of cake. Gently press chopped pecans onto sides of cake; arrange pecan halves on top. **Prep: 30 min., Bake: 25 min., Cool: 10 min.**

Butterscotch Filling:

MAKES 2 CUPS

- ½ cup firmly packed DOMINO Brown Sugar
- 2 tablespoons butter
- 1 cup milk, divided
- 3 tablespoons all-purpose flour
- ½ teaspoon salt
- 2 large eggs, lightly beaten
- ¼ cup chopped pecans, toasted
- ½ teaspoon vanilla extract

STIR together brown sugar and butter in a heavy saucepan over low heat, stirring constantly, until sugar melts and mixture is blended. Stir in ½ cup milk until blended.

WHISK together remaining ½ cup milk, flour, and salt; stir into brown sugar mixture, and cook, whisking constantly, over medium heat 5 minutes or until thickened. Gradually add eggs, and cook, whisking constantly, 2 minutes. Remove from heat, and let cool. Stir in pecans and vanilla. **Prep: 5 min., Cook: 10 min.**

Cream Cheese Frosting:

MAKES 3 CUPS

- 1 (8-ounce) package PHILADELPHIA Cream Cheese, softened
- ½ cup butter, softened
- 1 tablespoon vanilla extract
- 1 (16-ounce) package DOMINO 10-X Confectioners Sugar, unsifted

BEAT first 3 ingredients with an electric mixer until creamy. Add confectioners sugar, beating at low speed until blended. Beat at high speed until smooth. **Prep: 5 min.**

JULIANA BLACK
GARLAND, TEXAS

Judging Notes for Signature Desserts

Our rules defined the category as "any sweet creation that is the perfect ending to your casual or elegant gathering."

Donna Thomas's Pecan-Caramel Crunch Ice Cream caught the judges' attention because it was so easy to make and yet so GOOD. The judges liked the Southern touch offered by the pecans in the brown sugar-oat crunch mixture.

KIDS LOVE IT!

KIDS LOVE IT!
First Prize

BACON 'N' EGG BREAKFAST EMPANADAS

MAKES 4 SERVINGS (2 PER SERVING)

"My family wouldn't eat breakfast because they were always so busy," Sherry Little says. "I thought I'd come up with something better than fast food, something healthier." Sherry originally made these with sausage, but tailored her recipe to use Hormel bacon. Roll any leftover filling in a flour tortilla, if desired. *(pictured on page 303)*

- 6 ounces PHILADELPHIA Cream Cheese, softened
- 1½ tablespoons minced fresh parsley or 1½ teaspoons dried parsley flakes
- ¾ teaspoon seasoned salt
- ¼ teaspoon black pepper
- ⅔ cup shredded sharp Cheddar CHEESE
- 2 tablespoons butter
- 5 large eggs, lightly beaten
- 1 (16.3-ounce) can refrigerated jumbo flaky biscuits
- 8 HORMEL Black Label Bacon Slices, cooked and crumbled
- All Natural PAM Original Cooking Spray
- 1 egg white, lightly beaten
- 1 to 2 teaspoons sesame seeds (optional)

PREHEAT oven to 375°.
STIR together first 4 ingredients in a bowl until blended; stir in cheese.
MELT butter in a 9-inch skillet over medium heat; add eggs, and cook, without stirring, until eggs begin to set on bottom. Draw a spatula across bottom of skillet to form large curds. Continue cooking until eggs are slightly thickened but still moist. (Do not stir constantly.) Remove from heat, and let cool.
FLATTEN each biscuit into about a 5-inch circle. Spread cream cheese mixture evenly over tops of dough circles, leaving ½-inch border around edge. Top evenly with scrambled eggs and bacon.
FOLD dough circles in half over mixture, pinching edges to seal; place 2 inches apart in a 15- x 10-inch jellyroll pan coated with cooking spray. Brush tops evenly with egg white; press sealed edges with tines of a fork. Sprinkle with sesame seeds, if desired.
BAKE at 375° for 14 to 16 minutes or until golden brown. Remove to a wire rack. Serve warm. **Prep: 20 min., Cook: 5 min., Bake: 16 min.**

NOTE: Store leftover empanadas, completely cooled, in zip-top plastic bags or wrapped in plastic wrap in refrigerator. To reheat, wrap empanadas in paper towels and microwave at MEDIUM (50% power) 1 to 2 minutes or until thoroughly heated.

SHERRY LITTLE
SHERWOOD, ARKANSAS

BISQUICK® BAKING MIX
Brand Winner

BANANA-TOFFEE COFFEE CAKES

MAKES 12 SERVINGS

- 1 (12-muffin cup) DUPONT TEFLON NON-STICK muffin pan
- All Natural PAM Original Cooking Spray
- 2 cups BISQUICK Original All-Purpose Baking Mix
- ⅓ cup DOMINO Granulated Sugar
- 1 cup mashed ripe banana (about 2 large)
- ⅔ cup milk
- 1 large egg, lightly beaten
- ½ teaspoon McCORMICK Gourmet Collection Ground Allspice
- Streusel Topping
- ½ cup NESTLÉ TOLL HOUSE Premier White Chocolate Morsels
- 2 tablespoons whipping cream

PREHEAT oven to 400°. Coat cups in muffin pans with cooking spray.
STIR together baking mix and next 5 ingredients in a medium bowl until blended. Spoon batter evenly into prepared muffin pan; sprinkle batter evenly with Streusel Topping.
BAKE at 400° for 17 minutes or until a wooden pick inserted in center comes out clean. Cool in pan 10 minutes. Gently run a knife around edges of cakes; remove to wire rack to cool completely.
MICROWAVE white chocolate morsels and cream in a glass bowl at HIGH 30 to 60 seconds or until morsels melt; stir until smooth. Place wire rack with cakes on a large piece of wax paper. Drizzle white chocolate mixture back and forth over tops of cakes with tines of a fork. **Prep: 15 min., Bake: 17 min., Cool: 10 min.**

Streusel Topping:

MAKES ABOUT 1 CUP

- 3 tablespoons unsalted butter, melted
- ⅓ cup firmly packed DOMINO Light Brown Sugar
- ⅓ cup all-purpose flour
- ¼ teaspoon McCORMICK Gourmet Collection Saigon Cinnamon
- 2 (1.4-ounce) chocolate-covered toffee candy bars, finely chopped

STIR together all ingredients. **Prep: 5 min.**

BETH ROYALS
RICHMOND, VIRGINIA

Judging Notes for Kids Love It!

We confess that we had no idea what kinds of entries we'd receive in this category. Our rules simply said the entries needed to be recipes prepared by adults that make kids say "yummy." Note: For the 2003 Cook-Off, we're also inviting kids to enter this category.

BRAND WINNERS

These recipes won recognition for best use of a sponsor's product. Some of the brand winners were so outstanding they became category winners as well.

USA PEANUTS
Brand Winner

PEANUT BUTTER-TOFFEE TURTLE COOKIES

MAKES 3 DOZEN

- ½ cup unsalted butter, softened
- ½ cup DOMINO Granulated Sugar
- ½ cup firmly packed DOMINO Light Brown Sugar
- ⅔ cup creamy USA PEANUT Butter
- 1 large egg
- 2 cups BISQUICK Original All-Purpose Baking Mix
- ⅔ cup almond toffee bits
- ⅔ cup coarsely chopped USA PEANUTS
- ⅔ cup NESTLÉ TOLL HOUSE Milk Chocolate Morsels
- 10 ounces vanilla caramels
- 2 to 3 tablespoons whipping cream
- ½ teaspoon vanilla extract
- ⅔ cup NESTLÉ TOLL HOUSE Milk Chocolate Morsels, melted

PREHEAT oven to 350°.

BEAT first 4 ingredients at medium speed with an electric mixer until creamy. Add egg, beating until blended.

ADD baking mix, beating at low speed just until blended. Stir in toffee bits, peanuts, and ⅔ cup chocolate morsels.

DROP dough by rounded tablespoonfuls onto ungreased baking sheets; flatten dough with hand.

BAKE at 350° for 10 to 12 minutes or until golden brown. Cool cookies on baking sheets 1 minute, and remove to wire racks.

MICROWAVE caramels and 2 tablespoons cream in a glass bowl at HIGH 1 minute; stir. Continue to microwave at 30-second intervals, stirring until caramels melt and mixture is smooth; add remaining cream, if necessary. Stir in vanilla. Spoon caramel mixture evenly onto tops of cookies; drizzle evenly with melted chocolate. **Prep: 25 min., Bake: 12 min. per batch, Cool: 1 min.**

CAROLE HOLT
MENDOTA HEIGHTS, MINNESOTA

SPLENDA® NO CALORIE SWEETENER
Brand Winner

GEORGIE'S APPLE PIE

MAKES 8 SERVINGS

- 1 (15-ounce) package refrigerated piecrusts
- 1 cup SPLENDA Granular
- 1 tablespoon all-purpose flour
- 1 tablespoon ground cinnamon
- 6 to 8 Cortland apples, peeled and sliced*
- 1 tablespoon butter, cut up
- Milk
- Sugar-free ice cream or lite frozen whipped topping, thawed

LET piecrusts stand at room temperature according to package directions.

FIT 1 piecrust into a 9-inch pieplate. Stir together no-calorie sweetener, flour, and cinnamon. Sprinkle one-fourth of flour mixture over apples, tossing to coat. Spoon apple mixture into prepared pieplate, and dot with butter. Sprinkle with remaining flour mixture. Unfold remaining piecrust, and press out fold lines. Place over apple mixture, crimping edges; cut slits in top for steam to escape. Lightly brush with milk, and place pie on a baking sheet.

BAKE on lowest rack at 350° for 50 to 55 minutes or until golden. Serve warm with sugar-free ice cream or whipped topping. **Prep: 25 min., Bake: 55 min.**

JUNE ALLEN
FITCHBURG, MASSACHUSETTS

*Substitute 5 Granny Smith apples and 1 Golden Delicious apple, if desired.

More Brand-Winning Recipes

Look for these other brand-winning recipes that also won recognition in specific contest categories.

- **Bisquick® Baking Mix:** Banana-Toffee Coffee Cakes, page 324
- **Circulon® Cookware:** Peppered Sirloin With Cherry-Merlot Sauce and Gorgonzola, page 320
- **Hormel Meats:** Grilled Beef With Mashed Potatoes and Chipotle Cream, page 320
- **McCormick® Gourmet Collection™:** Jamaican Pork Tenderloin With Sauce Caribe, page 320
- **Nestlé® Toll House® Morsels:** That's Incredible, page 322
- **USA Peanuts:** Peanut Butter-Toffee Turtle Cookies, page 325

SUCCESS® & MAHATMA® RICE
Brand Winner

SKILLET HOPPIN' JOHN WITH SCALLION HOE CAKE MEDAILLONS

MAKES 6 SERVINGS

- 4 turkey bacon slices, chopped
- 1 tablespoon olive oil
- 1 medium onion, chopped
- 1 small red bell pepper, chopped
- 1½ teaspoons salt, divided
- ½ teaspoon dried thyme
- ¼ teaspoon freshly ground black pepper
- ⅛ teaspoon dried crushed red pepper
- ⅛ teaspoon ground chipotle chile pepper
- 2 cups cooked MAHATMA Valencia Short-grain Rice
- 1 (15-ounce) can black-eyed peas, rinsed and drained
- 2 cups white cornmeal
- ¼ cup butter or margarine, melted
- 2 cups boiling water
- 4 large scallions, finely chopped
- Vegetable oil
- 3 tablespoons fresh lime juice
- Garnish: sliced scallions

PREHEAT oven to 250°. Cook turkey bacon in 1 tablespoon hot oil in a large well-greased cast-iron skillet or oven-proof nonstick skillet over medium-high heat, stirring constantly, 5 minutes or until browned. Add onion; sauté 5 minutes. Add bell pepper; sauté 5 minutes or until tender. Stir in ½ teaspoon salt and next 4 ingredients until blended. Stir in rice and black-eyed peas; sauté 10 minutes or until thoroughly heated.

COVER skillet loosely with aluminum foil; place in preheated oven to keep warm.

COMBINE cornmeal, butter, and remaining 1 teaspoon salt in a large bowl. Gradually add boiling water, stirring until mixture resembles thickened grits. (Batter should be soft but not too thin. Add more water if mixture becomes too firm.) Fold in scallions.

DROP batter by tablespoonfuls, in batches, into ¼ cup hot oil in a large skillet over medium-high heat, and fry 3 minutes on each side or until golden, adding more oil as needed for each batch. Drain on paper towels; keep warm.

REMOVE rice mixture from oven; stir in lime juice. Serve with hoe cakes. Garnish, if desired. **Prep: 30 min., Fry: 6 min. per batch**

CATHERINE HUND
ST. LOUIS, MISSOURI

STOUFFER'S® FROZEN FOODS®
Brand Winner

APPLE-PECAN BISCUIT BRAID

MAKES 8 TO 10 SERVINGS

- 1 (12-ounce) package STOUFFER'S Escalloped Apples
- 1 (¼-ounce) envelope active dry yeast
- ½ cup warm water (100° to 110°)
- 2½ cups all-purpose baking mix
- 1¼ cups (6 ounces) shredded sharp Cheddar cheese
- 1 large egg, beaten
- Vegetable cooking spray
- 1 (8-ounce) package cream cheese, softened
- ¼ cup granulated sugar
- ½ teaspoon ground cinnamon
- ½ cup chopped pecans, toasted
- 3 tablespoons dark brown sugar
- 2 teaspoons all-purpose flour
- ¼ cup powdered sugar

THAW escalloped apples according to package directions; set aside.

COMBINE yeast and warm water in a large bowl; let stand 5 minutes. Stir in baking mix, cheese, and egg, stirring until a soft dough forms. Turn out onto a well-floured surface, and knead 20 times. Place in a bowl coated with cooking spray, turning to grease top. Cover; let stand 20 minutes.

PREHEAT oven to 350°.

STIR together cream cheese, granulated sugar, and cinnamon, and set aside. Stir together escalloped apples, pecans, brown sugar, and flour, and set aside.

ROLL or pat dough on a baking sheet coated with cooking spray into a 14- x 9-inch rectangle. Spread cream cheese mixture lengthwise down center of rectangle, leaving a 3-inch border on both long sides; spoon escalloped apples mixture over cream cheese mixture. Make horizontal cuts at 1-inch intervals into long sides (border) of rectangle, cutting to the filled center, to create dough strips.

FOLD dough strips in a slight downward angle over escalloped apples mixture, alternating sides and overlapping slightly to resemble a braid.

BAKE at 350° for 20 minutes or until golden brown; let cool slightly, and sift with powdered sugar. **Prep: 30 min., Stand: 25 min., Bake: 20 min.**

DIANE SPARROW
OSAGE, IOWA

EQUAL® SWEETENER
Brand Winner

SUGAR-FREE PEACHY CHEESECAKE PARFAITS

MAKES 8 SERVINGS

- 1 (8-ounce) package ⅓-less-fat cream cheese, softened
- 7 EQUAL Packets
- 1 (8-ounce) container sour cream
- 1 teaspoon vanilla extract
- 1 (8-ounce) container lite frozen whipped topping, thawed
- 3 ripe peaches
- 2 tablespoons graham cracker crumbs (optional)

BEAT cream cheese and no-calorie sweetener at medium speed with an electric mixer until light and fluffy. Add sour cream and vanilla, beating until blended. Stir in whipped topping. Peel peaches; cut into slices. Reserve 8 slices for garnish.

SPOON half of cream cheese mixture into 8 (4-ounce) parfait glasses; top evenly with remaining peach slices. Top with remaining cream cheese mixture; sprinkle with graham cracker crumbs, if desired.

TOP each with a reserved peach slice. Cover; chill 6 hours. **Prep: 20 min., Chill: 6 hrs.**

MARY MATLOCK
SHREVEPORT, LOUISIANA

REYNOLDS® POT LUX™ DISPOSABLE COOKWARE
Brand Winner

CREAM CHEESE-FILLED CINNAMON ROLLS

MAKES 12 TO 15 SERVINGS

- 5 to 6 cups all-purpose flour
- 1 (18.25-ounce) package white cake mix
- 2 (¼-ounce) envelopes rapid-rise yeast
- 2 cups warm milk (100° to 110°)
- 2 large eggs, lightly beaten
- ½ teaspoon salt
- 1 (8-ounce) package cream cheese, softened
- ½ cup sugar
- 1 tablespoon ground cinnamon
- ½ cup chopped pecans
- 1 REYNOLDS Pot Lux Cookware Pan With Lid (1½-quart size)
- 1 REYNOLDS Pot Lux Cookware Pan With Lid (9- x 12½-inch size)
- Vegetable cooking spray
- Frosting

STIR together 4 cups flour, cake mix, and next 4 ingredients in a large bowl; gradually add enough remaining flour to form a soft dough. (In our Test Kitchens, we used an additional ½ cup on a heavily floured surface; more may be used.)

TURN dough out onto a lightly floured surface, and knead until smooth and elastic (about 6 minutes).

ROLL into a 12- x 20-inch rectangle, and spread with cream cheese.

STIR together sugar and cinnamon, and sprinkle over cream cheese; sprinkle with pecans. Roll up, jellyroll fashion, starting at long edge. Cut into 1-inch slices. Coat pans with cooking spray; place slices in pans.

PREHEAT oven to 350°.

COVER and let rise in a warm place (85°), free from drafts, 15 minutes. Place each pan in center of a baking sheet.

BAKE, uncovered, at 350° for 15 to 20 minutes or until lightly browned. Remove baking sheets with pans from oven; spread warm rolls with Frosting.

Let pans stand on baking sheets 2 minutes before removing. **Prep:** 25 min., **Bake:** 20 min.

NOTE: To make ahead, freeze unbaked cinnamon rolls. Thaw completely, and bake as directed.

Frosting:

MAKES ¾ CUP

- ⅓ cup butter, softened
- 3 tablespoons milk
- ¼ teaspoon vanilla extract
- 1½ cups powdered sugar

STIR together first 3 ingredients; stir in powdered sugar, blending well. **Prep:** 5 min.

PAULA COX
TEXARKANA, TEXAS

GENUINE CALIFORNIA AVOCADOS
Brand Winner

SPICY SALMON FILLETS WITH AVOCADO MAYONNAISE

MAKES 6 SERVINGS

- 1 tablespoon brown sugar
- 2 teaspoons paprika
- 1½ teaspoons salt
- ½ teaspoon ground cumin
- ½ teaspoon chili powder
- ½ teaspoon ground black pepper
- 6 (6- to 8-ounce) salmon fillets
- 2 tablespoons olive oil
- 1 small very ripe GENUINE CALIFORNIA AVOCADO, peeled and cubed (about ½ cup)
- 2 teaspoons fresh lemon juice
- 5 tablespoons mayonnaise

PREHEAT broiler. Combine first 6 ingredients in a small bowl, and set aside.

RINSE salmon, and dry well. Place salmon, skin side down, in a broiler pan; brush each top with 1 teaspoon oil. Sprinkle evenly with brown sugar mixture.

BROIL 5 inches from heat 1½ to 2 minutes or until brown sugar mixture begins to caramelize. Reduce oven temperature to 425°, and bake 8 to 12 minutes or until fish flakes with a fork.

MASH avocado until smooth; stir in lemon juice. Whisk in mayonnaise until very smooth. Cover and chill until ready to serve. Serve with fillets. **Prep:** 15 min., **Broil:** 2 min., **Bake:** 12 min.

SUSAN FARRELLY
BEAVER, PENNSYLVANIA

KRAFT® VELVEETA®
Brand Winner

SPICY CHICKEN SPAGHETTI

MAKES 6 SERVINGS

- 1 (8-ounce) package spaghetti
- Vegetable cooking spray
- ¼ cup butter or margarine
- ½ large onion, chopped
- 1 (8-ounce) package VELVEETA Cheese, cubed
- 1 (10-ounce) can hot diced tomatoes and green chiles
- 4 skinned and boned cooked chicken breast halves, chopped
- 1 (10¾-ounce) can cream of chicken soup

PREHEAT oven to 350°. Cook spaghetti according to package directions; drain. Place spaghetti in a 13- x 9-inch baking dish coated with cooking spray.

MELT butter in a skillet over medium heat; add onion, and sauté 3 to 5 minutes or until tender. Add cheese and canned tomatoes and green chiles, stirring until cheese melts. Stir in chicken and soup, blending well. Pour over spaghetti in baking dish. Bake at 350° for 25 minutes or until bubbly. **Prep:** 20 min., **Bake:** 25 min.

DIANE CUTCHER
HARRISON, TENNESSEE

Metric Equivalents

The recipes that appear in this cookbook use the standard United States method for measuring liquid and dry or solid ingredients (teaspoons, tablespoons, and cups). The information on this chart is provided to help cooks outside the U.S. successfully use these recipes. All equivalents are approximate.

METRIC EQUIVALENTS FOR DIFFERENT TYPES OF INGREDIENTS

A standard cup measure of a dry or solid ingredient will vary in weight depending on the type of ingredient. A standard cup of liquid is the same volume for any type of liquid. Use the following chart when converting standard cup measures to grams (weight) or milliliters (volume).

Standard Cup	Fine Powder	Grain	Granular	Liquid Solids	Liquid
	(ex. flour)	(ex. rice)	(ex. sugar)	(ex. butter)	(ex. milk)
1	140 g	150 g	190 g	200 g	240 ml
¾	105 g	113 g	143 g	150 g	180 ml
⅔	93 g	100 g	125 g	133 g	160 ml
½	70 g	75 g	95 g	100 g	120 ml
⅓	47 g	50 g	63 g	67 g	80 ml
¼	35 g	38 g	48 g	50 g	60 ml
⅛	18 g	19 g	24 g	25 g	30 ml

USEFUL EQUIVALENTS FOR DRY INGREDIENTS BY WEIGHT

(To convert ounces to grams, multiply the number of ounces by 30.)

1 oz	=	¹⁄₁₆ lb	=	30 g
4 oz	=	¼ lb	=	120 g
8 oz	=	½ lb	=	240 g
12 oz	=	¾ lb	=	360 g
16 oz	=	1 lb	=	480 g

USEFUL EQUIVALENTS FOR LENGTH

(To convert inches to centimeters, multiply the number of inches by 2.5.)

1 in						=	2.5 cm		
6 in	=	½ ft	=		=	15 cm			
12 in	=	1 ft			=	30 cm			
36 in	=	3 ft	=	1 yd	=	90 cm			
40 in					=	100 cm	=	1 m	

USEFUL EQUIVALENTS FOR LIQUID INGREDIENTS BY VOLUME

¼ tsp	=							1 ml
½ tsp	=							2 ml
1 tsp	=							5 ml
3 tsp	=	1 tbls			=	½ fl oz	=	15 ml
	=	2 tbls	=	⅛ cup	=	1 fl oz	=	30 ml
	=	4 tbls	=	¼ cup	=	2 fl oz	=	60 ml
	=	5⅓ tbls	=	⅓ cup	=	3 fl oz	=	80 ml
	=	8 tbls	=	½ cup	=	4 fl oz	=	120 ml
	=	10⅔ tbls	=	⅔ cup	=	5 fl oz	=	160 ml
	=	12 tbls	=	¾ cup	=	6 fl oz	=	180 ml
	=	16 tbls	=	1 cup	=	8 fl oz	=	240 ml
	=	1 pt	=	2 cups	=	16 fl oz	=	480 ml
	=	1 qt	=	4 cups	=	32 fl oz	=	960 ml
						33 fl oz	=	1000 ml	= 1 l

USEFUL EQUIVALENTS FOR COOKING/OVEN TEMPERATURES

	Fahrenheit	Celsius	Gas Mark
Freeze Water	32° F	0° C	
Room Temperature	68° F	20° C	
Boil Water	212° F	100° C	
Bake	325° F	160° C	3
	350° F	180° C	4
	375° F	190° C	5
	400° F	200° C	6
	425° F	220° C	7
	450° F	230° C	8
Broil			Grill

Menu Index

This menu lists every menu by suggested occasion. Recipe in bold type are provided with the menu. Suggested accompaniments are in regular type.

MENUS FOR SPECIAL OCCASIONS

Valentine's Day Dinner
Serves 4
page 32
Cherry Tomato-Caper Salad
Chicken Cakes With Creole Sauce
Raspberry Shortbread   Chardonnay

Leprechauns' Breakfast
Serves 6
page 67
Boxty
Applesauce
Bacon, ham, or sausage
Pan-Fried Tomatoes
Irish Bread
Coffee   Orange juice

An Engaging Menu
Serves 8
page 118
Frances's Margaritas
Chimayó Cocktails   Assorted beers
Tomato Salsa   Guacamole   Tortilla chips
Beef and Chicken Fajitas
Red Rice   Frijoles
Pralines

Mother's Day Brunch
Serves 6
page 130
Gazpacho
Ham and Eggs Mornay
Cucumber-Salmon Sandwiches With Dill
Make-Ahead French Toast With Strawberry Sauce
Mimosas   Bloody Marys

Luau Menu
Serves 6
page 162
Fruit Punch
Macadamia-Mango Chicken
Peanut-Noodle Salad
Tropical Fruit Salad
Frozen Coffee Cooler
Banana-Coconut Ice Cream

Poolside Supper
Serves 6 to 8
page 164
Nutty Fruit-and-Cheese Spread
Pistachio Twists
Tuna Amandine
Crab-and-Scallop Cakes
Spinach-Stuffed Squash
Honey-Baked Tomatoes
Fig Cake

Mediterranean Menu
Serves 8
page 167
Grilled Lamb Patties
Persian Rice Pilaf
Marinated Cucumber-Tomato Salad

Ladies Luncheon
Serves 8
page 171
Chicken Tetrazzini
Miniature Date Muffins
Mocha Charlottes
Mint tea

MENUS FOR THE FAMILY

Family Night
Serves 4 to 6
page 18

Vegetable Dip   Sliced fresh vegetables
Rainbow Salad with Dijon Vinaigrette
or **Lite Herb Dressing**
Healthy Chicken Enchiladas   Black beans   Rice
Fresh fruit   Iced tea

Spaghetti and Meatballs Dinner
Serves 6 to 8
page 25

Country-Style Spaghetti   **Baked Meatballs**
Tossed green salad   **Vinaigrette Salad Dressing**
Buttery Garlic Bread

Southern Sunday Dinner
Serves 4
page 106

Our Best Southern Fried Chicken
Simple Turnip Greens   **Pepper Sauce**
Hearty Black-Eyed Peas
Hot-Water Cornbread
Classic Chess Pie   **Southern Sweet Tea**

Summer Fish Fry
Serves 10
page 166

Front-Porch Fried Catfish
Barbecue Beans
Creamy Coleslaw

Family-Pleasing Menu
Serves 6 to 8
page 178

Fruit Punch
Chicken Tetrazzini or **Easy Chicken Cordon Bleu**
Honey-Baked Tomatoes   Tossed green salad
Mixed-Berry Angel Cakes With Almond Sugar

Down-Home Menu
Serves 6
page 180

Mama's Fried Chicken
Barbecue Eggplant
Stuffed Summer Squash
Chocolate-Zucchini Cake
Peach Iced Tea

Mediterranean Menu
Serves 4
page 200

Stuffed Chicken Breasts With White Bean Puree
Tabbouleh Couscous
Easy Herb Focaccia
Lemon Ice   Pinot Grigio

Casual Supper
Serves 4
page 230

Tomato-Basil Bisque
Apple-Spinach Salad
Italian BLT Sandwiches
Ginger-Oatmeal Sorghum Cookies

A Taste of Italy
Serves 6 to 8
page 269

Caponata alla Siciliana
Hearty Chicken Cacciatore
Caesar Salad

Soul Food Supper
Serves 4 to 6
page 271

Down-Home Chicken and Onions
Hoppin' John
Fried Cabbage
Chocolate Quad

WHEN COMPANY IS COMING

Casual Southwestern Hospitality
Serves 10 to 12
page 86
Balsamic Strawberry Salsa   Tortilla chips
Texas White Sangría
Bacon-Mandarin Salad   **Chicken With Polenta**
Mocha Cake

Down-Home Gathering
Serves 6 to 8
page 88
Baked Vidalia Onion Dip   Tortilla chips
Chocolate Martinis
Italian Pot Roast   **Roasted Zucchini**
Coco Loco Custard

A Friendly Feast
Serves 6
page 96
Asparagus, Roasted-Beet, and Goat Cheese Salad
Grilled Lamb Chops With Chipotle and Cilantro Oils
Onion Risotto   **Ginger Pound Cake**   Ice cream

Summer Garden Party
Serves 10 to 12
page 134
Lemon Flank Steak Skewers With Lemon Dipping Sauce
Chilled Shrimp With Rémoulade Sauce
Balsamic Marinated Olives   Crusty bread
Spicy Jack Cheese Crisps
Creamy Citrus Tartlets   **Mint Bellinis**

A Harvest Menu
Serves 6 to 8
page 242
Cream of Curried Peanut Soup
Spinach-and-Cranberry Salad With Warm Chutney Dressing
Sugar-and-Spice Cured Turkey
Crabmeat-and-Oyster Dressing   Cranberry sauce
Marinated Asparagus   **Brussels Sprouts With Apples**
Baked Sweet-and-Savory Mashed Potatoes   Rolls
Elegant Pumpkin-Walnut Layered Pie

Supper Club Menu
Serves 8
page 250
Gin-Marinated Pheasant
Point Clear Potatoes
Green Beans With Zucchini
Poinsettia Punch*

Progressive Dinner Party
Serves 8
page 254
Marinated Shrimp   **Cranberry-Apple Salad***
Garlic-and-Rosemary Beef Tenderloin
Green Beans With Roquefort Cheese and Walnuts*

Cooking With Friends
Serves 6 to 8
page 276
Dijon Rack of Lamb   **Cranberry Relish**
Gratin Potatoes
Braised Red Cabbage
Chocolate Mousse

Easy Holiday Menu
Serves 6
page 290
Molasses Pork Tenderloin With Red Wine Sauce
Creamy Leek Mashed Potatoes
Broccoli With Pimiento Cheese Sauce
Pepper Jelly-Glazed Carrots
Cranberry Congealed Salad
Two-Seed Bread Knots
Chocolate cake   Pinot noir

Lasting Impressions Dinner
Serves 8
page 310
Beef Fillets With Stilton-Portobello Sauce
Sweet Onion Pudding
Roasted Potato Trio
Sautéed green beans
Apple strudel

*Double recipe.

Recipe Title Index

This index alphabetically lists every recipe by exact title.
All microwave recipe page numbers are preceded by an "M."

Month-by-Month Index

This index alphabetically lists every food article and accompanying recipes by month. All microwave recipe page numbers are preceded by an "M."

General Recipe Index

This index lists every recipe by food category and/or major ingredient.
All microwave recipe page numbers are preceded by an "M."

CHAYOTES
  Mirliton Stew, 57
CHEESE. *See also* **Appetizers/Cheese;**
  Cheesecakes.
  Breads
    Biscuits, Cheese-Garlic, 260
    Biscuits With Beef and Horseradish-
      Chive Cream, Blue Cheese, 313
    Biscuits With Sun-Dried Tomato
      Spread and Bacon, Cream Cheese-
      and-Olive, 313
    Biscuits With Tapenade, Cream
      Cheese-and-Olive, 313
    Black-Eyed Pea Bread, 224
    Cornbread, Bacon-Cheddar Hot-
      Water, 107
    Cornbread, Southwestern Hot-
      Water, 107
    Cups, Bacon-Cheese, 219
    English Cheese Muffins, 41
    French Toast, Stuffed, 105
    French Toast With Strawberry Sauce,
      Make-Ahead, 131
    Muffins, Southwestern Corn, 212
    Rolls, Cream Cheese-Filled
      Cinnamon, 327
    Triangles, Savory, 54
  Casseroles
    Broccoli Supreme, 312
    Broccoli With Pimiento Cheese
      Sauce, 291
    Carrots, Scalloped, 129
    Chicken Cannelloni With Roasted Red
      Bell Pepper Sauce, 287
    Chicken Casserole, Jalapeño, 50
    Chicken Tetrazzini, 171
    Eggplant, Spinach-and-Basil
      Stuffed, 147
    Enchilada Casserole, Easy, 143
    Enchiladas, Chicken-Cheese, 236
    Grits, Mexican Cheese, 34
    King Ranch Casserole, 210
    Lasagna, Ellie's, 186
    Lasagna, Spinach-Black Bean, 44
    Macaroni and Cheese, Baked, 26
    Macaroni and Cheese,
      Broccoli, 36
    Macaroni and Cheese, Creamy, 26
    Macaroni With Blue Cheese and
      Walnuts, M208
    Pasta Bake, Cheesy, 161
    Potatoes Au Gratin, 197
    Potatoes, Baked Sweet-and-Savory
      Mashed, 244
    Potatoes, Cream Cheese Mashed, 35
    Spaghetti-and-Spinach Casserole, 199

Chicken Breasts With White Bean Puree,
  Stuffed, 200
Chicken Bundles, Southwestern, 215
Chicken, Cheesy Mexican, 91
Chicken in Phyllo, Cheesy, 308
Chicken Macaroni and Cheese,
  Spicy, 63
Chowder, Cheese-Vegetable, 305
Desserts
  Cake With Strawberries and Cream,
    Cream Cheese Pound, 104
  Cookies, Cream Cheese, 229
  Cookies, Cream Cheese-Chocolate
    Chip, 229
  Filling, Mascarpone, 146
  Frosting, Chocolate-Cream
    Cheese, 256
  Frosting, Cream Cheese, 83, 209, 323
  Frosting, Pecan-Cream Cheese, 294
  Noodle Casserole, Sweet, 238
  Pie, Cheddar-Pear, 197
  Pie, Coconut Cream, 92
  Pie, Lemon-Blueberry Cream, 92
  Pie, Mystery Pecan, 249
  Quad, Chocolate, 272
  Quesadillas, Dessert, 54
  Tart, Strawberry-Mascarpone, 146
  Tiramisù, 285
Dogs, Taco, M57
Dressing, Spinach Salad With Zesty Blue
  Cheese, 121
Enchiladas, Healthy Chicken, 19
Grits, Parmesan Cheese, 233
Grits, Smoked Gouda, 319
Ham and Eggs Mornay, 130
Macaroni and Cheese, Chicken, 63
Macaroni, Cheeseburger, 119
Monster Eyes, 222
Omelet, Ham-and-Cheese, 246
Omelet, Open-Faced Bacon-and-
  Potato, 246
Pasta Primavera, Peppery, 161
Peppers With Chicken and Corn,
  Stuffed, 147
Pizza, Broccoli Supreme, 312
Pizza Squares, Easy, 61
Pork Chops, Garlic-Parmesan, 61
Pork Chops, Stuffed, 204
Quiche, Chiles Rellenos, 321
Rosemary Cheese With Fig
  Preserves, 256
Salads
  Asparagus, Roasted-Beet, and Goat
    Cheese Salad, 96
  Blue Cheese Salad With Spicy
    Pecans, 300

Bluegrass Salad, 255
Cranberry Congealed Salad Parfaits,
  Frosted, 292
Italian House Salad, 300
Mozzarella-Tomato Basil Salad,
  Fresh, 110
Pasta Salad, Greek, 139
Ribbon Salad, Christmas, 257
Tortellini Pasta Salad, Cheese, 139
Sandwiches
  Hot Browns, Biscuit, 94
  Hot Browns, Kentucky, 94
  Hot Browns, Southwestern, 94
  Hot Browns With Fried Cheese
    Grits, 94
  Party Sandwiches, Duck, 48
  Party Sandwiches, Easter
    Bunny, 48
  Party Sandwiches, Easter Egg, 48
  Party Sandwiches, Flower, 48
  Quesadillas, Quick Fiesta, 246
  Roast Beef Slices, 246
Sauce, Cheese, 94
Sauce, Pimiento Cheese, 291
Sirloin With Cherry-Merlot Sauce and
  Gorgonzola, Peppered, 320
Spread, Horseradish, 53
Taco Stacks, Soft, 54
Topping, Breadcrumb, 233
Vegetables
  Asparagus Squares, 183
  Banana Peppers, Stuffed, 55
  Corn, Creamy Fried Confetti, 160
  Green Beans With Roquefort Cheese
    and Walnuts, 255
  Hash Browns, Smothered-
    Covered, 248
  Pie, Summer Garden, 182
  Potatoes, Cheesy Mashed, 98
  Potatoes, Cheesy Stuffed, 175
  Potatoes, Stuffed, 283
  Potatoes With Ham, Scalloped, 42
  Spinach, Easy Italian, 235
  Spinach-Gorgonzola Custards,
    Savory, 284
  Squash Pie, Italian, 183
  Sweet Potato Hash Browns,
    Cheesy, 248
  Tomato Stacks, Fried Green, 184
CHEESECAKES
  Ambrosia Cheesecake, 296
  Lemon Cheesecakes With Raspberry
    Sauce, Mini, 123
  Parfaits, Sugar-Free Peachy
    Cheesecake, 326
  Passover Cheesecake, Lemony, 51

From Our Kitchen/Recipe Preparation
(continued)

Favorite Recipes Journal

Jot down your family's and your favorite recipes for quick and handy reference. And don't forget to include the dishes that drew rave reviews when company came for dinner.

RECIPE	SOURCE/PAGE	REMARKS